BUSINESS ISSUES, COMPETITION AND ENTREPRENEURSHIP SERIES

HANDBOOK OF BUSINESS AND FINANCE: MULTINATIONAL COMPANIES, VENTURE CAPITAL AND NON-PROFIT ORGANIZATIONS

BUSINESS ISSUES, COMPETITION AND ENTREPRENEURSHIP SERIES

Improving Internet Access to Help Small Business Compete in a Global Economy
Hermann E. Walker (Editor)
2009. ISBN: 978-1-60692-515-7

Multinational Companies: Outsourcing, Conduct, and Taxes
Loran K. Cornejo (Editor)
2009. ISBN: 978-1-60741-260-1

Private Equity and its Impact
Spencer J. Fritz (Editor)
2009. ISBN: 978-1-60692-682-6

Progress in Management Engineering
Lucas P. Gragg and Jan M. Cassell (Editor)
2009. ISBN: 978-1-60741-310-3

Codes of Good Governance around the World
Felix J. Lopez Iturriaga (Editors)
2009. ISBN: 978-1-60741-141-3

Crisis Decision Making
*Chien-Ta Bruce Ho, KB Oh, Richard J. Pech, Geoffrey Durden
and Bret Slade*
2009. ISBN: 978-1-60876-073-2

Electronic Breadcrumbs: Issues in Tracking Consumers
Dmitar N. Kovac
2010. ISBN: 978-1-60741-600-5

**Handbook of Business and Finance: Multinational Companies, Venture Capital
and Non-Profit Organizations**
Matthaus Bergmann and Timotheus Faust (Editors)
2010. ISBN: 978-1-60692-855-4

BUSINESS ISSUES, COMPETITION AND ENTREPRENEURSHIP SERIES

HANDBOOK OF BUSINESS AND FINANCE: MULTINATIONAL COMPANIES, VENTURE CAPITAL AND NON-PROFIT ORGANIZATIONS

MATTHAUS BERGMANN
AND
TIMOTHEUS FAUST
EDITORS

Nova Science Publishers, Inc.
New York

Copyright © 2010 by Nova Science Publishers, Inc.

All rights reserved. No part of this book may be reproduced, stored in a retrieval system or transmitted in any form or by any means: electronic, electrostatic, magnetic, tape, mechanical photocopying, recording or otherwise without the written permission of the Publisher.

For permission to use material from this book please contact us:
Telephone 631-231-7269; Fax 631-231-8175
Web Site: http://www.novapublishers.com

NOTICE TO THE READER

The Publisher has taken reasonable care in the preparation of this book, but makes no expressed or implied warranty of any kind and assumes no responsibility for any errors or omissions. No liability is assumed for incidental or consequential damages in connection with or arising out of information contained in this book. The Publisher shall not be liable for any special, consequential, or exemplary damages resulting, in whole or in part, from the readers' use of, or reliance upon, this material. Any parts of this book based on government reports are so indicated and copyright is claimed for those parts to the extent applicable to compilations of such works.

Independent verification should be sought for any data, advice or recommendations contained in this book. In addition, no responsibility is assumed by the publisher for any injury and/or damage to persons or property arising from any methods, products, instructions, ideas or otherwise contained in this publication.

This publication is designed to provide accurate and authoritative information with regard to the subject matter covered herein. It is sold with the clear understanding that the Publisher is not engaged in rendering legal or any other professional services. If legal or any other expert assistance is required, the services of a competent person should be sought. FROM A DECLARATION OF PARTICIPANTS JOINTLY ADOPTED BY A COMMITTEE OF THE AMERICAN BAR ASSOCIATION AND A COMMITTEE OF PUBLISHERS.

LIBRARY OF CONGRESS CATALOGING-IN-PUBLICATION DATA

Handbook of business and finance : multinational companies, venture capital and non-profit organizations / [edited by] Matthaus Bergmann and Timotheus Faust.
    p. cm.
  Includes index.
  ISBN 978-1-60692-855-4 (hbk.)
  1. International business enterprises. 2. Nonprofit organizations. 3. Venture capital. 4. Corporations--Finance. I. Bergmann, Matthaus. II. Faust, Timotheus.
  HD2755.5.H367 2009
  658--dc22
          2009027057

Published by Nova Science Publishers, Inc. ✦ *New York*

CONTENTS

Preface   **vii**

Chapter 1   People Management Challenges to Multinational Companies   **1**
in Asia
Connie Zheng

Chapter 2   Alliance Portfolio Internationalization   **41**
Dovev Lavie and Stewart R. Miller

Chapter 3   Uniting the Service Trinity in Non-profit Community   **79**
Organisations: A Sequence of Studies, Reflections and
Implications for Theory and Practice in the Performing Arts
Margee Hume and Gillian Sullivan-Mort

Chapter 4   Explaining Individual Empowerment among Elderly Women   **101**
Volunteers in Nonprofit Organizations: The Israeli Case
Liat Kulik

Chapter 5   Local Outsourcing and Global Competition: The Case of New   **123**
Product Development in MNC Subsidiaries located in Brazil
Dirk Michael Boehe

Chapter 6   A Cost of Capital Analysis of the Gains   **147**
from Securitization
Hugh Thomas and Zhiqiang Wang

Chapter 7   National Museum Websites: Colonizing and De-Colonizing   **171**
Mary Leigh Morbey

Chapter 8   Is Staged Financing Designed for Alleviating Risks or Agency   **191**
Problems?
Lanfang Wang and Susheng Wang

Chapter 9   Syndication as a Management Strategy   **217**
Lanfang Wang and Susheng Wang

Chapter 10	The Economics of the Nonprofit Sector Toward the Self-sufficiency Paradigm *Vladislav Valentinov*	**241**
Chapter 11	M&A Impact on the Relationship between Business Definition and Corporate Growth *Koji Wakabayashi*	**259**
Chapter 12	Perils and Promises of Information and Communication Technology for Developing Countries: The ICT Services Outsourcing Boom in India *Tina Saebi, Geert Duysters and Bert Sadowski*	**281**
Chapter 13	Social Capital in the Capitalisation of New Ventures: Accessing, Lubricating and Fitting *Alistair R. Anderson, Sarah L. Jack and Sarah Drakopoulou Dodd*	**293**
Chapter 14	The Impact of Financial Services Firms Failures on the Careers of Financial Services Professionals *Monika Hamori*	**301**
Chapter 15	Do Organizational Types Behave Differently? Theories and Evidences from the Italian Hospital Sector *Monica Auteri*	**309**
Expert Commentary	*Margee Hume and Gillian Sullivan-Mort*	**321**
Index		**323**

PREFACE

This new book gathers the latest research from around the globe on business developments in multinational corporations, venture capital firms and non-profit organizations. The challenges of multinational companies (MNCs) in the particular areas of attraction and retention, training and career development of the local skilled labour workforce are analyzed using the data of 529 MNCs in six Asian countries. Also examined is the argument that the global coordination of MNC activities and possible local impacts on the subsidiary or host country level are connected. Furthermore, this book introduces the notion of alliance portfolio internationalization (API), which refers to the degree of foreignness of partners in a firm's collection of immediate alliance relationships. It is suggested that as a firm's API increases, financial performance is expected to initially decline, then improve, and finally decline again. Additionally, this book explores staged financing - a device very popular in reality, especially in venture capital financing. Over 90% of venture capital is invested through staged financing. Other chapters in this book examine the syndication of investment and its implications on the allocation of income rights and control rights, the current economics of nonprofit organizations, the impact of mergers and acquisitions (M&A) on the relationship between business definition and corporate growth, and an analysis of securitizations of corporate receivables, credit card debt, auto loans and leases, home equity loans, and non-agency guaranteed mortgages.

Chapter 1 discusses the contextual factors such as cultural and institutional settings that impact on effective people management practices in Asia. The challenges of multinational companies (MNCs) in the particular areas of attraction and retention, training and career development of the local skilled labour workforce are analyzed using the data of 529 MNCs in six Asian countries (namely Indonesia, Malaysia, Philippines, Singapore, Taiwan and Thailand). The degree of challenges varies by country and sector. The key conclusion drawn from the empirical research is that the culture and institutional theories, as well as the convergence and divergence theses can explain at best partially reasons behind the different outcomes of people management or human resource management (HRM) practices across MNCs in different operations in the region. There is a greater need to explore the impact of MNC's duality response to their global and local demands on the formation of their regional and international HRM strategies.

Alliance research has traditionally focused on structural and relational aspects of the networks in which firms are situated, paying less attention to the inherent characteristics of their partners. Chapter 2 introduces the notion of alliance portfolio internationalization (API), which refers to the degree of foreignness of partners in a firm's collection of immediate alliance relationships. The authors develop a framework to explain how API impacts firm performance. The authors suggest that as a firm's API increases, financial performance is expected to initially decline, then improve, and finally decline again. This sigmoid relationship between API and financial performance is ascribed to evolving learning effects that shape the net benefits of API. When the firm's alliance portfolio, on average, consists of proximate foreign partners, the firm may fail to recognize latent national differences, but at moderate levels of API, its absorptive capacity and specialized collaborative routines support the exchange of valuable network resources. Nevertheless, high levels of API undermine firm performance because of the failure of collaborative routines and mounting liabilities of cross-national differences. The authors test the framework using data on the alliance portfolios of U.S.-based software firms during the period from 1990 to 2001. The results provide support for the sigmoid relationship as well as for our predictions that firms which have gained experience with foreign partners and maintained wholly owned subsidiaries in their partners' countries of origin can overcome some of the liabilities of API and better leverage its benefits.

Services researchers suggest that implementing a multi-disciplinary approach to research will advance the domain of services research. The current approach to services research has minimized the nexus between marketing and operations and the importance of the implementation of strategy to achieve objectives. It is argued that failing to integrate service operations both practically and theoretically, into services research, in particular, applying multiple perspectives to customer re-purchase intentions research frameworks limits the potential effectiveness and practical applicability of findings. The research in Chapter 3 contributes to the field of service research by drawing from methods and theories offered in both service operations and services marketing fields. A mixed method implementing a series of three integrated studies was used to explore this context from both operations and marketing domains. This research identified the aspects of a performing arts encounter that are relevant to the customer by conducting a two-staged set of qualitative interviews. This process is based on the operations technique Service Transaction Analysis (STA). Consultant consumers and organizational personnel were used to formulate a consensus definition of a typical performing arts experience, and then 26 in-depth interviews were conducted with potential future consumers of the performing arts based on this description of the offering. A survey instrument was then conducted on 273 potential future consumers of the performing arts. The proposed model was then analyzed using the AMOS 5.0 Structural Equation Modeling package. Interestingly, the tested model found empirically that the subjective and experiential aspects of the service, such as the emotional and artistic quality of the show, did not have a significant and direct relationship with re-purchase intention. Offering further support, the tested model found service quality and show experience were mediated by value to satisfaction, with satisfaction in turn mediating the relationship between value and re-purchase intention. Collectively, these findings have led to several developments and contributions for both scholarship and practice. This exploration advanced the 'service management trinity', specifically strengthening the importance of the relationship between service marketing and service operations. By contributing to the field of service management and advancing enquiry in the field of services marketing and service operations, this project has offered a new perspective and practical approach to service marketing context analysis, making a valuable contribution to scholarship.

Chapter 4 aimed to explain the sense of empowerment in volunteer activity among Israeli women in middle and later life. The sample consisted of 146 women volunteering in social services in Israel. Based on Bronfenbrenner's ecological model of human adaptation to environments, the contribution of three ecological systems to explaining empowerment among volunteer women was examined: the ontogenic system, the microsystem, and the chronosystem. The women reported positive experiences with volunteering, as expressed in high levels of empowerment and family support for volunteer activity. In addition, the findings revealed high levels of satisfaction with rewards of volunteering and low levels of difficulty with the provider organization. The variables that contributed most to explaining empowerment in volunteering were those belonging to the ontogenic system: self-esteem and motives for volunteering. Of the microsystem variables, difficulties with the provider organization and rewards also contributed significantly to explaining empowerment.

Multinational companies' local impact may reveal itself as improvement of the competitive environment or crowding out of local companies, local supplier development, technological and managerial spill-over effects, among others. Chapter 5 focuses on a particular channel for technological or managerial linkages between MNCs and host countries: technical collaboration in the form of outsourcing between subsidiaries of multinational companies (MNC) and local host country partner organizations such as engineering firms, suppliers, universities or research institutes. For this reasons, I will discuss reasons of why MNC subsidiaries establish local outsourcing relationships in product. More specifically, I address the question of how MNC coordination mechanisms may influence the decision to keep new product development (NPD) activities in a local subsidiary (in-house) or to outsource it to local collaborators. Coordination mechanisms are implemented by headquarters and are defined as the process of integrating activities dispersed across subsidiaries. Thus, this study links global coordination mechanisms of MNCs with local collaboration (outsourcing). Hence, this chapter puts forward the argument that the global coordination of MNC activities and possible local impacts on the subsidiary or host country level are connected. Using a theoretic approach that combines literature on collaboration in R&D and NPD, headquarter-subsidiary as well as subsidiary-subsidiary relationships, this argument will be tested using structural equations modeling applied to a sample of 146 product development units located in Brazil. The results suggest that one of the coordination mechanisms, internal markets, has a positive effect on NPD outsourcing while the other coordination mechanism, global autonomy, has a positive effect on in-house NPD. Finally, I discuss several contributions to the scientific literature on MNCs. In particular, the study contributes to integrating the internal market construct with the coordination mechanism stream of literature. Moreover, I claim that future research and literature on multinational companies needs to increasingly treat both the external, host country part and the internal MNC part of subsidiaries' operational linkages in an integrated manner.

In Chapter 6 the authors study the gains that securitizing companies enjoy. They expressed the gains as a spread between two costs of capital, that weighted cost of capital of the asset selling firm and the all-in, weighted average cost of the securitization. The authors calculate the spread for 1,713 securitizations and regress those gains on asset seller characteristics. They show that they are increasing in size in the amount of asset backed securities originated but are decreasing in the percent of the balance sheet that the originator has outstanding. Companies that off-lay the risk of the sold assets (i.e., those retaining no subordinate interest in the SPV) pick their best assets to securitize. Companies that do not off-lay risk gain more from securitization the less liquid they are. The authors find that securitization is a substitute for leverage and that those companies that use more conventional leverage benefit less from securitization.

Internet communications technology (ICT) changes culture and therefore how a museum represents itself. Framed by the concepts of cybercolonialism and cyberglocalization, the chapter will critique and address, through case studies, a cybercolonizing by IBM of the State Hermitage Museum website, and cyberglocalizing processes in the Louvre Museum new website. Further, Chapter 7 examines the notion of de-colonization in relation to museum ICT and website development, particularly for countries in the Global South. Along with a discussion of virtual colonization, glocalization, and de-colonization, the chapter will attend to the place of virtual museum representation in light of Web 2.0 (interactive participation) and Web 3.0 (intelligent and semantic web) and relate these to Global South museum website development.

Staged financing is very popular in reality, especially in venture capital financing. Over 90% of venture capital is invested through staged financing. Why is staged financing so popular? There are many theoretical studies that focus on two major issues of venture capital: risks and agency problems. These studies find that staged financing is capable of controlling both risks and agency problems. In other words, staged financing can potentially be used as an effective mechanism in dealing with both risks and agency problems. In fact, the emphasis in the literature has been on the resolution of agency problems. What happens in reality? Is staged financing in reality mainly a device for alleviating risks, for coping with agency problems or both? This is an important empirical question. Surprisingly, no one has ever conducted such an investigation. Chapter 8 reports on an empirical study of the issue. To our surprise, the authors find that staged financing is almost exclusively a device in alleviating risks in venture capital financing. More specifically, the authors find a lot of evidence supporting staged financing as a mechanism in alleviating risks but not in coping with agency problems.

Syndication of investment exists in over 90% of venture capital backed companies. Syndication means that the investors form a group to invest jointly in a company. The existing literature emphasizes the benefits of investors from syndication through risk sharing and resource sharing. However, a few questions are left unanswered. First, does the manager of the firm also benefit from syndication? For example, with more sources of funding, the firm's future funding is more secure. Also, with competition among the investors, the manager may improve his bargaining position. Second, is syndication related to agency problems? There are no answers to these questions in the literature and empirical studies on syndication in venture capital are rare. By collecting data from 933 venture capital backed companies that went public in recent years, in Chapter 9 the authors conduct a detailed empirical study on syndication. It shows that (1) syndication is beneficial to both managers and investors for the purposes of risk sharing and potentially for alleviating agency problems; (2) syndication has clear implications on the allocations of income rights and control rights, implying a possible solution to or a result of agency problems.

The current economics of nonprofit organization has two interrelated problems. First, it is still marked by a logical separation between the demand-side and supply-side arguments for the existence of nonprofit firms. Second, it implicitly conceptualizes nonprofit organization as a nexus of contractual exchange relationships and thus overlooks the important element of noncontractibility associated with the not-for-profit motivation of nonprofit managers and entrepreneurs.

Chapter 10 presents an overview of the author's previous research aimed at addressing these problems. It is shown that both these problems can be solved by grounding the understanding of nonprofit organization in the theory of the division of labor. From the perspective of this theory, nonprofit organization is located outside the social division of labor since it is not based on profit making motivation. This fact implies that nonprofit organization must be treated as an institutional form of collective self-sufficiency, i.e., self-provision of stakeholder groups with the realization of nonprofit missions. The self-sufficiency view of nonprofit organization solves the first above mentioned problem since the notion of self-sufficient activity involves a harmony between the supply-side and demand-side motivations. Moreover, the notion of self-sufficiency presents a clear contrast with the institution of the for-profit firm that is rooted in the social division of labor. While the social division of labor requires economic organization based on contractual exchange, this is not the case with self-sufficiency, thus solving the second problem as well.

The self-sufficiency view of nonprofit organization yields two major organizational economics implications that are explored in this chapter. First, opportunism must be less important in the nonprofit sector than for-profit one, because of the harmony of demand-side and supply-side motivations of individuals practicing self-sufficiency. Hence, nonprofit firms economize on transaction cost primarily by reducing the cost of information processing and not by aligning incentives in order to minimize opportunism. Second, the relevant incentive alignment problem in nonprofit organization consists not of minimizing opportunism, but of preventing the crowding out of intrinsic motivation.

The paper concludes with exploring special rationales for nonprofit organization in agriculture and rural development. It is argued that rurality and agriculture are associated with special limitations on the ability of for-profit firms to satisfy the needs of rural dwellers, thus creating a niche for cooperatives and rural nonprofit firms. The last section summarizes the argument and presents the most important implications for further research.

In a previous study, the relationship between business definition and corporate performance has been explored, which is to prove the hypothesis drawn from Theodore Levitt's idea that a company could continue growing, if it properly defined its business by function (customer value), based on an empirical analysis of 50 electric/electronics companies. The relationship between 'functionality' (magnitude that function is contained) in the past business definitions rated by an evaluation panel and time series performance data until recently had been statistically analyzed and positive correlation between functionality and consolidated sales growth rate was found, which thus supported the hypothesis. However, the correlation coefficient was not large enough to sufficiently explain the trend in sales growth rate by the functionality. Chapter 11 is to further analyze the influence of the second explanatory variable, 'alignment degree' (magnitude of alignment in terms of function), based on the assumption that even the corporate business definition is functional, if the function is not fully aligned through the whole company, the growth rate still will be lower. The appearance frequency of the key words forming business definitions in new product press releases is measured as alignment degree with 25 selected companies by content analysis using text mining technique. As a result, a multiple regression model is identified with the companies of high and low ranges in functionality and it can explicitly explain growth rate by functionality and alignment degree. However, this regression model is not applicable to the companies of medium range in functionality including the ones that grow mainly through mergers and acquisitions (M&A). The reason is that short-term impact of M&A on sales growth is so substantial that it exceeds the scope of the regression model. Based on all those concerns, the impact of M&A on the relationship between business definition and corporate growth is the issue of the study to further explore by using some cases.

The case of India illustrates well how technological revolutions may bring unexpected opportunities for developing countries. To benefit from the recent outsourcing boom in ICT services, India's government has directed investments into the restructuring and expansion of the local ICT services sector, positioning the country among the most popular ICT services outsourcing destinations. Drawing on national innovation system theory and concepts of absorptive capacity, Chapter 12 questions the sustainability of India's success as a top ICT offshoring destination. In the immediate distance, eroding cost advantages and unsophisticated service exports are threatening India's top position. To avoid competition in the low-segments of ICT services exports, India would have to move up the value chain, requiring the expansion of the ICT services sector into higher spheres of software design and development. However, as this paper argues, the expansion of this industry is constrained by the enormous variation in inter-state levels of ICT education and infrastructure. The poor absorptive capacity of the remaining part of the country is found to severely limit the industry's expansion possibilities. As empirically shown, state efforts to build a learning system exclusively for the ICT sector have prevented a nation-wide investment in absorptive capacity. Therefore this paper proposes that resolving these inter-state disparities requires the development of learning capabilities outside the ICT industry; enabling the remaining economic sectors to absorb the benefits generated by the expansion of the ICT sector. However, until this aim is achieved, India's ICT sector may have long lost its competitive advantage.

As discussed in Chapter 13, new venture capitalisation demands the formation of the necessary financial resources to launch. Social capital - the potential resources to which individuals have access due to their position within specific social networks of relationships - also plays a significant role in new venture capitalisation in three main ways. Firstly, social capital provides *access*, and thus acts a means of securing other forms of capital. Secondly, social capital also *lubricates* relations between entrepreneur and others within the socio-economic environment, including financiers. Thirdly, social capital acts as a mechanism for *fitting* the entrepreneur and their new venture to the wider socio-economic environment.

Chapter 14 looks at the effect, on finance professionals' career moves to another employer, of six types of events in financial services firms: criticism of the firm in the business media; resignation of key individuals from the organization; downsizing; a drop in net income; lawsuits launched by public authorities, competitors, or customers; and lawsuits launched by employees. It samples over 900 financial services professionals who have worked for the five most prestigious financial services institutions on Wall Street. The results show that out of the six types of events, the ones that signal the decline of corporate performance are the most devastating for the career success of finance professionals who try to leave the firm in the wake of the event. Outsiders, on the other hand, are less sensitive to financial services firms' involvement in lawsuits launched by public authorities or employees. The events affect the career of every professional, irrespective of their level in the organization.

Scholars characterize the nonprofit sector according to several, often overlapping theories. Unfortunately, these theories, do not offer testable hypotheses and it is hard to tell whether nonprofits exist because of historical accident, path dependence, different organizational goals, consumer demand, or government regulation. Therefore, rather than trying to answer such broad questions about the role of the entire sector, in Chapter 15 the authors take a step toward filling a research gap by asking this simple question: Do ownership types behave differently? To answer this question, the authors test the provision of the Italian health care services. If ownership seems to matter, they then assess alternative explanations for those differences. They mainly consider whether ownership types have different objectives and then investigate whether hospital types behave differently.

In: Handbook of Business and Finance
Editors: M. Bergmann and T. Faust, pp. 1-39

ISBN: 978-1-60692-855-4
© 2010 Nova Science Publishers, Inc.

Chapter 1

PEOPLE MANAGEMENT CHALLENGES TO MULTINATIONAL COMPANIES IN ASIA

Connie Zheng
RMIT University, Melbourne, Australia

Abstract

This chapter discusses the contextual factors such as cultural and institutional settings that impact on effective people management practices in Asia. The challenges of multinational companies (MNCs) in the particular areas of attraction and retention, training and career development of the local skilled labour workforce are analyzed using the data of 529 MNCs in six Asian countries (namely Indonesia, Malaysia, Philippines, Singapore, Taiwan and Thailand). The degree of challenges varies by country and sector. The key conclusion drawn from the empirical research is that the culture and institutional theories, as well as the convergence and divergence theses can explain at best partially reasons behind the different outcomes of people management or human resource management (HRM) practices across MNCs in different operations in the region. There is a greater need to explore the impact of MNC's duality response to their global and local demands on the formation of their regional and international HRM strategies.

Introduction

Asia, with the half of the world population, has about 3 billion inhabitants over 20 economies[1][Bangladesh, Bhutan, Brunei, Cambodia, China (including Hong Kong and

---

[1] The term 'economy' or 'economies' may be contentious but it is commonly used in the APEC forums (Asia Pacific Economic Cooperation). The replacement of 'country' or 'nation' with 'economy' is intended to keep away from the confrontation between two different political, economic and social entities such as People's Republic of China (so called PRC or Mainland China) and Republic of China (ROC or Treasure Island Taiwan), similar to North and South Korea. Use of the term 'economy' is understandable as even though PRC and ROC may have inherited from the same historical and cultural traits (Hofstede and Bond, 1988, so have North and South Korea), they contain quite different sets of modern economic and social systems, such as currency, exchange rate, welfare and economic sectoral disparity, for example there is a higher proportion of service economy in Taiwan and South Korea than that in PR China.

Macau), India, Indonesia, Japan, North and South Korea, Lao, Malaysia, Myanmar, Nepal, Pakistan, Philippines, Singapore, Sri Lanka, Taiwan, Thailand and Vietnam]. This simple definition of 'Asia' may be subject to many debates. For example, Bruton and Lau (2008) reckon that Asia has a population of approximately 3.5 billion people in over 30 economies, covering some Middle East countries (eg. Iran, Israel, Jordan and Saudi Abrabia); and Caucasus (such as Armenia, Georgia and Azerbaijan and more of those newly established states which broke away from the former Soviet Unions since 1992). Hofstede (2007) jokingly argues that we can almost call Hong Kong East Asia and Holland West Asia, if the definition of 'Asia' was simply based on the geographical concept. Most of modern (and western) concept of 'Asia' tend to adopt the Ancient Greeks' view, whereby 'Asia was everything East of them....and Europe everything West of them' (Hofstede, 2007, p. 412). UNCTAD (2008) divided the 40 Asian economies into 13 Western Asian countries and the rest 27 either belonged to the South, or East or the South-East states. The rationale putting only 20 economies together is that they are not only geographically proximate, but culturally predominant by the influence of Buddhism and Confucianism, not to undermine the dominant presence of Islamism in some parts of the region (eg. Bangladesh, Indonesia, Malaysia and Pakistan).

The defined Asia region contains one of the world's largest economies (Japan) and two of the world's fastest growing economies (China and India). The economic impact of the region has been strong and continuously expanding, with a number of Asian economies having experienced unprecedented levels of economic growth that have contributed to the sustained 'global prosperity and stability' (Budhwar, 2004, p. 1). This claim was supported by the recent UNCTAD report on 'Development and Globalization' (2008, p. 9), which states that:

> ....only Eastern, Southern and South-Eastern Asia could significantly diminish the gap with developed economies in terms of per capita GDP in the last 20 years of the twentieth century. Per capita real GDP in that region almost tripled between 1980 and 2007 (although from very low levels), while it stagnated in other developing regions (such as Africa, the Americas, Western Asia and Oceania)...

The prosperity and rapid development of many Asian economies has been largely due to the globalization of businesses and the ability of these economies to successfully attract foreign direction investment (FDI) from the developed world. The Asia region has gained an impressive total FDI inflow of almost US$200 billion in 2006 (UNCTAD 2008). Among these FDI, China has topped the list, becoming the biggest host country with inflows of US$69 billion in 2006 (UNCTAD, 2007).

Today, more than half of 780,000 foreign affiliates owned by an estimated 78,000 multinational companies (MNCs) or transnational firms (TNCs) in the world are located in Asia. The number of employees in foreign affiliates worldwide has grown dramatically; it reached 73 million in 2006, up from 25 million in 1990, increased nearly threefold, with again China having the largest number of employees, estimated at 24 million (UNCTAD, 2007). Also, in a number of Asian economies, the share of employment in foreign affiliates compared to total employment rose during the same period. Sales by foreign affiliates quadrupled, from $6 trillion in 1990 to $25 trillion in 2006. MNCs' total assets reached $51 trillion (UNCTAD, 2007).

MNCs have increasingly dominated the world's product and labour markets. On one hand, MNCs have played an important role in harnessing the globalization of world economic activities. On the other hand, this process of globalization with free flow of FDI, different cohorts of employees and access to modern technology requires MNCs to develop new forms of transnational organizations and new ways of management thinking (Zhang, 2003; Schuler and Tarique, 2007). In particular, the ways in which MNCs effectively manage their global workforce across borders are increasingly viewed as critical to the success of their implementing global strategies (Barlett and Ghoshal, 1989). The increased number of MNCs has escalated the globalization process; yet globalization exerts pressure on management of global operations of MNCs because of different national culture and institutional settings. In Asia and the rest of the world, MNCs have been confronted with adopting and/or adapting to a variety of local HRM practices in their countries of operation (Friedman, 2007; Farndale and Paauwe, 2007). How to balance global and local HRM strategies presents a particular challenge for MNCs and it is the strategic choice MNCs must make in order to be successful and sustaining competitive in this part of the international market.

Although this book is about multinational companies and issues related to management, globalization and local impacts, I believe and concur with Hofstede's (2007) argument that 'management is always about people': 'getting things done through other people' and 'coordinating the efforts of people towards common goals' (p. 412). This is no exception for MNCs – addressing the management challenges for MNCs is all about addressing the international people management challenges. Hence, in this chapter, I seek to explain the cultural and institutional variables that are very much embedded in the strategic international human resource management (HRM) framework (eg. Schuler, De Cieri and Dowling, 1993; Schuler, Jackson and Luo, 2004; Schuler and Tarique, 2007). I will particularly focus on assessing the impact of these variables on the people management practices in Asia contexts[2]. I will then shed some lights on the theoretical discussion on convergent and divergent management practices around the globe as they are contained in the debates of cultural and institutional theories. The research evidence from my prior studies on the multinational companies operating in six Asia economies will be used to answer the following key research questions:

1) What are the key areas of IHRM challenges MNCs are confronting?
2) How have they managed to address these challenges?
3) Have the cultural and institutional variables affected much on the choice of IHRM policies and practices made by MNCs?
4) What are other key variables that have impacted on MNCs' choice of IHRM policies and practices?
5) What are the implications of these choices to local impacts and global diffusion of management practices?

Needless to say the limitations of my studies in answering all these important questions, to compensate this inadequacy, other empirical studies are also reviewed to capture more fully the key management challenges and issues faced by MNCs operating in Asia.

---

2 Bruton and Lau (2008) reviewed 306 articles that addressed Asian management issues during the ten-year period from 1996-2005 in the ten leading mainstream journals and found that culture theories and institutional theories were heavily employed to describe national cultural differences and explain new management phenomena (pp. 642-643).

Culture and Institutions in Asia

Even though Asia is generally defined as discussed earlier, it is important to acknowledge that each economy within the region has an independent set of cultural and institutional settings differing from one another in content and arising inevitably from the interplay of historical, social and economic relations unique to themselves (Budwar, 2004). Because management is always about people (Hofstede, 2007), and people are part of the culture and determinants of their society's institutional frameworks, there is a clear need to see the management phenomena as part and parcel of the distinctive political, cultural and institutional systems of each economy (Morishima, 1995).

Asia is as vast and diverse as a universe. Although the scope of this chapter does not warrant the space to summarise all different culture and institutional setting for each of the 20 Asian economies, this section will selectively introduce basic cultural and institutional frameworks in 8 economies. I choose China and India as these are two growing and important economies in the region and the world. Indonesia, Malaysia, Philippines, Singapore, Taiwan and Thailand are included because of two reasons. First, these economies were covered in my empirical research (so was China in the separate study). Secondly, the industrial relations (IR) and human resource management (HRM) practices in six economies plus China and India conform closely to the typical Asian models discussed in Kuruvilla and Venkataratnam (1996)[3] (see more discussion later). These chosen eight economies not only represent the Asia region in the general terms as they constitute the majority of GDP and population but they also offer a range of distinctive cultures and IR institutions that help better understand the complexity of human resource management contexts for MNCs in the region (Jackson and Schuler, 1995). Before the discussion of these economies' culture and institutional settings, the theories underpinning the impact of culture and institutions on business management are first introduced.

Culture Theory

The culture theory views organization and society as culturally specific entity with 'the collective programming of the mind' (Hofstede, 1980, p. 21) that is able to classify the organizational members of one group[4] or category of people in society from one and another (Hofstede, 1991; 2007). According to Kluckhohn and Strodbeck (1961), difference in culture is measured by value preference placed on certain affairs/matters over the others. For example, in one society, people may prefer to be identified in groups; whilst in another society, individualistic character is more valued. Similarly, an organization might have a culture of promoting teamwork or collective decision-making, whilst another organizational culture may encourage more of individual achievement, performance-based pays and

---

3 In fact, Kuruvilla and Venkitaratnam (1996) discussed six distinct stylized IR/HR models in Asia: the Japanese flexible-workplace model (although not discussed, Thailand seem following this model, as you would see from the discussion in this chapter), the tripartite Singapore model, the state-employer-dominated model (Malaysia and Indonesia), the pluralist decentralized and fragmented model (the Philippines), the politicized multiunion model (India and the rest of South Asia), and the transitory model (a catch-all category that includes South Korea, Taiwan, China and Vietnam) (Kuruvilla and Erickson, 2002, pp. 172-173).

4 Note that Hofstede always discusses culture from the national point of view, but I believe culture at the organizational level is similarly formed as continuous collective programming of a group of people's minds.

managerial discreet in hiring and firing employees (Robbins and Barnwell, 2006). In a society or an organization whereby relationships between people are always affected by the values, management of people within organization or society would be very much subject to cultural values that form part of 'the collective programming of people's minds', which in return, reinforce management practices in that organization and society over time. Consequently, as argued by Hofstede (2007), 'a management technique or philosophy that is appropriate in one national culture is not necessary appropriate in another' (p. 413). In another word, management practices instilled in one culture would also be hard to change and evolve in the short term.

In the context of multinational companies, the culture theory explains why organizations operating across borders tend to adopt international human resource management practices either influenced by country of origin effect (ie. national isomorphism) or by host country effect (ie. local isomorphism) (Laurent, 1986; Schneider, 1988; Ferner, 1997; Ferner et al., 2001). It is quite likely because of the dominant American culture values that an US multinational company may want to transfer their home country's HR and other management practices to one of their Asian operations. However, they may have to adopt HRM practices that reflect cultural and institutional conditions in the place of local operation (Evans, Pucik and Barsoux, 2002). Generally speaking, HRM practices of MNCs are not only affected by the culture values of the local subsidiary, but also are subject to the influence of both local and international institutional framework. The institutional theory, which is discussed next, asserts that two additional isomorphisms would influence the choice of HRM strategies made by MNCs.

Institutional Theory

The cultural and institutional theories are somewhat intertwined in the theoretical discussion (Chow, 2004). For instance, the institutional perspective argues that organizations as social entities must seek approval for their performances in the socially and culturally acceptable conditions in order to gain legitimacy and acceptance, which facilitates survival (Jackson and Schuler, 1995). Based on this argument, culture is clearly part of the institutional theory, even though the institutional theory addresses both internal and external institutions. Internal institutionalization constitutes those formalized structures and processes, as well as informal or emergent group and organization process (Meyer and Rowan, 1977; Zucker, 1987). External institutionalization includes those related to the national laws and regulations, the professional standards (eg. licensure and certification) and industry-wide benchmarks (Jackson and Schuler, 1995). Jackson and Schuler (1995) argue that regardless of the source of institutional pressures, there appear two central assertions of the institutional perspective, which are similar to those arising from the cultural arguments. One is that institutionalized activities (eg. HRM functions and activities of MNCs) are resistant to change. Secondly, organizations in the institutionalized environment are pressured to become similar.

From the first assertion of the institutional perspective, it seems that MNCs are required to accommodate local traditions and cultural values, yet at the same time, also subject to responding appropriately to their own internal structure and strategy. MNCs' strategy has often been conceptualized in terms of global integration or MNC standardization versus local responsiveness or MNC localization (Prahalad and Doz, 1987). The strategic choice determines the global HRM policies and practices in MNCs (Schuler et al., 1993). The emphasis on global integration would lead to a greater standardization of HRM practices, whilst differentiation strategy leads to a greater emphasis on localizing HRM practices. Nonetheless, subject to the pressure from the internal institutionalization, many well-known MNCs (eg. Lincoln Electric; Toyota; Hewlett Packard) tended to adopt the standardized HRM policies and practices in their global operation, in line with the concept of 'corporate isomorphism' as defined by Evan et al. (2002, p. 63). Bjorkman (2004) indicated a number of benefits MNCs may gain from using standardized HRM practices across the borders, such as equity among employees, increased collaboration, better control, effective use of resources and economic of scale and scope. Potential drawbacks to a standardized approach could however occur due to lacking responsiveness to the local cultural environment, neglecting different institutional settings and IR legal requirements, and failure to meet the local labour market needs and to develop the innovative HR solutions for the local units (Bjorkman, 2004). There appears a significant challenge for MNCs to strategically respond to both local and global needs of people and business (Sorge, 2005).

From the second assertion, it appears that similar HRM policies and practices may be adopted by MNCs globally or locally simply because other MNCs have done so. This argument is in line with what Evan et al. (2002) term as 'global intercorporate isomorphism' (p. 64) or De Cieri et al.'s (2007) claim for an 'imitation' approach to international HRM. The pressures to imitate may come from requirements to comply the laws and regulations and meet both professional and industry standards (Jackson and Schuler, 1995). Another pressure to conform could be from global diffusion of technology and management practices that force MNCs to constantly compare their practices with others and model their practices against the best practices in the given industry, sector or economy. At this point, we can not ignore the old debate about converging and diverging management practices around the world, including HRM practices as MNCs are at the heart of these debates (Farndale and Paauwe, 2007).

Convergence v. Divergence

The central themes to convergence and divergence debates are derived from the strategic HRM research (Delery and Doty, 1996). The convergent theists tend to adopt a universalistic perspective and argue that some HR practices are always better than the others and that all organizations should adopt these best practices to achieve better organizational outcomes in terms of productivity, return of investment and profits (eg. Huselid, 1995; Pfeffer, 1994). When considering multinational companies, as they are operating both at national and global levels, it would be at a low cost and low risk for them to imitate, adopt or reproduce a set of universal high performance work practices to improve efficiency and effectiveness, rather than leading 'managerial fads and fashions' to gain legitimacy and acceptance (Abrahmson, 1991; Jackson and Schuler, 1995; Farndale and Paauwe, 2007).

In contrast, the divergent theists are opt for a contingency view and believe that an organization's HR policies and practices must 'best fit' prevailing conditions whereby the firm is operating. The best fit or contingency perspective rejects the notion of one best way of doing things in all contexts (Delery and Doty, 1996). In reality, any organization would be much influenced by three strong institutional mechanism defined by DiMaggio and Powell

(1983) as *coercive, mimetic* and *normative* mechanisms. To apply these institutional mechanisms in the context of MNC's international HRM, *coercive* mechanisms at national and global levels could include the influence of social partners in HR management, such as the role of trade unions as well as national and international actors in the industrial relations (IR) systems. *Mimetic* mechanisms refer to benchmarking and the imitation of strategies of successful competitors. For instance, if a successful competitor in the local operation adopts more of local responsiveness strategy, even though this strategy may not be congruent with the best HRM practices, MNCs may want to benchmark and imitate such strategies in order to be successful, or at least to be acceptable within the local social and cultural context. *Normative* mechanisms include the impact of HR professional bodies and employers associations. Meeting the requirements of professional and industry standards in a given sector and economy also prevents MNCs from implementing the standardized HRM practices across borders.

What if these institutional mechanisms are becoming more and more similar? This is so called neo-institutional theory (Greenwood and Hinings, 1996) advocating that institutional isomorphism may cause the society look more and more alike and organizations to behaviour similarly. Thus, the convergence of both institutional IR framework and HRM practices is quite likely (Farndale and Paauwe, 2007; see also Bamber et al., 2000; 2004; and Kuruvilla and Erickson, 2002 for further discussion on the convergence of IR, ER and HR practices among the Asian economies). Nevertheless, according to the resource-based view of the firm (Barney, 1991), firms are unlikely to conform to these institutional isomorphic influences. In fact, firms are more likely to differentiate themselves from their competitors by cultivating their resources differently in order to achieve competitive advantages. In the cross-border operation, MNCs are inclined to adopt a divergent approach, selecting HRM practices that are contingent in building their tangible and intangible resources and capabilities required for product/market competition (Kamoche, 1996; Subramony, 2006). Interestingly, in recent years, cultural intelligence (cultural quotient or CQ) that signifies individual's ability to know what to do and being motivated to persist in getting it right in the cross-cultural contexts is regarded as an essential selection and assessment criteria for global executives and expatriate managers (Rosen et al, 2000; Schneider and Barsoux 2003; Earley and Mosakowski, 2004). Not only must MNCs need to differentiate in achieving their global competitiveness, but they also need to respond to the increasingly desegregated societies as a result of globalization. According to Vaclav Havel, former President of the Czech Republic,

> 'globalization often exacerbated nationalistic and ethnic rivalries. Rather than uniting people in a common global culture, a mass culture in which everyone wears the same jeans, eats the same fast food and listens to the same music doesn't inevitably bring people closer. Rather, it can make them less secure about who they are...'
> (p. 358, cited from Clinton, 2003).

Hence, having global managers with a high attribute of cultural quotients perhaps could help MNCs address these differences and achieve the balance. It is to this reason perhaps that a better understanding of people from different cultures and their national characteristics of the economy and business environment becomes essential for international managers working across cultures. Sorge (2005), in criticising the dominant convergence thesis, also supports the notion that that it is not possible that globalization leads inevitably to convergence across societies and economies. On the contrary, globalization feeds into both societal aggregation and desegregation, and cultural universality and specificity (Trompenaars, 1993). Therefore, it is important to have an overview of some cultural and institutional contexts in Asia where many MNCs are operating. The purpose of such review is to identify where the challenges could be sourced and also provide the contexts for answering the first research question, 'What are the key areas of IHRM challenges MNCs are confronting?' Potentially MNCs may find approaches to unravel the dilemma of responding to local needs and implementing their global strategy.

Snapshots of Cultural and Institutional Characteristics in 8 Asia Economies

In the economy cases below, I seek to identify the key culture characteristics, based on the cultural framework developed by Hofstede (1980) and Hofstede and Bond (1988). Because HRM philosophy and practices have deep historical roots and often are embedded in the national industrial relations system (Jackson and Schuler, 1995; Kuruvilla and Erickson, 2002), it is impossible to evaluate the impact of the cultural and institutional framework on people management without looking into the past and evolution of IR system in each of these economies. Hence, in this sub-section, each economy will be briefly introduced based on: 1) population (human resources); 2) cultural characteristics; 3) historical development of various institutions, in particular the IR system; and 4) current HRM practices.

Mainland China[5]

China has a population of 1.3 billion or over 20 percent of the world population. With a history of over 5,000 years, China belongs to the one of oldest and most complex civilizations. A large geographic region covers diverse customs and traditions spreading over 57 minority groups, predominated though by Hans with 91 percent of the population. Hans established the Chinese culture that has a dominant influence among many Chinese-speaking region in Asia and beyond the border of mainland China (CIA, 2008).

The Chinese culture is largely characterized by the Confucianism blended with moral teachings of the Taoism and Buddhism. The set of social values contained in the Confucianism is reflected in seven letters (*Li* – etiquette; *Yi* – righteousness; *Ren* – humanness; *Xiao* – familial love; *Xin* –trustworthy; *Zhi* – wisdom; and *Zhong* – loyalty). Evaluating this set of social values against Hofstede's (1980) national culture dimensions, it appears that the Chinese society generally scores high on collectivism and power distance because of its emphasis on loyalty and love to family, community and the state instead of self or individual interests. Besides, the dynamic Confucian values place many Chinese around the world on the far end of the 'long-term orientation' scale, according to Hosftede and Bond's (1988) study in 23 countries. This propensity of thinking in long term drives many Chinese as well as other Confucian value-oriented Asians (eg. Hong Kong, Taiwan, Japan, Korea, India, Singapore, Thailand etc) to focus on 'persistence and thrift' (Hofstede, 2007, p. 418). In contrast, people with the short-term orientation tend to value instant gratification

---

5 This is to distinguish two different economies – the People's Republic of China (PRC) and Island Economy of Taiwan, also called Republic of China. Mainland China hence excludes the small economies such as Hong Kong and Macau as these two economies represent different economic systems even though they are now parts of the PRC.

and seek pleasure without pain. Chinese, however knows the best how to persist against adversity and resist gratification that bring no long term benefits to family and society.

Such culture values are deeply rooted in the China's history. In particular for the past 100 years, as China experienced many ups and downs of social, economic and political changes. The current institutional system controlled by the Chinese Communist Party (CCP) has been the very product of the cultural evolution and values developed through many events happened in the past century. The dramatic events include the fall of Qing feudalistic dynasty, the brutality and humiliation of warfare (eg. the Opium) launched by the West and Wars and Japanese Invasion, as well as the prolonged civil wars between CCP and the Nationalist Party (KMT), leading eventually to the establishment of the People's Republic of China by CPC in mainland China and the Republic of China (ROC) by KMT in Taiwan since 1949 (Zhu, 2006). For the past 60 years under the rule of CCP, Chinese people have seen a period of relative stability without wars, but not without man-made disasters such as the Great Leap Forward with a massive famine killing 30 million in the period of 1958-1961(Becker, 2000); and the sweeping Cultural Revolution leaving almost every mainland Chinese with a 'Wild Swans[6]' story still to be recounted.

The economic reforms started in 1978 and subsequently the access to World Trade Organization (WTO) since 2001 have changed much the landscape of China's social and economic systems, though not significantly in the political system with still one Party's control of the government. Parallelled with the economic reforms, we've seen the changes of IR legislation such as re-establishing the Trade Unions Law (1992), the Labour Law (1995) and Labour Contract Law (2007). These laws and regulations mainly target at the foreign investment sector; the government's intention is to keep the basic labour protection and welfare as similar as possible to the state-owned sector (Kuruvilla and Erickson, 2002). Although the Trade Unions Law stipulates that every enterprise should have a union; and that union reps should attend the board meetings of the companies, in practice, the role of unions in many organizations has been limited to act as the Party's speaker, carrying out its economic reform agenda, instead of representing workers' interests (Zheng et al., 2006). However, on 15 July 2008, the Chairman of the Guangdong[7] branch of ACFTU (All China Federation of Trade Union – the only workers' organization in China) announced first time in history that from now on, China's Trade Union is going to represent 'the workers and no one else' and to 'place collective bargaining – previously a no-go area – at the core of the union's work' (China Labour Bulletin, 2008). This new move surely will have profound implications to MNCs operating in China, which requires further assessment.

Central to the enterprise reforms is the change of management practices, in particular the implementation of new policies and practices of HRM in China. Many authors (eg. Child, 1994; Warner, 1993; 1997; Zhu and Dowling, 2002; Cooke, 2004; 2005; Zhu, 2006) have taken into the account of these changes (for the most recent review, see Zheng and Lamond, in press). The key message derived from the argument of patterns and trends of the HRM

---

6 'Wild Swans Three Daughters of China' written by Jung Chang, Oxford Scholar, who won the 1992 NCR Book Award and the 1993 British Book of the Year Award. Many Chinese are unfortunately not able to write as well as Dr Chang, but their stories are equally compelling.

7 One needs to be aware that Guangdong was the first province in China to start the economic reform in the late 1970s and its model of success was copied thereafter by other parts of China. Perhaps this move shows Guangdong also in pioneering the China's political reform. Allowing unions the collective bargaining right signifies a move to true pluralist approach in managing industrial relations.

development in China is that the practices tend to be varied across enterprises with different ownership. Strategic HRM tends to be seen as weak, whilst functional HRM in the areas of market recruitment and selection, performance management through merit-based pay, training and development and reward systems were much in line with the recent development trends in the West to focus on high performance work practices (eg. Zheng et al., 2006) and increased numerical, functional and wage flexibility[8] to enhance enterprise competitiveness (Kuruvilla and Erickson, 2002).

India

Next to China, India is the second largest state with 1.1 billion people (CIA, 2008). Similar to China, India belongs to one of the oldest and most complex civilizations in the world, with folklores and sages well remembered by Indians as well as many connecting Asian neighbours. For example, in one of the folktales (eg. the Story of Monkey King[9]), the Chinese recounts the journey to India – the birthplace of Buddhism - for finding moral and spiritual guidance. Nowadays, the country is populated predominantly by Hindus (83 percent) with only 1 percent of Buddhists (Saini and Budhwar, 2004).

The unique social structure in India is the caste system that stratifies people into 3000 groups, even though the ancient Indian wisdom emphasising the equality of all human beings (Sen, 2005). The caste system was exacerbated by the rule of the British elitists over India for more than two hundred years since the seventeenth century. The values of hierarchy and subjugation initially disliked by Indians were gradually ingrained in 'the psyche of common people' (Saini and Budhwar, 2004, p. 120). By the time India broke away from the British rule in 1947, a culture of elitism has already taken the stronghold in the land. On the basis of Hofstede's (1980) culture dimensions, Kanungo and Mendonca (1994) conclude that India stands relatively high on uncertainty avoidance and power distance and relatively low on individualism and masculinity dimensions. This is understandable, as the Indian social and cultural environment would put primacy on strong family ties that dilute individualism, resulting in greater dependence on others. Relatively high uncertainty avoidance implies that the Indians are in general are reluctant to take risks and accept change They also hesitate to delegate or make independent decision (Saini and Budhwar, 2004).

As often commented, at least the British elitists left India with the largest democracy in the world. Nonetheless, the past democracy in India seemed having the negative connotation

---

8 Numerical flexibility refers to developing 'core and peripheral workers' who could be involved in part-time, temporary work or sub-contracting; functional flexibility involves the possession of 'flexible' skills by employees, together with their willingness to display flexibility by moving freely between tasks; and financial (wage) flexibility refers to using various ways of compensation strategy (eg. bonus, share options, performance-based pay) to boost productivity and efficiency (for more comprehensive introduction on these flexibility, see David Guest's well cited paper "Human Resource Management and Industrial Relations" published in 1987 in Journal of Management Studies 25(5): 503-521; or Karen Legge's book (1995) Human Resource Management: Rhetoric and Realities, London: Macmillan.

9 Monkey King, or known to the Chinese old and young as Xi You Ji (Journey to the West), is one of the renowned classical Chinese novels dated back some four hundred years ago, based on a true story of a famous monk, Xuan Zang of the Chinese Tang Dynasty (602-664). After a decade of trials and tribulations, he arrived on foot to what is today India, the birthplace of Buddhism. He was there for the true Buddhist holy scriptures. When he returned, Xuan Zang translated the Sutras into Chinese, thus making a great contribution to the development of Buddhism in China (from 'The Magic Lotus Lantern and Other Tales from the Han Chinese' by Yuan Hai Wang, published by Libraries Unlimited, Greenwood Publishing Group, Westport, 2006).

with dual system of elite and the general public, pluralism without prudence in decision making and multi-unionism without strong union membership (Kuruvilla and Erickson, 2002; Saini and Budhwar, 2004).

Recent changes in economic policies as a result of implementing the World Bank and IMF's 'bail-out' programs since the mid-1990s had helped India gradually develop into one of the world's largest economies. The Indian economy has responded positively to the various 'liberalization' reforms suggested by the World Bank and IMF (Saini and Budhwar, 2004). India has since become a favourite destination for many foreign investors who are particularly interested in the business process outsourcing (BPO) industry. More than 15,000 MNCs operating in India, of them, majority are in the BPO industry, posing the particular challenge of international HRM for MNCs operating in the dynamic culture and institutional environment (Dowling, Festing and Engel, 2008).

In terms of the IR system, India belongs to the politicized multi-union model (Kuruvilla and Erickson, 2002). The multi-union model was largely inherited from the British labour institutions and regulations that aimed at controlling industrial conflict via a plethora of protective labour legislations (DeSousa, 1999; see also Chatterjee, 2006 for more discussion on the multiple unions in India). The Industrial Dispute Act 1947, the Trade Unions Act 1926 and the Industrial Employment (Standing Orders) Act 1946 represent just a few of many IR laws that the Indian government has a major influence. However, the actual impact of such laws on protecting workers' rights is not evident. In fact, as suggested by Saini and Budhwar (2004), the laws are so obsolete that they have not served effectively the interests for both employers and employees. Yet, being a democracy, India finds it difficult to reform the IR system. The Indian IR systems is exhibiting the tensions as it attempts to break away from the rigid policies. The need to compete both domestically and globally with the best in the world has forced Indian employers to strive for increased numerical flexibility (Kuruvila and Erickson, 2002). The use of HRM as a broad model of workplace justice was proposed to combine the HRM and IR reform effort, yet the degree of the success of such application has only been shown in some software companies as observed by Saini and Budhwar (2004). There are many challenges for foreign firms to cope with the complexity of the Indian institutions, especially dealing with varieties of laws and regulations.

Similar to the firms operating in China, strategic HRM among Indian companies are seen as weak (see Budhwar and Sparrow, 1997; 2002), but the focus on the functional HRM such as pay determination, recruitment, training and development, industrial relations, health and safety and expansion/reduction decisions is noticeable (Saini and Budhwar, 2004).

Indonesia

As the forth most populous nation with 238 million people, Indonesia is the world's largest archipelagic state with 17,000 large and small islands. Indonesia is represented by diverse ethnic groups with different languages, customs and traditions. The main group is Javanese, representing 41 percent of the population. Indonesia was a Dutch colony for over 350 years before the WWII; currently, 86 percent of the population are Muslims (CIA, 2008).

It appears that Indonesia's cultural heritage has been formed from the variety and multiplicity of ethnic groupings and religions. The world's four major religions – Islam, Buddhism, Hinduism and Christianity benignly coexist in the land of Indonesia, with the guardian of '*pancasila*'. It is important to understand the Pancasila's social principles in order to understand the Indonesia's contemporary cultural and institutional settings.

Pancasila was set up by the nation's founding father President Sukarno, and was built into the Indonesian Constitution in 1945. In recognising the difficulty of managing a country with people from many faiths and ethnic groups, the then Sukarno government reinforced culturally acceptable code 'pancasila', that signifies five principles – namely belief in one god, just and civilized humanity, unity of Indonesia, democracy guided by representative government and social justice for all people of Indonesia (Patung, 2006). This has since become the nation's ideology in guiding social interaction, IR and workplace practices.

Table 1. Comparison of Transparency International Corruption Perceptions Index (CPI) 2007

Country rank	Country/territory	2007 CPI score*
	Most clean countries	
1	Denmark, Finland and NZ	9.4
4	Singapore	9.3
34	Taiwan	5.7
43	Malaysia	5.1
72	China	3.5
72	India	3.5
84	Thailand	3.3
131	Philippines	2.5
143	Indonesia	2.3
	Most corrupted countries	
178	Iraq	1.5
179	Myanmar (Burma) and Somalia	1.4

CPI score relates to perceptions of the degree of corruption as seen by business people and risk analysts, and ranges from between 10 (highly clean) and 0 (highly corrupt).
Source: adapted from the Transparency International Corruption Perceptions Index 2007 (www.transparency.org).

Relevant to MNCs in Indonesia are the four powerful representative business groups: the Javanese society, the Mingankabaah community of Sumatra (largely Muslim with businesses mainly managed by women), the Batak community of North Sumatra (influenced by patriarchal and Dutch Christians) and the Peranakan – Chinese Indonesians (many with successful big business enterprises) (Nankervis and Putra, 2006). These four stereotyped groups represent the diversity of values, behaviours and interaction styles in the main fabric of Indonesian society.

Regardless how much effort the Indonesian government has put into propagating the Pancasila principles, the society has been regarded as one of the most corrupted nations in the world in terms of its judicial system and social justice (Global Corruption Report 2007). Among 8 economies surveyed, Indonesia is perceived by business and risk analysts as the least transparent one (see Table 1).

Concurrent with these social and institutional issues, Indonesia also faces a high level of unemployment rate and a lack of skilled and qualified professional, technical and managerial personnel in many industry sectors (Zanko and Ngui, 2003) along with inequitable access to education and inadequate quality of educational infrastructure (Nankervis and Putra, 2006).

The current IR systems embedded in the Pancasila principles aim to build 'an ideal society with peace, stability, disciplined and dedicated workforce, increased productivity and a commitment to improve workers' welfare' (Suwarno and Elliot, 2000, p. 131). However, there is no clear legal obligation on the part of workers and employers to comply with the commitment. In fact, the pancasila IR system had promoted the underlying tension between employers and employees directed by the government with restriction of only one official union – The All Indonesian Union of Workers. The new and amended IR legislation were in place since the early 2000s. This indicated a significant move towards a pluralist approach, allowing employers and employees to directly negotiate employment conditions. However, according to Nankervis and Putra (2006), the government still has tight grip on the IR issues. The Pacansila principle of 'democracy as guided by the government' is still strongly evident.

Furthermore, Indonesian cultural characteristics also permeate into the workplace, whereby the HRM philosophy emphasises the moral obligation between employers and employees and overrates employee loyalty against performance (Habir and Lasarati, 1999). Strategic HRM has only been pursued by large organizations, especially those foreign-owned companies. Many functional HRM such as recruitment and selection, training and development and performance management are still in their infancy, underdeveloped and less sophisticated (Nankervis and Putra, 2006). Many of these HRM practices also reflect the cultural and institutional elements of 'nepotism' and 'cronyism'.

Malaysia

Compared to China, India and Indonesia, Malaysia is a relatively small country with a population of 25 million. About 50 percent of the population are Malay; the rest are Chinese (24 percent), Indian (7 percent) and other ethnic groups (CIA, 2008). Similar to Indonesia, Islam is the dominant religion with 60 percent being Muslim in the country.

Malaysia is seen as a multi-ethnic society with racial division clearly defined. Abdullah (1997) crudely commented the racial issue in Malaysia as 'race was identified according to economic activities..... Malays are paddy cultivators, Indians are rubber tappers and Chinese businessmen' (cited from Mellahi and Wood, 2004, p. 202). It appears that Chinese, though less populated, control the economic power. It is the Malays who nevertheless control the parliament.

The cultural and institutional heritage of Malaysia stems from various sources. For instance, the Islamic values and principles may have influenced the majority of Muslim population; whilst Chinese and Indians might have adopted values and philosophies generated from Confucianism, Hinduism or Buddhism. Some western values may also exhibit due to the extensive colonial rule of Great Britain on Malaysia between the late eighteenth and nineteenth centuries (CIA, 2008).

According to Mellahi and Wood (2004), in Malaysia, collectivism comes to equate with traditional values and individualism with western values (p. 207). Hofstede (1997) found that Malaysia scored the highest on his Power Distance Index (along with other five ASEAN economies: Philippines, Indonesia, Singapore and Thailand). This indicates a very strong emphasis on hierarchy. This is understandable as the teaching from Islam, Confucius and Buddha has common and unified message of 'respecting elders, leaders and authority'. Noordin et al. (2002) identify Malaysia as a collective society because of its strong social relations, self-sacrifice and commitment to help each other. The GLOBE study[10] indicates that Malaysia also scored high on uncertainty avoidance (Gupta et al., 2002). Whilst there is an argument on the accuracy of the Hofstede's measurement on Malaysia because of its multi-ethnic groups, Lim's (2001) study found no significant difference between the Malays and the Chinese in work-related values.

Malaysia IR system reflects some of these cultural values, whereby the state has the tight control, employers have the final say and conflicts are minimized. Historically, because of the British colonial influence, the provisions of collective bargaining and minimum working conditions were legalized. When Malaysia started implementing the export strategy in the 1970s, a cost-effective IR was promoted and several IR rules and regulations to restrict unions activities were enacted, leading to the ban of unions eventually in the 1980s (Mellahi and Wood, 2004). In the 1990s, the concern was not so much on the restriction of collective bargaining, but on human resource development. As observed by Kuruvilla and Erickson (2002), the passing of the Human Resource Development Act in 1992 that established the Human Resource Development Fund (HRDF) required manufacturing firms to contribute the equivalent of 1 percent of their payroll to the HRDF, which is then used to subsidize the training expenses of contributing firms. On the surface, it appears that this act helped Malaysia to upskill their human resources to address the pressing issues of skill shortages (Stahl and Zheng, 2002). In reality, training programs were found to be less effective as expected (Kuruvilla and Erickson, 2002; Mellahi and Wood, 2004; Zheng et al., 2007).

The role of HRM in Malaysia companies is subject to much debate. Some argue that even though the Malaysia government determined to give more emphasis to human resource management by setting up the Ministry of Human Resources, the limited professional ability of HR managers imposed some limitation on this ambition. According to Kurruvilla and Erickson (2002), the HR function tended to occupy a low status in Malaysia companies and HR managers had little influence on the strategic management process. On the contrary, Todd and Peetz (2001) found evidence of the increasing strategic integration of the HR function in the Malaysia companies. HRM has rapidly become a growing field in Malaysia. Many companies, including MNCs seek to identify more appropriate and imaginative HRM solutions to address the growing issues of attraction, retention, employment involvement, performance management in the context of the rapid development of Malaysia economy with very low unemployment rate and high employee turnover rate (Mellahi and Wood, 2004).

The Philippines

Similar to Indonesia, the Philippines is an island state with more than 7100 islands. Dissimilarly, it has 81 percent of population claiming Roman Catholic faith, as against 86 percent of the Muslim population in Indonesia. The Philippines with a total population of 96 millions (CIA 2008) is also a much diversified society with many ethnic groups living side by

---

10 GLOBE stands for Global leadership and Organization Behaviour Effectiveness. It is the global joint research project launched by Robert House in 1993, involved about 62 countries. For further information, check http://www.thunderbird.edu/wwwfiles/ms/globe/ or read Culture, Leadership and Organizations: The GLOBE Study of 62 Cultures, by RJ House and his colleagues, Thousands Oaks: SAGE.

side. The largest ethnic group is called Tagalog (28 percent). However, as claimed by Jimenez (1993), most Filipinos were descendants of Malays migrating to the Philippines long before the Spanish settlement in 1521AD. After the US won the Spain-American War in 1898, it took over the Philippines till 1935. Hence, the culture of the Philippines reflects both the indigenous civilizations, which were blended with Hinduism and Buddhism brought along by Chinese, Indian and Malay traders, and Spanish and American influences. The Hispanic influence in the Philippines are most visible in its folk music, dance, art and religion.

Nonetheless, according to Hofstede and Bond (1988), the Philippines ranked quite low in the cultural dimension of individualism and high on power distance; these indices are similar to the values held by the Asia economies discussed above. However, Hofstede (2007) commented that the Philippines was the only two Asian nations (the other being Pakistan) that rated high on the short-term orientation. This implies that the Filipinos may value less on 'persistence and thrift', but opt for extravagance[11] and tend to pursue short-term solutions to the country's many social and economic problems.

Consequently, with these set of conflicting social and cultural values, the underlying logic of the Filipino IR system is to promote industrial peace and harmony, but the IR framework also appears less stable and fragmented (Kuruvilla and Erickson, 2002). The state plays a significant role in the IR legislation. In particular, the Martial law stipulated in 1972 changed the nature of the Filipino IR, which was originally taken from the US model. Subsequently, the IR policy undergone several stages of changes: 1) suppressing labour and keep costs low to facilitate the country's export-oriented industrialization process in the late 1970s; 2) developing highly fragmented and decentralized unions to calm down the dissent and maintain stability in the 1980s; 3) revising laws and regulations favourable to employers and to attract FDI in the 1990s (Jimenez, 1993; Kuruvilla and Erickson, 2002). In recent years, it appears that the changes in the workplace drive the changes in Philippine IR. Kuruvilla and Erickson (2002) comment that the Philippines's highly fragmented labour relations focus more on accelerating the move toward numerical flexibility driven by the needs to cut costs, this is line with the overall economic development strategy in the Philippines based on the competitive advantage of low costs.

HRM practices at the firm level in the Philippines closely follow the US moves. The study of Galang (2004) clearly concludes that despite the country difference and cultural impact, the prevalent of practices in hiring, training and development, performance appraisal prescribed in Western management can be found in most of the responding leading 100 Filipinos firms. Audea et al (2005) support such conclusion from their study of 128 local and foreign owned companies, which indicated that there was, on average, a fairly high level of adoption of HRM practices by all companies surveyed and their impact on firm performance was also significant, consistent with a strategic approach discussed in the US textbook. The result showed that foreign-owned firms tended to show a slightly higher level of adoption of high performance work practices than the domestic firms (Audea et al., 2005).

---

11 One could clearly see such example in the widow of the former dictator president, Mrs Imelda R. Marcos who was notorious of expensive collection of shoe, gown and jewellery while the country was in die poverty.

Singapore

As a city-state, Singapore has a population of 4.6 million, predominated by Chinese (77 percent), Malay (14 percent) and Indian (8 percent). Although multiple religions are allowed to practice, Buddhists take up 43 percent of population (CIA, 2008). Hence, the cultural fabric in Singapore is much influenced by Confucian and Buddhist values. However, Singapore is unique as it has built a nation, within a short period of time, with the most admirable order, disciplined and military-type administrative system.

Three elements are discussed below to better understand the institutional system in Singapore. First is 'authoritarian capitalism' that represents the unique Singaporean economic and political model. Khatri (2004) describes 'authoritarian capitalism' as to 'combine a selective degree of economic freedom and private property rights with strong-armed control over political life' (p. 223). This implies that the government has an ultimate control over all economic activities. Secondly, the control over economic affairs often extends to the social sphere of individual citizen's life. Singapore is also called 'nanny state' in which every citizen does exactly as told by the government that in turn takes care of all people's needs (Khatri, 2004). The third unique character of the institutional system in Singapore is that of 'crony capitalism', which represents a system whereby politicians, businesses and banks develop close relationships and businesses have to depend heavily on their relationships with the ruling party (Khatri, 2004; Khatri et al., 2006). Naturally, based on these characteristics, the Singaporean IR system must be tightly controlled by the ruling People's Action Party. Under this system, employers were given more power in determining workplace issues such as transfers, promotions, job assignments, terminations and hiring (Kurrivalla and Erickson, 2002).

Even though Singapore was built on the 'crony capitalism', as many Asian economies have modelled, its intention to create a pro-business environment to attract foreign investment since 1965 had somehow helped build the nation with a very open, clean and trade-oriented economy. Singapore was ranked as the world top most transparent nation in terms of its cleanness in corruption (see Table 1).

Long before other Asian economies' realization of the importance of FDI to boost their economic growth, Singapore had established the favourable investment and other economic policies to attract multinational companies. By 2004, multinationals produced more than 70 percent of the manufacturing output in Singapore and about 95 percent of tis total export. It is the gathering of multinational companies that has made Singapore the key regional trading and finance centre as well as the world's busiest port (Khatri, 2004).

A mix of multinational companies from different continents has brought to Singapore various management philosophies and practices. However, a strong government intervention at firm level plus professional organizations' reinforcement has well facilitated the process of 'unquestioned selective imitation' of western management practices (Khatri, 2004, p. 226). This attitude of selective imitation also affects on HRM practices in Singapore companies. Nevertheless, the pervasive transformation of HRM and emphasis of strategic HRM is perhaps most evident in Singapore than in any other Asian economies, even though HR functions are still perceived as in transition (Khatri, 2004). The government's excessive stress on training and development, and employers' focus on gaining functional flexibility at firm level (Kuruvilla and Erickson, 2002) had led to the negligence of addressing other important HR issues of recruitment and selection and proper performance management. These might be the main causes of the high job hopping and job turnover persistently reported in Singapore (Khatri et al., 2001; Zheng and Stahl, 2002; Zheng and Hu, 2008).

Taiwan

As an island state, Taiwan has the same size of population as Australia does. But 22 million people living in 12,000 square metres make Taiwan one of the most densely populated areas in the world (Wu, 2004). Predominated by Hans[12] (including 84 percent of Taiwanese Chinese whose ancestors resided in Taiwan before the KMT took over in 1947; and 14 percent of mainland Chinese or '*wai sheng ren*'), the culture characteristics of Taiwan are much in line with the Confucian values (Chen et al, 2005). Taiwan scored high on the long-term orientation scale and low on individualism (Hofstede and Bond, 1988).

For the past two decades, Taiwan has experienced an unprecedented transformation of its political system, such as abolition of the martial law (1987), right of universal suffrage (1995), and the election of the Democratic Progressive Party (DPP) into the office (2000) (Lee, 2000). The change of the political system has effect on the industrial relations. In the past, the government did not pay much attention on IR issues, mostly allowing the employers to take control of employment conditions. Such a *laissez-faire* approach was also aimed at encouraging the development of family-oriented small businesses, and attracting FDI and high-tech multinational companies with management know-how. With the democracy movement in recent years, there has been a greater move towards government intervention in protecting employees rights and welfare. Several pieces of legislation were re-enforced and re-established as many were already there, but not strongly enforced by the government (Lee, 2000; Zhu, 2003). A special piece of revised legislation is the Fair Labour Standards Law (FLAL) (1984) along with the establishment of the Council of Labour Affairs (1987). These have put much pressure on employers. The FLAL includes many specific and detailed regulations on employment conditions which many employers find hard to comply.

It was to addressing the compliance issue that Taiwanese companies started to push the idea of HRM on the high agenda (Lee, 2000). This is also in line with Taiwan's ambition to become a more service-oriented and knowledge-based economy (Zheng and Hu, 2008). Managing a knowledge economy requires companies to build HRM capabilities of attracting, selecting, training and retaining skilled labour. Several studies (eg. Lin, 1997; Huang, 1998; Zhu, Chen and Warner, 2000; Chen et al. 2005; Chen, 2007) concluded that strategic HRM has been adopted by Taiwanese companies. There appears much convergence of HRM practices among Taiwanese companies with those in the West (Chen, 2007); however, cultural and institutional factors may have caused some divergent practices particularly in the area of performance-based pay and appraisal systems (Wu, 2004). I will turn to this point of discussion in the later part of the chapter.

---

12 Hans resided beyond the border of mainland China would like them to be called by their national and geographical distinction, for example, Taiwanese, Singaporean or Thai and Vietnamese Chinese, instead of just 'Chinese' or 'overseas Chinese'. Yeung (2006) argues that loosely use of the term 'Chinese' for those born and already claimed citizenship in another nation is not appropriate or politically correct. He continues reasoning that many overseas Chinese would have 'discomfort' of being called 'huaren' or 'huajiao' or simply 'Chinese' as they are connotative of being only residents 'who are considered to be compatriots living in parts of the territory of China temporarily outside mainland Chinese control' (Yeung, 2006, p. 230). For this reason, I use the ancestral connotation of 'Han' here to avoid any discomfort.

Thailand

Thailand, formerly known as Siam is the land of smiles, occupied by two major ethnic groups: 85 percent ethnic Thai and 14 percent Chinese. With a total population of 65 million, of which 95 percent claimed to be Buddhists, Thailand is regarded as a typical collective society influenced by Buddhist and Confucian values, resisting to confrontation (Holmes and Tangtongtavy 1995). Thailand is the only South East nation that has never been colonized by the European power between sixteenth and twentieth centuries (CIA, 2008)

According to Hofstede (1991), Thailand scored high on collectivism and power distance, which are consistent with the Thai cultural norms that tend to emphasise the hierarchical structure as well as being kind to each other (Siengthai and Bechter 2004). Kamoche (2000) indicates that Thai social values typically appear to focus on harmonious social relations and reciprocity of goodness. Hofstede and Bond (1988) examined Thailand against the Confucian dynamism and found that Thailand (perhaps some of the participants were Chinese) scaled similarly to those in China, Taiwan and Singapore, focusing on the long-term orientation valuing 'persistence and thrift'. However, as argued by Siengthai and Bechter (2004), the Buddhist teaching of 'take it easy' (*jai yen yen*) and 'never mind' (*mai pen rai*) prevents Thai people from being proactive and taking risks, but the teaching help Thai have a high degree of tolerance of uncertainty.

Thailand formally established as a constitutional monarchy in 1932. Predominantly as an agriculture society, Thailand had only started its mission to launch the economic and social development under the rule of General Sarit Thanarat, who encouraged the country to adopt the import-substitution strategy and to protect and encourage domestic manufacturing industries during the 1960s and 1970s (Manusphaibool, 1993). The industrialization has since taken place with further positive public policies to encourage foreign investment. Thailand has changed its economic structure from a dominant agricultural society to become an industrialized economy (Onishi, 2006). The rapid economic growth appeared in the 1980s when many Japanese companies set up subsidiaries. According to Siengthai and Bechter (2004), Thailand was the largest recipient of Japanese FDI in ASEAN. Since the 1990s, many firms from Europe and America also set foots in Thailand, bring along different management practices (Wailerdsak and Suehiro 2004).

Concerning the IR system in Thailand, Deyo (1997) argued that Thailand closely followed the Japanese flexible –workplace model (see also Kurrivila and Erickson, 2002) and adopted enterprise union in recent years. There was a period of time (1945-1997) whereby the antagonistic nature of labour-management relations dominated. The power of Thai trade unions has been much diminished after the economic crisis in 1997. The relationship between employers and employees has exhibited more of a cooperative nature in recent time (Shibata, 2008).

The role of government in the IR system tends to be on and off, depending on whether the junta sees the labour organization as a threat to its power base or not. A number of times, the Labour Relations Act (1956) was lifted or amended due to the public pressure, eg. students' demonstration in 1973; but was banned or revised to restrict unions movement as a result of seeing the growing power of multiple unions. In 1990, Thailand had 618 unions registered, most of them are enterprise unions in the private sector that are prevented from joining the national labour federations (Manusphaibool, 1993). The employers associations tend to have little success in bringing their members together and substantially influence the collective bargaining process at the national industry level. However, they were very successful to nominate representatives on government committees, hence influencing the government's decision on the IR issues.

Similar to Singapore, a mix of multinationals brought along diverse HR and management practices to Thailand. Shibata (2008) summarized four common features of HRM practices in Thailand; they are: 1) promotion based on qualification and hierarchy (eg. blue-collar workers without university degree cannot be promoted to positions higher than their supervisors; 2) use of on-the-job training for workers and clerks and off-the-job training for managers and engineers; 3) performance evaluation applied to all employees; and 4) clearly defined jobs and roles. Siengthai and Bechter (2004) argue that the strategic HRM was not evident in the context of Thai companies simply because no sufficient professional competencies exhibited among HR managers in Thailand. Yet, Lawler and Atmiyanandana (2003) provide some evidence of using high performance work practices in Thailand, though the practices were constrained by the distinct culture. In assessing the relationship between employer and employee relationship in Thailand, Manusphaibool (1993, p. 249) shares the similar view:

> The relationship can not be easily understood.... Cultural and ethnical considerations remain crucial factors...An attitude of trust, co-operation and compromise tends to mark these relations. The decision to employ and to promote employees may be based substantially on personal connections, and the employees respect and gratitude to the employers and managers may reduce any form of challenge to managerial authority.

Summary

It is my attempt to provide snapshots of cultural and institutional characteristics of these eight chosen economies. However, each of these economy presents itself rather unique and complex system, which a page or two could hardly comprehensively describe[13]. I am hoping that this non-exhaustive introduction may inspire readers to go in depth and conduct further study on how the peculiar cultures and institutions of each Asian economy may have impact on effectively implementing MNCs' global HRM strategies. Despite the particularity of each economy, the analysis of the eight economies surges with some common themes. I discuss these commonalities as 5Cs (collectivist culture, command/control by state, concern on social issues, change in practices and contestation in play) to frame the key areas of the challenges faced by MNCs in managing people in Asia.

The eight Asian economies examined exhibit clearly a *collectivist* culture regardless whether the nation has been influenced by Confucianism, Buddhism, Islamism or Christianity. The collectivist culture also tend to go hand-in-hand with high scores in power distance (Hofstede, 2007). Culture has a direct impact on individual work behaviour, organization structure and societal order (Lawler et al., 2008). People management challenge

---

13 I am very grateful to read Lincoln's (2008) book review on 'The Embedded Corporation' about changing HRM practices of American and Japanese multinational companies whereby the author Sanford Jacoby apparently failed to provide more comprehensive description of Japanese historical, cultural and social influence on HRM practices. Lincoln (2008) writes that 'Admittedly, any writer on the institutional and cultural peculiarities of a country with whose complex institutions most readers will have limited familiarity faces the difficult decision of how deep to go and how much background to provide.' (p. 558). What a relief to read such a gracious comment! For those readers interested in reading more about the provocative views on Asian cultures and values, please check Greg Sheridan's interesting book on 'Asian Values, Western Dreams', Allen and Unwin, 1999.

would be particular acute for those MNCs whose national culture may be on the other end of the spectrum, ie. individualism and low power distance, as directly oppose to the collectivist social values in Asia.

A strong collectivism with high power distance may have led to a society whereby the state is esteemed to keep order and control. This is why we also see the governments of most Asian economies play a significant role in *controlling* and *commanding* the shift of economic policies, business system and IR system in all time. As commented by Edwards and Rees (2006), some of IHRM challenges would be related to understanding of governments and their ability to control and regulate their national economy, in particular their ability to regulate or deregulate their labour markets.

It seems that rapid economic development in Asia has also subsequently born some social costs. With pressure coming from domestic workers/employees calling for more protection and from international institutions demanding multinational companies to be more socially responsible in their operating countries (Sachdev, 2006; Engle, 2007), there has been a greater *concern* on social aspect of employees' welfare among the Asian nations. These social concerns have led some Asian states to formalise their IR legislation and to *seemingly* allow more pluralist multi-union representation at workplace as well as at societal level, though still under the tight grip of the government (as in the case of Singapore and Indonesia). China, in particular, seems moving toward giving unions rights to participate in enterprise management and collective bargaining in the MNCs (but still not in the state-owned companies). This signifies the similar move toward a pluralist approach in managing industrial relations in the Asian context. How MNCs respond to the labour management at firm level could be an area of challenge. Yet, more research on these challenges and impacts must be further assessed.

The fourth common theme appears among the chosen eight Asian economies is the *changing* pattern of HRM practices. Even among the most mature economies such as Singapore and Taiwan with the influence of multinational management practices being most apparent, the overall HRM practices exhibit different and changing patterns. These changes tend to be in line with the fluctuation of domestic labour market and demographic changes. In many parts of Asia, strategic HRM has not been taken overtly seriously. The feature of HRM functions is also diverse, with one economy exhibiting highly converged with the Western practices (eg. the Philippines); another showing underdevelopment and lack of sophistication in design and practice (eg. Indonesia); and many still in transitionary stage – picking what is best suited for the country (eg. China, Singapore and Malaysia).

Lastly, even though there are common Asian cultural characteristics, each economy faces the contestable issues within, regardless whether the nation is big or small. The *contestation* in play is caused not only by the stages of economic development but also by multiple ethnic, religion or even age groups with different values, interests and priorities. For example, even in the smallest city state as Singapore, with a population of just a few million, managers have to deal with culturally diversified workforce as there are large representation of Malays, Indians and Euroasians, besides the predominant Han group (Lawler et al., 2008). Not to mention in China, with a vast difference of economic development between its east and west regions, and different work attitude and behevior of people from north and south, plus multiple ethnic issues, managing diversity would be one of key IHRM challenge for MNCs operating in China. The studies done by Bae and Lawler (2000) in Korea and Chen et al. (2005) in Taiwan indicate how younger generations in the affluent societies resist the traditional Confucian-style management and would prefer different or more of western management and leadership styles. Chow (2004) advised managers of MNCs (including even ethnic Chinese managers) to be acutely aware of the sub-cultural differences in Hong Kong, Taiwan and Mainland China as there are vastly different HRM practices among the seemingly cultural similar societies. Needless to mention, the outcomes of the contestable issues have caused the social and racial unrest within each of the Asia economies that put the issues of terrorism, border safety and security on the HRM agenda in recent times (Scullion et al., 2007).

How have multinational companies managed to address the above mentioned challenges? The answer to the second research questions can only be found in the empirical studies of multinational companies in the region. In the following section, I will draw some results from the previous research of 529 MNCs in six Asian economies my colleagues and I have conducted. References to other studies will also be employed to illustrate the extent to which multinational companies might have responded to the cultural and institutional pressures.

Empirical Evidence

There appears a limited research on specifically examining the response of MNCs to the cultural and institutional pressures. A handful of studies, however, were devoted to evaluate the degree of MNC standardization versus local adaptation of HRM in the context of Asia (Bjorkman, 2004). From these studies, we could see some determinants relating to the cultural and institutional factors that have directed MNCs to either pursue the global integration or the local differentiation of HRM strategies. For example, Bjorkman and Lu (2001) studied 63 Chinese-Western joint ventures (JVEs) and found that the HRM practices in all these JVEs were similar to those of their MNCs' parent companies, signifying a high degree of MNC standardization. Interestingly, the reasons for standardization explained by Bjorkman and Lu (2001) were actually related to the weak institutionalization of the then Chinese HRM and industrial relations framework. Most respondents believed that the MNC parent company's HRM practices were more effective in leading to better firm performance; whilst local Chinese management practices needed much improvement. These results were supported by our separate study of the effect of HRM practices on the 74 small and medium sized enterprises' (SMEs) performance in China (Zheng et al., 2006). Our results demonstrated that most foreign-owned companies exhibited the western HRM practices and achieved better firm performance outcomes; positive performance outcomes were also significantly associated with the newly established domestic owned enterprises that adopted more of the western HRM practices than the state-owned companies.

We argue for the ownership type as a strong factor that determines the differences in HRM practices (Zheng et al., 2006; in press-PR). This argument was consistent with the outcomes generated from the recent study of Chow (2004). Local HRM practices carried the distinctiveness of parent firms even among the culturally similar societies. Chow's (2004) personal interviews with 33 HR professionals/experts, consultants and professors in the HR field in China, Taiwan and Hong Kong led to the conclusion that ownership forms differentiated HRM practices. HRM practices in the Taiwanese firms were different from ones in Hong Kong firms which were influenced somehow by the British rule, and the direct transplant of Taiwanese HRM practices in their subsidiaries in China was found difficult (see also Huo and Von Glinow, 1995). Extending this argument to different types of MNCs operating in the same region, Ngo et al (1998) found that the effects of country of origin on HRM practices were particularly evident among firms owned by the USA, Great Britain, Japan and Hong Kong. Lawler et al (1994) suggested similar existence of MNC's home-country effects in affiliates of US, European and Japanese firms operating in Thailand.

Perhaps, the part of the reasons why the parent country effects on HRM practices were particularly strong in Asia could be due to the prolonged unwillingness of the local government and employer groups to institutionalise the IR system and HRM professional practice standards. For the past three decades, in China as well as in most of Asian economies, the government's key economic policy has been to attract foreign capitals and encourage the establishment of MNCs locally. Although foreign companies might be under pressure to comply with various laws and regulations concerning issues such as social security payments and approval of labour contracts (Warner, 1996), they were more able to determine their own approach to HRM as the laws and regulations tend to be subject to various interpretation. Local governments also tended to take a *laissez faire* approach not to intervene HRM practice at firm level. Therefore, it appears that MNCs in the region tend to adopt the standardization of HRM strategies. For instance, Braun and Warner (2002) examined 6 American and 6 European MNCs operating in China and found that their HRM practices were much in line with the parent firms. Similarly, Low (1984) studied several aspects of management practices in American affiliates and local firms in Singapore and her results supported the notion that the practices of American affiliates were hardly the same with those local firms, instead their practices were the miniature of their US headquarters. A study by Lawler et al. (1994) on a cross-national comparison of HRM by indigenous Thai firms and MNCs illustrated that the US firms had emphasized most on performance-based pay, Japanese firms provided local employees with extensive training and local Thai firms did not emphasise either. Most recently, Budhwar and Bjorkman (2003) investigated 65 top HR managers in foreign firms operating in India and found that these foreign firms were able to 'adopt their respective HR practices in their operations with minor modifications' (cf. Saini and Budhwar, 2004, p. 133).

These findings seem suggesting that the degree of MNC standardization of HRM practices tend to be greater than localization in the economies with weak institutions. In the case of facing strong institutions, Brewster (1995) argued that a greater adaptation to the local environment would be required; this has been the evidence of MNCs operating in many European countries with more formalized institutions. In Singapore and Malaysia, the governments strongly emphasized skill development and training and have since institutionalized these practices at firm level, MNCs must comply with their training and development regulations (Khatri, 2004; Mellahi and Woods, 2004). Our study of training practices of 529 MNCs in Indonesia, Malaysia, the Philippines, Singapore, Taiwan and Thailand indicates a significantly larger proportion of training investment and practices in these two countries compared with other nations that did not have such training regulations (Zheng et al., 2007; cf. Zheng and Stahl, 2002). Nonetheless, from another study on the relationship between training and employee turnover (Zheng and Wong, 2007), we found that in fact these training were not effective in improving employee commitments as the predominant western HRM literature suggested (see for example Arthur, 1994; Huselid, 1995). The more training offered; the high rate of employee turnover occurred (Zheng and Wong, 2007). Singapore and Taiwan were among the economies with a highest employee turnover rate, followed by Malaysia (Zheng and Stahl, 2002). The extensive training programs offered were not relevant, especially not linked to local employees' career development, which was seen as the key reasons for high employee turnover among managerial and professional staff (Zheng et al., 2007). Companies' training practices in Singapore were also criticized by Khatri (2004) as they were not linked to MNCs' overall organizational strategy.

Having to comply with the local institutional requirements, MNCs seem having little choices to do otherwise. Sometimes, MNCs deliberately choose to follow the local customs and patterns of management with the belief that the local knows the best what needs to be done. For example, a study by As-Saber et al (1998) found that Australian MNCs operating in India preferred filling up key managerial positions using host country nationals (HCNs). Khilji's (2002) finding in the context of MNCs in Pakistan shared the similar view that it was better to employ HCNs as HR managers for the local operation than expatriates sent from the parent country because these local managers can better understand local employees' values and work attitudes, manage complex relationships with the host government and ensure proper compliance with local laws and regulations. The study on the evaluation of the link between the proportion of expatriates sent and the local employees turnover rate among eight economies (6 plus two Latin American countries, Chile and Mexico) also support this line of argument (Zheng and Wong, 2007). More expatriates, especially those incompetent expatriates sent from the headquarters in fact contributed to lower employee commitment in the high context cultures such as those Asian and Spanish cultures, as locals not only find hard to relate to expatriates, but also see less career development opportunity as expatriates taking up most of managerial positions in the local subsidiaries.

Even though MNCs deliberately tried to overcome the cultural and institutional barriers in transplanting management practices directly from home country to the host subsidiary, difficulty might occur as happened to the Taiwanese and Japanese MNCs operating in China (see Huo and von Glinow, 1995; Taylor, 1999; 2001). In the most recent study, Shibata (2008) contends that the work attitude and different labour division among Thai employees as well as inability of Japanese expatriates to manage work practices in Thailand were the key reasons for unsuccessful transfer of Japanese HRM practices to manufacturing plants in Thailand. Similar results were presented by Amante (1995) and Wilkinson et al (2001) to illustrate how Japanese MNCs failed to effectively transfer management practices to the Philippines and Malaysia due to the cultural and institutional constraints in the two countries.

Thus, it appears that the answer to the third research question 'have the cultural and institutional variables affected much on the choice of IHRM policies and practices made by MNCs?' would be 'yes'. However, the answer to the second research question 'how have MNCs managed to address these challenges?' was a bit diverse according to the empirical evidence presented above. On one hand, MNCs would like to keep consistency by standardising their IHRM practices across different operations in order to 'achieve unity of purpose through all employees worldwide adopting corporate value and codes of conduct' (Dowling et al., 2008, p. 216). On the other hand, MNCs are required to be sensitive and adaptive to the various host country cultures and customs as well as institutions regarding workers attitudes and behaviour and other employment conditions (Dowling et al., 2008). Failing to respond to these local needs would imply, at best, difficulty to manage local employees, and at worst, unsuccessful business ventures in the local operations. This leads us to address the fourth research question: 'what are other key variables, besides culture and institutions, that have affected MNCs' choice of IHRM policies and practices?' I will address the question with 'a balancing art' as it is a real art for MNCs to balance standardization and localization. It requires a comprehensive understanding of the correct formula of mixing key ingredients (variables *per se*) to master such balance.

Balancing Standardization and Localization

In addition to cultural and institutional factors, several other variables should be considered by MNCs when they shape their choice of standardization or localization of HRM practices in their cross-border operation. In the remaining sections, I will first discuss the eight non-exhaustive variables MNCs need to consider. These are *equity, mode of entry/operation, ownership, transnationality index, industry, operational effectiveness, nationality and subsidiary role* as forming what I call 'EMOTIONS' management to signify the delicacy of people management across the border. I will then analyse the alternative approach apart from the standardization and localization of HRM practices and argue for some benefits of using a regional or 'regiocentric' approach in creating stronger local impacts and fastening the global management diffusion process.

Managing 'EMOTIONS'

There are several variables MNCs need to consider, apart from cultural and institutional variables, in making the strategic choice of designing and implementing HRM policies and practices cross border. The variables concern interests both at corporate and subsidiary level. The first is *equity* – how much assets, stocks or shares of the local subsidiary held by a MNC determines the direction of management control. Bjorkman (2004) explains the amount of equity held by the MNC as an important indicator on whether MNCs could transfer their standardized HRM practices to their affiliates. Similarly, non-equity resources provided by the parent organization to the subsidiary also influence the local practices. For example, Hannon et al (1995) found among MNCs' subsidiaries in Taiwan that the more dependent a subsidiary was on the parent organization, the more globally standardized the HRM practices were. Consideration of equity and non-equity resources is particularly important nowadays as mergers and acquisitions of companies across nations and industries have been the lasting trend for the past decade and MNCs are particularly facing the challenge of managing change of ownership and balance of equity (Evan et al., 2002; Aguilera and Dencker, 2004; Schuler and Tarique, 2007).

Relating to the equity issue, *mode of entry/operation* is another factor MNCs need to evaluate when considering the choice of standardization and localization. A MNC's entry into the local market can be in the form of setting up independent subsidiary (ie. green-site operation) or collaborating with local companies via joint venture or alliance. Even though the national culture affects the choice of entry mode (Kogut and Singh, 1988), it is the mode of operation eventually affect the HRM practices in the local subsidiary (Schuler and Tarique, 2007). Kopp (1994) indicated that Japanese MNCs tended to send more expatriates to manage their green-site operation. Buckley et al. (2003) displayed how Shanghai Bell with many joint ventured partners' influence, had to variate their management practices between those of the parent firm in Belgium and those Chinese in the early reform period in China. However,

Motorola entered into the China market much later, and was able to establish as a wholly foreign owned company in Tianjin. Consequently, they adopted the global strategy and utilised the standardized HRM practices with a few minor modifications (Buckley et al., 2003). Hence, the decision to joint-venture with local company or not may lead to either more standardized or localized HRM practices[14].

Some argue that the reasons why Motorola was able to adopt the global standardized HR practices are because they were *wholly* owned by the foreign entity (an US firm *per se*). I have discussed the important of ownership earlier in determining the different HRM practices even in the culturally similar societies (cf. Chow, 2004). Hence, *ownership* is agued to be another important indicator of whether HRM practices of MNCs can be standardized or not. Ownership refers to both public and private ownership. In the Asia context, publicly owned companies can be those state-owned (such as many Mainland Chinese or Singaporean companies) or groups (such as Korean *Chaebols* or Japanese *Kaizen*), whilst private-owned firms are mainly those family businesses. Publicly owned MNCs, when operating overseas, may need to consider the balance of interests between domestic and foreign partners, hence more likely to adopt a standardized approach to keep consistency and control; whilst privately-owned companies would be easier to adapt and adopt the local practices. This is why Dowling et al (2008) suggest that many Chinese state-owned multinationals may face significant people management challenges as their international activities expand. A similar view was expressed by Shen (2006) in his examination of 10 Chinese international firms. However, in most of Singaporean and South-east Asian family businesses, the reverse practices occurred. This happened when the firms operating overseas, especially in UK and USA in fact adopted the local practices, and transferred these practices back to their own country (Yeung, 2006), creating effective global management knowledge flows (Gupta and Govindarajan, 1991). I will come back to address this later point shortly.

The fourth variable MNCs need to measure is the *'transnationality index'*. The transnationality index is measured by 'an average of ratio of foreign assets to total assets; foreign sales to total sales and foreign employment to total employment' (Dowling et al. 2008, p. 14). The higher index means the lower level of MNC reliance on its home-country domestic market. Behaviour of MNCs and their resultant HRM practices are influenced by the extent of home market the MNCs rely on. In another words, a small home market may drive companies to go global and hence cause them to be more willing to adapt to host country's local conditions as the host market may become strategically important for firm survival and growth. On the contrary, a large home market reduces the need for MNCs to think and act locally. For example, comparing the world top 10 large sized MNCs, no US firms were found to be among the list with the high transnationality index (UNCTAD, 2007). Hence, the US firms were often found to be taking an ethnocentric approach in their IHRM as many heavily relied on the domestic market. Senior management team who likely formed the international HRM strategy were trained domestically and inclined to use what they know best and practice most in domestic setting and transfer them to other operations. In contrast, many European firms were reported to have a relatively higher transnationality index and less likely to transfer the HR system but adapt to the local customs and practices (Dowling et al., 2008).

---

14 The issues and concern related to international HRM among the IJVs are beyond the scope of current discussion, for further information, please read Schuler (2001) and Schuler and Tarique (2007).

Industry represents another factor in determining whether HRM practices in MNCs should be integrated or differentiated across the border. Porter (1986) in evaluating the changing pattern of international competition, particularly distinguished the strategies used in multi-domestic and global industry. Firms in the multi-domestic industry see their competition from the domestic vantage point independent from overseas; whilst firms in the global industry depend on and are heavily influenced by their competitive position worldwide. One can see the examples of the multi-domestic firms in retails, distribution, financial and insurance sectors and the examples of the global firms in commercial aircraft, semiconductors and high-tech industry. According to Dowling et al. (2008), it is imperative for the global firms to adopt the consistent and standardized HR functions in order to achieve a competitive advantage. In contrast, the multi-domestic MNCs may well be subcontracting out their HR services in one location whilst in another location they may simply adopt less sophisticated HRM practices. In the study of 248 manufacturing and 261 service MNCs spreading across six Asian economies (Zheng et al., 2008), we found that the service MNCs engaging in retail, wholesale, banking and insurance businesses were resembled those in the multi-domestic industry and MNCs in the manufacturing sector were producing clothing, electronic products and toys, of which their market base is more global, in line with the characteristics of the global industry. HRM practices in these two sectors were different too. For example, 'word of mouth' was used more frequently in the service sector, with 51 percent of firms surveyed reporting the use of this method in recruitment and selection, whereas only 30 percent of firms surveyed in the manufacturing sector practised the same (Zheng et al., 2008). In average, standardized training practices were also adopted more among the manufacturing firms than in the service firms (Zheng et al., 2007). These results support the notion that MNCs in the multi-domestic industry may be required to be locally adaptable in order to compete successfully in the subsidiary market; whilst the MNCs in the global industry would need to maintain the standardized HR policies and practices to support firms' global strategy.

Based on specific industry requirement, MNCs may choose different control mechanism to manage their subsidiary's performance, ensuring the *operational effectiveness* of local subsidiary. Operational effectiveness is achieved through formal and informal control by MNC's headquarter (Dowling, et al., 2008). Corresponding to the formal control, HRM activities such as selection, training and rewards across MNC's different operations could be standardized. Informal control also called social control or 'clan control' as phrased by Ouchi (1981) refers to the necessity of MNCs as they operate in 'a complex multi-product, multicultural environment' to rely on individual and group informal interaction and networks as a 'nimble' control mechanism in order to achieve satisfactory subsidiary performance results (Dowling et al., 2008, p. 41). According to Engle et al. (2001), the more informal control is used to manage subsidiary performance, the more likely HR practices and process will be customized. Some authors argue that poor subsidiary performance could induce more formalized control, leading to more standardized HRM practices used by MNCs. In contrast, operational effectiveness and efficiency achieved by the subsidiary may change the entire role of subsidiary, making it the organizational champion to lead the localization of HRM practices (Birkinshaw and Hood, 1998; Ambos and Reitsberger, 2004), assuming that the effectiveness and efficiency were generated through localized best practices not by formal control.

Adding to this balancing scale is another familiar ingredient tended to be overlooked, which is MNC's country of origin – *nationality*. It has been reported in a number of studies that nationality of MNCs determine the extent to which firms would pursue an integrated global approach to HRM practices (see Lawler et al., 1994; Evan et al., 2002; Dowling et al., 2008). Examining 253 MNCs operating in Australia, Walsh (2001) found that despite the strong IR institutional setting in the Australian context, those Japanese and American owned firms still adopt more of their own home country HRM practices than those European or Australian owned firms. European MNCs were generally reported to have adapted to local customs and modified management practices than directly transferred their home country practices to the local subsidiary. With an increased amount of mergers and acquisitions and cross-border alliances (Evan et al., 2002; Schuler and Tarique, 2007), it is probably harder to identify the source of the origin of a certain MNC. However, nationality of senior management team and their attitude towards international operations may influence the choice made by MNCs in their international HRM strategies.

The last but not the least important ingredient for the balancing act is to evaluate the *subsidiary role* of a MNC. This variable is particularly important when many MNCs are operating in the knowledge economy. Effective knowledge transfer and management has become an important part of HRM activities as MNCs move towards the transnational model (Kamoche, 1997; Harzing and Noorderhaven, 2006). If a MNC is taken as a transnational network of capital, product and knowledge flows, each of their subsidiaries and those members in it would be the best channel to receive or provide knowledge constantly (Dowling et al., 2008). According to Gupta and Govindarajan (1991), a subsidiary in the global knowledge flow process can be either act as a local and/or global innovator, or as local and/or global implementer, depending on the magnitude and direction of knowledge flows. The implementer tends to heavily rely on knowledge from the parent company, whilst the innovator creates relevant local and global specific knowledge. If a subsidiary is a local innovator, likely, its HRM system would be more localized as the subsidiary develops more specific and relevant HRM policies and practices to suit its local needs. The subsidiary role in the global knowledge transfer process would impact the balance of standardization and localization in HRM. The more powerful a subsidiary is in determining the magnitude and direction of knowledge transfer of the MNC, the more reliance of the MNC on the subsidiary, the more likely the subsidiary would be in the stronger position in influencing the standardization and localization balance (Dowling et al., 2008).

The '*EMOTIONS*' variables are neither exhaustive nor exclusive. In fact, they have to be inclusive and interactive. The link among the headquarter variables such as equity, ownership, transnationality index and nationality is so close that they must be complementarily measured. The variables such as mode of operation, industry characteristics, roles played by the subsidiary and operational effectiveness are more locally based, hence need to be considered as a set to interact with the corporate variables. Besides, interplay of MNCs' corporate and national cultures in and out of their headquarters as well as corporate institutionalization of HRM policies and practices interplay with the local institutionalization must also be included in measuring the pros and cons of standardization and localization of HRM practices. This is truly an art form of mix and mesh to ensure the balance, and it is not an easy task for any MNC.

To address the challenge of people management among MNCs across border with so many unbound variables to consider and combine, I argue for the use of a regiocentric approach as a balanced approach to alleviate the extreme of an ethnocentric (standardized) and polycentric approach (localized) to international HRM. Benefits of using a regiocentric approach might be greater than what is discussed in Dowling et al. (2008, p. 84) as in terms of allowing a greater interaction among host country national and executives in the regional quarters. It may create a greater local impact, facilitate global knowledge transfer and potentially contribute to building a global workforce for real globalization. Therefore, in the remaining section, I will explain why the regiocentric approach is a better way to manage employees in Asia. The discussion aims at answering the last research question 'what are the implication of MNC's HRM choice to local impacts and global diffusion of management practices?'

Regionalization: Link to Local Impacts and Global Diffusion of Management Practices

In the main IHRM literature, international staffing approaches used by MNCs were categorised into four types: ethnocentric, polycentric, regiocentric and geocentric (Perlmutter, 1969; Heenan and Perlmuter, 1979). Ethnocentric and geocentric approaches are closely linked to standandized or integrated HRM practices, whilst polycentric approach is inclined to favour the localized practices. Regiocentric approach emphasises the use of managers and professionals available in the region instead of expatriates from the parent company or employees recruited from the specific local subsidiary. The approach effectively acts as a link for a MNC to 'gradually move from a purely ethnocentric or polycentric approach to a geocentric approach' (cf. Dowling et al., 2008, p. 84). There are a number of reasons why regiocentric approach should be used to manage the people management challenges in the context of MNCs in Asia.

First, the use of the regiocentric approach is *in line with the emergence of the focus on regionalization instead of globalization* in recent years. Zheng and Stahl (2002) argue that 'regionalization may serve as a better option to maintain nation-state status in the world system' whilst 'globalization tends to erode the sovereignty of the nation' (p. 20, cf. Ohmae, 1995). Hence, many Asian economies prefer to trade and operate within the region. The rise of regionalization occurred along with the rapid development of a number of economic and political blocs such as EU (European Unions), NAFTA (North America Free Trade Agreement), ASEAN (Association of South-East Asian Nations) and APEC (Asia Pacific Economic Cooperation) in the past decades. As indicated by Ghemawat (2005), global companies also take regionalization seriously as 'an alternative to further their cross border economic integration' (p. 100). We see the evidence of such regionalization in our study of 625 MNCs operating in eight APEC economies (six plus two Latin American economies, Chile and Mexico). It was found that most MNCs came from Asia economies within. 52 percent of MNCs responded indicated that their country of origin was from one of Asia economies. Among those, 46 percent were Japanese MNCs (Zheng and Stahl, 2002).

In addition to the mounting evidence showing that foreign trade and FDI were concentrated regionally (Ghemawat, 2005; Collinson and Rugman, 2007; UNCTAD, 2007), it appears that most MNCs in practice have already chosen to operate their business in blocks among Asia Pacific, Europe or America with their regional headquarters in place. However, it is not certain whether firms have truly used a regiocentric approach with a corresponding regional strategy. It is easier to set up regional offices, but it is harder to articulate a regional structure and relevant HRM practices. As commented by Ghemawat (2005, p. 104), a company with no regional office may still use regions as the building blocks to develop its global strategy, whilst a company with many regional HQs may still not have a clear focus. Hence, a physical regional structure is not as important as a firm actually practices a regional approach in articulating its strategy and managing its people to implement the regional strategy.

Second, use of the regiocentric approach in international HRM would help MNCs better *motivate and retain local and regional employees*. As discussed earlier, even though there are diverse culture values among different Asian economies, there were five commonalities (collective culture, control by the state, concern on social issues, change in HR practices and contestation in play) emerged as the key themes for MNCs to master. Use of the regiocentric approach incorporating these five themes will be more effective for several reasons. First, Asia is probably one of the most mobile region in terms of labour mobility rate. Because of the shortage of both high- and low-skilled labour (Zheng and Hu, 2008), many Asian economies have an extensive state plan and incentive programs to attract skilled professionals and physical workers abroad to boost local economic growth. The World Migration Report (2005) suggests that the labour migration from and within Asia will expand further as those high flying managers and professionals continue contributing to the high labour mobility rate. In addition, the number of low-skilled but legal migrants from the Philippines, Indonesia and Thailand flowing to Singapore, Taiwan and Malaysia will further increase, as the later economies desperately need foreign workers ton their infrastructure projects or domestic odd jobs which locals are reluctant to do (Zheng et al., 2008). Hence, managing employees of MNCs in any particular Asian economy is really about managing diverse workforce from different nationality, culture and social background. With the consideration of those five common themes discussed earlier, an integrated regional HRM strategy could better cater for the needs of diversified employees. Managing and motivating these diversified groups of employees has presented a real challenge to many HR managers in an increasing number of Asian economies (Kahtri et al., 2001). This is probably the second reason why the regional approach to international HRM is better because Asian employees of MNCs can see more career opportunities at the regional level rather than at the global level. Anecdotic evidence shows that a number of Chinese high level managers (close friends to the author) of some large multinational corporations in the region would prefer working in an Asian location to being relocated to the headquarter or subsidiary of the MNCs in America or Europe. Use of the regional approach is more able to address career aspiration of Asian employees and at the same time to meet their cultural and social needs.

Third, use of the regiocentric approach to people management will also help MNCs *better manage 'EMOTIONS'* – the eight key corporate and subsidiary variables that MNCs need to measure when considering the choice of the standardization and localization of HRM practices as previously discussed. Utilizing the regional approach leads MNCs to be more focused on the analysis of the data at the regional level, in turn to help conduct a more accurate assessment of the choice made. For example, instead of calculating the transnationality index based on the global figure, the firm can calculate what I would call the 'regionality index' based on the regional assets against total assets, regional sales against total sales and regional employment against the total employment. Similarly, the assessment of equity and non-equity resources can be carried out at the regional level. Both measurements will capture a more comprehensive picture of how MNCs impact on local and regional economy as well as the employment level. The extensive focus on the regional employment and economic issues also help MNCs gain a better corporate image among various stakeholders (ie government, trade unions and other social partners) at the local levels and likely to be voted as employer of choice in the region. Adoption of the regional approach reflects MNC's sensitivity to local and regional conditions, plus the key managerial positions tend to be filled up by local or regional employees. There is a greater chance for MNCs to enhance their ability to recruit and retain the best and brightest in the region.

Fourth, the regiocentric approach to people management will *facilitate better knowledge transfer and flow among MNCs and ensure faster diffusion of global management practices.* In fact, the regional approach can act as a bridge to help a MNC move from adopting a purely standardized or localized HRM system to implementing a truly global HRM strategy. The subsidiary role as 'local or global innovator' discussed by Gupta and Govindarajan (1991) earlier can be applied to the regional 'centre of excellence'. For example, General Electric claimed that their 'regional teams are the key to their company's globalization initiative'; Toyoto has fully exploited 'the power of regionalized thinking' (cited from Ghemawat, 2005, p. 100); and Hitachi established a regional RandD centre in China to transfer and develop new knowledge about air conditioners (Ying, 2005). These are the examples of global MNCs that have used the regiocentric approach to facilitate their knowledge transfer and flow to expand their global business eventually.

Lastly, use of the regiocentric approach in people management will not only help MNCs address the issues of culture and institutions in the region, but also look beyond the culture and institutions and tackle the core organisational issues in managing people. Zheng and Lamond (forthcoming) recently compared the different HRM issues faced by Asian and non-Asian owned companies and found that there were no significant differences. In fact, both types of firms face the similar challenges of attraction and retention of skilled labour in the region. We expect that the companies owned by those with a strong Confucian influence would emphasise more of loyalty and commitment, hence they would have achieved low levels of employee turnover rates. Nevertheless, the link between parent source and turnover in not clear. Zheng and Lamond (forthcoming) challenge the conventional thinking that culture is an additional explanatory factor to influence human resource management practices. Too many empirical studies in identifying different HRM practices cross border seems falling into the trap of 'culture imperative' instead of 'organizational imperative' (Chang and Tam, 2004, p. 25). Our study found that people management challenges are not dissimilar among Asian and non-Asian MNCs. Hence, MNCs operating in the Asia region should be encouraged to address the people management issue from the organisational perspective, in addition to the cultural and institutional perspective. Use of the regiocentric approach by MNCs may well help solving the puzzle of balancing the standardization and localization of HRM practices at the organizational level, whilst use of cultural and institutional hypothesis may only direct MNCs to look at the core of puzzle. Of course, there may be some other innovative methods that could be used to manage people among MNCs in Asia and to evaluate the divergent practices and outcomes in different Asian economies. It is however very likely that in the current climate of regionalization, regiocentric approach in people management by MNCs operating in the region could be more effective in leading to firm competitive advantage.

Conclusion

This chapter discussed the contextual factors that have impacted on people management practices in Asia. Although cultural and institutional theories were widely used to justify the different HRM practices and outcomes in the region, the empirical evidence does not support the hypothses that MNCs chose standardization or localization of HRM practices entirely because of culture and institutions. Organizations also need to evaluate 'EMOTIONS' variables to balance the needs at the corporate and subsidiary levels. Instead of focusing on the polarized end of standardization and localization, a more balance approach of 'regiocentrism' was suggested to help MNCs focus more on creating local and regional impacts in Asia region first and thereafter diffusing global management knowledge aimed at building truly global companies. To do so, it is necessary to address people management issues for MNCs operating in any region from the multilevel lens, but first still at the organizational level, then at local and regional cultural, social and institutional level, and finally global.

References

Abrahmson, E (1991). Managerial fads and fashions: the diffusion and rejections of innovations. *Academy of Management Review* **16**: 586-612.

Amante, MSV (1995). Employment and wage practices of Japanese firms in the Philippines: Convergence with Filipino-Chinese and Western-owned firms. *The International Journal of Human Resource Management* **6**(3): 642-655.

Aquilera, RV and Dencker, JC (2004). The role of human resource management in cross-border mergers and acquisitions. *The International Journal of Human Resource Management* **15**(10): 1355-1370.

As-Saber, SN, Dowling, PJ and Liesch, PW (1998). The role of human resource management in international joint ventures: A study of Australian-Indian joint ventures. *International Journal of Human Resource Management* **9**(5): 751-766.

Audea, T, Teo, STT and Crawford, J (2005). HRM professionals and their perceptions of HRM and firm performance in the Philippines. *The International Journal of Human Resource Management* **16**(4): 532-552.

Bae, J and Lawler J (2000). Organizational and HRM strategies in Korea: Impact on firm performance in am emerging economy. *Academy of Management Journal* **43**: 502-517.

Bamber, GJ, Lansbury, RD and Wailes, N (2004). eds, *International and comparative employment relations: globalisation and the developed market economies*, 4th edition, Crows Nest: Allen and Unwin.

Bamber, GJ, Park, F, Lee, C, Ross, PK and Braodbent, K (2000). eds, *Employment Relations in the Asia Pacific: Changing Approaches*. St Leonards: Allen and Unwin.

Barney, JB (1991). Firm resources and sustained competitive advantage. *Journal of Management* **17**:99-120.

Bartlett, CA and Ghoshal, S (1989). *Managing across Borders: The Transnational Solution*. Harvard Business School Press, Boston, MA.

Becker, J (2000). *The Chinese*, London: John Murray.

Birkinshaw, J and Hood, N (1998). Multinational subsidiary evolution: Capability and charter change in foreign owned subsidiary companies. *Academy of Management Review* **23**(4): 773-795.

Ambos, B and Reitsberger, WD (2004). Offshore centres of excellence: Social control and success. *Management International Review* **44**: 51-66.

Bjorkman, I (2004). Transfer of HRM to MNC affiliates in Asia-Pacific, in P. Budhwar, ed. *Managing Human Resources in Asia-Pacific*. London: Routledge, pp. 253-267.

Bjorkman, I and Lu, Y (2001). Institutionalization and bargaining power explanations of human resource management practices in international joint ventures – the case of Chinese-Western joint venture. *Organization Studies* **22**: 491-512.

Braun, WH and Warner, M (2002). Strategic human resource management in western multinationals in China: the differentiation of practices across different ownership forms. *Personnel Review* **31**: 553-579.

Brewster, C (1995). Towards a 'European' model of human resource management. *Journal of International Business Studies* **26**: 1-22.

Bruton, GD and Lau, CM (2008). Asian management research: status today and future outlook. *Journal of Management Studies* **45**(3): 636-659.

Buckley, PJ, Clegg, J and Tan, H (2003). The art of knowledge transfer: Secondary and reverse transfer in China's telecommunications manufacturing industry. *Management International Review* **43**(2): 67-93.

Budhwar, PS (2004). ed. *Managing Human Resources in Asia-Pacific*. London: Routledge.

Budhwar, PS and Bjorkman, I (2003). A corporate perspective on the management of human resources in foreign firms operating in India. *2003 International HRM conference,* Limerick, Ireland.

Budhwar, PS and Sparrow, P (1997). Evaluating levels of strategic integration and development of human resource management in India. *International Journal of Human Resource Management* **8**: 476-494.

Budhwar, PS and Sparrow, P (2002). Strategic HRM through the cultural looking glass: Mapping cognition of British and Indian HR managers. *Organization Studies* **23**(4): 599-638.

Central Intelligence Agency (CIA) (2008). *The World Factbook*, www.cia.gov accessed 9 September, 2008.

Chang, LY and Tam, T (2004). The making of Chinese business culture: Culture versus organizational imperatives, from E. T. Gomez and H. H. M. Hsiao, eds, *Chinese Enterprise, Transnationalism, and Identity*, London: RoutledgeCurzon.

Chatterjee, S (2006). Human resource management in India, in A. Nankervis, S Chatterjee and J Coffey, eds. *Perspectives of Human Resource Management in the Asia Pacific*, Frenchs Forest: Pearson Education Australia, pp. 41-62.

Chen, SJ (2007). Human resource strategy and unionization: evidence from Taiwan. *The International Journal of Human Resource Management* **18**(6): 1116-1131.

Chen, SJ, Lawler, JJ and Bae, J (2005). Convergence in human resource systems: A comparison of locally owned and MNC subsidiaries in Taiwan. *Human Resource Management* **44**(3): 237-256.

Child, J (1994). *Management in China during the Age of Reform*. Cambridge: Cambridge University Press.

China Labour Bulletin (2008). A Turning Point for China's Trade Unions. www.clb.org.hk accessed 5 September, 2008

Chow, I (2004).The impact of institutional context on human resource management in three Chinese societies. *Employee Relations* **26**(6): 626-642.

Clinton, RH (2003). *Living History*. London: Headline.

Collinson, S and Rugman, AM (2007). The regional character of Asian multinational enterprises. *Asia Pacific Journal of Management* **24**: 429-446.

Cooke, FL (2004). Foreign firms in China: Modelling HRM in a toy manufacturing corporation. *Human Resource Management Journal* **14**: 31-52.

Cooke, FL (2005). Employment relations in small commercial businesses in China. *Industrial Relations Journal* **36**: 19-37.

De Cieri, H, Cox, JW and Fenwick, M (2007). A review of international human resource management: Integration, interrogation, imitation. *International Journal of Management Reviews* **9**(4): 281-302.

Delery, JE and Doty, DH (1996). Modes of theorizing in strategic human resource management: Tests of universalistic, contingency, and configurational performance predictions. *Academy of Management Journal* **39**(4): 802-835.

DeSousa, V (1999). Colonialism and industrial relations in India, in S Kuruvilla and B Mundell, eds. *The Institutionalization of Industrial Relations in Developing Nations*. Stamford: Jai Press.

Deyo, FC (1997). Labour and post-Fordist industrial restructuring in East and Southeast Asia. *Work and Occupations* **24**(1): 97-118.

DiMaggio, PJ and Powell, W (1983). The iron cage revisited: Institutional isomorphism and collective rationality in organizational fields. *American Sociological Review* **48**: 147-160.

Dowling, PJ, Festing, M and Engle, AD (Sr.) (2008). *International Human Resource Management*. 5th edition, South Melbourne: Thomson, Australia

Early, PC and Mosakowski, E (2004). Cultural intelligence. *Harvard Business Review* **82**(10): 139-146.

Edwards, T and Rees, C (2006).eds. *International Human Resource Management: Globalization, National Systems and Multinational Companies*. Harlow: Prentice Hall.

Engle, A, Mendenhall, M, Powers, R and Stedham, Y (2001). Conceptualizing the global competency cube: A transnational model of human resource. *Journal of European Industrial Training*, **25**(7): 15-23.

Engle, RL (2007). Corporate social responsibility in host countries: a perspective from American managers. *Corporate Social Responsibility and Environmental Management* **14**: 16-27.

Evans, P, Pucik, V and Barsoux, JL (2002). *The Global Challenge: Frameworks for International Human Resource Management*. Boston: McGraw-Hill Irwin.

Farndale, E and Paauwe, J (2007). Uncovering competitive and institutional drivers of HRM practices in multinational corporations. *Human Resource Management Journal*, **17**(4): 355-375.

Ferner, A (1997). Country of origin effects and HRM in multinational companies. *Human Resource Management Journal*, **7**(1): 19-37.

Ferner, A, Quintanilla, J and Varul, M (2001). Country of origin effects, host country effects and the management of HR in multinationals. *Journal of World Business* **36**(2): 107-127.

Friedman, BA (2007). Globalization implications fro human resource management roles. *Employment Responsibility Rights Journal* **19**: 157-171.

Galang, MC (2004). The transferability question: comparing HRM practices in the Philippines with the US and Canada. *The International Journal of Human Resource Management* **15**(7): 1207-1233.

Ghemawat, P (2001). Distance still matters: the hard reality of global expansion. *Harvard Business Review* **79**(8): 137-147.

Ghemawat, P (2005). Regional strategies for global leadership. *Harvard Business Review* **83**(12): 98-108.

Global Corruption Report (2007). www.transparency.org accessed on 5 September 2008.

Greenwood, R and Hinings, CR (1996). Understanding radical organizational change: Bringing together the old and the new institutionalism. *Academy of Management Review*, **21**(4): 1022–1054.

Gupta, AK and Govindarajan, V (1991). Knowledge flows and the structure of control within multinational corporations. *Academy of Management Review* **16**(4): 768–792.

Gupta, V, Surie, G, Javidian, M and Chhokar, J (2002). Southern Asia cluster: Where the old meets the new?. *Journal of World Business* **37**: 16-27.

Habir, A and Lasarati, A (1999). HRM as competitive advantage in the new millennium – An Indonesian perspective. *International Journal of Manpower* **20**(8): 548-562.

Hannon, JM, Huang, IC and Jaw, BS (1995). International human resource strategy and its determinants: The case of subsidiaries in Taiwan. *Journal of International Business Studies* **26**(3): 531-554.

Harzing, AW and Noorderhaven, N (2006). Knowledge flows in MNCs: An empirical test and extension of Gupta and Govindarajan's typology of subsidiary roles. *International Business Review* **15**(3): 195-214.

Hofstede, G (1980). *Culture's Consequences: International Differences in Work-Related Values*. Beverly Hills: Sage.

Hofstede, G (1991). *Cultures and organizations: Software of the mind*. London: McGraw Hill.

Hofstede, G (2007). Asian management in the 21st century. *Asia Pacific Journal of Management* **24**(4): 411-420.

Hofstede, G and Bond, MH (1988). The Confucius connection: from cultural roots to economic growth. *Organizational Dynamics* **16**(4): 4-21.

Holmes, H and Tangtongtavy, S (1995). *Working with the Thais: A guide to managing in Thailand*. Bangkok: White Lotus.

Huang, TC (1998). The strategic level of human resource management and organizational performance: An empirical investigation. *Asia Pacific Journal of Human Resources* **36**(2): 59-72.

Huo, PY and von Glinow, MA (1995). On transplanting human resource practices to China: A culture-driven approach. *International Journal of Manpower* **16**(9): 3-15.

Huselid, MA (1995). The impact of human resource management practices on turnover, productivity, and corporate financial performance. *Academy of Management Journal* **38**(3): 635-672.

Jackson, S and Schuler, RS (1995). Understanding human resource management in the context of organizations and their environment. *Annual Review of Psychology* **46**:237-264.

Jiminez, RT (1993). The Philippines, in SJ Deery and RJ Mitchell, eds. *Labour Law and Industrial Relations in Asia*. Melbourne: Longman Cheshire, pp. 209-240

Kamoche, K. (1996). Strategic human resource management within a resource-capability view of the firm. *Journal of Management Studies* **33**(2): 213-233.

Kamoche, K. (1997). Knowledge creation and learning in international HRM. *The International Journal of Human Resource Management* **8**(2): 213-225.

Kamoche, K. (2000). From boom to bust: The challenge of managing people in Thailand. *The International Journal of Human Resource Management* **11**(2): 452-468.

Kanungo, RN and Mendonca, M (1994). Culture and performance improvement. *Productivity* **35**(3): 447-453.

Khatri, N (2004). HRM in Singapore, in P. Budhwar, ed. *Managing Human Resources in Asia-Pacific*. London: Routledge, pp. 221-237.

Khatri, N., Chong, TF and Budhwar, P (2001). Explaining employee turnover in an Asian context. *Human Resource Management Journal* **11**(1): 54-74.

Khatri, N, Tsang, E and Begley, T (2006). Cronyism: a cross-cultural analysis. *Journal of International Business Studies* **37**(1): 61-75.

Khilji, SN (2002). Modes of convergence and divergence: An integrative view of multinational practices in Pakistan. *International Journal of Human Resource Management* **13**(2): 232-253.

Kluckhohn, F and Strodtbeck, F (1961). *Variations in Value Orientations*. Evanston: Row Peterson.

Kogut, B and Singh, H (1988). The effect of national culture on the choice of entry mode. *Journal of International Business Studies* **19**: 411-432.

Kopp, R (1994). International HR policies and practices in Japanese, European and US Multinationals. *Human Resource Management* **33**(4): 581–99.

Kuruvilla, S and Erickson, C (2002). Change and transformation in Asian industrial relations, *Industrial Relations* **41**(2): 171-227.

Kuruvilla, S and Venkataratnam, CS (1996). Economic development and industrial relations: The case of south and Southeast Asia. *Industrial Relations* **27**(1): 9-23.

Laurent, A (1986). The cross-cultural puzzle of international human resource management. *Human Resource Management* **25**: 91-102.

Lawler, J and Atmiyanandana, V (2003). Human resource management in Thailand: A post-1997 update. *Asia Pacific Business Review* **9**: 165-185.

Lawler, J, Atmiyanandana, V and Zaidi, M (1994). A cross-national comparison of human resource management in indigenous and multinational firms in Thailand, in D Mitchell and D Lewin, eds. *International Perspectives and Challenges in Human Resoruce Management*. LA: UCLA.

Lawler, JJ, Walumbwa, FO and Bai, B (2008). National culture and cultural effects, in Michael M. Harris, ed. *Handbook of Research in International Human Resource Management*, New York: Lawrence Erlbaum Associates – Taylor and Francis Group, pp. 5-28.

Lee, JS (2000). Changing approaches to employment relations in Taiwan, in G Bamber et al. eds, *Employment Relations in the Asia Pacific: Changing Approaches*. St Leonards: Allen and Unwin, pp. 100-116.

Lim, L (2001). Work-related values of Malays and Chinese Malaysians. *International Journal of Cross Cultural Management* **1**(2): 209-226.

Lin, CY (1997). Human resource management in Taiwan: A future perspective. *International Journal of Human Resource Management* **8**(1): 29-43.

Low, P (1984). Singapore-based subsidiaries of US multinational and Singapore firms: A comparative management study. *Asia Pacific Journal of Management* **2**(1): 29-39.

Manusphaibool, S (1993). Thailand, in SJ Deery and RJ Mitchell, eds. *Labour Law and Industrial Relations in Asia*. Melbourne: Longman Cheshire, pp. 241-269.

Mellahi, K and Wood, GT (2004). HRM in Malaysia, in P. Budhwar, ed. *Managing Human Resources in Asia-Pacific*. London: Routledge, pp. 201-220.

Meyer, JW and Rowan, B (1977). Institutionalized organizations: formal structure as myth and ceremony. *American Journal of Sociology* **83**: 340-363.

Morishima, M (1995). Embedding HRM in a social context, *British Journal of Industrial Relations* **33**: 617-640.

Nankervis, AR and Putra, AG (2006). Human resource management in Indonesia, in A. Nankervis, S Chatterjee and J Coffey, eds. *Perspectives of Human Resource Management in the Asia Pacific*, Frenchs Forest: Pearson Education Australia, pp. 179-200.

Noordin, F, Willuiams, T and Zimmer, C (2002). Career commitment in collectivist and individualist cultures: A comparative study. *International Journal of Human Resource Management* **13**(1): 35-54.

Ohmae, K (1995). *The End of Nation State: The Rise of Regional Economies*. London: HaperCollins.

Onishi, J (2006). The transferability of Japanese HRM practices to Thailand. *Asia Pacific Journal of Human Resources* **44**(3): 260-275.

Ouchi, WG (1981). *Theory Z: How American Business can Meet the Japanese Challenge*. Reading: Addison-Wesley.

Patung (2006), Pancasila, accessed on 9 September 2008, http://www.indonesiamatters.com.

Perlmutter, HV (1969). The tortuous evolution of the multinational corporation. *Columbia Journal of World Business* **4**:9-18

Heenan, DA and Perlmutter, HV (1979). *Multinational Organization Development*. Reading: Addison-Wesley.

Pfeffer, J (1994). *Competitive Advantage through People: Unleashing the Power of the Workforce*. Boston: Harvard Business School Press.

Porter, ME (1986). Changing patterns of international competition. *California Management Review* **28**(2): 9-40.

Prahalad, CK. and Doz, Y (1987) *The Multinational Mission: Balancing Global Demands and Global Vision*, New York: Free Press.

Robbins, SP and Barnwell, N (2006). *Organization Theory: Concepts and Cases*, 5th Edition, Frenchs Forest: Pearson Education Australia.

Rosen, R, Digh, P, Singer, M and Phillips, C (2000). *Global Literacies – Lessons on Business Leadership and National Cultures*. New York: Simon and Schuster.

Sachdev, S (2006). Chapter 13: International corporate social responsibility and employment relations, in T Edwards and C Rees eds. *International Human Resource Management: Globalization, National Systems and Multinational Companies*. Harlow: Prentice Hall, pp. 262-286.

Saini, DS and Budhwar, PS (2006). HRM in India, in P Budhwar (2004). ed. *Managing Human Resources in Asia-Pacific*. London: Routledge, pp. 113-140.

Schneider, SC (1988). National versus corporate culture: implications for human resource management. *Human Resource Management* **27**: 231-246.

Schneider, SC and Barsoux, JL (2003). *Managing Across Cultures.* 2nd edition, Harlow: Prentice Hall.

Schuler, RS (2001). Human resource issue and activities in international joint ventures. *International Journal of Human Resource Management* **12**(1): 1-52.

Schuler, RS and Tarique, I (2007). International human resource management: a North American perspective, a thematic update and suggestions for future research. *The International Journal of Human Resource Management* **18**(5): 717-744.

Schuler, RS, Dowling, PJ and De Cieri, H (1993). An integrative framework of strategic international human resource management. *Journal of Management* **19**: 419-459.

Schuler, RS, Jackson, S and Luo, Y. (2004). *Managing Human Resources in Cross-Border Alliances.* London: Routledge.

Scullion, H, Collings, D and Gunnigle, P (2007). International human resource management in the 21st century: emerging themes and contemporary debates. *Human Resource Management Journal* **17**(4): 309-319.

Sen, A (2005). *The Argumentative Indian: Writings on Indian History, Culture and Identity.* London: Penguin,

Shen, J. (2006). Factors affecting international staffing in Chinese multinationals (MNEs). *The International Journal of Human Resource Management* **17**: 295-315.

Shibata, H (2008). The transfer of Japanese work practices to plants in Thailand. *International Journal Human Resource Management* **19**(2): 330-345.

Siengthai, S and Bechter, C (2004). HRM in Thailand, in P Budhwar (2004). ed. *Managing Human Resources in Asia-Pacific.* London: Routledge, pp. 141-172.

Sorge, A (2005). *The Global and the Local: Understanding the Dialectics of Business Systems.* New York: Oxford University Press.

Subramony, M (2006). Why organizations adopt some human resource management practices and reject others: An exploration of rationales. *Human Resource Management,* **45**(2): 195-210.

Suwarno, S and Elliott, J (2000). Changing approaches to employment relations in Indonesia, in G Bamber et al. eds, *Employment Relations in the Asia Pacific: Changing Approaches.* St Leonards: Allen and Unwin, pp. 129-144.

Taylor, B (1999). Patterns of control within Japanese manufacturing plants in China: Doubts about Japanization in Asia. *Journal of Management Studies* **36**(6): 853-73.

Taylor, B (2001). The management of labour in Japanese manufacturing plants in China. *International Journal of Human Resource Management* **12**(4): 601-620.

Taylor, S (2006). Emerging motivations for global HRM integration. In A. Ferner, J. Quintanilla and C. Sanchez-Runda (Eds.), *Multinationals, Institutions and the Construction of Transnational Practices.* New York: Palgrave, pp. 109-130.

Todd, P and Peetz, D (2001). Malaysian industrial relations at century's turn: Vision 2020 or a spector of the past?. *International Journal of Human Resource Management* **12**(8): 1365-1382.

Trompenaars, F (1993). *Riding the Waves of Culture: Understanding Diversity in Global Business.* New York: Irwin.

UNCTAD (2007). *World Investment Report 2007: Transnational Corporations, Extractive Industries and Development.* www.untad.org, accessed 3 September, 2008.

UNCTAD (2008). *Development and Globalization: Facts and Figures.* www.untad.org, accessed 3 September, 2008.

Wailerdsak, N and Suehiro, A (2004). Promotion systems and career development in Thailand: A case study of Siam cement. *International Journal Human Resource Management* **15**(1): 196-218.

Walsh, J (2001). Human resource management in foreign owned workplaces: evidence from Australia. *International Journal of Human Resource Management* **12**(3): 425-444.

Wang, D, Tsui, AS, Zhang, Y and Ma, L (2003). Employment relationships and firm performance: Evidence from an emerging economy. *Journal of Organizational Behaviour* **24**(5): 511.

Warner, M (1993). Human resource management 'with Chinese characteristics'. *International Journal of Human Resource Management* **4**(1): 151-170.

Warner, M (1996). Managing China's enterprise reforms: A new agenda for the 1990s. *Journal of General Management* **21**(3): 1-18.

Warner, M (1997). Management-labour relations in the new Chinese economy. *Human Resource Management Journal* **7**(4): 30-43.

Wilkinson, B, Gamble, J, Humphrey, J, Morris, J and Anthony, D (2001). The new international division of labour in Asian electronics: Work organization and human resources in Japan and Malaysia. *Journal of Management Studies* **38**(5): 675-695.

World Migration Report (2005), published by the International Organisation for Migration (IOM), http://www.iom.int/en/news/prwmr2005_presskit_en.shtml.

Wu, PC (2004). HRM in Taiwan, in P Budhwar (2004). ed. *Managing Human Resources in Asia-Pacific.* London: Routledge, pp. 93-112.

Yeung, HWC (2006). Change and continuity in Southeast Asian ethnic Chinese businesses. *Asia Pacific Journal of Management* **23**: 229-254.

Ying, T (2005). Electronics giant to open R and D company. *China Daily,* p. 4

Zanko, M and Ngui, M (2003), eds. *The Handbook of HRM Policies and Practices in Asia-Pacific Economies.* Volumes 1 and 2, Cheltenham: Edward Elgar.

Zhang, M (2003). Transferring human resource management across national boundaries: the case of the Chinese multinational companies in the UK. *Employee Relations* **25**: 613-626.

Zheng , C and Hu, MC (2008). Challenge to ICT manpower planning under the economic restructuring: empirical evidence from MNCs in Singapore and Taiwan. *Technology Forecasting and Social Change* **75**: 834-853.

Zheng, C and Lamond, D (in press). A critical review of human resource management studies in China. *International Journal of Human Resource Management.*

Zheng , C and Lamond, D (forthcoming). Organizational determinants of employee turnover for multinational companies in Asia. Special Issue, *Asia Pacific Journal of Management.*

Zheng , C and Wong, HY (2007). Company training reduces employee turnover, or does it?". *International Journal of Business and Management* **2**(6): 28-35.

Zheng , C, Hyland, P and Soosay, C (2007). Training practices of multinational companies in Asia. *Journal of European Industrial Training* **31**(6): 472-494.

Zheng , C, Soosay, . and Hyland, . (2008). Manufacturing to Asia: Who will win the emerging battle for talent between Dragons and Tigers? *Journal of Manufacturing Technology Management* **19**(1): 52-72.

Zheng, C and Stahl, C (2002). A Synthesis Report, in Stahl and Zheng, edited, *Skill Shortages, Training Needs and HRD Strategies of Multinational Companies in APEC Member Economies*. Singapore: APEC Secretariat.

Zheng, C, Morrison, M and O'Neill, G (2006). An empirical study of high performance work practices of Chinese SMEs. *The International Journal of Human Resource Management* **17**(10): 1772-1803.

Zhu, CJ (2006). Human Resource Management in China, in A. Nankervis, C Samir and J Coffey, eds. *Perspectives of Human Resource Management in the Asia Pacific*, Frenchs Forest: Pearson Education Australia, pp. 12-40.

Zhu, CJ and Dowling, PJ (2002). Staffing practices in transition: Some empirical evidence from China. *The International Journal of Human Resource Management* **13**: 569-597.

Zhu, Y (2003). The post-Asian financial crisis: changes in HRM in Taiwanese enterprises. Asia Pacific Business Review **9**(4):147-164.

Zhu, Y, Chen, I and Warner, M (2000). HRM in Taiwan: an empirical case study. *Human Resource Management Journal* **10**(4): 32-44.

Zucker, LG (1987). Institutional theories of organization. *Annual Review of Sociology* **13**: 443-464.

In: Handbook of Business and Finance
Editors: M. Bergmann and T. Faust, pp. 41-78

ISBN: 978-1-60692-855-4
© 2010 Nova Science Publishers, Inc.

Chapter 2

ALLIANCE PORTFOLIO INTERNATIONALIZATION[♦]

Dovev Lavie[1,] and Stewart R. Miller[2,•]*
[1] Faculty of Industrial Engineering and Management,
Technion – Israel Institute of Technology, Israel
[2] Department of Management, College of Business,
The University of Texas at San Antonio, San Antonio, USA

Abstract

Alliance research has traditionally focused on structural and relational aspects of the networks in which firms are situated, paying less attention to the inherent characteristics of their partners. This study introduces the notion of alliance portfolio internationalization (API), which refers to the degree of foreignness of partners in a firm's collection of immediate alliance relationships. We develop a framework to explain how API impacts firm performance. We suggest that as a firm's API increases, financial performance is expected to initially decline, then improve, and finally decline again. This sigmoid relationship between API and financial performance is ascribed to evolving learning effects that shape the net benefits of API. When the firm's alliance portfolio, on average, consists of proximate foreign partners, the firm may fail to recognize latent national differences, but at moderate levels of API, its absorptive capacity and specialized collaborative routines support the exchange of

---

[♦] The authors acknowledge the financial support received from CIBER - The U.S. Department of Education and the McCombs School of Business at the University of Texas at Austin. We appreciate the feedback received from Mason Carpenter, Ari Dotan, Avi Fiegenbaum, Niron Hashai, Jeff Loewenstein, Muir Macpherson, Gerry McNamara, Jim Westphal, and Gautam Ahuja. We also thank Ashu Manohar and Ekant Kohli for their research assistance. This chapter is based on a paper published in *Organization Science*, titled "Alliance Portfolio Internationalization and Firm Performance". This research was presented at the 2008 Sloan Industry Studies Conference in Boston, the 2008 Conference on Organizational Networks in Haifa University, the 2007 Strategic Management Society Conference in San Diego, and the 2007 Israel Strategy Conference in Jerusalem. A prior version of this chapter was presented at the 2006 Academy of Management Conference in Atlanta, the 2005 Copenhagen Conference on Strategic Management, and the Israeli Strategy and Entrepreneurship Forum held in 2005. Additional feedback was received from seminar participants at the University of Texas at Austin, University of Illinois-Urbana-Champaign and the Technion. Dovev Lavie acknowledges the financial support received from the Sloan Industry Studies program of the Alfred. P. Sloan Foundation and of the Landau Fellowship which is supported by the Taub Foundation.

[*] E-mail address: dlavie@ie.technion.ac.il, Tel: 972-4-8294435, Fax: 972-4-8295688. Address: Haifa 32000, Israel.

[•] E-mail address: stewart. miller@utsa.edu, Tel: 210-458-6868, Fax: 210-458-6868. Address: One UTSA Circle, San Antonio, TX 78249, USA.

valuable network resources. Nevertheless, high levels of API undermine firm performance because of the failure of collaborative routines and mounting liabilities of cross-national differences. We test the framework using data on the alliance portfolios of U.S.-based software firms during the period from 1990 to 2001. The results provide support for the sigmoid relationship as well as for our predictions that firms which have gained experience with foreign partners and maintained wholly owned subsidiaries in their partners' countries of origin can overcome some of the liabilities of API and better leverage its benefits.

Introduction

As interfirm alliances have gained in popularity, scholars have researched their performance implications. Traditionally, they have focused on structural and relational properties of alliance portfolios (Burt 1992, Coleman 1990, Granovetter 1985), paying less attention to the characteristic profile of firms' partners. We advance recent research that has begun to consider the characteristics of partners (e.g., Stuart 2000) by studying how the foreignness of partners in a firm's alliance portfolio affects the firm's performance.

Researchers long have argued that interorganizational relationships may affect economic outcomes (Granovetter 1985). This notion has been applied to the study of interfirm alliances, which are voluntary arrangements among independent firms that exchange or share resources and engage in the co-development or provision of products, services, or technologies (Gulati 1998). Alliances serve various purposes and take different forms, such as joint ventures, affiliation in research consortia, collaborative RandD, and joint marketing efforts. A firm's collection of immediate alliance partners thus can be referred to as an alliance portfolio. Prior research on alliance portfolios has studied the impact of the overall structure and nature of alliance relationships on firm-level outcomes. For example, several studies revealed how the number of alliances, and properties such as network density and structural holes, affect a firm's innovation output, new product development, revenue growth, market value, and profitability (Ahuja 2000a, Baum et al. 2000, Rothaermel 2001, Rowley et al. 2000, Stuart et al. 1999). Other studies demonstrated the performance implications of the evolving interfirm trust and strength of ties to partners (Granovetter 1985, Podolny 1994, Powell 1990, Uzzi 1996). In addition to these structural and relational aspects, recent research has investigated the resources, capabilities, and reputation of partners (Gulati and Higgins 2003, Lavie 2007, Rothaermel 2001, Stuart 2000, Stuart et al. 1999), acknowledging that the qualities of partners in the alliance portfolio may influence firm performance.

Within this research stream, however, the degree of foreignness of partners in a firm's alliance portfolio has remained unexplored. Despite the surge in scholarly work on cross-national alliances with foreign partners (e.g., Barkema and Vermeulen 1997, Das et al. 1998, Inkpen and Beamish 1997, Makino and Beamish 1998, Osborn and Baughn 1990, Reuer and Leiblein 2000, Steensma et al. 2005, Yan and Zeng 1999), scholars have neglected the overall level of internationalization of alliance portfolios while focusing on the benefits and costs of individual alliances with foreign partners. For example, prior studies have demonstrated that cross-national alliances typically generate lower market returns than domestic ones. We claim, however, that the contribution of a cross-national alliance to firm performance cannot be examined independently of the overall level of internationalization, which adjusts the liabilities and benefits associated with these alliances. Furthermore, whereas the internationalization literature has identified alliances as a mode of entry that can alleviate some of the liabilities of foreignness entailed by subsidiary-based internationalization (Contractor and Lorange 1988), we show that foreignness still creates unique challenges and opportunities for firms that internationalize their alliance portfolios.[1]

We introduce the concept of alliance portfolio internationalization (API) to describe the degree of foreignness of partners in a firm's alliance portfolio as defined by the cross-national differences between the firm's home country and its partners' countries of origin. Such dissimilarities include, for instance, cultural differences, geographical distance, institutional differences, and dissimilarities in levels of economic development (Ghemawat 2001). Adopting this definition, we examine how API influences the focal firm's financial performance and how the firm can increase the returns on API by leveraging its partnering experience and configuration of wholly owned subsidiaries in foreign countries.

In addressing the above issues we draw from the literature on absorptive capacity and organizational learning (Cohen and Levinthal 1990, Levitt and March 1988), which has been applied in the study of alliance management (Anand and Khanna 2000, Kale et al. 2002, Sampson 2005, Simonin 1997, Zollo et al. 2002) and internationalization (Barkema et al. 1996, Lane et al. 2001, Shenkar and Li 1999). We focus on the impact of national differences on the effectiveness of collaboration with foreign partners and study how firms learn to bridge national differences in their alliance portfolios.

We argue that firm performance varies with the level of API, following a sigmoid pattern. When a firm approaches proximate foreign partners its performance is likely to decline with API because of unobserved national differences. Then, as API increases to a moderate level, the firm's relative absorptive capacity and specialized interorganizational routines can support effective collaboration and resource exchange, which leads to a positive association between firm performance and API. However, at high levels of API, the alliance portfolio renders these collaborative routines ineffective and thus undermines firm performance. We further argue that learning from the firm's own experience with foreign partners and the ability to rely on the firm's own foreign subsidiaries in partners' countries of origin assist in bridging cross-national differences between the firm and its foreign partners, thus enhancing the value of API while restricting its drawbacks. Hence, our study complements recent research on the sigmoid performance effects of internationalization through wholly owned subsidiaries (Contractor et al. 2003, Lu and Beamish 2004) by considering internationalization of alliance portfolios and shifting from a focus on the number or dispersion of subsidiaries to the role of cross-national differences in pursuing internationalization. We explain the performance implications of API by following a learning perspective that highlights the role of collaborative routines for alliance management instead of resorting to explanations based on economies of scale and scope or coordination challenges associated with complexity and bounded rationality. Therefore, we offer a more fine-grained perspective that takes into account the characteristics of partners' countries of origin instead of simply referring to the distribution of countries of operation. We suggest that besides the need to coordinate partnering activities across countries, a firm's ability to learn how to bridge cross-national differences is essential for leveraging its international alliance portfolio.

---

[1] Our objective is to study the implications of international alliance portfolios relative to portfolios of alliances with domestic partners. We do not intend to examine the broader phenomenon of internationalization or the merits of alliances versus acquisitions or de novo establishments in foreign countries, which have been discussed elsewhere.

We advance alliance portfolio research by highlighting the degree of foreignness of partners in a firm's alliance portfolio. Our findings underscore the merits of identifying partners with desirable characteristics, and thus complement prior research that has emphasized structural and relational embeddedness in networks (e.g., Rowley et al. 2000). Unlike prior studies that examined the independent characteristics of partners (e.g., Stuart 2000), we focus on dissimilarities between partners' characteristics and those of the focal firm, and reveal a complex association between firm performance and API. Our analysis of national differences extends the alliance management literature, which has previously concentrated on the inherent abilities of firms to manage their alliances (e.g., Kale et al. 2002). We do so by suggesting that learning from partnering experience and coordination via organizational subsidiaries enhance the firm's ability to bridge cross-national differences and thus set boundary conditions for the API effect. Hence, this study advances our understanding of the desirable level of API and the means by which firms can cope with the challenges of managing international alliance portfolios. It integrates and extends frameworks of alliance portfolios and internationalization.

Theory

The implications of national differences have been primarily studied in the context of foreign direct investment, where it has been suggested that multinational firms suffer from liabilities of foreignness when entering foreign countries because of their unfamiliarity with the local business environment and their need to coordinate activities across spatial distance as well as coping with cultural, institutional, and economic differences between their home countries and the foreign countries they enter (Buckley and Casson 1976, Eden and Miller 2004, Hymer 1976, Zaheer 1995). Cross-national alliances have been considered an alternative mode of entry that can mitigate some of these liabilities (Contractor and Lorange 1988, Woodcock et al. 1994). Yet little attention has been paid to the configuration of the alliance portfolio and the implications of its degree of foreignness. Although some firms ally mostly with domestic partners of the same national background, other firms seek foreign partners with whom they maintain substantial cross-national differences. The notion of API refers to national differences between a firm's home country and its partners' countries of origin with respect to national culture, geographic location, institutional systems, and economic development. Hence, API embodies a dynamic learning process in which the firm gathers country-related information and interprets it in order to better understand its partners and facilitate collaboration. We proceed by reviewing the literature on types of benefits and liabilities associated with cross-national alliances (sections 2.1 and 2.2) and then conjecturing that these implications vary with the level of API (section 2.3), so that the relationship between firm performance and API follows a sigmoid pattern.

The Benefits of Cross-National Alliances

With mounting pressures for globalization, cross-national alliances extend the range of partnering benefits relative to alliances with domestic partners by bridging national boundaries and leveraging a firm's competitive advantage in foreign markets. Thus, international alliance portfolios may provide greater flexibility, responsiveness, adaptability to global market conditions, and reduction of risk and uncertainty (Eisenhardt and Schoonhoven 1996, Hagedoorn 1993, Harrigan 1988, Kogut and Kulatilaka 1993, Powell et al. 1996, Teece 1992) compared to domestic alliance portfolios. In particular, downstream alliances with foreign partners extend the firm's market reach to new product markets (Contractor and Lorange 1988). Upstream alliances with foreign partners offer new sources of attractive technologies and resources that are in short supply in the firm's home country (Eisenhardt and Schoonhoven 1996, Hagedoorn 1993). Thus, foreign partners can offer unique opportunities that domestic partners may be unable to furnish.

Therefore, API introduces unique partners to the alliance portfolio that provide access to network resources that may in turn spur innovation and organizational capabilities (Gulati 1999). For instance, scientific knowledge tends to be specialized, localized, and spatially concentrated (Jaffe et al. 1993), while firms' operations and practices are institutionalized by national business systems (Gertler 2001). Hence, a firm that approaches partners in remote countries and is exposed to the needs of distinctive foreign markets can extend the scope of its accessible knowledge base. Network resources that foreign partners offer can dislodge a firm from its own competency traps and stimulate innovations, new solutions, and new skills (Levinthal and March 1993). The firm may learn more from foreign partners with dissimilar national backgrounds and cultures than from domestic partners that have emerged in the same national environment and thus share national resources, values, beliefs, and social norms. Finally, collaboration with geographically distant partners relaxes proximity constraints, enabling the firm to coordinate activities and allocate them to qualified partners that enjoy comparative advantage in certain domains (Porter 1990), thus capitalizing on differential skills and asset costs. Furthermore, it enables the firm to distribute value-adding activities across different time zones, and thus enhance its responsiveness, shorten product development cycles, and operate more efficiently, especially in technology and service industries (Zaheer 2000). These benefits can enhance the firm's financial performance.

The Liabilities of Cross-National Alliances

Notwithstanding the above benefits, cross-national alliances entail unique challenges. Compared with domestic partners, collaboration with foreign partners requires greater investments in means of communication and transportation to support interaction. The firm's RandD investments may also increase when foreign partners require customization of products and technologies in accordance with local preferences and standards. Furthermore, the risk of undesirable resource spillover and misappropriation of value by the foreign partner (Hamel 1991, Lavie 2006) increases with the disparity in levels of economic development and appropriability regimes in partners' home countries. Information asymmetries may be exploited by foreign partners that possess superior knowledge of local customers' preferences, the positions of local competitors, and the regulatory environment in their countries (Yan and Gray 1994). In turn, the firm's alliance governance costs increase and its share of alliance proceeds decreases (Khanna et al. 1998). While cross-national alliances alleviate some of the liabilities of foreignness that wholly owned subsidiaries may face in foreign countries (Hymer 1976), they increase the firm's dependence on foreign partners (Lu and Beamish 2006) and make learning more challenging (Steensma and Lyles 2000).

Additionally, differences in national culture between the focal firm and its partners limit the scope of shared values and goals that are needed to elicit positive attitudes, reduce coordination costs, and facilitate social exchange in alliances (Parkhe 1991). Specifically, when a firm establishes alliances with foreign partners, differences in national culture and institutional environments limit familiarity and thus impair interfirm trust (Gulati 1995). Differences in value systems and behavioral tendencies of culturally distant partners may result in divergence in priorities and expectations and eventually in lack of commitment and irresolvable conflicts (Lane and Beamish 1990). Thus, unlike domestic alliances, cross-national alliances suffer from "double layered acculturation," which entails adjustment both to a foreign country and to an alien corporate culture (Barkema et al. 1996). These acculturation challenges may inhibit the informal chemistry that is essential for coordination and ongoing conflict resolution in alliances (Kale et al. 2000). They also result in relational ambiguities and mistrust that impair learning (Parkhe 1991, Simonin 1999) because they impede communication channels (Szulanski 1996) and weaken the firm's ability to absorb its partners' resources (Lane et al. 2001). Overall, these liabilities reduce the effectiveness of collaboration with foreign partners (Barkema et al. 1996, Kumar and Nti 1998, Lane and Lubatkin 1998) and weaken the firm's ability to effectively operate these alliances (Barkema et al. 1997, Pothukuchi et al. 2002), which can impair the firm's financial performance.

The Sigmoid Effect of Alliance Portfolio Internationalization on Firm Performance

The national differences between the focal firm and its foreign partners create opportunities for accessing unique network resources but also impose barriers to efficient resource exchange. These ambivalent influences imply that the association between API and firm performance may vary with the level of API.

At low levels of API, the benefits of internationalization are fairly limited since foreign partners, on average, are geographically and culturally proximate to the firm. Given the economic and institutional similarities in national environments, these partners' resources and skills may not be fully differentiated from those of domestic partners, and thus such foreign partners offer marginal opportunities to the focal firm. The firm's domestic partners can most likely offer access to similar resources and markets at reasonable premiums. Thus, API benefits are moderately accumulated at this stage. Moreover, although understanding of the national background of proximate foreign partners is considered straightforward, the firm may find it challenging to manage alliances with foreign partners because unwarranted assumptions of isomorphism can prevent recognition of critical national differences. This notion is known as the psychic distance paradox (O'Grady and Lane 1996), according to which perceived similarities between the firm's home country and proximate countries reduce managers' uncertainty about the nature of the foreign environment and thus lead them to believe that conducting business in these countries would be relatively easy (Kogut and Singh 1988). Consequently, managers pay limited attention to latent yet critical national differences, which hinders their ability to fully understand the foreign countries from which their partners originate, resulting in underperforming cross-national alliances. This suboptimal outcome is a reflection of negative transfer (Novick 1988), that is, the misapplication of a behavior learned in a familiar situation to a superficially similar situation, which yields poor outcomes. Thus, at low levels of API, perceived familiarity with partners' national backgrounds may in fact hinder rather than facilitate learning by masking potential barriers to collaboration with foreign partners. Instead of identifying, understanding, and bridging subtle national differences by learning about partners' countries of origin, the firm may tend to implement managerial practices used in its domestic alliances under the assumption that these practices would be applicable in its alliances with proximate foreign partners.

Even though the firm and its partners are likely to operate in similar environments at low levels of API, insensitivity to marginal national differences will limit the firm's attempts to identify and assimilate network resources emerging in its alliance portfolio (Lane et al. 2001). With inadequate understanding of national differences, the firm may avoid even minor modifications to its collaborative practices (Jensen and Szulanski 2004), which will hinder its capacity to effectively act upon opportunities for resource exchange (Szulanski 2000). Hence, impediments to communication and resource sharing, the inability to adapt to the foreign context, and inappropriate application of collaborative routines will impair firm performance (Baum and Ingram 1998). Untreated cross-national dissonance and its consequent negative implications will intensify with the level of API until a threshold is reached beyond which the firm begins to acknowledge meaningful national differences in its alliance portfolio. Therefore, at low levels of API, there will be a negative association between API and firm performance.

At moderate levels of API, wherein national differences are perceptible but not excessive, the firm can overcome the psychic distance paradox and consciously manage its internationalization by recognizing and pursuing opportunities to leverage its ties to foreign partners. Once unfamiliarity with the foreign environment and national differences are acknowledged, the firm and its partners can develop co-specialized assets and collaborative routines to overcome noticeable barriers to collaboration (Dyer and Singh 1998; Zollo et al. 2002) and to boost performance by supplanting misapplied domestic routines employed at low levels of API. Additionally, at moderate levels of API, foreign partners provide access to network resources that are sufficiently distinctive yet related to the focal firm's knowledge base. According to Cohen and Levinthal, such partial overlap facilitates interaction (1990: 133–134):

> Assuming a sufficient level of knowledge overlap to ensure effective communication, interactions across individuals who each possess diverse and different knowledge structure will augment the organization's capacity for making novel linkages and associations....The observation that the ideal knowledge structure for an organizational subunit should reflect only partially overlapping knowledge complemented by nonoverlapping diverse knowledge suggests an organizational tradeoff between diversity and communality of knowledge across individuals. While common knowledge improves communication, commonality should not be carried so far that diversity across individuals is substantially diminished.

In the interorganizational context, a firm operating at moderate levels of API is likely to both recognize the value of network resources and rely on partial communalities with its partners' national environments to facilitate collaboration and enhance the assimilation and use of external knowledge. The firm's relative absorptive capacity is context-specific and thus depends not only on the firm's own knowledge base but on the cultural compatibility with its foreign partners (Lane et al. 2001). Thus, at moderate levels of API, the firm and its foreign partners can still communicate and engage in effective collaboration, while identifying and bridging cognitive, normative, and regulatory institutional gaps that may impede resource exchange (Kostova and Zaheer 1999). This allows the firm to capitalize on valuable network resources (Gulati 1999, Lavie 2006) and realize the benefits of API. As API increases, the value of partners' network resources appreciates, with partners extending the firm's market scope and providing access to unique or low-cost assets, technologies, and products. Overall, these dynamics account for the positive association between firm performance and API at moderate levels of API.

Finally, high levels of API are likely to adversely affect performance. As cross-national distance in the alliance portfolio, on average, becomes extensive, substantial national dissimilarities with partners limit the effectiveness of standard organizational routines for managing alliances with highly distant partners. A firm must invest more in coping with national differences and develop idiosyncratic procedures for working with a pool of cross-nationally distant partners. Consequently, the benefits of collaboration may be suppressed by the liabilities of API, especially if the firm had first sought partners in proximate countries (Contractor et al. 2003, Johanson and Vahlne 1977) and thus lacks relevant collaborative routines for managing alliances with nationally distant partners.

Beyond a certain threshold, geographical, cultural, institutional, and economic differences between the firm and its foreign partners cause coordination costs to overshadow the marginal benefits of sharing resources and leveraging market opportunities with foreign partners (Hitt et al. 1997). The firm's alliance portfolio may then be dominated by irresolvable conflict, mistrust, lack of commitment, and ineffective interactions (Lane and Beamish 1990). Even when nationally distant partners offer access to unique opportunities and novel network resources, these resources become less relevant because of insufficient overlap between the knowledge bases and national backgrounds of the firm and its foreign partners (Cohen and Levinthal 1990). The firm's ability to absorb and use valuable network resources of peripheral partners is severely constrained owing to geographical, regulatory, and technical dissimilarities (Phene et al. 2006). Impediments to interorganizational learning and collaboration become exorbitant as relative absorptive capacity diminishes with increases in the cross-national differences between the firm and its foreign partners in the course of internationalization (Lane et al. 2001). With weakened relative absorptive capacity and extensive national differences, the firm may be incapable of overcoming unfamiliarity, nurturing interorganizational trust, and engaging in knowledge-sharing, adaptation, and coordination of value-adding activities with its foreign partners. Therefore, at high levels of API, the liabilities of API outweigh the benefits and negatively influence firm performance.

In sum, we suggest a sigmoid relationship between API and a firm's financial performance. Firm performance is expected to decline at low levels of API because of negative transfer effects, improve at moderate levels of API in which the firm maintains a balance between the value of network resources and the efficiency of its relative absorptive capacity, and finally decline again at high levels of API when national differences become unbridgeable.

> Hypothesis 1. Alliance portfolio internationalization will produce a sigmoid impact on financial performance, with performance first declining, then improving, and finally declining again with increases in alliance portfolio internationalization.

Alliance Portfolio Internationalization and Foreign Partnering Experience

Thus far we have argued that the benefits and liabilities of API vary with the extent of national differences between the firm and partners in its alliance portfolio. However, the firm's capacity to extract API benefits and cope with API liabilities may also depend on its past experience. In particular, the firm's accumulated experience with foreign partners can help the firm recognize national differences, bridge cultural, geographical, institutional, and economic differences, identify and assimilate valuable network resources, and leverage ties to nationally distant partners. In this sense, API involves experiential learning (Cyert and March 1963, Levitt and March 1988, Martin and Salomon 2003, Nelson and Winter 1982, Pennings et al. 1994) that can enhance the firm's capacity to manage its international alliance portfolio by nurturing collaborative routines. Prior research suggests that learning from the firm's accumulated partnering experience contributes to the firm's capacity to identify partnering opportunities, develop alliance relationships, and establish relational mechanisms that involve knowledge sharing, investments in relation-specific assets, complementary partner resources, and informal safeguards (Dyer and Singh 1998, Kale et al. 2000, Lorenzoni and Lipparini 1999). Thus, partnering experience assists in attracting prospective partners and learning how to collaborate more effectively, which reduces the costs of coordinating activities with partners and facilitates resource sharing in alliances (Das and Teng 1998).

Partnering experience is most valuable when it is applied in relevant domains. With increasing API, the firm faces rising difficulties in accessing and properly interpreting relevant information, in part because its experience with domestic partners becomes less useful when applied in cross-national alliances (Eriksson et al. 1997). The ability to overcome API challenges derives not simply from the general experience of the firm with any prior partners, but specifically from its experience in managing cross-national alliances. The firm's experience in foreign direct investment would also be of limited assistance in managing cross-national alliances, since such experience leads to the formalization of hierarchical governance procedures rather than to the emergence of collaborative routines. In turn, foreign partnering experience can assist in overcoming relational impediments that arise because of unfamiliarity and national differences between the firm and its partners at any level of API. The firm's accumulated foreign partnering experience offers a relevant context for developing collaborative routines that can then be applied in the firm's new alliances with foreign partners. Experience with foreign partners enables the firm to learn how to identify subtle differences in foreign environments, overcome cultural distance and communication barriers, build interorganizational trust, and improve the governance of its relationships with foreign partners. It can also enhance the firm's ability to seek foreign partners, coordinate activities with them and allocate activities to them, and resolve emerging conflicts when managing cross-national alliances. Thus, foreign partnering experience contributes to the evolution of collaborative routines that assist the firm in coping with the challenges imposed by cross-national distance to partners in its international alliance portfolio.

Besides nurturing the firm's collaborative routines, foreign partnering experience shapes the firm's relative absorptive capacity. The firm's absorptive capacity is cumulative in that the ability to identify, evaluate, assimilate, and apply external knowledge depends on the firm's past experience in relevant domains (Zahra and George 2002). Thus, the firm's experience in forming alliances with a pool of nationally distant partners reinforces its capacity to understand its partners' national environments and collaborate with partners that are increasingly distinctive in their characteristics (Lavie and Rosenkopf 2006). The more extensive the firm's experience with foreign partners, the greater its familiarity with diverse foreign environments, and the more developed its means for exploring external opportunities with foreign partners. The firm's expanding knowledge base and attention to national differences, which evolve with absorptive capacity, enhance its ability to communicate and interact with outsiders (Levitt and March 1988). Thus, accumulated experience with foreign partners exposes the firm to foreign environments (Barkema et al. 1996), which improves its ability to discern national idiosyncrasies and develop unique procedures for working with nationally distant foreign partners.

In sum, accumulated foreign partnering experience enhances a firm's relative absorptive capacity and leads to positive transfer effects in situations that would otherwise produce negative transfer of learned behavior (Novick 1988). Foreign partnering experience establishes familiarity with foreign environments and specialization in cross-national alliances, which enable the firm to develop and successfully apply collaborative routines in the internationalization process. The more extensive the firm's foreign partnering experience, the better it can cope with the challenges and leverage the benefits of API at any level of API, resulting in an enhanced performance trajectory.

> Hypothesis 2. Foreign partnering experience will positively moderate the trajectory of the relationship between financial performance and alliance portfolio internationalization.

Alliance Portfolio Internationalization and Subsidiary-Country Overlap

The notion of subsidiary-country overlap refers to the case in which a firm maintains wholly owned subsidiaries in the home countries of its foreign partners.[2] From a learning perspective, prior research notes that cross-national alliances may be disadvantaged relative to wholly owned subsidiaries because of firms' need to adjust to both organizational and national cultural environments when allying with foreign partners (Barkema et al. 1996). However, scholars have not considered the implications of simultaneously maintaining wholly owned subsidiaries and cross-national alliances in the same countries. We suggest that such subsidiary-country overlap can facilitate learning and enables the firm to neutralize API impediments, resulting in enhanced financial performance. Whereas foreign partnering experience helps the firm to cope with cross-national differences, subsidiary-country overlap bridges such differences.

To the extent that a firm maintains wholly owned subsidiaries in its partners' countries of origin, it can temper the effects of double-layered acculturation. By hiring local personnel and becoming familiar with national cultures and institutional environments through its subsidiaries, the firm can reduce, in a sense, its cultural, geographical, institutional, and economic distances to partners in those countries in which its subsidiaries are located. Even when a subsidiary is not directly involved in managing alliances with foreign partners, it can provide support to the corporate alliance function in its dealings

---

[2] From a transaction costs economics perspective (Williamson 1991), subsidiary-country overlap may be considered undesirable, because a transaction can be consummated more efficiently either internally, via the market, or through a hybrid mode, i.e., alliance. However, the literature on quasi-integration (Monteverde and Teece 1982) suggests that complementary use of alternative governance structures can mitigate opportunistic behavior while enhancing bargaining power and flexibility. These issues remain beyond the scope of our study.

with foreign partners that are based in the subsidiary's country of operation. Despite administrative inefficiencies and redundancies arising from subsidiary-country overlap, the firm can more effectively govern its alliances with foreign partners by relying on interorganizational trust and informal safeguards (Dyer and Singh 1998) that emerge as a result of more immediate interfirm relationships. The firm can maintain a closer relationship with foreign partners, increase face-to-face interaction, and respond more promptly to emerging conflicts (Kale et al. 2000). Frequent communication and embedded interpersonal relationships create opportunities for building trust, enhancing familiarity, sharing resources, and solving problems (Dyer and Nobeoka 2000, Uzzi 1996), thus reducing the effective distance between the firm and its foreign partners. The firm's foreign subsidiaries can collaborate more efficiently with foreign partners as a result of shorter travel distances, more straightforward communication, and increased cultural alignment. Their familiarity with the local administration and legal systems in its partners' home countries can prevent conflicts with partners or aid their resolution. Thus, by nurturing embedded relationships with foreign partners, subsidiary-country overlap moderates some unfamiliarity and learning impediments that API creates.

In addition, the presence of wholly owned subsidiaries in foreign countries assists the firm in its search for prospective foreign partners and facilitates access to their network resources. Subsidiary-country overlap enables the firm to overcome communication barriers as well as facilitates coordination and exchange of resources, so that the firm can better exploit partnering opportunities abroad and internalize its foreign partners' network resources (Lane et al. 2001, Szulanski 1996). Alliances with foreign partners are likely to receive greater attention as a result of the country-specific responsibilities of the firm's subsidiaries in partners' countries of origin. The direct or indirect involvement of foreign subsidiaries in such alliances facilitates knowledge flows between the parent firm and its foreign partners (Kurokawa et al. 2007), and thus improves the effectiveness of collaboration.

Essentially, subsidiary-country overlap circumvents national differences by bringing the firm closer to partners in its alliance portfolio, thus eliminating resistance to cooperation and supporting richer flows of specialized resources such as tacit knowledge. The local presence of the firm in its foreign partners' countries of origin can assist in overcoming cognitive constraints and facilitate interaction by reducing complexity and ambiguity surrounding the firm's collaborative engagements with these partners. In this sense, the firm decentralizes collaboration and relies on the local absorptive capacity of its subsidiaries, which enjoy greater familiarity with the environments of foreign partners. By relying on these subsidiaries' local understanding of foreign environments, the firm can better identify subtle national differences, bridge these differences by means of organizational adaptation, and determine the applicability of collaborative routines in the countries in which it operates. This, in turn, reduces the likelihood of negative transfer effects and enhances the effectiveness of collaboration with foreign partners. The more extensive the firm's subsidiary-country overlap, the better it can bridge cross-national differences and thus attenuate the challenges and leverage the benefits of API at any level of API, resulting in an enhanced performance trajectory.

Hypothesis 3. Subsidiary-country overlap will positively moderate the trajectory of the relationship between financial performance and alliance portfolio internationalization.

Methods

Data and Sample

We designed our study as a pooled time-series analysis of 330 U.S.-based firms in the software industry (SICs 7371 through 7374).[3] The dynamic and intensive alliance formation in this industry enhances the meaningfulness, reliability, and variance of our variables. Our interviews with industry experts suggested that firms in this industry historically derive 30%-40% of their revenues from alliances, which is higher than the 26% revenue contribution reported in an Andersen Consulting survey of Fortune 500 firms (Kalmbach and Roussel 1999). The software industry features a high proportion of publicly traded firms, ensuring the accessibility of financial information and reducing potential size- and age-related biases. For example, 40% of the 4,199 initial public offerings between 1990 and 2000 were issued by information technology firms (Loughran and Ritter 2004). Finally, the worldwide software industry is dominated by U.S.-based firms. For instance, a Standard and Poor's industry survey indicated that 23 of the top 25 software vendors are headquartered in the United States, with U.S.-based software firms accounting for half of the worldwide software market (Rudy 2000). Since our study focuses on a leading national industry, we control for the national comparative advantage of the home country (Porter 1990).

This study's timeframe spanned 1990 to 2001, with historical alliances tracked back to 1985 in order to incorporate information on active alliances that were formed before 1990. This five-year window follows standard assumptions regarding the typical duration of alliances (Stuart 2000), which in our sample was shorter than five years (1.823 years on average). The initial sample included all 367 U.S.-based publicly traded software firms that were active in the year 2001, had at least five years of records in the Compustat database, and engaged in at least one alliance during the timeframe of the study.[4]

Alliance records first were compiled from the SDC database and then extracted from alliance announcements and status reports in press releases and partner listings posted on the Factiva database, corporate websites, and Edgar SEC filings. Most announcements were cross-validated by at least two independent sources. By relying on multiple sources and tracking follow-up announcements and status reports, we minimized the occurrence of alliances that were announced but not realized. To further validate our data, we reviewed some of our alliance listings with a select group of corporate executives in charge of alliances. Following these procedures, alliance records were corroborated, corrected, added, or

---

[3] Most of the focal firms were single business firms. Specifically, 84% of the firms had only a primary SIC code, 10% had a single secondary SIC code, 5% had two secondary SIC codes, and less than 1% had three or four secondary SIC codes. Thus, it is appropriate to define the industry based on the primary SIC code.

[4] We determined that the focus on U.S.-based firms that were active in 2001 and had at least five Compustat records is not likely to introduce a selection bias based on the lack of differences between the sampled firms and the remaining 297 publicly traded firms in the industry in terms of total assets ($t = 1.43$, $p = 0.15$), revenues ($t = 0.53$, $p = 0.60$), number of employees ($t = 0.27$, $p = 0.79$), net income ($t = 1.48$, $p = 0.14$), cash ($t = 1.51$, $p = 0.13$), long-term debt ($t = 0.07$, $p = 0.95$), stock price ($t = 1.27$, $p = 0.20$), and other relevant measures. We further minimized potential selection bias in firms' decisions to engage in cross-national alliances by including firms that did not engage in alliances with foreign partners and those that engaged in any alliances in some years but not in others. Additionally, in the sample of publicly traded software firms that were active in 2001 and had at least five years of records in the Compustat database, only five firms had no alliances during the timeframe of the study. Thus, when we corrected for the above selection biases using a two-stage Heckman procedure, our findings were not significantly affected.

eliminated. For instance, we dropped several resale, licensing, and supply relationships that resembled arm's-length transactions rather than collaborative alliances. In total, 20,779 alliances involving 8,801 unique partners from various industries were identified. The 2,884 identified publicly traded partners in the sample accounted for 66% of the alliances. For each alliance we coded the announcement date, pre-specified duration or termination date,[5] number of participating partners, partners' identities, public status, and countries of origin as well as the strategic significance of the alliance, whether it was a joint venture, and its classification to categories of agreements: RandD, manufacturing, original equipment manufacturing/value-added resale, marketing and service, licensing, royalties, or supply. A given alliance could involve more than one type of agreement. Firm-specific data, such as SIC code, total assets, revenues, long-term debt, RandD expenses, and net income, were extracted on an annual basis from Compustat. Finally, listings of foreign subsidiaries were extracted from the Corporate Affiliations database.

The firm-year was used as the unit of analysis, because the dependent variable was defined at the firm level. The data for the 20,779 alliances were transformed to 52,739 alliance-year records by replicating alliance records for active years of alliance duration and by updating all time-variant variables. These records were transformed to 2,595 firm-year observations corresponding to the years 1990–2000 by pooling the data for all alliances in a firm's portfolio in a given year. Because of the lagging of variables and missing data, and because not all of the sampled firms engaged in alliances throughout the study's timeframe, the effective sample size used in multivariate analysis was restricted to 1,929 observations.[6] Of the 330 sampled firms with non-missing data, 288 had alliances with foreign partners (87%). At the firm-year level, 69% of the 1,929 observations corresponded to portfolios involving foreign partners.

Measures

Dependent Variable — Financial Performance. Following prior research on the performance implications of international operations (Contractor et al. 2003, Tallman and Li 1996), we used profitability as our financial performance measure. This measure is consistent with our net benefit analysis of API. We measured profitability by computing the firm's return on assets (ROA), which is a common measure used in financial performance studies (Brush et al. 2000, Hitt et al. 1997). ROA was calculated as the ratio of net income

---

[5] Alliance termination dates were unavailable for many alliances, because firms rarely announce alliance termination and occasionally maintain inactive alliances. If the date of alliance termination was unavailable from archival sources, when possible it was calculated based on alliance extension announcements and reports of active alliance status in a given year. For example, an alliance partner that was mentioned in a press release, in a 10K SEC form, or in listings of partners posted on the firm's corporate website was coded as active during the year in which such report was found. Alliance termination dates were available for 23% of the alliances. Remaining alliances were assumed to have a three-year duration based on the average specified duration of other alliances in the sample as well as assessments of industry experts. The imputation of alliance termination dates is a conventional practice in alliance research. For example, Stuart (2000) imputed alliance duration for all alliances using a linear depreciating weighting for alliances with an earlier date of formation. In our study, the use of imputation was reduced by searching alliance status reports and recording alliance termination dates when available. We controlled for the implications of this imputation procedure by including a separate control for the average age of alliances.

[6] Missing values occurred in several variables. For instance, information on R&D investments was missing for many firms that were not required to report these figures by SEC regulations.

to total assets in a given year and was updated annually for each focal firm. In line with Hitt et al. (1997), ROA was preferred to alternative measures of profitability such as return on equity, which is susceptible to capital structure differences across firms, and return on sales, which is based on revenue figures that are less relevant for software firms in the early stages of product development. Still, the three profitability measures were positively correlated in our sample ($p< 0.001$). We lagged all the explanatory variables and controls by one year relative to the dependent variable in our models in order to facilitate causal interpretation of our findings.

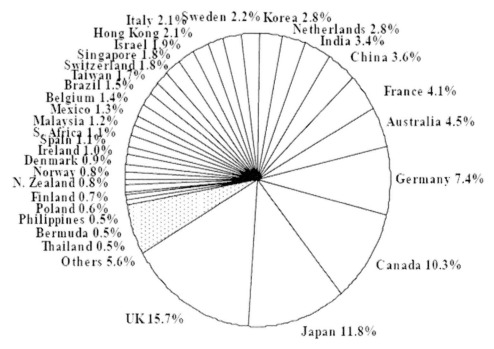

Figure 1. Distribution of Foreign Partners by Country of Origin.

Independent Variable — Alliance Portfolio Internationalization. API has not been studied nor measured in prior alliance research. For this reason, we have developed a robust measure of API that takes into account the cultural, geographical, institutional, and economic national differences between the focal firm and its partners (Ghemawat 2001). A partner's country of origin was defined based on the national location of its corporate headquarters (Erramilli 1996, Kogut and Singh 1988, Makino and Beamish 1998). Country of origin information was extracted from Compustat for publicly traded partners and from multiple sources, including Factiva, Hoover's, Mergent, SDC Platinum, and corporate websites, for privately held partners (see Figure 1 for the distribution of foreign partners' countries of origin).

Following the internationalization literature (Barkema et al. 1996, Johanson and Vahlne 1977), our first API indicator accounted for cross-country cultural differences in the alliance portfolio by incorporating information on the cultural distance between partners' countries of origin and the United States. Cultural distance was computed using Kogut and Singh's (1988) composite index of Hofstede's (1980) culture dimensions of uncertainty avoidance, individuality, tolerance of power distance, and masculinity-femininity. These dimensions are associated with national differences in administrative procedures, incentive systems, and cognitive, regulatory, and normative environments (e.g., Jensen and Szulanski 2004, Shane 1992). Despite its acknowledged limitations (Shenkar 2001), this measure has been employed extensively in internationalization studies (for a review, see Tihanyi et al. 2005), and the internationalization literature has yet to offer a better proxy for cultural national differences. The cultural distance between country c and the United States was indicated by $\sum_{d=1}^{4}(I_{dc} - I_{du})^2/4V_d$, where I_{dc} is the value of the Hofstede index for cultural dimension d of country c, u indicates the United States, and V_d represents the inter-country variance of the Hofstede index along dimension d. Accordingly, we computed the cultural distance of the alliance portfolio as the average cultural distance of firm i's partners in year t.

Our second API indicator captured the geographical distance in the alliance portfolio by calculating the average city-to-city great-circle distance in thousands of miles between the capital of the focal firm's country of origin and the capitals of its partners' countries in year t. Geographical distance often relates to transportation, communication, and other transactional activities that a firm conducts when collaborating with partners (Eden and Miller 2004) and has implications for partner familiarity and the governance of alliances (Grinblatt and Keloharju 2001, Gulati and Singh 1998).

A third set of indicators measured the institutional distance between the focal firm and its partners, assuming that differences in partners' administrative and political national environments can impact the effectiveness of collaboration. Specifically, regulatory, cognitive, and normative institutional differences may impact firms' legitimacy, resource transfer, organizational behavior, and investments across borders (Eden and Miller 2004, Henisz 2000, Jensen and Szulanski 2004, Kostova 1997, Kostova and Zaheer 1999, Xu and Shenkar 2002). We used World Bank data, which offered six aggregate country governance indicators: voice and accountability (VA), political stability and absence of violence (PV), government effectiveness (GE), regulatory quality (RQ), rule of law (RL), and control of corruption (CC) (Kaufmann et al. 2006).[7] For each of these k=6 indicators GI_k, we computed

---

[7] Voice and accountability (VA) measures the extent to which a country's citizens can elect their government, and enjoy freedom of expression, freedom of association, and free media. Political stability and absence of violence (PV) measures expectations that the government will be destabilized by unconstitutional or violent means. Government effectiveness (GE) measures the quality of public and civil services, and their independence from political pressures, as well as the quality of policy formulation and implementation, and the credibility of the government. Regulatory quality (RQ) measures the ability of the government to formulate and implement sound policies and regulations that permit and promote private sector development. Rule of law (RL) measures the extent to which agents have confidence in and abide by the rules of society, including the quality of contract enforcement, the police, and the courts, as well as the hazards of crime and violence. Control of corruption (CC) measures the extent to which public power is exercised for private gain, including both petty and grand forms of corruption, as well as "capture" of the state by elites and private interests. These six aggregated indicators were based on 276 items from 31 different sources. They were constructed using an unobserved components methodology and ranged between -2.5 and 2.5, with higher values corresponding to better governance outcomes. The aggregated indicators were measured in the years 1996, 1998, and 2000.

institutional distance measures using the formula $\sum_{j=1}^{n_{it}} \left| GI_{kc_j} - GI_{ku} \right| / n_{it}$, where c_j refers to partner j's country of origin, u indicates the United States, and n_{it} is the number of partners in firm i's portfolio in year t.

Finally, we incorporated information on economic distance, which refers to the relative economic development of partners' countries in the alliance portfolio. The national level of economic development is associated with local demand patterns and the utility of national resources (Haggard 1990) as well as with the nature of institutional regimes (Bollen and Jackman 1985, Kanungo and Jaeger 1990). We used the World Bank's World Development Indicators data on countries' gross domestic product per capita (GDPpc). The third API indicator was then calculated using the formula $\log\left(1 + \sum_{j=1}^{n_{it}} \left| GDPpc_{c_j} - GDPpc_u \right| / n_{it}\right)$, where c_j refers to partner j's country of origin, u indicates the United States, and n_{it} is the number of partners in firm i's portfolio in year t.

We constructed a composite API measure based on the factor score derived from the above nine indicators, which were highly correlated (see Table 1). We used principal components factor analysis with varimax rotation, which produced a single factor score with an eigenvalue of 7.321 and a standardized Cronbach alpha of 0.977. The resultant API measure was centered with the mean equal to 0 and standard deviation equal to 1. High values of this variable indicate a high degree of foreignness of partners.

Moderating Variables. The foreign partnering experience of firm i in year t was measured as the accumulated number of alliances that the firm formed with foreign partners between 1985 and the year t-1.8 Per hypothesis 2, this variable was expected to positively moderate the linear effect of API on financial performance. Subsidiary-country overlap was computed based on a series of dummy indicators that for each foreign partner j in firm i's alliance portfolio received a value of 1 if firm i operated a wholly owned subsidiary in partner j's country of origin during year t and a value of 0 otherwise. The subsidiary-country overlap was then calculated as the sum of these indicators divided by nit (the total number of foreign partners in firm i's alliance portfolio in year t). High values of this measure indicate greater overlap in the locations of the firm's subsidiaries and its partners' countries of origin. Per hypothesis 3, this variable was expected to positively moderate the linear effect of API.

Control Variables. We controlled for inter-industry variation by studying a single industry.9 Inter-temporal trends were controlled for with year dummy indicators. The remaining controls included annually updated firm- and portfolio-level variables. Firm-level controls included firm size as measured by the value of total assets, firm RandD intensity as measured by RandD investments divided by revenues, and firm solvency as measured by the

---

Interpolation was used to compute the 1997 and 1999 values, while values for years prior to 1996 were set to 1996 values. This approximation is consistent with the relative stability in countries' institutional environments (Kaufmann et al. 2006).

[8] The use of firm fixed effects and year dummies precluded age-related biases in the calculation of foreign partnering experience. In addition, only 20 cross-national alliances were tracked during the years 1985-1989, an annual average of 0.011 alliances per firm compared to 0.908 during the years 1990-2001. This finding reflects the surge in alliance formation during the 1990s and the fact that many of the firms in our sample did not commence operations before 1990. In fact, only 11 of the sampled firms engaged in cross-national alliances between 1985 and 1989, which mitigates concerns of potential left-censoring bias in the foreign partnering experience measure.

[9] An indicator of the firm's 4-digit SIC segment was not included as a control variable because of redundancy and the occurrence of complete separation when the firm fixed effects were also included in the tested models.

log-transformed ratio of cash to long-term debt. We included an indicator of whether the firm operated wholly owned subsidiaries in foreign countries because such subsidiaries can substitute for API as a mode of foreign market entry (e.g., Anderson and Gatignon 1986). All remaining interfirm heterogeneity was controlled for with firm fixed effects.

Portfolio-level controls included the adjusted size of the alliance portfolio (Ahuja 2000a, Baum et al. 2000, Stuart et al. 1999), which was computed by taking the logarithm of the number of alliances divided by the firm's total assets. Multi-partner alliances were decomposed to dyads for the purpose of calculating this control variable, which captures the firm's propensity to form alliances. We also controlled for the proportion of technology alliances to capture the type of alliances in the firm's portfolio. To control for changes in the contributions of alliances as they mature, we measured the average age of alliances in the portfolio. We controlled for the complexity of alliances in the portfolio by including a measure of the proportion of different agreement types per alliance. We included a measure of the percentage of equity joint ventures in the alliance portfolio to control for the alliance governance structure. The strategic significance of alliances was controlled by measuring the percentage of alliances that were identified as strategic in alliance announcements. In addition, we controlled for the similarity between the firm and its partners' businesses by calculating the proportion of alliances in which the partners operated in the same primary 4-digit SIC as the focal firm.

In order to further isolate the contribution of API to firm performance, we controlled for the firm's tendency to ally with foreign partners by measuring the number of foreign partners in the focal firm's alliance portfolio. Finally, we controlled for the diversity of partners' countries of origin (Goerzen and Beamish 2005, Tallman and Li 1996) using an inversed

Herfindahl index. For each firm i in year t, we used the formula $1 - \sum_{c=1}^{70} \left(n_{itc} / n_{it} \right)^2$, where n_{itc} is the number of firm i's partners that were headquartered in country c, and n_{it} is the total number of partners in firm i's alliance portfolio in year t. High values of this measure suggest that the firm's partners are dispersed across many countries.

Analysis

Table 1 provides descriptive statistics. Correlations were relatively low, with few exceptions. Firm size, the number of foreign partners, and foreign partnering experience were highly correlated, but we were able to isolate the influence of foreign partnering experience by controlling for firm size and the number of foreign partners. Similarly, subsidiary-country overlap was highly correlated with the indicator of a firm's foreign subsidiaries, since owning subsidiaries is a necessary condition for such overlap. Finally, the diversity of partners' countries of origin was highly correlated with our API indicators, which suggests that firms that extend their reach to distant foreign partners also tend to diversify their alliance portfolio across many countries. We isolated API effects by controlling for these related tendencies in all models. The standardized API measure ranged between -0.731 and 14.133, as illustrated in Figures 2-4.

Table 1. Descriptive Statistics and Pairwise Correlations for Sampled Firms during 1990-2000

Variable	N	Mean	S.D.	1.	2.	3.	4.	5.	6.	7.	8.	9.	10.	11.	12.
1. ROA_{t+1}	2388	-0.239	0.636												
2. Firm Age	2595	13.912	8.288	0.157***											
3. Firm Size	2310	0.412	2.005	0.048*	0.073***										
4. Firm R&D Intensity	2068	0.392	1.893	-0.257***	-0.078***	-0.024									
5. Firm Solvency	2295	4.506	4.516	0.088***	-0.113***	0.010	0.003								
6. Size of Alliance Portfolio	2595	-0.832	3.293	-0.183***	-0.276***	-0.293***	0.114***	0.036†							
7. % Technology Alliances	2595	0.477	0.315	0.070***	-0.009	0.025	0.030	0.084***	0.007						
8. Alliance Age	2595	1.823	0.633	0.063**	0.183***	0.025	-0.049*	0.013	-0.089***	-0.018					
9. Agreements Types/Alliance	2595	0.060	0.064	0.028	0.001	-0.013	0.015	0.031	-0.038†	0.394***	0.029				
10. % Joint Ventures	2595	0.043	0.141	0.015	0.094***	0.063**	-0.019	-0.165***	-0.065***	0.003	0.119***	0.043*			
11. % Strategic Alliances	2595	0.312	0.297	0.080***	0.061***	0.106***	-0.015	-0.020	-0.113***	0.178***	-0.013	0.283***	-0.081***		
12. Firm-Partner Industry Match	2445	0.253	0.294	0.050*	-0.112***	-0.025	0.016	0.215***	0.076***	0.138***	-0.064**	0.035†	-0.118***	0.009	
13. Firm Foreign Subsidiaries	2595	0.150	0.357	0.097***	0.307***	0.233***	-0.053*	-0.058**	-0.258***	0.062**	0.114***	0.036†	0.064**	0.153***	-0.018
14. Portfolio Internationalized	2595	0.615	0.487	-0.013***	-0.042*	0.116***	-0.033	0.137***	-0.131***	-0.009	0.088***	-0.001	0.041*	0.021	0.020
15. Number of Foreign Partners	2595	2.878	7.478	0.025	0.009	0.736***	-0.017	0.152***	-0.112***	0.052**	0.047*	-0.015	0.004	0.060**	0.024
16. Partner Country Diversity	2595	0.222	0.225	-0.010	-0.046*	0.051*	-0.015	0.097***	-0.074***	0.036	0.081***	0.003	0.001	0.004	-0.048*
17. Foreign Partnering Experience	2595	6.685	16.79	0.034†	0.047*	0.644***	-0.011	0.188***	-0.151***	0.092***	0.136***	0.004	-0.009	0.085***	0.030
18. Subsidiary-Country Overlap	2595	0.059	0.210	0.053**	0.089***	0.258***	-0.027	0.011	-0.151***	0.060**	0.077***	0.023	0.013	0.115***	0.001
19. Partner Cultural Distance	2595	0.296	0.485	0.139	-0.036†	0.008	-0.009	0.055**	0.004	-0.017	0.049*	0.091***	0.117***	0.059**	-0.123***
20. Partner Geographical Distance	2595	0.869	1.231	0.004	-0.035†	-0.000	-0.009	0.023	-0.017	-0.034†	0.046*	0.121***	0.143***	0.022	-0.121***
21. Partner Instit. VA Distance	2595	0.066	0.139	0.021	-0.160	0.013	-0.018	-0.021	-0.036†	-0.043*	0.062**	0.013	0.156***	-0.091***	-0.091***
22. Partner Instit. PV Distance	2595	0.052	0.129	0.009	0.002	0.013	-0.003	-0.025	-0.075***	-0.038†	0.060**	-0.021	0.055**	-0.040*	-0.022
23. Partner Instit. GE Distance	2595	0.100	0.183	0.014	-0.025	0.009	-0.013	-0.011	-0.039*	-0.062**	0.049*	0.027	0.176***	0.005	-0.109***
24. Partner Instit. RQ Distance	2595	0.083	0.137	0.007	-0.030	0.012	-0.004	0.033	-0.021	-0.036†	0.037†	0.054**	0.160***	0.013	-0.107***
25. Partner Instit. RL Distance	2595	0.066	0.148	0.005	-0.010	0.015	-0.008	-0.028	-0.057**	-0.057**	0.061**	-0.017	0.143***	-0.015	-0.058**
26. Partner Instit. CC Distance	2595	0.108	0.183	0.004	-0.022	0.012	-0.011	0.005	-0.044*	-0.054**	0.064**	0.008	0.162***	-0.016	-0.088***
27. Partner Economic Distance	2595	0.717	0.757	-0.009	-0.058**	0.060**	-0.028	0.053*	-0.062**	-0.029	0.065***	0.046*	0.121***	0.013	-0.077**

Table 1. Continued

Variable	13.	14.	15.	16.	17.	18.	19.	20.	21.	22.	23.	24.	25.	26.
28. Portfolio Internationalized	0.154***													
29. Number of Foreign Partners	0.216***	0.303***												
30. Partner Country Diversity	0.109***	0.782***	0.335***											
31. Foreign Partnering Experience	0.251***	0.226***	0.808***	0.225***										
32. Subsidiary-Country Overlap	0.601***	0.223***	0.287***	0.193**	0.310***									
33. Partner Cultural Distance	0.071***	0.483***	0.173***	0.561***	0.098***	0.062**								
34. Partner Geographical Distance	0.058**	0.558***	0.189***	0.630***	0.102***	0.072***	0.876***							
35. Partner Instit. VA Distance	0.048*	0.373***	0.119***	0.4301***	0.053**	0.034†	0.754***	0.717***						
36. Partner Instit. PV Distance	0.033†	0.317***	0.107***	0.383***	0.055**	0.040*	0.467***	0.527***	0.760***					
37. Partner Instit. GE Distance	0.054**	0.430***	0.134***	0.465***	0.065**	0.047*	0.775***	0.779***	0.890***	0.794***				
38. Partner Instit. RQ Distance	0.075**	0.481***	0.163***	0.519***	0.087***	0.065**	0.877***	0.851***	0.855***	0.683***	0.936***			
39. Partner Instit. RL Distance	0.046*	0.350***	0.115***	0.407***	0.049*	0.039*	0.597***	0.610***	0.892***	0.902***	0.909***	0.811***		
40. Partner Instit. CC Distance	0.053**	0.469***	0.155***	0.527***	0.079***	0.056**	0.754***	0.759***	0.896***	0.817***	0.960***	0.921***	0.939***	
41. Partner Economic Distance	0.114***	0.749***	0.284***	0.793***	0.184***	0.139***	0.762***	0.829***	0.692***	0.535***	0.768***	0.803***	0.632***	0.777***

Significance levels: $†$ p<0.1, * p<0.05, ** p<0.01, *** p<0.001.

Table 2. Probit Panel GEE Model for the Alliance Portfolio Internationalization

Dependent Variable: Portfolio Internationalized	First-Stage Model
Intercept	0.092 (0.454)
SIC 7371 Computer Programming Services	0.726 (0.259)
SIC 7372 Prepackaged Software	0.965* (0.434)
SIC 7373 Computer Integrated Systems Design	0.176 (0.452)
Year 1990	-1.662*** (0.407)
Year 1991	-1.180*** (0.334)
Year 1992	-1.033*** (0.277)
Year 1993	-1.021*** (0.269)
Year 1994	-0.777** (0.261)
Year 1995	-1.040*** (0.236)
Year 1996	-0.803*** (0.223)
Year 1997	-0.466* (0.213)
Year 1998	-0.149 (0.188)
Year 1999	-0.016 (0.158)
Firm Age	-0.026** (0.008)
Firm Size	2.776** (0.994)
Firm R&D Intensity	-0.035 (0.023)
Firm Solvency	0.037* (0.019)
Firm Foreign Subsidiaries	0.459 (0.299)
Foreign Partnering Experience	0.056* (0.024)
N Firm-Years	2062
N Firms	334
-2Log Likelihood	2153.0

Significance levels: † $p<0.1$, * $p<0.05$, ** $p<0.01$, *** $p<0.001$.

We used two-stage analysis for handling potential self-selection bias in firms' decisions to internationalize their alliance portfolios. Firms' internationalization strategies derive from their attributes and industry conditions, and thus are self-selected (Shaver 1998). Models that fail to take such biases into account may lead to erroneous conclusions. Specifically, firms' decisions to engage in alliances with foreign partners may vary by industry sector and depend on the availability of technological and financial resources. Whereas prior experience with foreign partners may encourage the use of alliances for pursuing internationalization, reliance on wholly owned subsidiaries as a mode of entry to foreign countries may attenuate this tendency. If firms self-select whether to engage in alliances with foreign partners, this self-selection may bias the estimates of API effects. Following Heckman (1979) we estimated two models. For the first stage we used a probit model that predicts whether or not the alliance portfolio of a firm is internationalized, i.e., includes at least one foreign partner in a particular year. This choice variable was regressed on the firm's industry sector (4-digit SIC), age, RandD intensity, and solvency, as well as on an indicator of whether it operated wholly owned foreign subsidiaries and a measure of its foreign partnering experience, while accounting for the panel structure of the data and controlling for year fixed effects (see Table 2). In the second-stage model we considered the firm's financial performance as our dependent variable while controlling for the inverse mills ratio (Lambda) to estimate the impact of self-selection based on the predicted values from the first-stage model.[10]

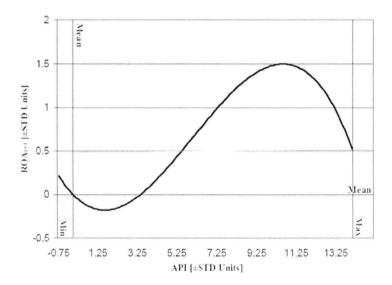

Figure 2. Predicted Profitability by API (Model 7).

---

[10] We considered alternative modeling techniques in order to account for unobserved heterogeneity and endogeneity. For lack of appropriate instruments that could serve for capturing the richness of our API construct, we did not use an instrumental variable approach. A two-stage Tobit model with selectivity, which can be considered a special case of the Heckman model, was inapplicable because our API variable was not zero-bounded. Finally, matched sampling techniques were of limited use because our sample already included the population of active U.S.-based publicly traded software firms with sufficient Compustat records. We have minimized unobserved heterogeneity and potential endogeneity by incorporating a multi-item measure of API that makes full use of the available data such as information on domestic alliances, as well as by following the two-stage Heckman procedure, including firm and year fixed effects, lagging the predictors, incorporating an extensive number of controls, and running numerous robustness tests.

Table 3. Fixed Effects Panel AR(1) Models for Financial Performance

Dependent Variable: ROA$_{t+1}$	Model 1	Model 2	Model 3	Model 4	Model 5	Model 6	Model 7
Intercept	0.065	0.060	-0.027	0.083	0.084	0.101	0.006
	(0.284)	(0.283)	(0.283)	(0.283)	(0.283)	(0.283)	(0.283)
Firm and Year Fixed Effects	Included	Included	Included	Included	Included	Included	Included
Firm Size	-0.023†	-0.024†	-0.023†	-0.032*	-0.025†	-0.032*	-0.310*
	(0.013)	(0.013)	(0.013)	(0.013)	(0.013)	(0.013)	(0.013)
Firm R&D Intensity	-0.064***	-0.065***	-0.064***	-0.065***	-0.065***	-0.066***	-0.065***
	(0.007)	(0.007)	(0.007)	(0.007)	(0.007)	(0.007)	(0.007)
Firm Solvency	0.008*	0.008*	0.008*	0.008*	0.008*	0.008*	0.008*
	(0.004)	(0.004)	(0.004)	(0.004)	(0.004)	(0.004)	(0.004)
Size of Alliance Portfolio	0.078***	0.076***	0.078***	0.079***	0.076***	0.079***	0.081***
	(0.015)	(0.015)	(0.015)	(0.015)	(0.015)	(0.015)	(0.015)
% Technology Alliances	0.012	0.012	0.009	0.008	0.011	0.007	0.002
	(0.058)	(0.058)	(0.058)	(0.058)	(0.058)	(0.058)	(0.057)
Alliance Age	0.051*	0.055*	0.057*	0.049*	0.057*	0.051*	0.052*
	(0.024)	(0.024)	(0.024)	(0.024)	(0.024)	(0.024)	(0.024)
Agreements Types per Alliance	-0.082	-0.072	-0.031	-0.035	-0.067	-0.036	0.019
	(0.283)	(0.283)	(0.281)	(0.283)	(0.283)	(0.283)	(0.281)
% Joint Ventures	-0.162	-0.136	-0.149	-0.132	-0.136	-0.132	-0.145
	(0.139)	(0.140)	(0.140)	(0.140)	(0.140)	(0.140)	(0.140)
% Strategic Alliances	-0.125*	-0.120*	-0.118†	-0.111†	-0.122*	-0.113†	-0.110†
	(0.061)	(0.061)	(0.060)	(0.061)	(0.061)	(0.061)	(0.060)
Firm-Partner Industry Match	0.071	0.067	0.055	0.056	0.068	0.058	0.044
	(0.061)	(0.061)	(0.061)	(0.061)	(0.061)	(0.061)	(0.061)
Firm Foreign Subsidiaries	0.013	0.016	0.015	0.014	0.017	0.015	0.019
	(0.050)	(0.050)	(0.050)	(0.050)	(0.055)	(0.055)	(0.055)
Number of Foreign Partners	0.003	0.004	0.003	-0.003	0.003	-0.003	-0.003
	(0.003)	(0.003)	(0.003)	(0.004)	(0.003)	(0.004)	(0.004)
Partner Country Diversity	-0.126†	-0.063	0.218†	-0.027	-0.071	-0.033	0.283*
	(0.071)	(0.083)	(0.118)	(0.087)	(0.084)	(0.087)	(0.121)
API		-0.025	-0.155***	-0.038*	-0.031†	-0.040*	-0.192***
		(0.017)	(0.042)	(0.018)	(0.017)	(0.018)	(0.044)
API^2			0.047**				0.053***
			(0.015)				(0.015)
API^3			-0.003**				-0.003**
			(0.001)				(0.001)
Foreign Partnering Experience				0.003†		0.003†	0.002
				(0.001)		(0.001)	(0.001)
API x Foreign Partnering Experience				0.004**		0.003**	0.004**
				(0.001)		(0.001)	(0.001)
Subsidiary-Country Overlap					-0.004	-0.002	-0.018
					(0.077)	(0.077)	(0.076)
API x Subsidiary-Country Overlap					0.210**	0.174*	0.190*
					(0.079)	(0.081)	(0.081)
Correction for Self-Selection (λ)	-0.484**	-0.510**	-0.491**	-0.518**	-0.535**	-0.540***	-0.520**
	(0.168)	(0.169)	(0.168)	(0.169)	(0.169)	(0.170)	(0.169)
AR(1) Parameter	-0.029	-0.030	-0.036	-0.025	-0.030	-0.024	-0.032
N Firm-Years	1929	1929	1929	1929	1929	1929	1929
N Firms	330	330	330	330	330	330	330
-2Log Likelihood	2231.1	2228.9	2217.7	2219.2	2221.9	2214.6	2200.2
Δ -2LL		2.2	13.4**	11.9**	9.2*	16.5**	30.9***

Significance levels: $\dagger$ p<0.1, * p<0.05, ** p<0.01, *** p<0.001.

We implemented our second-stage models using cross-section time-series regressions with firm fixed effects. Fixed effects models control for unobserved heterogeneity in the form of time-invariant variables and in our case were found to be superior to random effects models based on the Hausman (1978) test ($\chi^2_{df=21} = 230.37$, $p < 0.001$). The inclusion of firm fixed effects suggests that the reported models explain within-firm variation in performance over time rather than interfirm variation in performance. In addition, the analysis of panel data raises concerns about serial correlation of errors within cross-sections, which may deflate standard errors and inflate significance levels. Autocorrelation was treated by incorporating first-order autoregressive errors in the tested models, assuming correlation of errors across adjacent years.[11] Thus, the tested models took the form: $y_{i,t+1} = \alpha + \beta x_{i,t} + u_i + \varepsilon_{i,t}$, where $\varepsilon_{i,t} = \rho \varepsilon_{i,t-1} + \mu_{i,t}$ and $-1 < \rho < 1$. In this equation, u_i represents the firm fixed effects and ρ is the autoregressive AR(1) parameter, which has a zero mean, homoskedastic, and serially uncorrelated error term $\mu_{i,t}$. These models were estimated using maximum likelihood estimators, with missing values subject to listwise deletion. The results are reported in Table 3 in which Model 1 is the baseline model that includes the control variables. Model 2 introduces the linear term of API, while Model 3 adds the quadratic and cubic terms of API in order to test hypothesis 1. Models 4 and 5 correspondingly introduce the interaction terms of API with foreign partnering experience and subsidiary-country overlap in order to test hypotheses 2 and 3. Model 6 includes both interactions, with Model 7 serving as the full model.

We relied on the partial models for testing our hypotheses, since tests for potential multicollinearity indicated that the maximum VIF index in the full model (Model 7) exceeds the critical value of 10 (Kleinbaum et al. 1998). The high VIF values were ascribed to the multiple occurrences of the main effect (API) in the explanatory variables and interactions, and thus fell to conventional levels when the quadratic and cubic terms of API were dropped (Model 6). Still, no symptoms of multicollinearity were present in the full model (Maddala 2001). The contributions of API and its related interaction effects were evaluated using log likelihood ratio tests comparing each model to the baseline model.

Results

Table 2 reports the results of the first-stage model, predicting the likelihood of the alliance portfolio becoming internationalized. The internationalization of alliance portfolios has gradually gained popularity in recent years as indicated by year effects, primarily in the prepackaged software sector ($\beta = 0.965$, $p < 0.001$). As firms grow in size ($\beta = 2.776$, $p < 0.01$), gain financial strength ($\beta = 0.037$, $p < 0.05$), and accumulate experience with foreign partners ($\beta = 0.056$, $p < 0.05$), they are more likely to engage in alliances with foreign partners. However, firms were also likely to internationalize their alliance portfolios when they were younger ($\beta = -0.026$, $p < 0.01$), perhaps as a low-commitment entry mode that precedes the use of wholly owned subsidiaries (Johanson and Vahlne 1977). Hence, self-selection in firms' decisions to internationalize their alliance portfolios was significant (see parameter λ in Table 3).

---

[11] Potential contemporaneous (cross-sectional) correlation across firms in the panel data was also tested and ruled out after the additional covariance parameter turned out to be insignificant.

Table 3 reports the results of the second-stage models. Model 1 indicates that financial performance improves with solvency ($\beta = 0.008$, $p < 0.05$), the age of alliances ($\beta = 0.051$, $p < 0.05$), and the overall propensity to form alliances as captured by the adjusted size of the alliance portfolio ($\beta = 0.078$, $p < 0.001$). In turn, financial performance declines with the firm's RandD intensity ($\beta = -0.064$, $p < 0.001$). Hence, firms that invest heavily in RandD but otherwise lack efficient access to internal and external network resources suffer losses. Additionally, performance declined with the proportion of alliances classified as strategic ($\beta = -0.125$, $p < 0.05$). Presumably, strategic alliances consume substantial resources or, perhaps, firms may have been misusing the term "strategic" in their alliance announcements.

Model 2 reveals no significant effect of the linear term of API on financial performance, but its negative effect becomes significant in Model 3 ($\beta = -0.155$, $p < 0.001$) which includes the quadratic and cubic terms of API. In this model, the quadratic effect is positive ($\beta = 0.047$, $p < 0.01$) and the cubic effect is negative ($\beta = -0.003$, $p < 0.01$), in support of hypothesis 1 that suggested a sigmoid relationship between financial performance and API. Model 4 reveals a positive coefficient for the interaction effect of API and foreign partnering experience on financial performance ($\beta = 0.004$, $p < 0.01$) in support of hypothesis 2. Finally, Model 5 reveals a significant positive interaction effect of API and subsidiary-country overlap on financial performance ($\beta = 0.210$, $p < 0.01$), consistent with hypothesis 3. Our results remain significant when the two interactions are introduced simultaneously in Model 6 and also in the full model (Model 7). These results suggest that subsidiary-country overlap is not merely a reflection of the firm's internationalization capability as captured by its foreign partnering experience.

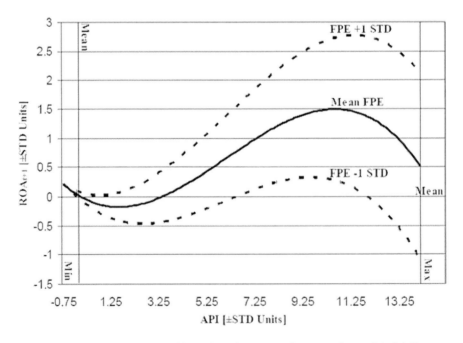

Figure 3. The Moderating Effect of Foreign Partnering Experience (Model 7).

We illustrate our findings with Figures 2-4, which depict the predicted profitability based on Model 7. In these figures, the variables of interest are represented in standard deviation units while all remaining variables are held at their mean levels. Figure 2 captures the sigmoid curve characterizing the performance implications of API, showing how profitability initially declines as API increases up to 1.6 standard deviation units above the mean. Then, it increases until API reaches 10.6 standard deviations above the mean, followed by a subsequent decline. Figures 3 and 4 correspondingly illustrate how the effect of API on profitability shifts with one standard deviation change in the firm's foreign partnering experience and subsidiary-country overlap.

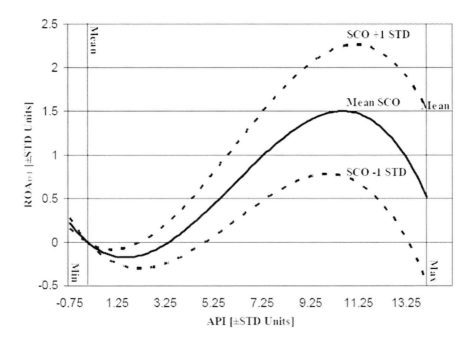

Figure 4. The Moderating Effect of Subsidiary-Country Overlap (Model 7).

Robustness Tests

We conducted several auxiliary analyses to test the robustness of our findings by considering alternative operationalizations of our variables and implementing alternative models. First, we tested variations of our dependent variable, such as a profitability measure based on a moving average of two years (t+1, t+2). In this model, the main effects and interactions remained significant, although the interaction with subsidiary-country overlap became marginally significant. We expect API effects to fade away over longer time horizons because of the transient nature of alliances. With respect to our independent variable, we separately analyzed each of the nine indicators in the composite API measure. This auxiliary analysis revealed that with only a few exceptions, most of the reported API effects and interactions remain significant when using these individual indicators of API.[12]

---

[12] API indicators based on economic distance and based on differences in political stability and absence of violence (PV) produced linear negative effects on financial performance. The interaction effect of institutional distance (PV) with foreign partnering experience as well as the interaction between differences in voice and

We then considered alternative operationalizations of API based on the proportion of foreign partners in the alliance portfolio and the diversity of partners' countries of origin. The proportion of foreign partners did not directly affect firm performance, but its interaction effects with foreign partnering experience and subsidiary-country overlap were significant, per hypotheses 2 and 3. Still, these interaction effects became insignificant when adding the interactions with our original API measure, which reinforces our operationalization. Models based on the diversity of partners' countries of origin produced significant results consistent with hypotheses 1 and 3, but these results were deemed unstable because of potential multicollinearity. Despite this caveat, when we simultaneously introduced our original API measure with the alternative measure based on partner country diversity, all the effects incorporating the original API measure remained significant. In addition, we tested an alternative measure of diversity in the cultural, geographical, institutional, and economic development attributes of partners' countries of origin based on a factor analysis of standard deviations in these indicators. This composite diversity measure produced a significant negative effect on financial performance as well as an interaction effect with foreign partnering experience, in accordance with hypothesis 2. Thus, foreign partnering experience assists not only in coping with national differences but also in managing a nationally diverse alliance portfolio. Our reported results (Table 3) remained unchanged when this composite diversity measure was included as an additional control variable.

Next, we considered alternative operationalizations of our moderators, such as limited experience windows and weighted partnering experience measures, which produced consistent results per hypothesis 2. Because of the high correlation of foreign partnering experience with the current number of foreign partners, we verified that the interaction of API with foreign partnering experience becomes insignificant when the number of foreign partners is used as an alternative moderator. Similarly, the interaction of API with foreign partnering experience remained significant when an interaction of API with domestic partnering experience was introduced (Barkema et al. 1997). This result suggests that only the experience with foreign partners rather than more general partnering experience enhances the contribution of API to firm performance. Eventually, we excluded the control for domestic partnering experience, because its direct and moderating effects were insignificant and their inclusion raised concerns about multicollinearity due to this measure's high correlation with foreign partnering experience. Moreover, we considered the implications of the firm's broader international experience by adding the number of foreign subsidiaries as a moderator of API. This interaction effect turned out to be insignificant, while the interaction of API with foreign partnering experience remained significant as predicted by hypothesis 2.

In addition, we verified that the interaction of API with subsidiary-country overlap remains significant when the measure is computed on a country-by-country basis rather than on a partner-by-partner basis, i.e., when assigning an equal weight to each country rather than to each partner in the aggregated measure. Moreover, we considered the possibility that the benefits of subsidiary-country overlap diminish with the number of partners that each subsidiary serves by dividing our overlap dummy indicators by the number of foreign partners operating in the same country of origin before averaging the indicators at the firm-year level. The resultant measure was highly correlated with our original measure ($r = 0.931$,

---

accountability (VA) and subsidiary-country overlap were insignificant. All the other effects of the individual API indicators were significant in accordance with our hypotheses.

$p < 0.001$), and thus our reported results remained virtually unchanged when this alternative measure was used. We next considered the possibility that subsidiary-country overlap takes place in the United States rather than abroad when foreign partners maintain wholly owned subsidiaries in the United States. When we used this alternative overlap measure or a combined measure that allows for overlap either in the home country of the focal firm or in its partners' foreign countries, the interaction of API with subsidiary-country overlap became insignificant. Thus, we conclude that subsidiary-country overlap attenuates the negative implications of API when it involves the focal firm's own subsidiaries. Perhaps partners' subsidiaries help them overcome their own API challenges without necessarily contributing to the performance of the focal firm.

Moreover, we substantiate our argument that subsidiary-country overlap facilitates learning and reduces unfamiliarity by demonstrating that most foreign subsidiaries were established prior to the formation of cross-national alliances. We found that in 81% of the cases, firms operated wholly owned subsidiaries in the year prior to the recorded overlap year. However, when we operationalized subsidiary-country overlap based on whether a firm has operated a wholly owned subsidiary in the foreign partner's country in the year prior to the year in which an alliance was active, the interaction effect with API became insignificant, which suggests that the subsidiary must operate concurrently with the alliance in order to realize the overlap benefits. Similarly, we considered the possibility that the interaction effect of API with subsidiary-country overlap captures benefits to the firm's network of subsidiaries by including an interaction of subsidiary-country overlap with an indicator of the firm's number of wholly owned foreign subsidiaries. This interaction was insignificant, while the interaction of API with subsidiary-country overlap remained significant.

Next, we examined the implications of regional overlap (e.g., can a subsidiary in Sweden assist in bridging cross-national distance to a Norwegian partner?). We classified the 70 countries of origin to 16 geographical regions using composition schemes of the United Nations Statistics Division. A subsidiary region overlap indicator measured the availability of wholly owned subsidiaries in the geographical region of each foreign partner; we computed the mean value of this indicator across a firm's partners. The resultant variable served as a moderator of API that produced an insignificant effect on financial performance. When this variable was included as a moderator in addition to our original subsidiary-country overlap moderator, the interaction effect of the subsidiary region overlap remained insignificant while the moderation effect of our original measure was significant. Hence, we conclude that the presence of a firm's subsidiaries in its partners' home countries is essential for bridging cross-national differences.

To further test the robustness of our findings we considered additional controls, such as a count of the overall number of foreign subsidiaries that the firm owned, which turned out to be insignificant. Following Contractor et al. (2003), we also considered the impact of the squared and cubic terms of this foreign subsidiaries variable. While the coefficients of these additional controls were insignificant, our reported findings were robust to the introduction of these additional controls. We did not include these insignificant controls in our reported models because of potential multicollinearity concerns. In addition, we examined the implications of the firm's involvement in multi-partner alliances by controlling for the number of partners involved in each alliance. This added control produced an insignificant effect without influencing the significance of our findings. In auxiliary analysis we also included interaction terms between our control variables and API, which produced insignificant effects. For instance, our findings were insensitive to the distinction between technology and marketing alliances. Interactions of API with firm size and financial strength also were insignificant, suggesting that internationalizing the alliance portfolio is not necessarily a dominant strategy for smaller or weaker firms that may lack the resources to establish wholly owned subsidiaries. Similarly, profitability did not affect the likelihood of API when incorporated in the first-stage model. Additionally, we examined whether foreign partnering experience and subsidiary-country overlap attenuate the overall non-linear relationship between financial performance and API by including interactions with the quadratic and cubic terms of API. The additional interactions were insignificant while our reported effects remained significant. We thus conclude that consistent with our hypotheses, the moderating effects of foreign partnering experience and subsidiary-country overlap persist linearly at various levels of API.

Moreover, since the extrema of the API function (see Figure 1) occurred at relatively high levels of API, we verified that the sigmoid impact on performance is not driven by outliers in our data. Based on multivariate outlier analysis of our API indicators we excluded 1% of the observations with the highest jackknifed residuals. All terms of the sigmoid function in Model 3 were significant in the remaining sub-sample, albeit the significance level of the cubic term of API dropped to 5%. We conclude that in the context of the U.S.-based software industry, most cross-national differences can be dealt with quite effectively so that the ultimate decline in performance occurs only when partners have very distinctive national background. Firms in other industries may require more substantial and tighter coordination of activities with partners, which would bring an ultimate decline in performance at lower levels of API.

Conclusion

Our study advances alliance portfolio research by revealing the ramifications of cross-national distance between the firm and partners in its alliance portfolio. Prior research has either considered the benefits and drawbacks of independently forming dyadic alliances with foreign partners (e.g., Barkema and Vermeulen 1997, Das et al. 1998, Inkpen and Beamish 1997, Makino and Beamish 1998, Reuer and Leiblein 2000) or studied alliance portfolios with little attention to internationalization. With only a few exceptions of recent studies that examine the diversity of partners' resources, lines of business, and identities (Baum et al. 2000, Goerzen and Beamish 2005), researchers have paid little attention to how the composition of partners in alliance portfolios affects firm performance. We contribute to this avenue of research by introducing the notion of API and uncovering its performance implications as well as some moderating effects.

Our study highlights the foreignness of partners as an aspect of interorganizational relationships that may affect economic outcomes (Granovetter 1985). We suggest that national dissimilarities between a firm and its partners shape the contribution of the alliance portfolio to its performance. We demonstrate how a firm that collaborates with a pool of relatively proximate foreign partners may face declining performance as it increases its API. We ascribe this downturn to subtle yet critical national differences between the firm and its partners, which remain unnoticed and prevent successful adaptation of collaborative routines. When the firm's API reaches moderate levels, the firm's performance is likely to improve.

We attribute these effects to the partial overlap in the national profiles of the firm and its foreign partners, which enables the firm to leverage its relative absorptive capacity, understand these partners' background, efficiently adjust its collaborative routines, and benefit from access to network resources and markets. However, at high levels of API, internationalization precludes successful adaptation to nationally distant partners, because the firm's collaborative routines are ineffective in bridging geographical, cultural, institutional, and economic differences. We posit that these impediments account for the negative association between firm performance and over-internationalization. Our findings reveal that in the case of software firms, the ultimate decline in performance due to over-internationalization of the alliance portfolio occurs at very high levels of cross-national distance, and even then, the predicted performance is typically better than expected for firms with purely domestic alliance portfolios. While firms should proceed with caution when their portfolio consists primarily of distant partners, our findings underscore the merits of API. In a global economy, collaboration with foreign partners is necessary for expanding firms' market reach and resource pools given the greater commitment, rigidity, and risk entailed by internationalization through wholly owned subsidiaries.

The evolution of alliance portfolios depends on internal inducements and external partnering opportunities (Ahuja 2000b). Yet, a firm may enhance the contribution of its alliance portfolio by modifying its level of API. The transition points between API levels may be industry-, firm-, and even country-specific. Hence, exploration through trial and error (Levitt and March 1988, Nelson and Winter 1982) may be needed to identify the optimal level of API. Our study can guide this exploration, for instance, by encouraging firms that suffer decline in performance following limited API efforts to extend rather than retract API so as to reach the threshold beyond which API enhances performance. Still, managers should consider the challenges of bridging national differences, the switching costs between partners, resource allocation constraints, and the alignment with the firm's overall internationalization strategy. For instance, a firm's API investments can generate indirect returns from its existing network of wholly owned subsidiaries or by creating a low-cost alternative to the expansion of such a network, but some firms may lack the expertise to swiftly extend API or substitute domestic partners for foreign ones.

Examining moderators that set boundary conditions for API effects, we found that the liabilities of API can be mitigated and financial performance can be enhanced if a firm is experienced in managing cross-national alliances and relies on its internal network of foreign subsidiaries when collaborating with foreign partners. Whereas the firm's accumulated experience with foreign partners contributes to its general ability to manage an international alliance portfolio, the availability of wholly owned subsidiaries enhances the firm's ability to overcome cross-national differences in the particular countries from which its foreign partners originate. We extend prior research on subsidiary-based internationalization experience (Eriksson et al. 1997) by demonstrating how firms that leverage their experience in cross-national alliances can avoid negative transfer effects and improve their performance. We thus infer that API entails experiential learning (Cyert and March 1963, Nelson and Winter 1982) and that the capacity to collaborate with foreign partners is experience-driven (Anand and Khanna 2000, Kale et al. 2002). We extend Kale et al.'s (2002) perspective on the role of the corporate alliance function by showing that a decentralized organization of wholly owned subsidiaries in foreign partners' home countries can facilitate collaboration by circumventing geographical, cultural, institutional, and economic differences.

Our study contributes to the alliance management literature by demonstrating that while embeddedness in networks facilitates interorganizational exchange (e.g., Baum and Ingram 1998, Powell et al. 1996), there remains variation in firms' abilities to interact and exchange resources within such networks as a function of their cultural, institutional, geographic, and economic distances to partners. Hence, the prospects of alliances depend not only on the motivations and abilities of the parties to engage in exchange (Szulanski 1996), but also on similarities in their national backgrounds. Dissimilarities prevent a firm from effectively accessing and leveraging network resources even when it has an absorptive capacity (Cohen and Levinthal 1990), since failure to recognize subtle national differences leads to underutilized absorptive capacity, whereas extensive differences result in misapplication of collaborative routines. A firm can overcome these negative transfer effects by learning from its partnering experience how to detect relevant national dissimilarities as well as develop and apply appropriate collaborative routines. It can also leverage the local absorptive capacity of its subsidiaries in its partners' countries of origin to reduce its effective distance to them. The study of cross-national differences in alliance portfolios thus advances our understanding of the contribution of partner fit (Kale et al. 2000) for learning and collaboration in alliance portfolios.

Our study also offers ramifications for internationalization theories (e.g., Johanson and Vahlne 1977). Our findings complement recent research that has revealed a sigmoid performance effect of internationalization through wholly owned subsidiaries (Contractor et al. 2003, Lu and Beamish 2004). Whereas these studies tested the propensity to engage in internationalization by measuring the number and size of foreign subsidiaries or the dispersion of subsidiaries across countries, we focused on the cross-national differences between the firm and its partners, while accounting for the firm's network of subsidiaries. Hence, we attribute the sigmoid pattern to negative transfer effects, relative absorptive capacity, and application of collaborative routines. In turn, prior research on subsidiary-based internationalization ascribes the initial decline in performance to setup costs and liabilities of foreignness, noting that performance will then improve due to economies of scale and scope and international optimization of the network configuration (Porter 1990). Finally, the subsequent decline in performance is related to complexity and bounded rationality that contribute to coordination costs. This three-stage model (Contractor et al. 2003, Lu and Beamish 2004) cannot be bluntly applied in our study because we consider national differences as the mode of internationalization and since cross-national alliances differ from wholly owned subsidiaries. Alliances enable firms to overcome some liabilities of foreignness associated with foreign direct investment (Contractor and Lorange 1988, Eden and Miller 2004), whereas wholly owned subsidiaries overcome double-layered acculturation that alliances face (Barkema et al. 1996). Thus, the negative ramifications of national differences manifest in the first stage of subsidiary-based internationalization but become eminent only in the third stage of API.

One of the implications of our study is that API can complement subsidiary-based internationalization. Firms may need to coordinate their activities across wholly owned subsidiaries and alliances in foreign countries in order to identify optimal modes and levels of internationalization. We call for future research to further analyze the interplay between subsidiaries and alliances as means for international expansion. We highlight the benefits of simultaneously maintaining foreign subsidiaries and alliances in the same country, yet a better understanding of the inherent tradeoffs may be needed.

Future research may also address some of this study's limitations. First, we focused on the software industry during the 1990s, which may not be representative. Other industries may lack the modularity and complementarity features of software development processes or may involve combinations of more tangible resources. To the extent that collaboration leads to greater task complexity and need for coordination (Argote and Ingram 2000), the liabilities of API may intensify. Future research may test our framework in less dynamic or more financially stable industries, bearing in mind, however, that transition points between levels of API may vary by industry. Second, the shape of the sigmoid API effect may reflect the fact that the United States has a comparative advantage in the software industry. Firms originating in countries with small home markets and a limited pool of domestic partners may benefit more from API. Hence, future research may examine whether comparative advantage of the focal firm's home country augments the negative performance implications of API.

Third, our focus on national differences highlights the depth aspect of API. Although we controlled for the number of foreign partners and dispersion of partners' countries, future research may examine the diversification of foreign subsidiaries (Contractor et al. 2003, Hitt et al. 1997, Lu and Beamish 2004, Tallman and Li 1996, Thomas and Eden 2004) and study the interplay between API and the diversity of foreign partners in alliance portfolios.[13] Fourth, to isolate the mechanisms that drive our results, future research may furnish evidence from case studies and surveys that directly measure learning from experience and absorptive capacity, which remain latent in our study. By considering intermediate outcomes at the alliance level, researchers may gain new insights on the processes through which firms learn how to manage international alliance portfolios. Finally, we studied the implications of API for profitability, which is a short-term accounting-based measure. It is possible that while API constrains performance in the short term, it contributes to long-term growth prospects. Future research may examine long-term performance implications by considering alternative performance measures.

In conclusion, our study advances alliance portfolio research by analyzing the prospects of forming alliances with foreign partners. The outcomes of alliance-based internationalization depend not only on the number of foreign partners and their configuration in the alliance portfolio but also on the physical and psychic distances to these partners. Firms that develop relational capabilities (Kale et al. 2002) that enable them to detect national differences, adjust collaborative routines, and properly apply them in cross-national alliances can better leverage their relative absorptive capacity and avoid competency traps. There is an optimal level of API that enables firms to leverage their absorptive capacity in order to bridge national differences and extract valuable network resources from moderately distant foreign partners. To reach this optimal level, firms can exploit their prior experience with foreign partners as well as engage in experimentation as they fine-tune their API. Another approach for enhancing the returns on API involves bridging cross-national differences by forming alliances in countries where the firm already operates wholly owned subsidiaries. The foreignness of partners in the alliance portfolio can become either a liability or an opportunity

---

[13] An immediate implication of diversity of foreign partners in the alliance portfolio concerns the hypothetical case of a firm that maintains dual focus on nationally proximate and distant foreign partners. In such a case the firm is likely to develop a broad range of collaborative routines and nurture an absorptive capacity that enable it to sensitively identify and bridge national differences in its alliance portfolio. Hence, the diversity of foreign partners may lead to positive performance implications at moderate levels of API, as our theory predicts.

depending on whether firms proactively manage their alliance portfolios and engage in concurrent learning within and across their organizational boundaries.

References

Ahuja, G. (2000a). Collaboration networks, structural holes, and innovation: A longitudinal study. *Administrative Science Quarterly*, **45**(3), 425-455.

Ahuja, G. (2000b). The duality of collaboration: Inducements and opportunities in the formation of interfirm linkages. *Strategic Management Journal*, **21**(Special Issue), 317-343.

Anand, B. N., and Khanna, T. (2000). Do firms learn to create value? The case of alliances. *Strategic Management Journal*, **21**, 295-317.

Anderson, E., and Gatignon, H. (1986). Modes of foreign entry: A transaction cost analysis and propositions. *Journal of International Business Studies*, **17**(3), 1-26.

Argote, L. and Ingram, P. (2000). Knowledge transfer: A basis for competitive advantage in firms. *Organizational Behavior and Human Decision Processes*, **82**(1), 150–169.

Barkema, H., Bell, J., and Pennings, J. (1996). Foreign entry, cultural barriers, and learning. *Strategic Management Journal*, **17**, 151-166.

Barkema, H., Shenkar, O., Vermeulen, F., and Bell, J. (1997). Working abroad, working with others: How firms learn to operate international joint ventures. *Academy of Management Journal*, **40**, 426-442.

Barkema, H. G. and Vermeulen, F. (1997). What differences in the cultural background of partners are detrimental for international joint ventures? *Journal of Internaitonal Business Studies*, **28**(4) 845–864.

Baum, J. A. C., Calabrese, T., and Silverman, B. S. (2000). Don't go it alone: Alliance network composition and startups' performance in Canadian biotechnology. *Strategic Management Journal*, **21**, 267-294.

Baum, J. A. C., and Ingram, P. (1998). Survival-enhancing learning in the Manhattan hotel industry, 1898-1980. *Management Science*, **44**, 996-1016.

Bollen, K. A., and Jackman, R. W. (1985). Economic and non-economic determinants of political democracy in the 1960s. *Research in Political Sociology*, **1**, 27–48.

Brush, T. H., Bromiley, P., and Hendrickx, M. (2000). The free cash flow hypothesis for sales growth and firm performance. *Strategic Management Journal*, **21**(4), 455-472.

Buckley, P. J., and Casson, M. (1976). The Economic Theory of the Multinational Enterprise. London: Macmillan.

Burt, R. S. (1992). *Structural Holes: The Social Structure of Competition*. Cambridge, MA.: Harvard University Press.

Cohen, W. M., and Levinthal, D. A. (1990). Absorptive capacity: A new perspective on learning and innovation. *Administrative Science Quarterly*, **35**, 128-152.

Coleman, J. S. (1990). Foundations of social theory. Cambridge, MA: Harvard University Press.

Contractor, F., Kundu, S., and Hsu, C.-C. (2003). A three-stage theory of international expansion: The link between multinationality and performance in the service sector. *Journal of International Business Studies*, **34**, 5-18.

Contractor, F. J., and Lorange, P. (1988). *Cooperative Strategies in International Business*. Lexington, MA: Lexington Books.

Cyert, R. M., and March, J. G. (1963). *A Behavioral Theory of the Firm* (2nd ed.). Englewood Cliffs, NJ: Prentice-Hall.

Das, S., Sen, P. K., and Sengupta, S. (1998). Impact of strategic alliances on firm valuation. *Academy of Management Journal*, **41**(1), 27-41.

Das, T. K., and Teng, B.-S. (1998). Between trust and control: Developing confidence in partner cooperation in alliances. *Academy of Management Review*, **23**(3), 491-512.

Dyer, J. H., and Nobeoka, K. (2000). Creating and managing a high-performance knowledge-sharing network: The Toyota case. *Strategic Management Journal*, **21**(3), 345-367.

Dyer, J. H., and Singh, H. (1998). The relational view: Cooperative strategies and sources of interorganizational competitive advantage. *Academy of Management Review*, **23**(4), 660-679.

Eden, L., and Miller, S.R. (2004). Distance matters: Liability of foreignness, institutional distance and ownership strategy. *Advances in International Management*, **16**, 187-221.

Eisenhardt, K. M., and Schoonhoven, C. B. (1996). Resource-based view of strategic alliance formation: Strategic and social effects in entrepreneurial firms. *Organization Science*, **7**(2), 136-150.

Eriksson, K., Johanson, J., Majkgard, A., and Sharma, D.D. (1997). Experiential knowledge and cost in the internationalization process. *Journal of International Business Studies*, **28**(2), 337-360.

Erramilli, K. (1996). Nationality and subsidiary ownership patterns in multinational corporations. *Journal of International Business Studies*, **27**, 225–248.

Gertler, M. (2001). Best practice? Geography, learning and the institutional limits to strong convergence. *Journal of economic geography*, **1**, 5-26.

Ghemawat, P. (2001). Distance still matters: The hard reality of global expansion. *Harvard Business Review*, **79**(8), 137-147.

Goerzen, A., and Beamish, P. W. (2005). The effect of alliance network diversity on multinational enterprise performance. *Strategic Management Journal*, **26**, 333-354.

Granovetter, M. (1985). Economic action and social structure: The problem of embeddedness. *American Journal of Sociology*, **91**, 481-510.

Grinblatt, M., and Keloharju, M. (2001). How distance, language, and culture influence stockholdings and trades. *Journal of Finance*, **17**(3), 769-809.

Gulati, R. (1995). Does familiarity breed trust? The implications of repeated ties for contractual choices. *Academy of Management Journal*, **35**(4), 85-112.

Gulati, R. (1998). Alliances and networks. *Strategic Management Journal*, **19**(4), 293-317.

Gulati, R. (1999). Network location and learning: The influence of network resources and firm capabilities on alliance formation. *Strategic Management Journal*, **20**(5), 397-420.

Gulati, R., and Higgins, M. C. (2003). Which ties matter when? The contingent effects of interorganizational partnerships on IPO success. *Strategic Management Journal*, **24**(2), 127-144.

Gulati, R., and Singh, H. (1998). The architecture of cooperation: Managing coordination costs and appropriation concerns in strategic alliances. *Administrative Science Quarterly*, **43**(4), 781-814.

Hagedoorn, J. (1993). Understanding the rationale of strategic technology partnering. *Strategic Management Journal*, **14**(5), 371-385.

Haggard, S. (1990). Pathways from the periphery: The politics of growth in the newly industrialized countries. Ithaca: Cornell University Press.

Hamel, G. (1991). Competition for competence and interpartner learning within international strategic alliances. *Strategic Management Journal*, **12**(Summer Special Issue), 83-103.

Harrigan, K. R. (1988). Joint ventures and competitive strategy. *Strategic Management Journal*, 9, 361-398.

Hausman, J. (1978). Specification tests in econometrics. *Econometrica*, **46**, 1251–1271.

Heckman, J. (1979). Sample selection bias as a specification error. *Econometrica*, **47**, 153-161.

Henisz, W. J. (2000). The institutional environment for economic growth. *Economics and Politics*, **12**(1), 1-31.

Hitt, M. A., Hoskisson, R. E., and Kim, H. (1997). International diversification: Effects on innovation and firm performance in product-diversified firms. *Academy of Management Journal*, **40**, 767-798.

Hofstede, G. (1980). Culture's consequences: International differences in work-related values. Beverly Hills: Sage Publications.

Hymer, S. H. (1976). The international operations of national firms: A study of foreign direct investment. Cambridge, MA: MIT Press.

Inkpen, A. C., and Beamish, P. W. (1997). Knowledge, bargaining power, and the instability of international joint ventures. *Academy of Management Review*, **22**(1), 177–202.

Jaffe, A. B., Trajtenberg, M., and Henderson, R. (1993). Geographic location of knowledge spillovers as evidenced by patent citations. *Quarterly Journal of Economics*, **108**(3), 577-598.

Jensen, R., and Szulanski, G. (2004). Stickiness and the adaptation of organizational practices in cross-border knowledge transfers. *Journal of International Business Studies*, **35**(6), 508-523.

Johanson, J., and Vahlne, J.-E. (1977). The internationalization process of the firm: A model of knowledge development and increasing foreign market commitments. *Journal of International Business Studies*, **8**, 23-32.

Kale, P., Dyer, J. H., and Singh, H. (2002). Alliance capability, stock market response, and long-term alliance success: The role of the alliance function. *Strategic Management Journal*, **23**(8), 747-767.

Kale, P., Singh, H., and Perlmutter, H. (2000). Learning and protection of proprietary assets in strategic alliances: Building relational capital. *Strategic Management Journal*, **21**(3), 217-237.

Kalmbach, C. J., and Roussel, C. (1999). Dispelling the Myths of Alliances. Outlook, October(Special Edition), 5-32.

Kanungo, R. N., and Jaeger, A. M. (1990). Chapter 1: Introduction. In A. M. Jaeger, and R. N. Kanungo (Eds.), Management in Developing Countries, 1-19. London: Routledge.

Kaufmann, D., Kraay, A., and Mastruzzi, M. (2006). Governance matters V: Aggregate and individual governance indicators for 1996-2005. Washington, D.C.: The World Bank.

Khanna, T., Gulati, R., and Nohria, N. (1998). The dynamics of learning alliances: competition, cooperation, and relative scope. *Strategic Management Journal*, **19**(3), 193-210.

Kleinbaum, D. G., Lawrence, L. K., Muller, K. E., and Nizam, A. (1998). Applied regression analysis and other multivariable methods (3rd ed.). Pacific Grove, CA: Brooks/Cole Publishing Company.

Kogut, B., and Kulatilaka, N. (1993). Operating flexibility, global manufacturing, and the option value of a multinational network. *Management Science*, **39**(11), 123-139.

Kogut, B., and Singh, H. (1988). The effect of national culture on the choice of entry mode. *Journal of International Business Studies*, **19**(3), 411-432.

Kostova, T. (1997). Country institutional profile: Concept and measurement. *Best Paper Proceedings of the Academy of Management*, 180-184.

Kostova, T., and Zaheer, S. (1999). Organizational legitimacy under conditions of complexity: The case of the multinational enterprise. *Academy of Management Review*, **24**, 64-81.

Kumar, R. and Nti, K. O. (1998). Differential learning and interaction in alliance dynamics: A process and outcome discrepancy model. *Organization Science*, **9**(3), 356–367.

Kurokawa, S., Iwata, S. and Roberts, E. B. (2007). Global RandD activities of Japanese MNCs in the US: A triangulation approach. *Research Policy*, **36**, 3–36.

Lane, H. W., and Beamish, P. W. (1990). Cross-cultural cooperative behavior in joint ventures in LCDs. *Management International Review*(**30**), 87-102.

Lane, P. J., Salk, J. E., and Lyles, M. A. (2001). Absorptive capacity, learning, and performance in international joint ventures. *Strategic Management Journal*, **22**, 1139-1161.

Lane, P. J., and Lubatkin, M. (1998). Relative absorptive capacity and interorganizational learning. *Strategic Management Journal*, **19**(5), 461–477.

Lane, P. J., Salk, J. E., and Lyles M. A. (2001). Absorptive capacity, learning, and performance in international joint ventures. *Strategic Management Journal*, **22**, 1139–1161.

Lavie, D. (2006). The competitive advantage of interconnected firms: An extension of the resource-based view. *Academy of Management Review*, **31**(3), 638-658.

Lavie, D., and Rosenkopf, L. (2006). Balancing exploration and exploitation in alliance formation. *Academy of Management Journal*, **49**(6), 797-818.

Lavie, D. (2007). Alliance portfolios and firm performance: A study of value creation and appropriation in the U.S. software industry. *Strategic Management Journal*, **28**(12), 1187-1212.

Levinthal, D. A., and March, J. G. (1993). The myopia of learning. *Strategic Management Journal*, **14**(special issue), 95-112.

Levitt, B., and March, J. G. (1988). Organizational learning. In W. R. Scott, and J. F. Short (Eds.), *Annual Review of Sociology*, Vol. 14, 319-340. Palo Alto, CA: Annual Reviews.

Lorenzoni, G., and Lipparini, A. (1999). The leveraging of interfirm relationships as a distinctive organizational capability: A longitudinal study. *Strategic Management Journal*, **20**, 317-338.

Loughran, T., and Ritter, J. R. (2004). Why has IPO underwriting changed over time? *Financial Management*, **33**(3), 5-37.

Lu, J., and Beamish, P. W. (2006). Partnering strategies and performance of SMEs' international joint ventures. *Journal of Business Venturing*, **21**, 461-486.

Lu, J. W., and Beamish, P. W. (2004). International diversification and firm performance: The s-curve hypothesis. *Academy of Management Journal*, **47**(4), 598-609.

Maddala, G. S. (2001). Introduction to Econometrics (3rd ed.). New York, NY: John Wiley and Sons.

Makino, S., and Beamish, P. W. (1998). Performance and survival of joint ventures with non-conventional ownership structures. *Journal of International Business Studies*, **29**, 797–818.

Martin, X., and Salomon, R. (2003). Tacitness, learning, and international expansion: A study of foreign direct investment in a knowledge-intensive industry. *Organization Science*, **14**, 297-311.

Monteverde, K., and Teece, D. (1982). Appropriable rents and quasi-vertical integration. *Journal of Law and Economics*, 321-328.

Nelson, R., and Winter, S. (1982). *An evolutionary theory of economic change.* Cambridge, MA: Belknap Press of Harvard University Press.

Novick, L. R. (1988). Analogical transfer, problem similarity, and expertise. *Journal of Experimental Psychology, Learning, Memory, and Cognition,* **14**, 510-520.

O'Grady, S., and Lane, H. W. (1996). The psychic distance paradox. *Journal of International Business Studies,* **27**(2), 309-333.

Osborn, R. N., and Baughn, C. (1990). Forms of interorganizational governance for multinational alliances. *Academy of Management Journal*, **33**, 503-519.

Parkhe, A. (1991). Interfirm diversity, organizational learning, and longevity in global strategic alliances. *Journal of International Business Studies*, **22**(4), 579-601.

Pennings, J., Barkema, H., and Douma, S. (1994). Organizational learning and diversification. *Academy of Management Journal*, **37**, 608-640.

Phene, A., Fladmoe-Lindquist, K., and Marsh, L. (2006). Breakthrough innovations in the U.S. biotechnology industry: The effects of technological space and geographic origin. *Strategic Management Journal*, **27**, 369-388.

Podolny, J. M. (1994). Market uncertainty and the social character of economic exchange. *Administrative Science Quarterly*, **39**, 458-483.

Porter, M. E. (1990). The competitive advantage of nations. *Harvard Business Review*, **68**(2), 73-91.

Pothukuchi, V., Damanpour, F., Choi, J., Chen, C. C., and Park, S. H. (2002). National and organizational culture differences and international joint venture performance. *Journal of International Business Studies*, **33**(2), 243–265.

Powell, W. (1990). Neither market nor hierarchy: Network forms of organization. *Research in Organizational Behavior,* **12**(295-336).

Powell, W. W., Koput, K. W., and Smith-Doerr, L. (1996). Interorganizational collaboration and the locus of innovation: Networks of learning in biotechnology. *Administrative Science Quarterly*, **41**(1), 116-145.

Reuer, J. J., and Leiblein, M. J. (2000). Downside risk implications of multinationality and international joint ventures. *Academy of Management Journal*, **43**, 201-214.

Rothaermel, F. T. (2001). Incumbent's advantage through exploiting complementary assets via interfirm cooperation. *Strategic Management Journal*, **22**, 687-699.

Rowley, T., Behrens, D., and Krackhardt, D. (2000). Redundant governance structures: An analysis of structural and relational embeddedness in the steel and semiconductor industries. *Strategic Management Journal*, **21**, 369-386.

Rudy, J. (2000). *Standard and Poor's Industry Surveys - Computers: Software*, 1-38.

Sampson, R. C. (2005). Experience effects and collaborative returns in RandD alliances. *Strategic Management Journal, 26*, 1009-1031.

Shane, S. (1992). Why do some societies invest more than others? *Journal of Business Venturing, 7*(1), 29-46.

Shaver, M. J. (1998). Accounting for endogeneity: When assessing strategy performance: Does entry mode choice affect FDI survival? *Management Science, 44*(4), 571-585.

Shenkar, O. (2001). Cultural distance revisited: Towards a more rigorous conceptualization and measurement of cultural differences. *Journal of International Business Studies, 32*, 519-535.

Shenkar, O., and Li, J. T. (1999). Knowledge search in international cooperative ventures. *Organization Science, 10*(2), 134-143.

Simonin, B. L. (1997). The importance of collaborative know-how: An empirical test of the learning organization. *Academy of Management Journal, 40*(5), 1150-1174.

Simonin, B. L. (1999). Ambiguity and the process of knowledge transfer in strategic alliances. *Strategic Management Journal, 20*, 595-623.

Steensma, H. K., and Lyles, M. A. (2000). Explaining IJV survival in a transitional economy through social exchange and knowledge-based perspectives. *Strategic Management Journal, 21*, 831-851.

Steensma, H. K., Tihanyi, L., Lyles, M. A., and Dhanaraj, C. (2005). The evolving value of foreign partnerships in transitioning economies. *Academy of Management Journal, 48*(2), 213-235.

Stuart, T. E. (2000). Interorganizational alliances and the performance of firms: A study of growth and innovation rates in a high-technology industry. *Strategic Management Journal, 21*(8), 719-811.

Stuart, T. E., Hoang, H., and Hybels, R. (1999). Interorganizational endorsements and the performance of entrepreneurial ventures. *Administrative Science Quarterly, 44*, 315-349.

Szulanski, G. (1996). Exploring internal stickiness: Impediments to the transfer of best practice within the firm. *Strategic Management Journal, 17*(Winter Special Issue), 27-43.

Szulanski, G. (2000). The process of knowledge transfer: A dichronic analysis of stickiness. *Organizational Behavior and Human Decision Processes, 82*(1), 9-27.

Tallman, S., and Li, J. (1996). Effects of international diversity and product diversity on the performance of multinational firms. *Academy of Management Journal, 39*(1), 179-196.

Teece, D. (1992). Competition, cooperation, and innovation. *Journal of Economic Behavior and Organization, 18*, 1-25.

Thomas, D., and Eden, L. (2004). What is the shape of the multinationality-performance relationship? *Multinational Business Review, 12*, 89-110.

Tihanyi, L., Griffith, D. A., and Russell, C. J. (2005). The effect of cultural distance on entry mode choice, international diversification, and MNE performance: A meta-analysis. *Journal of International Business Studies, 36*(3), 270-283.

Uzzi, B. (1996). The sources and consequences of embeddedness for the economic performance of organizations: The network effect. *American Sociological Review, 61*, 674-698.

Williamson, O. E. (1991). Comparative economic organization: the analysis of discrete structural alternatives. *Administrative Science Quarterly, 36*, 269-296.

Woodcock, C. P., Beamish, P. W., and Makino, S. (1994). Ownership based entry mode strategies and international performance. *Journal of International Business Studies*, **2**, 253-272.

Yan, A., and Gray, B. (1994). Bargaining power, management control, and performance in United States - Chinese joint ventures: a comparative case study. *Academy of Management Journal*, **37**(6), 1478-1517.

Yan, A. M., and Zeng, M. (1999). International joint venture instability: A critique of previous research, a reconceptualization, and directions for future research. *Journal of International Business Studies*, **30**(2), 397–414.

Zaheer, S. (1995). Overcoming the liability of foreignness. *Academy of Management Journal*, **38**, 341-363.

Zaheer, S. (2000). Time zone economics and managerial work in a global world. In P. C. Earley, and H. Singh (Eds.), *Innovations in international and cross-cultural management*, 339-353. Thousand Oaks, CA: Sage Publications.

Zahra, S. A., and George, G. (2002). Absorptive capacity: A review, reconceptualization, and extension. *Academy of Management Review*, **27**(2), 185-203.

Zollo, M., Reuer, J. J., and Singh, H. (2002). Interorganizational routines and performance in strategic alliances. *Organization Science,* **13**(6), 701-713.

In: Handbook of Business and Finance
Editors: M. Bergmann and T. Faust, pp. 79-99

ISBN: 978-1-60692-855-4
© 2010 Nova Science Publishers, Inc.

Chapter 3

UNITING THE SERVICE TRINITY IN NON-PROFIT COMMUNITY ORGANISATIONS: A SEQUENCE OF STUDIES, REFLECTIONS AND IMPLICATIONS FOR THEORY AND PRACTICE IN THE PERFORMING ARTS

Margee Hume and Gillian Sullivan-Mort*
Department of Marketing, Griffith University

Abstract

Services researchers suggest that implementing a multi-disciplinary approach to research will advance the domain of services research. The current approach to services research has minimized the nexus between marketing and operations and the importance of the implementation of strategy to achieve objectives. It is argued that failing to integrate service operations both practically and theoretically, into services research, in particular, applying multiple perspectives to customer re-purchase intentions research frameworks limits the potential effectiveness and practical applicability of findings. This research contributes to the field of service research by drawing from methods and theories offered in both service operations and services marketing fields. A mixed method implementing a series of three integrated studies was used to explore this context from both operations and marketing domains. This research identified the aspects of a performing arts encounter that are relevant to the customer by conducting a two-staged set of qualitative interviews. This process is based on the operations technique Service Transaction Analysis (STA). Consultant consumers and organizational personnel were used to formulate a consensus definition of a typical performing arts experience, and then 26 in-depth interviews were conducted with potential future consumers of the performing arts based on this description of the offering. A survey instrument was then conducted on 273 potential future consumers of the performing arts. The proposed model was then analyzed using the AMOS 5.0 Structural Equation Modeling package. Interestingly, the tested model found empirically that the subjective and experiential aspects of the service, such as the emotional and artistic quality of the show, did not have a significant and direct relationship with re-purchase intention. Offering further support, the

---

* E-mail address: m.hume@griffith.edu.au, Nathan Campus Nathan Qld 4111.

tested model found service quality and show experience were mediated by value to satisfaction, with satisfaction in turn mediating the relationship between value and re-purchase intention. Collectively, these findings have led to several developments and contributions for both scholarship and practice. This exploration advanced the 'service management trinity', specifically strengthening the importance of the relationship between service marketing and service operations. By contributing to the field of service management and advancing enquiry in the field of services marketing and service operations, this project has offered a new perspective and practical approach to service marketing context analysis, making a valuable contribution to scholarship.

Format of this Chapter: A Series of Integrated Studies and Papers Informing Reflections and Implications

In contrast to many other approaches, this chapter's style originates and distinguishes itself by the presentation of the research contributions using set of author papers rather than adopting a traditional narrative approach. The set of papers is integrated and based on the data set developed by the three linked studies aimed at the overall research question and will inform the reflections and implications offered. Moreover, the papers in this research are based on the progressive results of the authors' research and offer an integrated set of findings and discussions. The papers are not mutually exclusive but interrelated to comprehensively elucidate the central research themes of the research. In developing each paper, only subsets of the overall literature review and data relevant to the papers' overall contribution will be presented.

Introduction

Research into the performing arts has most recently set out to advance theory on the nature of re-purchase intention in this experiential service context. Moreover, research has aimed to amalgamate the fields of operations management and services marketing by using theories and approaches from both fields. Using aspects from both fields has assisted in obtaining a deeper understanding of the issues facing this sector with respect to RI (Hume, Sullivan Mort, Liesch and Winzar, 2006).

This chapter will present a set of related findings from recent research, leading to reflections and implications for theory and practice. This chapter will offer some limitations of current research and the direction for the future research in this sector paving the way for a future research agenda for scholars and practitioners. The findings of this research highlight several areas of consideration for managers of performing arts organisations. Importantly, these findings are applicable to the performing arts but are likely to have implications for other non-profit service organisations and non-experiential services.

The purpose of this chapter is to discuss current research related to theory development in the non-profit cultural performing arts, in particularly related to increasing visitation and intent to revisit. Services researchers suggest implementing a multi-disciplinary approach to research using theories and methods from several of the management fields in order to advance the domain of services research. This chapter aims to contribute to the discipline of service research and the sub-discipline of non-profit experiential services by drawing from methods and theories from service operations and services marketing fields. To date, service research has been preoccupied primarily with consumer behaviour aspects of services marketing such as satisfaction but underestimates the importance of constructs such as re-purchase intention and the subsequent implications for strategy formulation and implementation. Further to this, the current approach to services research has overlooked the nexus between marketing and operations and the importance of the implementation of strategy to achieve objectives. It is argued that failing to integrate service operations both practically and theoretically into the re-purchase intention research framework confines its potential effectiveness.

By contributing to the field of service management and advancing enquiry in the field of services marketing and service operations, this research offers a new perspective and practical approach to service marketing context analysis making a valuable contribution to scholarship. This approach is based on improving organisational performance in experiential services specifically by applying operations and marketing theory from a customer-perspective. By doing this, findings inform organisations of ways to better meet the needs and wants of consumers through design, delivery and marketing. Moreover, the findings assist researchers in further advancing the field of services research. This research positions the future research program to focus on continuing the advancement of service management by examining the higher order constructs of service quality and show experience and examining the impact of additional customer motivations such as emotional goal attainment and involvement in experiential settings.

In addition, the lack of specific service context application has been identified as a significant oversight in previous services research. Construct measurements and findings have been difficult to replicate across contexts and contextual examination of constructs and relationships has been suggested as a solution. One such context deserving of attention is that of the non-profit experiential services, specifically the performing arts. Developing and the using measures and theories developed specifically for this context, will offer a more comprehensive approach to re-purchase intention research in a performing arts setting. This chapter will offer an overview of a set of studies and research that adopted a mixed method approach uniting operations and marketing fields in the examination of non-profit performing arts. This chapter discusses several papers published in the area of performing arts culminating in the presentation of a set of managerial reflections and implications for non-profit performing arts managers.

Consolidating issues such as the need for research in the performing arts sector, the limited research identifying the drivers of re-purchase intention in experiential services, the importance of re-purchase intention as a driver of profitability, the need for contextual research to clarify constructs and the need to integrate operations management approaches into services research, it is evident that a research agenda in this field warrants reporting.

In view of this, this chapter will present research related to the following research objectives and questions:

How organisations and customers define and describe a typical performing arts encounter? (Hume et al, 2006).
The factors that contribute to re-purchase intention in the performing arts (Hume et al, 2007 and Hume 2008a).

How do the encounter dimensions/factors of service quality, show experience, value and customer satisfaction interacts to create positive re-purchase intention? (Hume et al, 2008, Hume, 2008b).

Experiential Consumption and the Performing Arts

Decreased government financial support and increased competition for donors, grants and sponsor support (Sullivan Mort, Weerawardena and Carnegie, 2003) have increased the pressure on cultural arts organizations to raise funds from ticket sales to improve financial returns on show performances. Rentschler, Radbourne, Carr and Rickard (2002) suggest the primary objectives of cultural arts organizations must focus on audience development and increased ticket sales to achieve improved profitability and performance. It is evident however, that past and present marketing efforts focusing on subscriptions, venue management and attendance are not meeting organizational profit performance objectives and new strategies need to be identified (Cutts and Drozd, 1995; Rentschler *et al.*, 2002).

Performing arts research has positioned arts management and arts consumption as specialist fields of consumer behavior research (Bouder-Pailler, 1999). The performing arts have measured performance not only in ticket sales but also in overall artistic effectiveness and contribution to the arts (Bendixen, 2000). This research has focused on the experiential nature of the cultural arts and the emotional motives of consumers (Bouder-Pailler, 1999). These motives have included personal intrinsic goals such as emotional and intellectual developments (Bouder-Pailler, 1999) and social goals. Social goals are more extrinsic, such as social contact and membership (Garbarino and Johnson, 1999). This research does not recognise consumer goals outside the sphere of hedonism and focuses only on experiential service aspects (Bendixen, 2000; Bouder-Pailler, 1999; Cavenago, Francesconi and Santuari, 2002).

Marketing approaches that seek to nurture greater contact between the audience and the core service (the show) have been introduced to this field (Bouder-Pailler, 1999); however, these strategies have not addressed the entire service offering from pre-arrival to post-departure (Danaher and Mattsson, 1994) which includes contacts with all facilitating and supplementary services (Cooper-Martin, 1991; Lovelock, Patterson and Walker, 2001). Motivations for attending the theatre have been explored (Scheff, 1999), but the judgments influencing re-consumption such as satisfaction and value have not been clarified. Artistic appreciation of the cultural arts seems to increase with consumption (Cavenago *et al.*, 2002). Whether increased appreciation results in increased rates of re-consumption, has not been explored. Research has suggested that increased customer familiarity does alter the drivers of re-consumption (Soderlund, 2002), but how this applies in this context has not been explored. Overall, this research stream focuses on artistic value and technical show quality and overlooks the utilitarian or more functional dimensions of service quality and process (Grönroos, 1990).

Until recently, it has been suggested that success of the performing arts service offering is dependent on the ability of the show/service to evoke emotion and arouse subjective reactions (Hirschman, 1982; Holbrook and Hirschman, 1982; Holbrook, 2000; Addis and Holbrook, 2001). Consequently, the primary intent and core of the service offering has been the delivery of these components to meet subjective needs. Under this paradigm, it is suggested that consumers do not use comparison standards to measure the encounter. Rather, they look to risk-reducing strategies to avoid poor consumption experiences, such as attending movies featuring a favorite actor or receiving favorable reviews by critics.

More recently, it is suggested that the higher the experiential component and consumer involvement, the greater the emphasis not only on subjective or emotional aspects but also on objective aspects (Holbrook, 2000; Addis and Holbrook, 2001) of consumption. This suggests that the emphasis should not be on either experiential or utilitarian functional aspects but on how the consumer weighs these attributes in their overall judgments (Pine and Gilmore, 1999; Addis and Holbrook, 2001). Some researchers have suggested that experiential outcomes of the service offering are not the economic offering. They highlight the importance of subtleties, such as augmented service attributes, and suggest it is these that drive value and satisfaction judgments (Johnston, 1999; Pine and Gilmore, 1999) and subsequently re-purchase or re-consumption intention.

There has been a great deal of focus on post-purchase constructs such as satisfaction, service quality and perceived value and the evaluation process in recent service marketing research. Moreover, the relationship of these constructs to re-purchase intention has been of interest to marketing practitioners and scholars for many years. Researchers (Henning-Thurau and Klee, 1997; Bahia, Paulin and Perrien, 2000) aim to explain the phenomenon of what makes us as customers return to re-purchase a product or a service. For organisations adopting market-based learning in practice, the answer to this question drives the strategies used to market and brand the product and service. This information is invaluable to the owners, manufacturers and marketers of products and services as it is directly linked to organisational performance, market share, growth and survival. The research discussed in this chapter couples the journey to further advance the current knowledge of post-purchase evaluations and re-purchase intention (RI) with the examination of a sector of the business community that has many constraints and complexities such as limited funding, social and education responsibilities, non-profit status and perishability, the cultural performing arts industry.

The non-profit performing arts sector is complex in its operation with some organisations operating as both venue owners and show producers, or singularly as show brokers, show creators, or proprietors. The strategies each uses to survive are many and diverse; however, a number of factors are important to the industry as a whole. First, competition has increased dramatically in the recent years with sport and other entertainment offerings improving in presentation and gaining greater popularity. Second, the industry supports many smaller struggling supplementary industries such as costume hire, audio sound technicians and musicians placing emphasis on its economic survival. Third, most organisations, irrespective of size, rely heavily on government support through grants, budget allocation and supportive strategies such as tax incentives. This type of government support is diminishing in recent years while the competition for this form of support increases. Fourth, on a more theoretical level, the performing arts industry as an experiential service, is complicated by intangible elements. It is deeply entrenched with emotion and sensory stimuli and little research has been conducted specifically in this sector to understand the impact of these factors on RI. Finally, the focus of operations and marketing strategy in this sector has remained on the delivery of artistic value with very few organisations expanding strategic focus to fully appreciate the broader role of satisfaction, service quality, show experience and perceived value on customer RI. Clarifying the RI judgments and the relationship of post-purchase behavioural constructs on RI will offer insight into new strategies required to develop this sector while advancing service marketing and service operations theory.

Introducing Repurchase Intention in the Performing Arts Sector

The focus on constructs that lead to positive re-purchase intention and post-purchase behaviour such as value, quality and satisfaction (Caurana, Money and Berthon, 2000) has increased in services research (Henning-Thurau and Klee, 1997; Albrecht, 1992; Anderson, Fornell and Lehmann, 1994; Anderson and Sullivan, 1993; Broetzmann, Kemp, Rossano and Marwaha, 1995; Fornell, 1992; Heskett, Lovemann and Sasser and Schlesinger, 1994). For many years, the services research agenda was preoccupied with understanding the satisfaction construct and the antecedents of satisfaction. While, this research has been beneficial, it has not fully disclosed the nature of consumer's post-purchase behaviour, only their attitude toward satisfaction. Positive post-purchase behaviour, repeat re-purchase intention in particular, drives profitability. Constructs such as value, customer satisfaction and service quality (Bahia, Paulin and Perrien, 2000; Brady and Robertson, 2001) are associated with the customer intention to re-purchase. Therefore, to comprehensively examine and inform services research, focus on post-purchase behaviour, in particular, re-purchase intention, should be refined.

Services research initially grouped all services in order to develop the field of research and create generalised definitions (Brown, Fisk and Bitner, 1994). Service classifications have subsequently emerged in research (Silvestro, 1990; Lovelock, 1983) to recognise some of the subtle and observable differences of service types. Now more than 10 years on from the Brown, Fisk and Bitner (1994), researchers are questioning how the contextual differences of services may in fact alter the nature and relationships of constructs and influence the nature of post-purchase evaluation (Bahia, Paulin and Perrien, 2000) of differing service types and this warrants specific attention in research. Recent research has suggested that the causal relationship of satisfaction, perceived quality and re-purchase intention is dependent on contextual factors such as the nature of the service, the customer type and personality, time dimension, duration of relationships and corporate image (Bahia, Paulin and Perrien, 2000; Brady and Robertson, 2001; Monfort, Masurel and Van Rijn, 2000). It is suggested that the contextual differences of services may explain the inability to replicate findings across a broad range of services (Bahia, Paulin and Perrien, 2000) and that different service types could benefit from specific research.

One specific type of service context that will benefit from research is the experiential context (Addis and Holbrook, 2002) such as the performing arts. Research into post-service evaluation in this field has been rudimentary at best. This service context type is of interest due to its complexity. It is rich in emotional and intangible attributes (Addis and Holbrook, 2002; Holbrook and Hirschman, 1993) and irrespective of the physical and process elements needed to deliver the services, these intangibles have been the primary focus of research in the past and have overlooked customer evaluation judgments encompassing other aspects. Experiential service research has primarily focused on the delivery of emotional goals and the influence of these subjective factors on service satisfaction and how hedonistic aspects may drive consumption. This concentration has overlooked the relationship of service constructs such as service quality to subjective experiential factors. Moreover, research devoted to re-purchase drivers, and in particular, the examination of the relationship of comparison standards of utility measures and service quality to experiential variables, such as emotion as predictors of RI, has not been developed significantly. The specific nature of traditional constructs in experiential settings is also undeveloped. As such, this research intends to examine positive re-purchase intention in an experiential setting using the performing arts experience as an archetype of an experiential setting.

Understanding re-purchase intention drivers will advance research in this sector. Performing arts researchers have suggested, for the survival of the cultural arts, it is essential that audience retention and growth be increased and attention is given to audience development (Rentschler, Radbourne, Carr and Rickard, 2002). In order to do this, it must first be understood why customers return and do not return to performing arts performances. Performing arts research has primarily focused on attendance drivers such as critic reviews and segmenting patrons' degree of love of the performing arts (Bouder-Pailler, 1998). However, re-purchase judgments and continued attendance has not been specifically addressed. By better understanding the drivers of re-purchase intention such as what constitutes perceived value, show experience, service quality, satisfaction and re-purchase intention, this sector could begin to design services, programs and program delivery which best retain and enhance audience numbers and provide services which assist in developing audiences for long term survival. Identifying the varied measures and relationships present in the consumer mindset will assist cultural arts managers in better segmenting and customizing the offering and delivery of the service experience as well as innovating for future sustainability.

Services research has focused on the marketing field often minimizing the importance of service operations and services management. Specific service operations research in a performing arts or experiential service setting is extremely limited highlighting the need for examination in this sector. Moreover, the use of operations techniques in examining repurchase intention and visitation are essential to ensure that service delivery and service process aspects are fully examined. This research draws upon the fields of operations and marketing, thereby advancing and endorsing the importance of the once proposed, "service management trinity" (Lovelock Patterson and Walker, 1998). The 'trinity' recognises the importance of the interrelationship of operations management, marketing and human resources in successful business practices in the services sector.

The Research Program, Design, and Method

As a multidisciplinary approach to the understanding of RI in experiential settings has not been adopted previously in services research, the Study 1 and Study 2 research programs were exploratory, descriptive, and qualitative. They were orientated toward conceptualisation and theory building. In order to extract rich and substantial descriptions of a typical performing arts experience, several managerial decision makers and consultant customers were interviewed. This process resulted in clarification and identification of the boundaries of the service experience offered and an expected service experience as seen by the providing organisation and the customer. The aim of this Study was to clarify the baseline phenomena for observation. The overarching research question focused on the primary aim: "How do organisations and customers define and describe a typical performing arts encounter?" Sub-questions included "How do performing arts service providers evaluate their offering?" and "How does the performing arts consumer observe and evaluate the performing arts service experience and the process of service delivery?" This study informed the structure of several key constructs to be investigated, including the service description from the provider and customer perspectives, and the service process and service design from the provider and customer perspectives. .

The second study focused on using the definitions gained in Study 1 to extract thick description from current and potential performing arts customers. It consisted of 26 in-depth interviews with a sample of past and potential performing arts customers. Research questions addressed included:

"What are the attributes that contribute to re-purchase in the performing arts?"
"What factors drive satisfaction and dissatisfaction?"
"What factors are critical in a performing arts experience?"
"What factors do not affect your overall value perception of the experience?"
"What role does emotion play in the overall service delivery?"

The objective of this investigation was to systematically disclose the hierarchy of factors that consumers assessed in their decision to return to another performing arts experience. The interviews were used to gather thick description of the critical factors and non-critical factors (Johnston and Heineke, 1998) such as interactions with contact employees, service scripts, and tangible and intangible service aspects that drive performance measures such as satisfaction and value in a performing arts experience. Moreover, this study identified why consumers have chosen to consume other activities instead of the performing arts. This third study in this program used structural equation modeling to test the model of RI proposed for this investigation. A survey instrument was developed primarily from known marketing scales and modified to fit the performing arts context. After undergoing purification and pre-testing, it was administered to a sample of 273 candidates.

The research process offered collectively by the papers discussed, includes a set of three integrated and triangulated approaches that builds on each other to offer a rigorous set of contributions. The first process is based on the operations technique Service Transaction Analysis (STA). First, consultant consumers and organisational personnel were used to formulate a consensus definition of a typical performing arts experience and, second, 26 in-depth interviews were conducted with potential future Qualitative work undertaken identified the service experience description. The survey measured and tested the key constructs of service quality, show experience, value, satisfaction and the significance of the researched pathways to re-purchase intention. The proposed model was then analysed using the AMOS 5.0 Structural Equation Modelling package.

Overall, the format of the research program reported in this research can be divided into two segments; conceptualisation and theory building and testing. Study 1 and Study 2 are deeply entrenched in conceptualisation, developing theory to be tested in Study 3. Study 3 of this program focuses on theory testing, specifically, the relationships of service quality, show experience, customer satisfaction and value to re-purchase intention in a performing arts setting. This work has lead to other constructs being examined including emotion and involvement and the findings and discussion of these papers can be found in Hume and Sullivan Mort (2009a) and (2009b).

The Papers

This section offers a short summary of each of the papers used in this chapter. Moreover, this section highlights how the studies map on to each of the papers presented. Paper 1 (Hume, Sullivan Mort, Liesch and Winzar, 2006) titled *"Understanding Service Experience in Non-Profit Performing Arts: Implications for Operations and Service Management"* discusses the operations field and uses an operations analytical approach applied to the performing arts. This paper specifically addresses Study 1 and Study 2. This paper focuses analysis from an operations management perspective of the performing arts and aims to first develop a baseline definition and description of the performing arts. It accomplishes this by comparing the descriptions offered by both organisational representatives and consultant customers (Study 1) and then uses this baseline description to interview 26 potential entertainment consumers about their attitude to performing arts consumption and evaluation. This paper reports that arts managers have a truncated description of the encounter in comparison to the consultant customers. This highlights the limited focus of arts managers on issues other that artistic delivery. Further to this, the paper offers insight into the service attributes customers value as satisfiers, dissatisfies and critical factors in service delivery in this context. The findings highlight the importance of service factors such as service quality and personnel interactions and emphasise the importance of considering this in service strategy. Moreover, the paper identifies several segments of consumers, which have not been previously considered by performing arts management. The paper offers managerial recommendations for these groups and performing arts managers focusing on standardised mass customisation.

Extending these findings and arguments developed in Hume et al. (2006), Hume et al. (2007) *Exploring re-purchase intention in a performing arts context: Who comes? And why do they come back?"* and Hume 2008a (not specifically discussed in this chapter) takes a marketing approach to the 26 qualitative interviews conducted in Study 2 and presents the experiential and utilitarian aspects identified in a performing arts setting which the candidates identified as driving re-purchase. This paper further develops the integrated and progressive discussion central to the research questions of this research. The identified attributes were coded to experiential or utilitarian attributes and it was made evident that utilitarian aspects such as service quality are of primary importance to the majority of candidates. Moreover, this paper reported that consumers identified that hedonic and experiential aspects may drive consumption, however, the utility aspects were more strongly suggested as driving re-purchase. This paper suggests candidates did not regard experiential and emotional aspects of the encounter as drivers of re-purchase intention, emotion was given little attention as a predictive construct of re-purchase intention in the tested models used in Study 3, and reported in Hume (2008a and 2008b) and Hume and Sullivan Mort (2008). It further examines and reports the issues of involvement, emotion and subscription and how these interact and persuade the consumer's decisions to consume and re-purchase. [This work informed the development of examination into the influence of involvement and emotion on the intent to revisit (Hume and Sullivan Mort, 2009a and 2009b)].

Moreover, the second paper further covers consumer's experiences of a typical performing arts service to identify the predictors of positive re-purchase intention. This paper reports that functional factors, especially value and service qualities, are extremely important to candidates when deciding to re-purchase in this setting. Factors such as emotional attainment and show experience, which have been the primary focus of current strategy, were found to play a lesser role in overall desire to re-purchase. This paper then identifies specific psychological segments of consumers and explores the specific attributes driving re-purchase for each group. The focus of this paper was to observe issues not previously developed in any depth in Hume et al. (2006) such as involvement, subscription and emotional outcomes. Together, these two papers offer comprehensive coverage of both the marketing and operations topics offered by the 26 candidates' interviews. Moreover, these papers contribute to consolidating the fields of operations management and marketing in this context and reflect the close relationship as depicted by the service management trinity (Lovelock Patterson and Walker, 2000). The papers build on each other and create a progressive and informative argument on the nature of re-purchase intention in an experiential setting.

Hume and Sullivan Mort (2008) and Hume (2008b) respectively report the structure and findings of Study 3. As the relationships of service quality, show experience, satisfaction and value are unclear in extant research, it was seen as prudent to first test these inter-relationships and clearly define each construct prior to testing the re-purchase intention model. Hume et al. (2008) is specifically concerned with the role of value and satisfaction in a performing arts setting and is titled: *"Satisfaction in a performing arts context: What role does value play?"*. The paper found that value was derived from both service quality and the show experience with no direct relationship of these constructs to satisfaction. The model found value mediated the relationship of service quality and show experience to satisfaction and reported strategies for ensuring that consumers perceive a value experience. Hume (2008b) *"Understanding core and peripheral service quality in customer repurchase of the performing arts"* covers the full system of relationships that Study 3 investigates. This paper examines the relationships of service quality, show experience, value and satisfaction to re-purchase intention and reports that the independent variables of service quality and show experience have a positive and indirect relationship with RI with a positive and direct relationship to value. The paper reports that satisfaction mediates the value relationship to re-purchase intention and that no direct relationship exists between service quality and show experience to satisfaction and re-purchase intention. These constructs are reported to be mediated by value to satisfaction to re-purchase intention in the context of the performing arts.

Interestingly, the tested model found empirically that the subjective and experiential aspects of the service, such as the emotional and artistic quality of the show, did not have a significant and direct relationship with re-purchase intention. This finding is of interest, in particular, to scholars of experiential consumption and marketing practitioners offering these types of services. Previous research has supported the desire to fulfil experiential needs as driving the initial purchase. Conversely, this finding suggests that the desire to visit again is driven by utility and value. As customer maintenance and repeat patronage are of utmost importance to practice, this is an exciting development. Offering further support, the tested model found service quality and show experience were mediated by value to satisfaction, with satisfaction inturn mediating the relationship between value and re-purchase intention. Collectively, these findings have lead to several developments and contributions for both scholarship and practice. The contributions to knowledge of this research highlight five main theoretical contributions and four main managerial implications which will be discussed in this implications and reflections section of this chapter.

At a summary level, these findings encompass the critical need for performing arts managers to increase efforts to understand their markets and customers (current and potential) and the necessary engagement that must occur with their respective organisations and their service offerings. The need for professional managers in non-profit organisations, particularly the performing arts, who possess the requisite graduate management training and experience, must be emphasised. Loyalty, "a love of the arts" and/or longevity of involvement, whilst desirable credentials, should be secondary attributes to engaging and/or employing management professionals to guide the performing arts organisations through the increasing competitive entertainment landscape. Moreover, focusing the design and delivery of the performing arts service from a practice of cultural exhibition to a consumer-driven service offering is a fundamental that must transform performing arts organisations to ensure their future survival.

Contribution to the Scholarship of Non-profit Research and Performing Arts: Reflections and Limitations for Non-profit Performing Arts Managers

The contributions to scholarship of this research consist of managerial implications and theoretical contributions. These contributions are discussed and presented in the reflections and implications section. The managerial recommendations proposed include market segmentation and targeting, service positioning strategy, operations service design, streamlining delivery through standardised mass customisation and providing customer value. The theoretical contributions include first, advancing the service management trinity (Lovelock, Patterson and Walker, 2000) and strengthening the importance of the relationship between service marketing and service operations. Using operations techniques in this research program assists in identifying a more accurate profile of consumer needs and expectations. Second, development of the construct of RI and research of the predictors of this construct especially pertinent to the cultural arts (Jones and Suh, 2000; Patterson and Spreng, 1997; Butcher, Sparks, O'Callaghan, 2002, Soderlund, 2002, Anderson and Sullivan, 1993, Slogland and Siguaw, 2004, Bagozzi, Gopinath and Nyer, 1999; Liljander and Mattsson, 2002) is achieved.

This sector has received little research focus examining these specific constructs. Research into this sector will be advanced by further increasing knowledge in this area. Finally, contributions to service management in experiential settings will be gained through advancing the measures of construct, testing their relevance and offering an extended description of the service to inform design theory. Specifically, incorporating utilitarian attributes into performing arts and experiential research (Addis and Holbrook, 2002) will be accomplished, advancing experiential research. The following discussion highlights the full set of reflections for performing art managers including both the theoretical and practical operations management and services marketing contributions that have been highlighted throughout this research program. These contributions are identified as theoretical contributions and managerial implications.

Theoretical Contributions and Implications

This section will discuss in more depth each of these contributions.

Contribution 1: Operations, Marketing and the Service Trinity

Strengthening and amalgamating management fields of service operations and service marketing in service management this research strengthens various aspects of the significance of the service management trinity (Lovelock, Patterson and Walker, 1998) and recommends scholars look to operations management theory and practice when examining service settings. Figure 1 depicts the service management trinity revealing the interrelationships between service operations, human resources, and service marketing and how each of these interact and affect the customer.

The dotted pathways identify the links between marketing and operations management that have been strengthened by this research program. Service marketing and service operations are not mutually exclusive, they are interrelated and they are essential components of each other. Hume et al. (2006) titled "Understanding Service Experience in Non-Profit Performing Arts: Implications for Operations and Service Management" highlighted the use of Service Transaction Analysis (Johnston, 1999) and showed the important contribution of adopting an operations management approach in informing service management and marketing. By performing consultant customer and organisational interviews, this paper advanced service research by mutually reinforcing aspects of these two fields, offering a multifaceted and more thorough approach to encounter analysis than has been the norm to date.

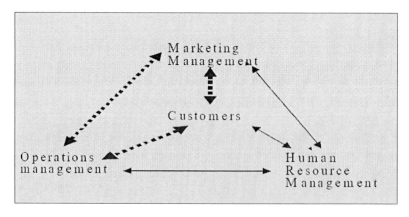

Figure 7.1. Service Management Trinity.

Contribution 2: Enhancing the Definition of Service Offering

The primary implication of the research findings in Hume, Sullivan Mort, Liesch and Winzar (2006) was the need to understand the customer's definition and perception of the service on offer. Understanding definition and description is tantamount to identifying primary expectations of the service and are important to reducing gap conflict (Berry,

Parasuraman and Zeithaml, 1990) between the service/s expected and the service/s delivered. Using gap analysis and Service Transaction Analysis (Johnston, 1999) complemented by the use of in-depth interviews has assisted in informing managers of the encounter requirements perceived by customers. Gaining sound understanding of the expectations and perceptions of the service on offer assists in unraveling the consumption and re-consumption behaviours of all potential target markets. This process and the strategic recommendations offered, in particular elements of customisation strategy, highlight the importance of the service management trinity (Lovelock, Patterson and Walker, 1998) and the interrelationship of operations management and service marketing. Highlighting the importance of the service management trinity, this research emphasises the need for cross-field research in the services arena.

Contribution 3: Experiential Consumption and Re-purchase

The collation of scholarly contributions presented in this chapter and the research investigation has advanced research into experiential service settings (Addis and Holbrook, 2002), specifically in cultural arts marketing and management. Researchers of experiential consumption posit that satisfying the emotional requirements of the customer is the key to satisfaction (Addis and Holbrook, 2002). However, it is evident from the research program that the nature of RI in the performing arts is not one-dimensional but rather it is a complex multidimensional process of factors complicated by consumer definition of the context. This research has identified that consumers define the service through their own needs and measure subjective and objective experience attributes accordingly related to their perception of what the experience is and what it means to them.

As reported, it was found, that desired service was dependent on how the customer perceived the service as either high or low contact, as general entertainment or as artistic or an emotionally charged experience. Satisfaction was then derived from a measurement of the technical qualities of the show with the overall show experience being strongly related to emotion. Moreover, the functional quality of the service delivery and venue quality and the level of satisfaction with the "performance" of these desired factors, also led to satisfaction and satisfaction led to RI. Therefore, the intent to re-purchase was decided by the degree of satisfaction derived from desired level of performance with functional and/or technical quality. From a theoretical perspective, the findings of the qualitative research (Hume et al, 2006; Hume Sullivan Mort and Winzar, 2007) support experiential aspects as motivators of consumption in certain customer segments, but challenge them as the keys drivers of satisfaction and RI in others.

Contribution 4: Re-purchase Intention and its Antecedents

Current theory in RI has been extended through the clarification of RI, the measure of the antecedents of RI and by testing their inter-relationships. This research has examined how service quality and show experience interact with satisfaction and value to directly and /or indirectly measure and predict re-purchase intention. Each of these constructs had been shown in previous research to have some form of direct or indirect relationship with RI. To briefly review the highlights of previous research, value has been positioned as a direct antecedent of both loyalty and RI and to act indirectly as a moderator of service quality and satisfaction (Caruana, Money and Berthon, 2000). This relationship was not supported by this research. Further research offered value to be entirely mediated through satisfaction to RI (Patterson and Spreng, 1997). This relationship was supported. Slogland and Siguaw (2004) offered service quality as a direct antecedent of RI but this was not supported by this research. Service quality has also been shown to affect customer satisfaction (Harvey, 1998) and therefore was proposed to indirectly influence RI.

This research found that in a performing arts setting, service quality was mediated by value to satisfaction. Interestingly, the experiential nature and the need for the attainment of subjective emotional goals (Bagozzi *et al.,* 1999) in the performing arts are suggested to complicate the nature of service. This was not confirmed by the qualitative research (Hume et al, 2006 and Hume et al, 2007) and was subsequently not tested in the structural model due to this weak association. The relationships that were found significant in this performing arts setting included service quality and show experience as predictors of value, however these constructs had no direct relationship with re-purchase. Value was shown to mediate the relationship between these constructs and satisfaction. Satisfaction mediated the relationship between value and re-purchase intention.

Interestingly, it was found that service quality was a stronger predictor of value in a performing arts setting than was show experience, positioning it as an important construct for consideration in future performing arts audience and market development research. Discovering this, in an experiential sector that has focused on subjective factors, has advanced experiential and performing arts research into a new regime that could be innovative and exciting research. Finding service quality to have a stronger relationship with value by no means suggests that the show experience is not an important construct, it merely presents the construct, value, in a performing arts setting as a multidimensional measure of the show and the service quality. In sum, it was found that the antecedents of RI are multiple and complex, including utilitarian aspects rather than focusing purely on experiential and emotional aspects. This finding contributes to a more comprehensive understanding of the nature of RI in a performing arts experiential service setting.

Contribution 5: Providing Value and Satisfaction

Not only did this research identify the above-mentioned relationships as important elements of re-purchase intention but also it supported a positive relationship between satisfaction and RI supporting the application of Patterson and Spreng (1997) in an experiential cultural arts setting. This research offered insight into the nature of customer satisfaction and the role that service quality factors play in deriving satisfaction. The main theme raised throughout this investigation was the relationship between utilitarian and experiential service aspects and the relationship of these to customer satisfaction in this setting. Performing arts management has focused on the delivery of artistic value and content, often minimizing the importance of service and venue quality. This investigation has found that it is a strategic imperative for arts managers to understand the complexity of the satisfaction equation and to ensure that service delivery; service quality and venue quality are given the commensurate emphasis in strategic development and implementation as artistic content.

Managerial Contributions and Implications

The following discussion highlights the practical operations management and marketing contributions that have been highlighted throughout this research program as areas of consideration. These managerial contributions include:

Implication 1: Segmentation and Targeting Strategies

It is evident throughout studies 1 and 2 presented in (Hume et al, 2006; Hume, Sullivan Mort and Winzar, 2007) respectively, that distinct market segments exist, each with differing needs and measures of performance that are not currently being maximised. The importance of profiling market potential to understand the market's attractiveness and achieve optimal service design is not new in service research (Verma *et al..*, 2001). However, CEO in-depth interviews suggested that it is not widely practiced. It is imperative that the performing arts sector expands their target market definition and advances the approach to current segmentation practices. Consequently, it is recommended that managers explore other market segments, identify their potential, understand the dimensions and requirements required by each potential segment and design services to satisfy the new market/s needs. Hume et al. (2006) argued that more focus needs to be given to the deeper complexities of the performing arts sector such as the wider competitive market identified by customers and the importance of consumer's utility and service quality. These factors are important criteria available to the segmentation and targeting process.

It is apparent from the research presented in Hume et al. (2006) that the performing arts need to elaborate the positioning statement of the service from a purely cultural offering. At the very least, including the more complete entertainment offering will start to re-position the service. The entertainment sector has grown in recent years to include sport consumption, movies and other cultural pursuits. The communication of the service position of the performing arts needs greater breadth and depth to capitalise on the potential of this expanded market definition to compete with other entertainment forms. The objective of this re-positioning is to attract new customer segments to protect and maximise the financial returns.

Implication 2: Customer Value Frameworks

Strategists have often overlooked the heterogeneous nature of customer value perceptions and generally try to satisfy them generically on a mass level. By virtue of this, and the belief that the show experience is the most important aspect of providing value, service quality is often overlooked in strategic development. The findings of this research suggest the need for a significant shift in managerial practice away from solely focusing on the show delivery to an increased comprehension and delivery of the factors that make up customer perceived value that influence satisfaction and that influence the desire to re-purchase in this context. It is evident from the research that this practice needs to be expanded to include the elements of service quality that the customer identifies as the factors of financial and temporal value.

This research reveals that consumers evaluate the extrinsic and augmented aspects of the experience such as assurance, trust and reliability as important measures of value and they must be satisfied with the performance of these to have satisfaction and positive RI. Cultural arts managers must balance the delivery of quality service aspects, especially the contact points with personnel, and the price quality perception with the time and budget invested in show development. Once establishing the predictors of value, the cultural arts manager needs to design programs and delivery processes that attain the satisfaction of the customer. It is evident that service design will play an important role in the delivery of a value experience.

The service design process needs to integrate not only the core technical quality factors of the performing arts and their delivery but also the functional quality, supplementary and facilitating services customer segments suggested as important performance measures. It is evident that the differing segments did emphasize different elements of service design, thus bestowing a level of complexity to the design process. Functional quality aspects have been demonstrated in this research to be a more important measure to the broader potential segments. Finally, it is evident there will be cost considerations when innovating and implementing changes and these changes need to achieve positive returns through positive behavioral responses of the potential segments.

Implication 3: Operations Service Design and Creation Strategies

A basic premise of strategic planning is that an organisation must determine its objectives before formulating competitive strategies and organising its operations resources and capabilities to deliver them. Identifying, defining and quantifying the strategic objectives are often very difficult for many organisations, including mature industry players such as the performing arts. In particular, determining the functional operations strategies such as marketing, human resources, finance and the more intricate functions of design, delivery and fulfillment to achieve strategic objectives must be supported by a thorough understanding of the service description and offering. This is the basic premise of strategic alignment (Johnston and Heineke, 1998). Decisions including the depth and breadth of service offering such as specific genres to be presented, the diversity of genre offering and subsets offered within genres will all be affected by the description and defined service offering.

Moreover, the measurement of organisational capability to meet the desired breadth and depth decisions and the complexities of design and delivery will also be influenced by the actual description of the service offering. The performing arts sector and many of the diverse organisations it houses would undoubtedly benefit from a greater comprehension of the specific description and desired offering as perceived by the customer. Furthermore, using customer integrated design procedures would enhance in translating the customer's service description and desired service offering into service strategy; this ideally leading to satisfied customers with a positive intent to re-purchase.

Implication 4: Streamlining Delivery through Standardised Mass Customisation

The use of a mass customisation strategy is recommended for performing arts organisations to provide a well-designed system of delivery for its many customer profiles. However, the costs of implementing this strategy, in an industry sector facing intense competition, may outweigh the benefits obtained. A proposed approach to implementing mass customisation in this setting is to offer multiple quality-standardised processes that can be *self-customised* according to the segment profile of consumption desires and judgment processes of each customer. More specifically, each customer can consume the aspects of the service they desire. This standardised mass customisation approach is proposed as a cost effective alternative to pure mass customisation and is suggested as the most appropriate for the performing arts to cater to high volumes of diverse customers allowing for variety in consumption patterns (Stevenson, 2002) while controlling costs.

Conclusion

This research program and chapter discussion has focused primarily on a general non profit performing arts organizational definition extracted from consumer and CEO interviews and has not intentionally selected particular organisational segments nor organisational categories for survey. This was as a result of the research design selected in each of the studies and the envisaged need of a strong foundation context for examination. Future research could adopt a different research design and specifically select another organisational description based on some other secondary source. Research could be conducted using organisational types such as small troupes, large multiple genre venues and small niche venues. Furthermore, this research purposively selected entertainment customers in order to understand why potential performing arts customers chose between entertainment offerings and why they returned to the performing arts. Other specific customer types, as examined in popular arts research such as regular, subscriber and infrequent users (Garbarino and Johnson, 1999) observing in particular, levels of involvement and commitment, could also provide an interesting and worthwhile approach for future research.

As research of this type, in this sector, has been limited in the past, compared to other service sectors and generally in the non-profit sectors, there are many additional themes and topics for future research. Future themes could include an examination of performing arts organisations and their business performance, considering the governance and function of the organisation i.e. rather than focusing on large government-owned and managed venues, research could be conducted with smaller community-based non-profit troupes investigating whether internal function and type is considered by the customer and influences their tolerance and judgments. This style of research could highlight whether or not customers perceive large venue based organisations to be different to smaller troupe style performers and performances. It is often suggested in arts research that the venue and the performance are perceived as separate (Cuadrado and Molla, 2000; Cowan, 2001 and Bouder-Pailler, 1999). The participants in this investigation did not put forward this, in fact they saw each as a part of the other. However, in different performing arts settings with different customer types, customers may offer opposing views. Research based on organisational structure and type and differing customer type could test this conjecture.

This research was not specific to show selection i.e. a general approach to genre was adopted. Implementing genre specific research program, comparing responses in popular genres versus non-popular genres, could further develop research findings. In addition to researching different service types within the cultural arts, research could examine whether or not value and satisfaction measure differently in other different physical settings such as sporting venues and entertainment event management and whether the relationships confirmed in this research could also exist in other non-experiential contexts.

The model adopted in this program was based on the current literature for RI. One construct which received little attention, however is discussed, is emotion. In Studies 1 and 2 of this program, consumers focused little attention on this construct. Emotion or the need for emotion was suggested as a part of the show experience by a small number of emotionally driven customers, and not addressed at all by the majority. These customers grouped it as a small part of the show. Therefore, emotion was not considered in the main model developed for testing [Emotion has subsequently been tested in Hume and Sullivan Mort (2009a)]. Future research could develop this construct more, considering additional pathways such as emotion as a predictor of value, satisfaction and/or RI and further examine the group of consumers who appear to be emotionally charged. Moreover, other specific higher-order factors of other constructs such as service quality and show experience could also be examined to further inform management strategy, service creation and delivery strategy. Testing higher-order factors relationships would offer deeper understanding of the nature and measurement of the constructs developed in this investigation.

The research conducted in this program did not examine the third arm of the service management trinity, human resource management. The service management trinity unites operations, human resource and services marketing and suggests the three fields interact to define strategy. Focusing on human resource strategy could provide an interesting area of future research and elaborate strategic innovations in this area. Some candidates saw the cultural performing arts as high contact and in this case human resource management would play a role in the measure of value, satisfaction and RI.

Overall, this research project focused on measuring re-purchase intention in a cultural performing arts setting. The composition of the context definition was extracted from a set of consultant customers and organisational CEOs. These candidates formulated a general description that formed the basis for research in Study 2 and Study 3. This description may not be reflective of all performing arts venues and organisations nor can results be generalised to all performing arts venues without further research. However, this research has broadened the managerial and theoretical underpinning of enquiry in this area and has advanced the model of RI in this context. The performing arts have not been a popular choice of service context in business research and have not received the same attention from rigorous business researchers as has health, professional services and telecommunications. This program has offered rich investigation that will assist in the future development of audience retention strategies, service creation and delivery in this sector. It has offered developmental strategies that can begin to establish the survival and growth strategies for the future of this sector and bridge a previously unexplored nexus of services marketing and operations management. Moreover, this research contributes to the domains of academic researchers, artistic managers and business managers in the performing arts sector.

References

Addis, M., Holbrook, M.B. (2001). "On the conceptual link between mass customisation and experiential consumption: An explosion of subjectivity", *Journal of Consumer Behaviour,* **1**(1):50-66.

Albrecht, K. (1992) *The Only Thing That Matters, Bringing the Power of the Customer Into the Centre Of Your Business,* New York, Harper Business.

Anderson, E., Fornell, C., and Lehmann, D. (1994) "Customer satisfaction, market share, and profitability: Findings from Sweden", *Journal of Marketing,* **58**:53-66.

Anderson, E.W. and Sullivan, M. (1993) "The antecedents and consequences of customer satisfaction for firms", *Marketing Science,* **12**:125-43.

Bagozzi, R., Gopinath, M., and Nyer, P. (1999) 'The role of emotions in marketing', *Academy of Marketing Science,* **27**(2):184-206.

Bahia, K., Paulin, M., and Perrien, J. (2000) "Reconciliating literature about client satisfaction and perceived service quality", *Journal of Professional Services Marketing,* **12**(2):21-41.

Berry, L., Zeithaml, V., Parasuraman, A. (1990). "Five imperatives for improving service quality", *Sloan Management Review,* **31**(4) Summer: 29-38.

Bouder-Pailler, D. (1999). "A model for measuring the goals of theatre attendance", *International Journal of Arts Management,* **1**(2): 4-15.

Brady, M.K., Robertson, C.J.. (2001). "Searching for a consensus on the antecedent role of service quality and satisfaction: An exploratory cross national study", *Journal of Business Research,* **51**:53-60.

Broetzmann, S.M., Kemp, J., Rossano, M., and Marwaha, J. (1995) "Customer satisfaction – lip service or management tool?", *Managing Service Quality,* **5**(2):13-18.

Brown, S., Fisk, R., Bitner, M. (1994), "The development and emergence of services marketing thought", *International Journal of Service Industry Management,* Vol. 1 pp.21-48.

Butcher, K., Sparks, B., and O'Callaghan, F. (2002) 'Effect of social influence on repurchase intention', *Journal of Services Marketing,* **16**(6):503-515.

Caruana, A., Money, A., and Berthon, P. (2000) "Service quality and satisfaction- the moderating role of value", *European Journal of Marketing,* **34**(11/12):1338-1256.

Cavenago, D., Francesconi, A., Santuari, A. (2002). "The shift in cultural management from government agencies to non-for-profit organizations: An Italian case study", *International Journal of Arts Management,* **4**(2):16-24.

Cooper-Martin, E. (1991). "Consumers and motives: Some findings on experiential products." *Advances in Consumer Research,* 18 (1):372-379.

Cowan, D. (2001) 'The art of business', *Accountancy,* **127**(1293):68-73.

Cuadrado, M., Molla, A. (2000) "Grouping performing arts consumers according to attendance goals", *International Journal of Arts Management,* **2**(3): 54-60.

Cutts, C. and Drozd, F. (1995) "Managing the performing arts", *Business Quarterly,* **59**(3):62.

Danaher, P. and Mattsson, J. (1994). "Cumulative encounter satisfaction in the hotel conference process", *International Journal Service Industry Management,* **5**(4):69-80.

Fornell, C. (1992) "A national satisfaction barometer: The Swedish experience", *Journal of Marketing,* **56**(1):6-21.

Fornell, C. and Johnson, M.D. (1993) "Differentiation as a basis for explaining customer satisfaction across industries", *Journal of Economic Psychology*, December 1993, **14**(4):681-696.

Garbarino, E. and Johnson, M.S. (1999) "The different roles of satisfaction, trust, and commitment in customer relationships", *Journal of Marketing*, **63**(2):70-87.

Grönroos, C. (1990) "Relationship approach to marketing in service contexts: The marketing and organizational behaviour interface", *Journal of Business Research*, **20**(1):3-11.

Harvey, J. (1998). "Service Quality: A tutorial.", *Journal of Operations Management*, **16**(5):583-597.

Hennig-Thurau, T. and Klee, A. (1997) "The impact of customer satisfaction and relationship quality on customer retention: A critical reassessment and model development", *Psychology and Marketing*, **14**(8):737-764.

Heskett, J.L., Jones, T.O., Loveman, G.W., Sasser, W.E. Jr, and Schlesinger, L.A. (1994) "Putting the service-profit chain to work", *Harvard Business Review*, **72**(2):164-172.

Hirschman, E.C. (1982) "Hedonic consumption: Emerging concepts, method and propositions", *Journal of Marketing*, **46**(3):92-102.

Holbrook, M. and Hirschman, E. (1982) "The experiential aspects of consumption: Consumer fantasies, feelings and fun", *Journal of Consumer Research*, (**4**):132-140.

Holbrook, M.B. (2000). "The millennial consumer in the text of our times: Experience and entertainment", *Journal of Macromarketing*, **20**(2):178-192.

Hume, M., Sullivan Mort, G.(2009a) "Understanding the role of involvement in customer repurchase of the performing arts" *Journal of Nonprofit and Public Sector Marketing* **21**, (1)

Hume M., and Sullivan Mort. G., (2009b) "The consequence of appraisal emotion, service quality, value and satisfaction on repurchase intention in the performing arts" *The Journal of Services Marketing* editors letter received 7th April 2008

Hume M. (2008a) "Conceptualising a behavioural model of repeaters in the performing arts: the role of emotion, core service and peripheral service delivery" *International Journal of Arts Management.*, **10**(2) Winter 2008

Hume, M., (2008b)"Understanding core and peripheral service quality in customer repurchase of the performing arts. " *Managing Service Quality* Vol. 18 No. 4, 2008

Hume M., and Sullivan Mort. G., (2008)"Repurchase in a performing arts context: What role does value play?" *European Journal of Marketing*

Hume, M., Sullivan Mort, G., and Winzar, H. (2007). "Exploring Repurchase Intention in a Performing Arts Context: Who comes? And why do they come back?, *International Journal of Not-Profit and Voluntary Sector Marketing* accepted for publication 2007

Hume, M., Sullivan Mort, G., Liesch, P., and Winzar, H.(2006) "Understanding Service Experience I Non-Profit Performing Arts: Implications for Operations and Service Management", Journal *of Operations Management, Special Issue: Not for Profit, Government and Voluntary Sector Management.*

Johnston, R. (1999) "Service transaction analysis: Assessing and improving the customer's experience", *Managing Service Quality*, **9**(2):102-109.

Johnston, R., Heineke, J. (1998) "Exploring the relationship between perception and performance: Priorities for action", *The Services Industry Journal*, **18**(1):101-109.

Jones, M. and Suh, J. (2000) "Transaction-specific satisfaction and overall satisfaction: An empirical analysis", *The Journal of Services Marketing*, **14**(2):147-168.

Lovelock, Christopher (1983) "Classifying services to gain strategic marketing insights", *Journal of Marketing, American Marketing Association Chicago*, **47**(9):20.

Lovelock, C. and Patterson, P. and Walker, R. (1998) *Services Marketing - Australia and New Zealand*, Prentice Hall, Australia.

Monfort, K., Masurel, E., Van Rijn, I. (2000). "Service satisfaction: An empirical analysis of consumer satisfaction to financial services", *The Services Industries Journal*, **20**(3): 84-94.

Patterson, P.G. and Spreng, R.A. (1997). "Modelling of the relationship between value, satisfaction and repurchase intention in a business-to-business, professional services context: An empirical investigation", *International Journal of Service Industry Management*, **8**(5):414-438.

Pine, B., Gilmore, J. (1999) "Welcome to the experience economy", *Harvard Business Review*, .**76** (July/August):97-105.

Rentschler, R., Radbourne, J., Carr, R., and Rickard, J. (2002) "Relationship marketing, audience retention and performing arts organisations viability", *International Journal of Non-Profit and Voluntary Sector Marketing*, **7**(2):118-130.

Scheff, J. (1999). "Factors influencing subscription and single-purchases at performing arts organisations", *International Journal of Arts Management*, **1**(2):16-26.

Slogland, I. and Siguaw, J. (2004) "Are your satisfied customers loyal?", *Cornell Hotel and Restaurant Quarterly*, **45**(3):221-234.

Sonderlund, M. (2002) "Customer familiarity and its effects on satisfaction and behavioural intentions", *Psychology and Marketing*, **19**(10):861-871.

Stevenson, W.J. (2002). Operations Management, Seventh Edition, McGraw-Hill Irwin.

Sullivan Mort, G., Weerawardena, J., and Carnegie, K. (2003) "Social entrepreneurship: Towards conceptualisation", *International Journal of Non-Profit and Voluntary Sector Marketing*, **8**(1):76-90.

Verma, R., Thompson, G.M., Moore, W., Louviere, J.J., (2001) "Effective design of products/services: An approach based on integration of marketing and operations decisions", *Decision Sciences*, **32**(1):165-194.

Zikmund, W.G. (1997) Business Research Methods, Forth Worth TX, The Dryden Press.

In: Handbook of Business and Finance
Editors: M. Bergmann and T. Faust, pp. 101-122

ISBN: 978-1-60692-855-4
© 2010 Nova Science Publishers, Inc.

Chapter 4

EXPLAINING INDIVIDUAL EMPOWERMENT AMONG ELDERLY WOMEN VOLUNTEERS IN NONPROFIT ORGANIZATIONS: THE ISRAELI CASE

Liat Kulik[*]

School of Social Work, Bar Ilan University,
Ramat Gan, Israel

Abstract

The study aimed to explain the sense of empowerment in volunteer activity among Israeli women in middle and later life. The sample consisted of 146 women volunteering in social services in Israel. Based on Bronfenbrenner's ecological model of human adaptation to environments, the contribution of three ecological systems to explaining empowerment among volunteer women was examined: the ontogenic system, the microsystem, and the chronosystem. The women reported positive experiences with volunteering, as expressed in high levels of empowerment and family support for volunteer activity. In addition, the findings revealed high levels of satisfaction with rewards of volunteering and low levels of difficulty with the provider organization. The variables that contributed most to explaining empowerment in volunteering were those belonging to the ontogenic system: self-esteem and motives for volunteering. Of the microsystem variables, difficulties with the provider organization and rewards also contributed significantly to explaining empowerment.

Keywords: volunteering, women, midlife, late adulthood, ecological model

---

[*] E-mail address: kulikl@mail.biu. ac.il, Fax (School of Social Work): 972-3-5347228.

Explaining Individual Empowerment of Women Volunteers in Middle and Later Life

Over the past two centuries, women have played a major role in philanthropic and volunteer activities in a wide range of organizations throughout the world (Wilson, 2000). In the 19th century, for example, women's organizations in the United States promoted social reforms, particularly reforms aimed at enhancing the well-being of women and children. In the 19th and 20th centuries, women volunteered in various social organizations such as the sanitary commission, which cared for wounded soldiers during the Civil War in the United States. Jewish women's organizations have also sponsored charitable and philanthropic efforts on behalf of Jewish communities throughout the world (for a review, see Chambre, 2001). The first Zionist women's volunteer organizations were established between 1900 and 1903 in England, Austria, South Africa, and Ireland. In Israel, women's volunteer organizations such as WIZO and the Hadassah Women's Zionist organization were established as early as the beginning of the Zionist *Yishuv* (for a review see Herzog and Greenberg, 1978). The women belonging to those organizations were motivated mainly by a strong sense of public mission and social involvement, and their activities have made a substantial contribution to social action in Israel.

Today, women volunteers are more educated, more empowered, and have more personal and social skills than they did in the past. Moreover, women have developed higher levels of social and political awareness, and try to influence and shape policies in the organizations where they volunteer. Many women in Israel volunteer in social service organizations, and they constitute the absolute majority of volunteers in that sector (Kulik, 2004). The high proportion of women volunteers in welfare organizations can be attributed to the women's tendency to view volunteer activity as an extension of their traditional roles as mothers and wives (Negrey, 1993). It is commonly believed that women are empathic, and that they attach considerable importance to the value of altruism (Wilson and Musick, 1999). They feel guilty when they fail to show compassion for people who need their assistance (Flanagan, Bowes, Jonsson, Csapo, and Sheblanova, 1998), and believe that they are obligated to show concern for the personal and emotional needs of others (Daniels, 1988). Another reason for the high proportion of women volunteering in social service organizations is their tendency to engage more in "feminine" activities such as caregiving and nursing, than in activities of a political or public nature (Cable, 1992; Thompson, 1993). The central role of women volunteers in the fields of social welfare is evident in various countries (Gaskin and Smith, 1997), ethnic groups (Woodward, 1987), and age groups (Wuthnow, 1995; for a review, see also Wilson, 2000).

Most women who volunteer in social services in Israel have reached midlife or late adulthood. At those stages of life, women are gradually relieved of the responsibilities that they assumed at earlier stages. Especially after retirement, many of them choose volunteer activity as their main social role (Fisher and Schaffer, 1993). Some researchers argue that later life is accompanied by loss of resources, as well as by a decline in physical strength, health, economic resources, and social resources. The decline in resources, particularly after retirement, can lead to dependence on others and can affect several areas of life simultaneously (Cumming and Henry, 1961). However, other scholars argue that as of midlife women actually begin a process of growth and development. Although they still experience some decline in resources, they begin to perceive themselves as having more control over the environment, which alleviates the losses (Friedman, 1987). One of the factors that contributes to strengthening women in midlife and late adulthood is the reversal of gender roles, which begins when women are relieved of some of their parental responsibilities and become less dependent on their husbands (e.g., Gutmann, 1975). According to Jung (1933/1971), men often emphasize feminine aspects of their personality in late adulthood, which make them more dependent on their wives and further increase the women's perceived strength.

One of the prevalent terms that reflects the women's increased strength and independence over the life cycle is "empowerment". This term is particularly common among researchers with a feminist orientation, who encourage independence in women and promote egalitarian gender roles (Le-Bosse et al., 1999; Luks and Payne, 1991). In the present study, we examined the sense of empowerment in volunteering among women who volunteer in social services in Israel in midlife and late adulthood, as well as the variables that explain empowerment in those contexts.

On the Term "Empowerment"

In the early 1980s, the concept of empowerment was used in the social sciences in the context of therapeutic work with disadvantaged groups, as well as in rehabilitative care and special education. In this context, the concept was defined as an internal process, through which weak social groups acquire strength (Solomon, 1985). Today, the concept is used in a broader sense, and applies to contexts that are not necessarily characterized by weakness (Peterson and Hughey, 2002). Moreover, empowerment operates at various levels, including personal or individual, interpersonal, organizational, community, and collective (for a review, see Hur, 2006). Empowered people are characterized by a sense of authority and responsibility, and have a strong belief that they will succeed in attaining that goal. A low level of empowerment, however, is manifested in a sense of helplessness, loss, and lack of control over life and the environment (Rappaport, 1987). In the process of empowerment, individuals discover internal resources which enable them to generate new abilities such as helping others and developing leadership abilities in groups and organizations (Rappaport, Reisch, and Zimmerman, 1992). Researchers view empowerment as both a process and an outcome. Some researchers have used the term empowerment in reference to volunteers engaging in activities on behalf of the community and other beneficiaries. In that context, empowered individuals are confident of their ability to provide substantial assistance to needy persons and promote processes that benefit the community (Rodich, 2001).

In the present study, empowerment was examined as an outcome of volunteer activity among Israeli women in midlife and late adulthood. An attempt was made to explain sources of empowerment, based on a set of personal and situational variables. Toward that end, the author adopted the model developed by Wallach and Mueller (2006), which explains individual empowerment in the context of the work place. According to their model, the selection of variables that explain empowerment should reflect a multidimensional approach, which focuses on personal and environmental factors, e.g., resources available in the organizational context as well as stressors and difficulties encountered in the work place. Following that approach, a large set of variables was examined to explain women's personal sense of empowerment in volunteer activity. The explanatory variables, i.e., difficulties (stressors) and resources, were organized in the context of several systems belonging to Bronfenbrenner's (1979) ecological model.

The Conceptual Framework: The Ecological Approach

The underlying assumption of Bronfenbrenner's (1979) model is that human development occurs over a prolonged period in a continuing process of mutual interactions between individuals and their environment. These mutual interactions were initially described in the context of five systems: the microsystem, which reflects the relationships between individuals and their immediate environment; the mesosystem, which reflects the links between two or more microsystems in which the individual develops; the exosystem, which individuals do not belong to but has an indirect impact on their development; and the macrosystem, which includes the prevailing cultural values and norms that affect the development of the individual. Finally, the chronosystem (system of time), reflects the ongoing impact of experiences on the individual's development throughout the life cycle.

Various researchers have expanded Bronfenbrenner's ecological model, and added the dimension of the ontogenic (individual) system (Belsky, 1980; Garbarino, 1978), which includes psychological and emotional characteristics as well as objective demographic characteristics of individuals. The expanded model enables a more detailed analysis of personality traits that affect the adjustment and behavior of individuals, and has been adopted by researchers in the field. Even though Bronfenbrenner's (1979) model is not considered an actual theory, its principles and assumptions constitute an appropriate conceptual framework for organizing the variables that explain human development and attitudes in various spheres of life (Corcoran, Franklin, and Bennett, 2002).

Because it is difficult to examine all five of the ecological systems of Bronfenbrenner's model simultaneously, researchers usually examine only some of those systems in any given study (e.g., Huebner and Mancini, 2003). Consistent with this approach, we adopted three of the ecological systems of Bronfenbrenner's expanded model: the ontogenic (individual) system, the microsystem, and the chronosystem.

The Ontogenic System

The ontogenic system variables examined in this study were education, self-esteem, and motives for volunteering. We chose these variables to represent the ontogenic system because they reflect personality as well as sociodemographic background.

Education. Researchers have found a relationship between education and experience with volunteer activity (Rosenthal, Feiring, and Lewis, 1998). For example, researchers have argued that there is a relationship between education and the individual's tendency to volunteer. Specifically, it has been found that education increases social awareness and self-esteem which, in turn, enhance the individual's ability to help others (McPherson and Rotolo, 1996). However, there is a lack of research on the relationship between education and empowerment in volunteering, although studies have revealed a relationship between women's education and empowerment in other domains such as work (Izraeli, 1999). Evidently, because women with higher education have more professional skills than those with lower levels of education, they have a greater sense of control over their environment, which generates a higher level of empowerment at work. Consistent with these findings, we assume that in the context of volunteering, as in the workplace, there will be a relationship between women's education and their sense of empowerment.

Self-esteem. Self-esteem was defined by Rosenberg (1965) as a system of beliefs and attitudes that individuals have about themselves, their value, their abilities, and their social status. These beliefs are shaped through comparisons that individuals make with others in a process of social interaction, and usually determine their perceptions of events, their behavior, and the extent of their aspirations (Tuttle, 1984). Thus, the belief in one's ability to contribute to others and attain worthy goals is related to high self-esteem and a sense of control: the higher a person's self-esteem, the more that person's behavior will include intensive involvement with the environment (Ayalowitz, 1988). Based on this perspective, high self-esteem can be viewed as a personal resource that enhances empowerment.

Motives for volunteer activity. Motives can be considered a resource that may enhance the individual's ability to cope with stressors in volunteer activity. Strong motives can alleviate feelings of incompetence among volunteers, and enable them to perform tasks successfully. In this context, Fisher and Schaffer (1993) mention two main types of motives that affect the functioning of volunteers. One type of motive relates to personal benefits, which are reflected in a desire to gain prestige and achieve professional goals. The most prevalent personal motives are expressed in a desire to gain recognition from the community, to alleviate guilt feelings, to alleviate anxiety, or to resolve internal conflicts by helping others (Clary and Snyder, 1991). The other type of motive is social, and expresses a desire to help others (Francies, 1983; Smith, 1982). Because these motives provide an incentive for volunteer activity, it can be assumed that women with high motivation are better able to cope with difficulties that arise in volunteering than are those with low motivation. Therefore, women with high motivation will also adjust better to volunteer activity, and will have higher levels of empowerment.

The Microsystem

In the present study, we examined two types of microsystem variables: family context (the extent to which family members support the participants in their volunteer activity), and the organizational context of volunteering (rewards of volunteering, and perceived difficulties in relations with the provider organization). We chose these variables to represent the microsystem, because they reflect two distinctive aspects of the relationship between the individual and his or her immediate environment. Family support and perceived rewards of volunteering are resources that can increase adjustment to volunteer activity, as reflected in the women's sense of empowerment. Difficulties in relations with the provider organization, however, are considered to be stressors that can reduce the woman's sense of empowerment in volunteer activity.

Family support for volunteering. The family plays an important role in encouraging volunteer activity by creating an atmosphere that emphasizes values of altruism and contributing to society (Fogelman, 1997; Wuthnow, 1995). Thus, researchers have argued that the tendency to engage in volunteer activity increases when another family member volunteers (Freeman, 1997; Rosenthal et al., 1998). At the same time, however, family members can also discourage volunteering, and even exert pressure to discontinue volunteer activity (Blake and Jefferson, 1992). In the case of women in midlife and late adulthood, family support for volunteer activity can give them legitimation to invest time and energy in volunteering, and thus serve as a social resource that will help them cope with difficulties encountered in the context of volunteering and enhance their sense of empowerment.

Rewards of volunteering. Research has revealed that the two main types of rewards in volunteering, as in the workplace, are intrinsic and extrinsic rewards. Intrinsic rewards are related to the content of volunteering, such as challenge, diversity, personal growth, and opportunities to learn (Luks and Payne, 1991). Extrinsic rewards are related to the conditions of volunteer activity, and derive from the volunteers' interaction with their environment, e.g., appreciation by the organization, or social relations with other volunteers (Fogelman, 1981; Hulbert and Chase, 1991). The literature indicates that when volunteers are satisfied with their activity and with the rewards derived from it, their sense of well-being is better than among other volunteers as expressed in health and life satisfaction (Hulbert and Chase, 1991; Tobis et al., 1991). Therefore, we also assumed that rewards would be related to higher levels of empowerment in volunteering.

Difficulty in relations with the provider organization. The literature on volunteerism examines a wide range of difficulties between volunteers and the provider organization. In a comprehensive study, Fisher and Schaffer (1993) found that volunteers may experience ambiguity resulting from a discrepancy between their own ideology and goals on the one hand, and those of the organization on the other. Moreover, they may experience frustration when the organization lacks resources necessary for ongoing activity, or when they feel stuck (Chau-wai Yan and So-kum Tang, 2003). Researchers have also found that volunteer activity in the community may conflict with other commitments in the lives of the volunteers, such as paid work and family life (Blake and Jefferson, 1992; Omoto and Snyder, 1993). The wide range of difficulties that can be encountered in the volunteer context are a source of stress, which can detract from a woman's adjustment to volunteer activity in general and reduce her sense of empowerment in volunteer activity in particular.

The Chronosystem

The chronosystem relates to the dimension of time, and includes the effects of events and experiences during the lifetime of the individual. Because the study deals with volunteering, the dimension of time is represented by measures that are relevant to volunteer activity, i.e., hours of volunteer activity per week, and the number of years that the woman has been volunteering. Studies have revealed a significant relationship between years of experience in community volunteer activity and sense of empowerment (Le-Bosse et al., 1999).

The research model encompasses three ecological systems – the ontogenic system, the microsystem, and the chronosystem. The ontogenic system comprises three personal variables: level of education, self-esteem, and motives for volunteering. The microsystem comprises two sets of environmental variables: family context variables (family support for volunteer activity); and variables related to the volunteer context (rewards of volunteering, and difficulties in relations with the provider organization). The chronosystem comprises two variables related to experience with volunteer activity: years of volunteer experience, and hours of volunteer activity per week.

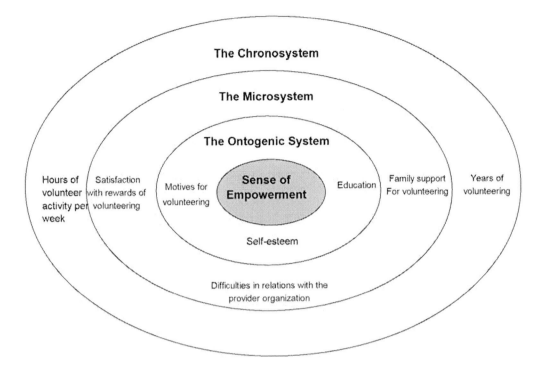

Figure 1. The Research Model.

Research Goals

The main goal of the study was to find the specific relationships between the various ecological system variables and empowerment of women who volunteer in midlife and late adulthood. Another goal was to examine the combined contribution of the different ecological systems to explaining perceived empowerment among the volunteer women, as well as to find the relationships between the variables in the three ecological systems.

Based on the theoretical and empirical background, several hypotheses are put forth regarding women's sense of empowerment in volunteer activity.

Research Hypotheses

The Ontogenic System

1. The higher the women's level of education, the greater their sense of empowerment in volunteering will be.
2. The higher the women's self-esteem, the greater their sense of empowerment in volunteering will be.
3. The higher the women's motivation to engage in volunteer activity, the greater their sense of empowerment in volunteering will be.

The Microsystem

4. The more women perceive the family as supporting their volunteer activity, the greater their sense of empowerment in volunteering will be.
5. The more positive the women's perceptions of the rewards of volunteer activity, the greater their sense of empowerment in volunteering will be.
6. The more the women perceive themselves as experiencing difficulties in their relations with the provider organization, the lower their sense of empowerment in volunteering will be.

The Chronosystem

7. The more years the women have engaged in volunteer activity, and the more hours they devote to volunteering, the greater their sense of empowerment in volunteering will be.

In addition, we examined the combined contribution of the variables belonging to the three ecological systems to explaining women's empowerment in volunteering.

Method

Sample

The research sample comprised 146 women ranging from 46 to 85 years of age. Of the women in the sample, 34.5% were Israeli-born, 44.1% were European-American born, and 21.4% were Asian-African born; 58.2% of them were married, and the remaining 41.8% were unmarried (of those, 97.3% were widows, and 2.7% had never been married). Regarding education, 30.8% of the women had partial secondary education, 45.2% had a high school diploma, and 24.0% had post-secondary education (academic or other). As for level of religiosity, 47.9% of the women defined themselves as secular, 37.5% defined themselves as traditionally religious, and 14.6% defined themselves as Orthodox. Regarding employment, 14.4% of the women worked for pay outside of the home, and 85.6% did not work for pay (they were either retired or had never worked for pay). In terms of self-assessed financial situation, 4.7% of the women assessed their situation as below average, 71% assessed their situation as average, and 24.3% assessed their situation as above average.

Instruments

Empowerment. Originally developed by Spreitzer (1995), the instrument aims to measure empowerment in the context of work and was adapted to context of volunteer activity for the present study. Women were asked to indicate the extent to which 12 statements apply to their experience with volunteer activity, e.g., "I am sure I have the appropriate skills to do my job". Responses were based on a 5-point scale ranging from 1 (not at all) to 5 (to a great extent). One score was derived by computing the mean of the scores on the questionnaire: the higher the score, the greater the participant's sense of empowerment. The Cronbach's alpha reliability value for the questionnaire was .75.

Self-esteem. The instrument was developed by Rosenberg (1965), and included a series of 10 questions concerning feelings about self-worth (e.g., "I feel I am just as worthy a person as others," "I feel I don't have many things I can be proud of," and "I have a positive view of myself"). Responses were based on a 5-point scale ranging from 1 (strongly agree) to 5 (strongly disagree). One score was derived by computing the mean of the items on the questionnaire: the higher the score, the higher the participant's self-esteem. The questionnaire has been validated in previous studies, which have found that it distinguishes between various population groups (Demo, Small, and Savin-Williams, 1987). The Cronbach's alpha internal reliability value for the questionnaire was .88, similar to the value found in other studies (Demo, 1985)

Motives for volunteer activity. The instrument was based on Cnaan and Goldberg-Glen's (1991) questionnaire, which consists of 16 items. Responses were based on a scale ranging from 1 (never) to 5 (always). The higher the score, the stronger the motive for volunteer activity. Principal component analysis of the items on the questionnaire revealed four components that combined to explain 54.5 % of the variance in motives for volunteering (Eigenvalue>1). The criterion used for component retention was the scree plot. The first component explained 27% of the variance, and included motives that express a desire to conform to social norms of behavior regarding volunteer activity (henceforth "conformist motives", e.g., "most people in my community volunteer"). The Cronbach's alpha value for this component was .79. The second component explained 10.3% of the variance in this variable, and included motives that express a desire to help others without expecting direct compensation (henceforth "altruistic motives", e.g., "volunteer activity leads to a better society"). The Cronbach's alpha value for this component was .75. The third component explained 8.9% of the variance, and included items that express a desire for personal development through volunteer activity (henceforth the "personal growth motive", e.g., "I want to broaden my horizons"). The Cronbach's alpha value for this component was .60. The fourth component explained 8.3% of the variance, and included items that express a desire to fill free time (henceforth the "free time motive", e.g., "I don't have anything to do in my free time"). The Cronbach's alpha value for this component was .60. For each component, one score was derived by calculating the mean of the items related to it.

Family support for volunteer activity. The questionnaire was constructed for the current study, and consisted of five statements related to various aspects of social support that family members provide volunteers, such as appreciation ("I feel that my family appreciates my work"; emotional support ("my family encourages me to volunteer"); and instrumental support ("when volunteer activity conflicts with my family life, the family helps me"). Kulik (2004) found that family support for volunteering correlated positively with satisfaction in volunteering, and negatively with burnout. Responses were based on a 5-point scale, ranging from 1 (never) to 5 (frequently). One overall score was derived by calculating the mean of the items on the questionnaire: the higher the score, the greater the extent of support from family members. The Cronbach's alpha reliability value for the questionnaire was .75.

Perceived rewards of volunteer activity. The questionnaire was based on Gidron and Griffel's (1981) questionnaire, which examined the extent to which volunteers believe that volunteer activity provides them with rewards. The questionnaire consisted of 13 items, which represent different types of rewards, such as challenge, diversity, and personal development. Responses were based on a 5-point scale ranging from 1 (not at all) to 5 (to a great extent): the higher the score, the greater the extent of perceived rewards in volunteer activity. One score was derived by calculating the mean of the items on the questionnaire. The Cronbach's alpha reliability value for the questionnaire was .88.

Difficulty in relations with the provider organization. The instrument was based on Gidron and Griffel's (1981) 17-item questionnaire, which examined various areas of difficulty that volunteers might encounter in their work. Responses were based on a scale ranging from 1 (never) to 5 (always). Principal component analysis revealed three components that describe distinctive content areas, and combine to explain 49.5% of the variance in difficulty in relations with provider organizations (Eigenvalue>1.0). The criterion used for component retention was scree plot.The first component explained 19.2% of the variance, and included items related to ambiguity about the tasks to be performed, such as "I don't know exactly what I am supposed to do" (henceforth "ambiguity"). The Cronbach's alpha coefficient for this component was .82. The second component explained 15.7% of the variance, and included items related to inefficient utilization of time, such as "I spend a lot of time doing administrative jobs instead of dealing with clients" (henceforth "wasting time"). The Cronbach's alpha coefficient for this component was .83. The third component explained 14.6% of the variance, and included items that reflect lack of appreciation by the provider organization, such as "the organization I work for doesn't appreciate what I do" (henceforth "lack of appreciation"). Because this component consisted of only two items, a Pearson's correlation was calculated, which amounted to .42. One score was derived for each factor by calculating the mean of the items for that component: the higher the score, the greater the participant's perceived difficulty in relations with the provider organization.

Background questionnaire. The questionnaire included sociodemographic information such as age, country of birth, marital status, education level (from 1=elementary to 6=Master's degree and above), level of religiosity, employment status, and self-assessed financial situation (from 1= considerably below average to 5=considerably above average).

Data Collection

The study reported here was part of a larger project on various issues related to volunteer activity conducted at a university in Israel. Data were collected between January and May 2003, and the sample included men as well as women. In this paper, we will relate only to reports of women. Data were derived from a convenience sample of volunteers in organizations run by the Ministry of Welfare, the National Insurance Institute, the Ministry of Education, municipalities, and other voluntary nonprofit organizations. The volunteers were recruited for the study through social service departments in the community as well as by the snowball method. Questionnaires were distributed by volunteer activity coordinators in those organizations, filled out by the participants at home, and returned to the coordinators. The average amount of time required to complete the questionnaire was about 30 minutes, and the response rate was about 75%.

Table 1. Research Variables Description (N=146)

Variables	Mean	SD	Min	Max	Scale
Empowerment	3.83	.64	2.50	5.00	1-5
Education	3.38	1.39	1.00	6.00	1-6
Self-esteem	4.29	.90	2.00	5.00	1-5
Altruistic motives	3.62	.81	1.00	5.00	1-5
Conformist motives	2.49	1.03	1.00	5.00	1-5
Personal growth	2.04	.93	1.00	5.00	1-5
Free time	2.42	.94	1.00	5.00	1-5
Family support	3.69	.85	1.00	5.00	1-5
Rewards	3.86	.80	1.00	5.00	1-5
Lack of appreciation	1.38	.67	1.00	5.00	1-5
Wasting time	1.41	.49	1.00	3.50	1-5
Ambiguity	1.99	.84	1.00	4.00	1-5
Hours of volunteering	6.91	3.20	1.00	43	-
Years of volunteering	4.77	2.55	0.00	35	-

Data Processing

To test the research hypotheses, the correlations between each of the ecological system variables and sense of empowerment were calculated. In addition, to determine the overall contribution of the ecological systems to explaining empowerment, stepwise hierarchical regression analyses were carried out.

Results

a. Description of the Research Variables

The level of empowerment among women in the research group was far above midpoint 3 on the 5-point scale used for the measures in the study (M=3.83, SD=.64). Regarding motives, the strongest one was altruism (M=3.62, SD=.81), followed by conformism (M=2.49, SD=1.03), free time (M=2.42, SD=.94), and finally personal growth (M=2.04, SD=.93). Family support and self-esteem were also above midpoint 3 (M=3.69, SD=.85, and M=4.29, SD=.90, respectively). However, difficulties in relations with the provider organization were far below midpoint 3. The highest level of difficulty was found with regard to ambiguity in organizational demands (M=1.99, SD=.84), followed by wasting time (M=1.41, SD=.49), and lack of appreciation by the provider organization (M=1.38, SD=.67). As for rewards of volunteering, levels were far above midpoint 3 (M=3.86, SD=.80) (see Table 1).

Table 2. Pearson's Correlations between the Research Variables

	1 Empower-ment	2 Rewards	3 Education	4 Altruistic motives	5 Conformist motives	6 Personal growth	7 Free time	8 Self-esteem	9 Family support	10 Lack of appreciation	11 Wasting time	12 Ambiguity	13 Hours of volunteering	14 Years of volunteering
1	-	-	-	-	-	-	-	-	-	-	-	-	-	-
2	**50.	-	-	-	-	-	-	-	-	-	-	-	-	-
3	**19.-	**18.-	-	-	-	-	-	-	-	-	-	-	-	-
4	**50.	**47.	03.	-	-	-	-	-	-	-	-	-	-	-
5	**31.	**46.	**25.-	***59.	-	-	-	-	-	-	-	-	-	-
6	**21.	*16.	07.	***33.	**29.	-	-	-	-	-	-	-	-	-
7	*17.	07.	**24.-	**18.	*13.	*13.	-	-	-	-	-	-	-	-
8	***40.	***30.	**25.	**19.	13. *	12.	13.*	-	-	-	-	-	-	-
9	**27.	***37.	**23.-	**24.	***30.	10.	01.	**27.	-	-	-	-	-	-
10	*17.-	01.	04.	*16.	***33.	03.	03.	*18.-	10.	-	-	-	-	-
11	03.	13.	08.	06.	11.	05.	09.	*19.-	*13.-	**20.	-	-	-	-
12	**20.-	**17.-	04.	01.	01.	*14.	01.	**20.-	12.-	10.	15.*	-	-	-
13	**19	*16.	10.-	08.	04.	01.	12.	**18.	.11.	05.	**23.	**25.-	-	-
14	*15.	08.	06.	08.	05.	02.	.07	**18.	06.	07.	15*.	**21.-	.01	-

* $p<.05$, ** $p<.01$, *** $p<.001$.

b. Correlations between Empowerment and Ecological System Variables

The Ontogenic System

Regarding the ontogenic system variables (education, self-esteem, and motives for volunteer activity), a low significant negative correlation was found between level of education and empowerment: the higher the women's education, the lower their sense of empowerment. In addition, a positive correlation was found between self-esteem and empowerment: the higher the women's self-esteem, the greater their sense of empowerment. Regarding motives for volunteer activity, a positive correlation was found between each of the motives and the women's sense of empowerment: the stronger the motives of altruism, conformism, personal growth, and free time, the greater the women's sense of empowerment. Comparison of the four correlations reveals that altruistic motives correlated most strongly with empowerment, followed by conformism, personal growth, and free time (see Table 2).

Microsystem

The microsystem variables focused on the family context and on the volunteer context (for a detailed description, see the Instruments section). Regarding family context variables, family support for volunteering correlated significantly with the women's sense of empowerment: the more support the women received from their families, the greater their sense of empowerment. In addition, the findings revealed low negative correlations between two areas of difficulty in relations with the provider organization and sense of empowerment: the higher the level of ambiguity related to the organization's demands, the lower the volunteers' sense of empowerment, and the less appreciation the organization showed for volunteer activity, the lower the women's sense of empowerment. Perceived rewards of volunteering correlated positively with empowerment: the higher the women's assessments of the rewards received from volunteering, the greater their sense of empowerment.

Chronosystem

Regarding the two aspects of the chronosystem examined in the study (years of volunteering, and hours of volunteering per week), there were low positive correlations with empowerment: the more hours per week the women devoted to volunteer activity, and the more years of experience they had in volunteering, the greater their sense of empowerment.

In sum, most of the research variables in the three ecological systems correlated with empowerment in volunteering.

c. Correlations among the Variables in the Ecological Systems

Table 2 shows several significant correlations between the variables in the ecological systems (explanatory variables) – particularly among the three variables that are resources (self-esteem, family support for volunteering, and education) and the other research variables (see Table 2). Self-esteem correlated positively with altruistic motives: the higher the women's self-esteem, the stronger their altruistic motive for volunteering. In addition, the greater the perceived rewards of volunteering and the more hours the women devoted to volunteer activity per week, the higher their self-esteem. Self-esteem also correlated negatively with difficulty due to ambiguity in the demands of the provider organization: the higher the women's self-esteem, the lower the levels of perceived ambiguity in the demands of the provider organization. Regarding family support for volunteer activity, a positive correlation was found with social motives for volunteering: the greater the extent of family support for volunteer activity, the stronger the women's social motives for volunteering (altruistic and conformist). As for the third resource, education, significant negative correlations were found with some of the explanatory variables: the higher the women's levels of education, the weaker the motives of conformism and free time, the lower the levels of family support, and the lower their assessments of rewards.

Regarding the chronosystem variables, women with fewer years of volunteering experience expressed higher levels of perceived ambiguity in volunteer activity. In a similar vein, the more hours the women devoted to volunteer activity per week, the higher the levels of perceived rewards.

Finally, significant correlations were found between motives for volunteering and perceived rewards of volunteer activity: the stronger the motives for volunteering (altruism, conformism, and personal growth), the higher the levels of perceived rewards.

d. The Combined Contribution of the Research Variables to Explaining Empowerment in Volunteering

To examine the combined contribution of the variables in the various ecological systems to explaining the women's sense of empowerment in volunteering, stepwise hierarchical regression analyses were conducted. The regression analyses conformed to basic standards such as homoscedasticity, normal distribution of the dependent variable, and interval scales for variables. Intercorrelations between the independent variables were not too high (up to .59), so that collinearity was avoided (see Table 2); and the ratio of number of participants to number of variables was appropriate (at least 10 participants for each variable examined). Because the ontogenic system is closest to the individual, we entered education level and personal background variables (self-esteem and motives for volunteering) in the early steps. In the first step, we entered level of education, in order to partial out its contribution from that of the variables that were entered in subsequent steps of the regression. In the second step, we entered personal-psychological variables (self-esteem and motives for volunteering); in the third step we entered the microsystem variables (family support for volunteering, rewards of volunteer activity, and difficulties in relations with the provider organization); in the fourth step, we entered the chronosystem variables (years of experience with volunteering, and hours of volunteer activity per week).

Table 3 presents the results of the regression analysis, and indicates that all of the ecological system variables examined in the study explained substantial percentages (as high as 49%) of the variance in empowerment. The ontogenic system variables contributed more than the variables in the other two systems to explaining the women's sense of empowerment (about 37%). Of the ontogenic system variables, altruistic motives and self-esteem contributed most to explaining the women's sense of empowerment: the stronger women's altruistic motives and the higher their self-esteem, the greater their sense of empowerment.

Univariate analysis also revealed correlations between the other motives and empowerment (see section "b" of the Results and Table 2). However, altruism was the only motive to enter the regression equation, because it had the highest correlation with empowerment. A significant negative correlation was found between the women's level of education and their level of perceived empowerment. However, the correlation was no longer significant in the second step, when other variables were entered into the regression equation.

Table 3. Hierarchical Regression Coefficients (β) Explaining Women's Empowerment in Volunteering

	B	SEB	β	t
Step 1				
Education	-.09	-.04	-11*	-.234
$R^2 = .03$				
F = 5.49*				
Step 2				
Education	-.04	.03	-.09	-.31
Self-esteem	.38	..09	.38***	4.07
Altruistic motives	.27	.07	.34***	3.76
Conformist motives	.07	.05	.12	1.33
Personal growth	.00	.05	.05	.06
Free time	.04	.05	.06	.86
$R^2 = .37$				
F = 14.20***				
Step 3				
Education	-.03	.03	-.06	-.87
Self-esteem	.33	.09	.24**	3.57
Altruistic motives	.18	.07	.24**	2.51
Conformist motives	-.02	.05	.03	-.38
Personal growth	.03	.05	.04	.65
Free time	.08	.04	.12	1.84
Family support	-.00	.05	.02	-.02
Rewards	.30	.06	.36***	4.47
Lack of appreciation	.14	.06	-.14**	2.01
Wasting time	.01	.09	.08	.11
Ambiguity	-.07	.05	.09	-1.39
$R^2 = .48$				
F = 5.63***				
Step 4				
Education	-.03	.03	-.06	-.68
Self-esteem	.32	.09	.24**	3.52
Altruistic motives	.17	.07	.21**	2.37
Conformist motives	-.02	.06	.03	-.34
Personal growth	.03	.05	.04	.66
Free time	.09	.04	.13	1.88
Family support	-.00	.05	.07	-.10
Rewards	.30	.06	.36***	4.43
Lack of appreciation	.14	.07	-.14**	2.07
Wasting time	-.00	.09	.03	-.04
Ambiguity	-.06	.08	.07	-1.06
Hours of volunteering	.00	.00	.01	.27
Years of volunteering	.00	.00	.07	1.19
$R^2 = .49$				
F = .64				

* $p<.05$, ** $p<.01$, *** $p<.001$.

The microsystem variables explained 11% of the variance in empowerment, over and above the variance explained by the ontogenic system variables. Of the microsystem variables, two contributed significantly to explaining the variance in empowerment: difficulties due to lack of appreciation, and rewards of volunteering. Beta coefficients indicate that the more the women felt difficulty due to lack of appreciation, the lower their levels of empowerment; and the more positive their perceptions of the rewards of volunteering, the greater their sense of empowerment. With regard to the chronosystem, after the variables from the other ecological systems entered the regression equation, neither years of experience with volunteering nor hours of volunteering per week contributed significantly to explaining empowerment.

Discussion

This study adopted an ecological approach to examine the sources of individual empowerment in volunteering among middle-aged and elderly Israeli women volunteers in social service organizations. Understanding the sources of empowerment among women in those stages of life is important for several reasons. First, in later stages of life, when people no longer engage in the same activities as they did at earlier stages, volunteering often plays a role as a major source of satisfaction and as an outlet for self-expression. Therefore, empowerment in volunteering at later stages of life can contribute to the volunteer's general sense of well-being. Moreover, the experience of empowerment in volunteering can enhance the volunteers' sense of involvement in the community, and motivate them to help people in need of their assistance. Before discussing the specific research hypotheses, several general results of the study are worthy of mention.

The research findings suggest that the experience of volunteering is a positive one for women in middle and later life, as reflected in the high sense of empowerment reported by the participants in the study. In addition, the women had personal resources such as self-esteem as well as environmental resources such as family support and rewards from volunteer activity, as reflected in appreciation by the provider organization and performance of challenging tasks. Moreover, they were not particularly concerned with difficulties in relations with the provider organization.

Another major finding relates to the correlation between the women's level of education and the other study variables. Level of education correlated negatively with sense of empowerment, so that women with higher education felt less empowered than those with lower levels of education (refuting Hypothesis 1). This unexpected finding contradicts the results of other studies, which have shown that women with higher education usually feel more empowered than other women in places of employment (Hertz-Lazarowitz and Shapira, 2005). Evidently, the differences in levels of empowerment among educated women in paid work and in volunteer activity are due to the distinct nature of each domain. In workplaces, the employee's level of education is usually taken into account as a criterion for determining the amount of compensation received. Thus, employed women with higher education receive different rewards (instrumental and intrinsic) in accordance with their skills and education, and their expectations in this area can usually be fulfilled. In the context of volunteering, however, there is less emphasis on women's skills and education and more emphasis on the needs of the target population. Therefore, educated women do not always utilize their professional skills in volunteer activity, and the disillusionment they feel when their expectations are not fulfilled reduces their sense of empowerment. This explanation is also supported by the negative correlation between the women's level of education and their perceptions of the rewards they receive from volunteer activity: the higher the women's education, the more negative their perceptions of rewards. Furthermore, regarding the negative correlation between education and empowerment, the contribution of education to explaining women's empowerment in volunteering was no longer significant when the other study variables were partialled out. Therefore, it is possible that the contribution of education to explaining empowerment can be attributed to other variables that correlated with education.

Regarding the specific variables in the ecological systems, the findings indicate that the ontogenic system, which is closest to the individual, contributes most to explaining perceived empowerment among middle-aged and elderly volunteer women. Of the ontogenic variables examined in the study, the psychological aspects (self-esteem and motives for volunteering) were found to be particularly significant. Apparently, these resources strengthen the woman and facilitate coping with difficulties that might inhibit empowerment in volunteering (supporting Hypotheses 2 and 3).

As for the microsystem variables, the findings revealed a correlation between family support for volunteering and the women's sense of empowerment (supporting Hypothesis 4). Because the family is a primary group in the individual's environment, support from family members in the form of appreciation, encouragement, legitimation, and relief from some household responsibilities can enhance women's success in volunteer activity and increase their sense of empowerment. Hence in the context of volunteer activity, as in other contexts such as work, family support can be considered a resource that contributes to positive adjustment and enhances the volunteer's sense of empowerment. As expected, rewards correlated significantly with empowerment. This suggests that rewards from volunteer activity enhance the women's feelings of success, and give them a greater sense of control and influence over their environment (supporting Hypothesis 5). With regard to difficulty in relations with the provider organization, the finding that lack of appreciation and ambiguity correlated negatively with empowerment can be attributed to the feelings of stress and tension aroused by those difficulties, which in turn undermine the women's sense of control and weaken their levels of empowerment (supporting Hypothesis 6).

Finally, the correlation between the chronosystem variables (years of experience with volunteering and hours of volunteer activity per week) suggest that the more the women establish a presence in the volunteer environment, the more successful they feel in their activity (supporting Hypothesis 7). However, because the present study was correlative, there is no way of determining the direction of the effect among chronosystem variables and empowerment. Specifically, it is unclear whether longevity and intensity in volunteer activity enhance empowerment, or whether the sense of empowerment causes women to volunteer more frequently and continue longer with their activity.

Besides the correlations between the ecological system variables and empowerment, the correlations among the variables in the three systems can provide further insight into the experience of women in middle and later life. Significant correlations were found between level of education and the other research variables – most notably, education correlated negatively with conformist motives and family support for volunteer activity. A possible explanation for the negative correlation between education and conformist motives is that education enhances the individual's sense of security, so that women with higher education feel less of a need to gain approval and conform to social norms. Regarding the negative correlation between education and family support for volunteer activity, it can be argued that because educated women derive satisfaction from a broad range of activities, their families do not feel obligated to support them in their volunteer efforts. By contrast, women with lower levels of education view volunteering as an outlet for self-fulfillment and creativity, which also generates family support. Furthermore, the correlations between family support and motives for volunteering indicate that legitimation from the family can enhance motivation to volunteer.

Before concluding, two limitations of the study should be noted. First, as mentioned, because the study was correlative, longitudinal research should be conducted in order to identify the causal relationship between the ecological system variables and women's sense of empowerment. A longitudinal design would make it possible to examine the dependent and independent variables over time rather than simultaneously. For example, the women's motives for volunteering and their self-esteem can be evaluated at a given point in time, and then their sense of empowerment can be evaluated at a later point, as determined in the research plan. This research design would provide a more valid basis than a correlative study for establishing a causal relationship between motives for volunteering and self-esteem on the one hand, and empowerment in volunteering on the other.

The second limitation relates to the research sample, which was a convenience sample and did not represent all women who volunteer in social services in midlife and late adulthood. Therefore, future studies should adopt a sampling method which is more representative of the population of women who engage in volunteer activity at those stages of life.

In sum, the research findings support the ecological model underlying the study, and indicate that the women's sense of empowerment in volunteering is shaped by a combination of ecological systems. Thus, to understand the sources of women's empowerment in volunteering it is important to examine a wide range of variables from different systems. Some of the variables are personal characteristics such as self-esteem, motives, and education. Other variables are environmental, such as family support, rewards, and difficulties in relations with the provider organization. Some of these variables enhance the women's sense of empowerment, and others inhibit it. Finally, the study highlights the importance of motives for volunteering in enhancing the volunteer's sense of empowerment.

Practical Recommendations

The research findings elicit several practical recommendations for organizations that engage volunteers. First, emphasis should be placed on strengthening motives for volunteering by appropriate socialization, which includes training and guidance. In addition, volunteers should receive rewards such as challenging and diverse tasks, as well as appreciation for their efforts, which might enhance their motivation to continue volunteering. Another way of enhancing motivation to volunteer is to set realistic goals, so that it will be possible to avoid difficulties in performance of assigned tasks.

Furthermore, the finding that family support enhances empowerment and motivation to volunteer highlights the need to gain support from the family for volunteer activity. One way to increase family for volunteering support is to involve family members in social activities that provider organizations sponsor in honor of volunteers. In addition, it would be worthwhile to devote more attention to educated women, who expressed lower levels of empowerment, were less motivated to volunteer, and felt that they were less rewarded than women with lower levels of education. Specifically, the needs and expectations of women with higher education should be addressed at the stage of screening and placement in volunteer jobs. In this connection, the broad approach of adjustment to the workplace (Dawis and Lofquist, 1969), which highlights the importance of coordinating the needs of employees with the needs of the organization, can be applied to the volunteer context. In the same vein, besides the needs of the beneficiaries, it is necessary to focus on the needs and desires of women who volunteer. In this way, it might be possible to create a more challenging, rewarding, and empowering volunteering environment for women with various personality traits and background characteristics.

Acknowledgement

The author would like to thank Mimi Schneiderman for her editorial assistance.

References

Ayalowitz, T. (1988). Mehuyavut al-ishit bebituy ubema'aseh vehakesher shela bahayim lehavayot hiyuviyot ulatehushot coherentiyut bekerev mitbagrim [Personal commitment in words and action, and their relationships to positive experiences and to a sense of coherence among adolescents]. Unpublished Master's thesis, Tel Aviv University (Hebrew).

Belsky, J. (1980). Child maltreatment: An ecological integration. *American Psychologist*, **35**, 320-335.

Blake, R., and Jefferson, S. (1992). Defection... why? An insight into the reasons for volunteers leaving.. York, England: Kestrecourt Ltd.

Bronfenbrenner, U. (1979). The ecology of human development: Experiment By nature and design. Cambridge, MA: Harvard University Press.

Cable, S. (1992). Women's social movement involvement: The role of structural availability in recruitment and participation processes. *Sociological Quarterly*, **33**, 35-50.

Chambre, S. M. (2001). Parallel power structures, invisible careers, and the changing nature of American Jewish women's philanthropy. In K.D. McCarthy (Ed.), Women, philanthropy, and civil society (pp. 169-186). Bloomington, IA: Indiana University Press.

Chau-wai Yan, E., and So-kum Tang, C. (2003). The role of individual, interpersonal and organizational factors in mitigating burnout among elderly Chinese volunteers. *International Journal of Geriatric Psychiatry*, **18**, 795-802.

Clary, E.G., and Snyder, M. (1991). A functional analysis of altruism and prosocial behavior: The case of volunteerism. *Review of Personality and Social Psychology*, **12**, 119-147.

Cnaan, R.A., and Goldberg-Glen, R.S. (1991). Measuring motivation to volunteer in human services. *Journal of Behavioral Science*, **27**, 269-284.

Corcoran, J., Franklin, C., and Bennett, P. (2002). Ecological factors associated with adolescent pregnancy and parenting. Social Work Research, **24**, 29-39.

Cumming, E., and Henry, W. E. (1961). *Growing old: The process of disengagement.* New York: Basic Books.

Daniels, A. (1988). *Invisible careers: Women civic leaders from the volunteer world.* Chicago, IL: University of Chicago Press.

Dawis, R.V., and Lofquist, L.H. (1969). Adjustment to work. New York: Appleton-Century-Crofts.

Demo, D.H. (1985). Self-esteem and family cohesion: The child's perspective and adjustment. *Journal of Marriage and the Family*, **45**, 153-159.

Demo, D.H., Small, S.A., and Savin-Williams, R.C. (1987). Family relations and the self-esteem of adolescents and their parents. *Journal of Marriage and the Family*, **49**, 705-715.

Fisher, L. R., and Schaffer, K. B. (1993). *Older volunteers: A guide to research and practice.* Newbury Park, CA: Sage.

Flanagan, C., Bowes, J., Jonsson, B., Csapo, B., and Sheblanova, E. (1998). Ties that bind: Correlates of adolescents' civic commitments in seven countries. *Journal of Social Issues,* **54**, 457-475.

Fogelman, C. J. (1981). Being a volunteer: Some effects on older people. *Generations*, **49**, 24-25.

Fogelman, E. (1997). What motivates rescuers? In *J. Michalczyk, Resisters, rescuers and refugees* (pp. 147-154). Kansas City, KA: Sheed and Ward.

Francies, R.G. (1983). The Volunteer Needs Profile: A tool for reducing turnover. *The Journal of Volunteer Administration,* **16**(2), 17-33.

Freeman, R. (1997). Working for nothing: The supply of volunteer labor. *Journal of Labor Economics*, 140-167.

Friedman, A. (1987). Getting powerful with age: Changes in women over the life cycle. *Israel Social Science Research*, **5**, 76-86.

Garbarino, J. (1978). The social maps of children approaching adolescence: Studying the ecology of youth development. *Journal of Youth and Adolescence*, 7, 417-428.

Gaskin, K., and Smith, J. (1997). A new civic Europe? A study of the extent and role of volunteering. London: National Centre for Volunteering.

Gidron, B., and Griffel, A. (1981). Tagmulim, sve'ut ratzon btokhnit lehakhsharat menahalim vesegel bakhir bemerkazim kehilati'im al shem Schwartz [Rewards and satisfaction in the Schwartz Program for Training Directors and Senior Staff in Community Centers]. Unpublished Master's Thesis, The Paul Baerwald School of Social Work, The Hebrew University of Jerusalem (Hebrew).

Gutmann, D. (1975). Parenthood: A key to the comparative study of the life cycle. In N. Datan and L.H. Ginsberg (Eds.), Life span developmental psychology: Normative life crises (pp. 167-184). New York: Academic Press.

Hertz-Lazarowitz, R., and Shapira, T. (2005). Muslim women's life stories: Building leadership. *Anthropology and Education Quarterly*, **36**, 165-181.

Herzog, H., and Greenberg, O. (1978). A voluntary women's organisation in a society in the making: WIZO's contribution to Israeli society. Tel Aviv: Tel Aviv University Institute of Social Research, Faculty of Sociology and Anthropology.

Huebner, A. J., and Mancini, J. A. (2003). Shaping structured out of school time use among youth: The effects of self, family, and friend systems. *Journal of Youth and Adolescence*, **32**, 453-463.

Hulbert, J. R., and Chase, R. A. (1991). *Retiree volunteers and the agencies they serve: A national survey.* Report prepared for the National Retiree Volunteer Center. St. Paul, MN: Amherst H. Wilder Foundation.

Hur, M. H. (2006). Empowerment in terms of theoretical perspectives: Exploring a typology of the process and components across disciplines. *Journal of Community Pasychology*, **34**, 523.

Izraeli, D. N. (1999). Nashim bemakom ha'avodah [Women in the work place]. In D.N. Izraeli, A. Friedman, H. Dahan-Kalev, S. Fogiel-Bijaoui, H. Herzog, M. Hasan, and R. Naveh (Eds.), *Sex, gender, politics: Women in Israel* (pp. 167-216). Tel Aviv: Hakibbutz Hameuhad (Hebrew).

Jung, C.G. (1933/1971). The stage of life. In *J. Camble* (Ed.), The portable Jung (pp. 3-22). New York: Viking.

Kulik, L. (2004). Hevdelim bein gvarim venashim beshika behitnadvut :Doh Mekhkar [Gender differences in burnout in volunteering]. Research Report, the National Insurance Institute, Jerusalem Israel (Hebrew).

Le-Bosse, Y., Lavallee, M., Lacerte, D., Dube, N., Nadeau, J., Porcher, E., and Vandette, L. (1999). Is community participation empirical evidence for psychological empowerment? A distinction between passive and active participation. *Social Work and Social Sciences Review*, **8**, 59-82.

Luks, A., and Payne, P. (1991). The healing power of doing good. New York: Fawcett Columbine.

McPherson J., and Rotolo, T. (1996). Diversity and change in voluntary groups. *American Sociological Review*, **61**,179-202.

Negrey, C. (1993). Gender, time, and reduced work. Albany, NY: State University of New York Press.

Omoto, A. N., and Snyder, M. (1993). AIDS volunteers and their motivations: Theoretical issues and practical concerns. *Nonprofit Management and Leadership*, **4**, 157-176.

Peterson, A. C., and Hughey, J. (2002). Tailoring organizational characteristics for empowerment: Accommodating individual economic resources. *Journal of Community Practice*, **10**(3), 41-60.

Rappaport, J. (1987). Terms of empowerment / exemplars of prevention: Toward a theory for community psychology. *American Journal of Community Psychology*, **15**, 121-148.

Rappaport, J., Reisch,T., and Zimmerman, M. (1992). Mutual help mechanisms in the empowerment of former mental patients. In D. Saleebey, (Ed.), The strengths perspective in social work practice (pp. 84-97). White Plains, NY: Allyn and Bacon.

Rodich, V. (2001). Hakesher ben hahsharat mitnadvim gimla'im leven tehushat ha'haatzama shelahem, midat sve'ut haratzon shelahem vehamehuyavut ha'ishit. [Training pensioners to volunteer and its impact on their sense of empowerment, satisfaction with volunteering, and sense of personal commitment]. Unpublished Master's thesis, School of Social Work, Bar Ilan University, Ramat Gan (Hebrew).

Rosenberg, M. (1965). *Society and adolescents' self image*. Princeton, NJ: Princeton University Press.

Rosenthal, S., Feiring, C., and Lewis, M. (1998). Political volunteering from late adolescence to young adulthood: Patterns and predictors. *Journal of Social Issues*, **54**, 477-494.

Smith, D. A. (1982). Altruism, volunteers and volunteerism. In J.D. Harmon (Ed.). Volunteerism in the eighties: *Fundamental issues in voluntary action* (pp. 23-44). Washington, D.C.: University Press of America.

Solomon, B. B. (1985). How to really empower families? New strategies for social practitioners. Family Resource Coalition, **3**, 2-3.

Spreitzer, G. M. (1995). An empirical test of a comprehensive model of interpersonal empowerment in the workplace. *American Journal of Community Psychology*, **23**, 601-629.

Thompson, A. (1993). Rural emergency medical volunteers and their communities: A demographic comparison. *Journal of Community Health*, **18**, 379-392.

Tobis, J. S., Crinella, F. M., Ashurst, J. T., Rook, K. S., Sandman, C. A. A., Wilson, A. F., Mosko, S. S., Swanson, J. M., and Reisch, S. (1991). *Intervention effects on psychobiological decline in aging* (Final Report of Program Project HP01AGO3975). Washington, D.C.: National Institute of Aging.

Tuttle, D. W. (1984). *Self-esteem and adjusting with blindness*. Springfield, IL: Charles C. Thomas.

Wallach, V.A., and Mueller, C. W. (2006). Job characteristics and organizational predictors of psychological empowerment among paraprofessionals within human service organizations: An exploratory study. *Administration in Social Work*, **30**, 95-116.

Wilson, J. (2000). Volunteering. *Annual Review of Sociology*, **26**, 215-240.

Wilson, J., and Musick, M. (1999). Attachment to volunteering. Social Forum, **14**, 243-272.

Woodward, M. (1987). Voluntary association membership among black Americans. *Sociological Quarterly*, **28**, 285-301.

Wuthnow, R. (1995). Learning to care. New York: Oxford University Press.

In: Handbook of Business and Finance
Editors: M. Bergmann and T. Faust, pp. 123-145

ISBN: 978-1-60692-855-4
© 2010 Nova Science Publishers, Inc.

Chapter 5

LOCAL OUTSOURCING AND GLOBAL COMPETITION: THE CASE OF NEW PRODUCT DEVELOPMENT IN MNC SUBSIDIARIES LOCATED IN BRAZIL

Dirk Michael Boehe

Insper Institute of Education and Research, São Paulo, Brazil[*]

Abstract

Multinational companies' local impact may reveal itself as improvement of the competitive environment or crowding out of local companies, local supplier development, technological and managerial spill-over effects, among others. This chapter focuses on a particular channel for technological or managerial linkages between MNCs and host countries: technical collaboration in the form of outsourcing between subsidiaries of multinational companies (MNC) and local host country partner organizations such as engineering firms, suppliers, universities or research institutes. For this reasons, I will discuss reasons of why MNC subsidiaries establish local outsourcing relationships in product. More specifically, I address the question of how MNC coordination mechanisms may influence the decision to keep new product development (NPD) activities in a local subsidiary (in-house) or to outsource it to local collaborators. Coordination mechanisms are implemented by headquarters and are defined as the process of integrating activities dispersed across subsidiaries. Thus, this study links global coordination mechanisms of MNCs with local collaboration (outsourcing). Hence, this chapter puts forward the argument that the global coordination of MNC activities and possible local impacts on the subsidiary or host country level are connected. Using a theoretic approach that combines literature on collaboration in R&D and NPD, headquarter-subsidiary as well as subsidiary-subsidiary relationships, this argument will be tested using structural equations modeling applied to a sample of 146 product development units located in Brazil. The results suggest that one of the coordination mechanisms, internal markets, has a positive effect on NPD outsourcing while the other coordination mechanism, global autonomy, has a positive effect on in-house NPD. Finally, I discuss several contributions to the scientific literature on MNCs. In particular, the study contributes to integrating the internal market construct with the coordination mechanism stream of literature. Moreover, I claim that future research and literature on multinational companies needs to increasingly treat both the

---

[*] E-mail address: http://www.insper.org.br.

external, host country part and the internal MNC part of subsidiaries' operational linkages in an integrated manner.

Keywords: New product development, coordination mechanisms, decision-making autonomy, internal market, local outsourcing

1. Introduction

Many R&D units of MNC subsidiaries find themselves in a situation of survival pressure. As headquarters strive to enhance the cost efficiency of their global network of R&D sites, minor, duplicated or less well performing R&D units face the risk to be eliminated (Birkinshaw and Hood, 1998). In response, R&D units may attempt to claim their stake exploiting new market opportunities, both within the MNC, i.e. selling technological services and R&D projects to peer subsidiaries, and developing products for external clients beyond the subsidiary's host country market. However, exploiting such market opportunities requires that the MNC uses coordination mechanisms which permit and incentive subsidiaries to carry out R&D and product development for internal and external global clients. At the same time, MNCs may take advantage of the external collaborator network of their subsidiaries in different host countries. Such a network of collaborators, for instance, outsourcing partners such as engineering firms, universities, research institutes, technology centers or supplier firms, may enhance and complement subsidiaries' internal capabilities and capacities. If this happened, local collaborators would be directly or indirectly integrated into global innovation networks. Thus, the question is to what extent MNC coordination mechanism might influence a subsidiary to exploit internal and external global market opportunities and to what extent this may trigger collaboration in NPD on the host country level.

Therefore, this paper focuses on such coordination mechanisms, defined as the process of integrating activities dispersed across subsidiaries (Martinez and Jarillo, 1991); more specifically, focus is on how MNC coordination mechanisms influence subsidiaries' new product development (NPD) activities and by extension, in-house and outsourced NPD activities on the subsidiary level. Yet, host country related factors that may also influence subsidiaries' NPD activities such as government incentives, local market demand, and the like, are not considered here, due to reasons of space and scope of this chapter. Accordingly, this chapter is concerned with the corporate environment, i.e. the headquarter-subsidiary and subsidiary-subsidiary relationships, and its potential effect on a focal subsidiary's in-house and outsourced NPD activities.

Literature on headquarter-subsidiary and subsidiary-subsidiary relationship has primarily examined formal coordination mechanisms, such as centralization of decision-making at main or divisional headquarters, formalization, planning, performance control, and informal mechanisms, such as informal communication, socialization, normative integration, particularly, transfer of knowledge, people, goods and services among MNC units, R&D co-practice, inter-unit networking (Bartlett and Ghoshal, 1989; Fischer and Behrman, 1979; Ghoshal and Nohria, 1993; Martinez and Jarillo, 1991; Gupta and Govindarajan, 1991 and 1994; Nobel and Birkinshaw, 1998; Persaud, Kumar and Kumar, 2002; Frost and Pedersen, 2002; Frost and Zhou, 2005). This stream of literature has been mainly concerned with conciliating strong globalization and localization pressures, being decision-making control (autonomy) the most researched coordination mechanism. However, it does not reflect on competitive or market-like relationships among MNC units as coordination mechanism.

A second stream of literature directly focuses on such competitive or market-like relationships also known as internal markets (Birkinshaw and Fey, 2000; Birkinshaw, 2001; Birkinshaw and Lingblad, 2001 and 2005); however, their arguments have rarely been submitted to empirical tests. Moreover, to my knowledge, research has not explicitly addressed the combined influence of different coordination mechanisms on subsidiaries' new product development (NPD) activities.

Thus, by hypothesizing and testing a model which examines the combined effect of autonomy and internal markets on a subsidiary's in-house and outsourced new product development activities, we attempt to contribute to theory development on coordination mechanisms.

Both coordination mechanisms can expose subsidiaries to higher (internal and external) market pressures. Thus, they provide incentives for learning and innovation, a relationship in line with the evolutionary theoretic perspective (Nelson and Winter, 1982). While existing research has focused either on coordination mechanism in MNCs or on the configuration (in-house vs. outsourcing) of NPD activities, the original contribution of the present study consists in assessing the proposed link between coordination mechanisms (internal and external market pressures) and the configuration (in-house vs. outsourcing) of subsidiary NPD activities.

The introduction of market-like elements in hierarchical governance forms has become a more frequent phenomenon due to rationalization and efficiency seeking by MNC headquarters and reduced communications, information and control costs (Zenger and Hesterly, 1997). Another phenomenon which motivates this study is decentralization of R&D itself (Pearce, 1999) which has prompted many subsidiaries to develop new products for markets beyond their original host countries. Several factors such as cost advantages and technological learning account for these new subsidiary roles; cost advantages of low and medium wage countries with reasonable technological infrastructure and technological learning performance make it profitable to use them not only as global production platforms but also as 'global R&D platforms'. A prominent example is GM which decentralized its global product development in five major centers located in Australia, Brazil, Germany, South Korea and the US, each of them being specialized in particular vehicle platforms. The Brazilian and South Korean centers, for example, combine competitive development costs with considerable technological capabilities and integrated local supply chains.

In the following section, I review the literature and develop my conceptual model exploring the question of how global decision-making autonomy and internal markets may influence subsidiaries' in-house and outsourced new product development (NPD) activities via the exposure to global market forces. The model consists of several testable hypotheses regarding the relationships between the decision-making autonomy construct and the internal market construct on the one hand and in-house and outsourced new product development on the other. After the method section, results from structural equations modeling are presented. Finally, I discuss the contributions of the results to literature on MNC coordination mechanisms and subsidiary development.

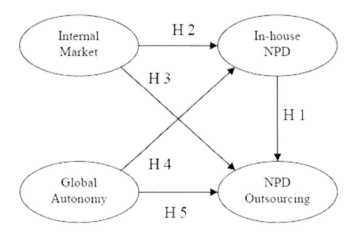

Figure 1. Hypothesized Structural Model.

2. Subsidiary Coordination Model

The basic idea of the model is that headquarters may use two different coordination mechanisms in order to expose its subsidiaries to internal and external market forces which, in turn, will create incentives for different organizational configurations in NPD. Figure 1 identifies two coordination mechanisms (left hand), internal markets and global autonomy, which are hypothesized to influence two organizational configurations in NPD (right hand), in-house NPD and NPD outsourcing.

In the next subsection, I describe the two elements of NPD configuration, in-house and outsourcing of NPD and the relationship between them. Then, I concentrate on the two coordination mechanisms, i.e. the mechanisms which headquarters applies (consciously or not) to manage its R&D network and to expose their units to more or less competition. Finally, all four elements will be integrated into a conceptual model which will be tested subsequently.

2.1. NPD Configuration in Foreign Subsidiaries

In-house NPD. While there are different concepts of product development processes, operations researcher seem to agree that its heart constitutes the design-build-test cycle (Clark e Fujimoto, 1991; Wheelwright e Clark, 1992). During this cycle – which may be repeated until a satisfactory solution is found or until it is abandoned – physical or virtual prototypes are built from a new product design. The prototypes are tested and results fed back into the design stage. This cycle can be complemented by additional stages such as concept development and product planning, process development or applied research. Management may choose to carry out all or only some stages in-house and to complement in-house activities with externally contracted product development services.

NPD outsourcing. Outsourcing refers to short-term, arms-length relationships between a customer and a supplier, were the customer passes design, prototype or test specifications to a technical service supplier. Outsourcing has been found to be more common than cooperation in R&D and is generally carried out under the following conditions: (a) it has to be cost effective, (b) it must not threaten the firm's competitive advantage and (c) various substitutable sources of outsourcing must be available (Narula, 2001).

Whether outsourcing and in-house product development activities are related is questionable from a theoretical point of view: whereas a transaction cost economics perspective would suggest that in-house NPD (hierarchy) and NPD outsourcing (market transaction) are discrete structural alternatives (Williamson, 1991), they may be seen as complementary from a resource-based view perspective (Veugeler and Cassiman, 1999). In the following, I will discuss these contradictory perspectives.

From a transaction cost economics approach, a firm may refrain from outsourcing for several reasons: to avoid the hold-up problem, outsourcing is recommended when multiple substitutable outsourcing partners are available (Pisano, 1990; Narula, 2001). In the same vein, Veugelers and Cassiman (1999) point out that outsourcing will be limited to generic, non-specific and routine activities due to transaction costs, the hold-up problem and reduced control possibilities. Therefore, NPD outsourcing requires that projects can be easily separated into strategic in-house components on the one hand and outsourcable routine activities on the other.

Even if these conditions were satisfied, a firm with all internal resources employed may lack sufficient resources to identify outsourcing partners for special needs, to coordinate and supervise the relationships with these partners. Hence, outsourcing may be discarded when transaction costs are too high compared to available resources and compared to the costs of organizing the same activities in-house (Williamson, 1985).

In line with this, empirical studies have found that the likelihood to combine in-house NPD with NPD outsourcing depends on firm size: while smaller firms tend to opt for either or strategies, larger firms tend to combine both forms of innovation (Veugeler and Cassiman, 1999) as they probably dispose over sufficient resources to identify, coordinate and control the fulfilment of contracts. Furthermore, NPD outsourcing is also said to be preferred when projects are of low duration, low geographical scope and when they involve a low number of partners and technologies (Croisier, 1998) as this would keep information, coordination and control costs low. Hence, outsourcing would make sense only under a limited set of conditions.

However, from a resource-based perspective, complementarity of resources is key to understanding the motivations for outsourcing. Outsourcing and in-house NPD can become complementary in several respects (competence, capacity, flexibility, speed and cost) which will be detailed below:

When a firm seeks to complement its own knowledge and competence base by knowledge owned by third parties, then outsourcing is driven by a lack of own competence or a lack of specialized knowledge. The rapid development and diffusion of new technologies implies that more and more technology needs to be sourced externally. However, internal NPD benefits more from outsourcing when sufficient absorptive capacity is present (Veugelers, 1997).

Firms focussing on its core competences limit their in-house NPD to what they know to do best and outsource what third parties can do more efficiently and at lower costs. Based on the corporate technology profile framework proposed by Granstrand, Patel and Pavitt (1997), firms tend to opt for outsourcing of R&D or NPD in areas where their technological competences are low (called background or marginal competences). Conversely, they carry out in-house R&D in areas where their competences are high (called distinctive and niche competences) (Narula, 2001).

When the problem is a lack of internal capacity, a firm might search for partners that could compensate their capacity shortage. A special case may come about when headquarters intends to reduce headcounts (cost reduction by rationalization): subsidiaries may then choose to substitute outsourcing for in-house NPD or channel increasing NPD demand directly to outsourcing partners.

Flexibility drivers can be compared to real options which a firm can buy (or rent) and exercise under conditions of uncertainty when more capacity or more competences are needed. Following this reasoning, a firm would do well building a network of existing or potential outsourcing partnerships that might be contracted or put on hold in response to market demand. In this latter sense, Narula (2001, p. 380) argues that outsourcing is used in order to 'smooth-out cyclical variations in demand'. In addition to increased flexibility, firms may gain efficiency since adding external capacity or external knowledge on demand is neutral with respect to fixed costs.

Sometimes, product development projects can be separated into modules. Thus, parallel development of separable modules by several outsourcing partners in addition to in-house NPD may contribute to shortening development lead time (Fujimoto, 2000).

Thus, an increase of NPD activities may prompt an increase of outsourced product development activities. In particular, higher in-house NPD may reveal bottlenecks, shortages of capacity or technological competence which may be covered by outsourcing. Besides, higher competition may force the firm to reduce lead-times and costs as well as to increase flexibility which may be achieved combining in-house NPD with outsourcing. Hence, I posit that:

Hypothesis 1. In-house NPD is positively related to NPD outsourcing.

2.2. MNC Coordination Mechanisms

Coordination mechanisms may influence both in-house NPD and NPD outsourcing, exposing the subsidiary to stronger or weaker market forces. In this section, I discuss two coordination mechanisms; first, the degree of market-like internal competition among product development units for project allocation by peer subsidiaries and headquarters; second, subsidiary autonomy as regards decision-making about initiating product development for and launching new products to global markets. As suggested by previous MNC research (Birkinshaw, 1997; Birkinshaw and Fey, 2000; Paterson and Brock, 2002; Young and Tavares, 2004), both mechanisms are essential to advance understanding of MNC coordination. Both coordination mechanisms expose subsidiaries to two different types of market forces. While internal market forces refer to competition among MNC units located in different countries, competition between an MNC unit and third companies in different markets is referred to as external market forces.

Internal Markets. After a major increase of mergers and acquisitions in the 1980s, inefficiencies of big organizations became notorious and a counter-movement took place which resulted in the deverticalization of many industrial conglomerates (Halal, 1994). Academia responded crafting an emerging research field on new organizational forms which combine characteristics of markets and hierarchy, a challenge to Williamson's (1991) 'discrete structural alternatives'. Indeed, the idea of market-like governance forms within the MNC hierarchy goes back to earlier work, Hedlund (1986, p. 14), for instance, refining Perlmutters polycentric MNC, states that:

'The tendency in terms of control mode is to move toward looser coupling between units and from hierarchy (…) of ethnocentrism to market solutions. Transfer pricing based on market prices rather than internal costs, freedom to choose external suppliers, rewards and punishment in monetary terms and elaborate bonus payment systems accompany greater turnover rates of personnel and organizational units being sold off and bought.'

Apart from the polycentric MNC, Market-like governance is also present in Hedlund's (1986) heterarchy were it coexists with hierarchical governance.

Deverticalization of firms into smaller business units and information technology encourages the infusion of markets into hierarchies, so called internal hybrids, or of hierarchies into markets, so called external hybrids (Zenger and Hesterly, 1997). I concentrate on the former which are also known as internal markets. Several scholars cite reduced coordination costs, high-powered incentives which reward internal organizational units in compliance with their output, better means to measure performance, superior flexibility, stronger intrapreneurial capabilities, among others, as the main advantages of internal markets (Birkinshaw, 1998, Halal, 1994). In particular, the use of hierarchical control and the price system in the same firm reduces the negative properties both of hierarchy and of the price mechanism (Hennart, 1993).

Internal markets can be understood as a practice during which several business units compete for resources, orders or projects (Birkinshaw, 1998; Birkinshaw and Fey, 2000)[1]. Thus, an internal market in an MNC R&D network implies that R&D or product development units negotiate and sell their research and technical services to peer subsidiaries or to headquarters. In this sense, an internal market does not entail the complete recreation of market forces within a firm; rather, incentives and some market-like elements are introduced, such as competition, a price-system, bidding for projects, orders or investments (resources). This means that different R&D units possess comparable capabilities and resources enabling them to compete for projects.

In the following I examine two hypotheses based on two alternative assumptions. The first assumption is that R&D or product development units, the players in the internal market, possess similar resources and capabilities in the same high competence fields. In other words, these units own basically the same distinctive or niche competences of their MNC. The diffusion of knowledge and competences across the entire MNC R&D network has been made increasingly feasible by knowledge management systems accessible MNC wide and by improved mechanisms of tacit knowledge transfer (Schulz and Jobe, 2001; Ernst and Kim, 2002).

Consequently, MNC product development units in different countries can compete for projects in these high competence fields. As soon as such a project has been assigned to a

---

[1] It is important to note that the concept of *internal markets* is different from the concept of *intra-firm competition*. The letter refers to a state in which two or more organizational units undertake duplicate activities, such as parallel development of competing solutions for the same problem or the coexistence of two or more products and brands targeting the same market (Galunic and Eisenhardt, 1996; Birkinshaw, 2001; Birkinshaw and Lingblad, 2001; Birkinshaw and Lingblad, 2005, p. 676).

product development unit, the bulk of NPD work is likely to be carried out in-house, because distinctive or niche competences are not considered subject to outsourcing (Narula, 2001). This means that internal market competition tends to increase innovative activities in-house. Thus, I hypothesize that

Hypothesis 2. The degree of internal market competition is positively related to in-house new product development.

The second assumption is that MNC subsidiaries, the players in the internal market, possess dissimilar resources and capabilities. Consequently, NPD projects are concentrated in centers of excellence or global subsidiary mandates, depending on the resources and capabilities required for project execution. This reasoning is based on center of excellence research (Birkinshaw and Hood, 1998; Andersson and Forsgren, 2000; Holm and Pedersen, 2000; Roth and Morrison, 1992; Frost, Birkinshaw and Ensign, 2002). Hence, what can be shifted from one product development unit or one subsidiary to another are NPD projects or modules of projects that are mainly based on background or marginal competences. Being not of highest strategic importance to the MNC, the bulk of these projects or modules can be outsourced locally in order to reap cost, flexibility, lead-time or specialization advantages (see section 2.1 on the expected benefits of NPD outsourcing). In other words, local outsourcing contributes then to increased NPD efficiency. In addition, outsourcing partners may contribute with complementary services and knowledge which may strengthen the unit's portfolio of technical services as well as the capacity to be offered to business units and subsidiaries abroad. As internal markets provide opportunities to offer product development services to peer subsidiaries, the focal product development unit has an incentive to increase its portfolio of services and to make its services more competitive vis-à-vis peer product development units. Thus, I hypothesize that

Hypothesis 3. The degree of internal market competition is positively related to new product development outsourcing.

Global Decision-Making Autonomy. High headquarters control over its subsidiaries is reflected in low decision-making autonomy perceived by subsidiary management and vice-versa. The concept dates back to sociological work on control in organizations (Crozier, 1981) and has been incorporated by theoretical work on MNCs which associates different levels of autonomy with different organizational structures (Perlmutter, 1969; Hedlund, 1986). The concept of autonomy is also one of the most discussed in empirical literature on MNC subsidiaries (e.g. Ghoshal e Bartlett, 1988; Birkinshaw e Morrison, 1995; Taggart, 1997; Nobel and Birkinshaw, 1998; Gupta e Govindarajan, 1994; Zahra, Darwadkar e George, 2000; Asakawa, 2001; Frost, Birkinshaw and Ensign, 2002) and several literature reviews have dedicated special attention to it (e.g. Paterson e Brock, 2002; Young e Tavares, 2004).

The positive relationship between local decision-making autonomy, this is a subsidiary's autonomy regarding activities within its host country, and (product or process) innovation seems to be reasonably well established in literature (Ghoshal and Bartlett, 1988; Holm and Pedersen, 2000; Young and Tavares, 2004). Conceptual work on global subsidiary mandates, such as 'product specialists' or 'strategic independent' subsidiaries has posited a positive relationship between global decision-making autonomy, i.e. autonomy regarding global markets (excluding the internal market of the MNC), and innovation (White and Poynter, 1984). However, empirical evidence on this relationship is mixed (Roth and Morrison, 1992; Birkinshaw, 1997); therefore, I revisit the relationship and attempt to integrate it into my conceptual framework.

Again, the following two hypotheses are based on two alternative assumptions. The first assumption supposes that the subsidiary carries out original NPD in areas of high technological competences, which Granstrand, Patel and Pavitt (1997) call distinctive or niche competences. If a subsidiary possesses decision-making autonomy to develop and launch products on global markets (and not just on its local market), it faces a whole range of new market opportunities. These opportunities and the freedom to exploit them may expose the subsidiary and its R&D department to a more diverse landscape of client requirements and competition. As a consequence, these opportunities may translate into powerful incentives to enhance innovative new product development activities. Given this, NPD is most likely to be carried out in-house for strategic reasons and to protect knowledge (Narula, 2001; Veugelers and Cassiman, 1999). Hence, I posit that:

Hypothesis 4. The degree of global decision-making autonomy is positively related to in-house new product development.

The opposite assumption supposes that the subsidiary focuses on a sort of NPD in areas where high technological competences are not needed, for instance in low-tech areas. If headquarters has conceded global decision-making autonomy to the product development unit, the latter is exposed to incentives to exploit opportunities on the global market. As the unit is assumed to focus on the development of low-tech products for global markets, competitiveness is not so much based on innovation but on efficiency. As argued in section 2.1, local outsourcing can contribute to efficiency gains, for instance, increasing capacity and sourcing generic technologies maintaining fix costs constant, reducing costs reaping economies of scale, reducing development lead-time, among others. Assuming that the product development unit focuses low-tech products, NPD mainly consists of generic, non-specific and routine activities (Veugelers and Cassiman 1999). Therefore, the unit will then primarily use NPD outsourcing which is the preferred mode when R&D or NPD activities rely on lower levels of competences (Narula, 2001; Veugelers and Cassiman, 1999). Thus, I hypothesize that:

Hypothesis 5. The degree of global decision-making autonomy is positively related to new product development outsourcing.

In sum, I posit that both concepts, internal markets and global decision-making autonomy, may have positive complementary effects on subsidiaries' in-house NPD and NPD outsourcing. This argument is represented by my conceptual model which encompasses all four concepts and the above-mentioned five hypotheses (see Figure 1 above).

3. Method

3.1. Key Informants

The unit of analysis chosen for this study is a product development or R&D unit in a wholly foreign-owned MNC subsidiary. Since there was no database of reasonable size with MNC product development units available, I built my own sample frame based on secondary material, such as other (smaller) survey sample frames, a government data-base, databases from industry associations, information from newspapers and web research. These product development managers – key informants – were contacted by phone in order to present the research, to convince them to take part in the survey and to check for their hierarchical position within the product development department. One additional criterion of respondent selection was that he/she should be in a position to keep direct working contact with other MNC units abroad. If the managers were responsible for several product families within their division, they were asked to limit their response to the product family most important to the subsidiary or division.

3.2. Sample

The sample was collected in Brazil due to the following reasons: first, Brazil continues to be one major destination of FDI-inflows with an economy were close to half of the GDP is generated by foreign owned MNCs. Correspondingly, roughly 48% of business R&D spending is generated by MNC subsidiaries (United Nations, 2005, p. 127). Furthermore, Brazil is also home of several regional headquarters and R&D centers with responsibilities for the Latin American region or even third countries, which makes it an interesting setting for a study using the concept of global decision-making autonomy as predictor variable.

Altogether, 269 e-mails with hyperlinks to the server hosted questionnaires as well as self-executing questionnaire-files (in case corporate firewalls blocked web-access to questionnaires) were sent to key informants. The researchers obtained 146 valid questionnaires which resulting in a response rate of 54%. This response rate can be considered very high for web-surveys.

Two procedures for outlier detection were used. I considered extreme scores with more than three standard deviations off the mean as univariate outliers and deleted these observations. Multivariate outliers were detected using the procedures offered by Amos 5.0 (Build 5138), in particular, Mahalanobis distance and Mardias coefficient of multivariate kurtosis. As a result, sample size shrank to 136 observations.

I checked for potential non-response bias using the extrapolation method (Armstrong and Overton, 1977). For this purpose, I calculated the time between the response date of the questionnaire and the first request to respond. Then the first and the last quartile of respondents were compared (t-tests for equality of means). I found no significant mean differences.

3.3. Measures

In-house New Product Development (NPD). In order to capture the extent to which a product development unit within a subsidiary carries out new product development activities, I asked the unit manager whether or not his unit carries out the following activities: new product designs, prototyping of new products and prototype tests. These indicators represent the main stages of the design-build-test cycle (Clark e Fujimoto, 1991; Wheelwright e Clark, 1992). A five-item Likert scale was used ranging from '1 – activity is never performed' through '5 – activity is always performed'. For reasons of parsimony, the last item (prototype tests) was eliminated from the overall model despite its high item validity. Overall scale reliability is acceptable (α= 0.77). The questionnaire extract is provided in Annex A.

New Product Development Outsourcing. Outsourcing of new product development activities implies that the focal product development unit passes on specifications (development agreements) to a subcontractor who carries out new product design, builds prototypes or performs tests of the prototypes. Applying the same reasoning as above, three indicators which represent the main stages of the design-build-test cycle were used. Using the same Likert scale as above, respondents were asked to what extent their unit orders services of new product designs, prototyping of new products, prototype tests from local entities be they companies, technology centres or universities. The reliability for outsourcing of design and prototyping is also quite reasonable (Cronbach alpha = 0.68 for the two indicator based construct). Although alpha coefficients above 0.7 are recommendable, reliabilities around 0.6 suffice for initial stages of basic research (Nunally, 1967 apud Churchill, 1979, p. 68).

Internal market. Internal competition was operationalised using three items proposed by the Birkinshaw and Fey (2000) case study research on internal markets in R&D organizations. The measures had to be adapted to the context of subsidiary research, since the original questionnaire items were applied to headquarters staff. A five item scale ("1 – fully disagree" through "5 – fully agree") was applied to statements such as competition for product development projects among PDUs in different countries, market like bidding for projects, commercialization of product development services to other units. The reasoning is as follows: if key informants agree that there is competition among units, bidding for projects and selling of product development related services to other units and subsidiaries occurs in the MNC, then they perceive essential characteristics of an internal market like organizational mechanism. Reliability for a two item construct was deemed acceptable for early stage construct development (Cronbach alpha = 0.67).

Global decision-making autonomy. I operationalized the global decision-making autonomy of the PDU using two items, the decision to initiate new product development projects for the global market and the decision to launch these projects on the global market. This construct is inspired by Foss (2003, p. 336), Nobel and Birkinshaw (1998) and Anderson and Forsgren (1996) who proposed similar items. A five point Likert scale was used with '1 – Headquarters decides alone' through '5 – this subsidiary decides alone'. The scale reliability was high (α = 0.89).

Table 1. Correlations

Observed variables	1	2	3	4	5	6	7	8
1 In-house design (DESI)	1							
2 In-house prototyping (PROTI)	0.63**	1						
3 Design outsourcing (DESO)	0.19*	0.20*	1					
4 Prototype outsourcing (PROTO)	0.16	0.17*	0.52**	1				
5 Global project initiation (NPDEX)	0.25**	0.29**	0.03	-0.03	1			
6 Global product launch (LAUNEX)	0.19*	0.30**	0.02	0.00	0.81**	1		
7 Internal competition (COMPET)	0.00	-0.05	0.14	0.17*	-0.10	-0.06	1	
8 Bidding process (INTMKT)	0.09	-0.05	0.15	0.18*	-0.01	-0.04	0.39**	1

* significant at 0.05.

** significant at 0.01.

Note: all indicators were standardized (z-scores) with mean = 0 and standard deviation = 1.

Table 2. Constructs and reliabilities

Construct	Indicators	Factor Loading	Error terms	C.R.	R^2	Reliability	AVE
Internal Market	COMPET	0.64	0.59	-	0.41	0.60	0.43
	INTMKT	0.67	0.55	2.269	0.45		
Global Autonomy	NPDEX	0.85	0.29	4.810	0.71	0.90	0.81
	LAUNEX	0.95	0.09	-	0.91		
In-house NPD	PROTI	0.83	0.31	-	0.69	0.77	0.63
	DESI	0.75	0.44	4.438	0.56		
NPD outsourcing	PROTO	0.72	0.48	3.595	0.52	0.68	0.52
	DESO	0.72	0.48	-	0.52		

3.4. Data Analysis

I used AMOS 5.0 software with the maximum likelihood algorithm to fit the hypothesized structural model (see Figure 2 below). Altogether, 30 parameters were freely estimated (the others were fixed). Considering the sample size of 136 observations, the ratio between freely estimable parameters and observations is 1:4.5 which is slightly below the recommended minimum benchmark of 1:5. However, maximum likelihood modeling 'is justifiable when the sample size minus the number of parameters to be estimated is greater than 50' (Bagozzi, 1981, p. 380) or as soon as sample size exceeds 100 observations. Fixing

Local Outsourcing and Global Competition

three parameters of the model with standardized estimates close to '0' lifted the ratio above the benchmark of '1:5' while all other parameters remain close to the original estimates.

4. Results

Table 1 provides correlations for all indicators used in this study. The profile of the sample can be described as follows: the most important countries of origin of the subsidiaries were the US (34.6% of the sample), Germany (26.5%), France (7.4%), Japan (6.6%), UK (5.2%) and Sweden (5.9%). The main industrial sectors included in the survey were the automotive industry (36%), electronic industry (36%), machinery industry (12.5%) and chemical industry (5%). Some industries such as the pharmaceutical, agricultural, construction or service industry have been excluded because of their unique characteristics or irrelevance for industrial product development in Brazil.

4.1. Measurement Model

Following Fornell and Larcker (1981) I calculated composite reliability and average variance extracted (AVE). None of the composite reliabilities (7th column of Table 2) fell below the benchmark of 0.6 (Bagozzi and Yi, 1988). The average variance extracted (8th column of Table 2) measures the amount of variance captured by the construct compared to the variance due to measurement error (Fornell and Larcker, 1981, p. 45). Though one AVE dropped slightly below the recommended benchmark of 0.5, I decided to maintain the internal market construct, since other measures were acceptable (similar factor loadings and all of them above 0.5, R^2 above 0.4, significant critical values, i.e. above 1.96 indicating that factor loadings were significant at least at the 0.05 level). Altogether, data suggests that the four constructs exhibit acceptable levels of reliability.

The correlations between constructs and its indicators (see Table 3 below) show satisfactory discriminant validity, as correlations between constructs and their defining indicators are significant and high while correlations between indicators and the remaining constructs are low and non-significant.

Following the recommendations compiled by Podsakoff et al. (2003) I addressed potential common method bias by guaranteeing confidential treatment of questionnaire data, by separating the items of the four constructs by at least two pages of the questionnaire. In addition, I used three different scales for the dependent and independent variables, ranging from 'never' (1) to 'always' (5), from 'totally disagree' (1) to 'totally agree' (5) and from 'headquarter decides alone' (1) to 'this subsidiary decides alone' (5). Furthermore, questionnaire items were worded carefully and were checked by several faculty staff (marketing and technology management professors), postgraduate students and subsidiary R&D staff. Though there is no definite test of common method bias, I applied Harman's single factor test; principal component analysis separated the four constructs.

Table 3. Discriminant Validity - Correlations between Constructs and indicators

	Global Autonomy	In-house NPD	NPD Outsourcing	Internal Market
In-house Design (DESI)	0.11	0.90**	0.09	0.07
In-house Prototyping (PROTI)	0.13	0.87**	0.15	-0.10
Design outsourcing (DESO)	0.01	0.13	0.86**	0.09
Prototyping outsourcing (PROTO)	-0.03	0.09	0.86**	0.12
Global Autonomy/project initiation (NPDEX)	0.94**	0.15	-0.02	-0.03
Global Autonomy/product launch (LAUNEX)	0.95**	0.10	0.00	-0.03
Competition for PD projects (COMPET)	-0.05	-0.02	0.09	0.83**
Bidding for NPD projects (INTMKT)	-0.01	0.01	0.11	0.84**

** significant at 0.01.

4.2. Structural Model

The fit indices give strong support for the whole structural model. The chi-square (χ^2=8.535) statistic for the model is low and insignificant (p=0.86), suggesting that the covariance matrix of the eight observed indicators fits well the hypothesized structural model (Figure 2). Adjusting for degrees of freedom (DF=14), the ratio χ^2/df (0.61) drops well below the maximum value of 3 recommended by Kline (1998, p. 128), indicating a good model fit.

The incremental fit indices, the normed fit index (NFI) and the comparative fit index (CFI) show values well above the minimum benchmark of 0.9, suggesting that the model fit is at least 90% better than the null model. The CFI takes the special characteristics of small samples into account.

The root mean square error of approximation (RMSEA) indicates very good fit and there is a probability of 90% that the RMSEA value falls between 0.0 and 0.045.

Hoelter's critical N indicates the largest sample size for which a model would be correct; thus it focuses directly on the adequacy of sample size (Byrne, 2001). A critical N of 375 at the 0.05 significance level implies that the present model would be correct with a sample size up to n=375.

Additionally, I checked the standardized residual covariances on the AMOS output table. According to Joreskog and Sorbom (1988 cited by in Byrne, p. 89), standardizes residual covariances should not exceed 2.58. As no residual was greater than 1.175, Joreskog and Sorbom's criterion is fulfilled. Modification indices are low and do not exceeding 4.2 and the implied parameter change is also low (0.11) which is why no action was taken.

I also examined whether alternative relationships between the two independent variables, internal market and global decision-making autonomy, and the two dependent variables, in-house NPD and NPD outsourcing, would lead to an improvement of fit. For this purpose, two alternative models were estimated. In Model II, I set the parameter between internal market and NPD outsourcing to '0' and in Model III I set the parameter between global decision-making autonomy and in-house NPD to '0'. Though both alternative models would not be rejected by fit statistics, they are considerably weaker than the unrestricted Model I as chi-square (χ^2) rises from 8.535 to 15.560 and 17.691 respectively. Therefore, only the original model should be maintained.

As for hypothesis tests, I examined the critical values and path coefficients between the four latent constructs. Critical values above 1.96 indicate statistical significance at 0.05 level and critical values above 2.58 indicate statistical significance at 0.01 level. Three of five hypotheses were supported (see Figure 2).

The relationship between in-house NPD and NPD outsourcing is positive (path coefficient = 0.39) and significant (critical value = 2.796) which supports hypothesis H1.

Internal Market has no significant impact on in-house NPD (path coefficient = -0.009, critical value = -0.075) which rejects hypothesis H2. However, internal market has a significant positive relationship with NPD outsourcing, with a path coefficient of 0.36 and a critical value of 2.237. Hence, there is support for hypothesis H3.

There is a significant positive relationship between global decision-making autonomy and in-house NPD (path coefficient = 0.31; critical value = 2.849), thus, supporting hypothesis H4. The fifth hypothesis H5 posits a positive relationship between global decision-making autonomy and NPD outsourcing. This hypothesis was not supported (path coefficient = -0.1; critical value of -0.883).

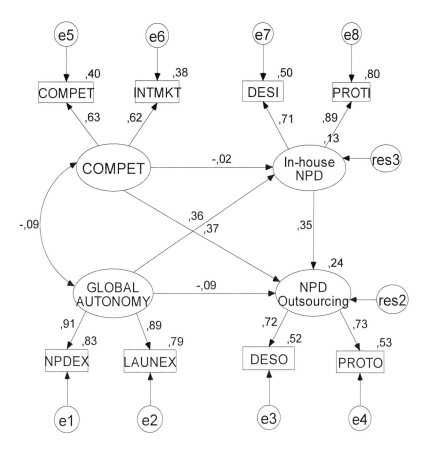

Figure 2. Path Model.

5. Conclusions

This research has examined the question of how MNC coordination mechanisms influence subsidiaries' in-house and outsourced new product development (NPD) activities. More specifically, how two essential coordination mechanisms, global decision-making autonomy and internal markets, influence NPD intensity exposing R&D units to internal and external global market forces. Evolutionary theory suggests that market competition influences favorably organizational and technological learning in general and innovation in particular. However, it has not been empirically examined yet how MNCs can utilize coordination mechanisms in order to expose its R&D units both to internal and to external competition and how this influences the NPD activities of the latter. This study fills this gap in that it proposes a model which hypothesizes the impact of two coordination mechanisms, a) decision-making autonomy regarding product development for global markets and b) internal markets on the intensity of in-house NPD and NPD outsourcing. The results suggest that the exposure to internal markets increases the intensity of NPD outsourcing which in turn is positively related to in-house NPD. Furthermore, the findings indicate that the exposure to global markets (conceding autonomy) directly increases the intensity of in-house new product development.

5.1. Contributions

Thus, this paper makes several contributions to literature on MNC coordination mechanisms and to the development of subsidiary R&D.

First of all, I extend literature on headquarters-subsidiary and subsidiary-subsidiary coordination mechanisms by testing a model which integrates the construct of internal markets along with the construct of global decision-making autonomy. Both can be considered as formal coordination mechanisms, although internal markets may have both formal or informal qualities depending on the degree to which they are put into practice and to whether headquarter has made its use explicit or not. Adding this dimension to the coordination mechanisms stream of literature is important because the intrusion of market-like elements into hierarchy seems to become an increasingly frequent practice which has been underscored by this research.

Second, I extend subsidiary level literature on R&D activities by differentiating between in-house NPD and NPD outsourcing. This is important because firms may leverage their NPD activities combining in-house and outsourced NPD activities. Hypotheses H2, H3, H4 and H5 were developed to test which coordination mechanism is more likely to influence in-house NPD or NPD outsourcing. In fact, the model suggests that the increase of in-house NPD is influenced by global autonomy while NPD outsourcing is influenced by internal markets. How can these finding be explained?

A possible explanation is that PDUs react differently to global internal and external market opportunities. As follows from the literature review, internal market opportunities can be characterized as new product development according to specifications defined by other MNC units. Thus, performance is likely to be measured in efficiency terms (costs, quality, time-to-market, etc.). Outsourcing of technological services may contribute to efficiency, since fixed costs can be maintained stable while capacity becomes enhanced. Outsourcing may also permit to yield specialization advantages and thus contribute to economies of scale and quality. Moreover, outsourcing may speed-up product development, because project stages can be carried out in parallel by different entities, thus reducing overall project lead time.

As for the direct effect of global autonomy on in-house NPD, the conquest of new markets beyond the host country implies more diverse and demanding client requirements. Thus, performance is likely to be evaluated in terms of effectiveness; this is the innovativeness of new products launched. However, outsourcing does not necessarily favor the development and market introduction of new pathbreaking products (Kessler, Bierly and Gopalakrishnan, 2000; Birkinshaw and Fey, 2001). Similarly, strategic and market relevant knowledge tends to be kept in-house, less strategic routine work is likely to be outsourced (Narula, 2001). Therefore, global market opportunities may translate directly into an increase of strategically relevant in-house rather than NPD outsourcing.

The positive relationship between in-house NPD and NPD outsourcing makes now even more sense, as internal markets may result in a re-distribution of the NPD related activities carried out internally and externally: outsourcing of less strategically relevant and activities with a high impact on NPD efficiency may free capacity for an increase of strategically relevant, more innovative NPD in-house, which explains my first hypothesis.

Another related point is the time horizon of NPD activities. The short-term orientation of internal market opportunities compared to global market opportunities may provide a further explanation of the empirical findings. Internal opportunities may arise when other MNC units work at the upper limit of capacity. Hence, it would be wise to deal with these projects in a flexible manner, i.e. without increasing fixed costs, which favors NPD outsourcing. Still, exploiting global market opportunities may imply a more proactive and long-term management orientation which would justify maintaining projects in-house.

Third, this chapter's findings also refine the literature on subsidiary development. Birkinshaw and Hood (1998, p. 787) claim that 'competitive internal resource allocation (…) provides a motivation for them (subsidiaries) to continually upgrade their capabilities'. Further, they propose that competitive internal resource allocation mechanism positively influences the likelihood that a subsidiary management takes initiatives to enlarge or reinforce its charter, i.e. its temporary market or product responsibility. The same rational applies to decentralization of decision-making which is also seen as positively related to subsidiary capability building and charter enlargement or reinforcement. Though not exactly focused on product development or R&D, Birkinshaw and Hood's (1998) theoretical propositions are compatible with my empirical findings, because an increase in NPD can be regarded as a manifestation of subsidiary capability building and as a prerequisite of charter enlargement or reinforcement.

Fourth, the study suggests that local impacts of multinational corporations may be, at least partly, a function of their global coordination mechanisms. This is a novel finding because previous research has given more emphasis to host country industrial policy and regulations which might 'oblige' subsidiaries to contribute to host country development, for example by partnering with local organizations. Moreover, previous research has also focused on specific host country market opportunities or the potential to tap into foreign knowledge sources.

Finally, the study contributes in that it operationalizes the internal market construct in a large scale survey which has not been done previously. Thus, the study fills an important void, i.e. the empirical test of a construct related to subsidiary development and MNC coordination mechanism literature.

5.2. Managerial Implications

If different coordination mechanisms indeed expose subsidiaries to internal and external market forces, then subsidiary management should proactively organize its R&D unit for rising market opportunities. When MNCs use internal markets as coordination mechanism, then subsidiary management should prepare its R&D unit for arising internal market opportunities by identifying, evaluating and establishing business relationships with potential outsourcing partners. In response to increasing or decreasing use of internal market coordination, such a local outsourcing network could be relied on in a flexible way.

Likewise, when MNCs use global market decision-making autonomy as a coordination mechanism, subsidiary management should prepare its R&D unit by developing technological capabilities that enable it to take advantage of upcoming opportunities in global markets. This is not new by itself, but may appear in new light when considered together with the relationship between internal market and outsourcing.

The substantial relationship between NPD outsourcing and in-house NPD, may imply that subsidiary management needs to develop a methodology for smoothly and efficiently combining in-house NPD and external (outsourced) NPD capacities, particularly when exposed to both internal and external market forces. Furthermore, subsidiaries may be advised to develop a local collaborator network if they intend to strengthen their competitive position within their MNC.

5.3. Limitations and Future Research

This research has tested a model using a country-specific data-set. Though, construct operationalization has not been linked to country-specific characteristics, further research should ensure the generalization of the model to other contexts, both low cost and high cost countries. This is important as the substantial effect of internal market coordination on NPD outsourcing may be due to the particular cost advantages of a medium cost country like Brazil vis-à-vis high cost countries where competing peer subsidiaries are located.

Due to limits imposed by sample-size, only two coordination mechanisms were included into my model. Though both coordination mechanisms may be of primary relevance as they represent two main dimensions of organizational economics (market and hierarchy), future research should advance studying interaction effects with other formal and informal coordination mechanisms. Thus, theory development about coordination mechanisms would benefit from a more comprehensive modeling approach. A further step in future research could then add host country related factors and thus provide us with a more comprehensive model.

Appendix

Questionnaire (translated from Portuguese)

In-house NPD
Does your unit carry out some of the following activities? Please use a scale from '1' (never) through '5' (always).

1. Design of new products (DESI)
2. Prototyping of new products (PROTI)

NPD Outsourcing
Does your unit commission some of the following activities from other organizations (universities, companies, technology centers) located in Brazil? Please use a scale from '1' (never) through '5' (always).

3. Design of new products (DESO)
4. Prototyping of new products (PROTO)

Decision-making autonomy in product development activities
"With respect to the product development activities of your unit, please indicate how the following decisions are taken. Use a scale from "1" (headquarters decides alone) through "5" (this subsidiary decides alone)."

5. Start of new product development projects for foreign markets (NPDEX)
6. Launch of new products abroad (LAUNEX)

Internal Market
"Please indicate whether you agree or disagree with the following affirmations with regard to the product development activities of your unit. Use a scale from "1" (totally disagree) through "5" (totally agree).

7. There is competition for the allocation of new product development projects with our corporation's units located abroad. (COMPET)
8. Product development projects are allocated using a bidding system among our corporation's units located in different countries. (MKTINT)

References

Andersson, U. and Forsgren, M., 2000. In search of centre of excellence: network embeddedness and subsidiary roles in multinational companies. *Management International Review,* **40** (4): 329–350.

Andersson, U., and Forsgren, M. 1996. Subsidiary embeddedness and control in the multinational corporation. *International business review,* **5**(5): 487-508.

Armstrong, S., and Overton, T. 1977. Estimating nonresponse bias in mail surveys. *Journal of Marketing Research,* **14**(3): 396-402.

Asakawa, K. 2001. Evolving headquarters-subsidiary dynamics in international R&D: the case of Japanese multinationals. *R&D Management,* **31** (1): 1-14.

Bagozzi, R. P. 1981. Evaluating Structural Equation Models With Unobservable Variables and Measurement Error: A Comment, *Journal of Marketing Research,* **18**(3): 375-381.

Bagozzi, R. P., and Yi, Y. On the Evaluation of Structural Equation Models. *Journal of the Academy* of *Marketing Science,* Spring88, **16** (1):74-95.

Bartlett, C., and Ghoshal, S. 1989. *Managing across borders: The transnational solution.* Boston: Harvard Business School Press.

Birkinshaw, J., and Fey, C. 2001. 'External sources of knowledge and performance in R&D organizations', *LBS Working Paper Series Strategic and International Management,* London: Business School. Retrieved February 15, 2007 from http://forum.london.edu/lbsfacpubs.nsf/(httpPublications)/093D62E4C408F78880256B37005847EE/$file/SIM03.pdf

Birkinshaw, J., and Fey, C. 2000. Building an internal market system: Insights from five R&D organizations. In J. Birkinshaw and P. Hagstrom (Eds.), *The flexible firm: Capability management in network organizations*: 149-175. Oxford: Oxford University Press.

Birkinshaw, J., and Morrison, A. 1995. Configurations of strategy and structure in subsidiaries of multinational corporations. *Journal of International Business Studies,* **26**(4): 729-754.

Birkinshaw, J., and Hood, N. 1998. Multinational subsidiary evolution: Capability and charter change in foreign-owned subsidiary companies. *The Academy of Management Review,* **23**(4): 773-796.

Birkinshaw, J. 1997. Entrepreneurship in multinational corporations: The characteristics of subsidiary initiatives, *Strategic Management Journal,* **18**(3): 207-229.

Birkinshaw, J. 1998. Corporate entrepreneurship in network organizations: How subsidiary initiative drives internal market efficiency. *European Management Journal,* **16**(3): 355-364.

Birkinshaw, J. 2001. Strategies for managing internal competition, *California: Management Review,* **44**(1): 21-39.

Birkinshaw, J., and Lingblad, M. 2005. Intra-Firm Competition and Charter Evolution in The Multi-Business Firm, *Organization Science,* **16** (6): 674-686.

Birkinshaw, J., and Lingblad, M. 2001. An Evolutionary Theory of Intra-Organisational Competition. Retrieved August 5, 2009 from http://www.druid.dk/conferences/nw/paper1/lingblad.pdf

Byrne, B. 2001. *Structural Equation Modeling with AMOS: Basic Concepts, Applications, and Programming,* Lawrence Erlbaum Associates Publishers: Mahwah.

Churchill, G. 1979. A paradigm for developing better measures of marketing constructs, *Journal of Marketing Research,* **16**: 64-73.

Clark, K. B., and Fujimoto, T. 1991. *Product development performance: strategy, organisation and management in the world auto industry.* In: Harvard Business School Press. Boston, Massachusetts.

Croisier, B. 1998. The governance of external research: empirical test of some transaction-cost related factors, *R&D Management,* **28**(4): 289-298.

Crozier, M. 1981. *O fenômeno burocrático*. Editora Universidade de Brasília, Brasília. (original edition in French from 1963).

Dillman, D. A., and Bowker, D. K. 2001. The web questionnaire challenge to survey methodologists. In U. D. Reips and M. Bosnjak (Eds.), *Dimensions of internet science*. Retrieved February 14, 2005 from http://survey.sesrc.wsu.edu/dillman/zuma_paper_ dillman_bowker.pdf

Ernst, D. and Kim, L. 2002. Global production networks, knowledge diffusion, and local capability formation, *Research Policy*, **31**(1): 1417–1429.

Foss, N. 2003. Selective Intervention and Internal Hybrids: Interpreting and Learning from the Rise and Decline of the Oticon Spaghetti Organization, *Organization Science*, **14**(3): 331-349.

Fischer, W., and Behrman, J. 1979. *The Coordination of Foreign R&D Activities by Transnational Corporations*, **10** (3): 28-35.

Fornell, C., and Larcker, D. 1981. Evaluating Structural Equation Models with Unobservable Variables and Measurement Error, *Journal of Marketing Research*, **18**(1): 39-50.

Frost, T., Birkinshaw, J., and Ensign, P. 2002. Centers of excellence in multinational corporations. *Strategic Management Journal*, **23**: 997-1018.

Frost, T. and Pedersen, T. 2002. Transferring knowledge in MNCs: The role of sources of subsidiary knowledge and organizational context, *Journal of International Management*, **8**: 49–67.

Frost, T. and Zhou, C. 2005. R&D co-practice and 'reverse' knowledge integration in multinational firms, *Journal of International Business Studies*, **36**: 676–687.

Fujimoto, T. 2000. Shortening Lead Time through Early Problem-solving – A New Round of Capability-building Competition in the Auto Industry, in Jürgens, U. (Ed.), New Product Development and Production Networks, Berlin, Springer: 23-53.

Galunic, D. C., and Eisenhardt, K. M. 1996. The Evolution of Intracorporate Domains: Divisional Charter Losses in High-Technology, Multidivisional Corporations, *Organization Science*, **7**(3): 255-282.

Ghoshal, S., and Bartlett, C. 1988. Creation, adoption and diffusion of innovations by subsidiaries of multinational companies. *Journal of International Business Studies*, **19**(3): 365-388.

Granstrand, O., Patel, P. and Pavitt, K. 1997. Multi-Technology Corporations: Why They Have "Distributed" rather than "Distinctive Core" Competencies. *California Management Review*, **39**(4): 8-25.

Gupta, A., and Govindarajan, V. 1991. Knowledge flows and the structure of control within multinational corporations. *Academy of Management Review*, **16**(4): 768-792.

Gupta, A., and Govindarajan, V. 1994. Organizing for knowledge flows within MNCs. *International Business Review*, **3**(4): 443-457.

Halal, W. 1994. From hierarchy to enterprise: Internal markets are the new foundation of management. *The Academy of Management Executive*, **8**(4): 69-83.

Hedlund, G. 1986. The hypermodern MNC - A heterarchy? *Human Resource Management*, **25**(1): 9-35.

Hennart, J.F. 1993. The swollen middle: a mix of market and hierarchy. *Organization Science*, **4** (4): 529-547.

Holm, U., and Pedersen, T. 2000. *The Emergence and impact of MNC centers of excellence: A subsidiary perspective*. London: McMillan Press.

Kessler, E. H., Bierly, P.E., and Gopalakrishnan, S. 2000. Internal and external learning in new product development: effects on speed, costs and competitive advantage. *R&D Management*, **30** (3): 213-233.

Kline, R. 1998. *Principles and practice of structural equation modeling.* New York: Guilford Press.

Martinez, J., and Jarillo, C. 1991. Coordination demands of international strategies, *Journal of International Business Studies*, **22**: 429-444.

Narula, R. 2001. Choosing Between Internal and Non-internal R&D Activities: Some Technological and Economic Factors, *Technology Analysis and Strategic Management,* **13** (3): 365-387.

Nobel, R., and Birkinshaw, J. 1998. Innovation in multinational corporations: control and communication patterns in international R&D operations. *Strategic Management Journal*, **19**: 479-496.

Paterson, S.L., and Brock, D.M. 2002. The development of subsidiary management research: review and theoretical analysis. *International Business Review*, **11**: 139-163.

Pearce, Robert. 1999. Decentralized R&D and strategic competitiveness: globalised approaches to generation and use of technology in multinational enterprises (MNEs). *Research Policy*, **28**: 157-178.

Perlmutter, H. 1969. The tortuous evolution of the multinational corporation. *Columbia Journal of World Business:* 9-18.

Persaud, A., Kumar, U., and Kumar, V. 2002. Coordination structures and innovative performance. *Canadian Journal of Administrative Sciences*, **19**(1): 57-75.

Pisano, G. 1990. The R&D boundaries of the Firm: an empirical analysis, *Administrative Science Quarterly*, **35**: 153-176.

Podsakoff, P.M., Mackenzie, S., Lee, J.Y., and Podsakoff, N. 2003. Common Method Biases in Behavioral Research: A Critical Review of the Literature and Recommended Remedies, *Journal of Applied Psychology,* doi:10.1037/0021-9010.88.5.879.

Roth, K., and Morrison, A.J. 1992. Implementing global strategy: Characteristics of global subsidiary mandates. *Journal of International Business Studies*, **23**(4): 715-736.

Rugman, A., and Hodgetts, R. 2000. The End of Global Strategy. *European Management Journal,* **19**(4): 333-343.

Schulz, M. and Jobe, L. 2001. Codification and tacitness as knowledge management strategies an empirical exploration, *Journal of High Technology Management Research*, **12**: 139-165.

Schütte, H. 1998. Between headquarters and subsidiaries: The RHQ solution. In: J. Birkinshaw and N. Hood (Eds.) *Multinational corporate evolution and subsidiary development:* 189-212. Basingstroke: McMillan.

Taggart, J. 1997. Autonomy and procedural justice: A framework for evaluating subsidiary strategy. *Journal of International Business Studies*, **28**(1): 51-76.

United Nations 2005. *World Investment Report 2005 – Transnational Corporations and the Internationalization of R&D.* New York and Geneva: United Nations.

Veugelers, R., Cassiman, B., 1999. Make and buy in innovation strategies: evidence from Belgian manufacturing firms, *Research Policy*, **28**(1), 63-80.

Williamson, O.E. 1991. Comparative economic organization: The analysis of discrete structural alternatives. *Administrative Science quarterly,* **36**(2): 269-296.

Wheelwright, S., and Clark, K. 1992. *Revolutionizing product development: quantum leaps in speed, efficiency and quality.* New York, Free Press.

Whithe, R., and Poynter, T. 1984. Strategies for Foreign-Owned Subsidiaries in Canada. *Business Quarterly,* **49**(2): 59-70.

Young, S., and Tavares, A. T. 2004. Centralization and autonomy: back to the future. *International Business Review*, **13**: 215-237.

Zahra, S., Dharwadkar, R., and George, G. 2000. *Entrepreneurship in Multinational Subsidiaries: The Effects of Corporate and Local Environmental Contexts.* Retrieved April 28, 2003 from http://www.ciber.gatech.edu/workingpaper/99_00-27.pdf

Zenger, T., and Hesterly, W. 1997.The disaggregation of corporations: Selective intervention, high-powered incentives, and molecular units. *Organization Science,* **8**(3): 209-222.

In: Handbook of Business and Finance
Editors: M. Bergmann and T. Faust, pp. 147-170

ISBN: 978-1-60692-855-4
© 2010 Nova Science Publishers, Inc.

Chapter 6

A COST OF CAPITAL ANALYSIS OF THE GAINS FROM SECURITIZATION

Hugh Thomas[1,] and Zhiqiang Wang[2]*
[1] The Chinese University of Hong Kong, Shatin,
NT, Hong Kong SAR, China
[2] Dongbei University of Finance and Economics,
Dalian, Liaoning, China

Abstract

In this paper we study the gains that securitizing companies enjoy. We expressed the gains as a spread between two costs of capital, that weighted cost of capital of the asset selling firm and the all-in, weighted average cost of the securitization. We calculate the spread for 1,713 securitizations and regress those gains on asset seller characteristics. We show that they are increasing in size in the amount of asset backed securities originated but are decreasing in the percent of the balance sheet that the originator has outstanding. Companies that off-lay the risk of the sold assets (i.e., those retaining no subordinate interest in the SPV) pick their best assets to securitize. Companies that do not off-lay risk gain more from securitization the less liquid they are. We find that securitization is a substitute for leverage and that those companies that use more conventional leverage benefit less from securitization.

A Cost of Capital Analysis of the Gains from Securitization

Securitization, the sale of fixed income assets into bankruptcy-remote, special purpose vehicles (SPVs) funded by the issuance of new asset backed securities (ABS)[1], has achieved

---

[*] E-mail address: Hugh-Thomas@cuhk.edu.hk (Corresponding Author).
[1] We use the term asset backed securities (ABS) to include all debt securities issued by bankruptcy remote special purpose entities backed primarily by fixed income assets. The term includes both pass-through securities including traditional mortgage backed securities (MBS) as well as pay-through securities. The SPV is a shell with no assets but the fixed income financial assets. It can be a limited liability company, a limited partnership or a trust account We use the term "fixed income" in a loose sense, encompassing not only traditional debt securities, but also near fixed income cash flows such as toll road revenues, lease payments. These flows must

tremendous popularity. From 1985 through 2003, ABS issues enjoyed an 18 percent per annum compound growth rate and rose to become the dominant fixed income security in the world. Today global outstanding ABS issues total approximately US$9 trillion. In the US, which accounts for about $7 trillion, half of all ABS are agency-based mortgaged backed securities. This article concerns the other, faster growing half, including securitizations of corporate receivables, credit card debt, auto loans and leases, home equity loans, non-agency guaranteed mortgages, etc., is approximately the same size as the treasury markets and exceeds the size of the corporate bond markets.

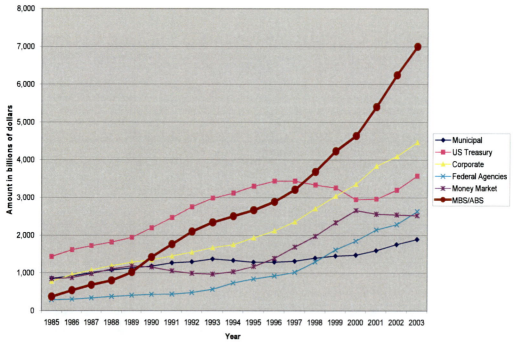

(in billions of dollars).
Source: U.S. Federal Research Board.

Figure 1. US Debt by Category.

Securitization, is a fundamental device changing the relationships between banks (and other financial institutions), non-financial corporations and financial markets. In this paper, we investigate how securitization adds value to the asset sellers through a direct measurement of cost of capital. We do this to lend light to the banking literature that has several divergent views of securitization. In their banking text, Greenbuam and Thakor (1995) observe that securitization permits banks to unbundled the traditional lending function, allowing them to specialize in the more basic activities in which they enjoy comparative advantages. In their signaling model Greenbaum and Thakor (1987) show that grains are available to borrowers with private knowledge of their individual credit quality who can signal that quality by purchasing credit enhancements from banks in securitization. Pennacchi (1988) models a securitization like contract of a bank that sells loans but, to alleviate the moral hazard of

---

be sufficiently predictable to allow the largely debt-financed SPV's debt to attract sufficiently high debt ratings to allow the transaction to proceed economically.

selling fully the loans retain the risk of the loan in a credit enhancement, or "equity position" in the sold loan. Securitization alters the capital structure of the originator. Perry (1995) states that for banks in general and for thinly capitalized banks in particular being both originator and credit enhancer increases the risk of the bank. Securitizations circumvent the bankruptcy process, possibly to the detriment of unsecured creditors (see Lupica (2000)). Leland and Skarabot (2003) provide a simulation model for how securitization can improve an originator's capital structure as long as the volatility of securitized assets is substantially different from the volatility of the assets that remain on balance sheet.

Within this literature, there are several concerns voiced about securitization. If it is used as a crutch for the weak banks, or to appropriate wealth from debt-holders, or for capital arbitrage, or to deceive equity holders about the true risk of a corporation, then it should be curtailed if not abolished. Bank regulators are especially concerned with the credit, liquidity and operational risk retention and risk off-lay effects of bank securitizations on the originating bank. The disclosures prescribed by FAS 140 (Financial Accounting Standards Board (2000)), determine whether or not a securitized asset should be shown on-balance sheet by applying the test of whether effective control is retained. This attempt to show the true assets of the firm takes on even more importance in the post-Enron environment, because Enron management used securitization to hide the risks it purported to sell but in fact retained. See Burroughs et al (2002) and Skipworth (2001).

Our tests in this paper follow in the tradition of Lockwood et al (1996) and Thomas (2001), who measure gains to securitization to the asset originator using event studies. The former finds increases to shareholder wealth in well-capitalized banks, but find no effect in thinly capitalized banks while the latter finds positive to securitizations in years when banks were not under pressure to increase capital levels. A recent paper by Ambrose, LaCour-Little and Sanders (2004) asks the question "does regulatory capital arbitrage, reputation or asymmetric information drive securitization?" and comes to the conclusion that capital arbitrage or reputation is driving it.

Investment bankers promoting securitization, however, answer the question of what drives securitization without hesitation. Securitization has grown rapidly because it provides companies with cheap financing.[2] In this paper, we estimate the gains in corporate wealth from this cheap financing by estimating the percentage differential costs of capital. We analyze these gains and show that they are increasing in size in the amount of ABS originated but are decreasing in the percent of the balance sheet that the originator has outstanding. Companies that off-lay the risk of the sold assets (i.e., those retaining no subordinate interest in the SPV) pick their best assets to securitize. Companies that do not off-lay risk (i.e., those who retain the concentrated first loss tranches that make up substantially all of the asset risk) gain more from securitization the less liquid they are. Securitization is a substitute for leverage; hence, those companies that use more conventional leverage benefit less from securitization.

The gains to securitization can be expressed as a spread between two costs of capital, that weighted cost of capital (WACC) of the asset selling firm and the all-in, weighted average cost of the securitization k_s.

---

[2] For example, Raynes and Rutledge (2003) who decry the inefficiencies of the ABS market, explained to the author the persistence of these efficiencies by their observation that corporate treasures make so much money for their firms by securitization that they are not concerned by the money left on the table by inefficient structures of the SPVs.

$$Spread = WACC - k_s \tag{1}$$

This paper has a very limited purpose. We calculate the spread to demonstrate its importance; run a series of linear regressions to determine the factors that influence the spread and discuss the implications of our simple tests on further studies of securitization.

Calculating Costs of Capital

We use costs of capital to estimate gains to securitization because corporate treasurers securitize to lower their costs of capital[3]. In most securitizations with single asset sellers, the value left in the SPV after payment of all fees and principal and interest claims of the ABS purchasers reverts back to the asset seller. This entitlement to residual cash-flows is analogous to the residual rights of the equity holder if the assets remain under the ownership of the asset seller; hence, securitization can be viewed as off-balance-sheet asset financing.

We calculate the weighted average cost of capital of the asset seller as follows

(2)

$$WACC = \frac{LTD}{A} \bullet k_{LTD} + \frac{STD}{A} \bullet k_{STD} + \frac{E}{A} \bullet k_E$$

where $WACC$ is the weighted average cost of capital of the asset seller; LTD is the value of the firm's long-term debts; STD is the value of the firm's short-term financial debts (i.e., excluding trade and other payables); E is the value of the firm's equity and $A = LTD + STD + E$. The terms k_{LTD}, k_{STD} and k_E denote the costs of long term debt, short term debt and equity respectively.

SPVs issue several classes of debt securities: A-Class (typically structured to be awarded a triple A bond rating), M-Class (high rated subordinate debt), B-Class (lower rated subordinate) and R-Class (unrated reserve trances)[4]. Each securitization is structured to maximize the amount of funding in the senior, rated class, whose yields are the lowest. The SPV is like a very simple, single purpose financial institution where management has extremely limited discretion in managing the fixed income assets. Although SPVs tend to be

---

3 Some securitizations are justified solely on the basis of increasing liquidity at the cost of increasing the cost of capital, reducing concentrations in certain risks to rebalance the credit risk of the portfolio, freeing up regulatory capital, meeting regulatory concentration limits, or improving the accounting appearance of the company, regardless of costs of capital considerations. Others are tax-motivated. But the vast majority of securitizations are justified on the basis of cost.

4 Our terms are consistent with those of ABSNet (www.absnet.net). ABSNet is a partnership between Lewtan Technolgies and Standard and Poor's, that provides the most comprehensive database of ABS deal performance data currently available. It was set up to meet the needs of institutional investors who wish to have up-to-date information on the quality of their investments. The website gives the current performance data and structure of outstanding ABS issues.

4 GMAC is a wholly owned subsidiary of General Motors set up to finance dealer inventories of automobiles. It has since expanded into consumer auto finance, insurance and mortgage financing to become one of the leading finance companies in the world with assets of $250 billion. Reflecting its lack bank deposit bases and relatively poor credit rating, it fund itself partly in the ABS markets with securitizations reported as $98 billion with $5 billion in continuing interests in securitizations (i.e., first loss tranches). See GMAC's 2003 10K

far more highly levered than regular financial institutions, SPVs do have an equity component. This equity component is credit support, made up of two components, a funded, un-rated reserve class, often retained by the asset seller and an "un-funded" portion. The unfunded portion usually includes over-collateralization, injected either when the SPV was formed or built up from the excess spread between the realized yield of the assets and the funds paid out to in fees and payments to the ABS holders and can also include partial guarantees.

We compute the cost of securitization as follows:

$$k_S = \sum_{i=1}^{n} \frac{D_i}{\sum_{i=1}^{n} D_i + E_R} \bullet k_i + \left[\frac{E_R}{\sum_{i=1}^{n} D_i + E_R} \bullet k_E + \frac{E_C}{\sum_{i=1}^{n} D_i + E_R} \bullet (k_E - r_f) \right] + fees \quad (2)$$

where k_S is the SPV's all-in cost of capital, k_i is the interest rate of the i-th class and k_E is the cost of equity of the asset seller as calculated above; D_i is the dollar amount of the i-th class of the securitization, E_R and E_C denote the amount in dollars of reserve and over-collateralization, respectively; r_f is risk-free rate and *fees* denotes the out of pocket front-end and annual fees to run the securitization expressed as an annuity in terms of percentage of the securitization.

In this equation, the first term calculates the weighted cost of debt; the second term (in square brackets) calculates the weighted cost of equity of the SPV and the third term adds the floatation costs. We use the term equity somewhat loosely. E_R is legally subordinate debt, constituting the bottom of the waterfall of subordination. E_C is the portion of the credit support, made up of partial guarantees, paid in surplus and/or accumulated surpluses. Since it is not included in the ABS claims on the SPV (i.e., in the denominator $\left(\sum_{i=1}^{n} D_i + E_R \right)$), we cost it as an unfunded in cost of capital equation by subtracting off the risk-free rate. If both E_R and E_C are owned by the asset seller who also is the residual claimant, then, clearly the asset seller retains the concentrated risk of the securitization.

We assume that the cost of equity is the same for the SPV and the seller. This is likely to be an overestimation of the cost of equity of the SPV for the following reason. The costs of debt k_i of the ABS are typically less than the costs of debt of the asset seller; therefore, the equity cushion made up of E_R and E_C provides no less of a cushion to debt holders than the equity of the asset seller provides to the debt-holders of the asset seller. Therefore, the equity of the SPV should be no more expensive than the equity of the asset seller. Unfortunately, since the equity of the SPV is not traded in public markets, we do not have information on its pricing.

An investment banker giving indicative pricing to a potential asset seller would typically quote the weighted average coupon plus the cost of fees to quote an all-in-cost of securitization. In our equation, this corresponds to the first and third terms and would ignore the second term (i.e., the cost of equity[5]). Since the costs of debt of the securitization are given by the coupons, but the cost of the equity is implicit, ignoring the second term is a convenient simplification. But can be a useful simplification: if the transaction involves no appreciable risk off-lay – i.e., if the first loss classes ($E_R + E_C$) are retained by the asset seller and if the capital at risk of the securitized assets is less than or equal to the first loss classes, then one can calculate the gains to securitization simply by comparing the weighted average coupon plus floatation costs with the cost of on-balance-sheet debt.

Potential Sources of Gains From Securitization

Using a no-arbitrage Modigiani and Miller (1959) argument, one can show that there *should* be no increase in value to a firm simply by altering its capital structure – through securitization or through any other device. If one separated the assets of a firm into two pools and financed those two pools separately, the costs of capital would differ as long as the risk characteristics of those two pools differed. Unless there are tax differences, bankruptcy cost differences, or differences in the performance of the firm induced by the separation of assets into the two pools, however, the weighted average cost of capital of the combined pools should be the same as that of the company prior to separation.

The largest violation of Modiglianni and Miller invariance is the interest rate tax shield of debt. Viewing securitization as an off-balance-sheet substitute for debt, a greater use of leverage to gain the benefits of tax shields will reduce the scope for using securitization to use the same tax shields in an off-balance sheet financing.

Leyland and Skarabot (2003), following Leyland (1993) look at the case where securitization involves full sale of assets (without residual risk kept by the asset seller) where tax differences and bankruptcy costs impact on optimal capital structure achieved through securitization. Using a Merton (1974) framework and specifying that the corporation has two portfolios with different but stable asset volatilities, recovery rates in default, and correlation of returns, they show that optimal securitization conditions are those under which the merged firm has a less efficient capital structure than the separate capital structures of the two different firms. This explains the phenomenon that securitization favors sale of a firm's lowest volatility assets[6]. The sale leads to an increase in risk in the asset seller by the act of securitization that increase the seller's cost of capital and appropriates wealth from the asset seller's creditors. The differential in asset volatility within the portfolio gives rise to the gains from securitization flowing from savings of bankruptcy costs. The bankruptcy costs, are calculated as a constant fraction of the bankrupt regardless of the portfolio.

Saving bankruptcy costs are probably a richer source of securitization's gains than modeled by Leyland and Skarabot. Not only are SPVs are structured to be bankruptcy remote[7], they are structured so that they will not go bankrupt themselves. In the event that the

---

[5] If the reserve tranche were purchased by an external party, its cost would also be included in the weighted average coupon. In our formula, we consider it in the cost of equity under the assumption that it is retained by the asset seller. The stated coupon, then, is irrelevant because residual cash-flow reverts to the seller.

[6] Greenbaum and Thakor (1987)'s signaling model came to a similar conclusion.

[7] See Cohn (1998) for a discussion of bankruptcy remoteness. The degree to which a bankruptcy court can reach into SPVs to recover value for the bankruptcy trustee of the asset seller was illustrated in Conseco in 2002-3.

SPV is unable to make payment on its obligations, there is no incentive for claimholders to put the SPV itself into bankruptcy (assuming it is a corporate entity). By enforcing strict priority of payout without recourse to the courts, SPV's financial claimants gain from this structure.

If securitization were a pure value transfer play from bondholders to stockholders, information of a securitization should be greeted as bad news to bondholders.

Empirical support for the proposition that securitization expropriates creditors, however is mixed. In his event study of shareholder and bondholder reactions to securitizations, Thomas (2001) finds appropriation occurs among non-investment rated asset sellers but no such effect is evident among investment grade asset sellers. Most asset sellers are investment grade.

Gains to securitization might accrue from changes in managerial incentives accompanied by creation of the SPV. SPVs are very simple business entities where management of the assets of the entity is almost entirely devoid of discretion. Unlike the managers of a corporation, who must decide marketing, personnel, logistics, manufacturing, financing and strategic policies, the administrators of an SPV need only administer the assets to realize the intrinsic value of their expected cash flows. If business management activities can be broadly divided into entrepreneurship and stewardship, then management of an SPV is largely stewardship. The separation of non-discretionary stewardship from discretionary entrepreneurship may reduce agency costs in the former achieving a more optimal capital structure in the separated (securitized) structure.

Some perceive securitization to be the realm of rascals. Lupica (2000) describes it as a scheme to rob the uninformed unsecured investor. The collapse of Enron (Timmons (2002) and Conseco has forced regulators pay increasing interest to securitization. Were this the case, the worst performing firms to gain most from securitization.

With this discussion in mind, we look at five potential sources of the gains from securitization: size, liquidity, risk, leverage and performance of the asset originator. The effect of size is obvious. Securitization is expensive in terms of front end fees. Moreover, buyers of ABS are interested in homogeneity and liquidity; hence, one would expect economies of scale to be reflected in greater gains to larger asset sellers. These gains to size, however, may be a function of the amount of securitization that the asset seller does (assuming that purchasers look to the SPV alone) or of the size of the asset seller itself.

If an asset seller is illiquid, one would expect that liquidity constraint to be evident in its higher on-balance sheet costs of capital. Hence, lower liquidity of the asset seller should be associated with greater gains to securitization. Mindful of the fact that most of our sample are financial institutions, we avoid the commonly used current ratio in place of a liquidity ratio (liquid assets to total assets) which can be used for both financial and non-financial companies.

Following the Leyland and Skarabot, the higher the risk of the asset seller, given that securitized assets are of constant risk, the higher the gains that should be available to

---

After purchasing the sub-prme securitiztion asset originator Green Tree, Conseco went bankrupt partly because of the decline in creditworhthiness of sub-prime lending and the fall in value of the residual first loss tranches. The bankruptcy court ruled that the service fees paid to Conseco by the SPVs were inadequate and raised the fees, imparing the creditworthiness of a large number of ABS issues, causing the some of the greatest losses in the recent history of ABS and calling into question bankruptcy-remoteness.Donovan (2003).

securitization. We use the CAPM beta as our risk measure. The sign on leverage is expected to be negative if one views securitization as an off-balance sheet substitute for debt.

Table 1. Top 15 Issuers of ABS: March 2004 Outstanding Series

Issuer	Number of debt series outstanding	Total Principal ($ millions)
Residential Funding Mortgage Securities I, Inc (GMAC)	297	100,805.5
Ford Credit Auto Owner Trust	33	90,075.6
SLM Funding Corporation (Sallie Mae)	44	77,446.1
Conseco Finance Corp.	142	71,456.1
Countrywide Home Loans, Inc.	128	63,910.8
Citibank Credit Card Master Trust I	43	57,266.5
MBNA Master Credit Card Trust II	106	56,104.3
Prudential Home Mortgage Company	153	47,435.7
Residential Asset Securities Corporation (GMAC)	55	45,072.0
Capital Auto Receivables Asset Trust (GMAC)	21	44,236.0
CS First Boston Mortgage Securities Corp.	46	43,079.1
Discover Card Master Trust I	52	42,941.6
Chase Credit Card Master Trust	44	41,518.0
Wells Fargo Mortgage Backed Securities	81	41,400.2
Washington Mutual Mortgage Securities Corp.	24	38,650.5

The above table summarizes the top issuers listed by ABSNet within the total 6,470 outstanding issues before reduction of sample size for matching with originators. The name in brackets gives main asset originator in instances where it is not obvious from the title.

Source: ABSNet March 2004.

Table 2. Summary Statistics

Panel A: Total Sample of 120 Asset Sellers						
Variable	Mean	Std Dev	Skewness	Kurtosis	Minimum	Maximum
Cost of Securitization	5.39	2.60	0.75	0.02	1.43	12.70
WACC	6.63	2.47	3.28	17.64	2.77	23.27
Spread	1.24	3.41	1.37	7.08	-5.64	20.33
Total Securitization	6.34	14.64	4.07	17.77	0.003	91.41
Securitize Ratio	0.46	1.35	4.43	21.23	0.00	9.25
Beta	0.82	0.52	0.86	1.31	-0.28	2.88
Size	10.20	2.10	-0.30	-0.84	5.15	13.59
Leverage	87.43	13.01	-2.47	6.16	32.98	98.17
Liquid Asset Ratio	47.87	33.42	-0.35	-1.30	0.00	98.86
Assets Growth Rate	11.33	18.39	-0.52	9.38	-89.99	86.63
ROE	11.14	14.66	-1.68	9.86	-63.75	63.77

A Cost of Capital Analysis of the Gains from Securitization

Table 2. Continued

Panel A: Total Sample of 120 Asset Sellers						
Variable	**Mean**	**Std Dev**	**Skewness**	**Kurtosis**	**Minimum**	**Maximum**
I1	0.51	0.50	-0.03	-2.03	0.00	1.00
I2	0.29	0.46	0.93	-1.16	0.00	1.00
I3	0.20	0.40	1.52	0.31	0.00	1.00
Panel B: Sub-Sample of 63 Assets Sellers without Retention of Equity Risk						
Variable	**Mean**	**Std Dev**	**Skewness**	**Kurtosis**	**Minimum**	**Maximum**
Cost of Securitization	5.64	2.62	0.57	-0.34	1.70	11.89
WACC	6.53	2.81	3.80	20.48	2.77	23.27
Spread	0.90	3.84	2.01	9.44	-5.45	20.33
Total Securitization	2.37	3.23	1.94	3.93	0.003	15.37
Securitize Ratio	0.53	1.61	4.14	17.66	0.00	9.25
Beta	0.73	0.51	1.28	3.80	-0.28	2.88
Size	9.86	2.24	-0.19	-1.09	5.15	13.49
Leverage	88.17	12.31	-2.50	6.08	37.08	97.61
Liquid Asset Ratio	44.17	35.31	-0.13	-1.54	0.00	98.86
Assets Growth Rate	10.44	18.67	-1.41	4.34	-28.06	86.63
ROE	8.77	17.03	-1.75	8.87	-63.75	63.77
I1	0.48	0.50	0.10	-2.06	0.00	1.00
I2	0.37	0.49	0.57	-1.73	0.00	1.00
I3	0.16	0.37	1.91	1.72	0.00	1.00
Panel C: Sub-Sample of 57 Asset Sellers with Retention of Equity Risk						
Variable	**Mean**	**Std Dev**	**Skewness**	**Kurtosis**	**Minimum**	**Maximum**
Cost of Securitization	5.12	2.58	0.99	0.73	1.43	12.70
WACC	6.73	2.07	1.74	4.32	3.94	14.87
Spread	1.61	2.85	-0.05	-0.24	-5.64	8.34
Total Securitization	10.74	20.16	2.70	7.02	0.044	91.41
Securitize Ratio	0.39	1.00	4.09	17.84	0.00	5.62
Beta	0.92	0.52	0.52	-0.32	0.04	2.11
Size	10.59	1.87	-0.27	-0.66	6.79	13.59
Leverage	86.62	13.80	-2.47	6.47	32.98	98.17
Liquid Asset Ratio	51.95	30.99	-0.62	-0.82	0.00	98.32
Assets Growth Rate	12.31	18.19	-2.85	17.77	-89.99	54.22
ROE	13.77	11.05	-0.37	3.69	-21.53	46.37
I1	0.54	0.50	-0.18	-2.04	0.00	1.00
I2	0.21	0.41	1.46	0.13	0.00	1.00
I3	0.25	0.43	1.21	-0.55	0.00	1.00

Table 2. Continued

Panel D: Test of Difference Between Means of Sub-Samples					
Variable	Without Equity Risk	Without Equity Risk	Difference	t Value	Pr >|t|
Cost of Securitization	5.64	5.12	0.52	1.09	0.28
WACC	6.53	6.73	-0.20	-0.44	0.66
Spread	0.90	1.61	-0.71	-1.17	0.25
Total Securitization	2.37	10.74	-7.37	-3.10***	0.00
Securitize Ratio	0.53	0.39	0.14	0.61	0.54
Beta	0.73	0.92	-0.19	-2.03**	0.04
Size	9.86	10.59	-0.73	-1.95*	0.05
Leverage	88.17	86.62	1.55	0.65	0.52
Liquid Asset Ratio	44.17	51.95	-7.78	-1.28	0.20
Assets Growth Rate	10.44	12.31	-1.87	-0.55	0.58
ROE	8.77	13.77	-5.00	-1.93*	0.06
I1	0.48	0.54	-0.06	-0.74	0.46
I2	0.37	0.21	0.16	1.89*	0.06
I3	0.16	0.25	-0.09	-1.18	0.24

Note: Sample statistics of 1,713 series with a total outstanding principal of $810 billions sponsored by 120 asset sellers. Panel B sub-sample shows sellers who did not retain equity risk being the first-loss reserve tranche and/or other guarantees. Panel C subsample shows sellers who did retain equity risk being the first loss reserve tranche and/or other guarantees. *Spread* is WACC – cost of securitization; *Total securitization* is the total principal of outstanding securitized assets of the asset seller expressed in billions of dollars; *Securitize Ratio* is the outstanding amount of securitized assets expressed as a percent of total seller assets; *Beta* is the CAPM Beta of the seller as provided by Compustat; *Size* is the natural logarithm of total assets of the seller in millions of dollars; *Leverage* is Total Liabilities / Total Assets of the seller; *Current Ratio* is current assets / current liabilities of the seller; *Liquid Asset Ratio* is Liquid Assets /Total Assets of the seller; *Assets Growth Rate* is the one year growth rate of the sellers assets for the previous year; *ROE* is the return on equity of the seller in the last year.

If securitization is a tool used by astute managers to maximize shareholder wealth, we would expect to see a positive correlation between performance and gains to securitization. If it is the preserve of rascals, however, we would expect the reverse. We use two performance measures: growth and return on equity.

Finally, since there are three distinct industries – banking, non-banking financial intermediation and non-financial industries – in which securitization operates, we control for industry effects.

Data

We downloaded securitization data from ABSNet [8] in March 2004. There were 6,470 issues outstanding, with a then-current principal amount of $5,226 billions. The largest number of issues, however, were issued by a smaller number of SPVs who were originated by a still smaller number of corporate asset sellers. Table 1 shows, that the largest single issuer,

---

8 ABSNetTM (www.absnet.net) is a partnership between Lewtan Technolgies and Standard and Poor's, that provides the most comprehensive database of ABS deal performance data currently available. It was set up to meet the needs of institutional investors who wish to have up-to-date information on the quality of their investments. The website gives the current performance data and structure of outstanding ABS issues.

with 297 issues outstanding, comprising a total original principal of \$100 billion, was Residential Funding Mortgage Securities I, Inc. a corporate SPV set up by GMAC[9] to fund residential mortgages. Within the largest 15 issuers shown in Table 1, two other GMAC-sponsored SPVs are featured – Residential Asset Securities Corporation and Capital Auto Receivables Asset Trust. Each debt series is separately followed and rated by bond ratings agencies[10]. These large SPVs are conduits that issue ABS series from time to time to meet funding needs of newly purchased assets.

From the original sample, we excluded issues that were entirely retired as of March 2004 as well as those with no listed asset seller and those with incomplete or clearly incorrect data[11] and matched them with corporate, publicly listed sellers whose data was available in the WRDS/Compustat database. This left us with 1713 issues having an aggregate principal outstanding of \$810 billion originated by 120 asset sellers composed of 61 banks, 35 non-bank financial institutions and 24 non-financial companies. From these companies, we obtained information about their securitization activity, liquidity, profitability, risk and performance. We considered the 1,713 issues in aggregate as if they were a single securitization for each of the 120 asset sellers by weighting them by outstanding principal amount as of March 2004.

Costs of capital are calculated for each of the asset sellers by using the bond rating for the asset seller's long term debt and short term debt respectively and the average yield of such rated securities in March 2004 as provided by Datastream. Costs of capital of the securitization are given by the coupons on each of the classes in each of the securitizations as reported by ABSNet. The cost of equity for both the asset seller and the securitization is calculated by using the capital asset pricing model and betas given by WRDS/Compustat. We use a risk premium of eight percent[12] and the risk free rate of the 10-year bond rate in March 2004.

Results

Summary Statistics. Gains from securitization can be read directly from Table 2. The average cost of securitization is 5.39 percent. The average cost of capital is 6.63 percent.

---

9 GMAC is a wholly owned subsidiary of General Motors set up to finance dealer inventories of automobiles. It has since expanded into consumer auto finance, insurance and mortgage financing to become one of the leading finance companies in the world with assets of \$250 billion. Reflecting its lack bank deposit bases and relatively poor credit rating, it fund itself partly in the ABS markets with securitizations reported as \$98 billion with \$5 billion in continuing interests in securitizations (i.e., first loss tranches). See GMAC's 2003 10K.

10 Neither GNMA nor FNMA issues would feature among the largest 15 issuers because GNMA and FNMA - pools are individually much smaller than the ones listed in Table 1. Note that we did not include agency issues in this analysis and that ABSNet does not list the issue characteristics of the limited GNMA and FNMA issues given in their database. This may be because the database is constructed largely to assist in portfolio credit risk management for investors; however, the risk of agency issues is considered quasi-sovereign.

11 For example, we excluded transactions where the cost of securitization was less than 1 percent. The deal summary contains information on the closing date, the original amount, remittance frequency, placement type, lead managers and trustee. For each class in each deal, information includes the class name, currency, original balance of outstanding securities, current balance of outstanding securities and original subordination (in terms of classes below the class in question that can be viewed as a cushion), current subordination, collateral type, original weighted average maturity, asset seller and asset servicer. Data are also given on initial and current credit support, broken down into over-collateralization, excess spread, etc., and the classes to which the credit support applies. The database gives information on delinquencies, loss rate, prepayment rate and the collateral pool balances.

12 Varying the equity market premium from five percent to eight percent did not substantially alter the results.

The 1.24 percent difference is the gain. If one multiplies the average spread by total sample securitized principal of $810 billion, the annual savings are a not inconsiderable $10 billion.

Although GMAC described above is one of the most active originators of securitizations, it is by no means an outliner among the 120. The average principal of ABS outstanding for each asset seller is $6.3 billion, being 46 percent of on-balance sheet assets of the asset sellers. The most active asset sellers (in terms of outstanding ABS as a proportion of assets) raise more than nine times their on-balance sheet funding with securitization. On average, the asset sellers exhibit lower than one betas. Their high leverage (87 percent debt) reflects the fact that most members of the sample are banks or non-bank financial institutions. Liquidity varies widely. On average the firms are profitable (11.33 percent return on equity) and enjoying a moderately rapid growth of 11.14 percent per annum.

It is instructive to compare two sub-samples based on risk retention versus risk off-lay. Just over half of the asset sellers (52.5 percent) sell off their risk exposure to their assets when they securitize them. Their summary statistics are reported in Panel B as "Asset Sellers without Retention of Equity Risk". The other 57 asset originators, reported in Panel C, retain equity risk, i.e., the first loss classes that contribute credit support in securitizations. Although the risk retention group contains only 47.5 percent of the asset sellers by number, it accounts for 80.4 percent of the ABS by dollar amount of principal outstanding. In this important aspect, the vast majority of securitizations involve no substantial off-lay of risk of the securitized assets: for them securitization is simply an off-balance sheet, debt-financing technique. As Table 2 Panel D shows, the asset sellers without retention of equity risk are significantly smaller, securitize less assets, are less risky (in terms of beta) and are less profitable than those that retain the equity risk of the assets securitized. The asset sellers that do not retain equity risk have substantially lower gains from securitization measured by the spread between the asset seller WACC and the SPV cost of securitization, (90 basis points versus 161 basis points), but this substantial difference is not statistically significant. The asset sellers that do not retain equity risk are more likely to be non-bank financial institutions (non-bank financial institutions make up about one third of the sup-sample compared with about one fifth of the equity risk retention sub-sample). In other respects, however, the sub-samples are not much different.

Sources of Gains in total sample. Table 3 presents the regression where the dependent variable is the spread between the WACC of the asset seller and the cost of securitization and a set of independent variables. Since the spread is the difference between two costs of capital which themselves are combinations of similar independent variables, we present the regression equations for the WACC and the cost of securitization as well as the spread. We only discuss the regressions for the spread.

Size counts. The higher the dollar amount of ABS outstanding originated by the asset seller, the greater the spread enjoyed by the asset seller. An increase from $6 billion ABS to $16 billion in ABS outstanding is associated with a very significant and economically substantial rise of 59 basis points[13]. The market appears to be rewarding the liquidity of aggregate ABS issued, not the size of the asset seller (which is measured by the log of the

---

[13] The size factors are in natural logs of the ABE outstanding expressed in thousands of dollars . The average principal of ABS outstanding for each asset seller is $6.3 billion or 15.6 expressed in natural logs. Increasing the coefficient to 16.6 to is an increase to $16.2 billion dollars.

asset seller's assets, an independent variable that remains insignificant). But a rise in the *proportion* of assets that an asset seller securitizes leads to a significant fall in the spread. Remembering that the average asset seller has ABS outstanding of about 46 percent of on-balance-sheet assets, raising that one standard deviation to 180 percent would lower the spread by over 100 basis points, wiping out the positive spread to securitization. Too much securitization – i.e., securitization out of proportion to the asset seller – is penalized by the market.

The higher the leverage of the asset seller the lower the gains from securitization, lending support to the view that gains from on-balance sheet leverage of debt and the off-balance securitization are substitutes for each other.

We hypothesized that the riskier the company, the higher the gains to securitization. The sign of the beta coefficient is correct, but insignificant.

Finally, asset sellers that are less liquidity-constrained have less to gain from securitization. An increase in the liquid asset ratio from the average 48 percent to 58 percent will decrease spreads by 20 basis points.

There is no significant effect for either performance or industry.

With or Without Equity Risk Retention. We gain greater insight by dividing our sample into two sub-samples: those asset sellers who do not retain equity risk of the assets sold and those who do retain equity risk. Turn first to liquidity. Among those asset sellers who retain equity risk (Table 3 Panel C), liquidity becomes the most significant determinant of gains to securitization. This group has a high 52 percent average liquidity. Decreasing that liquidity to 42 percent leads to a 40 basis point improvement in spread gains. For this sub-sample, too, the on-balance sheet – off-balance-sheet substitution of leverage is strongly evident. A company that retains the risk of assets whether or not it securitizes them can take the interest rate tax shield of debt with either on or off the balance sheet financing.

Turn now to Table 3 Panel B, the larger sub-sample in terms of number of asset sellers, but the much smaller sub-sample in terms of total ABS dollar volume, where the asset sellers off-lay the equity risk when the sell assets. Here liquidity is an insignificant explainer of gains to securitization and leverage drops substantially in terms of significance. Return on equity, however, takes on a significant negative sign, and the securitization ratio's sign is large and negative. Both of these signs lend support to the hypothesis that securitization that truly isolates two parts of the formerly integrated portfolio of the asset seller is a method by which poorly performing companies can gain by selling their best assets into SPVs. Their gains, measured in the lower cost of capital of the securitization comes possibly at the expense of existing asset seller creditors. These companies correspond more to the theoretical models of securitization of Leyland and Skarabot which model SPVs and post securitization asset sellers as truly separated. The highly negative and significant sign on the securitization ratio (not evident in Panel C) may be interpreted as the market's increasing doubt in the quality of the assets sold as the ratio of securitized assets increases.

Table 3. Sources of Gains from Securitization

	Panel A: Total Sample of 120 Asset Sellers										

Dependent Variable	Independent Variables										
	Intercept	Log (Assets)	Log (Securitization)	Securitize Ratio	Beta	Leverage	Liquid Asset Ratio	Assets Growth Rate	ROE	Dummy Variable I1	Dummy Variable I2
Cost of Securitization	10.17***	-0.24	0.52***	0.73***	1.81***	0.04	0.01	0.00	0.01	-0.42	-1.44**
	4.57	-1.49	3.58	2.67	3.75	1.56	1.64	0.17	0.56	-0.62	-2.03
WACC	12.03***	-0.36***	0.07	-0.21	2.81***	-0.05***	-0.00	-0.00	-0.02	0.06	0.00
	6.63	-2.79	0.60	-0.95	7.14	-2.69	-0.83	-0.37	-1.42	0.10	0.01
Spread	1.86	-0.13	0.59***	-0.94**	1.00	-0.09***	-0.02*	-0.01	-0.03	0.48	1.44
	0.62	-0.58	3.00	-2.54	1.53	-2.77	-1.71	-0.35	-1.27	0.52	1.50

	Panel B: Sub-Sample of 63 Assets Sellers without Retention of equity Risk										

Dependent Variable	Independent Variables										
	Intercept	Log (Assets)	Log (Securitization)	Securitize Ratio	Beta	Leverage	Liquid Asset Ratio	Assets Growth Rate	ROE	Dummy Variable I1	Dummy Variable I2
Cost of Securitization	10.95***	-0.53**	-0.37*	0.56	2.32***	0.05	-0.01	0.01	0.04	-2.00*	-2.51*
	2.84	-2.38	-1.73	1.38	3.05	1.41	-0.64	0.69	1.67	-1.71	-2.01
WACC	10.98***	-0.46**	0.20	-0.81**	2.85***	-0.05	-0.01	-0.01	-0.04*	0.64	1.65
	3.09	-2.23	1.01	-2.18	4.09	-1.43	-0.97	-0.33	-1.77	0.60	1.44
Spread	0.03	0.07	0.58*	-1.38**	0.53	-0.11*	-0.00	-0.02	-0.07**	2.64	4.16**
	0.01	0.22	1.78	-2.28	0.47	-1.83	-0.16	-0.67	-2.21	1.51	2.24

Table 3. Continued

	Panel C: Subsample of 57 Asset Sellers with Retention of equity Risk										
Dependent Variable	**Independent Variables**										
	Intercept	**Log (Assets)**	**Log (Securitization)**	**Securitize Ratio**	**Beta**	**Leverage**	**Liquid Asset Ratio**	**Assets Growth Rate**	**ROE**	**Dummy Variable I1**	**Dummy Variable I2**
Cost of Securitization	**10.26*****	**-0.29**	**0.49****	**0.79***	**2.25*****	**0.01**	**0.03*****	**-0.02**	**-0.04**	**1.08**	**-0.66**
	3.89	-1.08	2.27	1.88	3.33	0.50	3.31	-0.87	-1.33	1.25	-0.72
WACC	**13.15*****	**-0.16**	**0.01**	**0.46***	**2.03*****	**-0.07*****	**-0.01**	**-0.00**	**-0.00**	**-0.10**	**-1.45*****
	8.79	-1.07	0.06	1.96	5.30	-4.18	-1.26	-0.20	-0.16	-0.21	-2.79
Spread	**2.88**	**0.13**	**0.49****	**-0.32**	**-0.22**	**-0.08****	**-0.04*****	**0.01**	**0.04**	**-1.18**	**-0.79**
	1.00	0.43	2.10	-0.70	-0.29	-2.62	-3.67	0.69	1.13	-1.25	-0.78

Notes: The bold-faced number in each line is the coefficient estimates below which T statistics are given. *, **, *** significant in a 2-tailed test at the 10 percent, 5 percent and 1 percent levels of confidence.

Spread is WACC – cost of securitization; Total securitization is the total principal of outstanding securitized assets by the asset seller expressed in billions of dollars; Securitize Ratio is the outstanding amount of securitized assets expressed as a percent of total seller assets; Beta is the CAPM Beta of the seller as provided by Compustat; Size is the natural logarithm of total assets of the seller in millions of dollars; Leverage is Total Liabilities / Total Assets of the seller; Current Ratio is current assets / current liabilities of the seller; Liquid Asset Ratio is Liquid Assets /Total Assets of the seller; Assets Growth Rate is the one year growth rate of the sellers assets for the previous year; ROE is the return on equity of the seller in the last year; Bank is a dummy variable that equals 1 when the asset seller is a bank and zero otherwise; Non-Bank FI is a dummy variable that equals 1 when the asset seller is a non-bank financial institution and zero otherwise.

The R-squared for the three regressions are: for Panel A 0.29, 0.47 and 0.24; for Panel B 0.30, 0.48 and 0.28l and for Panel C 0.47, 0.74 and 0.48, respectively.

The Chow Test's that F value (Pr>F) are 1.65(0.0956), 1.69(0.0858) and 1.39(0.1919).

Table 4. Sources of Gains from Securitization: Industry Subsamples

Panel A: Banks								
Dependent Variable	**Independent Variables**							
	Intercept	**Log (Assets)**	**Log**	**Securitize**	**Beta**	**Leverage**	**Liquid Asset**	**Assets Growth**	**ROE**
Cost of Securitization	**16.01**	**-0.39**	**-0.40**	**-1.32**	**3.12*****	**-0.04**	**0.02**	**-0.01**	**-0.04**
	1.18	-1.58	-1.50	-0.65	3.44	-0.24	1.57	-0.34	-1.05
WACC	**13.54*****	**0.06**	**-0.14**	**1.33***	**2.05*****	**-0.08**	**-0.01****	**-0.00**	**0.00**
	3.05	0.68	-1.66	2.00	6.94	-1.66	-2.56	-0.36	0.23
Spread	**-2.46**	**0.45***	**0.25**	**2.64**	**-1.07**	**-0.04**	**-0.03****	**0.01**	**0.04**
	-0.18	1.80	0.96	1.30	-1.18	-0.30	-2.41	0.22	1.12
Panel B: Non-Bank Financial Institutions								
Dependent Variable	**Independent Variables**							
	Intercept	**Log (Assets)**	**Log**	**Securitize**	**Beta**	**Leverage**	**Liquid Asset**	**Assets Growth**	**ROE**
Cost of Securitization	**6.82**	**-0.29**	**-0.45**	**0.60***	**1.07**	**0.07***	**0.00**	**0.00**	**-0.02**
	1.59	-0.89	-1.46	1.74	1.44	1.75	0.11	0.23	-0.71
WACC	**12.93****	**-1.27****	**0.22**	**-0.83***	**3.60*****	**0.03**	**-0.02**	**-0.00**	**-0.04**
	2.15	-2.73	0.51	-1.71	3.45	0.48	-0.79	-0.09	-1.06
Spread	**6.10**	**-0.98**	**0.68**	**-1.43****	**2.54**	**-0.05**	**-0.02**	**-0.01**	**-0.02**
	0.71	-1.47	1.09	-2.06	1.70	-0.54	-0.61	-0.18	-0.39
Panel C: Non-FI Company								
Dependent Variable	**Independent Variables**							
	Intercept	**Log (Assets)**	**Log**	**Securitize**	**Beta**	**Leverage**	**Liquid Asset**	**Assets Growth**	**ROE**
Cost of Securitization	**9.85***	**-0.93**	**-0.25**	**1.31***	**1.64**	**0.09**	**-0.02**	**0.02**	**0.03**
	1.94	-1.44	-0.49	1.82	1.00	1.55	-0.33	0.62	0.93
WACC	**9.87*****	**-0.02**	**0.13**	**0.43**	**3.66*****	**-0.08*****	**-0.03**	**-0.00**	**-0.02**
	4.72	-0.06	0.64	1.46	5.40	-3.31	-1.33	-0.32	-1.56
Spread	**0.02**	**0.92**	**0.38**	**-0.87**	**2.02**	**-0.17****	**-0.01**	**-0.02**	**-0.06**
	0.00	1.21	0.65	-1.05	1.05	-2.50	-0.19	-0.64	-1.35

The R-squared for the three regressions are: for Panel A 0.33,0.61 and 0.35; for Panel B 0.32,0.51 and 0.32; and for Panel 0.52,0.86 and 0.33, respectively.

Table 5. Tests of Structural Change: Chow Test

Difference between	Dependent Variable	F Value	Pr> F
Banks and Non-Bank Financial Institutions	Cost of Securitization	0.85	0.5693
	WACC	2.07	0.0425
	Spread	1.44	0.1863
Non-Bank Financial Institutions and Non-FI Companies	Cost of Securitization	1.16	0.3448
	WACC	0.96	0.4894
	Spread	0.52	0.8490
Banks and Non-FI Companies	Cost of Securitization	0.48	0.8819
	WACC	1.31	0.2469
	Spread	0.95	0.4888

Note: These tests measure the joint hypothesis that all coefficients *except the intercept* are the same.

Industry Sub-samples. In the above analysis, we have treated the 61 asset-selling banks identically to the 35 non-bank financial institutions and the 24 non-financial institutions. We used no more than a dummy variable to separate their average spread effects. Although we cannot reject the null hypothesis that jointly these three types of corporations gains from securitization are the same (See Table 5). The strong tradition of academic banking literature that views banks as special leads us to examine industry sub-samples. Table 4 presents the industry sub-samples' regressions. Panel A suggests that liquidity and liquidity alone explains the gains to securitizations that banks enjoy. The less liquid the bank, the more it gains from securitization.

The 35 non-bank financial institutions drive the sample results that show gains to securitization decreasing in the securitization ratio. If the reduced benefits for increased proportion of the balance sheet in securitized assets is a market penalty for suspected lower quality assets being securitized (and, from Table 3 Panel B, securitized without retention of equity risk by the asset seller), then suspicions are falling on the non-bank financial institutions.

Turning to the smallest sub-sample, the 24 non-financial institutions, gains to securitization are strongly and significantly decreasing in leverage. Given the higher leverage that banks and other financial institutions display, and the greater differential between typical fixed income securitized assets and the typical on-balance-sheet assets of non-financial corporations, it is not surprising that we observe the tradeoff between on balance sheet and off balance sheet leverage to be greatest among the non-financial institutions.

These industry conclusions, however are tentative, because we have insufficiently large samples to allow division of our sub-samples by the criteria of both Table 3 and Table 4.

Finally, our sample contains both US and foreign asset sellers. We ran separate regressions of gains from securitization of the 74 US asset sellers and the 46 non-US asset sellers in Table 6. As one would expect from the reduced sample size, the non US sample shows reduced significance of all coefficients, with only the size variables retaining significance: as with the overall sample, gains to securitization are increasing in the amount of ABS issued by an issuer but decreasing in the securitization outstanding as a percentage of assets. An interesting change occurs with the (larger) US sample, however. Throughout the sample, the previous tests, the risk of the asset seller measured by beta had no significant effect on the gains to securitization. For US securitizes, when isolated in their own sample, however the riskier the asset seller, the greater the gains to securitization.

Table 6. Sources of Gains from Securitization

Panel A: Sub-Sample of 74 Assets Sellers from US											
Dependent Variable	Independent Variables										
	Intercept	Log (Assets)	Log (Securitization)	Securitize Ratio	Beta	Leverage	Liquid Asset Ratio	Assets Growth Rate	ROE	Dummy Variable I1	Dummy Variable I2
Cost of Securitization	12.74***	-0.12	-0.54***	0.48**	1.02*	0.01	0.02	0.01	0.00	-1.55	-2.43***
	5.00	-0.59	-3.00	2.04	1.73	0.40	1.31	0.87	0.01	-1.66	-2.68
WACC	13.82***	-0.54**	0.13	-0.31	3.03***	-0.08***	0.01	-0.01	-0.01	0.50	0.35
	5.53	-2.62	0.72	-1.35	5.26	-2.81	0.70	-0.38	-0.26	0.55	0.39
Spread	1.08	-0.41	0.66**	-0.78**	2.01**	-0.09**	-0.01	-0.02	-0.01	2.06	2.78**
	0.28	-1.32	2.47	-2.23	2.28	-2.11	-0.42	-0.83	-0.17	1.46	2.04

Note: The R-squared for the three regressions are 0.32, 0.53 and 0.29, respectively.

Panel B: Subsample of 46 Asset Sellers from non-US											
Dependent Variable	Independent Variables										
	Intercept	Log (Assets)	Log (Securitization)	Securitize Ratio	Beta	Leverage	Liquid Asset Ratio	Assets Growth Rate	ROE	Dummy Variable I1	Dummy Variable I2
Cost of Securitization	7.81	-0.08	-0.56	1.05	3.09***	0.03	-0.00	-0.02	0.01	0.09	-0.51
	1.27	-0.22	-1.53	0.41	3.03	0.70	-0.06	-0.76	0.31	0.08	-0.34
WACC	6.42***	-0.18	0.14	-0.74	2.20***	-0.01	-0.00	-0.01	-0.01	-0.46	1.09*
	2.92	-1.40	1.04	-0.81	6.04	-0.63	-0.50	-0.68	-0.89	-1.11	2.01
Spread	-1.39	-0.10	0.69*	-1.79	-0.89	-0.05	-0.00	0.01	-0.02	-0.55	1.60
	-0.21	-0.26	1.76	-0.65	-0.80	-0.86	-0.11	0.48	-0.57	-0.43	0.98

Note: The R-squared for the three regressions are 0.27, 0.66 and 0.21, respectively.
The Chow Test's F value (Pr>F) are 1.06(0.4010), 1.33(0.2208) and 1.02(0.4322).

Conclusion

Our paper has contributed to the literature in several respects. We have shown that gains from securitization are considerable. This is not surprising, given securitization's rapid rise to become the largest fixed income asset class in the world. Gains to the asset seller are increasing in the size (and hence liquidity) of the amount of an asset seller's ABS outstanding. Further analysis of the gains, however, take into consideration differences between securitization where the asset seller retains (versus off-lays) equity risk.

The vast majority of securitizations by dollar volume (80 percent) are in the former category where the asset originator enjoys no off-lay of the equity risk of the sold assets. Because the sellers retain the equity of the SPV, these securitizations are really off-balance sheet debt financing. These asset sellers primarily source their gains from liquidity. These asset sellers can substitution of on-balance leverage with off-balance sheet leverage. This phenomenon is especially evident among non-financial institutions.

Some 20 percent of securitizations by dollar volume, but slightly over half by asset seller number, involve asset sellers off-laying equity risk of the sold assets. These securitizations resemble more closely non-recourse securitization modeled in the optimal capital structure literature. Here the declining returns to performance and the securitization ratio suggest that investor concerns of asset quality and the potential for wealth transfers from creditors to equity holders are substantial.

We undertook this research to publish and analyzing the magnitude of the gains from securitization. Our metric for calculating those gains, suggested by the investment banking method of reporting securitizations costs as a cost of capital, has we believe provided some insights. But our conclusions are limited by our lack of theortical development. Theories of optimal capital structure can and should be expanded to include structured finance. The special purpose entities of structured finance – securitizations, real estate investment trusts, project finance, mutual funds, hedge funds etc. – give academics rich empirical testing grounds on which we can increase our understanding of the determinants of optimal capital structure.

Appendix: 120 Securitizing Companies with Average Sizes of Securitization Tranches

Company Name	Industry	Country	Total Securitization	Senior Class (%)	Subordinate Class (%)	Other Class (%)	Credit Support (%)
AAMES FINANCIAL CORP.	2	United States	410,871	0.6733	0.3016	0.0252	0.0000
ABBEY NATIONAL PLC - ADR	1	England	884,820	0.7909	0.1045	0.1045	0.0300
ABN AMRO HLDG N V - SPON ADR	1	Netherlands	2,265,361	0.8217	0.0656	0.1128	0.0272
ACE LIMITED	2	Cayman Islands	1,073,690	0.7895	0.2105	0.0000	0.0000
ADVANTA CORP -CL B	2	United States	229,275	1.0000	0.0000	0.0000	0.0000
AEGON NV	2	Netherlands	2,848,772	0.9341	0.0319	0.0340	0.0000
AMERICAN EXPRESS	2	United States	15,372,188	0.8576	0.0753	0.0671	0.0000

Appendix. Continued

Company Name	Industry	Country	Total Securitization	Senior Class (%)	Subordinate Class (%)	Other Class (%)	Credit Support (%)
AMSOUTH BANCORPORATION	1	United States	94,362	0.5467	0.3021	0.1511	0.0823
ANGLO IRISH BANK	1	Ireland	575,367	0.6737	0.1328	0.1935	0.0301
AUTONATION INC	3	United States	177,071	1.0000	0.0000	0.0000	0.0000
BANCA ANTONVENETA POPOLARE	1	Italy	717,890	0.8976	0.0334	0.0689	0.0000
BANCA INTESA SPA	1	Italy	2,239,635	0.8728	0.0421	0.0851	0.0120
BANCA POPOLARE DI BERGAMO	1	Italy	738,686	0.9222	0.0778	0.0000	0.0306
BANCA POPOLARE DI MILANO	1	Italy	851,958	0.9105	0.0596	0.0299	0.0157
BANCA POPOLARE DI VERONA	1	Italy	373,227	0.9237	0.0697	0.0067	0.0204
BANCO COMERCIAL PORTGE -ADR	1	Portugal	2,436,089	0.9151	0.0448	0.0400	0.0189
BANCO GUIPUZCOANO	1	Spain	889,898	0.9490	0.0510	0.0000	0.0000
BANCO PASTOR	1	Spain	803,642	0.9468	0.0453	0.0079	0.0000
BANCO POPULAR ESPANOL	1	Spain	432,566	0.9458	0.0542	0.0000	0.0000
BANCO SANTANDER CENT -ADR	1	Spain	1,080,000	0.9000	0.0350	0.0650	0.0170
BANK OF AMERICA CORP	1	United States	10,679,721	0.3690	0.0974	0.5335	0.0000
BANK OF NOVA SCOTIA	3	Canada	294,750	0.9500	0.0195	0.0305	0.0000
BANK ONE CORP	1	United States	752,667	0.9756	0.0244	0.0000	0.0030
BANKINTER	1	Spain	5,099,273	0.9099	0.0303	0.0599	0.0136
BARCLAYS PLC/ENGLAND - ADR	1	England	2,631,993	0.9692	0.0308	0.0000	0.0147
BEAR STEARNS COMPANIES INC	2	United States	6,094,611	0.5511	0.0292	0.4197	0.0000
BMW-BAYER MOTOREN WERKE AG	3	Germany	2,344,520	0.9522	0.0478	0.0000	0.0184
BNL-BANCA NAZIONALE LAVORO	1	Italy	3,040,507	0.8068	0.0425	0.1507	0.0000
BOMBARDIER INC	3	Canada	1,571,868	0.7968	0.2032	0.0000	0.0013
CANADIAN IMPERIAL BANK	1	Canada	3,075,000	1.0000	0.0000	0.0000	0.0000
CANADIAN TIRE CORP	3	Canada	2,362,500	0.0000	0.0000	1.0000	0.0000
CAPITAL ONE FINL CORP	2	United States	91,414,812	0.7996	0.1019	0.0985	0.0025
CAPITALIA SPA	1	Italy	3,495,758	0.2619	0.1445	0.5937	0.0000
CAPSTEAD MORTGAGE CORP	2	United States	10,436	0.0000	0.7127	0.2873	0.0000
CARMAX INC	3	United States	5,157,735	0.9115	0.0273	0.0611	0.0174
CATERPILLAR INC	3	United States	2,356,311	0.8976	0.0615	0.0409	0.0474
CENDANT CORP	2	United States	1,691,280	0.8016	0.1958	0.0026	0.0002
CENTEX CORP	3	United States	10,553,295	0.6452	0.1409	0.2139	0.0000
CENTRO PROPERTIES GROUP	2	Australia	1,031,300	0.9280	0.0720	0.0000	0.0126

A Cost of Capital Analysis of the Gains from Securitization

Appendix. Continued

Company Name	Industry	Country	Total Securitization	Senior Class (%)	Subordinate Class (%)	Other Class (%)	Credit Support (%)
CHARMING SHOPPES	3	United States	500,000	0.6470	0.1740	0.1790	0.0000
CITICORP	1	United States	14,253,706	0.8983	0.0974	0.0044	0.0504
CITY NATIONAL CORP	1	United States	448,107	0.9280	0.0532	0.0188	0.0248
CNH GLOBAL NV	3	Netherlands	3,092,736	0.8898	0.0330	0.0772	0.0000
COLONIAL BANCGROUP	1	United States	472,815	0.9603	0.0397	0.0000	0.0000
COLONIAL PROPERTIES TRUST	2	United States	251,000	0.7100	0.2050	0.0850	0.0464
COUNTRYWIDE FINANCIAL CORP	2	United States	31,518,423	0.3072	0.0713	0.6215	0.0000
CREDIT AGRICOLE INDOSUEZ	1	France	43,705	0.8645	0.1355	0.0000	0.0000
CREDIT LYONNAIS SA	1	France	400,442	0.7967	0.2033	0.0000	0.0000
CREDIT SUISSE FIRST BOS USA	2	United States	9,653,397	0.9327	0.0466	0.0207	0.0000
DAIMLERCHRYSLER AG	3	Germany	27,393,340	0.6426	0.0000	0.3574	0.0012
DEUTSCHE BANK AG	1	Germany	6,469,731	0.8785	0.1019	0.0196	0.0189
DVI INC	2	United States	1,853,869	0.8709	0.0162	0.1129	0.0053
EGG PLC	1	United Kingdom	500,000	0.8700	0.0500	0.0800	0.0000
EMC INSURANCE GROUP INC	2	United States	6,242,178	0.4901	0.1895	0.3204	0.0000
ENI S P A -SPON ADR	3	Italy	6,637,000	0.7900	0.1293	0.0808	0.0000
EUROHYPO AG	1	Germany	674,826	0.1843	0.2464	0.5693	0.0000
FEDERAL HOME LOAN MORTG CORP	2	United States	40,685	1.0000	0.0000	0.0000	0.0000
FIAT SPA -ADR	3	Italy	850,005	0.9000	0.1000	0.0000	0.0000
FIRST ACTIVE PLC	1	Ireland	6,843,393	0.9276	0.0724	0.0000	0.0220
FIRST KEYSTONE FINL INC	1	United States	195,312	0.2567	0.7433	0.0000	0.0000
FIRST UNION RE EQ and MTG INV	2	United States	1,011,799	0.6336	0.0765	0.2899	0.0000
FLEETBOSTON FINANCIAL CORP	1	United States	7,680,100	0.8394	0.0606	0.1000	0.0035
FLEETWOOD ENTERPRISES	3	United States	34,822	0.9650	0.0350	0.0000	0.0000
FORD MOTOR CO	3	United States	22,084,746	0.8404	0.0675	0.0921	0.0109
FREMONT GENERAL CORP	2	United States	712,356	0.1404	0.1650	0.6946	0.0000
GENERAL ELECTRIC CAPITAL SVC	2	United States	242,550	0.5517	0.2988	0.1494	0.0000
GENERAL MOTORS CORP	3	United States	65,643,254	0.8552	0.0324	0.1124	0.0127
GREENPOINT FINANCIAL CORP	1	United States	1,846,205	0.3742	0.1438	0.4820	0.0015
HARLEY-DAVIDSON INC	3	United States	2,384,351	0.9387	0.0483	0.0129	0.0098
HONDA MOTOR LTD -AM SHARES	3	Japan	9,036,282	0.9673	0.0000	0.0327	0.0114
HOUSEHOLD FINANCE CORP	2	United States	13,799,854	0.8921	0.0670	0.0409	0.0154
HUNTINGTON BANCSHARES	1	United States	3,185	0.0000	0.0603	0.9397	0.0000

Appendix. Continued

Company Name	Industry	Country	Total Securitization	Senior Class (%)	Subordinate Class (%)	Other Class (%)	Credit Support (%)
HYUNDAI MOTOR CO LTD	3	Korea	640,737	0.8568	0.0609	0.0822	0.0082
IKON OFFICE SOLUTIONS	3	United States	1,273,363	1.0000	0.0000	0.0000	0.0245
IMPAC MORTGAGE HLDGS INC	2	United States	4,503,112	0.4164	0.1131	0.4704	0.0000
INDEPENDENT BANK CORP/MA	1	United States	149,178	0.0740	0.2627	0.6633	0.0000
INDYMAC BANCORP INC	2	United States	1,244,053	0.4024	0.2309	0.3666	0.0000
IRWIN FINL CORP	1	United States	468,645	0.4515	0.2347	0.3138	0.0000
J P MORGAN CHASE and CO	1	United States	80,341,023	0.8015	0.0671	0.1314	0.0044
KEYCORP	1	United States	774,177	0.6922	0.0388	0.2690	0.0127
KREDITANSTALT FUER WIEDERAUF	1	Germany	164,725	0.4688	0.2793	0.2519	0.0000
LEHMAN BROTHERS HOLDINGS INC	2	United States	17,380,347	0.7006	0.2113	0.0881	0.0009
MACQUARIE BANK LTD	1	Australia	700,000	0.9750	0.0250	0.0000	0.0000
MARSHALL and ILSLEY CORP	1	United States	298,670	0.9256	0.0744	0.0000	0.0175
MBIA INC	2	United States	60,040	0.0000	0.0000	1.0000	0.0201
MBNA CORP	1	United States	63,877,006	0.8365	0.0768	0.0867	0.0014
MELLON FINANCIAL CORP	1	United States	1,270,113	0.7365	0.0345	0.2290	0.0000
MERRILL LYNCH and CO	2	United States	7,144,618	0.4563	0.0922	0.4515	0.0000
METRIS COMPANIES INC	2	United States	5,984,789	0.7844	0.1038	0.1118	0.0000
MID-STATE BANCSHARES	1	United States	605,991	0.6544	0.3456	0.0000	0.0033
MORGAN STANLEY	2	United States	11,537,741	0.6629	0.2231	0.1139	0.0002
NATIONAL BANK CANADA	3	Canada	5,115,192	0.5961	0.0273	0.3766	0.0025
NEW CENTURY FINANCIAL CORP	2	United States	10,638,675	0.8102	0.1882	0.0016	0.0008
NORTHERN ROCK PLC	1	United Kingdom	24,788,765	0.8986	0.0522	0.0492	0.0045
NOVASTAR FINANCIAL INC	2	United States	4,237,120	0.8901	0.0765	0.0334	0.0000
ONYX ACCEPTANCE CORP	2	United States	2,362,054	1.0000	0.0000	0.0000	0.0000
POPULAR INC	1	United States	4,699,374	0.4044	0.1032	0.4925	0.0000
PROVIDENT FINL HLDGS INC	1	United States	380,420	1.0000	0.0000	0.0000	0.0000
PRUDENTIAL PLC -ADR	2	England	163,118	0.7736	0.2264	0.0000	0.0000
PSB BANCORP INC	1	United States	36,832	0.1915	0.8085	0.0000	0.0000
REGIONS FINL CORP	1	United States	1,333,060	0.9283	0.0404	0.0313	0.0194
ROYAL BANK OF CANADA	3	Canada	2,675,000	0.0000	0.0000	1.0000	0.0000
SAXON CAPITAL INC	2	United States	989,288	0.6984	0.3011	0.0005	0.0000
SKY FINANCIAL GROUP INC	1	United States	344,574	1.0000	0.0000	0.0000	0.0443
SLM CORP	2	United States	42,443,938	0.9376	0.0315	0.0308	0.0022
ST GEORGE BANK LTD	1	Australia	4,803,282	0.8946	0.0401	0.0653	0.0000
STERLING BANCORP/NY	1	United States	44,355	0.9422	0.0578	0.0000	0.0062

A Cost of Capital Analysis of the Gains from Securitization

Appendix. Continued

Company Name	Industry	Country	Total Securitization	Senior Class (%)	Subordinate Class (%)	Other Class (%)	Credit Support (%)
SUPERIOR FINANCIAL CORP DE	1	United States	100,714	0.5736	0.4264	0.0000	0.0000
SYNOVUS FINANCIAL CP	1	United States	65,519	0.0750	0.1919	0.7331	0.0000
TEXTRON FINANCIAL CORP	2	United States	212,875	0.8866	0.1134	0.0000	0.0000
UNIPOL	2	Italy	149,552	0.7939	0.0843	0.1219	0.0000
UNITED COMMUNITY FINL CORP	1	United States	185,284	0.6292	0.3708	0.0000	0.0233
WACHOVIA CORP	1	United States	4,447,901	0.9137	0.0434	0.0429	0.0000
WASHINGTON MUTUAL INC	1	United States	7,539,417	0.4295	0.0432	0.5273	0.0000
WELLS FARGO and CO	1	United States	12,639,919	0.4494	0.0450	0.5056	0.0005
WESTCORP	1	United States	300,781	1.0000	0.0000	0.0000	0.0879
WILSHIRE FINL SVCS GROUP INC	1	United States	302,805	0.9270	0.0565	0.0164	0.0000
XEROX CORP	3	United States	57,010	0.0000	0.0000	1.0000	0.1312
YAMAHA MOTOR CO LTD	3	Japan	200,000	0.8550	0.0600	0.0850	0.0306
ZIONS BANCORPORATION	1	United States	579,381	0.9025	0.0975	0.0000	0.0000

Note: For Industry, 1,2,3 denote bank, non-bank financial institution, and other industry (non-financial institution), respectively.

Acknowledgment

We gratefully acknowledge the support of an Earmark Grant from the Hong Kong Research Grants Council that made this research possible.

References

Ambrose, Brent W., Michael LaCour-Little and Anthony Saunders (2004) "Does Regulatory Capital Arbitrage, Reputation or Asymmetric Information Drive Securitization?" *working paper* August 24.

Burroughs, Katherine, Robert Grady and Kathleen Bailey (2002). "Select Recent Bankruptcy Cases Affecting Commercial Real Estate Finance and Securitization." *Finance and Real Estate* (July), Dechert, www.dechert.com.

Cohn, Michael J. (1998) "Asset Securitization: How Remote Is Bankruptcy Remote?" *Hofstra Law Review* **26**: 4 Summer.

Donovan, Kevin.(2003) "Conseco Bankruptcy Heats Up: ABS players fight fee-related sleight of hand" *The Investment Dealers' Digest : IDD*. New York (Feb 24) 1.

Financial Accounting Standards Board (2000). "Statement No. 140:Accounting for Transfers and Servicing of Financial Assets and Extinguishments of Liabilities." Norwalk, CT (September 2000).

Greenbaum, Stuart and Anjan Thakor (1987). "bank lending models: securitization versus deposits". *Journal of Banking and Finance* **11** (3) 379-401.

-- -- (1995). *Contemporary Financial Intermediation* Dryden. Fort Worth.

Leyland, Hayne and Jure Skarabot (2003) "On Purely Financial Synergies and the Optimal Scope of the Firm: Implications for Mergers, Spin-offs and Structured Finance" *working paper*.

Leyland, Hayne (1994) "Corporate Debt Value, Bond Covenants and Optimal Capital Structure" *The Journal of Finance* **49**:4, 1213-1252.

Leland, Hayne and Jure Skarabot (2003). "On purely financial synergies and the optimal scope of the firm: implications for mergers, spinoffs and off-balance sheet finance." working paper.

Lockwood, Larry, Ronald Rutherford and Martin Herrera (1996). "Wealth Effects of Asset Securitization." *Journal of Banking and Finance* **20**, 151-164.

Lupica, Lois (2000). "Circumvention of the bankruptcy process: the statutory institutionalization of securitization." *Connecticut Law Review* **33**: 199.

LaCour-Little and Sanders (2004) asks the question "does regulatory capital arbitrage, reputation or asymmetric information drive securitization?" and comes to the conclusion that capital arbitrage or reputation is driving it.

Merton, RC. (1974) "On the pricing of corporate debt: The risk structure of interest rates" *The Journal of Finance* **29**(2): 449-70.

Modigliani, F., and M. H. Miller(1959). "Corporation Finance, and the Theory of Investment: Reply." *American Economic Review*, vol. 49, no. 4 (September): 655–669.

Pennacchi, George (1988). "Loan Sales and the Cost of Bank Capital." *The Journal of Finance* **43**:2, 375-96.

Perry, Debra (1995). "Can asset securitization squeeze any juice out of your capital structure?" Speech for the Investors Forum on Asset Securitization given on October 23, 1995 in Bermuda reprinted in Moody's Investor Service Special Comment.

Raynes, Sylvain and Ann Rutledge (2003). *The Analysis of Structured Securities: precise risk measurement and capital allocation* Oxford University Press, New York.

Skipworth, Douglas (2001). "Statement 140: a study of securitization disclosure." FASB Study, December 26.

Thomas, Hugh (2001). "Effects of Asset Securitization on Seller Claimants." *Journal of Financial Intermediation* **10**, 306-330.

Timmons, Heather (2002) Everybody out of the risk pool? Enron and other problems are taking a toll on the structured-finance business" *Business Week* New York (September 2, 2002) 3797, 86.

In: Handbook of Business and Finance
Editors: M. Bergmann and T. Faust, pp. 171-189

ISBN: 978-1-60692-855-4
© 2010 Nova Science Publishers, Inc.

Chapter 7

NATIONAL MUSEUM WEBSITES: COLONIZING AND DE-COLONIZING

Mary Leigh Morbey
York University, Toronto, Canada

Abstract

Internet communications technology (ICT) changes culture and therefore how a museum represents itself. Framed by the concepts of cybercolonialism and cyberglocalization, the chapter will critique and address, through case studies, a cybercolonizing by IBM of the State Hermitage Museum website, and cyberglocalizing processes in the Louvre Museum new website. Further, the chapter examines the notion of de-colonization in relation to museum ICT and website development, particularly for countries in the Global South. Along with a discussion of virtual colonization, glocalization, and de-colonization, the chapter will attend to the place of virtual museum representation in light of Web 2.0 (interactive participation) and Web 3.0 (intelligent and semantic web) and relate these to Global South museum website development.

Introduction

Internet communications technology (ICT) can change culture (Bowers, 2000, 2001, 2006; Lessig, 2002; Marcus, 2002, 2006; Parekh, 2000) and subsequently how a museum represents itself. This is particularly so as national museum websites transform how we view, understand, and interact with the cultural artifacts they represent virtually on the World Wide Web. We are only beginning to discover the un-researched assumptions about ICT ideas, models, interaction, and appearance on museum websites and this is an important challenge before us.

Framed by the concepts of cybercolonialism, a colonizing of cultures and cultural artifacts by an array of computing ideologies, and cyberglocalization, an adapting of global cyber processes to local situations, the chapter will critique and address, through case studies, a cybercolonizing by IBM of the State Hermitage Museum (St. Petersburg, Russia) website at http://www.hermitagemuseum.org/, and cyberglocalizing processes in the context of the

Louvre Museum (Paris) new website development located at http://www.louvre.fr/llv/commun/home.jsp?bmLocale=en. The case studies ask: How are ideological influences, cultural pressures, and structural constraints giving shape to theoretical, cultural, and applied website developments by the two museums?

Further, in light of a working of cybercolonialism in the Hermitage Museum case study, the chapter advances the notion of de-colonization, a contestation of colonial domination and the legacies of colonialism, in relation to museum ICT and website development and particularly for countries in the Global South. Along with critique and discussion of the notions of virtual colonization, glocalization, and de-colonization, the chapter will attend to the place of virtual museum representation in light of Web 2.0 (interactive with an architecture of participation) and Web 3.0 (third generation of Internet services that comprise the intelligent web). Since the State Hermitage Museum site illustrates Web 1.0 (point and click) and The Louvre site Web 1.5 (with some interactive participation), suggestions will be offered as to how to move museum development towards Web 2.0 and 3.0 possibilities, with attention to open access, glocalization, de-colonization, and local impact in website development for museums located in the Global South.

Literature and Theoretical Framing

There are questions about the Internet's ideological flavour, not only at the levels of content and context but in its very design (Marcus, 2002, 2006). The design and programs that comprise particular computing applications (such as the Internet and the World Wide Web) are dominated by an arguably narrow range of ideological viewpoints, often emanating from the United States. This chapter takes the position that no ideology or influence is neutral, and therefore ideologies are value-laden and direction shaping (Bowers, 1988, 2000, 2001, 2006; Franklin, 1999; Morbey, 1996, 2000, 2003, 2006; Morbey and Granger, 2002; Penley and Ross, 1991).

As information communications technology becomes dominant in shaping the transition from industrial-based to digital-based information cultures, the relationship between processes of colonialism and post-colonialism to the designs and encounters in cyberspace grows in significance. There exists an expanding body of research and literature on the concept of cybercolonialism (Chesher, 1994; Ebo, 2001; Fernandez, 1999; Marchart, 1998; Morbey, 1998, 2000, 2003, 2006; Morbey and Granger, 2002; Sardar and Ravetz, 1996). This work emerges from the concept of Discourse Analysis of Colonialism, first developed in Edward Said's salient 1978 work *Orientalism* (Said, 1978, 1994). There Said argues that the "orient" is constructed by Western discourses as "other" and represented as primitive, dependent upon Western expertise and in need of being controlled. Analogous to this understanding is the West's, and particularly the United States', historical global domination of computing expertise.

Two particular ideological viewpoints are key players in cybercolonizing roles: the "American New Frontier" notion, deployed in narratives of cyberspace and standing in the tradition of one of the American founding myths of conquering new geographic spaces, and Japanese "techno-orientalism," a technical inter-discourse consisting mainly of "oriental" consumer technologies and objects (Marchart, 1998). The American New Frontier notion, as illustrated through various narratives such as American Revolution literature about colonial movement westward across the North American continent that foreground the emptying and subsequent re-territorialization of geographic spaces, can be understood in relation to electronic spaces which can themselves be de- and re-colonized. Techno-orientalism can be described as a more expansive aesthetic or cultural orientalism that "seeks to re-code Western consumer products into an oriental trend" (Marchart, 1998, p. 57). Morley and Robins (1995) contend that "Japan has become synonymous with technologies of the future – with screens, networks, cybernetics, robotics, artificial intelligence, simulation" (p.168). In the techno-orientalizing process, the Internet and the web, as technological objects, replace other artifacts of popular culture (Marchart, 1998). The case study of the State Hermitage Museum comprises a deeper investigation of the notion of cybercolonialism and its influence.

In contrast to the cybercolonization that will be pointed to in the context of the Hermitage, the notion of cyberglocalization (Friedman, 2000; Robertson, 1995, 2000; Seerveld, 2003) will be illustrated through developments in the Louvre Museum new website launched on June 6, 2005. The notion of glocalization being argued here follows Roland Robertson's articulation of the global not counter posed to the local but rather the inclusion of the local within the global; affirming that globalization can enhance traditional culture (Robertson, 1995, 2000). Glocalization in this respect then is a linking of localities (Robertson, 1995). Robertson (2000) views globalization as a compression of the world, recognizing it is as a multidimensional process which simultaneously is cultural, economic, and political. Adapting his conceptualization from the Japanese word *dockakuka* with a meaning roughly akin to "global localization," Robertson (2000) posits that glocalization encompasses worldwide processes adapted to local circumstances. Robertson's delineation of glocalization given a cyber designation brings new possibilities for cyber spaces interlinking with centuries old geographic and culturally defined spaces. The Louvre Museum website provides an example of adapting global cyber processes to local circumstances and is done in a way that richly expresses French history and culture.

The notion of de-colonlization articulated by Mahmood Mamdani (1996, 2005), in his work on the generation that inherited Africa's colonial legacy, posits that knowledge exchange between developing countries and the developing world often have been organized in colonial terms. Complementing Mamdani's colonizing concern is Linda Tuhiwai Smith's (1999) offering of decolonizing methodologies for theses kinds of working relationships. Although Tuhiwai Smith's work is an extensive critique of Western paradigms and knowledge from the position of indigenous and colonized Maori woman and argumentation for a new agenda of indigenous research, her thinking assists in understanding possibilities for de-colonization of mainly Western paradigms shaping ICT conceptualizations and applications for website development in the Global South. The critical understandings of Mandani (2005) and Tuhiwai Smith (1999) of the underlying assumptions, motivations, and values that inform research methods and practices parallels Aaron Marcus' (2006) emphasis upon uncovering un-researched assumptions about ICT ideas, models, interaction, and appearance. These notions will be engaged in initial conceptualization and design of Global South museum websites and online presence engaging Web 2.0 and an emergent Web 3.0. There is a lack of needed research and literature regarding critical underlying understandings of non-colonizing website development for museums in the Global South. We are only beginning to discover the un-researched assumptions about ICT and de-colonizing ideas, models, interaction, and appearance on museum websites; this is an important and timely 21st century challenge before us.

Methodological Processes

A multi-pronged methodological design for the two museum website case studies (Yin, 2002), as well as future non-Western museum website development, are structured to capture the complexity of ICT ideas and influences. Historical tracings of website development in each museum were recorded. Philosophical analysis uses a hermeneutical approach to decipher the notion of de-colonization in relation to museum website development for the Global South as well as to bring insight to the convergence of text and image in museum websites employing Bolter and Grusin's (1999) notion of remediation, that is, new media re-fashioning old media in web communication. Ethnographic onsite field observations (Spradley, 1980, 1997; Yow, 1994), pre-structured open-ended interviews (Creswell, 1998), and ongoing discussions online and face-to-face with six Hermitage ICT related personnel and three of the Louvre Service Internet combined in field data collection for the parallel case studies (Yin, 2002). The face-to-face interview process gives voice to museum personnel working with ICT and the museum websites.

Onsite field data collection at the Hermitage in 2001-2004, the first case study, and at the Louvre in 2003-2005, the second study, engaged ICT website related personnel in qualitative pre-structured, open-ended, taped interviews of about one hour in length. The Hermitage interview questions numbered eight, and the Louvre, eight, with similar questions asked of personnel at both sites. Those interviewed were invited to query the interview questions as well as to add pertinent information not overtly sought in questions asked. Several ICT personnel of both museums were interviewed several times as further inqueries arose in the ongoing collection of research data. The taped interviews were transcribed and analyzed. Along with the interview texts, ethnographic notes were taken onsite noting museum ICT procedures and practices. Subsequent conversations and emails with personnel of the two museums continue to clarify particular ICT engagements.

Transcribed interviews were analyzed qualitatively and coded, both manually and employing Atlas.ti qualitative software, to track themes and locate patterns, with a coding synthesis of transcriptions using an inductive grounded theory (Glaser and Strauss, 1967; Strauss and Corbin, 1998) approach to coding to structure a system for understanding and framing these to produce meaningful knowledge. Analysis of the full data collection searched out themes and patterns of web employments with cross-museum comparisons made (Hantrais and Mangen, 1996; Ragin, 1991).

The two museum website histories, website interpretation using the Bolter-Grusin remediation notion, and multiple onsite field data were analyzed and pressed forward by two questions. First, how is information communications technology changing each museum's representation of itself on the web? And second, can these changes be understood as a playing out of underlying ideologies?

Further, the conceptualization of de-colonization in museum website development for countries of the Global South is emergent and important to initiate research literature as well as website experimentation and development.

The Hermitage Story

Historically the Hermitage has been represented virtually through two websites. The first, a large website with text errors, was created in 1995 by the museum with available Russian technology and expertise because its director, Dr. Mikhail Piotrovsky, understood the importance of the Hermitage having an online presence which would give the possibility for a global sharing of Russian history, culture, and treasures collected in the Hermitage (R. Shabaltas, personal communication, May 11, 2001). In June of 1999, the administrations of the Hermitage and IBM, through the work of Rebecca Kerr of Global IBM, jointly launched a second and IBM-sponsored Web 1.0 (point and click) site with IBM giving certain specified equipment and lending particular expertise. The original agreement however, took a long time to evolve because Ms Kerr had to convince IBM that this would be a good step for the company to take since it did not want to lose money. Many within the museum view the second website, run by an IBM server located in the United States, as superior to the initial site. The story of the current Hermitage site is told in three sections: 1) interpreting museum website representation, 2) problems within the IBM technological shell, and 3) a question of reciprocity.

Interpreting Museum Website Representation

Before proceeding to a critical analysis of ICT and cybercolonial shapings in the current IBM sponsored Hermitage website, a brief review of the concept of remediation assists in understanding what is transpiring on screen as one views the Hermitage site. In their influential 1999 text *Remediation: Understanding New Media*, Jay Bolter and Richard Grusin posit that the World Wide Web favours ongoing re-mediation, that is ways new media – computer graphics, virtual reality, and the web – define and refashion old media – painting, photography, film, and TV – and vice versa. Their remediation theory provides a hermeneutic, a way to interpret and understand what is transpiring on a website and applies to both the Hermitage and Louvre discussions, as well as other museum websites whether employing Web 1.0, 2.0, or 3.0.

The web offers a constant promise of live interactivity through the flexibility of networked communication. Bolter and Grusin (1999) argue this instantaneously engaging immediacy – a style of visual representation which aims at erasing the medium to make the viewer believe they are in the direct web presence of the represented objects – dictates the medium. Immediacy is created through the underlying contributing layers of media labeled hypermediacy – a visual style that offers fragmented and heterogeneous representation and gives the viewer simultaneous access to the multiple media. The web has become an increasingly salient remediator, a reconfigurer, of all sorts of information which readily absorbs and integrates almost all other visual and verbal media.

This refashioning occurs in convincing manner, for example, in viewing the "Big" French ornate ceremonial carriage located on the Hermitage's first floor atop the main public entrance stairwell in the Field Marshalls' Hall (http://www.hermitagemuseum. org/html_En/08/hm88_0_1_22.html). The carriage (early 1720s, Gobelins factory), commissioned by Peter I in Paris in 1717, was used in the coronation ceremonies of Catherine I (1724) and Catherine the Great (1762). An immediacy of one's presence in the virtual web space depends on hypermediacy arranging text, graphics, digitized imagery, video, and other media in multiple panes and windows, and joining them with programming and hyperlinks to generate the live sensation of moving around the Field Marshall's Hall and viewing the carriage much celebrated in Russian eighteenth century history. "HotMedia" (facilitates a virtual tour) and "Zoom View" (enables a zooming in on detail) Java-based technology provide movement about the room to create an instantaneous engagement of the on-screen visitor. The Hermitage website was a first to use HotMedia. The "live" experience of the ceremonial carriage is that of the working of the interface, enabling one's immediate presence and movement about the Hermitage hall. In contrast however to the immediate "liveness" of HotMedia and Zoom View leading one about the room, are the hidden layers of the other media, hypermediated, which enable and facilitate the lively immediacy for the viewer. The two live together in contemporary media such as the Hermitage site and are mutually dependent (Bolter and Grusin, 1999). Both old and more current media that comprise the Hermitage website – traditional graphic design, digitized imagery, composites of paintings, text, video, HotMedia, Zoom View, etc. – co-exist in the remediation process, which provides a vantage point through which to understand what happens in the IBM technological shell.

Problems within the IBM Technological Shell

The current IBM sponsored Hermitage website bears a striking resemblance to the websites of various other national museums, notably the National Gallery of Art in Washington, DC (http://www.nga.gov/) on which it is modeled. The employment of a museum website design following that of a US American national museum at first received unquestioned acceptance by those engaged in the development of the Hermitage site, with little concern about whether the use of a website design following that of a US American national museum developed through the technology and website structuring of a US American company to represent a Russian national museum was problematic. The Museum IBM Project Head however, points to a possible limiting of Russian cultural representation in his observation that "it will take a long time to answer this question .... I cannot say that we have problems with the Western design, but you can see the influence of IBM on this project" (A. Grigoryev, personal communication, May 10, 2001). The Hermitage web specialist commented on the sources of the information appearing on the new website and the relationship that brought it about:

> Most of this information [came] from the collections called life section, history section, and education section, and was brought [forward] from the old [web] version. The main structure and the ideology of the site, the targeting of the site, and design styles were developed by IBM staff, managers, and designers. They developed the structure and we brought [the static information from the first web site] (R. Shabaltas, personal communication, May 11, 2001).

Along with IBM hardware, software, and expertise donated to facilitate the new website development came the import of an IBM American English e-business advertisement situated beneath the blue IBM logo located on each site page in both Russian and English sections. The e-business underlay (http://www-03.ibm.com/innovation/us) contains the Executive Interaction Channel with a variety of IBM e-business choices; a click on Home at the left top page sends the viewer to the IBM US homepage (http://www.ibm.com/us/). The "About the Site" page accessible only in English on the homepage clearly articulates IBM's involvement and goals for the project, namely

> to do much more than just provide technology to the Hermitage Museum. We aimed to transform how people around the world experience the Hermitage Museum and its collections. The partnership with a world class cultural institution like the Hermitage marks IBM's web debut in the cultural arena and represents another powerful opportunity for IBM to demonstrate its leadership in providing leading edge e-business solutions to help customers leverage their existing assets ... (http://www.hermitagemuseum.org/html_En/00/hm0_8.html).

This text, which does not appear in Russian, is an advertisement for IBM's e-business. It consists of a statement of the corporation's business goals for *its* project with the Hermitage, which is positioned as a commodity to be exploited, a museum to be cybernetically colonized, and invites the important question of precisely how IBM benefits (vis-à-vis its global business) from involving itself in such a project?

The Museum IBM Project Head indicated what he believes is a key question directing the museum's web development: What [is the] goal [for people who] use this website?" This query about the goal, or perhaps goals, for potential website users raises further questions because the majority of the Hermitage web visitors, to date, come from outside Russia and from mainly the Western world. If the primary goals directing the website design and content are ease of use, so articulated by the Museum Project Head, with an underlying expansion of IBM e-business and for mainly Western site visitors, does this then not lead to the creation of an e-communication which moves the cultural museum artifacts towards commodification? And is this movement not from the West and for the West?

The overall consensus within the Hermitage ICT related administration seems to be that while IBM provided the technological framework for the new website, the content was provided by the employees of the museum. Content from the original Russian-based website was incorporated into the new site within the IBM technological shell. What is most interesting about this, however, is the relationship between the technological framework and the content. The distinction could be made delineating a separation of technological design and content, however the actuality of what historically occurred appears to be to the contrary. The Museum IBM Project Head succinctly described this relationship in noting that because we already had a new technology we had to make new content. "We did not have the full technology [for the old website] but we tried to prepare everything for [the new website], so when we got it we could fill it.... We create[d] data for [the] new technology" (A. Grigoryev, personal communication, May 10, 2001).

This is a clear indication of how a change in technological framework – the form – began to drive the content of the website. What is important to note is first that the shift came about, and second that it came about as a result of IBM's involvement in the training of Hermitage staff and the application to their work of its technical and corporate standards: web design formats including an e-business underlay, guidance in cultural content presented, direction of aesthetic design decisions, technical standards, and quality control demands. This is not particularly unique for museums that have acquired computer management systems have discovered it is neither a straight forward nor simple task to shift content and data from a previous website. The Museum IBM Project Head's pragmatic acknowledgement that the working of the technology is primary, along with his initial contention that the site be easy to use, suggests however a clear acceptance of the superiority of IBM formats, standards, and procedures in the shaping of the content.

To state that the choice of design does not matter as long as it pragmatically works is to ignore or to fail to see the ways in which the structures that make the site easy to use and accessible to the onsite visitor are not neutral; there are underlying ideologies and directions at work. Applications of information communications technology embody the underlying structure – and in this case IBM and its configurations – that forms the technology, therefore the application of a particular information and communications technology is not an act of neutrality (Morbey, 2000).

A Question of Reciprocity

Querying the relationship between the Hermitage and IBM, and particularly in relation to website development, maintenance, and sustainability, is it one of reciprocity in which each party benefits to a similar degree or is one party likely to be advantaged more than the other as the relationship unfolds? Within the interview transcripts, ongoing conversations with museum personnel, museum ethnographic observations, and website analysis, there are certainly moments when a perception of reciprocity is specifically noted in website decisions and what appears onscreen. Clearly, the enthusiasm with which many of the Hermitage ICT related staff has become involved in the IBM project reveals that they believe it is beneficial for them. In fact, the Museum IBM Project Head relates that it is good for both the museum and IBM. Other museum ICT related personnel in more recent discussion, reflecting about their thoughts prior to the Hermitage-IBM partnership and what might happen to Russian cultural content in an IBM-shaped website, strongly believed that Russian content and context would be minimized in relation to the first museum website with emphasis given towards IBM site objectives. They now confirm this is the case. There are three areas in which cybercolonizing aspects of IBM's work with the Hermitage website can fairly easily be demonstrated. These include: (1) the subtle shaping by a US corporation of the structure and ideology underlying the website, (2) the changes ICT and the website have brought to ways people experience (and think about experiencing) the museum, and (3) the question of language choice and usages, including corporate e-business language as well as American English branding on the website.

In considering the question of cybercolonizing influences on the Hermitage website on the part of IBM, it is important to examine not only the overt concepts but also events that symptomize the process. We must look at how both the concepts – website ideology and structure – and events become naturalized in the users of technology. There is a clear indication across data findings of the IBM developed website to support the view that members of the Hermitage ICT related web staff have begun to accept as given, particular forms subtle cybercolonization has taken with respect to their work. It seems quite natural for museum personnel to accept: the website structure incorporating US American New Frontier "take over" and techno-oriental consumer coding influences; a website structure and appearance resembling strongly that of a US American national museum; aesthetic decisions, content realignment, quality control, and technical standards of IBM; and the site's marketing component – the goal of attracting more visitors to the museum where they can transact US American English IBM e-business as well as purchase goods in the Hermitage Museum Shop and museum entry tickets. Put differently, such naturalization – a subtle and penetrating influence that views technological and economic ideologies as neutral with no underlying shaping – might help to account for the overall enthusiasm on the part of Hermitage ICT personnel for the joint museum-IBM project. Technology has become naturalized, that is neutralized, to such an extent that it can no longer be viewed as other than pragmatically useful, even when it has the potential to change profoundly the ways the museum represents itself, and the artifacts it houses, on the web and is experienced by the website users.

A fore fronting of IBM's goals is also made evident in relation to the question of language on the website. The fact that English is chosen as the second language is not surprising since it is the language of approximately half the individuals who access the website. Moreover IBM is a US based company, and US English is its language of operation. What is curious, however, is the fact observed by the site web specialist that IBM was determined the English used on the website be *American* English. This demand resulted in heated debate between the Hermitage's English translators, who use standard British English and have done so for decades, and IBM management, who wondered why British English was being used. American English, rather than British English, is the second website language.

With the creation of the website, the objective is not one of solely wishing to attract virtual visitors who come and go. Of course the administration of the Hermitage is aware that the website and its content provide only visual republication of the museum's artifacts. The hope exists for the viewer to some day visit the Hermitage to view and interact with the original artifacts beyond the remediated immediacy which draws them into the website. This leads one however to wonder whether the Hermitage website, with IBM shaping web structure and directing ideologies, aesthetics, content alignment, technical standards, and e-business underlay and US American English overlay, alters through remediation an understanding of the museum and its artifacts towards IBM techno-objects. The techno-orientalization process recodes the museum and its cultural artifacts, Russian and otherwise, into products for consumption and towards the consumer driven e-business underlay, and away from Russian culture and history which brought the viewer to the website. Are not the agreed upon IBM American New Frontier web structure and design subtly, very subtly, both de- and re-colonizing the representation of Hermitage content?

The Louvre Tale

The first official Louvre website was launched in 1995. Then in 1999 the Louvre Museum President-Director Pierre Rosenberg realized the importance of a new website that employed the Internet in more contemporary and meaningful ways to engage viewers around the world. His leadership initiated a minor new website development. It was his successor, Henri Loyrette, who inherited this vision in 2001 and made the development of a new and different kind of website a key emphasis of the museum for at least the next half decade. The new site was launched June 6, 2005 using Web 1.5 with some interactive participation, and its guiding premises illustrate a playing out of the notion of cyberglocalization. The museum's new website development will be elaborated in three parts: 1) collaborative conceptualization, 2) differing curatorial and educational objectives, and 3) a French cultural heritage scripted for global communication.

Collaborative Conceptualization

Under the new leadership in 2001 of President-Director Loyrette, the Service Internet team headed by Director Dr. Myriam Prot was struck to develop a new website conceptualization for the museum. From the outset Loyrette made the new site a top Louvre priority with the goal of employing contemporary web ideas to change the Louvre cybernetically in relation to global visitors, and to change communication, relationships, and collaborative engagement across Louvre departments and personnel vis-à-vis its internal life and internal service. The new Director wanted an open system within the Louvre; his vision encompasses openness, communication, and new technology (M. Prot, personal communication, July 16, 2003). A July 28, 2008 (Gumbel) *Time Magazine* article on Loyrette and the Louvre discusses his vision of the museum as a "beacon of culture that is both accessible and global" (p. 38). Loyrette's mission is one of pulling the venerable institution into a new era, financially through fundraising, and as reflected in Prot's interview commentary as a player in the 21st century cyberworld.

Following Loyrette's vision, collaboration with and input from all sectors of the museum were imperative for the new site development – curation to museum restoration to Service Internet to museum education to online ticketing. The Service Internet Director Prot clearly articulates the Louvre new website vision, "… we spent a lot of time, to define [through interaction] with lots of different [museum personnel] what they could contribute to the new website. [We looked for what] they could invent as new services that [did not exist] on the old website, [what] they could create with their own knowledge. It took almost a year just to meet people, talk with them, and imagine all these new services for the next generation site. This is new for the Louvre, and very important! The [Museum Director] decided it was one of the main priorities for the Louvre" (M. Prot, personal communication, July 16, 2003). This vision led to an emphasis on the Internet and the development of innovative strategies for its implementation. It has engaged others, not just technology personnel, in getting used to working with the Internet; a collaboration of researchers, art historians, curators, educators, and technology personnel which has become part of everyday life in the museum. Following the launching of the new website version 1.5 on June 6, 2005, the different museum sectors remain collaboratively and integrally involved in ongoing input and development.

The new site is financially supported by Credit Lyonnais with a monetary gift of four million euros, by in kind sponsorship of Accenture with personnel contributions to assist in building the Louvre new site strategy, and by technology from US-based Blue Martini providing the platform software. These sponsors have been openly engaged in the site conceptualization and development conversations. The French corporation Gapgemini assisted with strategies and implementation of the Blue Martini platform, tailored to the unique requirements of the Louvre. The Gapgemini connection came through a juried competition run by the French Ministry of Culture and was chosen for its ability to bring large French corporate expertise to the project. French bureaucratic procedures slowed the museum's collaborative process which contributed to a site launching two years later than initially planned. Descriptive website wording attached to each key supporter is carefully chosen so to clearly reflect each company's precise contribution to the website development.

It is the practice of software companies globally to sell a museum software at the full price and then to return 90%. French Napoleonic law, however, declares there can be corporate contributions to French national museums which are 100% philanthropic with no monies paid to a particular corporation; "they do not ask for anything in return" (M. Prot, personal communication, July 16, 2003). Under French law a violation is serious and can result in what the French call "mis en examen," which translated means "subject to investigation". To elaborate the concept and why it is advantageous for the Louvre, corporate supporters of the museum may receive gift tickets or other kinds of gifts, however, a request cannot be made asking for a payment for software or computer work of which a certain percentage is returned to the museum. If this is transgressed "mis en examen" comes about where an official examination is opened. A corporation can be questioned as a suspect if there is serious evidence brought forward in which monies are requested from the Louvre in relation to a corporate contribution, and can be sent before the *tribunal correctional* or *cour d'assises.* This means that the kind of relationship that IBM had with the Hermitage would not be possible in France.

Along with integral internal museum website development assisted by sponsors, the Service Internet realized that the approach to those outside of Paris, and particularly outside France and the French language, needed to be engaging in design, content, a variety of languages, and for diverse cultures and age ranges. With a vision and strategy in place to bring about these possibilities, the Service Internet and contributing sectors remain constant to an embedding of French history and culture in their open collaborative site.

Differing Curatorial and Educational Objectives

With the advent of the vision and strategy for the new website, the Service Internet and sectors across the museum view the employment of the Internet as a cultural medium rather than as a financial tool, a way to offer cultural and historical context to the museum and its artifacts. The outreach of the site is two-fold: global visitors and the French population. Two-thirds of those who visit the museum are foreign visitors, with one-third coming from within France.

Since the majority of visitors are non-French, the Service Internet realizes a need to develop strategies to engage in a "user-friendly" manner the dominate groupings of non-French visitors in their own languages. Website 2005 includes the French and English languages, however as the site continues development Spanish and Japanese will be added. An emphasis exists to represent the dominate languages present on the Internet, which also would include Chinese.

The new site focuses on two objectives directed by the sectors of curation and education: 1) a more intellectual understanding of the artifacts, and 2) real museum visitation preparation that brings forward an intellectual purpose for the visit, engagement with guided tours online, key points about the main art works that will be encountered, and museum navigation. A thematic teaching approach is offered through five "Thematic Trails" located at http://www.louvre.fr/llv/activite/liste_parcours.jsp?bmLocale=en, for the exploration of a particular theme, movement, or period in depth. For example, the "Masterpieces of the Louvre in Search of Ideal Beauty" offering encouraged for a first visit, includes the three key museum works of Venus de Milo, the Victory of Samonthrace, and La Gioconda – the Mona Lisa, with a reflection upon the indefinable notion of masterpiece.

Engagement, in particular, by the Curatorial Department on the new site focuses on providing the public with another kind of experience other than tourism. The curators wish to offer engaging venues for the museum's large global public that present the museum intellectually and culturally with the curators writing for a large general audience. This is a far cry from the elitism of Louvre curators of a decade ago.

A French Cultural Heritage Scripted for Global Communication

A directing philosophy of the new site vision is one of global communication. With entry onto the site homepage, along with brief acknowledgments of the three key sponsors and a link to http://www.culture.fr/, the visitor is introduced to and can choose to click on the four groupings which comprise the Louvre community: Membership, Professionals, Young People, and Support the Louvre. The sub-groupings include a broad range of ways to be involved with and to support the museum. The administration, acknowledging that two-thirds of its visitors real and virtual come from outside France, is reaching out globally to engage and to educate its many visitors. The once elite world renowned museum has altered what it was about to interconnect with, on diverse levels, the large global population that wishes to learn about the museum, its history and culture, and the artifacts it houses. What has changed is the development of a vision and strategies to do this in ways that engage, communicate with, and educate the many non-French visitors. Strategies to involve the French, Parisian or otherwise, are also in place. In the next website versions, there is planning for the development of an open research community as well as more personalized service so that one can collect and save information on the site. This change in the contemporary Louvre is movement towards an "open system," reflecting Director Loyrette's priorities of openness, communication, and new technology.

Along with its goal of global cyber engagement online, the Service Internet has built in website layers of French culture and history relevant to the Louvre. This is done in four ways. First, the site is developed so that the virtual visitor will feel more comfortable and familiar with the real Louvre the day they come for a visit so the web design of the museum layout and navigation is close to that of the real museum. Second, the Louvre in actuality is a palace. For the website user it is important to explain the history and culture of the Louvre so on the site there is an historical explanation of the palace. Third, many of the items on the site have been taken from ideas on other websites, however, the Louvre site possesses its own competencies which show what the Louvre is and that it could not be another museum. Fourth, within the site design and the 1015 artifact explanations thus far represented, the code layering includes title, image, details, information, cultural explanation, text, guided tour, and so on with interactive links throughout. In this way the site design more subtly embeds historical and cultural information, and explanation important to the museum and its representation of French history and culture. The Louvre website, an open system built on internal and external communication for the French and for the world, is a striking cyberglocal example of adapting global cyber processes to a particular local museum context.

Differing Ideological Visions of Two National Museums

The key similarity of the two national museum website case studies is the impetus and vision for each site comes from the museum director, although how each has gone about directing website development is considerably different. Piotrovsky initiated both Hermitage websites. In 1997 conversations with Global IBM about what it could bring to the Hermitage, in light of the lack of financial and technical support within Russia to bring contemporary ICT to the museum to substantially improve the first site, Piotrovsky invited in the sponsorship of IBM with its accompanying baggage of influence to insure the Hermitage would have a quality global presence online. Louvre Director Loyrette, when taking over the directorship in 2001, set as a top priority the development of an open and collaborative website engaging all sectors of the museum in its development and with more user-friendly educational and intellectual engagement of its visitors through a diverse range of languages. Both directors pressed forward a website vision realizing the importance of the Internet for the global presence of their museum.

The content of these visions however, play out in substantially different ways. Because of its Communist direction for decades and a lack of money and contemporary technological equipment, design, and expertise, the approach to Piotrovsky by Global IBM provided a way to concretize his vision to have the Hermitage on the web in a manner globally respected. He accepted IBM's sponsorship with its influences and shapings which may have altered the Hermitage's internal ICT related choices. The American New Frontier and techno-oriental influences manifest in web structure, design, aesthetic decisions, content realignment, quality control, technical standards, US American language branding, and IBM e-business underlay of the site, came with the agreement. Personnel within the museum, ICT related and otherwise, confirm the reality that Russian cultural and historical sensitivity inherent in the first website was minimized in the second IBM sponsored site. The Hermitage website perhaps is ultimately a financial and communication tool where much of what it is about is US corporate branding.

The Louvre site embodying Loyrette's vision of an open system emphasizing internal and external communication and new technology differs considerably from that of the Hermitage. Although museums regularly are in need of more funding as is also the case at the Louvre, the museum is one of the world's wealthiest so internal goals can be other than continually money generating. The website development came from the viewpoint of global openness and inclusivity in structure, strategy, and design while at the same time overtly embedding French culture and history, and with sensitivity towards the French people. Once the vision was established, Loyrette passed the baton over to the newly formed Service Internet and Director Prot to develop a team to engage all museum sectors in the site vision, strategic planning, and cultivation with an emphasis on internal and external communications. Differing museum sectors continue to develop and make ongoing website changes. The site, with its open collaborative conceptualization and development, with its curatorial and educative goals of engaging in a non-elite manner the virtual visitor to foster more intellectual understanding of the museum and its artifacts, and with French cultural heritage embedded so to communicate to the French as well as global visitors, provides a model of how the notion of cyberglocalization can be worked out meaningfully in the context of a large national museum.

While the Hermitage website holds a US American IBM corporate overlay and language branding, the Louvre website is more open, collaborative, and communicative engaging all sectors of the museum as well as an array of sponsors in new educative and cultural visions. The need for financial assistance most probably directed the Hermitage choices towards IBM and its influences leading to a subtle cybercolonization of the museum site as IBM met its economically-based objectives and the Hermitage seemingly received what it needed. The

Louvre on the other hand, led by a vision of openness, communication, and engagement embedding French culture within the development of the new website, made from its Paris-based home a site that engages on local and French national levels, and reaches out in a diverse, user-friendly, multilingual manner to engage those from around the globe. The Louvre website offers an example of the development of a museum site in the vein of cyberglocalization, providing an alternative to cybercolonizing influences and particularly so for less affluent national museums located in the Global South. The two case studies illuminate then, in tellingly different ways, the premise that information communications technology is a cultural construction, and it carries and generates cultural discourse related to its construction and place of application.

Conclusion: Global South Museum Web 2.0 Development

The Hermitage and Louvre Museum studies well illustrate that information communications technology holds the potential to change how a museum presents itself and the artifacts it houses online and subsequently the culture it embodies and represents (Bowers, 2000, 2001, 2006; Lessig, 2002; Marcus, 2002, 2006; Parekh, 2000). With the two historical case studies in place and an awareness of the ideological visions played out on the museum websites, in 2009 we face the question, in light of cybercolonial and cyberglocal influences, of how a Global South national museum might envision website development. This brings to the fore the importance of careful attention to ideological envisioning and website conceptualization by museums for web representation and presentation. In light of the two case studies and with a view towards the Global South, for example the continent of Africa and its various national museums, ideological visioning from a de-cybercolonizing viewpoint (Tuhiwai Smith, 1999; Mandani, 1996, 2005), taking into account local and global possibilities (Robertson, 1995, 2000), is key. These ideological considerations, rather than ones of overt or subtle colonization, guiding website design, artifact representation, and technological and electrical structural sustainability development, offer an approach that may enable non-Western museums possibilities to develop what they envision important to their culture. It is imperative in emergent Global South museum website development to attend to, as urged by Mamdani (1996, 2005), Marcus (2006), and Tuhiwai Smith (1999), the underlying assumptions about ICT and de-colonizing ideas, methodological approaches, models, interactions, and appearance in website conceptualization, development, and sustainability.

Before moving on to a discussion of Global South museum Web 2.0 and emergent Web 3.0 possibilities, the two Web categories need elaboration. Web 2.0 describes the current trend in World Wide Web technology and design which aims to enhance creativity, information sharing, and collaboration among users. These concepts have led to the development of web-based communities such as the social networking sites of Facebook, Second Life, Twitter, and YouTube as well as wikis and blogs. According to Tim O'Reilly (2006), "Web 2.0 is the business revolution in the computer industry caused by the move to the Internet, and an attempt to understand the rules for success on the new platform". It is about changes in the ways software developers and end-users adapt the Web. As Web 2.0 refers to current transformations in Web usage, Web 3.0 hypothesizes about a future wave in Internet innovation. Although there is much debate and variation of what Web 3.0 will be,

John Markoff of *The New York Times* coined the phrase in 2006. Markoff's Web 3.0 refers to a supposed third generation of Internet-based services that collectively comprise what might be called "the intelligent Web". It is envisioned as an era when machines start to do intelligent things (Markoff, 2006). Web 3.0 will include the semantic Web, microformats, natural language search, data-mining, machine learning, artificial intelligence technologies, and emphasize machine facilitated understanding of information to provide a more productive and intuitive user experience.

Recent data about four national museums websites on the website alexa.com alerts us to the need for new museum website development to move beyond Web 1.0 towards Web 2.0. The graph that follows is from the recognized internet traffic ranking website. Web traffic statistics are compiled for four museum websites: The Louvre Museum at http://www.louvre.fr/llv/commun/home.jsp?bmLocale=en, The State Hermitage Museum at http://www.hermitagemuseum.org, The National Gallery of Art (NGA), Washington, DC, at http://www.nga.gov, and the Royal Ontario Museum (ROM) at http://www.rom.on.ca. It captures web traffic comparables of the four museums from 2006-2008. The line graph illustrates a three year trend of "Daily Reach," which is described as the "Percent of global Internet users who visit [the noted] site". It is clear that the Louvre (blue line) and the NGA (yellow line) websites are more active compared to the Hermitage (red line) and ROM (turquoise line) websites. This appears to suggest an obvious relationship between superior web design and traffic on a website. However, through closer inspection, you will notice that there is a global trend of declining visits to both the Louvre and the NGA websites since 2006. Meanwhile, the Hermitage site has been relatively consistent in terms of traffic. It is also interesting to note that the Louvre and the NGA websites were re-introduced sometime during 2006, which suggests that the initial high traffic might be associated with hype, press releases, and advertising of the new websites. The decline in website hits regarding the four museums also corresponds with the rise of Web 2.0 which more interactively engages as participants contemporary web savvy users. Current Web 2.0 development, with an architecture of participation in which users generate, share, and curate content, may well facilitate museum 2.0 website conceptualizations (Yasko, 2007) and development for the Global South that can embrace the de-colonizing ideas of Tuhiwai Smith (1999) and Mamdani (2005) as well as underlying ICT assumptions of Marcus (2006). An awareness of de-colonizing and glocalizing ideas in conjunction with Web 2.0 offers rich possibilities for Global South museum website development, with museums probably free of old and out-dated communication philosophies that may now hamper famed Western museums in a movement towards Web 2.0.

In querying what a Web 2.0 museum website might look like, a few working definitions help clarify the terminology in play. Website "content" is what is being discussed, shared, shown, and explored. "Interaction" describes how the user(s) engages the site. "Network" is the interconnection of users. "Social benefit" delineates the value a user receives from the participation of other users. "Collective action" illuminates how much users work together. With a vocabulary of key components in place, what might a contemporary museum 2.0 website look like? A strong example, although from North America rather than the Global South, is the Brooklyn Museum in New York City located at http://www.brooklynmuseum. org/.

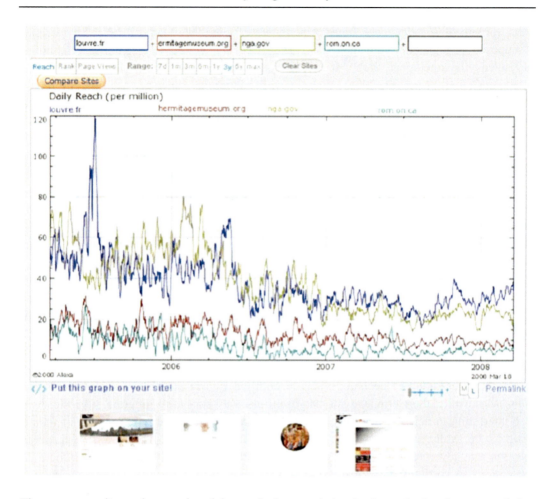

The museum site embraces the elaborated characteristics in its web development of the "Brooklyn Museum on Facebook" at http://www.brooklynmuseum.org/community/ blogosphere/bloggers/2007/11/08/artshare-on-facebook/, and the "YouTube Contest" at http://wwwbrooklynmuseum.org/community/wc/ with museum "Lessons Learned" from the YouTube competition at http://www.brooklynmuseum.org/community/blogosphere/bloggers/ 2007/11/07/video-competition-lessons-learned/ (Barazadi, 2008). The Brooklyn Museum's 2.0 website, moving towards Web 3.0 innovations, illuminates key stages to successful interactive Web projects: stimulate interest, engage, guide, communicate, educate, and create, as seen in its online social networking community on Facebook and its participatory YouTube contest. Both engage savvy, and often youthful, Web 2.0 users. The Brooklyn Museum site is not the older "point and click" Web 1.0 used by most museums. With this example in mind, and working with researched underlying assumptions of ICT and de-colonizing ideas delineated by Mamdani (2005), Marcus (2006), and Tuhiwai Smith (1999), museums of the Global South can move forward in website creation in which the website ideas and conceptualization capture what is of importance to the museum and the cultural artifacts it houses, employing its technological and sustainable capabilities. This is the challenge ahead.

References

Barazadi, L., (2008, March). *Architecture of participation: Museum and online communities.* Paper presented at the Digital Dimensions York University Seminar for Advanced Research, University of Toronto, Toronto.

Bolter, J., and Grusin, R. (1999). *Remediation: Understanding new media.* Cambridge, MA: MIT Press.

Bowers, C. (1988). *The cultural dimensions of educational computing: Understanding the non-neutrality of technology.* New York: Teachers College Press.

Bowers, C. (2000). *Let them eat data: How computers affect education, cultural diversity and the prospects of ecological sustainability.* Athens GA: University of Georgia Press.

Bowers, C. (2001, September 1). Culture clubbed: The social impact of technology. *CIO Magazine.* Retrieved August 9, 2009, from http://www.cio.com/archive/090101/diff.html

Bowers, C. (2006). *Revitalizing the commons: Cultural and educational sites of resistance and affirmation.* Lanham,. MD: Rowman and Littlefield.

Chesher, C. (1994). Colonizing virtual reality. Construction of the discourse of virtual reality, 1982–1992. *Cultronix, 1*(1). Retrieved August 24, 2009, from http://eserver.org/cultronix/chesher/

Creswell, J. (1998). *Qualitative inquiry and research design: Choosing among five traditions.* Thousand Oaks, CA: Sage Publications.

Ebo, B. (2001). *Cyberimperialism?: Global relations in the new electronic frontier.* Westport, CT: Praeger.

Fernandez, M. (1999). Postcolonial media theory. *Art Journal,* **58**(3), 58-73.

Franklin, U. (1999). *The real world of technology.* Toronto: Anansi Press.

Friedman, T. (2000). *The lexus and the olive tree: Understanding globalization.* New York: Anchor Books.

Glaser, B., and Strauss, A. (1967). *The discovery of grounded theory: Strategies for qualitative research.* Chicago: Aldine de Gruyter.

Gumbel, P. (2008, July 28). The Louvre Inc. *Time Magazine,* **172**(4), 34-38.

Hantrais, L., and Mangen, S. (1996). *Cross-national research methods in the social sciences.* New York: Pinter.

Lessig, L. (2002). *The future of ideas: The fate of the commons in a connected world.* New York: Vintage Books.

Mamdani, M. (1996). *Citizen and subject: Contemporary Africa and the legacy of late colonialism.* Princeton: Princeton University Press.

Mamdani, M. (2005, December). Political identity, citizenship and ethnicity in post-colonial Africa. Keynote address presented at the World Bank Conference on New Frontiers of Social Policy: Development in a Globalizing World, Arusha, Tanzania.

Marchart, O. (1998). The east, the west and the rest: Central and eastern Europe between techno-orientalism and the new electronic frontier. *Convergence: The Journal of Research into New Media Technologies,* **4**(2), 56-75.

Marcus, A. (2002). Globalization, localization, and cross-cultural communication in user-interface design. In J. Jacko, and A. Spears (Eds.), *Handbook of human-computer interaction* (pp. 441-463). New York: Lawrence Erlbaum Publishers.

Marcus, A. (2006). Culture: Wanted? Alive or dead? *Journal of Usability Studies,* **1**(2), 62-63.

Markoff, J. (2006, November 12). Entrepreneurs see a web guided by common sense. *The New York Times.* Retrieved August 24, 2009, from http://www.nytimes.com/11/12/business/12web.html?pagewanted=all

Morbey, M. L. (1996). Getting women wired: New connections in art and technology. *The Bridge: SIGGRAPH 96 Visual Proceedings,* 52-55.

Morbey, M. L. (Guest Ed.). (1998). Advancing neo-colonialism: Emerging theory and the changing work of art in the age of information technology. *Astrolabe: Ethical Navigations through Virtual Technologies,* 2-7. Retrieved August 24, 2009, from http://www.accad.ohio-state.edu/Astrolabe/journal/inaugural/inaugural.html

Morbey, M. L. (2000). Academic computing and beyond: New opportunities for women, minority populations, and the new media arts. *Convergence: The Journal of Research into New Media Technologies,* **6**(4), 54-77.

Morbey, M. L. (2003, October). Real and virtual spaces of world national musea. Paper presented at the Symposium on International Education and Globalization, York University, Toronto.

Morbey, M. L. (2006). Killing a culture softly: Corporate partnership with a Russian Museum. *Museum Management and Curatorship,* 21(4), 267-282.

Morbey, M. L., and Granger, C. (2002). Cybercolonialism in the State Hermitage Museum, St. Petersburg, Russia: Does it matter? *Proceedings of Electronic Imaging and the Visual Arts 2002 Moscow,* Russia, 45-52 (English version). Retrieved August 24, 2009, from http://www.evarussia.ru/eva2002/english/dok_652.html

Morley, D., and Robins, K. (1995). *Spaces of identity: Global media, electronic landscapes and cultural boundaries.* New York: Routledge.

Museum 2.0. Retrieved August 24, 2009, from http://museumtwo.blogspot.com/

O'Reilly, T. (2006). Web 2.0 compact definition: Trying again. Retrieved August 24, 2009, from http://radar.oreilly.com/archives/2006/12/web_20_compact.html

Parekh, B. (2000). *Rethinking multiculturalism: Cultural diversity and political theory.* Cambridge, MA: Harvard University Press.

Penley, C., and Ross, A. (Eds). (1991). *Technoculture.* Minneapolis: University of Minnesota Press.

Ragin, C. (1991). *Issues and alternatives in comparative social research.* Leiden: Brill.

Robertson, R. (1995). Glocalization: Time-space and homogeneity-heterogeneity. In M. Featherstone, S. Lash, and R. Robertson (Eds.), *Global modernities* (pp. 25-44). London: Sage Publications.

Robertson, R. (2000). Globalization and the future of "traditional religion". In M Stackhouse and P. Paris (Eds.), *Religion and the powers of common life* (pp. 53-69). Harrisburg, PA: Trinity Press International.

Said, E. (1978). *Orientalism.* London: Routledge and Kegan.

Said, E. (1994). *Culture and imperialism.* New York: Vintage.

Sardar, Z., and Ravetz, J. (Eds.). (1996). *Cyberfutures: Culture and politics on the information superhighway.* New York: New York University Press.

Seerveld. C. (2003, August). Glocal culture: Biblical vision and Christian mission within riven societies in God's world. Paper presented at the Symposium on Globalization, Doorn, The Netherlands.

Spradley, J. (1997). *The ethnographic interview.* Albany, NY: International Thomson Publishing.

Spradley, J. (1980). *Participant observation.* New York: Holt, Rinehart, and Winston.

Strauss, A., and Corbin, J. (1998). *Basics of qualitative research: Grounded theory procedures and techniques.* Thousand Oaks, CA: Sage Publications.

Tuhiwai Smith, L. (1999). *Decolonizing methodologies.* New York: Palgrave Macmillan.

Yasko, J. (2007). Museums and web 2.0. *Museum News,* **86**(4), 42-47, 72.

Yin, R. (2002). *Case study research: Design and methods.* Thousand Oaks, CA: Sage Publications.

Yow, V. (1994). *Recording oral history.* Thousand Oaks, CA: Sage Publications.

In: Handbook of Business and Finance
Editors: M. Bergmann and T. Faust, pp. 191-215

ISBN: 978-1-60692-855-4
© 2010 Nova Science Publishers, Inc.

Chapter 8

IS STAGED FINANCING DESIGNED FOR ALLEVIATING RISKS OR AGENCY PROBLEMS?[♦]

Lanfang Wang[1] and Susheng Wang[2,]*
[1] School of Accounting, Shanghai University of Finance and Economics,
Shanghai, China
[2] Department of Economics, Hong Kong University of Science and Technology,
Hong Kong, China

Abstract

Staged financing is very popular in reality, especially in venture capital financing. Over 90% of venture capital is invested through staged financing. Why is staged financing so popular? There are many theoretical studies that focus on two major issues of venture capital: risks and agency problems. These studies find that staged financing is capable of controlling both risks and agency problems. In other words, staged financing can potentially be used as an effective mechanism in dealing with both risks and agency problems. In fact, the emphasis in the literature has been on the resolution of agency problems. What happens in reality? Is staged financing in reality mainly a device for alleviating risks, for coping with agency problems or both? This is an important empirical question. Surprisingly, no one has ever conducted such an investigation. This paper reports on an empirical study of the issue. To our surprise, we find that staged financing is almost exclusively a device in alleviating risks in venture capital financing. More specifically, we find a lot of evidence supporting staged financing as a mechanism in alleviating risks but not in coping with agency problems.

JEL Classification: *G24, G31, G34*

Keywords: *Staged financing, Venture Capital, Incentives, Risks*

[♦] We gratefully acknowledge the support of a grant from the Shanghai Pujiang Program.
[*] E-mail address: wang.lanfang@mail.shufe.edu.cn, s.wang@ust.hk.

1. Introduction

Over the past two decades, the venture capital industry in the U.S. has experienced dramatic growth. The pool of U.S. venture capital funds grew from less than $1 billion in 1976 to over $250 billion in 2001. The percentage of venture capital backed IPOs was 50%, 34.6%, and 24.7% of all IPOs in 2000, 2001, and 2002, respectively (Gompers and Lerner 2004). Venture capital backed companies have created close to one-third of the total market value of all public companies in the United States.

Venture capital is predominantly used to finance startup enterprises with high growth potential and high risks. One dominant feature in venture capital financing is that almost every venture capitalist (VC) employs staged financing. With staged financing, VCs can stage the commitment of capital and preserve the option to abandon or to switch to equity. Staged financing allows VCs to monitor the firm before they make a refinancing decision. The information acquired through such monitoring helps VCs avoid throwing money at bad projects. It reduces losses from inefficient continuation and creates an exit option for VCs.

One key characteristic of many new startup companies in high-tech industries is the high risk due to the great uncertainty about returns, the lack of substantial tangible assets, the lack of a track record in operations, and possibly many years of negative earnings. According to Bergemann and Hege (1998), the fraction of such projects for which investors can successfully cash out, mostly through IPOs, is twenty percent or less. Given this situation, banks and other traditional intermediaries are reluctant to or even prohibited from lending money to such firms. Furthermore, these financial institutions usually lack expertise in investing in young and high-risk companies. Consequently, startups often seek involvement of VCs by offering various securities, principally convertible securities.

Another key characteristic of venture capital is the incentive problem of entrepreneurs (EN). Several agency problems may exist in such a joint venture. If cash flows are not completely verifiable, ENs may appropriate investments; if effort is not verifiable, ENs may shirk job responsibilities; also, if there are private benefits from continuing a project, ENs may keep the project going even if it has negative expected profits. By monitoring in stages and credibly threatening termination, VCs can have effective control over potential moral hazards. Besides staged financing, VCs can utilize the board of directors and the influence of major shareholders. Each new round of investment implies a change of the board composition and ownership structure. These mechanisms also have important monitoring power on the EN, since they can potentially block some plans by the EN and even dismiss the EN. Evidence shows a correlation of the timing of CEO turnover and an increase of the board representation of VCs (Gompers and Lerner, 2004).

There is a relatively small and recent literature on venture capital. Sahlman (1990) discusses various aspects of venture capital, in which the agency problem is emphasized. Sahlman focuses on legal definitions, organizational forms, and relationships among VCs, other investors and ENs. Admati and Perry (1991) consider a situation in which enforceable contracts are not possible and investments are sunk as soon as they are committed. In such a case, staged financing is used as a way to reduce the cost of commitment. Hellmann (1994) argues that staged financing triggers the EN's short-term behavior. To deal with this short-termism, the VC is allocated a larger share, which induces an incentive to monitor the EN. Gompers (1995) provides an empirical study on the factors affecting the structure of staged financing when moral hazard exists. He shows that, in financing high-risk companies with pervasive moral hazards, staged financing allows VCs to gather information and to monitor the progress of projects while maintaining the option to quit. Repullo and Suarez (1998) derive an optimal contract that resembles a convertible preferred stock in a model with double moral hazard and two-stage financing. Bergemann and Hege (1998) emphasize the learning of the true potential of a venture through staged financing. The effort input from the EN is not considered in their model, while an incentive condition for no stealing is considered. Neher (1999) studies staged financing in mitigating the EN's commitment problem in a model without risks and agency problems. By staging, early rounds of investment create collateral that protects the VC's claim from being renegotiated downward in the future. Kockesen and Ozerturk (2002) present the "real option" view of staged financing. They show that VCs do not use staged financing as a mechanism to mitigate agency problems. Instead, staged financing embodies a real option value. The initial financier's ability to provide further financing at less competitive terms than outsiders can is a key feature that sustains staging as a superior investment mechanism. Wang and Zhou (2004) show that staged financing can act as an effective complementary mechanism to contracting in controlling agency problems. With staged financing, many projects, which may otherwise be abandoned under upfront financing, become profitable. For highly promising enterprises, staged financing tends to the first-best solution. Cuny and Talmor (2005) emphasize milestone financing as opposed to staged financing. They show that four main factors affect the optimal contract and the choice of the financing method: EN effort, VC effort, VC's preference for liquid investments, and heterogeneous expectations about the feasibility of the underlying technology. Cases of the superiority of milestone financing over staged financing are characterized. However, Wang (2006) shows that milestone financing is actually an equilibrium phenomenon of staged financing. That is, staged financing can be carried out in milestones in equilibrium.

Empirical studies on staged financing are few. Besides Gompers (1995) whom we have mentioned above, Davila et al (2003) empirically study the roles that the first and follow-on rounds play in venture capital investment. The first round is to solve the cash-constrained problem and establish an agency relationship between the EN and VC. The follow-on rounds are intended to mitigate the agency costs associated with this relationship. Based on this idea, the paper utilizes a unique data set with employee-level and firm-level information to investigate the contributions of the first and follow-up rounds.

As the above literature review indicates, staged financing has been found in theory to be an effective device in dealing with both risks and agency problems. In fact, most theoretical studies focus on agency problems. What about empirical evidence? Is staged financing in reality mainly a device for alleviating risks, for coping with agency problems or both? This is an important empirical question. Surprisingly, no one has yet conducted such an investigation. This paper reports on an empirical study of this topic. We investigate sample data from 974 VC-backed companies that are mostly registered in the United States. We empirically examine various aspects of staged financing in venture capital financing, including its roles in alleviating risks and in coping with agency problems. To our surprise, we find that, after isolating its effects on expected performance, expected growth, size, and nature of technology, staged financing for these companies is almost exclusively a device for alleviating risks. In other words, our empirical study finds a lot of evidence for staged financing being used for alleviating risks but not for coping with agency problems.[1]

This paper proceeds as follows. In Section 2, we describe the factors affecting staged financing, particularly risk and agency factors. In Section 3, we present some stylized facts from the data. In Section 4, we present the hypotheses, the econometric model, and our regression results. Finally, we conclude the paper in Section 5 with a concluding summary.

2. Factors in Staged Financing

Staged financing means that a VC agrees to a total investment but invests portions of the total in stages. The VC has the option to abandon the project anytime without a penalty. Evidence shows that over 90% of all VC-backed firms are financed by staged financing. No matter which development stage the firm is in when a VC starts her investment, she generally invests in stages.

Staged financing can be implemented by milestone strategies and by various forms of convertible securities, debt, and equity. The key to staged financing is that a VC has the option to stop further investments at anytime. For example, if staged financing is implemented by a convertible security (in this case, staging is a phenomenon and the convertible security is the instrument), investment is made in the form of debt, but the VC has certain rights, including the right to convert her investment into equity at anytime.

Staged financing is believed to be used for and shown in theory to be capable of reducing risks and mitigating agency problems. It is an empirical question to see if indeed staged financing is a mechanism in handling both risks and agency problems or either. A key choice variable in staged financing is the initial investment. The choice of this variable may depend on the firm's risk situation and the severity of potential agency problems.

2.1. Risk Factors

Due to a large proportion of intangible asset, substantial RandD expenses, and the lack of steady cash flows, startups in high-tech industries are very risky. Such a firm has no history to examine and is difficult to evaluate. Hence, banks and other traditional intermediaries are reluctant to or even prohibited from lending money to such firms. However, VCs are specialized in investing in these firms. VCs look for high growth potential and they develop strategies to deal with risks. For example, to control risks, VCs tend to invest in stages. It makes sense that the more risky a firm is, the less the VC invests initially.

A firm has many characteristics to indicate its risk level. For example, a firm in an early stage (startup/seed and early stages) is riskier than a firm in a later stage (B/A, expansion and later stages). Also, the higher proportion of intangible assets, especially RandD expense, and the tighter cash constraints are, the riskier a firm is.

---

1 A lack of data on certain aspects of the companies may result in a limitation on our conclusion. For example, due to the lack of information on all VC-backed private companies (including those that disappear before IPO), we have to focus on VC-backed public companies (those that successfully complete IPO). Successful companies are only a small portion in each VC's portfolio, about 10%. However, unsuccessful companies are likely to be more risky than successful ones and hence staged financing is likely to be focused more on risks. In other words, including unsuccessful companies in our regressions is likely to strengthen our conclusion in this paper.

An investor's behavior can also reflect risks. For example, syndication can be an indication of risks. When two or more VCs invest jointly in a firm, we say that the investment is syndicated. It is typical that syndication happens even though one VC can afford the entire capital requirement. An EN in a startup will typically invite one VC to be the lead VC, who coordinates a syndicate and invites other VCs to join. Syndication can be an effective way to share risks; more participation by VCs means fewer risks for each VC. Theoretical and empirical studies both show that syndication is an important and effective means to reduce risks, especially in the initial round (Lerner 1994, Brander et al. 2002, and Lockett–Wright 2001). However, although syndication implies risk sharing, it also implies profit sharing. Hence, no more VCs will be invited to join if the risk has reached an acceptable level. Therefore, when many VCs are involved in a syndicate, it may be an indication of high risks. This is consistent with the fact that syndication is generally observed in an environment of high risks.

Further, from the point of project selection, when there is a large turnover of VCs (VCs come in and out often), it may mean less confidence among VCs, which may be an indication of high risks or fluctuating performances. After early stages of investment, if VCs are quite sure about the company's expected performance, VCs may not be willing to invite more investors to join due to the unwillingness to share profits. On the opposite, if VCs still feel much uncertainty, VCs may invite more investors to participate and are more willing to seek other VCs' opinions and willingness to be involved.

2.2. Agency Factors

Several agency problems may exist in such a joint venture. If cash flows are not completely verifiable, the EN may appropriate investments; if effort is not verifiable, the EN may shirk job responsibilities; also, if there are private benefits from continuing a project, the EN may keep the project going even if it is expected to have a negative return. Due to these agency problems, VCs typically actively involve in a project's development and act as an active monitor. By monitoring in stages and credibly threatening termination, the VCs may have effective control over potential moral hazards. The more serious the agency problems are, the less proportion of the total capital may be committed initially and the more rounds the investment may last.

There are many other means to control agency problems. For example, participation in the board of directors allows the VC to wield influence over and to monitor the firm's major business decisions. A board member's rights include veto rights, the right to vote on the EN's pay package, the right to dismiss the EN, and the right to call for a vote. Lerner (1994) shows that VCs increase their board representation when the need for monitoring is greater. Due to the special rights it entails, board representation is considered as a key agency-controlling instrument.

Further, the chairman of the board wields special power and influence, the chairmanship is considered in the literature as a key factor in controlling agency problems. With a VC chairman (the chairman is a VC rather than the EN), agency problems could be well under control.

Another important method of monitoring is through equity holding, especially a major shareholder (or minority block shareholders). Real control is enjoyed by a minority block owner who can persuade other owners, maybe a sufficient fraction of them to create a dissenting majority, of the need for intervention. Hence, major shareholders can play an important role in monitoring and watching out the firm's activities. If a firm has serious agency problems, the syndicate of VCs involved in the firm may intentionally have a large number of major VC shareholders as a way to control agency problems. In other words, agency problems can be better controlled in a company with a larger number of major VC shareholders, leading to a higher initial investment.

Equity sharing has been used extensively in venture capital financing. It is generally embodied in convertible securities, which have a form of contingent equity sharing. The VC can acquire the equity share when she converts her debt to equity. Equity ownership not only yields a share of revenue, but also a share of voting rights. It hence has direct implications on the firm's allocation of income and control rights.

Two key features are involved in convertibles: equity sharing and a contingent option. Wang–Zhou (2004) show that equity sharing can be an effective complementary mechanism to staged financing in handling risks and agency problems. Schmidt (2003) shows that the contingent feature is useful in achieving efficiency with sequential investments. From a different angle, with simultaneous investments, Wang (2006) shows that the contingent feature is particularly useful in achieving efficiency in an environment in which default and bankruptcy are real possibilities.

Further, if a company is found to be riskier than expected after early stages of investment, the VCs may change their equity holdings, some VCs may exit, and more VCs may be invited. Hence, VCs' turnovers and their equity holdings at different stages of investment are indicators of agency problems.

Finally, according to Baker–Gompers (2003), a successful VC-backed company is likely to have an optimal board composition and ownership structure at the time of IPO. Hence, our data on the board composition and ownership structure are collected at IPO.

2.3. Control Variables in Regressions

Besides risk and agency factors, there are a few other factors that may influence the decision on staged financing. We must control these factors in our investigation of the risk and agency factors. Specifically, in our regressions, we control the expected performance (return on assets or ROA), the expected growth prospective (market to book ratio), and the nature of technology (the total number of investment rounds from the beginning of a company to its IPO).

3. Data Description

Our data set comes from SDC VentureXpert, SEC EDGER, and COMPUSTAT. It covers more than 90% of all venture investment (Gompers–Lerner, 2004). All the publicly listed VC-backed companies are selected if they went public during 1997-2006. We exclude the investment by M/A venture capital funds, individual angels and "undisclosed venture capital funds". A sample of 974 companies was gathered. In sequence of IPO years, 116 companies completed IPOs in 1997, 72 companies in 1998, 252 companies in 1999, 254 companies in

2000, 35 companies in 2001, 19 companies in 2002, 27 companies in 2003, 91 companies in 2004, 53 companies in 2005, and 55 companies in 2006.

Most of these companies have filing records in SEC EDGAR since most of these companies are listed and have addresses in the United States. Specifically, 942 companies are listed on the NASDAQ market, 22 companies on the New York Stock Exchange, 9 companies on the American Stock Exchange, and only 2 companies on stock exchanges of other countries. Also, we collect information on board composition and equity ownership structure from their IPO prospectuses. We gather financial data from COMPUSTAT. Over 90% of the companies have complete data on board composition, equity ownership and financial records.

3.1. General Information

Our sample data contain information on investment and management for almost all the available VC-backed companies that successfully completed IPOs in recent years. In particular, the data contain company general information and information on investment, VC funds, board of directors and equity ownership. We describe some stylized facts in the data in this section.[2]

The 974 sample companies received a total of 3,794 rounds and 37,188.44 million dollars from VCs during the period from December 1, 1974 to September 29, 2006. On average, each company receives about 4 rounds of funding. There are 2608 VC funds (11446 person-times) participated in the 3,794 rounds. On average, about 7 VC funds participated in each company and about 3 VC funds involved in each round through syndication. The sample data include only VC investments before each company's IPO; investments after IPO are complicated due to many outside factors. Data include: 1) name of company; 2) founding date; 3) IPO date; 4) current status; 5) industry code; 6) total amount of VC investments; 7) amount of venture capital committed in each round; 8) identities of VCs in each round (investment focus, industry focus, etc.); 9) a firm's development stage when a round of investment occurs (seed, start-up, etc.); 10) security type (convertible security, debt, warrants, etc.).

Table 1 through Table 4 list general information on some key characteristics of VC financing. First, Table 1 summarizes information on the age and performance for the 974 companies by industry. Industry classification is based on Venture Economics Industry Code (VEIC) from VentureXpert. High technology includes information technology (IT) and medical/health/life science, in which the IT industry includes the communication sector, computer related sector and semiconductor/electronics firms, while the medical/health/life science industry includes the biotechnology sector and medical/health sector. The non-high technology industry includes the consumer related sector, the industry/energy sector, transportation sector, business services, manufacturing, the agriculture/forestry/fishing sector, construction sector, utilities, and others. The average company age is about 3 years old at the time of receiving the first round of funding and about 7 years old at the time of IPO. The average market to book ratio,[3] which is used to indicate the growth prospective, is close to 8

---

2 The sample sizes in different tables may vary due to some incomplete records.

3 It is the ratio of the current share price to the book value per share. It measures how much a company's worth at present, in comparison with the amount of capital invested by current and past shareholders.

even though the actual performance in the IPO year is often not good (most ROA and ROE are negative).

Table 1. Age and Performance by Industry[4]

Industry	Number of Companies	Age at IPO (Year)	Age at First Round (Year)	ROE (%)	ROA (%)	Market to Book Ratio
Communications	117	5.62	2.12	-17.80	-15.87	10.62
	(12)	(4.60)	(1.24)	(-14.44)	(-11.10)	(4.70)
Computer Hardware	38	7.70	3.68	-5.97	-5.23	5.97
	(3.9)	(5.66)	(2.68)	(-3.62)	(-3.26)	(4.13)
Computer Software	162	7.51	3.92	-19.64	-19.42	10.66
	(16.62)	(6.4)	(2.75)	(-9.89)	(-10.08)	(5.49)
Internet Specific	258	4.83	2.10	-24.71	-35.55	10.72
	(26.46)	(3.86)	(1.25)	(-26.01)	(-27.45)	(5.60)
Computer Other	1	6.28	1.58	-35.49	-180.14	.26
	(0.1)	(6.28)	(1.58)	(-35.49)	(-180.14)	(.260)
Semiconductor/Electronics	62	8.74	3.37	2.62	.79	5.99
	(6.36)	(7.54)	(1.87)	(6.95)	(4.96)	(3.92)
Biotechnology	114	7.16	2.14	-42.59	-33.81	4.45
	(11.69)	(5.76)	(1.08)	(-34.45)	(-30.20)	(3.85)
Medical/Health	124	9.29	4.20	-22.52	-16.68	3.99
	(12.72)	(7.03)	(1.34)	(-17.72)	(-16.68)	(3.45)
Consumer Related	40	12.92	8.40	14.18	5.97	4.65
	(4.1)	(9.54)	(2.55)	(11.32)	(9.22)	(3.49)
Industry/Energy	22	10.71	7.02	-43.23	-5.90	5.73
	(2.26)	(5.91)	(2.08)	(-3.54)	(-4.01)	(3.39)
Transportation	3	29.90	24.78	21.33	16.93	3.16
	(0.31)	(9.94)	(8.33)	(21.33)	(16.93)	(3.16)
Financial Services	19	11.45	7.89	-1.36	15.71	4.35
	(1.95)	(9.39)	(3.96)	(16.70)	(14.55)	(4.32)
Business Services	9	6.55	3.82	-10.38	-6.57	8.07
	(0.92)	(5.30)	(2.83)	(10.01)	(9.87)	(7.13)
Manufacturing	2	4.03	.02	-13.33	40.08	1.60
	(0.21)	(4.03)	(.02)	(-13.33)	(40.08)	(1.60)
Agriculture/Forestry/Fishing	1	15.90	14.68	154.5	46.75	11.20
	(0.1)	(15.90)	(14.68)	(154.5)	(46.75)	(11.20)
Other	2	3.45	.21	12.14	25.21	1.73
	(0.21)	(3.45)	(.21)	(12.14)	(25.21)	(1.73)
Total	974	7.26	3.38	-21.21	-21.10	7.96
	(100)	(5.48)	(1.52)	(-16.82)	(-16.10)	(4.20)

Table 2 shows information on VC investment by development stage, by industry, and by investing year in panels A to C, respectively. The whole investment period is from December 1974 to March 2006. We divide the investment period into 6 groups, that is, years 1974 to 1980, years 1981 to 1985, years 1986 to 1990, years 1991 to 1995, years 1996 to 2000, and years 2001 to 2006. The development stage at the time of investment is from VentureXpert. Development stages of a company can be classified into 6 categories: startup/seed stage, early

---

4 ROA is the return on assets in the IPO year and ROE is the return on equity in the IPO year. The numbers in parentheses are the percentages in the first column and the median numbers in the rest.

stage, M/A stage, expansion stage, later stage, and other. In Panel A, VCs show a clear preference for certain development stages. A VC's first round of investment in a company is more likely to happen in the startup/seed and early stages (over 60%), while a follow-on round is likely to happen in the expansion and later stages. Panel B indicates the general growth pattern of VC investments. Most investments are made after 1995 (around 90%), which is consistent with the growth pattern of venture capital all over the world. Panel C shows that most funding went to high-technology sectors, especially sectors in communications, computer software, internet specific, biotechnology, and medical/health (over 60%). All these distributions are consistent with what have been reported in the literature (Gompers–Lerner 2004 and Sahlman 1990).

Table 2. VC Investments by Stage, Investing Year, Industry and IPO year[5]

	Panel A: Venture Capital Investment by Stage of Development			
Stage of Development	Number of Participating Funds (Person-times)	Amount of Investment ($mil)	Number of Rounds	Number of First Round
Startup/Seed	769 (6.72)	1445.82 (3.89)	331 (8.72)	221 (22.69)
Early Stage	1733 (15.14)	3968.31 (10.67)	701 (18.48)	376 (38.6)
Buyout/Acquisition	237 (2.07)	1448.53 (3.90)	112 (2.95)	29 (2.98)
Expansion	4827 (42.17)	16339.18 (43.94)	1488 (39.22)	274 (28.13)
Later Stage	3045 (26.6)	10154.48 (27.31)	747 (19.69)	51 (5.24)
Other	835 (7.30)	3832.11 (10.30)	415 (10.94)	23 (2.36)
Total	11446 (100)	37188.44 (100)	3794 (100)	974 (100)
	Panel B: Venture Capital Investments by Investing Year			
1974-1980	12 (0.1)	5.33 (.01)	5 (0.13)	
1981-1985	136 (1.19)	61.76 (.17)	39 (1.03)	
1986-1990	389 (3.40)	226.26 (.59)	127 (3.35)	
1991-1995	1329 (11.61)	2628.65 (7.00)	524 (13.81)	
1996-2000	7387 (64.54)	24897.92 (65.65)	2428 (63.70)	
2001-2006	2193 (19.16)	9368.53 (24.89)	671 (17.68)	
Total	11446 (100)	37188.44 (100)	3794 (100)	

---

5 The numbers in parentheses are percentages.

Table 2. Continued

Panel C: Venture Capital Investments by Industry

Communications	1567 (13.69)	5801.57 (15.60)	500 (13.18)
Computer Hardware	372 (3.25)	990.46 (2.66)	124 (3.27)
Computer Software	1756 (15.34)	4586.49 (12.33)	645 (17)
Internet Specific	2751 (24.03)	10023.68 (26.95)	934 (24.62)
Computer Other	22 (0.19)	45.53 (0.12)	4 (0.11)
Semiconductor/Electron ics	732 (6.40)	2663.67 (7.16)	231 (6.09)
Biotechnology	2004 (17.51)	5755.43 (15.48)	543 (14.31)
Medical/Health	1678 (14.66)	4133.56 (11.11)	543 (14.31)
Consumer Related	225 (1.97)	1279.51 (3.44)	119 (3.14)
Industry/Energy	188 (1.64)	557.88 (1.5)	68 (1.79)
Transportation	11 (0.1)	40.47 (0.11)	7 (0.18)
Financial Services	59 (0.52)	695.56 (1.87)	33 (0.87)
Business Services	41 (0.36)	232.89 (.63)	23 (0.61)
Manufacturing	15 (0.13)	188.91 (0.51)	10 (0.26)
Agriculture/Forestry/Fis hing	2 (0.02)	59.61 (0.16)	2 (0.05)
Other	23 (0.2)	133.22 (0.36)	8 (0.21)
Total	11446 (100)	37188.44 (100)	3794 (100)

Our sample data show strong evidence of staged financing. In total, only 31 companies (3.2%) receive upfront financing. Panel C of Table 2 shows the number of investment rounds occurred in each sector. If we divide them by the number of companies (shown in first column of Table 1), we find that each company receives about 4 rounds on average and there is not much difference among industry sectors.

Syndication is a widely observed phenomenon for the purpose of risk sharing. In total, only 103 companies (about 10%) receive all funding from one single VC fund and 1,334 rounds (about 35%) are made by one singe VC fund. Since we exclude M/A funds, individual angels and undisclosed VC funds, the actual degree of syndication should be much greater.[6]

---

6 We distinguish between a VC firm and a VC fund. A VC firm typically manages several VC funds. Several VC funds from a VC firm may separately invest in the same company.

As shown in Table 2, by dividing the numbers in column 1 by the numbers in column 3, we can find the average number of VC funds participated in each round. Clearly, syndication is widely observed in the sample companies. On average, three VC funds participate in each round.

Table 3. VC funds by Investment Focus[7]

Investment Focus	Number of VC Funds	Amount of investment ($mil)	Average Number of Funded Companies	Average Number of Participating Rounds
Seed Stage	79	16136.49	1.77	1.90
	(3.02)	(43.39)	(1)	(1)
Development Stage	7	26.12	1.43	1.14
	(.27)	(0.07)	(1)	(1)
Early Stage	870	9856.13	2.43	1.73
	(33.36)	(26.50)	(1)	(1)
Balanced Stage	1072	3384.10	2.74	1.60
	(41.1)	(9.10)	(1)	(1)
Expansion Stage	264	7366.10	2.18	1.44
	(10.12)	(19.81)	(1)	(1)
Later Stage	316	419.49	3.18	1.40
	(12.12)	(1.13)	(2)	(1)
Total	2608	37188.44	2.6	1.69
	(100)	(100)	(1)	(1)

Each VC fund tends to have a preference to invest in a company when the company is at a certain development stage.

Our sample data show strong evidence of staged financing. In total, only 31 companies (3.2%) receive upfront financing. Panel C of Table 2 shows the number of investment rounds occurred in each sector. If we divide them by the number of companies (shown in first column of Table 1), we find that each company receives about 4 rounds on average and there is not much difference among industry sectors.

Syndication is a widely observed phenomenon for the purpose of risk sharing. In total, only 103 companies (about 10%) receive all funding from one single VC fund and 1,334 rounds (about 35%) are made by one singe VC fund. Since we exclude M/A funds, individual angels and undisclosed VC funds, the actual degree of syndication should be much greater. As shown in Table 2, by dividing the numbers in column 1 by the numbers in column 3, we can find the average number of VC funds participated in each round. Clearly, syndication is widely observed in the sample companies. On average, three VC funds participate in each round.

Table 3 shows the information on VC funds' participation by their investment preferences, including seed stage, development stage, early stage, balanced stage, expansion stage, and later stage. As shown in

Our sample data show strong evidence of staged financing. In total, only 31 companies (3.2%) receive upfront financing. Panel C of Table 2 shows the number of investment rounds occurred in each sector. If we divide them by the number of companies (shown in first

---

7 The numbers in parentheses in the first two columns are percentages and in other two columns are median numbers.

column of Table 1), we find that each company receives about 4 rounds on average and there is not much difference among industry sectors.

Syndication is a widely observed phenomenon for the purpose of risk sharing. In total, only 103 companies (about 10%) receive all funding from one single VC fund and 1,334 rounds (about 35%) are made by one singe VC fund. Since we exclude M/A funds, individual angels and undisclosed VC funds, the actual degree of syndication should be much greater. As shown in Table 2, by dividing the numbers in column 1 by the numbers in column 3, we can find the average number of VC funds participated in each round. Clearly, syndication is widely observed in the sample companies. On average, three VC funds participate in each round.

Table 3, each fund on average participates in 1.7 rounds and 2.6 companies.

Table 4. Security Types by Industry[8]

Industry	Convertible Security (%)	Common Stock (%)	Debt (%)	Other (%)
Communications	87.95	7.26	1.61	3.17
	(100)	(0)	(0)	(0)
Computer Hardware	79.55	4.70	5.04	10.70
	(100)	(0)	(0)	(0)
Computer Software	88.66	4.09	4.01	2.60
	(100)	(0)	(0)	(0)
Internet Specific	90.80	4.63	1.86	2.71
	(100)	(0)	(0)	(0)
Computer Other	100	0	0	0
	(100)	(0)	(0)	(0)
Semiconductor/Electronics	93.46	0.89	0.81	3.22
	(100)	(0)	(0)	(0)
Biotechnology	90.21	7.02	1.56	1.13
	(100)	(0)	(0)	(0)
Medical/Health	85.75	7.46	1.78	5.00
	(100)	(0)	(0)	(0)
Consumer Related	82.51	7.68	3.22	6.60
	(100)	(0)	(0)	(0)
Industry/Energy	71.47	4.54	9.83	9.62
	(100)	(0)	(0)	(0)
Transportation	100	0	0	0
	(100)	(0)	(0)	(0)
Financial Services	73.64	5.26	0	5.30
	(100)	(0)	(0)	(0)
Business Services	88.89	0	0	11.11
	(100)	(0)	(0)	(0)
Manufacturing	56.89	2.24	40.88	0
	(56.89)	(2.24)	(40.88)	(0)

---

8 All the numbers are in percentage. The median numbers are in parentheses.

Table 4. Continued

Industry	Convertible Security (%)	Common Stock (%)	Debt (%)	Other (%)
Agriculture/Forestry/Fishing	0.45 (0.45)	0 (0)	0 (0)	99.55 (99.55)
Other	94.54 (94.54)	1.15 (1.15)	0 (0)	4.31 (4.31)
Total	87.88 (100)	5.32 (0)	2.45 (0)	3.73 (0)

Table 5. Board Composition by Industry[9]

Industry	Average Board Size	Average Number of Executive Directors	Average Number of VC Directors	Number of Companies with a VC Chairman
Communications	6.88 (7)	3.66 (1)	2.09 (2)	11 (9.82)
Computer Hardware	6.16 (6)	1.66 (2)	1.71 (2)	3 (7.89)
Computer Software	6.78 (6)	1.63 (2)	2.02 (2)	10 (6.58)
Internet Specific	6.73 (7)	1.51 (1)	2.18 (2)	17 (6.94)
Computer Other	8 (8)	1 (1)	5 (5)	1 (100)
Semiconductor/Electronics	6.27 (6)	1.5 (1)	1.37 (1)	6 (10)
Biotechnology	7.5 (8)	1.42 (1)	2.48 (2)	27 (25)
Medical/Health	6.87 (7)	1.44 (1)	2.07 (2)	24 (19.35)
Consumer Related	7.03 (7)	1.62 (2)	1.35 (1)	1 (2.70)
Industry/Energy	6.79 (7)	1.58 (1)	1.47 (1)	2 (10.53)
Transportation	7.33 (6)	2 (2)	1.67 (2)	0 (0.00)
Financial Services	7.61 (8.5)	2.17 (2)	0.94 (1)	0 (0.00)
Business Services	6.44 (6)	1.22 (1)	2 (2)	0 (0.00)
Manufacturing	5.5 (5.5)	2 (2)	2 (2)	0 (0.00)
Agriculture/Forestry/Fishing	6 (6)	2 (2)	0 (0)	0 (0.00)
Other	6 (6)	2 (2)	1 (1)	0 (0.00)
Total	6.84 (7)	1.79 (1)	2.02 (2)	102 (10.96)

9 The numbers in parentheses of the first three columns are the medians and that of the last column are the percentages.

VCs can also be distinguished by their choices of investment instruments or security types. The security types can be divided into 4 major categories: convertible security, common stock, debt, and other. VCs mainly choose convertible securities (around 88%). Table 4 lists the distribution of security types used by VCs by industry.

VCs can also be distinguished by their choices of investment instruments or security types. The security types can be divided into 4 major categories: convertible security, common stock, debt, and other. VCs mainly choose convertible securities (around 88%). Table 4 lists the distribution of security types used by VCs by industry.

Table 6. Equity Ownership by Industry[10]

Industry	Equity Owned by VCs (%)		Equity Owned by EN (%)		Number of major VC Stockholders		
	Just Prior IPO	Just After IPO	Just Prior IPO	Just After IPO	Over 10%	Over15%	Over 20%
Communications	38.95	31.2	19.83	15.64	1.59	0.8	0.39
	(40.2)	(32)	(13.60)	(10.91)	(1)	(1)	(0)
Computer Hardware	36.03	26.73	24.35	18.58	1.37	0.82	0.45
	(33.40)	(25.50)	(15.50)	(11.65)	(1)	(1)	(0)
Computer Software	40.08	31.04	26.11	19.89	1.6	0.85	0.48
	(38.29)	(28.96)	(19.95)	(15.40)	(1)	(1)	(0)
Internet Specific	20.59	30.45	22.00	16.94	1.54	0.88	0.49
	(36.80)	(28.50)	(16.40)	(13.29)	(1)	(1)	(0)
Computer Other	57.10	47.60	3.90	2.40	3	0	0
	(57.10)	(47.60)	(3.90)	(2.40)	(3)	(0)	(0)
Semiconductor/Electronics	29.31	22.31	25.51	19.28	1.05	0.56	0.29
	(23.40)	(18.11)	(17.62)	(13.85)	(1)	(0)	(0)
Biotechnology	43.97	32.01	11.56	8.53	1.83	0.84	0.42
	(43.10)	(31.60)	(6.90)	(4.75)	(2)	(1)	(0)
Medical/Health	24.52	32.79	15.45	11.68	1.63	0.96	0.53
	(40.70)	(31.30)	(10.08)	(7.25)	(1)	(1)	(0)
Consumer Related	28.65	19.73	25.64	17.142	0.86	0.49	0.29
	(27.95)	(19.58)	(24.20)	(13.52)	(1)	(0)	(0)
Industry/Energy	21.57	15.03	20.06	12.75	0.71	0.29	0.17
	(16.15)	(11)	(8.30)	(5.50)	(1)	(0)	(0)
Transportation	27.90	17.00	26.80	18.23	1	1	1
	(29.30)	(17.40)	(21.90)	(11.30)	(1)	(1)	(0)
Financial Services	23.79	12.75	32.03	24.17	0.89	0.61	0.22
	(19.63)	(14.25)	(23.94)	(15.20)	(1)	(0.5)	(0)
Business Services	43.72	31.73	24.06	17.79	1.22	1.22	0.89
	(36.60)	(28.10)	(17.60)	(13.40)	(1)	(1)	(1)
Manufacturing	60.85	48.35	3.2	2.8	1	1	1
	(60.85)	(48.35)	(3.2)	(2.8)	(1)	(1)	(1)
Agriculture/Forestry/Fishing			13.2	6.60	0	0	0
			(13.2)	(6.60)	(0)	(0)	(0)
Other	42.90	23.50	9.29	5.77	0.50	0.50	0.5
	(42.90)	(23.50)	(9.29)	(5.77)	(0.50)	(0.50)	(0.50)
Total	38.81	29.50	20.96	15.86	1.49	0.82	0.44
	(36.9)	(27.6)	(14.7)	(10.75)	(1)	(1)	(0)

10 The numbers in parentheses are the medians.

The above tables provide some general information on VC investments. Generally speaking, VC funds tend to focus on high-risk startup companies with a good expected growth prospective. VC funds tend to choose convertible securities as investment instruments. Staged financing is widely observed and syndication is popular.

Table 7. Initial Investment Proportion by Development Stage

Development Stage	Mean	Median	S.D
Startup/Seed	9.69	3.70	17.03
Early Stage	14.18	6.58	18.44
Buyout/Acquisition	36.08	23.84	33.91
Expansion	31.96	17.5	32.02
Later Stage	33.53	24.05	30.66
Other	18.16	0.80	29.46
Total	19.90	8.32	26.04

3.2. Investor Involvement

We now turn attention to VCs' active involvement in a company. Investing in a high-risk company requires a set of involvement, not just a financing strategy. A VC may need to be involved in the board, exercise her voting rights, coordinate with other VCs in a syndicate, and design her investment in stages. Table 5 and Table 6 provide information on board composition and ownership structure at IPO. The information includes: (1) each director's name, position, age and education, (2) whether the director is appointed by or related to VCs (called a VC director), (3) whether a director is an executive (called an executive director), and (4) equity shares owned by VCs and the EN.

Table 5 summarizes information on the board of directors by industry. The number and positions of VC directors are a consequence of bargaining between the EN and VCs. Table 5 indicates that VCs hold about 30% of the seats in the board and about 10% of the chairmanship of the board.

Table 6 shows information on equity ownership structure by industry around IPO. On average, VCs hold about 40% of a company's equity just before IPO and down to about 30% just after IPO, while the EN holds about 20% just before IPO and down to about 16% just after IPO. A major VC shareholder may be defined to be one who owns over 10% or 15% of a company's equity. Table 6 shows that a company on average has 1.5, 0.8 and 0.4 major shareholders who own over 10%, 15% and 20% of equity, respectively.

Finally, Table 7 shows the initial investment proportions by the companies' development stages. This proportion is on average about 20% of a VC's total investment in a company. When investing in a company in early stages of development (startup/seed and early stages), a VC tends to choose a lower initial investment proportion (mostly less than 10%). When investing a company in later stages of development (M/A, expansion and later stages), a VC tends to choose a higher initial investment proportion (mostly greater than 20%). The variation of the initial investment proportion is quite large (about 26), and even larger for later stages (over 30).

4. Regression Analysis

4.1. The Regression Model

The initial investment is the first investment that a VC offers to a company. We choose the VC's initial investment proportion (the initial investment as a proportion of the VC's total investment) as the variable representing staged financing. This is consistent with most theoretical models on staged financing. This proportion is the dependent variable in our model.

We test two hypotheses on the determination of the initial decision. First, when faced with risks, a VC may reduce early commitments in an attempt to control her risk exposure. That is, staged financing can be used to control risks.

Hypothesis 1. Staged financing is used to control risks.

To put pressure on the EN to expend more effort, a VC may withhold some investments until she sees good results. In other words, staged financing can be used as a mechanism to deal with agency problems. Hence, we expect the initial investment to be negatively related to the possibility of agency problems.[11]

Hypothesis 2. Staged financing is used to deal with agency problems.

The initial investment proportion is run against three sets of independent variables, including risk factors, agency factors, and control variables. The control variables are used to control some other factors that may affect the initial decision, such as the expected performance. That is, our regression model is

$$\text{Initial Investment Ratio} = \beta_0 + \beta_1 (\text{risk factors}) + \beta_2 (\text{agency factors})$$
$$+ \beta_3 (\text{control variables}) + \varepsilon,$$

where ε is the error term and the β_i's are parameters.

Table 8 lists the three sets of independent variables, including risk factors, agency factors, and control variables. Risk factors include the company age when a VC starts to invest in the company (the first round), whether or not a VC's first round of investment occurs in an early stage of a company's development, the number of VC funds participating in the first round (syndication at the first round), the number of VC funds involved in the whole investment period from the beginning of the company to IPO, the ratio of intangible assets to total assets, the ratio of RandD expense to total assets, and the ratio of cash and equivalents to total assets. The justification for the choice of these variables is as follows. The younger a company is, the more risky it is. Risks can be reflected by asset intangibilities, cash constraints and

---

11 Agency problems may or may not exist in equilibrium. Hence, our task is to identify the statistical relationship between the initial investment and the possibility of agency problems, rather than the relationship between the initial investment and the severity of agency problems. The same logic applies to risk factors as well.

syndication. The higher ratio of intangible assets to total assets or sales, especially the higher ratio of RandD expense to total asset or sales, the more risky it is. The greater cash constraints are (the smaller ratio of cash and equivalents to the total assets or sales), the more risky the firm is. The more participating VCs in the initial round, the less risky it is for each VC. Finally, fewer VCs involved in the whole investment period means less VC turnovers, implying confidence of participating VCs to stay with the company and hence an indication of less risk. Hence, the fewer VCs involved in the whole investment period, the less risky the firm is.

Agency variables (those variables used to control agency problems) consist mainly of board representation and major shareholders. Board representation and equity sharing are considered in the literature as two major mechanisms in dealing with agency problems. The chairman of the board is considered to possess special power and influence. Major shareholders have an interest to watch over the EN and to be actively involved in decision making and management of a company. We use a dummy variable to represent whether or not the chairman is a VC director and another three variables to represent the number of major VC shareholders. A VC chairman and a higher number of major VC shareholders mean that the VCs have more control rights and monitoring power over the company, implying a lower degree of agency problems.

Table 8. Independent Variables[12]

Type of Variable	Independent Variable
Risk Factors	Company age at the first round of investment
	Whether the first investment round occurred in early stages*
	Number of VC funds in the first round
	Number of VC funds involved in the whole investment period
	Ratio of intangible assets to total assets
	Ratio of RandD expense to total assets
	Ratio of cash and equivalents to total assets
Agency Factors	Whether or not the chairman of the board is a VC*
	Number of major VC shareholders (1) (those who owns over 10% of equity)
	Number of major VC shareholders (2) those who owns over 15% of equity)
	Number of major VC shareholders (3) (those who owns over 20% of equity)
Control Variables	Market to book ratio (for expected growth prospective)
	ROA (return on asset, for expected performance)
	Number of investment rounds

---

12 A star * here represents a dummy variable. When a VC starts to invest in a company, the company may have been in existence for a number of years. The "company age at the first round" is the company age when a VC offers the first installment. "Whether the first round occurred in early stages" indicates the occurrence in the company's startup/seed stage or early stage. The "number of VC funds in the first round" means the number of VCs who invest together in the first round. The "number of VC funds involved in the whole investment period" is the total number of VCs that have ever involved in the company from the company's startup to IPO. The "number of investment rounds" means the total number of rounds received from all VCs up to IPO.

In our regressions, we control three factors: the expected performance, the expected growth prospective and the total number of rounds[13]. The initial investment proportion is expected to be positively related to the expected performance and expected growth. We use the ROA (return on assets) and the market to book ratio in the IPO year to indicate the expected performance and expected growth, respectively. In addition, the total number of investment rounds is another control variable, which is related to the nature of business. Hence, we expect it to be negatively related to the initial investment proportion.

Table 9. Regressions on Risk and Agency Factors Separately[14]

Panel A: Regressions on Risk Factors				
	1	2	3	4
Control Variables:				
ROA	7.19 [4.03***]	8.42 [4.72***]	8.44 [4.54***]	7.57 [4.18***]
Market to book ratio	0.082 [1.77*]	0.047 [1.45]	0.044 [1.28]	0.080 [1.75*]
Number of investment rounds	-2.57 [-6.05***]	-2.69 [-6.70***]	-2.74 [-6.71***]	-2.53 [-5.91***]
Risk Factors:				
Company age at first investment round	0.001 [1.96**]	0.001 [1.89*]	0.001 [1.93*]	0.001 [2.00**]
Whether first investment round occurs in early stages*	-8.97 [-4.86***]	-10.02 [-5.72***]	-10.07 [-5.75***]	-8.94 [-4.80***]
Number of VCs participating in the first investment round	3.25 [5.72***]	3.00 [5.65***]	2.90 [5.46***]	3.20 [5.59***]
Number of VCs participating in the whole investment period	-0.97 [-6.43***]	-0.99 [-6.71***]	-1.00 [-6.59***]	-0.99 [-6.49***]
Ratio of RandD expense to total assets	-2.72 [-2.32**]			-2.60 [-1.96**]
Ratio of cash and equivalents to total assets		2.44 [1.87*]		1.28 [0.90]
Ratio of intangible assets to total assets			-9.04 [-1.52]	-12.39 [-1.58]
Constant	35.85 [12.07***]	37.16 [13.38***]	38.42 [13.64***]	36.28 [11.47***]
Number of Observations	650	745	735	642
R^2	37.91	37.08	36.97	38.09

---

13 Here, we have no need to have a variable for company size, since the variable for expected performance has already included the effect of company size (total assets).

14 The numbers in the square brackets are the t-values. The symbols *, ** and *** denote significance at the 10%, 5% and 1% level (two-sided), respectively.

Table 9. Continued

Panel B: Regressions on Agency Factors				
	5	6	7	8
Control Variables:				
Return on Assets	9.73 [4.07***]	9.39 [4.01***]	9.64 [4.04***]	9.58 [3.99***]
Market to Book Ratio	0.062 [1.83*]	0.060 [1.72*]	0.061 [1.81*]	0.063 [1.85*]
Number of investment rounds	-4.91 [-10.64***]	-4.79 [-10.01***]	-4.91 [-10.41***]	-4.92 [-10.52***]
Agency Factors:				
Whether the chairman of board is a VC	-2.12 [-1.28]	-1.60 [-0.95]	-2.12 [-1.26]	-2.22 [-1.29]
Number of Major VC shareholders (1)		-0.84 [0.28]		
Number of Major VC shareholders (2)			0.42 [0.41]	
Number of Major VC shareholders (3)				1.22 [0.83]
Constant	41.05 [17.17***]	41.73 [16.51***]	40.77 [16.40***]	40.58 [16.50***]
Number of Observations	606	595	595	595
R^2	27.98	27.99	27.89	27.96

4.2. Regression Results

To test the effect of risk and agency factors on the decision of staged financing (the initial investment proportion), we first run regressions on risk and agency factors separately. The regression results are listed separately in Panel A and Panel B of Table 9.

VCs are expected to invest more initially if they expect a better performance (ROA), better growth prospective (market to book ratio), and fewer investment rounds. These factors are controlled in our regressions. The regression results in Table 9 are largely consistent with these expected correlations, except that the market to book ratio is not very significant.

Panel A of Table 9 shows a strong and significant negative relationship between the initial investment and the risk factors. Specifically, we have the following observations:

- VCs invest less initially if the firm is young. A young firm is considered risky.
- VCs invest less initially if the firm is in an early stage of development. A firm in its early stages is considered very risky.
- More is invested initially when more VCs are involved in the first round. This is due to risk sharing among the VCs.
- Less is invested initially when more VCs are involved in the whole investment period. This is due to project selection. Typically, the participating VCs form a

syndicate with a lead VC as the coordinator. After the initial investment, if the company is considered less risky, fewer VCs will be invited due to the unwillingness to share profits; if the company is considered quite risky, to share risks, the lead VC tends to invite more investors to join the syndicate. A large syndicate means less risk for each, but it also means a smaller profit share for each. Due to the unwillingness to share profits, a risky company is likely to remain more risky than an average company even with a larger syndicate of VCs. Hence, a large syndicate indicates a risky company as well as high risk for each VC.

- As shown in regressions 1–3, less is invested initially when a company has more intangible assets, more RandD expense, and more cash constrains. Regression 4 suggests that the ratio of RandD expense to total assets is the most significant variable among the three asset ratios.

Hence, our regression results show strong evidence in support of Hypothesis 1.

Panel B of Table 9 shows the regression results on agency factors. We have the following observations:

- There is no significant relationship between the initial investment and the agency factors.
- The R^2 is substantially lower than that in Panel A. This indicates that the risk factors explain much more about the use of staged financing than the agency factors.

Hence, the evidence shows no support for Hypothesis 2.

In Table 10, we include both risk and agency factors together in a regression. We want to see the relative importance of these factors on the decision of staged financing.

Table 10. Regressions on Risk and Agency Factors Together

	1	2	3	4
Control Variables:				
ROA	5.87	7.00	6.96	6.87
	[2.90***]	[3.92***]	[3.91***]	[3.85***]
Market to Book Ratio	0.083	0.084	0.083	0.085
	[1.80*]	[1.86*]	[1.79*]	[1.82*]
Number of investment rounds	-2.70	-2.58	-2.61	-2.64
	[-5.28***]	[-5.87***]	[-5.88***]	[-5.94***]
Risk Factors:				
Company age at first investment round	0.002	0.0011	0.0011	0.0011
	[2.62***]	[1.87*]	[1.88*]	[1.84*]
Whether first investment round occurs in early stages	-8.80	-8.84	-8.96	-9.05
	[-4.26***]	[-4.65***]	[-4.73***]	[-4.80***]
Number of VCs participating in the first investment round	3.19	3.35	3.35	3.36
	[5.13***]	[5.70***]	[5.72***]	[5.72***]
Number of VCs participating in the whole investment period	-0.92	-0.99	-0.97	-0.95
	[-5.18***]	[-6.16***]	[-6.21***]	[-6.02]
Ratio of RandD expense to total assets	-3.21	-3.09	-3.10	-3.16
	[-2.48**]	[-2.62***]	[-2.64***]	[-2.68]

Table 10. Continued

	1	2	3	4
Agency Factors:				
Whether the chairman of board is a VC	0.40 [0.26]			
Number of Major VC shareholders (1)		0.30 [0.44]		
Number of Major VC shareholders (2)			1.00 [1.16]	
Number of Major VC shareholders (3)				2.11 [1.60]
Constant	35.37 [10.13***]	34.52 [11.38***]	34.21 [11.47***]	35.12 [1.58***]
Number of Observations	529	615	615	615
R^2	38.07	37.54	37.63	37.80

	5	6	7
Control Variables:			
ROA	6.06 [2.93***]	6.04 [2.95***]	5.92 [2.86***]
Market to Book Ratio	0.084 [1.83*]	0.081 [1.72*]	0.084 [1.76*]
Number of investment rounds	-2.72 [-5.20***]	-2.75 [-5.21***]	-2.77 [-5.28***]
Risk Factors:			
Company age at first investment round	0.002 [2.62***]	0.002 [2.68***]	0.002 [2.67***]
Whether first investment round occurs in early stages	-8.96 [-4.30***]	-9.08 [-4.37***]	-9.15 [-4.42***]
Number of VCs participating in the first investment round	3.23 [5.14***]	3.22 [5.12***]	3.25 [5.13***]
Number of VCs participating in the whole investment period	-0.95 [-4.95***]	-0.91 [-4.98***]	-0.89 [-4.78***]
Ratio of RandD expense to total assets	-3.23 [-2.39**]	-3.22 [-2.39**]	-3.31 [-2.46**]
Agency Factors:			
Whether the chairman of board is a VC	0.33 [0.21]	0.21 [0.13]	0.12 [0.08]
Number of Major VC shareholders (1)	0.50 [0.62]		
Number of Major VC shareholders (2)		1.33 [1.33]	
Number of Major VC shareholders (3)			2.31 [1.59]

Table 10. Continued.

	5	6	7
Constant	35.00 [9.84***]	34.66 [9.93***]	34.60 [10.02***]
Number of Observations	524	524	524
R^2	38.03	38.16	38.29

We have the following observations from Table 10:

- There is still a strong negative and significant relationship between the initial investment and the risk factors (mostly at 1% level). This significance is not reduced after the agency factors are included.[15] Hence, the evidence offers a strong support for Hypothesis 1.
- For the agency factors, all the signs in the regressions of Table 10 are consistent with Hypothesis 2. In particular, since less initial investment can put pressure on the company to perform, the initial investment proportion should be negatively associated with the degree of agency problems. A greater control, such as having a VC board chairman and more major shareholders, should lead to fewer agency problems. Hence, a greater control should be associated with a higher initial investment. However, in our regressions, there are no significant relationships between the initial investment proportion and the agency factors. Further, the R^2 increases only slightly in comparison with Panel A of Table 9 after the agency variables are added, indicating that the agency factors explain little about the use of staged financing. Hence, the evidence again offers little support for Hypothesis 2.

Note that, although the evidence shows no support for staged financing to be used in dealing with agency problems, it is not in contradiction with the argument that the chairmanship and major shareholders play an important role in combating agency problems. Having the chairmanship and/or a large group of major shareholders may have sufficiently alleviated agency problems so that staged financing is no longer needed as an instrument in controlling agency problems.

In summary, on the question of risk vs agency factors, our regression results indicate that (1) risk factors are the dominant factors in explaining the use of staged financing, and (2) staged financing is not used as a means in dealing with agency problems. That is, our results support Hypothesis 1 but reject Hypothesis 2.

4.3. Heteroskedasticity and Multicollinearity

All our regressions are based on the robust standard error approach, which effectively eliminates the possibility of heteroskedasticity.

---

15 Since the most significant variable among the three asset ratios is the ratio of R&D expense to total assets, we have reported regressions with this ratio only.

Another possible econometric problem is multicollinearity. Multicollinearity can be tested by calculating the variance inflation factors (VIF or tolerance) for each of the independent variables. According to the rules of Chatterjee, Hadi and Price (2000), there is evidence of multicollinearity if

(a) The largest VIF is greater than 10 (they choose a more conservative threshold of 30).
(b) The mean of all the VIFs is considerably larger than 1.

In Table 11, we list all the VIFs for all our independent variables and for all our regressions. We can see that none of the VIFs is greater than 10 and none of the means is considerably larger than 1. Hence, multicollinearity does not exist in all our regressions.

Table 11. VIF Test for Multicollinearity

	1	2	3	4	5	6	7	8
ROA	1.06	1.08	1.08	1.08	1.02	1.03	1.02	1.02
Market to book ratio	1.01	1.01	1.01	1.01	1.00	1.00	1.00	1.00
Number of investment rounds	1.95	2.02	2.01	1.99	1.07	1.16	1.09	1.08
Company age at the first investment round	1.12	1.12	1.12	1.13				
Whether the first investment round occurred in early stages*	1.16	1.16	1.16	1.17				
Number of VC funds participating in the first investment round	1.25	1.25	1.25	1.26				
Number of VC funds participating in the whole investment period	2.17	2.24	2.27	2.20				
Ratio of RandD expense to total assets	1.05			1.23				
Ratio of cash and equivalents to total assets		1.03		1.20				
Ratio of intangible assets to total assets			1.04	1.04				
Whether chairman of the board is a VC*					1.05	1.08	1.07	1.06
Number of major VC shareholders (1)						1.16		
Number of major VC shareholders (2)							1.04	
Number of major VC shareholders (3)								1.02
Mean VIF	1.35	1.36	1.37	1.33	1.04	1.09	1.04	1.04

Table 11. Continued

	9	10	11	12	13	14	15
Control Variables:							
ROA	1.07	1.06	1.06	1.06	1.07	1.07	1.07
Market to book ratio	1.02	1.01	1.01	1.01	1.02	1.02	1.02
Number of investment rounds	2.01	1.95	1.96	1.96	2.03	2.04	2.04
Risk Factors:							
Company age at the first investment round	1.18	1.13	1.12	1.12	1.18	1.18	1.18
Whether the first investment round occurred in early stages*	1.20	1.18	1.17	1.17	1.21	1.21	1.21
Number of VC funds participating in the first investment round	1.21	1.24	1.24	1.24	1.20	1.20	1.20
Number of VC funds participating in the whole investment period	2.31	2.24	2.17	2.18	2.39	2.31	2.33
Ratio of RandD expense to total assets	1.05	1.05	1.05	1.05	1.05	1.05	1.05
Agency Factors:							
Whether chairman of the board is a VC*	1.11				1.12	1.11	1.11
Number of major VC shareholders (1)		1.19			1.23		
Number of major VC shareholders (2)			1.05			1.06	
Number of major VC shareholders (3)				1.03			1.05
Mean VIF	1.35	1.34	1.31	1.31	1.35	1.33	1.33

5. Concluding Summary

With over 90% of all VC financing being carried out through staged financing, it is important to understand the role of staged financing in reality. There are some theoretical studies on staged financing that have mostly focused on agency problems. But, the rational for staged financing has rarely been investigated by empirical studies. In particular, the role of staged financing in controlling agency problems in reality has never been verified.

By exploring sample data from 974 VC-backed public companies, we conducted an empirical study on the use of staged financing in venture capital financing. Our empirical results show a strong relationship between staged financing and risk factors, but little evidence on a relationship between staged financing and agency factors. In other words, we find strong evidence that staged financing is used to cope with risks but not to control agency problems. Therefore, our main conclusion is that staged financing is mainly used to handle risks, while agency problems may be handled by many other mechanisms such as equity sharing, the board of directors, major shareholders, and the chairmanship of the board.

References

Admati, A.R. and M. Perry (1991), "Joint Projects without Commitment", *Review of Economic Studies,* **58**, 259–276.

Baker, M. and P.A. Gompers (2003), "The Determinants of Board Structure at the Initial Public Offering", *Journal of Law and Economics,* **46**, 569–598.

Bergemann, D. and U. Hege (1998), "Venture Capital Financing, Moral Hazard, and Learning," *Journal of Banking and Finance,* **22**, 703–735.

Chatterjee, S., A.S. Hadi, and B. Price (2000), *Regression Analysis by Example*, John Wiley and Sons.

Cuny, C.J. and E. Talmor (2005), "The Staging of Venture Capital Financing: Milestone vs. Rounds," Working Paper, Texas A and M University.

Davila, A., G. Foster and M. Gupta (2003), "Staging Venture Capital: Empirical Evidence on The Differential Roles of Early Versus Late Rounds," *Working Paper*, Stanford University.

Gompers, P.A. (1995), "Optimal Investment, Monitoring, and the Staging of Venture Capital," *Journal of Finance,* **50** (5), 1461–1489.

Gompers, P. A. and J. Lerner (2004), *The Venture Capital Cycle*, MIT press.

Hellmann, T. (1994), "Financial Structure and Control in Venture Capital," Chapter 2 of Ph.D Dissertation, Stanford University.

Kockesen, L., and S. Ozerturk (2002), "Staged Financing and Endogenous Lock-In: A Model of Start-up Finance," Working Paper, Columbia University.

Lerner, J. (1994), "The Syndication of Venture Capital Investments," *Financial Management,* **23** (3), 16–27.

Neher, D.V. (1999), "Staged Financing: An Agency Perspective," *Review of Economic Studies,* **66**, 255–274.

Repullo, R. and J. Suarez (1998): "Venture Capital Finance: A Security Design Approach," Working Paper #9804, CEMFI.

Sahlman, W. (1990), "The Structure and Governance of Venture Capital Organizations," *Journal of Financial Economics,* **27**, 473–524.

Schmidt, Klaus M. (2003): "Convertible Securities and Venture Capital Finance", *Journal of Finance*, **LVIII** (3), 1139–1166.

Wang, L. (2005), *Four Essays on Corporate Finance,* Ph.D Thesis, HKUST.

Wang, S. (2006), "Convertibles and Milestones in Staged Financing," *Review of* Finance, forthcoming.

Wang, L. and S. Wang (2006): "Syndication in Venture Capital: Risk Sharing and Bargaining Positions," *Working Paper*, HKUST.

Wang, L. and S. Wang (2008): "Convertibles in Staged Financing," *Journal of Economics and Finance*, forthcoming.

Wang, S., and H. Zhou (2004), "Staged Financing in Venture Capital: Moral Hazard and Risks," *Journal of Corporate Finance,* **10**, 131–151.

In: Handbook of Business and Finance
Editors: M. Bergmann and T. Faust, pp. 217-239

ISBN: 978-1-60692-855-4
© 2010 Nova Science Publishers, Inc.

Chapter 9

SYNDICATION AS A MANAGEMENT STRATEGY[♦]

Lanfang Wang[1] and Susheng Wang[2,]*

[1] School of Accounting, Shanghai University of Finance and Economics,
Shanghai, China
[2] Department of Economics, Hong Kong University of Science and Technology,
Hong Kong, China

Abstract

Syndication of investment exists in over 90% of venture capital backed companies. Syndication means that the investors form a group to invest jointly in a company. The existing literature emphasizes the benefits of investors from syndication through risk sharing and resource sharing. However, a few questions are left unanswered. First, does the manager of the firm also benefit from syndication? For example, with more sources of funding, the firm's future funding is more secure. Also, with competition among the investors, the manager may improve his bargaining position. Second, is syndication related to agency problems? There are no answers to these questions in the literature and empirical studies on syndication in venture capital are rare. By collecting data from 933 venture capital backed companies that went public in recent years, we conduct a detailed empirical study on syndication. It shows that (1) syndication is beneficial to both managers and investors for the purposes of risk sharing and potentially for alleviating agency problems; (2) syndication has clear implications on the allocations of income rights and control rights, implying a possible solution to or a result of agency problems.

Keywords: Syndication, Risk Sharing, Resource Sharing, Income Rights, Control Rights

1. Introduction

Venture capital has played a crucial role in economic growth in the past few decades, especially in the United States. Venture capital backed companies create close to one-third of the total market value of all public companies in the United States. Especially in the past two

---

[♦] We gratefully acknowledge the support of a grant from the Shanghai Pujiang Program.
[*] E-mail address: wang.lanfang@mail.shufe.edu.cn, s.wang@ust.hk.

decades, the venture capital industry in the U.S. has experienced dramatic growth. The pool of U.S. venture capital funds grew from less than \$1 billion in 1976 to over \$250 billion in 2001. The percentage of venture capital backed IPOs was 50%, 34.6%, and 24.7% of all IPOs in 2000, 2001, and 2002, respectively (Gompers–Lerner 2004).

Due to its importance, it is necessary for us to understand various issues in venture capital. Startup enterprises with high growth potential and high risks depend primarily on venture capital for financing. Large investors in these startups are typically venture-capital firms, called venture capitalists (VCs).[1] Syndication is a prominent feature in venture capital financing and has been gaining popularity in recent years. Syndication means that several VCs form a group with a lead VC as the coordinator to invest jointly in a company. Venture capital financing is plagued with agency problems. Sahlman's (1990) extensive field study points out three key control mechanisms employed to manage agency costs in venture capital financing: (1) the use of convertibles; (2) staged financing; and (3) syndication of investment. The first two mechanisms have been extensively studied in the literature. But, the study for the last mechanism is rare in the literature. The aim of this paper is to do an extensive empirical study on the third mechanism.

One key characteristic of many startup companies in high-tech industries is the high risk due to the great uncertainty about returns, the lack of substantial tangible assets, the lack of a track record in operations, and possibly many years of negative earnings. According to Bergemann–Hege (1998), the fraction of such projects for which investors can successfully cash out, mostly through IPO, is twenty percent or less. Given this situation, banks and other traditional intermediaries are reluctant to or even prohibited from lending money to such firms. Furthermore, these financial institutions usually lack expertise in investing in such high-risk companies. Consequently, startups often seek involvement of VCs by offering various securities, principally convertible securities. These convertibles provide certain guaranteed returns, contingent convertibility, and guaranteed or contingent equity shares. In addition, through syndication, allocations of income rights and control rights are well balanced among all parties.

Another key characteristic of venture capital is the incentive problem of entrepreneurs (ENs).[2] Several agency problems may exist in such a joint venture. If cash flows are not completely verifiable, the ENs may appropriate investments; if effort is not verifiable, the ENs may shirk job responsibilities; also, if there are private benefits from continuing a project, the ENs may keep the project going even if it has negative expected profits.

There is a relatively recent literature on venture capital. A good source for a general knowledge of venture capital is Sahlman (1990), who discusses various aspects of venture capital, including legal definitions, organizational forms, and relationships between VCs and ENs. Syndication is generally observed in a high-risk environment. Since participation by more VCs means less risk for each VC, a dominant view on syndication in the literature argues that syndication is the result of risk sharing by VCs (the risk-sharing theory).

---

1 Each venture-capital firm is typically divided into several venture-capital funds. These funds have different investment preferences, targets and objectives. Two funds from the same venture-capital firm may invest in one company in different rounds or even in the same round. When this happens, since the two funds must share information and experiences between them and behave in the best interest of their firm, we combine them together as one VC in our analysis.

2 Each VC-backed company has several ENs. All the ENs in each company are counted in the data. However, not all investors are reported in the data; only those investors who are VCs (venture capital firms) are counted in the data. Besides VCs, there are many individual investors, who typically have tiny stakes in the company.

Theoretical and empirical studies both show that syndication is an important and effective means to reduce risks, especially in the initial round of investment. A second view of syndication argues that a syndicate of VCs may share their resources, information and experiences (the resource-sharing theory). Syndication allows each VC to access certain resources from other VCs. Hence, syndication should improve a company's performance.

However, the existing literature on syndication focuses only on the VCs' rationales. Syndication is treated as a phenomenon in which the VCs band together to bargain with the ENs and to share risks, information and resources among themselves. Little is discussed about the ENs' rationale for syndication. In reality, however, it is the ENs in a company who initiate the formation of a syndicate by appointing a lead VC, delegating her to form a syndicate, and stipulating rewards for the lead VC for organizing the syndicate. Hence, the ENs must benefit from syndication.

A natural question is: how do the ENs benefit from syndication and what is the benefit? One obvious benefit is that, through the availability of more financial sources, the firm's funding is more secure. In fact, a constant problem for startups in reality is a delay in funding due to a change of mind by investors after the investors have agreed to provide funds. Also, VCs may provide the ENs with valuable contacts and advice. It is known that some ENs explicitly search for VCs who have funded a successful company before. That is, there is resource sharing between ENs and VCs. And, with more competition among the VCs for a stake in the company, the ENs may improve their bargaining positions with the VCs.

Further, the existing literature does not relate syndication to agency problems. As we find from our empirical study, syndication has clear implications on the allocation of income rights and the allocation of control rights, particularly on the composition of the board of directors. These factors are known in theory to be important in dealing with incentive problems. Hence, syndication can potentially play an important role in resolving agency problems.

Is syndication in reality mainly a device for risk sharing, for resource sharing, for alleviating agency problems or all three? This is an important empirical question. Surprisingly, no one has yet conducted an investigation to answer this question. This paper reports on an empirical study of this topic. With a cross-section data set of 933 VC-backed companies that went public during the period of 1997 to 2005, we conducted a detailed analysis of the rationale for syndication by testing three hypotheses: syndication is for risk sharing, for allocating income rights, or for allocating control rights. We pay particular attention to the implications of syndication on both ENs and VCs. Our empirical study shows that, after isolating its effects on performance, company size, types of technology and types of industry, syndication is beneficial to both VCs and ENs for risk sharing and potentially in alleviating agency problems.

This paper proceeds as follows. Section 2 gives a short literature review of the existing studies on syndication in venture capital. Section 3 presents our econometric model together with three hypotheses. Section 4 describes the sources of data and various variables used in our regressions, together with some stylized facts from the data set. Section 5 presents the regression results with some discussion. Section 6 tests model integrity. Finally, Section 7 concludes the paper with a summary.

2. A Literature Review

There are three distinct theories about syndication. The risk-sharing theory (or financial-motive theory) argues that syndication is mainly a strategy to reduce risks of VCs through portfolio diversification.[3] The resource-sharing theory (or value-added theory) argues that syndication allows the VCs to share information, resources, and managerial skills.[4] We propose a third theory: the agency theory. We argue that syndication has direct implications on the allocation of income rights and the allocation of control rights and hence it can potentially be used as a mechanism in dealing with agency problems.

2.1. The Risk-Sharing Theory

The risk-sharing theory is the dominant view in the literature. It views syndication as a way to share risks among VCs through portfolio diversification. There are two kinds of risks: market risks and firm-specific risks. Firm-specific risks can be reduced by portfolio diversification. Due to this, each VC tends to allocate their capital to many ventures.

Lockett–Wright (2001) present two more risk-sharing motives for syndication. One is due to the needs of maintaining a healthy cash flow for a VC fund. By maintaining the ability to raise funds when opportunities arrive in the future, the VC can be assured that she will not underperform her peers substantially. The other is due to the illiquidity of venture capital investments in comparison with stock market investments. The actual risk may not be known before a VC has committed to an investment and hence gained access to more information as an investor. With the illiquidity, it will be difficult to adjust the investment portfolio in the short term after the extent of the risk is fully revealed. Therefore, syndication provides a means of risk sharing on a deal-by-deal basis, which may help reduce the overall portfolio risk of a VC.

2.2. The Resource-Sharing Theory

Venture capital funds in reality typically diversify their portfolios at their fund level by investing in many different ventures across an industry. Why do they need to diversify again when they invest in a venture or even at a round of investment through syndication? The answer to this question leads to a second argument for syndication: sharing of information, experiences, resources, and managerial skills.

Resources are required to reduce various dimensions of firm-specific risks at both ex-ante and ex-post decision-making stages. Ex-ante decision making may relate to the selection of investment objectives, whereas ex-post decision making may relate to the subsequent management of the investments. A syndicate of VCs may allow the VCs to share their resources and experiences to improve efficiency and reduce costs in these decision-making activities.

In the literature, Brander et al. (2002) argue for the value-added motive of syndication. Different VCs have different skills and information, which can be helpful in different aspects

---

3 See Bygrave (1987), Smith–Smith (2000), and Lockett–Wright (2001).
4 See Lerner (1994), Brander et al. (2002), and Sorenson–Stuart (2001).

of the project, such as organizing production, human-resource management, and customer service, etc. Hence, VCs in a syndicate all add value to a project.

Lerner (1994) argues for the project-selection motive of syndication, which is in line with the resource-sharing motive. Before making a commitment to an investment, a VC may want to see a similar decision from others. Hence, syndication may lead to a good venture selection or a right continuation decision. This leads to the prediction that a syndicated project should perform better than a non-syndicated one.

We further argue that there is resource sharing between VCs and ENs. It is known in the venture-capital industry that some VCs play a crucial role in the success of a company by providing the ENs with valuable contacts and advice. A VC's contacts and advice can sometimes be more important than the VC's money. In fact, it is known in reality that ENs actively seek those VCs who have funded some successful ventures before. The experiences of the VCs can be an important asset.

2.3. The Agency Theory

We propose a third view: the agency theory. We argue that agency problems, which may exist between VCs and ENs, can potentially be reduced by syndication.

There are some studies in the literature that are somewhat in support of our view. In a model with multiple investment decisions, Admati–Pfleiderer (1994) show that, by becoming an insider through investment, a VC can effectively solve conflicts of interests and information asymmetry. In particular, the VC can make an optimal investment decision by holding a fixed-fraction contract, by which he receives a fixed fraction of the project's payoffs and provides the same fixed fraction of finance in future investments. That is, the VC obtains a fixed fraction α of the total payoffs of the project no matter what the continuation strategy is; if the project continues and an investment I is needed, then the VC puts up αI and the rest is financed by others. This is an equity-like contract, which can be implemented by syndication. This suggests a potential role for syndication as a means to prevent agency problems.

More importantly, if syndication has an effect on the bargaining positions of ENs and VCs, it can potentially be used as a mechanism to deal with agency problems. Kaplan–Strömberg (1999) argue that more VCs banding together to share information and resources rather than to compete against each other can result in an improvement in their bargaining positions with ENs. On the contrary, Fluck–Garrison–Myers (2004) show in a computational model that a commitment to syndicate is a way to ensure that the ENs have more favorable financing terms, which encourages the ENs to exert more effort.

Until now, most of the literature on syndication has been empirical, including Lerner (1994), Lockett–Wright (2001), Brander et al. (2002), and Manigart et al. (2002), who examine several potential roles of syndication. However, these empirical studies have so far tested only two possible rationales for syndication: risk sharing and resource sharing. There is still no empirical study on the agency view of syndication.

3. The Econometric Model

3.1. Hypotheses

We are interested in three hypotheses. First, syndication is a mechanism for risk sharing. The existing literature discusses the role of syndication in risk sharing among VCs. We are interested in risk sharing both among VCs and between VCs and ENs. When faced with a project with high risk, VCs will hesitate to join in, but ENs will have incentives to attract more VCs. By offering more attractive deals, the ENs can attract more VCs to reduce risks for both ENs and VCs. We state the first hypothesis as follows.

Hypothesis 1 (Risk-Sharing Theory). Syndication is for the purpose of risk sharing.

Second, syndication may have implications on the allocation of revenue shares and the allocation of control rights. These allocations are known to have important implications on agency problems, and hence they can be designed to deal with agency problems. As such, we argue that syndication can potentially be used as a mechanism to alleviate agency problems.

In what way can syndication play a role in solving agency problems? We argue that syndication helps alleviate agency problems by striking a balance in income and control rights between VCs and ENs. In fact, in theoretical papers on double moral hazards, the key to an efficient solution is to balance control and income rights between the two parties. For example, in a joint venture, Wang–Zhu (2005) find a pair of optimal allocations of control rights and income rights. Also, Wang (2006) shows that callable convertibles with proper call protection can achieve efficiency by striking a balance of control and income rights between the company and an investor. The existing literature has viewed syndication as a way by which the VCs band together to bargain with the ENs. We argue that syndication can also be a way by which the ENs introduce competition among the VCs to improve their own bargaining position. Hence, we expect syndication to be significantly related to allocations of both ENs' and VCs' control and income rights in our regressions. We state the third and fourth hypotheses as follows, with one focusing on control rights and the other on income rights.

Hypothesis 2 (Incomplete-Contract Theory). Syndication is for the purpose of allocating control rights.

Hypothesis 3 (Agency Theory). Syndication is for the purpose of allocating of income rights.

3.2. Regression Model

The Dependent Variable

We choose the number of principal VCs at IPO to represent syndication, where a principal VC is a VC who either holds over 5% of the company's equity or over 1% if she is a director. This number is called the syndication variable and it is chosen as the dependent variable in our regression model.

Why do we choose this number to represent syndication? The numbers of VCs at different stages are generally different. During the whole investment period (from the company's existence to IPO), VCs may join or quit from time to time. Those who stay until

IPO tend to be more committed VCs who are interested in the true value of the company. Besides, we will also include the so-called stage variables in our regression model to take into account the difference, where the stage variables are the numbers of VCs at various stages.

Our independent variables include various variables representing risk factors, control rights, and income rights. We also include some econometric control variables that control the stage factors and performance. The following is our regression model:

$$\text{syndication variable} = \beta_0 + \beta_1(\text{risk factors}) + \beta_2(\text{control rights})$$
$$+ \beta_3(\text{income rights}) + \beta_4(\text{control variables}) + \varepsilon,$$

where ε represents a random variable and $\beta_1, \beta_2, \beta_3$ and β_4 represent the coefficients for various factors. By running regressions with various sets of variables, we test the three hypotheses.

Risk Factors

Risk factors include the overall risk of the firm and the standard deviations of equity shares just before IPO. A company's overall risk is represented by three variables defined by whether or not a company belongs to a high-technology industry, whether or not a company belongs to an information-technology industry, and the company's average value during the whole investment period. A large company value means a large company, implying fewer potential risks.

The standard deviation indicates fluctuations or risk in income. Specifically in this case, the standard deviations of the equity shares owned by VCs and ENs represent the adjustment of risk sharing among and between VCs and ENs. If syndication serves as a mechanism for risk sharing, the standard deviations should be reduced as more VCs join in.

Control Rights

Syndication may help alleviate agency problems by striking a balance in the allocation of control rights among VCs and ENs. Board representation has a direct implication on control rights and the chairmanship in particular is considered in the literature to be critical to sound corporate governance (the so-called good and bad governance structures).

We use two variables to represent the allocation of control rights. (1) Since the Chairman of the board holds great influence and power, whether or not the Chairman is a VC is an important indicator of the VCs' collective position on the board. (2) The proportion of VC directors on the board is also an important indicator since this proportion represents the voting power of the VCs, where a VC director is a board member who is appointed by or related to VCs.

Income Rights

Syndication may help alleviate agency problems by striking a balance in the allocation of income rights among VCs and ENs. Equity sharing has a direct implication on the allocation of income rights. Many theoretical works show that equity sharing can be used as an effective mechanism in alleviating agency problems (e.g., Admati–Pfleiderer 1994 and Wang–Zhou 2004).

We use five variables to represent the allocation of income rights. (1) Equity sharing has direct implications on the allocation of revenue shares. Hence, the average equity shares of ENs and VCs are chosen as important indicators of income rights. (2) Similarly, the total equity shares held by ENs and VCs are chosen as well. (3) Finally, the relative equity share of VCs over ENs (the ratio of the VCs' to the ENs' equity share) is also chosen as an indicator of income rights.

Control Variables

Syndication has a clear timing pattern. Syndication occurs mostly in the expansion and later stages. The next most popular choice is the early stage, while the seed and startup stages are the third. There should be a strong correlation between the number of VCs at IPO and the numbers of VCs in these stages. Hence, we include the stage variables defined by the numbers of VCs in these stages in our regressions. These stage variables represent the degrees of syndication across the development stages.

Table 1. Independent Variables

Type	Variable
Risk factors	Whether High Technology*
	Whether Information Technology*
	Average Company Value across all Investment Rounds
	S.D. of the Equity Share Owned by ENs just before IPO
	S.D. of the Equity Share Owned by VCs just before IPO
Control Rights	Proportion of VC Directors
	Whether Chairman of the Board is a VC*
Income Rights	Average Equity Share Owned by ENs just before IPO
	Average Equity Share Owned by VCs just before IPO
	Total Equity Share Owned by ENs just before IPO
	Total Equity Share Owned by VCs just before IPO
	Relative Equity Share of VCs at IPO
Control Variables	Number of VCs in Expansion and Later Stages
	Number of VCs in the Early Stage
	Number of VCs in Seed and Startup Stages
	Annual Profit Growth Rate one year after IPO

We also need to control performance. According the resource-sharing theory, syndication should have effects on the chance of success and on the overall performance of a company. We choose the company's annual profit growth rate one year after IPO as the indicator of performance. Here, since the timing of our syndication variable is at IPO, the timing of the performance variable is chosen to be one year after IPO.

In summary, Table 1 lists all the independent variables in our regressions.

We have several notes on the definition of the variables.

1. A star * stands for a dummy variable.
2. S.D. stands for standard deviation.
3. We say "the ENs" instead of "the EN," since there are typically several ENs (the founders) in each VC-backed company. In theoretical models, these ENs are typically treated as one individual. We need to treat them as separate individuals.
4. The "average equity share of ENs" is the average of the equity shares among all the ENs in a company. The "total equity share of ENs" is the total share of equity summed over all the ENs in a company. The equity shares for VCs are similarly defined.
5. The sum of the total equity shares of ENs and VCs is less than 1, since individual investors are not counted in the data (see Footnote 2). In terms of equity holdings just before IPO, ENs count for about 25%, VCs about 45%, and individual investors about 30%.

4. Sample Data

The sample data comes from two sources: SDC VentureXpert and SEC EDGAR. The sample consists of 933 VC-backed companies that went public during 1997–2005. In sequence of offering years, 109 companies completed their IPOs in 1997, 79 companies in 1998, 265 companies in 1999, 263 companies in 2000, 39 companies in 2001, 24 companies in 2002, 29 companies in 2003, 93 companies in 2004, and 32 companies in 2005. Most of these companies have filing records in SEC EDGAR since most of these companies are listed and have addresses in the United States. In terms of stock exchanges, 871 companies are listed on the NASDAQ market, 27 companies on the New York Stock Exchange, 9 companies on the American Stock Exchange, and 26 companies on the exchange markets of other countries.

The sample data contain information on investment and management for almost all the available VC-backed companies that successfully completed IPOs in recent years. In particular, they contain the company general information and more specific information on investment rounds, VCs, and the board of directors. We describe some details of these four categories of information below. The sample sizes in different tables may vary due to incomplete records in the data.

Table 2. Summary of the Company's Age at IPO

IPO Year Age at IPO		1997	1998	1999	2000	2001	2002	2003	2004	2005	Total
	Mean	7.86	6.46	5.22	6.51	9.43	10.78	8.22	7.67	7.52	6.73
Age at IPO (Years)	S.D.	6.72	5.49	4.55	9.03	12.3	11.48	4.33	5.89	5.49	7.26
	Obs.	107	79	265	263	39	24	29	93	32	931

4.1. General Information

Based on the Venture Economics Industry Classifications (VEIC), all the firms in the data set can be classified either as a high-technology industry or a non-high-technology industry. Almost 90% of the companies are in the high-technology industry, in which the IT industry covers about 66% and the medical/health/life science industry covers 22%. In particular, the sectors that are larger than 10% are: communications (12.13%), computer software (16.36%), internet-specific (27.09%), biotechnology (10.40%), and medical/health (12.13%). This industry distribution is consistent with prior reports in the literature (Gompers 1995, Sahlman 1990).

VCs actively encouraged and helped their investing companies to go public and to complete a capital exit successfully from their portfolios. Hence, the ages of VC-backed companies tend to be young. As shown in Table 2, the average company age at IPO is about 6 to 7 years. Also, the performance of VC-backed companies is known to be significantly higher on average than that of non-VC-backed companies even after IPO (Brav and Gompers 1997). A young age and good performance are two important features of VC-backed companies. In Table 2, by listing companies by their IPO years, we summarize the mean and standard deviation of the company age at IPO, where *S.D.* is the standard deviation and *Obs.* is the number of observations.

4.2. Investment Rounds

The sample data set contains information on 3419 investment rounds for 909 companies. Table 3 andTable 4 summarize, respectively, the total number of VCs involved in each VC-backed company over the whole investment period (from startup to IPO) and the number of VCs involved in each investment round of the company. The information on investment rounds shows strong evidence of syndication. Syndication is not only strong over the whole investment period (before IPO), but also strong in each investment round. On average, about seven VCs are involved in each company over the whole investment period, and about three VCs participate in each investment round.

According to the sample, a company's development stages can be divided into Startup/ Seed Stage, Early Stage, Buyout/Acquisition Stage, Expansion Stage, Later Stage, and Other Stage, with each stage lasting just over one year on average. In particular, the seed /startup stage usually means the first year of the company's existence. Different VCs may prefer to join in investing in a company at different stages. Some development stages are more popular than are others. As a result, the degrees of syndication vary across stages. There are three major timing patterns in syndication (Brander et al. 2002). The most common pattern is that syndication occurs soon after an investment by the lead VC in the expansion or later stage. A second pattern is that the lead VC makes an investment at the seed or startup stage, followed by syndicated investments at a later stage. The least common pattern is that syndication occurs at the seed or startup stage. Table 5 lists the average number of VCs participating in each stage. We can see that most VCs participate in the expansion and later stages, and the next popular choice is the early stage.

Syndication as a Management Strategy

Table 3. Number of VCs Involved in Each Company

# of VCs IPO Year	Mean	S.D.	Obs.
1997	5.07	4.51	95
1998	4.79	3.68	78
1999	6.62	4.35	259
2000	7.9	5.23	261
2001	5.67	4.84	39
2002	5.65	4.90	23
2003	7.48	4.55	29
2004	7.72	5.6	93
2005	6.66	4.69	32
Total	6.75	4.88	909

Table 4. Number of VCs Participating in Each Investment Round

# of VCs IPO Year	Mean	S.D.	Obs.
1997	2.76	2.68	361
1998	2.78	2.25	257
1999	3.21	2.5	961
2000	3.6	3.03	1045
2001	3.13	2.86	121
2002	2.84	2.61	76
2003	3.81	2.93	121
2004	3.82	3.04	369
2005	3.55	2.97	108
Total	3.34	2.8	3419

Table 5. Average Number of VCs Involved in a Specific Stage

Stage IPO Year	Startup/ Seed	Early	Buyout/ Acquisition	Expansion/ Later	Other	Obs.
1997	1.06	1.64	0.17	3.84	0.53	95
1998	0.37	1.24	0.41	3.81	0.28	78
1999	0.78	1.45	0.28	5.6	0.38	258
2000	0.71	1.84	0.18	6.66	0.44	262
2001	0.31	1.74	0.26	4.62	0.33	39
2002	0.61	1.13	0.48	4.52	0.13	23
2003	0.59	2.31	0.03	6.59	0.69	29
2004	0.58	1.49	0.19	7.11	0.19	93
2005	0.28	1.44	0.06	5.75	0.38	32
Total	0.69	1.6	0.23	5.69	0.39	909

Table 6. Number of Rounds in Which Each VC Participates

# of Rounds IPO Year	Mean	S.D.	Obs.
1997	2.01	1.49	482
1998	1.88	1.45	373
1999	1.77	1.24	1713
2000	1.81	1.36	2059
2001	1.71	1.12	221
2002	1.67	1.21	130
2003	2.14	1.9	215
2004	1.95	1.36	718
2005	1.73	1.2	210
Total	1.84	1.35	6121

Each VC may participate in only one round or in several rounds over the whole investment period of a company. Table 6 lists the average number of rounds in which each VC participates. The table indicates that each VC participates in about two rounds.

Relating to our dependent variable, Table 7 lists the average number of those VCs who own over 5% equity or those VC directors who own over 1% equity at IPO. These VCs are likely to play an important role in syndication. On average, there are three to four participating VCs at IPO for each VC-backed company, which is about half of the VCs who have ever been involved with the company.

Table 7. Number of VCs at IPO for Each Company

# of VCs IPO Year	Mean	S.D.	Obs.
1997	2.78	1.87	106
1998	2.87	1.77	77
1999	3.46	1.84	255
2000	3.63	1.9	248
2001	2.84	1.7	38
2002	2.74	1.57	23
2003	4.04	1.37	24
2004	3.98	2.3	92
2005	3.34	1.82	32
Total	3.40	1.82	895

Table 8. Proportion of VC Directors in the Board (%)

Proportion IPO Year	Mean	S.D.	Obs.
1997	32.28	0.20	109
1998	36.56	0.17	79
1999	39.87	0.18	263
2000	37.73	0.18	252
2001	33.72	0.18	38
2002	31.57	0.18	23
2003	34.00	0.17	28
2004	36.46	0.19	93
2005	33.8	0.19	32
Total	37.7	0.19	917

4.3. Board Representation

The board composition of 917 companies at the time of IPO is available. VCs' active involvement is a critical characteristic of venture capital financing. Normally, about one-third of board members are VC directors. The number and positions of these appointed directors are a consequence of bargaining between the ENs and VCs. The board composition represents a key part of the VC's control rights. Through these directors, VCs can be well informed of and involved in decision making on daily management, governance, development strategy, etc. The proportions of VC directors in all the companies are summarized in Table 8. On average, about 37.7% of the board seats are controlled by VCs.

Table 9. Number of Companies with a VC Chairman

Number IPO Year	Number	Percentage	# of Obs.
1997	20	18.35	109
1998	11	13.92	79
1999	29	11.03	263
2000	39	15.48	252
2001	2	5.26	38
2002	3	13.04	23
2003	6	21.43	28
2004	18	19.35	93
2005	5	15.63	32
Total	133	14.5	917

Table 10. Equity Shares Owned by ENs and VCs Just Before IPO (%)

Equity Share IPO Year	Owned by ENs			Owned by VCs			Obs.
	Average	Total	S.D.	Average	Total	S.D.	
1997	8.13	26.67	7.65	18.63	41.93	7.06	105
1998	8.38	31.28	9.50	18.01	41.47	7.86	76
1999	6.44	25.62	6.66	15.72	45.65	8.05	251
2000	5.08	20.64	5.56	15.68	47.80	7.75	244
2001	4.62	22.28	6.89	18.54	43.46	9.13	34
2002	4.71	23.23	6.02	21.41	51.84	14.81	22
2003	2.94	16.02	3.46	13.74	53.84	8.50	24
2004	4.83	18.62	5.16	13.91	51.11	7.13	90
2005	6.21	20.33	6.38	14.26	49.00	7.72	28
Total	6.05	23.50	6.47	16.22	46.40	7.95	874

The chairman of the board is endowed with special power and influence. Table 9 indicates the number of companies whose chairmen are appointed by VCs and the percentage of such companies in all VC-backed companies. Roughly 14.5% of the companies' chairmen are appointed by VCs.

4.4. Equity Sharing

Equity sharing has been used extensively in venture capital financing. It is generally embodied in convertible securities, which is a form of contingent equity sharing. The VCs can acquire the pre-determined equity share when they convert debt to equity. We collect the equity shares owned by ENs and VCs just before IPO and immediately after IPO from 874 companies, assuming full conversion of convertible securities. Table 10 and Table 11 summarize the average, the total, and the standard deviation of the equity shares owned by

Table 11. Equity Shares Owned by ENs and VCs Immediately After IPO (%)

Equity Share IPO Year	Owned by ENs			Owned by VCs			Obs.
	Average	Total	S.D.	Average	Total	S.D.	
1997	5.67	18.43	5.25	12.89	29.83	4.92	105
1998	5.98	22.44	6.73	13.16	30.76	6.29	76
1999	5.11	20.39	5.27	12.32	36.31	6.49	251
2000	4.03	16.45	4.41	12.35	37.96	6.13	244
2001	3.65	17.30	5.57	13.62	32.12	6.46	34
2002	3.46	17.23	4.49	15.00	36.87	10.56	22
2003	2.14	11.72	2.60	9.72	39.03	6.43	24
2004	3.65	14.26	3.99	10.16	37.70	5.46	90
2005	4.81	16.07	5.15	9.77	35.62	5.72	28
Total	4.61	18.03	4.94	12.21	35.56	6.17	874

ENs and VCs for each VC-backed company just before IPO and immediately after IPO, respectively. We can see that the total equity shares of ENs and VCs are respectively about 25% and 45% just before IPO and about 18% and 35% immediately after IPO.

Finally, Table 12 summarizes the relative equity share of VCs for each company. On average, the equity share owned by VCs is five to six times that of ENs.

Table 12. Relative Equity Share of VCs for Each VC-Backed Company

Relative equity share IPO Year	Mean	S.D.	Obs.
1997	4.33	6.28	105
1998	3.55	5.80	77
1999	4.42	8.79	254
2000	7.78	19.92	245
2001	6.24	14.39	35
2002	6.04	10.8	22
2003	6.68	5.27	24
2004	6.58	7.82	91
2005	5.93	6.56	29
Total	5.71	12.70	882

5. Regression Results

5.1. Regressions on Risk Sharing

The regression results on those independent variables representing risk factors are listed in Table 14, where the numbers in the square brackets are the t-values.

We have the following observations. First, syndication is negatively related to risky technologies (high technology and information technology). This is because when the technology is viewed as risky, VCs are less willing to invest in the company. As a result, a risky technology implies less syndication.

Second, syndication is negatively related to the company value. A large company value means a large company, implying fewer risks. Hence, the ENs have less incentive to invite many VCs. As a result, a large company value implies less syndication.

Syndication is determined in equilibrium by a balance of bargaining positions from the ENs and VCs. For the case with a risky technology, the ENs will encourage syndication with certain compensation for high risk, but the VCs will be reluctant to join. The equilibrium degree of syndication is a balance of these two forces. Which force is dominant is a matter of empirical evidence. Our regressions indicate a reduction in syndication in this case, which means that the VCs' reluctance is the dominant factor. However, for the case with a large company value, the balance tips over to the ENs' side. In this case, with fewer risks, the ENs may not want to share revenue with too many VCs, although the VCs are more willing to participate. Again, which force is dominant is a matter of empirical evidence. Our regressions indicate a reduction in syndication, which means that the ENs' incentive is the dominant factor in this case. This same situation happens to other regression variables, but we mention only the dominant factor from now on.

Table 13. Regressions on Risk Sharing

	Regression # Independent Variables	1	2	3	4	5
Risk Variables	Whether High Technology Industry	-0.39584 [-2.22]			-0.5752 [-2.68]	
	Whether Information Technology		-0.4512 [-4.23]	-0.47325 [-4.25]		-0.3519 [-2.74]
	Average Company Value for all Investment Rounds	-0.00178 [-4.20]	-0.00165 [-3.93]	-0.00119 [-2.11]	-0.0015 [-2.54]	-0.00138 [-2.34]
	S.D. of Equity Shares Owned by ENs just before IPO			-0.04111 [-4.56]		
	S.D. of Equity Shares Owned by VCs just before IPO			-0.03931 [-5.13]		
Control Variables	Number of VCs in Expansion and Later Stages	0.21287 [19.43]	0.21211 [19.69]	0.15125 [13]	0.20961 [15.91]	0.21018 [15.94]
	Number of VCs in the Early Stage	0.19305 [7.97]	0.18537 [7.71]	0.11583 [4.87]	0.16952 [6.29]	0.16224 [6.00]
	Number of VCs in Startup and Seed Stages	0.18634 [5.54]	0.17873 [5.34]	0.12927 [3.98]	0.19514 [4.75]	0.18752 [4.55]
	Annual Profit Growth Rate One Year after IPO				0.005549 [2.16]	0.005414 [2.1]
	Constant	2.34418 [13.02]	2.29811 [19.81]	3.60506 [21.12]	2.49839 [11.29]	2.21923 [15.95]
	# of Observations	788	788	661	560	560
	R^2	0.4447	0.4537	0.406	0.4446	0.4449

Asymmetric information may play a role here. The technology type is usually well known to the public (to VCs), while the company value is less well known to the public. For the case of a risky technology, the VCs are fully aware of the risk; and for the case with a large company value, the ENs are more aware of the rewards. This information difference may play a role in identifying the dominant factor.

Finally, fluctuations in equity shares among ENs and VCs represent another dimension of risk. Regression 3 includes the two variables representing the standard deviation. It shows a negative relationship between syndication and the standard deviations. This is due to the VCs' reluctance to participate when facing undue risks.

In summary, our regression results support Hypothesis 1.

Table 14. Regressions on Control Rights

	Regression # Independent Variables	6	7	8	9
Risk Variables	Whether Information Technology	-0.46648 [-4.67]	-0.48563 [-4.58]	-0.4549547 [-4.49]	-0.36881 [-3.01]
	Average Company Value for all Investment Rounds	-0.00147 [-3.76]	-0.00119 [-2.21]	-0.00114 [-2.31]	-0.00123 [-2.18]
	Annual Profit Growth Rate One Year after IPO				0.00513 [2.12]
	S.D. of Equity Shares Owned by ENs just before IPO		-0.02895 [-3.32]	-0.02118 [-3.01]	-0.01711 [-2.09]
	S.D. of Equity Shares Owned by VCs just before IPO		-0.045421 [-6.19]		
Control Rights	Proportion of VC directors	3.09675 [10.59]	2.63568 [8.19]	2.97476 [9.80]	2.89417 [8.09]
	Whether Chairman of the Board is a VC	-0.56229 [-2.32]		-0.58054 [-2.36]	
Control Variables	Number of VCs in Expansion and Later Stages	0.18114 [17.25]	0.13395 [11.87]	0.17142 [15.73]	0.17442 [13.10]
	Number of VCs in the Early Stage	0.15428 [6.80]	0.10083 [4.44]	0.14710 [6.41]	0.13068 [5.05]
	Number of VCs in Startup and Seed Stages	0.14240 [4.52]	0.10496 [3.38]	0.13318 [4.20]	0.13299 [3.35]
	Constant	1.38426 [9.89]	2.67577 [13.49]	1.61795 [9.86]	1.53307 [7.97]
	# of Observations	788	661	765	543
	R^2	0.5233	0.4615	0.528	0.5126

5.2. Regressions on Control Rights

In our model, two sets of variables represent the two allocations: the allocation of control rights and the allocation of income rights. Board representation has a direct implication for control rights. We hence adopt the two board-representation variables: the proportion of VC directors and whether or not the Chairman is a VC director. The regression results are given in Table 14, where the numbers in the square brackets are the t-values.

We have the following observations. First, syndication is positively related to the proportion of VC directors. This result is quite understandable. A higher degree of syndication means greater VC involvement, implying greater VC representation in the board.

Second, syndication is negatively related to the holding of chairmanship. This indicates that the greater VC participation, and hence the greater proportional representation of VCs on the board, the less likely the Chairman is a VC director. With a sufficient representation of VCs on the board, the agency problem may well be under control and monitoring may be sufficient, implying a less desire for the chairmanship by the VCs.

As known in the literature, efficiency in a double-moral-hazard model requires a balance of control rights between the two sides. The balance between proportional representation and the chairmanship from our regression results is consistent with this theoretical justification for efficiency. Hence, these regression results support Hypothesis 2.

5.3. Regression on Income Rights

Equity sharing has direct implications on the allocation of income rights. We hence add various equity sharing variables into the regression model. The regression results are in Table 15, where the numbers in the square brackets are the t-values.

We have the following observations. First, syndication is negatively related to the average equity shares of both the ENs and the VCs (Regressions 10 and 11). This means that greater VC participation implies a smaller equity share for everyone, including both the VCs and ENs. This evidence is counter to the perception in the literature that the VCs in a syndicate band together to bargain with the ENs for income shares.

Table 15. Regressions on Income Rights

	Regression # Independent Variables	10	11	12	13	14	15	16
Risk Variables	Whether Information Technology	-0.45667 [-4.84]	-0.36617 [-3.18]	-0.39149 [-3.88]	-0.28945 [-2.36]	-0.21010 [-2.48]	-0.4165 [-4.19]	-0.31197 [-2.60]
	Average Company Value during for all Investment Rounds	-0.00156 [-4.24]	-0.00144 [-2.71]	-0.00144 [-3.67]	-0.00131 [-2.34]		-0.00164 [-4.19]	-0.00131 [-2.37]
	Annual Profit Growth Rate One Year after IPO		0.004934 [2.16]		0.00489 [2.03]			0.00496 [2.08]
Control Rights	Proportion of VC directors	3.50412 [12.58]	3.35245 [10.14]	2.81365 [9.42]	2.64072 [7.47]	0.98079 [3.53]	2.81613 [9.49]	2.64367 [7.61]
	Whether Chairman of the Board is a VC	-0.52281 [-2.32]		-0.56672 [-2.36]		-0.50616 [2.52]	-0.54849 [-2.30]	
Income Rights	Average Equity Share Owned by ENs just before IPO	-0.02899 [-4.06]	-0.02627 [-3.27]					
	Average Equity Share Owned by VCs just before IPO	-0.04888 [-10.29]	-0.04484 [-8.13]					
	Total Equity Share Owned by ENs just before IPO			-0.01160 [-4.00]	-0.00991 [-3.00]			
	Total Equity Share Owned by VCs just before IPO					0.02901 [14.36]		
	Relative Equity Share of VCs						0.02456 [4.64]	0.02619 [4.31]
Control Variables	Number of VCs in Expansion and Later Stages	0.13552 [12.64]	0.13647 [10.27]	0.16940 [15.65]	0.173159 [13.07]	0.17801 [19.81]	0.17685 [17.02]	0.17906 [14.16]
	Number of VCs in the Early Stage	0.11519 [5.36]	0.10696 [4.38]	0.14258 [6.28]	0.12815 [4.98]	0.13463 [7.07]	0.14815 [6.61]	0.13262 [5.25]
	Number of VCs in Startup and Seed Stages	0.10954 [3.71]	0.115112 [3.11]	0.13218 [4.22]	0.13385 [3.42]	0.12406 [4.51]	0.13928 [4.49]	0.13789 [3.57]
	Constant	2.51331 [14.79]	2.37009 [11.85]	1.80288 [10.38]	1.70736 [8.24]	0.55639 [4.76]	1.38544 [10.03]	1.31399 [7.95]
	# of Observations	780	555	786	558	875	785	557
	R^2	0.586	0.5678	0.5317	0.5144	0.6260	0.5369	0.525

Second, what happens if we treat the ENs and the VCs as two groups? Regressions 12 and 13 show that syndication is negatively related to the total equity share of ENs, and Regression 14 shows that syndication is positively related to the total equity share of VCs. Regressions 15 and 16 further show a positive relationship between syndication and the relative equity share of VCs. Hence, the VCs as a group obtain a higher equity share through syndication. This evidence indicates that the ENs as a group use equity shares as a means to attract more VCs when necessary. This is consistent with the theoretical prediction that equity shares can be used as an effective complementary mechanism in alleviating agency problems (e.g., Admati–Pfleiderer 1994 and Wang–Zhou 2004).

Finally, we see a substantial increase in R^2 from Table 13 to Table 14 and from Table 13 to Table 15, implying a substantial improvement in the model's ability to explain the data when the variables relating to control rights and income rights are included. This means that syndication is closely related to the allocations of control rights and income rights and that syndication must play an important role beyond risk sharing.

Hence, our regression results point to a general tendency of syndication to a balanced allocation of income rights. Our regression results support Hypothesis 3.

In summary, syndication can be used or is likely to have been used as a mechanism for alleviating agency problems. We indeed find evidence of syndication's role in risk sharing (Table 13). More importantly, we also find strong evidence of syndication's role in deciding the allocations of income and control rights (Table 14 and Table 15).

6. Model Integrity

To ensure that our results are reliable, we tested for possible heteroskedasticity and multicollinearity problems in our regressions.

Heteroskedasticity

Using the Cook-Weisberg test (C-W test), we check for heteroskedasticity in our regressions. It turns out that, since the p-value is strictly less than 0.04, we can accept the null hypothesis of a constant variance for all our regressions in Tables 13–15. Hence, there is no evidence of heteroskedasticity in any of our regressions.

Multicollinearity

We tested for multicollinearity in our regressions by calculating the variance inflation factors (VIF) for each of the independent variables. According to the rules of Chatterjee, Hadi, and Price (2000), there is evidence of multicollinearity if:

i) The largest VIF is greater than 10 (they choose a more conservative threshold of 30).
ii) The mean of all the VIFs is considerably larger than 1.

In Table 16 and Table 17, we list all the VIFs for all our independent variables in all our regressions. We can see that none of the VIFs is greater than 10 and none of the means is considerably larger than 1. Hence, multicollinearity does not exist in any of our regressions.

Table 16. VIF Test for Multicollinearity (I)

Regression # Independent Variable	1	2	3	4	5	6	7	8	9
Number of VCs in Expansion and Later Stages	1.1	1.08	1.19	1.10	1.11	1.17	1.23	1.24	1.24
Number of VCs in the Early Stage	1.05	1.05	1.05	1.07	1.07	1.07	1.05	1.08	1.10
Number of VCs in Startup and Seed Stages	1.04	1.05	1.05	1.07	1.08	1.06	1.06	1.07	1.11
Whether High Technology Industry	1.03			1.01					
Whether Information Technology		1.01	1.03		1.03	1.01	1.03	1.02	1.04
Average Company Value for all Investment Rounds	1.02	1.01	1.02	1.01	1.01	1.02	1.02	1.02	1.02
S.D. of Equity Share Owned by ENs just before IPO			1.18				1.21	1.21	1.20
S.D. of Equity Share Owned by VCs just before IPO			1.07				1.09		
Annual Profit Growth Rate One Year after IPO				1.01	1.01				1.01
Proportion of VC directors						1.17	1.14	1.22	1.18
Whether Chairman of the Board is a VC						1.02		1.02	
Mean VIF	1.05	1.04	1.08	1.04	1.05	1.07	1.10	1.11	1.11

Table 17. VIF Test for Multicollinearity (II)

Regression # Independent Variable	10	11	12	13	14	15	16
Number of VCs in Expansion and Later Stages	1.40	1.43	1.27	1.27	1.21	1.18	1.18
Number of VCs in the Early Stage	1.10	1.11	1.09	1.11	1.09	1.07	1.09
Number of VCs in Startup and Seed Stages	1.07	1.11	1.07	1.11	1.08	1.06	1.10
Whether Information Technology	1.03	1.05	1.05	1.07	1.04	1.03	1.05
Average Company Value for all Investment Rounds	1.02	1.01	1.02	1.01	1.02	1.03	1.01
Annual Profit Growth Rate One Year after IPO		1.01		1.01			1.01
Proportion of VC directors	1.21	1.18	1.24	1.21	1.58	1.23	1.19
Whether Chairman of the Board is a VC	1.02		1.02			1.02	
Average Equity Share Owned by ENs just before IPO	1.18	1.19					
Average Equity Share Owned by VCs just before IPO	1.17	1.18					
Total Equity Share Owned by ENs just before IPO			1.32	1.33			
Total Equity Share Owned by VCs just before IPO					1.50		
Relative Equity Share of VCs						1.12	1.09
Mean VIF	1.13	1.14	1.13	1.14	1.21	1.09	1.09

7. Concluding Summary

Most venture capital financing is carried out through syndication. But, the rationale for syndication is not fully understood yet. The existing literature has focused on the roles of syndication in risk sharing and resource sharing. No one has investigated a possible role of syndication in agency problems. Also, the existing literature has focused on the rationale of VCs in syndication. Syndication is treated as a phenomenon in which the VCs band together to bargain with the ENs and to share information and resources among themselves. Little is discussed about the ENs' rationale for syndication. In reality, it is the ENs who initiate and encourage syndication.

With a sample data set of 933 VC-backed companies, we conducted a detailed analysis on the rationale for syndication by testing three hypotheses: syndication is for risk-sharing, for allocating control rights, and for allocating income rights. We pay attention to both ENs and VCs in syndication.

In testing the risk-sharing hypothesis, we find strong relationships between syndication and risk variables. Our regression results support the risk-sharing hypothesis. We also notice that the standard deviations of the ENs' revenue shares are reduced by syndication, implying a reduction of risks for the ENs. That is, syndication plays a role in risk sharing not only among VCs but also among ENs and between ENs and VCs.

In testing the agency hypotheses, we first find a balance between chairmanship and proportional representation on the board. We also find a reduction of equity shares for everyone, including both VCs and ENs, when more VCs participate. These findings point out that, first, contrary to the existing view in the literature, syndication does not mean that the VCs band together to bargain with the ENs; second, the two sides try to strike a balance in the allocations of control rights and income rights through syndication. Hence, our regression results support the agency hypotheses.

One byproduct of our investigation on the board of directors is that it touches an interesting issue: how the governance structure is formed for a new company. The existing literature understands the importance of the board but has little discussion on how it is formed. Our empirical analysis suggests a close relationship between the formation of the investors' syndicate and the formation of the governance structure.

References

[1] Admati, A.R. and P. Pfleiderer (1994), "Robust Financial Contracting and the Role of VCs," *Journal of Finance*, **49**(2), 374–402.

[2] Bergemann, D. and U. Hege (1998), "VC Financing, Moral Hazard, and Learning," *Journal of Banking and Finance*, **22**, 703–735.

[3] Berger, A.N. and G. Udell (1998), "The Economics of Small Business Finance: the Role of Private Equity and Debt Markets in the Financial Growth Cycle," *Journal of Banking and Finance* **22**, 613–673.

[4] Brander, J.A., R. Amit and W. Antweiler (2002), "VC Syndication: Improved Venture Selection vs. the Value-Added Hypothesis," *Journal of Economics and Management Strategy,* **11**(3), 423–452.

[5] Brav, A. and P.A. Gompers (1997), "Myth or Reality? The Long-Run Underperformance of Initial Public Offerings: Evidence from Venture Capital and Nonventure Capital-Backed Companies," *Journal of Finance*, **52**, 1791–1822.

[6] Bygrave, W.D. (1987), "Syndicated Investments by Venture Capital Firms: A Networking Perspective," *Journal of Business Venturing*, **2**, 139–154.

[7] Campbell, T.L. and M.B. Frye (2004), "Venture Capitalist involvement and the long-run performance of IPOs," Working paper, University of Central Florida.

[8] Chatterjee, S., A.S. Hadi, and B. Price (2000), *Regression Analysis by Example*, John Wiley and Sons.

[9] Fluck, Z., K. Garrison, and S. Myers (2004), "Venture Capital: An Experiment in Computational Corporate Finance," Working Paper, Michigan State University.

[10] Gohrman, M. and W. Sahlman (1989), "What Do Venture capitalists Do?" *Journal of Business Venturing,* **4**, 231–248.

[11] Gompers, P. A. and J. Lerner (2004), *The Venture Capital Cycle*, the MIT press.

[12] Hellmann, T. (1994), "Financial Structure and Control in Venture Capital," Chapter 2 of Ph.D Dissertation, Stanford University.

[13] Hellmann, T., 1998, "The Allocation of Control Rights in Venture Capital Contracts," *RAND Journal of Economics,* **29**(1), 57–76.

[14] Hellmann, T., and M. Puri (2002), "On the Fundamental Role of Venture Capital," *Federal Reserve Bank of Atlanta Economic Review,* 2002 (Q4), 19–23.

[15] Hochberg, Y.V. (2003), "Venture Capital and Corporate Governance in the Newly Public Firm," Working Paper, Cornell University.

[16] Kaplan, S. N., and P. Strömberg (2003), "Financial Contracting Theory Meets the Real World: An Empirical Analysis of Venture Capital Contracts," *Review of Economic Studies,* **70**(2), 281–315.

[17] Lehmann, E.E. (2004), "Does Venture Capital Syndication Spur Employment Growth and Shareholder Value? Evidence from German IPO Data," Working Paper, University of Konstanz.

[18] Lerner, J. (1994), "The Syndication of Venture Capital Investments," *Financial Management*, **23**(3), 16–27.

[19] Lerner, J. (1995), "Venture Capitalists and the Oversight of Private Firms," *Journal of Finance*, **50**(1), 301–318.

[20] Lockett, A. and M. Wright (2001), "The Syndication of Venture Capital Investments," *International Journal of Management Science,* **29**, 375–390.

[21] Manigart, S., A. Lockett, M. Meuleman, M. Wright, H. Landström, H. Bruining, P. Desbrieres and U. Hommel (2002), "Why do European Venture Capital Companies Syndicate?" *Working Paper*, Vlerick Leuven Gent Management School and Ghent University.

[22] Sahlman, W. (1990), "The Structure and Governance of Venture Capital Organizations," *Journal of Financial Economics*, **27**, 473–524.

[23] Sapienza, H. J. and A. K. Gupta (1994), "Impact of Agency Risks and Task Uncertainty on Venture Capitalist-CEO Interaction," *Academy of Management Journal,* **37**(6), 1618–1632.

[24] Smith, R.L. and J.K. Smith (2000), *Entrepreneurial Finance*, New York, Wiley.

[25] Sorenson, O. and T.E. Stuart (2001), "Syndication Networks and the Spatial Distribution of Venture Capital Investments," *American Journal of Sociology*, **106**(6), 1546–1588.

[26] Wang, S. (2006), "Convertibles and Milestones in Staged Financing," *Review of Finance*, Revision and resubmission.

[27] Wang, S., and H. Zhou (2004), "Staged Financing in Venture Capital: Moral Hazard and Risks," *Journal of Corporate Finance,* **10**, 131–151.

[28] Wang, S. and T. Zhu (2005): "Control Allocation, Revenue Sharing, and Joint Ownership," *International Economic Review*, **46** (3), 895–915.

[29] Wright, M. and A. Lockett (2003), "The Structure and Management of Alliances: Syndication in the Venture Capital Industry," *Journal of Management Studies,* **40**(8), 2073–2102.

In: Handbook of Business and Finance
Editors: M. Bergmann and T. Faust, pp. 241-257

ISBN: 978-1-60692-855-4
© 2010 Nova Science Publishers, Inc.

Chapter 10

THE ECONOMICS OF THE NONPROFIT SECTOR: TOWARD THE SELF-SUFFICIENCY PARADIGM

Vladislav Valentinov

Leibniz Institute of Agricultural Development in Central and Eastern Europe, Halle, Germany

Abstract

The current economics of nonprofit organization has two interrelated problems. First, it is still marked by a logical separation between the demand-side and supply-side arguments for the existence of nonprofit firms. Second, it implicitly conceptualizes nonprofit organization as a nexus of contractual exchange relationships and thus overlooks the important element of noncontractibility associated with the not-for-profit motivation of nonprofit managers and entrepreneurs.

The present chapter presents an overview of the author's previous research aimed at addressing these problems. It is shown that both these problems can be solved by grounding the understanding of nonprofit organization in the theory of the division of labor. From the perspective of this theory, nonprofit organization is located outside the social division of labor since it is not based on profit making motivation. This fact implies that nonprofit organization must be treated as an institutional form of collective self-sufficiency, i.e., self-provision of stakeholder groups with the realization of nonprofit missions. The self-sufficiency view of nonprofit organization solves the first above mentioned problem since the notion of self-sufficient activity involves a harmony between the supply-side and demand-side motivations. Moreover, the notion of self-sufficiency presents a clear contrast with the institution of the for-profit firm that is rooted in the social division of labor. While the social division of labor requires economic organization based on contractual exchange, this is not the case with self-sufficiency, thus solving the second problem as well.

The self-sufficiency view of nonprofit organization yields two major organizational economics implications that are explored in this chapter. First, opportunism must be less important in the nonprofit sector than for-profit one, because of the harmony of demand-side and supply-side motivations of individuals practicing self-sufficiency. Hence, nonprofit firms economize on transaction cost primarily by reducing the cost of information processing and not by aligning incentives in order to minimize opportunism. Second, the relevant incentive alignment problem in nonprofit organization consists not of minimizing opportunism, but of preventing the crowding out of intrinsic motivation.

The paper concludes with exploring special rationales for nonprofit organization in agriculture and rural development. It is argued that rurality and agriculture are associated with special limitations on the ability of for-profit firms to satisfy the needs of rural dwellers, thus creating a niche for cooperatives and rural nonprofit firms. The last section summarizes the argument and presents the most important implications for further research.

Introduction

A basic theme of research in the economics of the nonprofit sector is that nonprofit firms compensate for the limitations in the ability of for-profit firms to satisfy consumers' needs. The economic theories of the nonprofit sector are concerned with identifying the precise nature of these limitations and the institutional advantages of nonprofit firms in addressing these. However, while the development of economic approaches to the nonprofit sector has been truly impressive over the last decades, the full implications of the above research theme do not seem to have been sufficiently explored.

Specifically, there are two reasons to argue that the economic theories of the nonprofit sector have not gone as far as this research theme would require them to go. First, these theories are still marked by a logical separation between the demand-side and supply-side arguments for the existence of nonprofit firms. Originally noted by Hansmann in 1987, this separation means that the reasons why customers or citizens need the outputs of nonprofit firms have little to do with the reasons why these firms are created by nonprofit entrepreneurs. Since Hansmann made this observation, economists have made substantial progress in integrating the demand-side and supply-side rationales for the nonprofit sector (e.g., Steinberg 2004; 2006). Yet, despite the development of several models uniting these rationales on the basis of highly stylized assumptions, there still does not exist a general and commonly accepted theoretical framework that would clearly derive the motivations of nonprofit entrepreneurs from those of customers or citizens.

While the problem of separation between the demand-side and supply-side arguments has definitely not been unrecognized in the literature (Hansmann 1987; Steinberg 1993), its significance for the theoretical understanding of the nonprofit sector appears to be underestimated. Indeed, it is this problem that prevents the for-profit sector from fully satisfying the needs of consumers. Profit making motivation of for-profit entrepreneurs is evidently different from the consumption motivation guiding the behavior of consumers. As illustrated by the theory of market failure, this difference in motivations may prevent for-profit entrepreneurs from producing product mixes most preferred by consumers. Crucially, it is this difference in motivations that creates a functional niche for the nonprofit sector. Hence, if nonprofit firms are to compensate for the limitations of for-profit firms, they must exhibit a better integration between the motivations of those who create them and those who consume their outputs. If this integration is not the case, then the ability of nonprofit firms to compensate for the limitations of the for-profit sector is undermined. Indeed, the lack of the required integration implies that although nonprofits may address the limitations of for-profits, they do not necessarily emerge when these limitations are particularly pronounced, and even nonprofits currently in existence do not necessarily exist for the purpose of addressing these limitations. This point does not seem to have been recognized in the literature, although it indicates a major deficit in the current state of theoretical literature on the economics of the nonprofit sector.

The second reason why the economic theories of the nonprofit sector do not appear to be radical enough is that they implicitly conceive of nonprofit organization as a nexus of contractual exchange relationships. The problem with this conception is that it is primarily applicable to the institutions of the market and of the for-profit firm (though heterodox institutional economics questions even this application (e.g. Hodgson 1988)). If the for-profit firm is constituted by a network of contractual exchange relationships (among factor suppliers, entrepreneurs, and consumers), and if this firm is limited in its ability to satisfy consumers' needs, there must be something about contractual exchange that prevents it from fully serving these needs. Consequently, if nonprofit organization is to address the limitations of for-profit firms, it must embody a logic of economic organization other than that of contractual exchange. This gives rise to a question on how to precisely define the 'non-exchange' nature of nonprofit organization. A related important question concerns reconciling the 'non-exchange' interpretation of nonprofit organization with the constitutional economics postulate of normative individualism that treats all forms of voluntary social interaction as exchange behavior.

The two indicated deficits in the current economic literature on nonprofit organization constitute the basic motivation for the present work. The present paper summarizes a new theoretical understanding of nonprofit organization that addresses both of these deficits at the same time. This understanding is based on the theory of the social division of labor. As the social division of labor is profit-motivated process, it cannot include nonprofit organization, in contrast to for-profit firms. As will be shown in this paper, elaborating this insight yields a theoretical mechanism for deriving the motivations of nonprofit entrepreneurs from those of consumers dissatisfied with for-profit firms, with this derivation being possible precisely by virtue of nonprofit organization being an institution transcending the logic of contractual exchange.

The rest of this paper is structured into four sections. The first section explicates the way nonprofit organization can be conceptualized from the perspective the theory of the social division of labor. This will permit integrating the demand-side and supply-side rationales for nonprofit organization and explicitly defining its 'non-exchange' nature. The second section examines the organizational economics implications of this argument by analyzing the transaction cost-economizing role of nonprofit organization, by viewing it as a governance mechanism comparable to market and hierarchy, and by contrasting the problems of incentive alignment in for-profit and nonprofit firms. The third section explores the peculiarities of nonprofit organization in agriculture and rural development, both of which are shown to create a special functional niche for it in view of the respective limitations in the operation of for-profit firms. The fourth section summarizes the argument and presents the most important implications for further research.

Nonprofit Organization as Self-sufficiency

The Approach of the Theory of the Division of Labor[1]

The theory of the division of labor defines this process as a shift of productive activities from households to for-profit firms (Locay 1990) and describes it in terms of two principal

---

[1] This section draws on my (2008e) paper, unless stated otherwise.

propositions. One is that the division of labor improves productivity due to the existence of gains from specialization; the other is that the division of labor is limited by a number of factors, such as the extent of the market (Smith 1981), transaction cost (Becker and Murphy 1992; Yang and Borland 1991), and availability of knowledge (Becker and Murphy 1992). Crucially, this theory suggests that there exist two basic and complementary mechanisms of gratification of human wants, exchange and self-sufficiency. The role of the limitations on the division of labor lies in drawing the boundary between those human wants (preferences) that can be gratified by relying on the division of labor, and those that cannot. The theory of the division of labor does not claim that the latter wants must remain ungratified; rather, it sees the mechanism of their gratification not in the division of labor and exchange, but in self-sufficiency which is understood as production for one's own consumption (e.g. Demsetz 1997: 7). Gratification of wants through the division of labor and exchange is superior in the sense that it permits the realization of gains from specialization. Yet, when the generation of these gains is precluded by substantial limitations on the division of labor, individuals nevertheless seek to gratify their wants through self-sufficiency, despite the higher cost of doing so (due to the impossibility of realizing gains from specialization).

By emphasizing the existence of two alternative mechanisms of gratification of human preferences, the theory of the division of labor creates the possibility to understand various institutions as relying on different mixtures of these mechanisms. This is particularly important in view of the market failure theories' tendency to reduce nonprofit organization to a mere network of contractual exchange relationships, thus treating it in the same way as for-profit firms (Adaman and Madra 2002). Given that exchange relationships are subject to failures specified in the above theories, the theory of the division of labor suggests that nonprofit organization, apart from exchange relationships, necessarily involves an element of self-sufficiency, and hence cannot be viewed as a purely contractual nexus. More specifically, the theory of the division of labor implies that nonprofit firms are self-sufficient with respect to the activity of mission realization, but not necessarily with respect to other activities that they make undertake. The proposed self-sufficiency view of nonprofit organization does not exclude the possibility of nonprofit firms acquiring inputs and selling outputs in the marketplace through regular market transactions, as long as the object of these transactions is not the activity of mission realization. Self-sufficiency embodied in nonprofit organization may be designated as partial, since it refers only to the latter activity.

The self-sufficiency view of nonprofit organization implies a difference in the market failure-addressing roles of for-profit and nonprofit firms (Valentinov 2009a). Specifically, for-profit firms address market failure by substituting internal organization for market exchange, as internal organization can, under specified conditions, be more efficient in aligning incentives of economic agents and improving information flows between them (Williamson 1971). Since for-profit firms are themselves participants in market exchange, they address market failure by facilitating this exchange (specifically, by lowering the transaction cost). In contrast, the self-sufficiency view of nonprofit organization suggests that nonprofit firms address market failure by replacing exchange with self-sufficiency. Therefore, it is more precise to argue that for-profit firms emerge as a consequence of market failure, while nonprofit ones are a consequence of the existence of constraints on the division of labor.

In my (2008a) paper I showed that the difference in the market failure-addressing roles of for-profit and nonprofit firms is helpful in explaining the institutional peculiarities of economic development of low-income countries. Specifically, according to Dorward et al. (2005), low-income countries are often characterized by the occurrence of high transaction costs constraining the scope of operation of for-profit firms and respectively giving rise to non-market organizations such as producer groups, community-based organizations, microfinance groups, and common property management resource groups. In a broad sense, these non-market organizations are nonprofit, and their role lies in reacting to transaction cost acting as a constraint on the division of labor. Nonprofit organizations thus gain prominence in low-income countries for the reason that the scope of operation of for-profit firms is particularly constrained. As transaction cost constrains the division of labor, it follows that the arguments of Coase (1937) and Williamson (1971) about the transaction cost-economizing capacity of for-profit firms appear to be less applicable to low-income countries than to well-developed ones.

Application to the Major Economic Theories of Nonprofit Organization[2]

This section demonstrates that the major economic theories of nonprofit organization are consistent with its designation as a form of self-sufficiency. Moreover, these theories will be shown to reveal specific reasons why certain kinds of market failures cannot be overcome by for-profit organizational arrangements. The section will be structured according to the major theories of the nonprofit sector, such as the public goods theory, consumer control theory, trustworthiness theory, and the supply-side theory.

The Public Goods Theory

The public goods theory of nonprofit organization, developed by Weisbrod (1991), argues that the government provides public goods to meet the needs of the median voter. If a fragment of the population happens to have a greater need for a certain public good than is the case with the median voter, or needs a particular variety of this good that is different from the standard variety, then nonprofit organization represents a mechanism for satisfying this residual demand by means of privately producing these public goods by those who need them. More importantly for the present discussion, this governmental failure also represents market failure, because for-profit firms are prevented from supplying the required public goods due to the free-rider problem. Private production of public goods by those who need these goods for consumption purpose represents the process of self-sufficiency, since the founders of respective firms produce these public goods for own consumption rather than for sale.

The commonly cited examples of these goods include helping the needy and organization of medical research (Steinberg 2006; Hansmann 1987; Slivinsky 2003). In the U.S., the corresponding missions are pursued by nonprofit firms such as CARE, the American Heart Association, the American Cancer Society, and the March of Dimes (Hansmann 1987). Through these organizations, interested individuals contribute their time or money to the production of those public goods that they prefer, and in this sense, provide these goods to themselves, thus engaging in partial collective self-sufficiency.

---

[2] This section draws on my (2008e) paper.

The Consumer Control Theory

A related type of market failure that nonprofit organization can theoretically correct is emphasized by the 'consumer control' theory, which argues that markets may not ensure sufficiently strong consumer control over the activities of for-profit firms (Ben-Ner 1986). Stricter consumer control may be necessary to resist opportunistic behavior by managers and to guarantee that products offered by for-profit firms are of a sufficiently high quality. Nonprofit firms emerge by means of consumers taking over control of these firms, thus transforming them into a variety of consumer cooperatives. For example, parents who are unsure about the quality of service received by their children in for-profit day-care centers may create nonprofit day-care centers in whose governance they play a more substantial role (ibid). This transformation indicates a partial substitution of the reliance on market exchange by the reliance on self-sufficiency. Indeed, instead of delegating the organization of respective production activities to for-profit firms, consumers need to organize them themselves. By organizing them on their own, they signal that they do not see an opportunity for gratifying their consumption preferences through market exchange institutions.

The Trustworthiness Theory

According to the trustworthiness theory of nonprofit organization, consumers may have limited ability to evaluate the quality of particular products, especially complex personal services, such as nursing care for the elderly, day care for young children, education, and hospital care. If these services are provided on the for-profit basis, the managers of firms supplying these services would have incentives to take opportunistic advantage of the uninformed consumers in order to earn additional profit. The nonprofit organizational form dampens incentives for this opportunistic behavior as the nondistribution constraint precludes the appropriation of profit (Hansmann 1987). The trustworthiness theory, however, is incomplete because it does not clarify the nature of entrepreneurial motivation. Specifically, given that entrepreneurs cannot appropriate profit, they must be guided by a certain nonpecuniary motivation, which may include practicing commitment, sympathy, reciprocity, or receiving private benefits such as prestige and pride (see e.g. Rose-Ackerman 1996: 714). Hence, nonprofit entrepreneurs obtaining the above utility from operating nursing homes, day-care centers, universities, and hospitals, are practicing self-sufficiency for the reason that they perform these activities themselves rather than delegate these to specialized suppliers through the system of market exchange. From a logical point of view, performing a directly utility-enhancing activity represents self-sufficiency in much the same way as producing public or private goods for the purpose of own consumption.

The Supply-Side Theory

The objective of the supply-side theory of nonprofit organization is to understand the motivation of entrepreneurs who choose to found nonprofit rather than for-profit firms. A central concept in the supply-side theory is that of ideological entrepreneurship, implying that nonprofit firms are created by those entrepreneurs who seek not to generate profit, but rather to practice or disseminate particular ideologies and beliefs. Empirically, James (1987) found out the most important type of ideological entrepreneurs is represented by religious groups creating nonprofit schools and voluntary hospitals in the U.S. and UK, Catholic schools in France and Latin America, missionary nonprofit organizations in the developing countries. Ideological preferences of these entrepreneurs motivate them to get personally involved in their realization of ideologies instead of delegating this activity to for-profit firms. In this case, the division of labor is constrained not by insufficient feasibility, but by its insufficient desirability on the part of ideologically motivated individuals. Hence, religion-driven and other ideological nonprofit organizations are self-sufficient with respect to practicing commitment to the respective ideologies.

Implications for Explaining the Nondistribution Constraint[3]

The nondistribution constraint is a key characteristic of nonprofit firms and refers to the prohibition to distribute residual earnings to individuals who exercise control over these firms, such as officers, directors, or members (Hansmann 1987). The currently common explanation of the nondistribution constraint is given by the trustworthiness theory developed by Henry Hansmann (1980). This theory argues that the nondistribution constraint makes nonprofit firms more trustworthy in the eyes of consumers and donors than for-profit firms. For donors, the enhanced trustworthiness facilitates donative financing by providing assurance that the donated funds will not be appropriated as profits. For consumers, the nondistribution constraint serves as a signal that the firms' owners have no incentives to cheat by 'cutting corners' on quality or by providing unnecessary services (ibid).

The trustworthiness theory has been traditionally criticized for exaggerating the significance of the nondistribution constraint (Steinberg 2006) and assuming its perfect enforcement (e.g., Ortmann/Schlesinger 2003). While the trustworthiness theory has survived these criticisms (Steinberg 2006), it has additional limitations highlighting its logical incompleteness. First, the trustworthiness theory does not explain why the nondistribution constraint does not destroy the entrepreneurial motivation. Second, the trustworthiness theory explains the nondistribution constraint only in terms of information asymmetry between firm managers and consumers and thus has little to say about the nondistribution constraint in nonprofit firms existing for reasons other than the above-mentioned information asymmetry. At the same time, other theories, such as the public goods theory (Weisbrod 1991), consumer control theory (Ben-Ner 1986), and supply-side theory (Steinberg 2006) identify the functions of nonprofit firms without explicit specification of the role played by the nondistribution constraint in ensuring the fulfillment of these functions. Therefore, the trustworthiness theory does not provide a complete or general explanation of the nondistribution constraint that would be logically interrelated and consistent with other major theories of nonprofit organization.

The self-sufficiency view of nonprofit organization eliminates these difficulties in explaining the nondistribution constraint. According to this view, the nondistribution constraint is a legal expression of the fact that at least some stakeholders of nonprofit firms are guided by the nonpecuniary motivation related to realizing these firms' missions. Moreover, this explanation of the nondistribution constraint is consistent with other theories of nonprofit organization as all of them involve the nonpecuniary motivation of nonprofit

---

[3] This section draws on my (2008f) paper.

managers and entrepreneurs. At the same time, the self-sufficiency view of nonprofit organization does not deny the possibility of the trustworthiness-enhancing effect of the nondistribution constraint. Rather, this view locates the main reason for the higher trustworthiness of nonprofit firms not in the nondistribution constraint itself, but in the credible nonpecuniary motivation of managers and entrepreneurs.

Constitutional Economics Implications

The Constitutional Economics View of Nonprofit Organization[4]

Constitutional economics posits that all voluntary forms of social interaction can be explained in terms of particular gains-from-trade that accrue to participating individuals. Buchanan assumes the process of trade, or exchange, to be of such a fundamental nature that its occurrence is not even hindered by transaction cost. The role of transaction cost lies, according to Buchanan (1999), in defining the character of the institutional setting of exchange, rather than in generally preventing exchange from taking place. In any given institutional setting, individuals may derive gains-from-trade as long as their freedom to enter into exchange is not artificially constrained. Following this reasoning, transaction cost can affect resource allocation patterns, but it is irrelevant to the derivation of gains-from-trade. These gains exist independently of whether trade is hindered by transaction cost or not.

The self-sufficiency view of nonprofit organization does not readily yield itself to reconstruction in terms of the concept of gains-from-trade. Indeed, nonprofit organizations arise in cases when regular market exchange involving the interaction of consumers and for-profit firms is prevented by high transaction cost (Krashinsky 1986; Hansmann 1980). While it is clear that individual involvement in nonprofit firms is motivated by some form of individual gain, it is questionable that this gain stems from trade, as trade in the proper sense of the term has been disabled by transaction cost, and it is precisely this disabling of trade that gives rise to the emergence of nonprofit organization.

It is, however, noteworthy that Buchanan's proposition for explaining social interaction in terms of gains-from-trade is primarily motivated by his adherence to normative individualism, which requires locating the source of value in individuals rather than in supra-individual entities. At the same time, adherence to normative individualism is evidently not impaired by recognizing that transaction cost may prevent trade from taking place. Transaction cost, by its very definition, stands in the way of trade and exchange, but it nevertheless hardly necessitates explaining social reality in terms of methodological collectivism. Indeed, scholars who pointed out that nonprofit organization constitutes an institutional response to high transaction cost did not believe these organizations to be supra-individual organic entities (Krashinsky 1986; Hansmann 1980). Given the basic consistence of normative individualism with the fact of trade being prevented by transaction cost and superseded by nonprofit organization, it may be argued that the exchange paradigm of constitutional economics can be qualified in such a way as to allow for distinguishing between the for-profit and nonprofit sectors.

---

[4] This section draws on my (2008c) paper.

The designation of nonprofit organization as an institutional form of self-sufficiency implies that the theory of the division of labor circumscribes the extent to which social interaction can be explained in terms of individual gains-from-trade. While this theory does not deny that individuals gain from their actions and interactions, it asserts that these gains do not always or necessarily stem from trade, as they may also arise from self-sufficient activity. The major implication of the theory of the division of labor for constitutional economics seems to be that exchange, as a mechanism for gratifying human wants, is subject to certain limitations and is therefore usefully supplemented with self-sufficiency. In the following subsection, the complementarity between exchange and self-sufficiency is illustrated on the example of socio-economic rules as the key category of constitutional economics.

Socio-economic Rules as an Object of Self-sufficiency[5]

Constitutional economics views the formulation and observation of rules as the object of political exchange among rational individuals. Buchanan argued that 'individuals choose to impose constraints or limits on their own behavior primarily, if not exclusively, as part of an exchange in which the restrictions on their own actions are sacrificed in return for the benefits that are anticipated from the reciprocally extended restrictions on the actions of others with whom they interact' (1999, p. 380). Hence, according to constitutional economics, any socio-economic rule on which individuals might agree can thus be interpreted as the object of an exchange relationship.

To compare the relevance of the concepts of exchange and self-sufficiency for describing the maintenance for social order, an additional clarification of these concepts is in order. Defining self-sufficiency as 'production for one's own consumption' (Demsetz 1997) requires defining exchange as production for the consumption of individuals other than the producer. Hence, a basic difference between self-sufficiency and exchange consists of the extent to which an individual participates in the production of an object he consumes. Given these definitions, maintaining social order represents collective self-sufficiency since it is predicated on each individual complying with the respective rules. Observing rules can be usefully contrasted with exchanging ordinary private goods in the marketplace. The process of market exchange presupposes the realization of production activity by some, rather than all, individuals in a society. Thus, market exchange enables individuals to enjoy the results of production undertaken by other individuals who derive gains from specializing in this production. In contrast, the production of social order by means of individual observation of the respective rules admits no comparable specialization; each individual is supposed to participate in this production to the same extent as any other member of the respective community.

Since the very concept of exchange is defined by the possibility of relieving economic agents of the need to participate in the production of the goods they consume, rule observation is more appropriately characterized as collective self-sufficiency rather than exchange. A broader implication of the proposed argument is that socio-economic institutions can be explained as embodying different mixes of exchange and self-sufficiency as the two basic mechanisms of human wants gratification. Given that various market institutions, which clearly build on the former mechanism, fail in various respects (such as market failures and

---

[5] This section draws on my (2008b) paper.

constraints on the division of labor), these failures supposedly may be compensated by other institutions embodying greater recourse to self-sufficiency than to exchange. Nonprofit organization and maintenance of social order are some examples of institutions involving self-sufficiency, but there may be many others still waiting to be discovered and analyzed.

Organizational Economics Approaches

Nonprofit Organization as a Governance Mechanism

In my (2006) paper, I explored whether nonprofit organization constitutes a governance mechanism comparable with those of market and hierarchy. While nonprofit firms often incorporate elements of hierarchical organization, their distinct identity is often located in their embodying collective action of free individuals (e.g., Lohmann 1992; Wex 2004). On this basis, I argued that nonprofit organization may be interpreted as a mechanism for governing transactions marked by a high commonness of transactional participants' interests. In contrast, the commonness of transactional participants' interests is lower for hierarchical organization in view of the principal-agent problems in the subordinate-superordinate relation, and is arguably lowest for market organization in view of the mutual opposition of buyers' and sellers' interests. Thus, the commonness of transactional participants' interests may be used as a criterion for representing market, hierarchy, and nonprofit organization as elements of a governance continuum. Whereas the conventional view of the governance continuum (Williamson 1991; Menard 2004) can be described as 'from markets through hybrids to hierarchies', the proposed alternative view implies a different sequence – from markets through hierarchies to nonprofit organization.

Revisiting the Transaction Cost View of Nonprofit Organization[6]

The transaction cost theory of the for-profit firm has provided an important tool in the construction of the economic theories of nonprofit organization, some of which can be readily restated in transaction cost-economizing terms. Krashinsky (1986) demonstrated that nonprofit organization's economic role is to ensure a more efficient economizing on transaction cost than could be achieved by alternative institutional arrangements for certain types of transactions involving information asymmetry. However, in my 2008d paper I argued that the transaction cost theory of the for-profit firm consists of two conceptually distinct strands of literature, only one of which has been adequately taken into account in the nonprofit economics literature.

These two strands can be designated as the incentive alignment approach and the Coasean approach. The former approach places the economic role of the for-profit firm in the structuring of the economic agents' incentives in such a way as to minimize opportunistic behavior, in spite of the existing information asymmetries. By contrast, according to the latter approach, the economic role of the for-profit firm lies not in minimizing opportunism, but in minimizing the cost of handling information (i.e., transaction cost in the Coasean

---

[6] This section draws on my (2008d) paper, unless stated otherwise.

understanding), without any recourse to opportunism and the need to align incentives. The latter approach has been initiated by Coase (1937) and continued in other writings emphasizing the role of the for-profit firm in reducing the cost of searching for, processing, and communicating information (e.g., Malmgren 1961; Radner 1992).

While transaction cost explanations of nonprofit organization have accentuated its role in discouraging opportunism, I argued that the major aspect of the transaction cost-economizing role of nonprofit firms refers to reducing the cost of handling information (Valentinov 2008d). This aspect is particularly important for intrinsically motivated stakeholders who are not willing to act opportunistically but are boundedly rational in the sense of Williamson (1985). For these stakeholders, nonprofit firms economize on transaction cost primarily by reducing the number of contracts that needs to be made among individual stakeholders and by replacing short-term contracts with long-term ones.

Moreover, for nonprofit firms, the cost of handling information involves a dimension that is not relevant to for-profit firms, and that concerns the cost of identifying individuals supporting a certain nonprofit mission. As this motivational characteristic is not readily observable, individuals supporting a specific nonprofit mission may need to incur non-trivial cost in identifying each other, while the monetary motivation underlying individual involvement in for-profit firm can be safely assumed as universally present. This search cost may therefore exceed that of for-profit firms. This cost can be economized by nonprofit firms if they actively inform the general public about their missions, activities, and resource requirements (particularly in the form of fundraising campaigns). The information provided to the general public reaches intrinsically motivated individuals (such as donors, volunteers, prospective employees willing to accept relatively low wages) thus enabling them to reduce their costs of individual search.

In my (2007b) paper, I made a similar argument by distinguishing between two types of transaction costs economized by nonprofit firms: opportunism-induced and bounded rationality-induced. I have shown that economizing on the latter type of transaction cost enables public benefit nonprofit firms to obtain more charitable contributions, and mutual benefit nonprofit firms – to extend membership to individuals with low intensities of need in specific public or collective goods. These arguments are confirmed by the fact that existing nonprofit firms are generally not free from opportunism, and it is therefore not clear if they achieve a significant reduction in opportunism-induced transaction costs. Economizing on bounded rationality-induced transaction costs is much more evident.

Toward an Incentive Alignment Theory of Nonprofit Organization

In my (2008g) paper, I have argued that intrinsic motivation of many nonprofit employees and other stakeholders indicates their lack of interest in behaving opportunistically toward the leadership of their nonprofit firms. Accordingly, and in contrast to for-profit firms, the incentive alignment problem of nonprofit organization lies not in minimizing opportunistic behavior of these stakeholders, but rather in preventing the crowding-out of their intrinsic motivation, primarily by the use of the nondistribution constraint and self-governance. These governance instruments are thus rationalized in terms of their switching off, respectively, of monetary and administrative incentives that are known to adversely affect intrinsic motivation.

However, opportunism in nonprofit firms can be practiced by those stakeholders who do not share the relevant intrinsic motivation but pretend that they do. The latter individuals may be attracted to nonprofit firms, in particular, by relaxed hierarchical control and supervision opening greater space for shirking. In turn, the need for relaxing hierarchical control may stem from the need for avoiding the crowding out of intrinsic motivation of those who have it. While ensuring a positive work atmosphere for mission-driven individuals, relaxed hierarchical control may thus entail an unintended consequence of encouraging opportunism which may endanger the nonprofit firms' survival.

Hence, nonprofit firms face the challenge of hindering external opportunists in getting engaged in nonprofit firms. This may be achieved by the use of screening devices, one of which is the practice of paying lower wages in the nonprofit sector than can be earned elsewhere (e.g. Preston 1989; Ballou and Weisbrod 2003; Leete 2006). On the cost side, this signalling device may make employment in the nonprofit sector impossible to individuals who are intrinsically motivated to work for a particular nonprofit mission yet have no alternative sources of income to support their existence.

Applications to Agriculture and Rural Development

An Organizational Economics Rationale for Agricultural Cooperatives[7]

Agricultural economists traditionally explain the dominance of family farms in the agriculture of Western (and developing) countries in terms of the low feasibility of hierarchical organization of agricultural production due to supervision and monitoring difficulties (Schmitt 1991; Pollak 1985). The use of hierarchical organization is a major characteristic of for-profit firms (Coase 1937; Williamson 1985); hence, this organization's low feasibility constrains the extent to which for-profit firms can operate in agriculture and thus creates a niche for nonprofit organization in the form of agricultural cooperatives. However, in my (2007X) paper I argue that agricultural cooperatives fill this niche not because they embody self-sufficiency, but rather because they address the organizational disadvantages of family farms. Since the size of family farms is constrained by the size of the family, they find it difficult to realize external economies of scale and to develop market power comparable to that of their up- and downstream trading partners. These disadvantages represent the major motives for the creation of agricultural cooperatives.

Thus, the role of agricultural cooperatives lies in enabling the realization of advantages of hierarchical organization in agriculture while avoiding the need to incur its transaction costs, which are prohibitively high in this sector. This explanation of agricultural cooperatives is sector-specific since it does not apply to sectors other than agriculture, as compared with other explanations pointing out the general ability of cooperatives to economize on transaction costs and to develop 'countervailing power'. While the latter explanations reveal the general institutional advantage of cooperative organization, the account of sectoral specificity clarifies why this advantage is of particular relevance for agriculture.

---

[7] This section draws on my (2007a) paper.

Toward a Theory of the Rural Nonprofit Sector[8]

In many countries of the world, the development of rural areas is actively supported by nonprofit organizations, such as local community organizations, mutual self-help groups, rural and agricultural cooperatives, rural partnerships, and NGOs (OECD, 2006; Uphoff, 1993). However, in spite of the generally recognized importance of the nonprofit sector in rural development, economists have not yet examined whether rurality can represent a distinct theoretical reason for the existence of rural nonprofits. In an unpublished manuscript, I build on the self-sufficiency view of nonprofit organization in order to argue that rurality can constitute such a reason. The applicability of the self-sufficiency view of nonprofit organization to explaining the existence of rural nonprofits is based on the fact that rural areas, in both developed and developing countries, have a number of socio-economic characteristics that result in high transaction cost hindering the development of the system of the division of labor. These characteristics of rural areas most importantly include relatively low population density, significant geographic dispersion of consumers and producers, and relatively poor infrastructure (Terluin 2001). Transaction cost stemming from these characteristics is 'rurality-specific'.

Transaction cost analyzed by the traditional transaction cost theory is able of being reduced (economized) by using the right governance mechanisms. In contrast, the above mentioned characteristics of rural areas represent 'brute facts' that cannot be altered by using any governance mechanism; hence, the rurality-specific transaction cost does not meaningfully yield itself to being economized. Evidently, the inability of the rurality-specific transaction cost of being economized explains the persistence of the rural development challenges throughout the world. Indeed, transaction cost obviously exists in urban regions as well, but there it can be relatively well economized by for-profit governance mechanisms, ranging from market through intermediate contracting to hierarchy. It is the relative absence of these governance mechanisms in rural areas that gives expression to the numerous rurality-specific problems that are supposed to be alleviated by the rural development policies. That for-profit governance mechanisms do not arise to economize on the rurality-specific transaction cost suggests that this cost is more appropriately conceived of as a constraint on the division of labor. As the division of labor in rural areas is subject to additional rurality-specific constraints, rural areas must exhibit greater recourse to self-sufficiency, specifically in the institutional form of nonprofit organization.

Conclusion

The contributions of this paper focus on three themes. The first theme concerns reconsidering nonprofit organization in the light of the theory of the social division of labor. From the perspective of this theory, nonprofit organization is an institutional form of collective self-sufficiency, i.e., self-provision of intrinsically motivated stakeholders with the realization of nonprofit missions. The notion of self-sufficient activity involves a harmony between the supply-side and demand-side motivations, thus integrating the supply-side and demand-side theories of the nonprofit sector. It also presents a clear contrast with the

---

[8] This section draws on my (2009b ~~forthcoming~~ paper).

institution of the for-profit firm that is rooted in the social division of labor. While the social division of labor is based on contractual exchange, this is not the case with self-sufficiency. Furthermore, it has been argued that the self-sufficiency view of nonprofit organization implies a need for the constitutional economics research program to replace the exchange interpretation of voluntary behavior ("the exchange paradigm") by a broader paradigm allowing for the possibility of voluntary self-sufficient activity.

The second theme concerns the organizational economics implications of the self-sufficiency view of nonprofit organization. The major idea here is that opportunism as an explanatory factor of economic organization is less important in the nonprofit sector than for-profit one, because of the harmony of demand-side and supply-side motivations of individuals practicing self-sufficiency. Accordingly, nonprofit firms economize on transaction cost primarily by reducing the cost of information processing rather than by aligning incentives in order to minimize opportunism. This contrasts with the mainstream theory of the firm literature emphasizing the crucial role of the for-profit firm in minimizing opportunism. Given the lesser importance of opportunism, the incentive alignment problem in nonprofit organization consists not of discouraging opportunism, but of preventing the crowding out of intrinsic motivation. Moreover, nonprofit organization can be conceived of as a governance mechanism comparable to market and hierarchy. As governance mechanisms, market, hierarchy, and nonprofit organization embody increasing commonness of interests of transactional participants.

The third theme encompasses applications of the self-sufficiency view of nonprofit organization to agriculture and rural development. The persistence of rural development challenges suggests that rurality and agriculture are associated with special limitations on the ability of for-profit firms to satisfy the needs of rural dwellers. Thus it has been shown that the peculiarities of agricultural production underlying the persistence of family farms result in higher transaction costs of using market and hierarchical organization in the agrifood sector. These costs are economized by partially replacing agricultural markets and hierarchies with cooperatives. Next, the rural dwellers' need for self-sufficiency embodied in nonprofit organization is enhanced by rurality-specific transaction costs constraining the process of the social division of labor in rural areas. These costs result from characteristics of rural areas such as geographical dispersion, poor infrastructure, and low population density. Rurality thus represents a distinct theoretical reason for the existence of the rural nonprofit sector.

The most important implications for further research arising from the developed theoretical propositions relate to their empirical verification. So far, the empirical research in nonprofit economics has followed the traditional separation between the market failure and supply-side theories. While both of these theories were subjected to respective empirical tests (e.g., Anheier/Salamon 2006; Salamon/Anheier 1998; James 1987), the proposed theoretical framework encompassing both the market failure and supply-side arguments has been missing and therefore could not underlie empirical research. At the same time, this framework yields the empirically testable implication of the causal relationship between the occurrence of market failures and nonpecuniary preferences of nonprofit managers and entrepreneurs. The further research must therefore investigate to what extent the proposed integration between the market failure and supply side theories of the nonprofit sector is empirically supportable.

Furthermore, while a number of empirical studies in nonprofit economics sought to compare the empirical relevance of alternative theories (ibid), the theoretical rationale for the nondistribution constraint has not yet been subjected to such empirical tests. This gap in empirical research has evidently been caused by the lack of the nondistribution constraint's theoretical explanations other than the trustworthiness theory. Now that the nondistribution constraint has been alternatively explained as a reflection of the nonpecuniary entrepreneurial and managerial motivation, it is possible to conduct empirical studies examining the relative validity of these two explanations.

Finally, both theoretical and empirical research are needed to fully elaborate the proposed ,rurality' theory of the rural nonprofit sector by operationalizing and verifying the effect of individual determinants of the rurality-specific transaction cost on the emergence of rural nonprofits. These determinants may primarily include low population density, geographic dispersion of consumers and producers, and poor infrastructure, but are not necessarily limited to these. The rurality theory of the rural nonprofit sector must additionally take account of rural areas' institutional environment, particularly legal framework and rural social capital, as these may affect the possibilities of creating and maintaining rural nonprofits.

References

Adaman, F., and Madra, Y. M. (2002). Theorizing the "Third Sphere": A Critique of the Persistence of the "Economistic Fallacy". *Journal of Economic Issues, 36*(4), 1045-1078.

Anheier, H. K., and Salamon, L. (2006). The Nonprofit Sector in Comparative Perspective. In W. W. Powell and R. Steinberg (Eds.), *The Nonprofit Sector: A Research Handbook* (pp. 89-114). New Haven et al.

Ballou, J., and Weisbrod, B. (2003). Managerial Rewards and the Behavior of For-Profit, Governmental, and Nonprofit Organizations: Evidence from the Hospital Industry. *Journal of Public Economics, 87*(9-10), 1895-1920.

Becker, G.S., and Murphy, K. (1992). The Division of Labor, Coordination Costs, and Knowledge. *Quarterly Journal of Economics, 107*(4), 1137-1160.

Ben-Ner, A. (1986). Nonprofit Organizations: Why Do They Exist in Market Economies? In The Economics of Nonprofit Institutions: Studies in Structure and Policy *(edited by Susan Rose-Ackerman). Oxford: Oxford University Press.*

Buchanan, J. (1999). *The Logical Foundations of Constitutional Liberty.* Indianapolis: Liberty Fund.

Coase, R. (1937). The nature of the firm. *Economica, 4,* 386-405.

Demsetz, H. (1997). The Economics of the Business Firm: Seven Critical Commentaries. *Cambridge: Cambridge University Press.*

Dorward, A., and Kydd, J., Morrison, J., and Poulton, C. (2005). Institutions, Markets and Economic Co-ordination: Linking Development Policy to Theory and Praxis. *Development and Change, 36*(1), 1-25.

Edwards, B., Goodwin, M., Pemberton, S., and Woods, M. (2000). *Partnership Working in Rural Regeneration.* Bristol: The Policy Press.

Hansmann, H. (1980). The role of nonprofit enterprise. *Yale Law Journal, 89*(5), 835-901.

Hansmann, H. (1987). Economic Theories of Nonprofit Organization. In W. W. Powell (Ed.), *The Nonprofit Sector: A Research Handbook* (pp. 27-42). New Haven et al.: Yale University Press.

Hodgson, G. (1988). *Economics and Institutions: A Manifesto for a Modern Institutional Economics.* Cambridge et al.: Polity Press.

James, E. (1987). The Nonprofit Sector in Comparative Perspective. In W. W. Powell (Ed.), *The Nonprofit Sector: A Research Handbook* (pp. 397-415). New Haven et al.: Yale University Press.

Krashinsky, M. (1986). *Transaction Costs and a Theory of the Nonprofit Organization. In The Economics of Nonprofit Institutions: Studies in Structure and Policy* (edited by Susan Rose-Ackerman). Oxford: Oxford University Press.

Leete, L. (2006). Work in the Nonprofit Sector. In W. W. Powell, and R. Steinberg (Eds.), *The Nonprofit Sector: A Research Handbook* (pp. 159-179). New Haven et al.: Yale University Press.

Locay, L. (1990). Economic Development and the Division of Production between Households and Markets. *Journal of Political Economy,* **98**(5), 965-982.

Lohmann, R. (1992). The Commons: A Multidisciplinary Approach to Nonprofit Organizations. *Nonprofit and Voluntary Sector Quarterly,* **21**(3), 309-324.

Malmgren, H. (1961). Information, expectations, and the theory of the firm. *Quarterly Journal of Economics,* **75**, 399-421.

Menard, C. (2004). The economics of hybrid organizations. *Journal of Institutional and Theoretical Economics,* **160**, 1-32.

Moseley, M. (2003*). Local Partnerships for Rural Development: The European Experience.* Wallingford: CABI Publishing.

OECD (2006). Das neue Paradigma für den ländlichen Raum: Politik und Governance. *Paris: OECD Publications.*

Ortmann, A., and Schlesinger, M. (2003). Trust, Repute, and the role of Nonprofit Enterprise. In H. Anheier and A. Ben-Ner (Eds.), *The Study of the Nonprofit Enterprise* (pp. 77-114). New York: Kluwer.

Pollak, R. (1985). A Transaction Cost Approach to Families and Households. Journal of Economic Literature, **23**, 581-608.

Preston, A. (1989). The nonprofit worker in a for-profit world. *Journal of Labor Economics,* **7**, 38-63.

Radner, R. (1992). Hierarchy: the economics of managing. *Journal of Economic Literature,* **30**, 1382-1415.

Rose-Ackerman, S. (1996). Altruism, Nonprofits, and Economic Theory. *Journal of Economic Literature,* **34**(2), 701-728.

Salamon, L., and Anheier, H. K. (1998). Social Origins of Civil Society: Explaining the Nonprofit Sector Cross-Nationally. *Voluntas: International Journal of Voluntary and Nonprofit Organizations,* **9**(3), 213-247.

Schmitt, G. (1991). Why Is the Agriculture of Advanced Western Economies Still Organized by Family Farms? Will This Continue To Be So in the Future*? European Review of Agricultural Economics,* **18**, 443-458.

Slivinsky, A. (2003). The Public Goods Theory Revisited. In H. K. Anheier, and A. Ben-Ner (Eds.), *The Study of the Nonprofit Enterprise* (pp. 67-74). New York et al.: Kluwer Academic.

Smith, A. (1981). *An Inquiry into the Nature and Causes of the Wealth of Nations: Vol. 1.* Indianapolis: Liberty Fund.

Steinberg, R. (1993). Public policy and the performance of nonprofit organizations: a general framework. *Nonprofit and Voluntary Sector Quarterly, 22,* 13-31.

Steinberg, R. (2004). Introduction. In R. Steinberg (Ed.), *The economics of nonprofit enterprises* (pp. xiii-xxx). Cheltenham: Edward Elgar.

Steinberg, R. (2006). Economic Theories of Nonprofit Organization. In W. W. Powell, and R. Steinberg (Eds.), *The Nonprofit Sector: A Research Handbook* (pp. 117-139). New Haven et al.: Yale University Press.

Terluin, I. (2001). *Rural regions in the EU: exploring differences in economic development.* Utrecht et al.: Koninklijk Nederlands Aardrijkskundig Genootschap.

Uphoff, N. (1993). Grassroots organizations and NGOs in rural development: opportunities with diminishing states and expanding markets. *World Development,* **21**(4), 607-622.

Valentinov, V. (2006). The logic of the nonprofit sector: an organizational economics perspective. *Zeitschrift für öffentliche und gemeinwirtschaftliche Unternehmen,* **29**(2), 214-226.

Valentinov, V. (2007a). Why are cooperatives important in agriculture? An organizational economics perspective. *Journal of Institutional Economics,* **3**(1), 55-69.

Valentinov, V. (2007b). Some reflections on the transaction cost theory of nonprofit organization. *Zeitschrift für öffentliche und gemeinwirtschaftliche Unternehmen,* **30**(1), 52-67.

Valentinov, V. (2008a). Non-market institutions in economic development: the role of the third sector. *Development and Change,* **39**(3), 477-485.

Valentinov, V. (2008b). On the origin of rules: between exchange and self-sufficiency. *Social Science Journal,* **45**(2), 145-151.

Valentinov, V. (2008c). The exchange paradigm of constitutional economics: implications for understanding the third sector. *Constitutional Political Economy,* **19**(1), 19-33.

Valentinov, V. (2008d). The transaction cost theory of the nonprofit firm: beyond opportunism. *Nonprofit and Voluntary Sector Quarterly,* **37**(1), 5-18.

Valentinov, V. (2008g). Toward an incentive alignment theory of nonprofit organization. *Evolutionary and Institutional Economics Review,* **5**(1), 189-196.

Valentinov, V. (2009a). Managerial nonpecuniary preferences in the market failure theories of nonprofit organization. *International Journal of Social Economics,* **36**(1), 81-92.

Valentinov, V. (2009b). Third sector organizations in rural development: a transaction cost perspective. *Agricultural and Food Science,* **18**(1), 3-15.

Valentinov, V.: (2008e). The economics of nonprofit organization: in search of an integrative theory. *Journal of Economic Issues,* **42**(3), 745-761.

Valentinov, V.: (2008f). The economics of the nondistribution constraint: a critical reappraisal. *Annals of Public and Cooperative Economics,* **79**(1), 35-52.

Weisbrod, B. (1991). *The Nonprofit Economy.* Cambridge, MA: Harvard University Press.

Wex, T. (2004). *Der Nonprofit-Sektor der Organisationsgesellschaft.* Wiesbaden: Gabler.

Williamson, O. (1971). The vertical integration of production: market failure considerations. *American Economic Review,* **61**(2), 112-23.

Williamson, O. (1985). *The economic institutions of capitalism: firms, markets, relational contracting.* New York: Free Press.

Williamson, O. (1991). Comparative economic organization: the analysis of discrete structural alternatives. *Administrative Science Quarterly,* **36**, 269-296.

Yang, X., and Borland, J. (1991). A Microeconomic Mechanism for Economic Growth. *Journal of Political Economy,* **99**(3), 460-482.

In: Handbook of Business and Finance
Editors: M. Bergmann and T. Faust, pp. 259-279

ISBN: 978-1-60692-855-4
© 2010 Nova Science Publishers, Inc.

Chapter 11

M&A IMPACT ON THE RELATIONSHIP BETWEEN BUSINESS DEFINITION AND CORPORATE GROWTH

Koji Wakabayashi[*]
Nihon University, Tokyo, Japan

Abstract

In a previous study, the relationship between business definition and corporate performance has been explored, which is to prove the hypothesis drawn from Theodore Levitt's idea that a company could continue growing, if it properly defined its business by function (customer value), based on an empirical analysis of 50 electric/electronics companies. The relationship between 'functionality' (magnitude that function is contained) in the past business definitions rated by an evaluation panel and time series performance data until recently had been statistically analyzed and positive correlation between functionality and consolidated sales growth rate was found, which thus supported the hypothesis. However, the correlation coefficient was not large enough to sufficiently explain the trend in sales growth rate by the functionality. The present study is to further analyze the influence of the second explanatory variable, 'alignment degree' (magnitude of alignment in terms of function), based on the assumption that even the corporate business definition is functional, if the function is not fully aligned through the whole company, the growth rate still will be lower. The appearance frequency of the key words forming business definitions in new product press releases is measured as alignment degree with 25 selected companies by content analysis using text mining technique. As a result, a multiple regression model is identified with the companies of high and low ranges in functionality and it can explicitly explain growth rate by functionality and alignment degree. However, this regression model is not applicable to the companies of medium range in functionality including the ones that grow mainly through mergers and acquisitions (M&A). The reason is that short-term impact of M&A on sales growth is so substantial that it exceeds the scope of the regression model. Based on all those concerns, the

---

[*] E-mail address: wakabayashi.koji@nihon-u.ac.jp. Address for Correspondence: Koji Wakabayashi, Graduate School of Business, Nihon University, 4-8-24, Kudan-Minami, Chiyoda-ku, Tokyo 102-8275, Japan.
Most of the research concept and data in this chapter except for the descriptions related to M&A issues is based on the author's doctoral research at Tokyo Institute of Technology (c.f. Wakabayashi, 2007).

impact of M&A on the relationship between business definition and corporate growth is the issue of the study to further explore by using some cases.

1. Introduction

Levitt (1960) argued that organizations stop their growth because they improperly define their businesses. Railroads companies in the USA stopped growing because they assumed themselves to be in 'railroad business' rather than in 'transportation business'. It happened not because the need for passenger and freight transportation declined, but they were product-oriented rather than customer-oriented (or customer value oriented). Levitt indicated that business should be defined in terms of 'function'[1], not 'products' to survive and grow continuously. In other words, companies could continue growth by redefining their businesses in terms of function. The examples of functional definitions are an 'entertainment business' rather than a 'movie business' and an 'energy business' rather than a 'petroleum business'.

In a previous study[2], the hypothesis drawn from Levitt's idea that companies could survive and grow continuously by functional business definitions was statistically proved, through the analysis of 'functionality' (magnitude that function is contained) scores for corporate business definitions evaluated by the panel formed from 29 business people and performance data of 50 companies[3] in Japanese electric/electronics industry.

Security reports and annual reports were used as sources of business definitions.

Electric/electronics industry was chosen for the following reasons:

1. As the business environment of the industry is rapidly changing to keep up with the development of information technology and fierce global competitions, the difference in performance that business definitions bring to the companies is greater than for firms in other industries.
2. Also, as it is one of the major industries of the Japanese economy, various types of companies are competing in diverse market segments.

A term of seven years was taken as the research duration, based on the following premises:

1. Business definitions are revised in accordance with top management's turnovers and the average tenure of top management (CEOs and presidents) of Japanese companies is seven to eight years.
2. Business definitions that appear in the sources are elements of long-rage plans or corporate missions, and the target term for long–range plans is usually more than five years.

How the business definition of 1998 (FY1997) influenced performance indicators of the years through 2004 (FY2003) had been analyzed.

---

1 The term 'function' is used as a synonym of customer value throughout this chapter, following Hofer and Schendel (1978) who called Levitt's 'customer value oriented' as 'functional'.
2 Wakabayashi (2005).
3 50 electric/electronics companies with largest (from the top to 50th) sales volume in FY 2003 excluding NEC Electronics founded in 2002, since it has no financial data before 2002. All the companies list their stocks in the industrial category of 'Electric Appliances' on the Tokyo Stock Exchange (c.f. Table 8).

As a result, a positive correlation between functionality in the corporate business definitions and growth rates in consolidated net sales and market value was identified. However, the correlation coefficients were not large enough to fully explain the causal relationship between the functionality and growth rate. Some of the results are depicted in Table 1, 2, and 8.

A possible reason for it is that even the corporate business definition in the mission or long–range plan of the whole company is functional, if the one in the strategy of each business unit is not functional enough, the function will not be realized in business processes such as developing products and selling them to customers, as a result, the growth rate will be lower.

Table 1. Correlation between functionality and performance of 50 Japanese electric/electronics companies

	Net Sales Growth Rate (FY97-03)	Net Sales Growth Rate (FY98-03)	Average Opt.Profit Rate (FY97-03)	Average Opt.Profit Rate (FY98-03)	Change in Opt.Profit Rate (FY97-03)	Change in Opt. Profit Rate (FY98-03)	Market Value (FY97)	Market Value (FY03)	Market Value Growth Rate (FY97-02)	Market Value Growth Rate (FY97-03)
Coefficients	.393 **	.384 **	.024	.027	-.025	-.096	-.090	.004	.338 *	.330 *

Notes: Net Sales Growth Rate (%) is consolidated average annual rate base. Average Opt. Profit Rate (%) denotes the average of consolidated operating profit/net sales in the term. Change in Opt. Profit Rate (FY97-03) (%) is obtained by consolidated operating profit rate in FY2003 minus that in FY1997. Market Value (million yen) is obtained from average stock price multiplied by the number of total stocks issued. Market Value Growth Rate (%) is average annual rate base.
** denotes significance level $p < 01$ and * denotes $p < 05$.
Sources: Wakabayashi (2005) and Wakabayashi (2007).

Table 2. Sales growth rates and test results

Subgroup (N)	FY1997-2003		FY1998-2003	
	Mean (%)	t statistic	Mean (%)	t statistic
High (10)	9.212	2.330*	10.761	2.166*
Low (10)	-2.311		-2.247	
High (20)	5.807	2.603*	7.560	2.641*
Low (20)	-1.064		-.652	
Total (50)	2.755		4.032	

Notes: Sales growth rates are average annual growth rates of consolidated net sales. High (10) denotes the group of 10 companies receiving the highest functionality scores from the top and Low (10) is the group of 10 companies receiving lowest functionality scores from the bottom. High (20) and Low (20) are ditto.
* denotes significance level $p < 05$.
Source: Wakabayashi (2005).

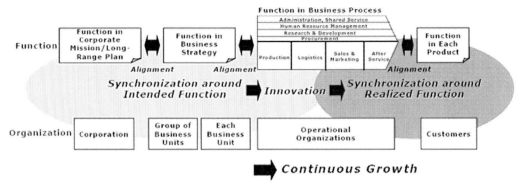

Source: Wakabayashi (2007).

Figure 1. Hypothetical mechanism of functional alignment and corporate growth.

In the present study, the hypothetical causal relationship is empirically tested that function in the corporate business definition is transferred through business units down to products/services, ultimately it brings continuous growth to the company, based on content analysis of the companies in the same industry.

Drucker (1974) mentioned, 'The innovation objective is the objective through which a company makes operational its definition of "what our business should be"'[4]. He also mentioned that 'innovation is not science or technology, but value'[5]. Labovitz & Rosansky (1997) argued that '[w]ith both the vertical (business strategy-people at work) and horizontal (processes-customer requirements) dimensions aligned, your strategy and your people are synchronized with customer focus and process capabilities'[6]. Based on those arguments, the following mechanism is assumed to underly the relationship among business definition, functional alignment (organizational alignment in terms of function), and corporate growth, as depicted in Figure 1. It means that in the company where common function is shared by the whole organization, synchronizations around the function among employees arise, innovation happens in each business process, and it makes the company provide customers with a clearer function (or customer value) through its products and services, and finally it brings continuous growth to the company.

Case studies based on interview or questionnaire surveys to the managers and employees of the companies are considered as the plausible methods to reveal the mechanism of the organizational behavior. And the elucidation of this hypothetical mechanism was tried in Wakabayashi (2008), based on the descriptive case studies of limited number of companies. However, interviews and questionnaires about past events inherently tend to be subjective and inaccurate, because they contain biases of interviewees and respondents, and the older the research events are, the vaguer their memories become.

In the present study, based on the presumption that the functional alignment in the whole company most explicitly appears as the alignment between the both ends, the corporate business definitions and the products/services, content analysis is used. Holsti (1969) defined content analysis as 'any technique for making inferences by objectively and systematically

---

4 p.107.
5 p.788.
6 p.37.

identifying specified characteristics of messages'[7]. Krippendorff (1980) defined it as 'a research technique for making replicable and valid inferences from data to their context'[8]. It is considered as a research technique to quantitatively recognize the appearance frequency of certain symbols or relationship among them in the text data. As computerized content analysis (or text mining) is superior in reliability, stability, and comparability, compared with human-coded content analysis, proved by Morris (1994), the text mining technique is used in the present study.

The content analysis used in the present study is to measure appearance frequency of the key words forming business definitions in the missions or long-rang plans in the new product press releases as 'alignment degree'. Security reports and annual reports are used as sources of the corporate business definitions, new product press releases are used as sources of the functions of the products and services, and they are compared each other.

2. Related Research and Literature

First, literatures related to the mechanism about business definitions, organizational alignment, and corporate performances are reviewed and then, those related to content analysis of strategies or management cognition are touched.

Abell (1980) proposed 'customer groups', 'customer functions', and 'alternative technologies', as the three axes to define the business. He analyzed the causal relationship of business definition and market share as the performance indicator through the case studies of the competitors in computer, ATM, CT scanners, and forestry skidders industries. However, his study is aimed at proving the efficiency of his three axes framework rather than investigating the causal mechanism of the business definition and performance.

Sakakibara, *et al.* (1989) studied the new business development processes at 3M, IBM, Xerox, NEC, etc. They analyzed the mechanism that business definitions in the corporate missions influence the product concepts through the new business development process. However, the study is based on the premise that corporate business definition spreads throughout the whole company, and the case that there might be misalignment in the organization is not considered.

Sakakibara (1992) hypothetically suggested the causal mechanism that the corporate business definition influences the performance through the consensus and synchronization on it between top management and employees, also between the company and customers or society surrounding it. However, there is no consideration on the common base in various levels from corporate mission to products/services.

Kaplan & Norton (2001) argued that strategy implementation requires that all business units, and employees be aligned and linked to the strategy. They advocate the cascade of strategy from the top to the bottom of organization as the framework to realize the alignment through financial, customer, internal business process, and learning and growth perspectives. However, they do not propose any clear and indispensable axis (or base) to align the whole organization.

---

7 p.14.
8 p.21.

In order to construct the really applicable theory related to business definition, it is necessary to deal with the linkage among corporate mission, business strategies, and products/services for customers. In this sense, the predecessor studies are not enough to respond to the needs in real businesses.

Bettman & Weitz (1983) studied the relationship between corporate performance and its causal reasoning. Based on the content analysis of 181 US companies' annual reports, they found that companies tend to attribute favorable outcomes to internal causes, while they attribute unfavorable outcomes to external, unstable, and uncontrollable causes. Their arguments on the superiority of the annual reports as sources of information, because of their comparability, objectivity, and standardized format, are impressive.

Pearce & David (1987) studied the correlation of financial performance (profit margin) and the appearance frequency of eight factors (cutomers/markets, products/services, geographic domain, core technologies, expression of commitment, company philosophy, company self-concept, and public image), based on content analysis of 61 Fortune 500 companies' mission statements. As a result, they found the company philosophy, company self-concept, and public images relate the corporate performance with statistical significance. However, they did not include function as the influential factor.

David (1989) followed Pearce and David (1987), and studied the correlation of financial performance (EPS, ROI, etc.) and the appearance frequency of nine factors, adding 'employees', based on content analysis of 75 Business Week 1000 companies' mission statements. However, function is not included as an explanatory variable.

There are very few studies that examine the alignment or consistency in two or more different kinds of sources by content analysis like the present study.

3. Research Methodology

The first hypothesis in the present study is as follows:

H1: among the companies with highly functional corporate business definitions, the ones that successfully align their corporate business definition, divisional business definitions, and products/services in terms of function continuously grow at a higher rate than the others that fail the alignment.

The second hypothesis is drawn from the first hypothesis, regarding the alignment between corporate business definition and products/services as follows:

H2:among the companies with highly functional corporate business definitions, the ones in which the common function is shared in the corporate business definitions and products/services continuously grow at a higher rate than those in which it is not fully shared.

'Corporate business definition' is usually the one that is defined in mission statement or long-range plan for the whole company. 'Corporation' is used as a synonym of the 'whole company' in this chapter.

'Divisional business definition' is the one that is defined in business strategy for each business unit or group of several business units.

As the general organizational structure of Japanese companies is slightly different from the counterpart of the Western companies in terms of financial autonomy of each division, hierarchical layers, etc., the elements of the two organization charts may not completely mach each other. In this chapter, the term 'business unit' is used for product division ('Jigyobu') of Japanese companies and 'group of business units' for the intermediate layer of management between the corporation and the business unit such as in-house company, product group ('Jigyohonbu'), product sector, and strategic business unit, based on the notations used by Prahalad & Bettis (1986), Watson & Wooldridge (2005), among others.

The entire research procedure is as follows:

STEP1. 10 companies of high range, eight companies of medium range[9], and seven companies of low range in functionality with the certain number[10] of press releases are picked up from the 50 electric/electronics companies analyzed in the previous study.

STEP2. For those 25 companies, security reports[11] and annual reports[12] issued during FY 1997 through FY 2003 are gathered. Based on those sources, the turn over date of the top managements and corporate business definitions are picked up, and the relationships among them are identified.

STEP3. The new product press releases of those 25 companies issued during FY 1998 to FY 2003 are gathered through their Internet home pages. They are transformed into the text files that enable the PC apply text search (search engine). With the companies that do not show the past press releases at their homepages, CD ROMs or hard copies of them are requested for their public relation departments. MS word or PDF files in the CD ROMs are transformed into text files. The hard copies are transformed into text files through scanners and the OCR software[13].

A press release is saved as a file and counted as one case or one analytical unit. A new technology press release is also counted as one case, in case that the estimated product release date is mentioned and it is within a year from the press release date.

STEP4. The appearance frequency of the key words forming business definitions is measured in the new products press releases as 'alignment degree'. Practically, the words[14] that form business definitions in security reports or annual reports of each company are picked up, and the numbers of files that contain those words and their synonyms are measured by text search software[15].

The alignment degree here is given by the following equation:

alignment degree = number of all the files that contain any of the words/number of all the files

When the business definition of a company changed in accordance with the change in top management during the research term, the new definition is used in the following years.

---

9 The mean functionality score of the 50 companies is .90 and medium range companies' scores scatter between .83 and 1.21 (c.f. Table 4 and 8).

10 at least 10, possibly more than 100 cases.

11 http://db.eol.co.jp/.

12 http://www.mergentonline.com/.

13 This part of the procedure is taken only with the 10 companies of high range in functionality. The press releases available through homepages are used with the other 15 companies.

14 nouns, verbs, adjectives, adverbs, and the compounds of them. General single words such as 'technology', 'product', 'customer', 'business', 'equipment', 'contribute', 'provide', 'suggest', 'create', 'audio', 'video', 'software', 'hardware' are excluded.

15 Sakura-editor (free software) is used.

As it is important to measure the frequency of semantic appearances, the files in which the key words are contained as corporate identity, slogans, and product names are excluded from the calculations.

STEP5. The alignment degrees combined with functionality scores[16] and growth rates[17] are analyzed all together based on the hypothetical framework that the functional alignment influences the growth rate of the company, in order to prove H2, accordingly H1. Whether the alignment degree between corporate business definition and products/services explains the residual of the growth rate that the functionality leaves unexplained is qualitatively tested. Multiple regression models with growth rate as a dependent variable, functionality and alignment degree as independent variables are tested.

4. Results

The content analysis results with the companies of high range in functionality explain the residual of the growth rate that the functionality leaves unexplained by the alignment degrees between corporate business definition and products/services (c.f. Table 3). For instance, the growth rates of Sony and Matsushita Electric Works, whose alignment degrees are relatively low, are lower than those of Pioneer, whose alignment degree is high. On the other hand, those of Koito, Stanley, Epson, etc., whose alignment degrees are high, are also high. The correlation coefficient between alignment degree and growth rate is .748 (p<.05) with the companies of this range.

The relationship between alignment degree and growth rate is identified with the seven companies of low range, too, in spite that the trend is not so clear as that of the 10 companies of high range in functionality (c.f. Table 5).

However, no clear tendency is identified with the eight companies of medium range in functionality (c.f. Table 4).

The results of the multiple regression analyses using growth rate as a dependent variable, functionality and alignment degree as independent (explanatory) variables are as follows:

A regression analysis applied for the 17 companies of high and low ranges in functionality draws remarkable results as depicted in Table 6. The regression model derived from this analysis well explains the growth rate by functionality and alignment degree, because R^2 and t statistics for explanatory variables are all high. The multicollinearity between functionality and alignment degree is negligible, as the VIF value is small (much less than 5).

---

16 scaled from .00 to 2.00, taken from Wakabayashi (2005) (c.f. Table 8).
17 average annual growth rate of consolidated net sales from FY 1997 to FY 2003, taken from Wakabayashi (2005) (c.f. Table 8).

Table 3. Content analysis results (1) (companies of high range in functionality)

Company	Business definitions	Keywords	Functionality score	Alignment degree	Growth rate
Alpine	Offer the finest in entertainment through innovative products for automobile environment Develop the mobile multimedia system of the future based on the concept of integrating sound, visual images, information and communication (Discovering the future of mobile media)	fun (.55), entertainment (.23), integration (.19)/fusion (.03) innovation (.19), multimedia (.13), mobile media (.00)	1.86	.65	4.02%
Epson	Saving Technology: to solve the customer's problem by integrating fineness and energy saving Color Imaging (Jan.2003-) Digital Image Innovation: offering advanced imaging solutions through the fusion of still and moving images	image (.41), saving (.34), moving image (.12), solution (.12), low power consumption (.11), fineness (.04), energy saving (.03), low power (.02), imaging (.02), color imaging (.01)	1.83	.75	4.88%
Koito Manufacturing Co.	Build the safe transportation systems (Shedding light on a global strategy for growth) Construct safe and comfortable society	light (.69), safety (.38), next generation (.13), transportation system (.00), comfort (.00), society (.00)	1.72	.75	6.73%
Sanyo	Create the comfortable living environment through clean energy business, and enrich the human life through multimedia products (creation of comfortable environment and propose the non-tedious lifestyle) (FY2001-) Digital, devices, energy, and ecology	environment (.34), comfort (.20), living (.16), space (.07), clean (.06), multimedia (.04), rich (.04), clean energy (.01), ecology (.01), tedious (.00), life (.00)	1.69	.57	5.14%
Ricoh	Building the equipment and systems essential to the modern networked office through Image Communication: superior imaging, open standard, appliance-like ease, workgroup support, and total office coverage	network (.36), image (.24), office (.21), easy operation (.20), group (.07), superior (.05), image communication (.01), color communication (.00), open standard (.00)	1.55	.64	4.04%
Stanley	Contribute to the improvements in car safety and enhance the joy of driving Explore the world of lightning as a creative provider of light products (FY2000-) Outshining lights. The five ways of creating value with light: creating light, sensing and recognizing with light, processing information with light, harnessing light's energy, and producing feeling with light	light (.82), safety (.18), comfort (.09), driving (.00), sensing (.00), recognizing (.00), feeling (.00)	1.55	.82	6.26%

Table 3. Continued

Company	Business definitions	Keywords	Functionality score	Alignment degree	Growth rate
Matsushita Electric Works	Amenity and intelligence: applying intelligence for amenity environments (Study the comfortable living, create the comfortable living environment) (Jan.2001-) Smart solutions by NAIS to respond in a timely fashion to needs arising from the IT revolution, aging society and global environment consciousness	environment (.33), comfort (.22), smart (.03), aging (.02), solution (.01)/problem solution (.00), amenity (.00), intelligence (.00), living (.00)	1.48	.42	2.78%
Pioneer	Move the heart and touch the soul, make audio/video entertainment ever more enlivening (Entertainment Creating Company)	fun (.70), entertainment (.10), more enlivening (.05), heart (.04), move (.03), entertainment (another orthography) (.01), soul (.00)	1.48	.73	3.82%
Sony	Create things for every kind of imagination Convey emotions and dreams to audiences by content, create hardware that achieves the highest standards possible by blending performance, quality, and design, and lead to a home network in which customers can access specific video and audio selections whenever they want, in order to make digital dreams come true	design (.35), high performance (.18), high quality (.05), access (.01), move (.01), home network (.01), whenever want (.01), dream (.00), digital dream (.00), video selection (.00), audio selection (.00)	1.41	.50	1.75%
Yokogawa	Provide 'enterprise technology solutions' that encompass resource management information, manufacturing execution information, and production control (supply solutions to industries and enterprise) Promote the quality, efficiency, and profitability of enterprise customers around the globe by providing total solutions and supplying the most reliable leading-edge instruments and control systems (provide a positive impact on a customer's business from the customer's point of view of management)	efficiency (.32), solution (.27)/problem solution (.00), quality (.22), reliability (.18), control system (.06), production control (.05), leading-edge (.04), management view (.01), resource management (.00), manufacturing execution (.00), profitability (.00)	1.31	.65	3.35%

Notes: Business definitions are mainly those in 1998. Figure in parenthesis denotes appearance frequency of each word during the research period. Functionality score and Growth rate are taken from Wakabayashi (2005). Functionality score is scaled from .00 to 2.00. Growth rate is the average annual growth rate of consolidated net sales from FY 1997 to FY 2003. The key words are not necessarily direct translations of original Japanese ones used in the actual content analysis for better understanding.

Source: Wakabayashi (2007).

Table 4. Content analysis results (2) (companies of medium range in functionality)

Company	Business definition	Key words	Functionality score	Alignment degree	Growth rate
Alps	Perfecting the art of electronics (Promote user-friendly communication between people and media) Create new values that satisfy stakeholders and are friendly to the earth	media (.13), user-friendly (.12), people (.05)/man (.03), earth (.03), value (.02), value creation (.01), art (.01), communication (.00), perfect (.00), friendly (.00)	1.21	.32	3.46%
Hitachi Maxell	(FY1998-) Memory and mobility (FY2000-) Storage media and battery-based energy solution	storage (.57), media (.35), memory (.06), mobile (.06), energy solution (.00)	1.14	.70	1.77%
Advantest	Support advanced technology at the cutting edge (FY2002-) Test and measurement	test (.63), measurement (.07), cutting edge (.07), advanced technology (.04), support (.00)	1.14	.70	-6.30%
Kyocera	(FY1998-) Create business in telecommunications and information processing, environmental protection, and quality of life (FY2000-) Strive for continuous growth by pursuing 'high-value-added' diversification	environment (.19), information (.16), value(.12), life(.12), telecommunication (.07), protection (.02), culture (.02), diversification (.02)	1.07	.61	7.84%
Oki	Help to shape the evolution of the information society with enterprising spirit (FY2001-) Move away from IT solutions toward e-business solutions A global manufacturer and marketer of leading-edge multimedia networks and services (Sept.1998-) Network solutions for a global society	network (.53), solution (.49)/problem solve (.00), multimedia (.21), leading edge (.09), e/E-business (.05), IT solution (.02), enterprising spirit (.00), information society (.00)	.97	.67	-2.57%
Hosiden	Timely provide with high quality products that market requires with leading-edge technology and contribute to the development of electronics industry (support the customer's corporate strategy) Keep wide-range of product line-ups, technologies that meet customers' diverse requirements, close services that best satisfy customers Meet the trend of miniaturization, multifunction, and power saving in electronics appliances	multifunction (.13), miniaturize (.03), leading edge (.00), quality (.00), timely (.00), corporate strategy (.00), line up (.00), diverse (.00), customer satisfaction (.00), close (.00), power saving (.00)	.97	.12	5.37%

Table 4. Continued

Company	Business definition	Key words	Functionality score	Alignment degree	Growth rate
Minebea	(FY1999-) Address the development of higher value-added products and the sophistication of product quality	quality (.00), sophistication (.00), value-added (.00)	.86	.00	-3.18%
Fuji Electric	(June2000-) Provide customers with highest satisfaction. The most valuable (optimum, high-quality) service provider, the most valuable components (of outstanding quality) provider	satisfaction(.17). optimum service (.00), valuable service (.00), quality (.00)	.83	.17	-2.27%

Notes: Business definitions are mainly those in 1998. Figure in parenthesis denotes appearance frequency of each word during the research period. Functionality score and Growth rate are taken from Wakabayashi (2005). Functionality score is scaled from .00 to 2.00. Growth rate is the average annual growth rate of consolidated net sales from FY 1997 to FY 2003. The business definitions and key words here are restricted to the researchable period with some companies that do not open all the press releases back to FY1998. The key words are not necessarily direct translations of original Japanese ones used in the actual content analysis for better understanding.

Source: Wakabayashi (2007).

Table 5. Content analysis results (3) (companies of low range in functionality)

Company	Business definition	Keywords	Functionality score	Alignment degree	Growth rate
Konica-Minolta	(Aug.2003-) From input to through output of the imaging field (the essentials of imaging). Continue to create inspiring products and services in the field of imaging and lead the market by advanced technology and reliability	reliability (.14), imaging (.11), inspiring (.03), from input to output (.00)	.38	.22	-3.64%
Omron	(May2001-) A provider of innovative solutions for industry, society and daily life, capitalizing on the core competencies in sensing and control	sensing (.25), control (.17), life (.17), industry (.08), solution (.08), social innovation (.00), innovation (.00)	.34	.67	-.75%
TDK	Contribute to culture and industry through creativity (FY2000-) e-material solution provider (Offer innovative components that solve specific customer needs on the expertise in electronic materials)	solution (.06), offer (.01), expertise in material (.01), cultural contribution (.00), industrial contribution (.00), e-material (.00), problem solve (.00), needs (.00), innovative (.00)	.24	.08	-.93%

Table 5. Continued

Company	Business definition	Keywords	Functionality score	Alignment degree	Growth rate
Meidensha	Powertronics: fusion of heavy electric technology with mechatronics and electronics (FY2002-) Not only provide products but also recommend the best solutions on the basis of what a customer values best (FY1999-) Contribute to society as a reliable solution provider to ensure that our technologies and products will be useful and effective in the creation of well-to-do society and a comfortable environment (FY2002-) Constantly in pursuit of innovation for new technologies and in contributing to the well-being of society at large	environment (.50), reliable (.25), solution (.17), powertronics (.00), well-to-do (.00), pursuit (.00), value (.00)	.21	.39	-3.35%
Kenwood	Work on advanced digital and networking technologies and actively develop new products and pioneer new businesses for the coming multimedia age (FY2003-) Establish the business domain of mobile and home multimedia systems, utilizing collective strength in audio and communications technologies	Mobile (.12), mobile (another expression) (.06), multimedia (.03), advanced digital (.00), networking (.00), home multimedia (.00)	.21	.04	-8.88%
Fujitsu General	Develop the products that lead the digital age. Develop the products with advanced features, innovative design, and environmental consciousness such as energy saving and recycling (FY2000-) Cope the environmental protection as a leading air conditioning equipment supplier by establishment of recycling technologies and creation of recycling society (FY2002-) Provide with unique and attractive products with high value based on advanced technologies	environment (.59), design (.50), earth (.26), recycle (.15), high value (.08), advanced technology (.04), recycling (.03), advanced function (.00), power saving (.00), environmental protection (.00), unique (.00), attractive (.00)	.14	.49	-2.57%
Mitsumi	An electronics parts specialist that strongly supports advancements in the international electronics industry. Steadily supply optimal electronic components that meet the needs of the market and develop unique anticipatory electronic components that open new vistas in electronics (FY1999-) Develop products that meet the needs and the technological innovation of IT-related market, and expand the manufacturing and sales network	international contribution (.00), market (.00), technological innovation (.00), market needs (.00), sales network (.00)	.10	.00	-3.40%

Notes: Business definitions are mainly those in 1998. Figure in parenthesis denotes appearance frequency of each word during the research period. Functionality score and Growth rate are taken from Wakabayashi (2005). Functionality score is scaled from .00 to 2.00. Growth rate is the average annual growth rate of consolidated net sales from FY 1997 to FY 2003. The business definitions and key words here are restricted to the researchable period with some companies that do not open all the press releases back to FY1998. The key words are not necessarily direct translations of original Japanese ones used in the actual content analysis for better understanding.

Source: Wakabayashi (2007).

A regression analysis of all the 25 companies including the ones of medium range in functionality does not draw a valid model. The regression results are depicted in Table 7. The R^2 and t statistics for explanatory variables are much worse than those with the 17 companies of high and low functionality ranges.

Table 6. Regression results with 17 companies of high and low ranges in functionality

R	R^2	Adjusted R^2	F statistic	p
.929	.864	.844	44.357	.000

	Non-normalized		Normalized Beta	t statistic	p	VIF
	Beta	Standard error				
Constant	-5.76	.905		-6.361	.000	
Functionality	4.00	.923	.646	4.338	.001	2.281
Alignment degree	5.63	2.464	.340	2.285	.038	2.281

Notes: VIF is variance-inflation factor to test the multicolinearity among explanatory variables.
Source: Wakabayashi (2007).

Table 7. Regression results with 25 companies

R	R^2	Adjusted R^2	F statistic	p
.743	.553	.512	13.596	.000

	Non-normalized		Normalized Beta	t statistic	p	VIF
	Beta	Standard error				
Constant	-5.13	1.373		-3.736	.001	
Functionality	5.18	1.424	.678	3.639	.001	1.709
Alignment degree	1.58	3.079	.095	.512	.614	1.709

Notes: VIF is variance-inflation factor to test the multicolinearity among explanatory variables.
Source: Wakabayashi (2007).

The possible reasons for this phenomenon are as follows:

1. As functions in the business definitions of those companies are generally vague[1], they are not fully interpreted by employees and accordingly not cascaded to products/services. Therefore, some companies' alignment degrees of this range are underestimated than their actual states. (e.g. Hosiden: 'Support the customer's corporate strategy', Alps: 'Create new values that satisfy stakeholders and are friendly to the earth', Fuji Electric: 'Provide customers with highest satisfaction',

---

1 evaluated as average.

M&A Impact on the Relationship between Business Definition...   273

Minebea: 'Address the development of higher value-added products and the sophistication of product quality')

2. There are many companies that grow mainly by mergers and acquisitions (M&A) of this range. The short-term impact of M&A on the growth rates is so large that it does not fit the regression types of analyses. Also, it is assumed that there are tendencies that those companies adopting M&A as main measures to grow do not give function a first priority in their business definitions (e.g. Kyocera, Nidec, Funai).

The impact of M&A on the relationship between business definition and corporate growth is studied by the following three companies of medium range in functionality, based on published data[2] and the results of the previous study[3]. By those cases, linkage between the business definitions in 1998 (or later years) and the M&A during FY1997 to FY2003 is analyzed and the influence to the performance of them is identified:

Kyocera. Kyocera Corporation is an electronics material, device, and equipment manufacturer originated in ceramic technology. Its major products are fine ceramic parts, semiconductor components, solar panels, crystal oscillators, cellular handsets, printers, copiers, digital cameras, etc.

Kyocera's functionality score is 1.07 (slightly higher than .9, the mean of 50 companies in the industry) and growth rate is 7.84% (nearly three times higher than the mean 2.75%). Its business definitions were to 'create business in telecommunications and information processing, environmental protection, and quality of life'[4] in 1998, and to 'strive for continuous growth by pursuing "high-value-added diversification"'[5] in 2000.

It acquired Kinseki, a quartz oscillator manufacturer, in 1998 (a wholly owned subsidiary of Kyocera in 2003), Mita, a photocopier and facsimile manufacturer, in 2000, Tycom, a cutting tool manufacturer, in 2001, Toshiba Chemical, a plastic and material maker for electronics components, in 2002, and Hotel Princess Kyoto, at present Hotel Nikko Princess operated as one of JAL Hotels' chain, in 2004.

Kyocera's M&A activities are characterized by the direction of upstream and downstream of its original product lines, namely in the fields from row materials and components to equipments for end-users.

Nidec. Nidec Corporation (Nihondensan) is a manufacturer of motors and related products. Its major products are HDD spindle motors, drive motors, precision fans, power supplies, etc. Nidec's functionality score is .79 (slightly lower than the mean) and growth rate is 19.03% (nearly seven times higher than the mean). Its business definition in the late 1990s was to 'concentrate on "turning and moving" products'[6].

Under that business definition Nidec had bought the shares of Tosok, a manufacturer of automotive parts and measuring devices, Read Electronics, a manufacturer of industrial

---

2 annual reports, security reports, press releases, Kyocera Corporation (1998), Kiriyama (2007), Watanabe & Amano (2007), etc.
3 c.f. Table 8.
4 Kyocera Security Report 1999, Kyocera Annual Report 1999.
5 Kyocera Security Report 2001, Kyocera Annual Report 2001.
6 *The Nikkei*, October 19, 1998, *The Nikkei Business Daily*, January 6, 1999, Nidec Annual Report 2001, Nidec Security Report 2001.

testers and measuring equipments, and Kyori Kogyo, a manufacturer of high speed presses and feeders, in 1997, Copal, an optical and precision instrument manufacturer, Copal Electronics, an electronics, optical, and mechanical parts manufacturer, and motor division of Shibaura Engineering Works that produced small and mid-sized motors, in 1998, Nemicon, a manufacturer of optical rotary encoders and sensors, in 1999, Y-E Drive, a manufacturer of mid- to small-sized drive motors, and manufacturing division of Seagate Technology (Thailand) that produced FDB (fluid dynamic bearing) spindle motors for HDD, in 2000, Sankyo Seiki Mfg., a manufacturer of small precision motors, optical pickups, magnetic card readers, industrial robots, etc., from 2003 to 2004.

All those companies are precision processing, testing, measuring, and press technology manufacturers. Nidec takes the steps in M&A starting from acquisition of small portion and gradually increasing its share. The one reason behind this procedure is to care for the investors' benefits and keep the market value high for financing the acquisition. The other reason is to restructure the business to improve its performance, while keeping original employees' minds motivated. It acquires the companies that potentially possess technical advantage in the deficit situation. Profitability, high growth rate, and high market value are the common objectives of the group companies after the acquisitions.

Nidec's M&A activities are based on the care for investors and employees, not customers, and all M&A cases are strictly within its technological business definition, to 'concentrate on "turning and moving" products'.

Funai. Funai Electric Corporation is a medium-sized audio video equipment manufacturer. Its major products are VCR/DVD recorders, LCD TVs, digital cameras, printers, DVD+RW drives, facsimiles, etc.

Funai's functionality score is .97 (slightly higher than the mean) and growth rate is 15.95% (nearly six times higher than the mean). Its business definitions in 1999 were to 'develop products to meet the needs of today's rapidly advancing digital technology- and network-oriented society' and to 'produce high-performance, high-quality products at the lowest cost'[7].

It acquired DX Antenna, a broadcast and communications equipment manufacturer, in 2001. After the acquisition, the consolidated net sales increased by 40.0% and the number of group's employees increased by 19.5 %. It acquired 2% of the issued shares in Chi Mei Optoelectronics of Taiwan, a liquid crystal display manufacturer, in 2001, too. It bought a portion of the shares in TeraRecon, a US based digital signal/image processor manufacturer, in 2003. Funai acquired the trademark use right of 'Emerson', a bankrupt old consumer electronics manufacturer in the US, as the exclusive distribution brand for Wal-Mart Stores at the beginning of 2001. Wal-Mart had accounted for nearly 50%[8] of Funai's North American sales, almost 70 %[9] of its world sales. Funai also allied with Sears Roebuck for the US distribution.

Funai's rapid growth largely depends on M&A in the direction of upstream, parts and basic technologies, and downstream, the distribution brand, of its original businesses.

---

7 Funai Security Report 1999, Funai Annual Report 2000.
8 48.3% in FY2002.
9 69.6% in FY1997 and 68.7% in FY 2003.

In Kyocere's case, it had acquired the companies up and downstream of its product lines in the direction of vertical integration. In Nidec's case, most of the acquired companies are in the scope of its technological business definition, 'turning and moving products'. In Funai's case, it has bought the companies up and downstream of the lines, too. The common trend in the M&A activitites of those three companies is to acquire the companies in the linkage of technologies or products, not function. Therefore functionality in business definitions has very little to do with the performance of those companies.

5. Conclusion

In the present study, the influence of the second explanatory variable, 'alignment degree' (magnitude of alignment in terms of function), is examined based on the assumption that even the corporate business definition is functional, if the function is not fully aligned through the whole company, the growth rate still will be lower, by content analysis to follow the previous statistic study.

A positive correlation between the alignment degree measured by an appearance frequency of key words composing business definitions in new product press releases and growth rate is identified with 10 companies of high range in functionality. The alignment degree clearly explains the difference in growth rate that is not explained by the difference in functionality. It explicitly supports H2, and thus H1 is proved.

The results of the previous and present studies jointly draw the conclusion that both the functionality in the business definition and the alignment in terms of function throughout the whole organization are essential for continuous growth of the companies.

It is also found that a multiple regression model is applicable to the companies of high and low ranges in functionality that well explains growth rate by functionality and alignment degree. The model forms the following equation:

$$\hat{G} = 4.00F + 5.63A - 5.76$$

where $\hat{G}=$ average annual growth rate of consolidated net sales (FY1997-FY2003) (%) (a theoretical value)

$F=$ functionality in corporate business definition (1998)

$A=$ alignment degree based on the content analysis of the new product press releases (FY1998-FY2003)

The regression results with the 25 companies including the eight companies of medium range in functionality do not bear a valid model. One of the reasons is that there are some companies of this range that grow mainly by M&A. The short-term impact of M&A on the corporate growth is so large that it distorts the regression analysis.

Table 8. Selected data for 50 Japanese electric/electronics companies

	Company	Sales FY2003	Sales FY1998	Sales FY1997	AAGR. Sales FY1997-03	AAGR. Sales FY1998-03	AOPR FY1997-03	AOPR FY1998-03	AAGR. market value FY1997-02	AAGR. market value FY1997-03	Functionality score
1	Hitachi	8,632,450	7,977,374	8,416,834	.42	1.59	1.55	1.39	-9.09	-9.91	.28
2	Sony	7,496,391	6,794,619	6,755,490	1.75	1.99	3.56	2.87	4.31	-3.75	1.41
3	Matsushita	7,479,744	7,640,119	7,890,662	-.89	-.42	1.81	1.40	-5.36	-6.10	.59
4	Toshiba	5,579,506	5,300,902	5,458,498	.37	1.03	1.54	1.55	-6.65	-6.63	1.14
5	N E C	4,906,821	4,759,412	4,901,122	.02	.61	2.11	1.82	-11.71	-9.47	.52
6	Fujitsu	4,766,888	5,242,986	4,985,382	-.74	-1.89	2.49	2.28	-12.99	-15.10	.52
7	Mitsubishi	3,309,651	3,794,063	3,801,344	-2.28	-2.69	1.31	1.53	-2.83	-1.95	.45
8	Canon	3,198,072	2,826,269	2,761,025	2.48	2.50	10.06	10.08	8.08	9.11	.69
9	Sanyo	2,599,939	1,882,439	1,924,675	5.14	6.67	3.20	3.19	.75	1.41	1.69
10	Sharp	2,257,273	1,745,537	1,790,542	3.94	5.28	4.14	4.32	2.21	3.36	1.24
11	Ricoh	1,780,245	1,425,999	1,403,348	4.04	4.54	6.91	7.00	7.09	5.12	1.55
12	Epson	1,413,243	1,057,020	1,062,016	4.88	5.98	5.75	5.75	-	-	1.83
13	Matsushita Electric Works	1,335,329	1,102,454	1,132,544	2.78	3.91	4.16	4.30	-8.56	-3.35	1.48
14	Kyocera	1,140,814	725,326	725,312	7.84	9.48	10.09	9.58	.05	-1.23	1.07
15	JVC	921,978	946,617	916,305	.10	-.53	.60	.55	-12.71	-5.01	.69
16	Konica-Minolta	860,420	1,090,416	1,074,659	-3.64	-4.63	5.40	5.64	4.22	8.64	.38
17	Fuji Electric	856,198	852,060	982,763	-2.27	.10	1.38	1.21	-6.52	-8.64	.83
18	Pioneer	700,885	568,857	559,841	3.82	4.26	3.81	3.96	-1.36	1.90	1.48
19	T D K	658,862	676,250	696,677	-.93	-.52	6.98	5.80	-10.63	-8.01	.24
20	Oki	654,214	673,170	764,596	-2.57	-.57	.08	-.13	-10.14	-1.71	.97
21	Alps	619,675	554,445	505,134	3.46	2.25	5.06	5.10	2.02	3.03	1.21
22	Omron	584,889	555,280	611,795	-.75	1.04	5.35	4.99	-6.87	-1.83	.34
23	Tokyo Electron	529,653	313,820	455,584	2.54	11.04	5.62	4.49	2.50	1.09	.76
24	Casio	523,528	451,141	502,012	.70	3.02	3.67	3.03	-9.00	-1.14	1.07
25	Murata	414,247	367,048	362,252	2.26	2.45	18.83	18.86	8.50	2.76	.41
26	Yokogawa	371,943	280,185	305,231	3.35	5.83	2.25	2.04	1.53	6.36	1.31
27	Rohm	355,630	328,631	335,922	.95	1.59	28.75	28.29	5.94	1.83	1.17
28	Toshiba Tec	355,112	296,926	293,630	3.22	3.64	3.39	3.19	-5.45	.61	.69

Table 8. Continued

	Company	Sales FY2003	Sales FY1998	Sales FY1997	AAGR. Sales FY1997-03	AAGR. Sales FY1998-03	AOPR FY1997-03	AOPR FY1998-03	AAGR. market value FY1997-02	AAGR. market value FY1997-03	Functionality score
29	Sumitomo Denso	345,599	209,903	218,481	7.94	10.49	2.10	2.15	-6.15	5.04	1.00
30	Funai	342,133	164,710	140,806	15.95	15.74	9.48	9.61	26.30	22.12	.97
31	Koito	334,254	275,934	226,134	6.73	3.91	3.64	3.72	-6.00	1.18	1.72
32	Nidec	329,003	132,594	115,662	19.03	19.93	9.07	8.66	24.29	22.79	.79
33	Japan Radio Co	278,571	276,226	276,056	.15	.17	2.55	2.39	-19.69	-14.70	.59
34	Stanley	278,300	180,676	193,344	6.26	9.02	6.24	6.82	21.75	26.76	1.55
35	Minebea	268,574	305,324	326,093	-3.18	-2.53	10.68	9.46	-12.20	-13.92	.86
36	Fanuc	264,832	226,070	230,788	2.32	3.22	29.94	30.00	4.55	5.29	.59
37	Yaskawa	263,045	227,457	268,642	-.35	2.95	2.48	2.06	1.23	6.78	.72
38	Kyoden	252,170	21,599	19,894	52.70	63.47	4.49	2.96	-6.10	.84	1.48
39	Hosiden	225,374	160,409	164,684	5.37	7.04	7.42	7.06	5.77	1.16	.97
40	Ibiden	220,540	132,399	118,295	10.94	10.74	7.30	7.05	-3.56	-4.74	.76
41	Mitsumi	214,216	249,178	263,691	-3.40	-2.98	4.12	3.48	-3.97	-7.82	.10
42	Alpine	213,019	176,311	168,146	4.02	3.86	4.02	4.13	.55	0.97	1.86
43	Hitachi Maxell	212,698	208,291	191,479	1.77	.42	5.61	5.71	-9.65	-8.47	1.14
44	Dainippon Screen	191,939	147,602	221,746	-2.38	5.39	.97	.31	-10.68	-3.40	.66
45	Meidensha	181,560	218,353	222,772	-3.35	-3.62	.84	1.13	-20.57	-11.12	.21
46	Kenwood	178,731	309,825	312,175	-8.88	-10.42	3.51	3.47	-8.12	3.64	.21
47	Advantest	174,218	141,714	257,418	-6.30	4.22	9.98	6.03	-2.03	-2.34	1.14
48	Yamatake	169,950	178,896	198,932	-2.59	-1.02	4.29	3.94	-17.15	-15.68	.72
49	Clarion	168,947	199,575	196,006	-2.45	-3.28	3.11	2.96	-11.14	-2.98	.61
50	Fujitsu General	168,678	193,298	197,169	-2.57	-2.69	1.68	1.61	-15.48	-8.75	.14
	Mean	1,391,599	1,291,314	1,318,072	2.75	4.03	5.67	5.38	-2.87	-.73	.90

Notes: 'Sales' denotes consolidated net sales in million yen. 'AAGR.sales' denotes average annual growth rate of consolidated net sales (%). 'AOPR' denotes average consolidated operating profit (%). 'AAGR.market value' denotes average annual growth rate of aggregate market value (%).

Regarding Konica-Minolta Holdings, sales for FY1997–2002 and market value for FY1997 were calculated by the aggregation of figures for the former Konica and Minolta. Accordingly, AAGR.sales FY1997–FY2003, AAGR.sales FY1998–FY2003, and AAGR.market value FY1997–FY2003 were derived on the basis of these aggregated figures.

Ranked by consolidated net sales in FY2003.

Source: Wakabayashi (2005).

The case study results of the three medium functionality companies, Kyocera, Nidec, and Funai, show the common trend in the series of M&A. The M&A of those companies had been adopted based on the linkage in technologies or products, and not function. Therefore functionality in business definitions has little to do with the performance of those companies. The impact of M&A on the relationship between business definition and corporate growth is not clearly identified from the perspective of function or customer value in the present study. However, if there is a tendency with those companies that they do not give function (customer value) a top priority in their business definitions, it will be difficult for them to continuously grow and their growth will be in short term, according to Levitt's arguments. In order to identify the real impact of M&A on the relationship between business definition and corporate growth, it is necessary to further study on it in the longer term.

The conclusions of the present study will draw a procedure to define businesses by text mining of text data in the field. The process of identifying key words in the corporate business definition is relatively simple because its length is short, and an exclusive text mining software is not necessary as it can be done by a search engine. However, in order to extract the key words from a bunch of new product press releases to newly formulate a corporate business definition, an exclusive text mining software is necessary for efficiency and accuracy. The detailed procedure will be the theme of the later study.

References

Abell, D. F. (1980). *Defining the Business: The Starting Point of Strategic Planning.* Englewood Cliffs, NJ: Prentice-Hall.

Bettman, J. R., & Weitz, B. A. (1983). Attributions in the Board Room: Causal Reasoning in Corporate Annual Reports. *Administrative Science Quarterly*, **28**, 165-183.

David, F. R. (1989). How Companies Define Their Mission. *Long Range Planning*, **22**(1), 90-97.

Drucker, P. F. (1974). *Management: Tasks, Responsibilities, Practices.* NY: Harper and Row.

Hofer, C. W., & Schendel, D. (1978). *Strategy Formulation: Analytical Concepts.* St. Paul, MN: West.

Holsti, O. R. (1969). *Content Analysis for the Social Sciences and Humanities.* Reading, MA: Addison-Wesley.

Kaplan, R.S., & Norton, D. P. (2001). *The Strategy Focused Organization.* Cambridge, MA: Harvard Business School Press.

Kiriyama, H. (2007). *Tetsuro Funai's Endless Challenge.* Tokyo: Kodansha (in Japanese).

Krippendorff, K. (1980). *Content Analysis: An Introduction to Its Methodology.* Beverly Hills, CA: Sage.

Kyocera Corporation (1998). *Strategic Direction.* Kyoto: Kyocera Corporation.

Labovitz, G., & Rosansky, V. (1997). *The Power of Alignment: How Great Companies Stay Centered and Accomplish Extraordinary Things.* NY: Wiley.

Levitt, T. (1960). Marketing Myopia. *Harvard Business Review*, **38**(4), 45-56.

Morris, R. (1994). Computerized Content Analysis in Management Research: A Demonstration of Advantages and Limitations. *Journal of Management*, **20**(4), 903-931.

Pearce, J. A., & David, F. (1987). Corporate Mission Statements: The Bottom Line. *Academy of Management Executive*, **1**(2), 109-116.

Prahalad, C. K., & Bettis, R. A. (1986). The Dominant Logic: a New Linkage Between Diversity and Performance. *Strategic Management Journal*, **7**, 485-501.

Sakakibara, K., Otaki, S., & Numagami, T. (1989). *Dynamics in Business Creation.* Tokyo: Hakuto-shobo (in Japanese).

Sakakibara, K. (1992). *The Strategic Concept of Corporate Domain.* Tokyo: Chuokoron-shinsha (in Japanese).

Wakabayashi, K. (2005). Relationship between Business Definition and the Long-Term Growth of Companies: Is Levitt Right? *Pacific Economic Review*, **10**(4), 577-589.

Wakabayashi, K. (2007). *A Study on the Relationship between Business Definition and Corporate Growth.* Doctoral thesis, Tokyo Institute of Technology, Tokyo (in Japanese).

Wakabayashi, K. (2008). Relationship between Business Definition and Corporate Growth: The Effect of Functional Alignment. *Pacific Economic Review*, **13**(5), 663-679.

Watanabe, W., & Amano, T. (2007). Nidec's M&A. In H. Miyajima (Ed.), *M&A in Japan* (pp.225-258). Tokyo: Toyo Keizai (in Japanese).

Watson, A., & Wooldridge, B., (2005). Business Unit Influence on Corporate-level Strategy Formulation. *Journal of Managerial Issues*, **17**(2), 147-161.

In: Handbook of Business and Finance
Editors: M. Bergmann and T. Faust, pp. 281-292

ISBN: 978-1-60692-855-4
© 2010 Nova Science Publishers, Inc.

Chapter 12

PERILS AND PROMISES OF INFORMATION AND COMMUNICATION TECHNOLOGY FOR DEVELOPING COUNTRIES: THE ICT SERVICES OUTSOURCING BOOM IN INDIA

Tina Saebi[1,•], Geert Duysters[1] and Bert Sadowski[2,]*
[1] UNU-MERIT, The Netherlands
[2] University of Technology Eindhoven, The Netherlands

Abstract

The case of India illustrates well how technological revolutions may bring unexpected opportunities for developing countries. To benefit from the recent outsourcing boom in ICT services, India's government has directed investments into the restructuring and expansion of the local ICT services sector, positioning the country among the most popular ICT services outsourcing destinations. Drawing on national innovation system theory and concepts of absorptive capacity, this paper questions the sustainability of India's success as a top ICT offshoring destination. In the immediate distance, eroding cost advantages and unsophisticated service exports are threatening India's top position. To avoid competition in the low-segments of ICT services exports, India would have to move up the value chain, requiring the expansion of the ICT services sector into higher spheres of software design and development. However, as this paper argues, the expansion of this industry is constrained by the enormous variation in inter-state levels of ICT education and infrastructure. The poor absorptive capacity of the remaining part of the country is found to severely limit the industry's expansion possibilities. As empirically shown, state efforts to build a learning system exclusively for the ICT sector have prevented a nation-wide investment in absorptive capacity. Therefore this paper proposes that resolving these inter-state disparities requires the development of learning capabilities outside the ICT industry; enabling the remaining economic sectors to absorb the benefits generated by the expansion of the ICT sector. However, until this aim is achieved, India's ICT sector may have long lost its competitive advantage.

• Keizer Karelplein 19, 6211 TC Maastricht, The Netherlands.
* Corresponding author: Tel.: 0031-402475510, Den Dolech 2, 5612 AZ Eindhoven, The Netherlands.

1. Introduction

'Information and communication technologies' (ICT) belong to the group of 'general purpose technologies', meaning that mastering this technology has the potential to generate impacts on the whole economy across several industrial sectors. ICT has the potential to enhance productivity of economic sectors by making the use of capital and labor more efficient; to restructure economic activities; to create markets that are more efficient, and to build new products and industries. Probably, the most visible impact of ICT has been on the tradability of services. The relocation of service functions was never regarded to be a feasible option until a decade ago. While the entire process of manufacturing has been fragmented into smaller tasks and distributed internationally, this could not be actualized for the production of services. A haircut, for instance, has and will always require physical proximity. While many corporate services have required face-to face interaction, due to either technical constraints or customs and habits, the latter have gradually altered as technical constraints have been solved by recent progresses in ICT (World Investment Report, 2004). When examining a corporate service as a totality, it appears to defy relocation (Dossani and Kenney, 2003). Yet, the use of ICT has enabled the digitization, codification and standardization of knowledge embodied in a service function. This in turn allows the production of a service to be fragmented into smaller components. Those components that require low levels of face-to-face interactivity are not bound to a certain location anymore; their production is increasingly subject to relocation - services became tradable.

With increased competition, – also a result of improved communication and transportation – companies increasingly opt to outsource their services activities to developing countries, where they achieve potential costs savings while retaining better quality than that currently provided by the developed nation facility (Dossani and Kenney 2003). Developing countries have responded by expanding their services sector as to take part in the production and exports of these services. Pursuing an export-oriented strategy in the information technology (IT) services sector promises increased export earnings and positive impacts on the labor force: job creation, higher wages and upgrading of skills. As the intensity of services activity in the economy is positively correlated with high GDP per capita, an offshoring boom in IT services is likely to result in rapid growth for these economies (Bajpai, Sachs, Arora and Khurana, 2004). Noteworthy, ICT has the *potential* to enhance productivity and competitiveness of industries. The extent, to which this potential can be exploited, is not equally distributed among countries or among industries within an economy. Empirical studies have shown that while ICT enhances the productivity of some industries, it has failed to do so for other parts of the economy (Joseph and Intarakumnerd 2004). For instance, India is well known for her success in developing an export sector for software and IT services (Kumar 2001; Joseph and Kumar 2004; Arora, Arunachalam, Asundi and Fernandes 2000; Dossani and Kenney 2003; Bajpai et al., 2004; Singh 2004). Yet, the achievements are less promising when it comes to the diffusion of this technology to other sectors of the Indian economy (Arora and Athreye 2002; Krishnan 2003; Desai 2000). Other economic sectors are still lagging behind in terms of economic growth and performance - in domestic as well as international dimensions (Economist Intelligence Unit (EIU), 2004).

Against this background, the question arises why ICT has been critical in India's outsourcing boom while the remaining parts of the country have not been able to benefit from this technology.

The answer to the first part of this question can be found in the literature on learning dynamics and technical change in developing countries (Viotti, 2002; Narula, 2003; Blomstrom et al., 2000; Patinbandla and Petersen, 2002). Here it is assumed that new technologies, such as ICT, originate in advanced industrialized nations. Section 2 describes firstly the process under which developing countries gain access to new technologies and secondly the conditions that determine if ICT is successfully integrated into the economy's learning system. Section 3 proposes that the remaining parts of an economy may not be able benefit from a new technology due to the country's development of learning capabilities in a lopsided manner. To illustrate this proposition, the case of India's IT services export industry is discussed in section 4. The last section sums up the discussion and underlines the dilemma between the perils and promises of ICT facing India.

2. Learning Dynamics and Conditions

Learning processes in developing countries are firstly based on the absorption of innovations produced elsewhere and secondly on the generation of improvements in the vicinity of acquired techniques (Viotti, 2002, p. 658). 'Absorption' refers to "the ability to internalize the knowledge created by others and modifying it to fit one's own specific applications, processes and routines" (Narula, 2003, p. 69). Absorption capacity is limited as companies are constrained in what they can learn by what they already know. The generation of improvements in the vicinity of acquired techniques is achieved by a learning process named learning-by-doing. It implies that companies acquire knowledge by exploring in the vicinity of their existing knowledge assets, by undertaking routines, which leads to incremental innovations (Narula, 2003). The extent to which these learning processes are successful depends on two conditions. The first condition claims that spillovers generated by multinational enterprises (MNE) activity have to be significant. The reasoning is as follows. By undertaking FDI, the MNE will equip its subsidiary with a stock of product and process technologies and implement the home country's management skills and knowledge base. Spillovers occur when indigenous firms are able to benefit from the MNE's superior knowledge of e.g. processes or markets. The MNE may improve *allocative efficiency* by entering into industries with high entry barriers and reducing monopolistic distortions or the MNE induces higher *technical efficiency* by demonstrating new technologies and training workers who later take employment in local firms. This may lead to increased competitive pressures, spurring local firms to more efficient use of existing resources (Blomstrom et al., 2000). To assess the significance of these spillovers, Blomstrom et al. (2000) suggest analyzing the nature and extent of linkages between the MNE and local firms. 'Backward linkages', for instance, arise as the MNE subsidiary sources some components and services from indigenous suppliers. It is in the MNE's own interest to provide technical support and assistance to its suppliers. The significance of spillovers depends very much on the 'level' the linkages are created. For instance, a MNE subsidiary that operates in the low-end of the market is unlikely to ask for challenging and complex input products. Hence, the supplier firm is not forced to employ its resources more efficiently to meet the MNE's product requirements. Moreover, operating in the lower end of the market does not require the MNE to equip its subsidiary with state-of the art technology. Thus, indigenous firms are prevented to gain access to superior technology. Patinbandla and Petersen (2002) confirm this reasoning by concluding that larger backward linkages of MNE with the local industry causes a higher level of spillovers than MNEs operating as islands in a developing economy. Further, a linkage between MNE and local firms at the higher-end of technologies benefits the industry.

The second condition requires the domestic sector to have the ability to absorb and diffuse the gained knowledge and technology. The ability to absorb depends on what the firms know. As mentioned before, firms are constrained in what they learn by what they know. "There thus exists a relationship between absorptive capacity and the stock of knowledge within any system" (Narula, 2003, p.70). Here, Narula (2003) refers to the system of national innovation. Yet, as argued by Viotti (2002), the ability to innovate is usually specific to advanced industrialized economies and thus a national system of learning is more appropriate to study technical change in developing countries. Nonetheless, the correlation between stock of knowledge and absorptive capacity is believed to hold in a learning system as well. This notion is captured in figure 1.

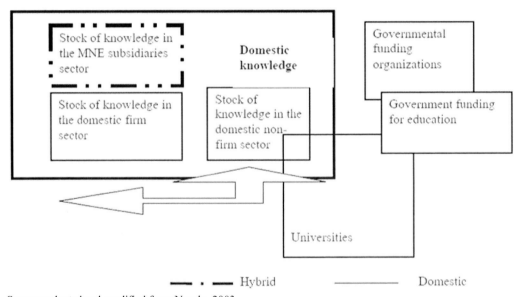

Source: adapted and modified from Narula, 2003.

Figure 1. Correlation between stock of knowledge and absorptive capacity in a learning system.

Starting on the right side of the figure, the role of the government is highlighted in providing an appropriate supply of human capital, which is associated with the non-firm sector. Non-firms, such as universities, determine the knowledge infrastructure that supports the process of incremental innovation inside a company. "They account for a certain portion of the stock of knowledge at the national level which may be regarded as 'general knowledge' in the sense that it has characteristics of a public good, and is potentially available to all firms that seek to internalize it for rent generation" (Narula, 2003, p.70). Absorptive capacity is not equally distributed amongst firms within an industry. Viotti (2002) introduces the concept of different technological capabilities to capture the notion of varying absorptive capacities. According to Patinbandla and Petersen (2002), it is the role of the government to enhance these technological capabilities, i.e. the production and improvement capabilities of indigenous firms. By investing in education and training of the labor force, the government can increase the knowledge and skills required for the process of production (production capability) and the knowledge and skills required for the continuous and incremental upgrading of product design, performance features and of process technology (improvement capability). These technological capabilities not only allow for the absorption of knowledge and technologies through spillovers, but also enable incremental innovations to take place in the domestic sector. Further, strategies have to be implemented to enhance knowledge flows across the domestic sector. However, networks to disseminate knowledge are not developed automatically, but have to be established by the government. Feinson (2003) concludes that governments have to play an essential role in establishing institution and networks that dissipate the tacit and codified knowledge underlying novel technological systems. The result is a complex network of actors involved in the learning process of developing countries.

3. Proposition on Uneven Learning Capability Development

Apparently, creating and running a system of learning requires large investments. This is especially the case for supporting and promoting a high-tech industry. For instance, as MNEs enter the ICT services sector of a host developing country, several investments by the government are required to fully take advantage of the foreign sources of knowledge. Firstly, investments are needed to maintain FDI inflows and to provide incentives to the MNE to build linkages with indigenous firms. This requires an adequate human endowment in the domestic sector that is able to absorb the generated spillovers. Therefore, the government has to provide higher levels of education and training in information and communication technology. Finally, investments in the infrastructure are needed, such as telecommunication and computer facilities as to allow for enhanced knowledge flows within the network of actors. As these conditions are fulfilled, even more MNEs are likely to enter the domestic sector and contribute their share of ICT and knowledge. Consequently, the dynamics inherent in the process of learning require a constant flow of investments to attract significant inflows of foreign sources of technology and to promote absorptive capacity.

Yet, this requirement of constant flow of investment strikes attention. Nations have finite resources, regardless of the size of the country. Investments in the IT sector may imply that certain areas (cities, states) of a country are promoted, while other parts of the country may not be similar recipients of such investments. This is likely to add to the absorptive capacity of the recipient areas as opposed to the remaining parts of the country. This paper proposes that inter-state disparity in absorptive capacity prevents a nation-wide ability to take full advantage of the new technology. Particularly, investments in the IT sector are proposed to widen the inter-state disparity in absorptive capacity and hence prevent other states and industries to benefit from the success in the IT sector.

To illustrate this proposition, India is taken as the country case of choice. India is well known for her success in developing an export sector for software and IT services (Kumar 2001; Joseph and Kumar 2004; Arora, Arunachalam, Asundi and Fernandes 2000; Dossani and Kenney 2003; Bajpai et al., 2004; Singh 2004). Yet, the achievements are less promising when it comes to the diffusion of this technology to other sectors of the Indian economy (Arora and Athreye 2002; Krishnan 2003; Desai 2000). Other economic sectors are still lagging behind in terms of economic growth and performance - in domestic as well as international dimensions (Economist Intelligence Unit (EIU), 2004). Further, the EIU report (2004) finds that states within India vary significantly in terms of infrastructure and levels of education and health. Therefore, section 4 firstly describes those state initiatives that are valued instrumental in the facilitation of India's IT success (Kumar and Joseph 2004; Singh, 2004), and further argues that these state initiatives contributed to the widening regional disparities in education, health and infrastructures across the country (Krishnan, 2003; Desai, 2000; Joseph and Intarakumnerd, 2004). These regional disparities mirror the lack of sufficient absorptive capacity as to allow for a further growth of the IT industry.

4. The Case of India's IT Services Export Industry

The recent IT services outsourcing boom in India was impossible to picture just two or three decades ago. Over half a century, the country has undergone severe changes in industrial strategy, from a heavily regulated and inward-oriented structure towards significant liberalization in both domestic and trade policy. Under the new regime, the progresses in ICT could be translated into significant spillovers to the services sector as a whole. Studying the Indian experience of liberalization gives us a unique opportunity to study what happens when an 'independent' country transforms to an 'integrationist'.

4.1. The Indian Learning System before Economic Liberalization

The outcome of rather domestic national learning systems has been investigated in extant literature (references) and the answer has not been straightforward at all. As Lall (1993) has highlighted, countries such as "Japan and the republic of Korea are clear examples of coherent and successful technological strategies based on a selective restriction of inward direct investment and developing local 'know-why" (p.16). Similarly, India had largely restricted inward direct investment to nurture the development of national learning capabilities. Yet, the outcome has not been similarly successful as for Japan or Korea. By the end of 1980s, India had one of the strongest bases of scientific and technical infrastructure for research and development. This enabled the country to make significant progress in strategic sectors such as atomic energy, defense and space research, resulting in some of the most advanced capabilities in these areas in the developing world (Krishnan, 2003). Yet this scientific and technological base did not translate into significant industrial innovation. This failure can be traced back to a highly protected and autarkic economic model characterizing India's industrialization policies since its independence in 1947. The local industry felt little need to innovate as they faced a high effective rate of protection (through physical constraints on imports and high import duties) together with industrial licensing (that constituted a major barrier to entry). Further, "constraints on growth also acted as a disincentive to innovative behavior. With a protected market, and a high cost structure, very few firms pursued exports or targeted external markets aggressively" (Krishnan, 2003).

Another similar fatal outcome of India's industrialization policies had been the emergence of a so-called 'dual economy'. In its aspiration of rapid industrialization, the state considered the development of heavy and basic manufacturing industries as the key to long-term growth (Kaplinsky, 1997, p. 682). Thus, state investments were then mainly focused on supporting the manufacturing industry opposed to agriculture. According to Krugman and Obstfeld (2000), in the 1980s, the total population of India counted 700 million people while only 6 million were employed in the manufacturing sector. However, the manufacturing workers produced more than 15% of the GNP and received wages that were six times as high as agricultural wages. Fact is that manufacturing is far more capital-intensive than agriculture. The government spending on capital equipment for the 'tiny' labor force of 6 million has consistently been larger than total investment in agriculture (Krugman and Obstfeld, 2000, p.263). Lall (1993) holds the restriction on FDI as well as on domestic private enterprises, conflicting policy objectives, inadequate inflows of foreign technology (in non-equity forms) and an ineffective educational and technology infrastructure responsible for the widespread technical lags and uneven capability development in India (Lall, 1993, p.16). Krishnan (2003) concludes that by the end of the 1980s, "the economy was largely stuck in the historical 'Hindu rate of growth' of about 3.5% and India had fallen significantly behind countries such as Korea that at one time had comparable per capita incomes" (p. 6).

4.2. The Economic Policy Reforms in the 1990s

Dissatisfied with former policies, the government took different steps to pursue lighter regulation and closer integration with the global economy. The 1990s experienced an impressive turn-around towards liberalization and openness, where economic growth should be stimulated by attracting foreign investment, removing licensing and 'monopoly' controls as well as allowing imports and encouraging exports (Parthasarathy, 2004). In 1991, the Industrial Policy Statement of the Government of India had among its objectives the development of indigenous competence for the efficient absorption of foreign technology (Krishnan, 2003). Around this time, the information technology revolution in the developed world had begun to take root and shortages of skilled programmers and IT professionals were beginning to develop, while tremendous pressures to cut costs forced corporations to offshore non-core activities (Arora, Arunachalam, Asundi and Fernandez, 2000). So to say, the Indian success story in software exports originates from a good sense of timing. "By the late 1980s, India was graduating approximately 150,000 English-speaking engineers and science graduates, with only a limited demand for their services from the rest of the economy. By this time, a number of Indians were working in very substantial numbers in US firms. Some of them played an important, although as yet undocumented role, in bridging the gap and matching the buyers in the US with the suppliers in India. Responding quickly to the growing demand, a number of Indian firms arose in quick time" (Arora et al., 2000, p.2). Indian software companies that used cost arbitrage as an entry strategy in an emerging business could fulfill the increasing demand for software services. The growth of local software companies was facilitated by "the fact that the software services model does not involve irreversible commitments on specialized resources and that the basic skills required are fairly generic" (Krishnan, 2003, p.16). "The State encouraged this growth by considerably simplifying the process for obtaining the numerous clearances and permits that any firm in the organized sector in India typically needs" (Arora et al., 2000, p.2). As to this writing, 18 state governments have also IT policies with a view to promote ICT growth in the respective states[1]. These policies include inter alia the removal of entry barriers for foreign companies and removal of restrictions on foreign technology transfer, measures to make faster and cheaper data communication facilities available as well as reduction and rationalization of taxes, duties and tariffs etc" (Kumar and Joseph, 2004).

4.3. The 'Indian' Critical Success Factors

The supply of trained manpower for software development has been one of the priorities on the policy agenda. To meet the demand for software personnel especially engineering graduates, state's effort has been in creating post-secondary engineering and management institutions such as the Indian Institute of Technology and Indian Institute of Management. Currently, India produces 3.1 million college graduates every year, where 200,000 of them graduate in engineering sciences (Singh, 2004). Other notable state interventions have been the promotion of spatial agglomeration of the IT sector. The case of Bangalore best visualizes this pattern. This city has been one of the most favored locations of multinationals. Bangalore is often referred to as the 'Silicon Valley of India', hosting headquarters of more than 120 companies as well as a high number of software centers. Bangalore has 30 engineering colleges out of 77 located in the Karnataka state, ensuring a steady supply of trained engineering manpower for the software houses. After the saturation of Bangalore in terms of available infrastructure and scarcity of space, the state government's promotional role has contributed to the emergence of Mumbai, Delhi, Hyderabad and Chennai as alternative software centers. These cities have shared a disproportionate share of significant agglomeration economies present in skills and knowledge intensive activities (Kumar and Joseph, 2004). To further enhance the Indian IT infrastructure, eighteen so called 'software technology parks' have been established in different parts of the country to provide the necessary infrastructure and training for software export[2].

And indeed, these critical success factors have resulted in impressive export earnings and in India's reputation as the most preferred destination for IT outsourcing (AT Kearney, 2004; Ernst and Young, 2004). India's software and IT services industry has been growing at 50 percent annually, starting from a small base in 1990. The country's value in exports of software and other services ($12 billion in 2003-2004) surpasses that of other competitors. India's figures on "the export intensity of the Indian software and IT service industry rose from 58% to 78%, and the share of these services in total exports from India increased from 3% to 21% between 1996 and 2003" indicating the country's growing popularity as an offshore destination (World Investment Report, 2004, p.169).

---

1 For the details of policies implemented by these different 18 state governments, the interested reader may like to visit www.Nasscom.org.

2 A software development park is in all respects similar to a free trade zone exclusively for the software industry. The specific objectives of the STPs are inter alia to establish and manage the infrastructural resources such as data communication facilities and core computer facilities, as well as to train professionals and to encourage design and development in the field of software technology and software engineering (Kumar and Joseph, 2004, p.11).

4.4. Regional Disparities in Infrastructure, Education, and Health Levels

Despite these praises, the Indian IT services export market has a long way ahead. Several studies have confirmed that India is still operating at the relatively lower end of the services chain (Evans, 1998; Arora et al., 2000; Singh, 2004; WIR, 2004; Joseph and Intarakumnerd, 2004; Dossani and Kenney, 2004). This issue is a very important with regard to emerging competition from China, Malaysia and Singapore. This is due to the reason that competition is likely to attack in the low segments of IT services outsourcing, meaning that the slogan 'went for cost, stayed for quality' will be applicable to many developing countries. According to Singh (2004), India is no longer the cheapest place to do business due to eroding cost advantages in the software clusters. Faced with eroding cost advantages in cities like Bangalore, Mumbai or New Delhi, the MNE would consider alternative locations for its subsidiaries in India. Yet, outside the clusters, the basic infrastructure required for large-scale growth of firms is simply not available, as the following illustrates. As a result, many MNEs have considered alternative offshoring destinations and willing targets are not far away.

Noteworthy, the very promotion of spatial agglomeration of the IT sector has clearly profited certain areas of the country at the expense of the remaining parts. Due to heavy state support, the southern and western cities of Chennai, Bangalore, Mumbai and Hyderabad have become preferred destinations for IT offshore outsourcing. Alertly, the rest of the country has not been the recipient for similar investments (Singh, 2004). Arora and Athreye (2003) claim that limited infrastructure outside the 'software clusters' constrain the growth of the software services industry. For the expansion of software services, sufficient availability of power and adequate quality of the telecommunications infrastructure has to be in place. Especially in rural areas, energy provision constitutes a major hindrance of growth. Many companies have to generate their own power. Regarding telecommunication infrastructure, limited bandwidth and telephone penetration are two major problems. For instance, "India has 15 main telephone lines per 1000 people, compared with 395 per 1000 for Ireland and 446 per 1000 for Israel. The situation is more serious when we consider the penetration of PCs in the total population: 1.5 computers per 1000 people versus 145 for Ireland and 117.6 for Israel" (Arora and Athreye, 2003, p. 259). The educational situation in India is a mixed picture. On the one hand, India has more than 225 universities, 6,800 affiliated colleges and 1,128 polytechnics. On the other hand, "India still lags behind in educational standards, both absolutely and compared with other developing countries: it has 17% of the world's population, but some 40% of the world's illiterate" (EIU, 2004, p. 22). Regional variations in literacy rates are striking and seem to correspond with the agglomeration process of the 'software clusters'. Similarly, regional disparities in healthcare are noteworthy. "Kerala has an infant mortality rate of 12 per 1,000, a figure not far short of high-income country standards, but Uttar Pradesh has an infant mortality rate of 85 per 1,000. Other states, such as Orissa and Madhya Pradesh, have even poorer rates" (EIU, 2004, p 23). Reducing poverty still poses a considerable challenge. "Two-thirds of India's labor force works in agriculture which, with forestry and fishing, accounts for around 25% of GDP. However, the majority of landholding is farmed at subsistence level, and many farming families live below the poverty line. India has some of the lowest human development indicators in the world, particularly in rural areas" (EIU, 2004, p. 28).

5. Implications for the Sustainability of India's IT Success

Currently, the software industry constitutes India's only viable competitive advantage. In view of emerging competition, it has to ensure that this will remain sustainable. The competition is likely to attack in the low segments of business outsourcing, meaning that the slogan 'went for cost, stayed for quality' will be applicable to many developing countries. According to Singh (2004), India is no longer the cheapest place to do business due to eroding cost advantages in the software clusters. "Quality of life has improved significantly, which has caused base salaries to increase substantially in places like Bangalore. This have has been exacerbated by MNEs coming to India, and recruiting the best and the brightest at a premium" (Singh, 2004, p.11). Faced with eroding cost advantages in cities like Bangalore, Mumbai or New Delhi, the MNE would consider alternative locations for its subsidiaries in India. Yet, outside the clusters, the basic infrastructure required for large-scale growth of firms is simply not available, not to mention the condition of rural areas. As a result, many MNEs have considered alternative offshoring destinations and willing targets were not far away. Here a brief overview of potential competitors. China ranks second on the 2004 offshore index and its position is relatively close to India's top position (AT Kearny, 2004). With its availability of a large pool of skilled people and low costs, the country is becoming a key product-development centre for companies like GE, Intel, Microsoft and Philips. Many industries are clustered in certain areas, with high-tech centers in Beijing and Shenzhen, financial services in Shanghai and Hong Kong as a global financial centre" (WIR, 2004 p.174). Similar close to India, Malaysia offers a "well–developed, low-cost infrastructure and strong government support" (AT Kearny, 2004, p.3). As a result, "the third-party call and contact centers are growing at the rate of 100-200% since 2000. BMW, Citigroup, Dell, DHL, Ericsson, Hewlett Packard, HSBC, IBM and Royal Dutch Shell have all set up regional service hubs in Malaysia"(WIR, 2004, p.174). With regard to Latin American countries, Argentina, Brazil, Mexico, Venezuela and Costa Rica are present on the 25 most preferred offshore destinations, offering relatively low labor costs and proximity (due to similar time zone) to the United States. The WIR (2004) predicts that countries such as Ghana, Mauritius, Morocco, Senegal and Tunisia will also be involved in the export of call centre and back office services, resulting in a 200% export increase until 2007. As it becomes obvious, competition is close by and the sustainability of India's IT success is endangered.

The case of India has illustrated that technological revolutions may bring unexpected opportunities for developing countries. MNEs have been the major source of this new technology for India and have encouraged the government to expand and restructure the software industry. The result has been indeed impressive. With a 50% annual growth rate over the last six years, India has earned the top position in the 2004 offshore index of the most popular IT services outsourcing destination. However, eroding cost advantages and unsophisticated service exports are threatening India's top position. To avoid competition in the low-segments of IT services exports India has to move up the value chain. This requires the growth of the IT services sector into higher spheres of software design and development. However, the growth of this industry is constrained by the enormous variation in inter-state levels of IT education and infrastructure. The government faces a dilemma that will prove difficult to solve. To beat competition, India would have to move up the value chain. Yet, the poor absorptive capacity of the remaining part of the country is severely limiting the industry's growth possibilities. As shown, other parts of the country suffer from under-investment and are unable to develop ICT learning capabilities. It seems as the efforts to build a learning system exclusively for the IT sector has prevented a nation-wide investment in absorptive capacity. Resolving these inter-state disparities requires investments over a long time horizon. These investments are necessary as to develop learning capabilities outside the software industry. Once this aim is achieved, the software industry has the ability to grow and other parts of the country will be able to absorb the benefits of ICT. However, until this aim is achieved, the software industry may have long lost its competitive advantage.

References

[1] Arora, A., Athreye, S., 2002, "The software industry and India's economic development", *Information Economics and Policy,* Vol. 14, pp. 253–273.

[2] Arora, A., Arunachalam, V.S., Asundi, J., and Fernandes R., 2000, "The Indian software services industry", *Research Policy*, Vol. 30, pp. 1267-1287.

[3] A.T. Kearny 2004, "Offshore Location Attractiveness Index".

[4] Bajpai, N., Sachs, J., Arora, R., and Khurana, H., 2004, "Global Services Sourcing: Issues of Cost and Quality", *CGSD Working Paper* No. 16.

[5] Blomstrom et al. 2000, "Multinational corporations and spillovers" in *foreign direct investment: Firm and host country strategies'* London, pp. 101-133.

[6] Desai, A.V. (2000) 'The Peril and the Promise: Broader Implications of the Indian presence in information technologies' *Centre for research on economic development and policy development, Working Paper* No.70

[7] Dossani, R., and Kenney, M., 2003, "Went for cost, stayed for quality: Moving the back office to India", http://APARC.standford.edu.

[8] Ernst and Young, 2004, "Survey on Offshore Outsourcing in India", www.ey.com

[9] Evans, P., 1998, "Transnational corporations and third World States: From the old internationalization to the new", in Kozul-Wright and Howtorn, Transnational corporations and the global economy London: Macmillan Press, 1998.

[10] Feinson, S., 2003, "National Innovation Systems Overview and Country Cases" *A Project for the Global Inclusion Program of the Rockefeller Foundation.*

[11] Joseph, K.J., Intarakumnerd, P., 2004, "GPTs and Innovation Systems in Developing Countries: A Comparative Analysis of ICT Experiences in India and Thailand".

[12] Krishnan, R.T., 2003, "The Evolution of a Developing Country Innovation System during Economic Liberalization: The Case of India", *Paper Presented at the First Globelics Conference* November 3-6, 2003.

[13] Kumar, N., 2001, "Indian Software Industry Development in International and National Development Perspective", #19/2001.

[14] Kumar, N., and Joseph, K.L., 2004, "The National Innovation System that Made India's IT Success Possible", *Research and Information System for the Non-Aligned and other developing countries.*

[15] Narula, R., 2003, "Globalization and Technology", UK: Polity Press.

[16] Patinbandla, M., and Petersen, B., 2002, "The Role of MNCs in the evolution of high-tech industries in developing economies: The case of India's software development", *World Development,* Vol. 30, No. 9, pp. 1561-1577.

[17] Singh, S., 2004, "IT Leadership in a Global Environment", *Lecture Notes* in 2004
[18] *The Economist Intelligence Unit*, 2004, "Country Profile: India", 15 Regent St, London SW1Y 4LR United Kingdom.
[19] Viotti, E., 2002, "National Learning Systems: A new approach on technological change in late industrializing economies", *Technological Forecasting and Social Change,* Vol.69, pp. 653-680.
[20] World Investment Report, 2004, "The Shift towards Services", *United Nations Conference on Trade and Development.*

In: Handbook of Business and Finance
Editors: M. Bergmann and T. Faust, pp. 293-300

ISBN: 978-1-60692-855-4
© 2010 Nova Science Publishers, Inc.

Chapter 13

SOCIAL CAPITAL IN THE CAPITALISATION OF NEW VENTURES: ACCESSING, LUBRICATING AND FITTING

Alistair R. Anderson[1,], Sarah L. Jack[2,•] and Sarah Drakopoulou Dodd[1,3,♦]*

[1] Centre for Entrepreneurship, Aberdeen Business School,
Robert Gordon University, Kaim House, Garthdee, Aberdeen
[2] Entrepreneurship, Institute for Entrepreneurship and
Enterprise Development, Lancaster University Management School, Lancaster
[3] Entrepreneurship, ALBA Graduate School of Business, Greece

Abstract

New venture capitalisation demands the formation of the necessary financial resources to launch. Social capital - the potential resources to which individuals have access due to their position within specific social networks of relationships - also plays a significant role in new venture capitalisation in three main ways. Firstly, social capital provides *access*, and thus acts a means of securing other forms of capital. Secondly, social capital also *lubricates* relations between entrepreneur and others within the socio-economic environment, including financiers. Thirdly, social capital acts as a mechanism for *fitting* the entrepreneur and their new venture to the wider socio-economic environment.

Introduction

The capitalisation of new ventures is traditionally seen as the formation of the necessary financial resources to launch the venture. In this chapter we argue that social capital can also

---

* E-mail address: a.r.anderson@rgu.ac.uk, Tel: +44 1224 263883, AB 24 7QE. Tel: +44 1224 263883.

• E-mail address: s.l.jack@lancaster.ac.uk, Tel: +44 1524 593540, LA1 4YX, Tel: +44 1524 593540.

♦ E-mail address: doddsarah@alba.edu.gr, Tel: +30 210 896 4531-8, Address: Athinas Ave. and 2A Areos Str., 166 71 Vouliagmeni, Greece (Corresponding Author: Sarah Drakopoulou Dodd).

play a significant role. Social capital can be considered as the potential resources to which individuals have access due to their position within specific social networks of relationships. We consider three important aspects of social capital for the capitalisation of new ventures. First, social capital provides access, and thus acts a means of securing other forms of capital, which typically include human and intellectual capital, as well as finance. Social capital acts as an accessing mechanism by providing a bridging function from the entrepreneur to the locus in their networked environment where these resources are located. Secondly, social capital itself also functions as a complementary entrepreneurial asset by lubricating relations between entrepreneur and others within the socio-economic environment, including financiers. A major element of the liability of newness is the lack of credibility, and its stable mate legitimacy. Yet such reputational goods are essential in the yet to be born business. The entrepreneur's social capital can provide this legitimacy and thus legitimise the emergence of new business. By signalling trust and similarity, as well as "guaranteeing" certain ethical and commercial norms, social capital enhances interactions between individuals linked by network relationships. Thirdly, social capital acts as a mechanism for "fitting" the entrepreneur and their new venture to the wider socio-economic environment. Just as knowledge, information and norms about the new venture are transmitted to the networked environment, so the responses of that environment to the new venture – and its entrepreneur – are returned to the entrepreneur. These "messages" may be explicit or tacit, written or oral, formal or informal.; from a raised eyebrow and a withheld smile, to an email suggesting potential clients. Taken together, and acted upon by the new entrepreneur, this dynamic flow of market signals, mediated through social capital, "fits" the new venture to market needs, norms, and nuances. We continue by discussing the role of the social in enterprise and go on to explain how social capital has these three important roles to play in new venture capitalisation, with special attention to venture capital.

The Social Nature of Entrepreneurship

Lindgren and Packendorff (2002) propose that most conceptual accounts of the entrepreneur are usually embodied in a single person, but they argue that entrepreneurship is not the result of what single individuals do; it is the consequence of collective organizing and social interaction. Drakopoulou Dodd and Anderson (2007) claim that given the strength of the evidence of how entrepreneurship involves networked individuals and the networking of individuals, it seems difficult to conceive of entrepreneurship as the isolated act of an individual. Indeed, Johannisson and Monsted (1997: 112) argue, it is very likely we should see 'contemporary venturing activities as a partial mobilization of a slowly changing overall network'. Moreover, the importance of networking to venture success is highlighted by recent evidence that it is the lead entrepreneur in team starts who takes responsibility for networking, or, perhaps, the key networker in a team who becomes the lead entrepreneur (Neergard, 2005). This all stands as evidence that entrepreneurship is not an individualistic act and clearly shows that at all of the key stages of new venture creation entrepreneurship appears to progress through interaction with others. In this way, entrepreneurship can be understood as a social activity, where the economic is deeply embedded in social interaction (Jack and Anderson, 2002).

Entrepreneurs, Networks and Social Capital

There is thus an increasingly accepted view that entrepreneurs are a product of their social environment and how opportunities are both perceived and realised is a consequence of social interaction and social background (Anderson and Miller, 2002). Although the actual process of entrepreneurship has been described as one in which "opportunities to bring into existence "future" goods and services are discovered, created and exploited" (Venkataraman, 1997: 120), more recently this process has been described as a social undertaking carried out within the context of social systems (Sarason et al, 2006). Entrepreneurs are embedded in a social context and in social situations (Steier and Greenwood, 1995; Kim and Aldrich, 2005). The role of relationships in organization formation has been widely examined (Larson, 1991; Larson and Starr, 1993; Steier and Greenwood, 1995; Hite, 2003; 2005). Studies have demonstrated that networks of relationships constitute a valuable resource for the entrepreneur (Nahapiet and Ghoshal, 1998; Davidsson and Honig, 2003; Batjargal and Liu, 2004). Consequently, the networks in which an entrepreneur is embedded; the ties he/she has to others, and the resources those ties can offer are important entrepreneurial venturing. Indeed Neergaard and Masden (2004) suggest that know who is as important as know how. Different clusters of ties offer "reservoirs of potential support" (Steier and Greenwood, 2000). So, a critical task for any entrepreneur is to make use of his/her existing network of relationships to mobilize necessary resources but also to work to enhance and strengthen that network of contacts (Steier and Greenwood, 2000). As Maula et al (2003) conclude, it makes sense for an entrepreneur to invest time and money to enable effective knowledge acquisition.

Accordingly, the central proposition of social capital theory is that networks of relationships constitute a valuable resource (Nahapiet and Ghoshal, 1998). By drawing on the social capital that exists in the network entrepreneurs are able to access other resources. But while possessing social capital might be useful, it is not a resource as such. The presence of social capital enables interactions which in turn may tap into resources (Anderson et al, 2007). Social capital represents a set of social resources embedded in relationships and which are available to people through their social connections (Baker, 1990; Coleman, 1990; Liao and Welsch, 2003; Lin, 2001; Kim and Aldrich, 2005; Anderson et al, 2007). It has been defined as "the features of social organisation, such as trust, norms and networks, that can improve the efficiency of society by facilitating coordinated actions" (Putnam, 1993; 167). Nahapiet and Ghoshal see social capital as "the sum of the actual and potential resources embedded within, available through and derived from the network of relationships possessed by individual or social units" (1998: 243). Similarly, for Bourdieu and Wacquant (1992: 119) social capital is "the sum of the resources, actual or virtual, that accrue to an individual or a group by virtue of possessing a durable network of more or less institutionalized relationships of mutual acquaintance and recognition". The underlying assumption is that "networks of relationships constitute, or lead to, resources that can be used for the good of the individual or the collective" (Dakhli and De Clecq, 2004: 110). So, within the entrepreneurial venturing context it is assumed that social connections are used to obtain resources that would otherwise be acquired through expending human or financial capital (Kim and Aldrich, 2005). Entrepreneurs must surely then invest in social relations because there is some kind of expected return in the marketplace (Lin, 2001).

Social capital is therefore a social asset, even though unlike other assets it can neither be owned or borrowed. It can only be produced, re-produced and shared within social interactions. Descriptions of the content and associations invariably talk of trust, relationships, associability, interdependencies and networks. Barbieri (2003) concludes that all of the many meanings proposed consider social capital to be connected with the system of relations and social belongings in which individuals are embedded. It is not based on market transactions, though it may support such transactions and is often described as a means of reducing the cost and moral hazard of interaction (Anderson et al, 2007). Trust and interdependency, key aspects of social exchange, are important for building, generating and developing social capital. Fukuyama (1999) talks of informal co-operation and reciprocity between individuals. Interdependency, the coins of social exchange, are also perceived to be important for building, generating and developing social capital (Anderson et al, 2007). The network facilitates these interactions.

Social Capital and Venture Capital

The financing of a new venture is central to the venturing process and given the importance of business creation to economic growth, it is important to understand how entrepreneurs obtain finance to exploit entrepreneurial opportunities (Timmons, 1994; Block and MacMillan, 1992; Steier and Greenwood, 2000; Shane and Cable, 2002). Aldrich and Martinez (2001) suggest that the resources required for creating a successful new firm consist of human capital, financial capital and social capital. As we explained above, social capital allows entrepreneurs access to other inputs that they do not possess. Liao and Welsch (2005) summarise this very well, talking about the general consensus that a high level of social capital built on a favourable reputation, expertise and personal direct contact often assists the enterprise in gaining access to venture capital.

This first role for social capital, "accessing" is well documented. Social capital has been described as a bridge (Anderson and Jack, 2002), a mechanism for connecting to assets that are not in the nascent entrepreneur's control, thus supplementing the entrepreneur's own resources. Social capital in networks improves entrepreneurial effectiveness by overcoming the liabilities of such resource constraints (Jack et al, 2004). Indeed, Davidsson and Honig (2002) argue that the presence of bridging and bonding social capital is a robust indicator of nascent entrepreneurship.

However the role of social capital is not limited to this direct "accessing" aspect. It also has two additional complementary functions; "lubricating" and "fitting". As a reputational good, social capital lubricates the interface between venture capitalists and the entrepreneur. Social capital can also provide a mechanism for fitting the proposed new business into the social, economic and technological landscape.

As a complementary asset, there is a growing realisation that social capital impacts on the decisions financiers make, particularly venture capitalists. Economic explanations for venture finance decisions are incomplete, undersocialised and ignore social ties (Shane and Cable, 2002). Financiers face difficult decisions when selecting who to support: entrepreneurs may act opportunitistically and of course, entrepreneurs vary in ability to identify and exploit opportunities (Macmillan et al, 1995). Thus seed-stage investors rely on social ties and relationships to select which ventures to fund, using social ties to overcome problems of information asymmetry (Venkataraman, 1997). Trust as Fukuyama (1995) explains is articulated in social capital. Nahapiet and Goshal (1998) explain the cognitive dimension of social capital as about shared values and shared meanings. Indeed Liao and Welsch (2005) discuss the similarities of this role to the institutional isomorphism of normative and mimetic forces described by Di Maggio and Powell (1993). In this sense, social capital allows and enables, as a signalling system, the drawing together of interests.

Indeed this connectedness can also be extended to see a governance mechanism. Drawing on the concept of embeddedness (Granovetter, 1985), Shane and Cable (2002) point out that organizational scholars have shown how social obligations between connected parties, and information transfer through social relationships, influence venture finance decisions. Anderson and Smith (2007), for example, describe how the moral dimension of entrepreneurship is both socially constructed and enacted, thus explaining social capital as a device for "approving" a new venture. Nonetheless, such explanations about the role of social relationships in venture finance have been criticised for being "unparsimonious and oversocialized". Furthermore, while investors might exploit social ties to gather private information, it does not follow that investors make investment decisions based on social obligations (Shane and Cable, 2002).

Nonetheless, social capital as a reputational good is powerful. Fried and Hisrich (1994: 21) argue that "while VCs receive many deals cold (without any introduction), they rarely invest in them....Most funded proposals come by referral". Shane and Cable (2002) argue that the reason why most funded proposals come by referral is that the referral provides information; and information about the individuals involved would seem to be key. Yet, to achieve this information, venture capitalists must surely draw on their networks of contacts. This implies that networks in which venture capitalists are embedded, their links to others and the social capital that resides within the network must impact on the venture capitalists decision making process. Moreover, Steier and Greenwood (1995) have illustrated that referrals can be critical in securing funding and that investors often participate in supporting a project because they have a relationship with a lead venture capitalist, "deal origination can be largely based on collaboration" (p.344). However, problems can also arise in that once involved, venture capitalists tend to take an active interest in promoting and managing the venture (Steier and Greenwood, 1995). Consequently, the relationship between the venture capitalist and entrepreneur can end up becoming about more than just finance and business advice as relationships become "multi-dimensional" exchange relationships (Macmillan et al, 1988; Timmons and Bygrave, 1986). Venture capitalists may providing access to other important networks which otherwise would be difficult to enter. (Steier and Greenwood, 1995). But, perhaps more importantly, relationships do not remain just social or economic by nature, instead friends become investors and investors become friends (Steier and Greenwood, 1995). As a result, friendships emerge, informal meetings and discussions take place and venture capitalists can become "personally troubled" when they have to withdraw funding from a venture: "the entrepreneurs had become their friends" (Steier and Greenwood, 1995, p.351). Through social interaction, social capital develops between the investor and the entrepreneur.

A final aspect of the complementarity of social capital is the aspect "fitting". By that we refer to how social capital can help shape a proposal, business idea or even an existing business to become more "attractive" to investors or stakeholders more generally (Jack et al, 2008). The ability of the new firm founder, as well as in the established firm, to capture external knowledge and expertise is vital, since no firm or individual is likely to own all such knowledge. Indeed, the employment of social capital in this conceptualisation is about transforming tacit knowledge, information and broad understandings into viable and appropriate applicable business acumen.

Conclusion

Figure 1 illustrates the roles we see for social capital. Such productions of social capital work with other forms of capital. Social capital is thus able to amplify, direct and focus the utility of other forms of capital. It may be seen as a complementary capital asset, but the operation of social capital works to overcome much of the liability of newness.

	Interpersonal Dimension	Community Dimension
Economic Aspects	Accessing- bridging to cash and other resources	Allocating– networked market function of getting resources to "right" loci and individuals
Legitimating Aspects	Lubricating – reputational good which smoothes relations and minimises information asymmetry	Norming – network level isomorphic effect of creating, transmitting and enacting locally legitimate norms
Knowledge Aspects	Learning- about norms and expectations	Fitting – community of practice shapes its members form and processes – perhaps especially new members – to fit.

Figure 1. Roles of Entrepreneurial Social Capital in the Capitalisation of New venture.

Moreover seen in this light, social capital is a convertible capital. It can be used to develop or tap into resources that would otherwise not be available. It may operate as a key to open doors which similarly, would not be accessible. It may also work to shape the emergent business to make it more attractive to venture capitalists. So social capital seems to play a critical role in the capitalisation of a new venture. It therefore follows that a critical task of any entrepreneur is to penetrate a venture capital network, to which there is a social dimension (Steier and Greenwood, 1995).

References

Anderson, A., Park, J. and Jack, S. (2007). Entrepreneurial social capital: conceptualizing social capital in new high-tech firms, *International Small Business Journal*, **25**(3): 245-272.

Baron, R.A., Markman, G.D. (2003) Beyond social capital: the role of entrepreneurs' social competence in their financial success, *Journal of Business Venturing*, Volume 18, Issue 1, Pages 41-60.

Bosma, N., van Praag, M., Thurik, R., de Wit, G (2004) The Value of Human and Social Capital Investments for the Business Performance of Startups, *Small Business Economics*, **23**: 227–236.

Bourdieu, P. (1985). "The Forms of Capital," in *Handbook of Theory and Research for Sociology of Education*. Ed J.G. Richardson, 241-258, Greenwood, New York.

Davidsson, P., Honig,, B. (2003) The role of social and human capital among nascent entrepreneurs, *Journal of Business Venturing*, Volume 18, Issue 3, Pages 301-331.

DiMaggio, P., and W. Powell (1983). "The Iron Cage Revisited: Institutional Isomorphism and Collective Rationality in Organizational Fields," *American Sociological Review* **48**:147–160.

Drakopoulou Dodd, S., Anderson, A.R. 2007, Mumpsimus and the Mything of the Individualistic Entrepreneur, *International Small Business Journal*, Vol. 25, No. 4, 341-360.

Fukuyama, F. (1995). *Trust: Social Virtues and the Creation of Prosperity*. London: Hamish Hamilton.

Jack, S. L. and Anderson, A. R. (2002) 'The Effects of Embeddedness on the Entrepreneurial Process', *Journal of Business Venturing* **17**(5): 467–87.

Jack S.L.; Dodd S.D.; Anderson A.R., 2004, Social structures and entrepreneurial networks: the strength of strong ties , *The International Journal of Entrepreneurship and Innovation*, Volume 5, Number 2, 107-120.

Jack,, S.L. Dodd, Dodd, S. D., Anderson, A. R. (2008) Change and the development of entrepreneurial networks over time: a processual perspective', *Entrepreneurship and Regional Development*, **20**:2,125 –159.

Johannisson, B. and Monsted, M. (1997) 'Contextualizing Entrepreneurial Networking', *International Journal of Management and Organization* **27**(3): 109–37.

Liao, J. Welsch, H2005, Roles of Social Capital in Venture Creation: Key Dimensions and Research Implications, *Journal of Small Business Management*, **43**(4), 345-362.

Macmillan, I.C., Siegel, R., Subba Narasimha, P.N., (1985) Criteria used by venture capitalists to evaluate new venture proposals, *Journal of Business Venturing*, Volume 1, Issue 1, Pages 119-128.

Markku, M., Erkko, M., Murray, G., (2003) Prerequisites for the creation of social capital and subsequent knowledge acquisition in corporate venture capital, *Venture Capital* **5**:2,117 – 134

Nahapiet, J., and S. Ghoshal (1998). Social Capital, Intellectual Capital and the Organizational Advantage, *Academy of Management Review* **23**(2), 242–266.

Neergaard, H. (2005) Networking Activities in Technology-based Entrepreneurial Teams, *International Small Business Journal* **23**(3): 257–78.

Neergaard, H., Madsen, H., 2004, Knowledge intensive entrepreneurship in a social capital perspective, *Journal of Enterprising Culture*, **12** (2), 105-125

Shane, S. and Cable, D. (2002). Network ties, reputation, and the financing of new ventures, *Management Science*, **48**(3): 364-381.

Steier, L. and Greenwood, R. (2000). Entrepreneurship and the evolution of angel financial networks, *Organization Studies*, **21**(1): 163-192.

Uzzi, B (1997). Social Structure and Competition in Interfirm Networks: The Paradox of Embeddedness, *Administrative Science Quarterly* **42** (March), 35–67.

In: Handbook of Business and Finance
Editors: M. Bergmann and T. Faust, pp. 301-307

ISBN: 978-1-60692-855-4
© 2010 Nova Science Publishers, Inc.

Chapter 14

THE IMPACT OF FINANCIAL SERVICES FIRMS FAILURES ON THE CAREERS OF FINANCIAL SERVICES PROFESSIONALS[1]

Monika Hamori[*]
IE Business School, Madrid, Spain

Abstract

I look at the effect, on finance professionals' career moves to another employer, of six types of events in financial services firms: criticism of the firm in the business media; resignation of key individuals from the organization; downsizing; a drop in net income; lawsuits launched by public authorities, competitors, or customers; and lawsuits launched by employees. I sample over 900 financial services professionals who have worked for the five most prestigious financial services institutions on Wall Street. The results show that out of the six types of events, the ones that signal the decline of corporate performance are the most devastating for the career success of finance professionals who try to leave the firm in the wake of the event. Outsiders, on the other hand, are less sensitive to financial services firms' involvement in lawsuits launched by public authorities or employees. The events affect the career of every professional, irrespective of their level in the organization.

Introduction

Corporate reputations have a significant impact on professionals' career paths and career success. Individuals moving out of organizations with an outstanding reputation manage to earn higher promotions upon transferring to a new employer than individuals affiliated with less reputable employers (Hamori, 2006). In addition, reputable organizations channel their employees toward the most important corporate posts in national economies. A survey of

---

[1] This commentary is a shortened and reworked version of "Career Success after Stigmatizing Organizational Events". Hamori, M. Human Resource Management, 46(4): 493-511. Copyright ©[2007] Wiley Periodicals, Inc.

[*] E-mail address: monika.hamori@ie.edu, Tel: +34 91568 9600 /ext. 1225, Fax: +34 91561 0930, Address: Maria de Molina 12, 5°, Madrid 28006 Spain.

chief financial officers (CFOs) shows that 89 percent of the CFOs of the largest US corporations started their career with such reputable employers as Bain Consultants, General Electric, General Motors, Pepsi, IBM or McKinsey and Co (O'Sullivan, 2004).

But what happens to individual careers when reputable organizations undergo crises? Do crises blight the career prospects of the professionals who are leaving in the wake of the crisis, or, on the contrary, do superior corporate reputations shield employees as they move to a new employer? The business press presents evidence for both scenarios: former employees of Arthur Andersen and Enron are advised by career counselors to "act humbly" and "minimize their ties" with the troubled organizations. At the same time, other accounts portray professionals at these firms to have easily found a new job due to the superior skills that they had acquired at the two corporations (Anders, 2004; Elmore, 2003).

Although empirical evidence exists on the effect of corporate scandals, fraud and suboptimal financial performance on the career paths of the CEO and the board of directors who have to leave their post in the wake of these events (Coughlan and Schmidt, 1985; Gilson, 1989; Huson, Malatesta and Parrino, 2004; Warner, Watts and Wruck, 1988; Weisbach, 1995), no empirical paper has looked at the effect of corporate crises on the subsequent careers of non-executive employees who are themselves cannot be held responsible for the crisis.

This Commentary examines the career of financial services professionals who move out of the five most reputable financial services firms on Wall Street in the wake of events that may negatively affect the perception of these organizations. The events fall under six types: a drop in the firm's net income, criticism of the organization in the business press, downsizing, the resignation of key executives from the organization, lawsuits launched by public authorities, competitors or customers and lawsuits launched by the employees of these firms.

Literature Review

Reputable Organizations and Their Impact on Employees

Reputation forms on the basis of the past actions of organizations and as a result of information exchange and influence among actors (Rindova, Pollock, and Hayward, 2006). Organizational reputation has a strong impact on the economic value of the firm (Rindova, Williamson, Petkova, and Sever, 2005) and also creates value for its employees. Individuals working for reputable organizations make more successful career moves upon leaving the firm (Hamori, 2006). Many CEOs of start-up firms are the former employees of firms with a superior reputation. Start-ups with such CEOs are more likely to receive external financing from private investors or from venture capital firms and they are more likely to get the endorsement of a prestigious investment bank in the IPO process (Burton, Sørensen, and Beckman, 2002; Higgins and Gulati, 2003). Small and resource-poor organizations resort to hiring the employees of reputable players in order to gain access to valuable human capital (Rao and Drazin, 2002).

Reputable organizations are so beneficial for individual careers because they provide their employees with work-related experience that is highly valued in the labor market. Higgins (2005) argues that reputable organizations bestow 4 types of benefits on their members. She labels these benefits *Capabilities* (skills, knowledge and know-how regarding work), *Confidence* (individual-level efficacy), *Cognition* (taken-for-granted beliefs and views regarding work) and *Connections* (work-related relationships inside and outside of the employer).

Failure in Organizations

While the events that are commonly associated with an organization's failure include bankruptcy and corporate scandals, in this paper we examine a broader range of events. Previous literature shows that corporate crises affect individuals both financially and psychologically (Stabile, 2002). Regarding their impact on careers with the firm, papers show that events such as suboptimal firm financial performance and stock performance, bankruptcy, securities class action lawsuits and lawsuits launched by the Securities and Exchange Commission for fraudulent financial statements trigger the dismissal of the CEO and of the top management team (Agrawal, Jaffe, and Karpoff, 1999; DeAngelo and DeAngelo, 1989; Fee and Hadlock, 2004; Gilson 1989 and 1990; Niehaus and Roth, 1999; Strahan, 1998).

In terms of their impact on top executives' subsequent careers, events like bankruptcy blight board of directors' career prospects by restricting them from acquiring board seats after the event (Gilson, 1990). Top managers who were dismissed due to the poor financial performance of their organization or their firm's involvement in securities class action (SCA) lawsuits did not find employment with publicly held firms within 3 years after the event even though they were not nearing retirement age (Gilson, 1989; Niehaus and Roth, 1999). It has to be noted, however, that this stream of papers examines only the key decision makers: the top executives in organizations, assuming that the negative effect of these events does not spill over to lower-level executives, managers and professionals who themselves may not be held accountable for it.

The Research Questions

The first question concerns whether events that signal a drop in the organization's performance and capabilities harm the subsequent career of its employees as they are leaving the organization for another employer. We examine six types of events. Out of them, we consider a drop in the firm's annual net income the most direct and straightforward signal of the decline in organizational capabilities and performance. Therefore a drop in net income will strongly impair career moves to another employer. We also propose that criticism of the organization in the business media will harm subsequent careers equally strongly, because such accounts shape the opinion and action of third parties in significant ways (Farrell and Whidbee, 2002). The link between two other types of events: employee layoffs and the resignation of key executives from the firm is less direct than is the link between a drop in the firm's net income or negative business press coverage and career outcomes. For this reason, we propose that layoffs and resignations impair the outcome of career moves less strongly than a drop in net income or negative coverage in the business press.

We also propose that lawsuits launched by public authorities, by the firm's competitors and customers and by the employees of the firm will also impair the career prospects of those who try to move out of the organization in the wake of the event, since lawsuits signal to outsiders that the members of the organization have violated ethical values.

Finally, we address the issue whether individuals' position in an organization affects the impact of the events listed above on career outcomes. Fieldwork by Higgins (2005) suggests that organizations transmit capabilities at every level of the organization and the events above will therefore affect employees equally. On the other hand, the "managerial ability" hypothesis (Fama, 1980) proposes that organizational characteristics and actions contain more information on the capabilities and efforts of the most highly-ranked executives. Therefore their career may be more severely affected by these events than the career of lower-level employees.

Methods

We test our propositions with the private dataset given to us by one of the largest multinational executive search firms in 2002. The dataset contains data on the current and previous job of 14,000 financial services professionals, the majority of them working in the New York metropolitan area. Our sample includes 916 individuals, who worked for one of the 5 most reputable financial services firms on Wall Street and made at least one career move between 1992 and 2002. We sample the most reputable organizations since their reputation often suffers more severely after corporate scandals, crises or other events than that of the less reputable firms (Ramirez and Yung, 2000). We use the news archives of the *Wall Street Journal* to identify the events that these firms faced between 1992 and 2002. We find an average of 404 articles on each firm. We dismiss "neutral" or "positive" news items (e.g. an organization buying a new business or launching a new financial product), and then we group the negative news stories into four categories: 1) items that are openly critical of the performance or actions of the organization; 2) items that state the resignation of key executives, 3) items that cover the lawsuits launched against the organizations by public authorities, competitors or customers and 4) items that cover lawsuits launched against the organization by the former or current employees of the firm. Each variable is the count measure of the number of news stories that were published on the organization in one of these categories annually. To determine whether the organization had experienced a drop in net income or had undergone downsizing, we consult the Compustat database.

In order to decide whether the events harmed individuals' career prospects upon changing employers, we measure the size of the promotion or demotion received by the individual (dependent variable). We code the current and the previous job titles of the individual (1-non-managerial employees, 2—associates, 3—managers, 4—directors, 5—vice presidents, 6—managing directors/executive directors, 7—senior vice-presidents, 8—heads of a division or function, 9—executive vice presidents, 10—chief operational officers, and 11—CEOs and top management team) and deduct the code of the former job from that of the current one. Negative numbers signify demotions, while positive numbers stand for promotions.

We run hierarchical ordinary least squares (OLS) regressions to test the propositions. In the analyses, we control for the size of the organization that the individual leaves as well as the industry segment in which the financial services firm is located, the individual's former job title and job function, the year in which the individual moved out of the firm and the number of years that the individual had spent in the organization before moving out of it.

Results

The descriptive statistics show that the *Wall Street Journal* published an annual average of 2.7 articles on each organization's involvement in lawsuits launched by public authorities, customers or competitors, 1.4 articles on lawsuits by current and former employees, and 2.8 articles that criticized the organization's performance. The average organization had a drop in net income every seven years and resorted to downsizing every four years.

The results reveal that individuals who depart from the organization in the wake of a net income drop experience very severe costs to their career. The resignation of key executives from the organization, negative news stories in the media and downsizing also significantly harm individuals' career prospects as they are changing employers, but their effect on the outcome of career moves is weaker than the effect of a net income drop. Interestingly, neither lawsuits by public authorities, competitors and customers, nor lawsuits by employees have any effect on the career prospects of those who are changing employers after these events. The results suggest that the events that directly (e.g. net income drop) or indirectly (e.g. resignation of key individuals) signal that the performance or capabilities of the organization have deteriorated are the most devastating for the careers of organization members.

Second, the analyses explore whether an individual's position or level in the organizational hierarchy affect the relationship between the various events and the outcome of his or her subsequent career moves. We find that with the exception of negative news stories in the business media (which has more severe consequences for the career prospects of the CEO than for lower-level executives), all the other events affect the career paths of individuals in a similar way, no matter where they are in the organizational hierarchy.

Conclusion

The results point to the fact that even superior corporate reputations do not shield the members of the organization from the judgment of outsiders in the wake of events. If the event suggests that the performance and capabilities of the organization have declined, even individuals affiliated with the most reputable companies incur a career-related penalty. Outsiders sensitively monitor reputable companies and are quick to adjust their judgment of these companies after such events. These findings reveal that the individual reputation of professionals, managers and executives is intertwined with the reputation of their employer. Outsiders often tend to equate individual competencies with organizational ones or weigh the signals related to an individual's organizations more heavily than the individual's performance in this organization. In addition, outsiders may be so sensitive to the cues coming from organizations that they change their perception not only after corporate scandals or crises, but also in the wake of events of a less radical nature such as a drop in the firm's earnings.

Counter to our propositions, lawsuits against the organization had no effect on the career of those who moved out of the organization. There may be two reasons for this finding. Apparently, outsiders do not attend to signals about the ethical or social conduct of the organization. This observation is consistent with research by Persons (2006) that shows that ethical factors do not have a significant impact on the turnover (dismissal) and compensation reduction of U.S. top executives and in general, ethics plays little part in boards' decisions.

Second, lawsuits may have no signaling effect because they do not represent an unusual event for financial services firms (the descriptive data reveal that the average firm in the dataset faced an annual 1.4 lawsuits between 1992 and 2002).

Finally, our results show that outsiders definitely see the firm's performance as a reflection of the ability and effort of its top executives. However, they also perceive that organizations imprint knowledge and skills on every level of employee irrespective of their position in the organizational hierarchy.

References

Agrawal, A., Jaffe, J. F., and Karpoff, J. M. (1999). Management turnover and governance changes following the revelation of fraud. *Journal of Law and Economics,* **42**, 309-342.

Anders, G. (2004). Moving on after Enron means being humble and minimizing role. *Wall Street Journal,* July 27, p. B1

Burton, D. M., Sørensen, J. B., and Beckman, C. M. (2002). Coming from good stock: Career histories and new venture formation. *Social Structure and Organizations Revisited,* **19**: 229-262.

Coughlan, A. T., and Schmidt, R. M. (1985). Executive compensation, management turnover and firm performance: An empirical investigation. *Journal of Accounting and Economics,* **7**, 43-66.

DeAngelo, H., and DeAngelo, L. (1989). Proxy contests and the governance of publicly held corporations. *Journal of Financial Economics,* **23**, 29-61.

Elmore, B. (2003). Life after Andersen. *Baylor Business Review,* **20**(1), 2-9.

Fama, E. (1980). Agency problems and the theory of the firm. *Journal of Political Economy,* **88**, 288-307.

Farrell, K. A., and Whidbee, D. A. (2002). Monitoring by the financial press and forced CEO turnover. *Journal of Banking and Finance,* **26**, 2249-2276.

Fee, C. E., and Hadlock, C. J. (2004). Management turnover across the corporate hierarchy. *Journal of Accounting and Economics,* **37**, 3-38.

Gilson, S. C. (1989). Management turnover and financial distress. *Journal of Financial Economics,* **25**(2), 241-262.

Gilson, S. C. (1990). Bankruptcy, boards, banks and blockholders: Evidence on changes in corporate ownership and control when firms default. *Journal of Financial Economics,* **27**, 355-388.

Hamori, M. (2006). Executive career advancement in career moves across employers: The role of organization-level predictors. *International Journal of Human Resource Management,* **17**, 1129-1151.

Higgins, M. C., and Gulati, R. (2003). Getting off to a good start: The effects of upper echelon affiliations on underwriter prestige. *Organization Science,* **14**(3), 244-264.

Higgins, M. (2005). *Career imprints: Creating leaders across an industry.* San Francisco, CA: Jossey-Bass.

Huson, M. R., Malatesta, P. H., and Parrino, R. (2004). Managerial succession and firm performance. *Journal of Financial Economics,* **74**, 237-275.

Niehaus, G., and Roth, G. (1999). Insider trading, equity issues, and CEO turnover in firms subject to Securities Class Action. *Financial Management,* **28**(4), 52-72.

O' Sulivan, S. (2004). Career tracks: Where CFOs got their start. *CFO Magazine*, November 1. http://www.cfo.com/article.cfm/3329154/c_3348416?f=magazine_featured

Persons, O. S. (2006). The effects of fraud and lawsuit revelation on U.S. executive turnover and compensation. *Journal of Business Ethics,* **64**(4), 405-419.

Ramirez, G. G., and Yung, K. K. (2000). Firm reputation and insider trading: The investment banking industry. *Quarterly Journal of Business and Economics,* **39**(3), 49-67.

Rao, H., and Drazin, R. (2002). Overcoming resource constraints on product innovation by recruiting talent from rivals: A study of the mutual fund industry, 1986-94. *Academy of Management Journal,* **45**(3), 491-507.

Rindova, V. P., Pollock, T. G., and Hayward, M. L. A. (2006). Celebrity firms: The social construction of market popularity. *Academy of Management Review,* **31**, 50-71.

Rindova, V. P., Williamson, I. O., Petkova, A. P., and Sever, J. M. (2005). Being good or being known: An empirical examination of the dimensions, antecedents and consequences of organizational reputation. *Academy of Management Journal,* **48**, 1033-1049.

Stabile, S. J. (2002). Enron, Global Crossing, and beyond: Implications for workers. *St. John's Law Review,* **76**(4), 815-834.

Strahan, P. (1998). Securities class actions, corporate governance and managerial agency problems. *Federal Reserve Bank of New York Research Paper* 9816.

Warner, J. B., Watts, R. L., and Wruck, K. (1988). Stock prices and top management changes. *Journal of Financial Economics,* **20**, 461-492.

Weigelt, K., and Camerer, C. (1998). Reputation and corporate strategy: A review of recent theory and applications. *Strategic Management Journal,* **9**, 443-454.

Weisbach, M. S. (1995). CEO turnover and the firm's investment decisions. *Journal of Financial Economics,* **37**: 159-188.

In: Handbook of Business and Finance
Editors: M. Bergmann and T. Faust, pp. 309-319

ISBN: 978-1-60692-855-4
© 2010 Nova Science Publishers, Inc.

Chapter 15

DO ORGANIZATIONAL TYPES BEHAVE DIFFERENTLY? THEORIES AND EVIDENCES FROM THE ITALIAN HOSPITAL SECTOR

Monica Auteri[*]
Dipartimento di Istituzioni Pubbliche, Economia e Società
Università Roma Tre and CREI, Italy

Abstract

Scholars characterize the nonprofit sector according to several, often overlapping theories. Unfortunately, these theories, do not offer testable hypotheses and it is hard to tell whether nonprofits exist because of historical accident, path dependence, different organizational goals, consumer demand, or government regulation. Therefore, rather than trying to answer such broad questions about the role of the entire sector, in this paper I take a step toward filling a research gap by asking this simple question: Do ownership types behave differently? To answer this question, I test the provision of the Italian health care services. If ownership seems to matter, I then assess alternative explanations for those differences. I mainly consider whether ownership types have different objectives and I then investigate whether hospital types behave differently.

JEL classifications: D23, G32, I11, I18, L31.

Keywords: economic calculation, entrepreneurship, governance, hospital behavior, nonprofit firms.

1. Introduction

Health and social services for a long time have been considered emblematic of public provision and production, because of the presence of market failures. Specifically hospital care is distinctive in two important respects. First, the product purchaser is often not well informed about the quality of the service being purchased and frequently is less informed

---

[*]E-mail address: mauteri@uniroma3.it

than the supplier. Moreover, the consumer often cannot experience the quality of the good. In other words, hospital care is a credence good (Emons, 1997). Second, consumers almost always pay out-of-pocket much less than the marginal cost of their care, and parties other than direct consumers foot the rest of the bill.

The Italian hospital industry provides a useful laboratory for comparing behavior of organizations having different ownership forms. Unlike in most other countries, for-profit organizations constitute a majority of firms supplying hospital care in Italy. According with the most recent data made available by the Census of industries and service (ISTAT, 2004) in 2001 in Italy nonprofit hospitals constituted only 23% of all general hospitals. By contrast 39% of hospitals were private for-profits and and the rest (38%), can be classified as public hospitals. Another stylized fact is that nowadays the Italian hospital sector appear as a good example of an attempt to create a quasi-market. All these hospital in fact compete with each others for the provision of the services and, after the changes that occurred after 1995, face the same reimbursement scheme. Therefore possible differences in behavior may be due solely to different ownership structures.

In general ownership has a relevant role in explaining economic performance, as different ownership structures create different incentives to economic actors. Private ownership, characterized by the presence of residual claimants, should represent a powerful incentive to economic efficiency and cost reduction (Alchian and Demsetz, 1972). However, in a nonprofit organization, it is not at all apparent what the managers are supposed to maximize. The literature has expressed differing views. Nonprofit may earn profits and many, including hospitals, do but are precluded from distributing profits to persons who exercise control over the firm. Whether nonprofits are thought to lack owners altogether (Hansmann, 1988) or whether the emphasis is placed on the diffuse character of ownership, as represented by Sloan (2000), the ill-defined ownership of nonprofit firms leads to technical inefficiency. A second set of theories do not support the claim of nonprofits inefficiency but explore the economic effect of prioritizing goals other than profit-making. For instance inefficiency may arise according to Steinberg (1986) in the nonprofit models from output maximization, while Smith et al. (1995) model it as arising from quality maximization. According to Weisbrod (1991) the nonprofit form is efficient to the extent that the increase in valuable behaviors offsets other responses that decrease welfare. Since property rights are attenuated, managers may purchase more non pecuniary benefits than managers of a profit-seeking firm would, such as nice offices, less supervision of employees, and prestige. When output is difficult for customers to measure, Weisbrod argued, it may not be efficient to reward easily monitored forms of behavior, but to allow for rewarding, or at least be more neutral to rewarding, less easily monitorable behavior. Pauly (1987) argues similarly, that because firms of different ownership structures coexist in the same market, there may be particular types of outputs for which certain types of firms are more suitable. If some dimension of quality cannot be observed well by consumers, and they are conscious of this problem, they may prefer to patronize the not-for-profit firm. A similar argument has been made by Hart et al. (1997) about circumstances under which government would provide a service directly or contract out for its provision. A government employee who manages a public enterprise cannot fully appropriate the gains from cost-reducing innovations. Hence, such a manager would be less likely to cut cost which in turn might adversely affect hard-to-monitor quality. In general, the larger are the potential adverse consequences of cost cutting on quality, the stronger is the argument for direct public provision.

Theories of nonprofit hospitals typically assume that hospital stakeholders maximize some objective function subject to a break-even constraint. Because there is no residual claimant in nonprofit hospitals, it is difficult to determine the hospital's objective function. Different theories have emphasized the interests of physicians (Pauly and Redisch, 1973), administrators (Newhouse, 1970), and the community at large (Ben-Ner, A., 1986) in shaping a hospital's objectives. An organizational difference between for-profit and nonprofit hospitals is the relationship between hospitals and doctors. The latter are typically not employees of the hospital, but rather are granted privileges to work there (Pauly, 1980). However, the alignment of incentives is somewhat different for for-profit hospitals. Some for-profit hospitals are owned outright by doctors and, recently in the USA, hospital companies have given some local doctors an explicit share of residual hospital income. Arrow (1963) explained the dominance of nonprofits in the USA hospital sector as a response to uncertainty and incomplete markets for risk. Because such organizations are not pure profit-seekers, they would not fully exploit their market power vis--vis a patient who experienced a major health shock. Furthermore, Glaeser (2003) suggests that competition can render nonprofit firms efficient despite their absence of explicit residual claimancy. These observations support the parasitic idea put forward by Auteri and Wagner (2007), that nonprofit firms interact with profit-seeking firms in order to receive signals from the market. This parasitic character of the relationship between the nonprofit association and the private firm explains how nonprofits solve problems of economic calculation. Then nonprofit firms are able to compete effectively against profit-seeking firms, as Thomsen and Rose (2004) observe.

2. The Italian Institutional Context

The hospital sector in Italy represents a good example of a recent trend common to other countries for the creation of quasi-markets in welfare industries. Services in the Italian hospital sector are supplied by a vast array of organizations that can be characterized as public, private for-profit and nonprofit. All of them compete with each other for the provision of services. Pricing and costing practices of hospital care in Italy derive from the nature of the Italian National Health Service (known as Servizio Sanitario Nazionale, hereafter INHS) and its recent developments. The INHS was established in 1978 with the aim to create an efficient and uniform health system covering the entire population, irrespective of income or contributions, employment or pre-existing health conditions. The INHS provides free or low cost health care to all residents, emergency care to visitors, irrespective of their nationality, hospital accommodation and treatment (including diagnostic tests, surgery and medication during hospitalization), free access to family doctors (GPs), specialist medical assistance, provided by paediatricians, obstetricians and other specialists, discounted medicines, laboratory services, appliances, ambulance services and free services at local health units. The organization is greatly decentralized and there are 3 levels of organization: national, regional and local. The institution at the national level is the Ministry of Health (Ministero della Salute). It is responsible for the overall INHS objectives (National Health Plan), for the control of the drug market and research (in conjunction with the Italian Drug Agency-Agenzia Italiana del Farmaco-AIFA), for national prevention programs (e.g. information on vaccination) and also for veterinary medicine. Moreover, it coordinates the Istituti di Ricovero e Cura a Carattere Scientifico (IRCCS) a cooperation of 40 public and private hospitals dedicated to research. The regional government is responsible for planning, financing, control and supervision, at a regional level, regarding efficiency, quality and provision of services through public and private health organizations. At a local level, the INHS is administered by more than 200 local health authorities (Azienda Sanitaria Locale/ASL).

The INHS largely relies on public production supplemented by privately licensed hospitals. Public hospitals are run by ASLs or by autonomous public trusts (Aziende Ospedaliere). Privately licensed hospitals can treat patients within the INHS, i.e. free of charge, and are afterwards refunded by the ASL to which the patient belongs. Hospital refunding is based on the prospective payment of each clinical episode. Clinical episodes are classified according to Diagnosis Related Groups (DRG), a classification scheme that assigns each episode in one out of 492 codified groups [1]. Each DRG is priced according to the amount of resources required for its treatment. Actually DRG is an isoresource classification scheme. Patients are completely free to choose their hospital; it may be public or privately licensed, both within or outside their assisting ASL or region. Patients are totally unaware of treatment costs and can choose freely among publicly financed hospitals, choice is essentially determined by distance from home, hospital specialization, waiting lists, and perceived quality. Publicly financed hospitals are strongly motivated to invest in quality and establish good reputation in order to attract patients and to maintain a continuous cash flow.

The funding mechanism of Italian hospitals changed significantly over time due to the difficulties in controlling public expenditures in this sector. In 1992, in order to favor competition among different providers, and to create quasi-markets in some areas of the health care industry, public hospitals were given some level of autonomy (some of the larger hospital were separated from the local health authorities and incorporated as self-governing public firms or Aziende Ospedaliere). Starting from 1995, the funding mechanism for hospitals operating in the National Health Service moved from a cost-based ex-post payment (for public hospitals) and bed-day rate (for private ones) to a prospective payment system based on diagnostic related groups (DRG) that applies to both types of hospitals. Initially DRG rates were defined at the national level, but then regional authorities have been allowed to divert from the definition made at the national level. The national DRG tariffs are set equal for all types of providers. The regions are free, however, to adopt changes if they wish to differentiate tariffs among various types of hospitals (e.g., between public and private hospitals or between teaching and non-teaching hospitals). Almost all regions apply different tariffs to different providers, classified according to various criteria. In the majority of cases those criteria refer to organizational features (e.g., presence of emergency room) and activities performed (e.g., case-mix complexity, research activities). Only in few regions tariffs are differentiated between public and private providers (Fattore and Torbica, 2006).

---

[1]While there are similarities between the DRG system in Italy and the prospective payment system in the United States, there are also important differences (Langiano, 1997). Because the SSN is essentially a single payer, all patients are included in the new financing scheme. By contrast to the system in the United States, payment for hospital-based physician services is included in the DRG rate in Italy (Langiano, 1997).

3. Nonprofit Organizations in the European Definition

As discussed above, services in the Italian hospital sector are supplied by a vast array of organizations that can be characterized as public, private for-profit and nonprofit. It is noteworthy that the European definition of nonprofit is in contrast with the internationally accepted definition of a Third Sector organization elaborated by the comparative nonprofit sector project directed by Salamon and Anheier (the Johns Hopkins Comparative Nonprofit Sector Project, JHCNSP). Drawing on existing definitions and empirical realities of various nations under study, the project developed what Anheier and Salamon term the structural-operational definition of the nonprofit sector (Salamon and Anheier, 1992), to allow sector demarcation across countries and facilitate comparative analysis. So defined, the nonprofit sector is a set of organizations that are formally constituted, independent of the government, self-governing, non-profit-distributing and voluntary. However the structural-operational definition does not effectively distinguish the nonprofit sector, as it excludes significant others such as mutual aid organizations. In short, this definition has an "American bias" (Borzaga, 1998) because it is based on the criterion of non-redistribution, underlying the American configuration of the sector. In contrast to this dominant international definition, the European approach takes a more analytical perspective, focusing more on generating nonprofit association typologies that highlight different models of action and the changes in them over time. The specific features of the European approach to the Third System can be summarized on the basis of three parameters: the type of organizations involved, the intermediary nature of the Third System within "welfare pluralism" or a mixed economy, and the systems sociopolitical dimension, which is as important as its economic dimension (Laville et al., 1999). The European definition is therefore broader and include co-operatives and mutual aid societies that can distribute some of their profits to members. [2] In other words, "the Third System includes all organizations with a legal status that place limits on private, individual acquisition of profits" (Laville et al., 1999, p.3). In short the criterion of non-redistribution, does not take into account the specific legal requirements of European countries for which the distinguishing criterion is the existence of limits on redistribution. Thus in this paper, given their ownership structure and according with ISTAT classification, (ISTAT, 2001), are classified as "nonprofit" research hospitals (Istituti di Ricovero e Cura a Carattere Scientifico, IRCCS), Hospitals run by religious bodies (Ospedali classificati),

---

[2]In Italy, on a legislative level, the most important changes in the definition of the new Third Sector began with Law 833/1978, which provides for a first reform of the health system and a redefinition of the institutional players involved in the welfare sector. There was then the Law on Non-governmental organization (NGO) 49/87, the Framework Law on the Voluntary Sector 266/91, the Law on Social Co-operatives 38/91 and finally the Law on Social Enterprise 118/2005. It is noteworthy that the first experiences of the Third Sector in Italy go back to the thirteenth and fourteenth centuries with the birth of the brotherhoods, whose purpose was to help the ill and the needy; this period when organizations devoted to charity and helping the needy flourished was also a time when the close-knit institutional network of the Church developed. However, until the 1970s the non-profit world was not linked to the territorial social economic dimension, but existed as a replacement for public intervention and was highly regulated by the State. In the twentieth century there arose mainly institutions with a religious background, mostly in the north of Italy, and as well as the imbalance between the South and the North of Italy there was a contrast expressing a political-idealistic direction, Catholic in Veneto and socialist in Emilia and Tuscany. In the 1990s more than half of the nonprofits active today started up. The typical scope of action of the Third Sector organizations in Italy includes social welfare, health care, charity, education, training, amateur sport.

and hospitals incorporated as public bodies (Istituti qualificati presidio ASL). I consider as "public", hospitals incorporated as public firms (Aziende Ospedaliere), local hospitals directly managed by Local Health authorities, the local branches of the INHS (Ospedali a gestione diretta ASL) and University hospitals (Policlinici Universitari).

4. Empirical Evidence

In Italy, patients are totally unaware of treatment costs and can choose freely among publicly financed hospitals; choice is essentially determined by distance from home, hospital specialization, waiting lists, and perceived quality. In addition, as previously stated, all hospitals, nowadays, face the same reimbursement scheme. Then unlike previous researches on hospital ownership, which focused primarily on financial measures, I examine whether and how organizational ownership is correlated with medical service provision. I ask whether hospital types behave differently and why they might do so. I categorize ownership into three types: nonprofit, government-owned, and for-profit, which is the omitted reference group due to lack of data. This study is based on data taken from the Italian National Ministry of Health. The sample consists of 625 hospitals providing health care services for the INHS, observed during the year 2005. Using a logit model I examine the theoretical predictions that hospitals with differences in governance, have different objectives and then they will make different choices with respect to the variables selected.

The logit model presents the propensity of an hospital to be incorporated under the nonprofit regulation, (i.e the probability that an hospital is a nonprofit) as depending on a linear combination of observed variables, with weights given by the coefficients. If we use x to denote the full set of explanatory variables, the goal of the logit model is to explain the effects of the x_i on the probability $P(NP = 1|x)$ as follows:

$$P(NP = 1|x) = \Phi\beta_0 + \beta_1 cmi + \beta_2 entr + \beta_3 pon + \beta_4 sud + \beta_5 or + \beta_5 alos \qquad (1)$$

NP is a binary response variable assuming value 1 if the hospital is a nonprofit and zero otherwise. The probability that an hospital is a nonprofit in 2005 depends on the organization objectives. CMI is the case mix index, the average diagnosis-related group weight for all Italian hospitals. If an hospital has a CMI greater than 1.00, their adjusted cost per patient or per day will be lowered and conversely if a hospital has a CMI less than 1.00, their adjusted cost will be higher. Therefore there should be detectable differences in terms of output case-mix with respect to the hospitals ownership structure. ENTR is "entropy". Low values of average entropy are desirable and imply that most of the mass in the frequency distribution of cases by DRG type is concentrated in a few values. Higher entropy values imply the cluster contains cases somewhat spread over more DRG types. PON is the "ratio physicians/nurses" reflecting the hospital choice of providing given levels of quality of care. The variable OR , "occupancy rate", provides a measure of health facility inpatient use, showing the percentage of beds occupied during the reporting period. It is determined by dividing patient days by licensed or available bed days (the number of beds multiplied by number of calendar days in reporting period). ALOS is the "average length of stay", defined as total number of occupied hospital bed-days divided by the total number of admissions. Finally hospital types are more prevalent in certain regions. There are more nonprofit in the Nord for example. Therefore, I included the SUD dummy variable to investigate the influence of geographic location on ownership choice. Table 1 presents the estimated coefficients of logit regressions. A positive coefficient indicates that an increase in the independent variable increases the probability of the nonprofit engaging in unrelated business activity. The standard errors are presented in parentheses below each coefficient. The results are generally consistent with expectations. From the empirical analysis, it appears that there is a positive correlation with ICM and the nonprofit ownership. Among real causes, the increase of case-mix complexity could be explained as a result of the tendency toward the increase of Day Hospital treatments. In addition according to Cerbo and Langiano (2004) a further factor impacting on case-mix is the incentive to "upcode" created by the introduction of DRG. The international empirical literature shows that for-profit hospitals tend to upcode patients more than private nonprofits, and nonprofits more than public ones (Dafny, 2005). The negative correlation between the dependent variable and ENTR is not surprising,reflecting the fact that public hospitals are more willing to deal with different DRG and are not interested in treating only specific patients. Surprisingly the variable PON is positively correlated with the dependent variable. This may be due to the specific objective of the organization to provide an higher level of quality care with respect to public hospitals. While the estimated coefficient OR differs statistically from zero, it implies a smaller absolute effect on the dependent variable than do the other estimated coefficients. Finally ALOS shows a negative sign. In fact while public hospitals are strongly motivated to invest in quality and establish good reputation in order to attract patients and to maintain a continuous cash flow, nonprofit are more interested than public hospital in decreasing ALOS. For-profit hospitals are most likely to respond to economic incentives (Danzon, 1982), avoid unprofitable patients (Barro, 1998), and up-code-that is, to inflate patients' diagnosis codes (e.g., complicated pneumonia rather than simple pneumonia) to generate higher reimbursements (Dafny and Dranov, 2006; Silverman and Skinner, 2001). At least in comparison to for-profits, government and nonprofit hospitals prioritize goals other than profit-making. Beyond profits, hospital objectives are likely to vary by hospital type. Empirical evidence shows then, that despite the fact that nonprofit and public hospitals have much in common, they make different choices. They use similar resources, operate under the same substantive health care regulations, employ professionals trained in the same manner, are governed by the same professional and ethical obligations to supply appropriate health care and their mission statements are often indistinguishable. The primary theoretical rationale for why different hospital types behave differently is that they adopt different objectives.

5. Conclusion

In this paper, I examined the proposition that ownership type leads to differences in the organization's objectives and governance. Hospitals are a natural place to examine for this proposition because they represent a set of organizations that are similar in many dimensions and exist simultaneously as a number of alternative ownership forms. Nonprofit organizations pose a dilemma for traditional economic analysis. In the case of a for-profit firm, the purpose of corporate governance is clear: the governance structure manages the process of maximizing this objective function through incentives and monitoring of the

Table 1. The Impact on ownership on medical services provision dependent variable NP=1

Independent Variables	Coefficient
C	-0,41
	(-1,01)
CMI	2,83
	(-0,82)
ENTR	-2,94
	(-0,35)
PON	2,17
	(-0,55)
SUD	-1,01
	(-0,33)
OR	0,01
	(0,00)
ALOS	-2,22
	(-2,79)

tot. obs 625
Obs. at one: 101
Obs. at zero: 524

Akaike info criterion	0,63
Schwarz criterion	0,68
S.E. of regression	0,30
Log likelihood	-189,04

top management. However, in a nonprofit organization, it is not at all apparent what the managers are supposed to maximize. The literature has expressed differing views and the general assumption is that nonprofits maximize some function other than the present value of profits. The identity of this function is not obvious, nor is it obvious how this objective function is chosen inside an organization. In this paper considers a sample of 625 hospitals in Italy to examine the hypothesis that hospitals with differences in governance have different objectives from one another. By focusing on a single industry, it is possible to isolate differences in governance due to likely differences in objectives. Moreover, the hospital industry is a good setting for this study since there are identifiable differences in ownership types. Some hospitals are owned by shareholders, or governments while others are nonprofit and are managed by various different groups such as religious organizations or groups of physicians. If different types of hospitals have systematically different objectives as well as different internal and external constituencies, then, as expected, systematic differences in term of medical services provision across ownership types have been found. Publicly financed hospitals are strongly motivated to invest in quality and establish good reputation in order to attract patients and to maintain a continuous cash flow while nonprofit are more interested than public hospital in decreasing ALOS. Both private and public hospitals receive their funds on the basis of the amount and the nature of services provided, and they should share a common incentive to decrease ALOS, thus the average cost of treatment with respect to the reference hospitals (i.e. those hospitals whose costs were used as a basis for setting reimbursement rates). Differences in efficiency are then be due solely to differences in behavior characterizing the two ownership structures, as the empirical evidence provided suggests.

References

Alchian, A. and Demsetz, H. (1972). Production, information costs, and economic organization, *American Economic Review* **62**(5): 777–795.

Arrow, K. (1963). Uncertainty and the welfare economics of medical care, *American Economic Review* **53**(5): 941–973.

Auteri, M. and Wagner, R. E. (2007). The organizational architecture of nonprofit governance: Economic calculation within an ecology of enterprises, *Public Organization Review* **7**(1): 57–68.

Barro, J. (1998). Hospital conversion to for-profit status: Causes and consequences, *working paper*, Harvard University.

Ben-Ner, A. (1986). Nonprofit organizations: Why do they exist in market economies, *in* S. Rose-Ackerman (ed.), *The Economics of Nonprofit Institutions: Studies in Structure and Policy*, Oxford University Press, pp. 94–113.

Borzaga, C. (1998). The economics of the Third Sector in Europe : The Italian experience, *Working paper*, Department of Economics, University of Trento.

Cerbo, M. and Langiano, T. (2004). L'impatto a livello nazionale del sistema di remunerazione, *in* N. Falcitelli and T. Langiano (eds), *Politiche innovative nel SSN: i primi dieci anni dei DRG in Italia,*, Il Mulino - Fondazione Smith Kline: Bologna.

Dafny, L. (2005). How do hospitals respond to price changes?, *American Economic Review* **95**(5): 1525–1547.

Dafny, L. and Dranov, D. (2006). Regulatory exploitation and the market for corporate controls, *Working Paper 12438*, National Bureau of Economic Research.
URL: *http://www.nber.org/papers/w12438*

Danzon, P. M. (1982). Hospital profits: The effects of reimbursement policies, j. health econ., *Journal of Health Economics* **1**(1): 29–52.

Emons, W. (1997). Credence goods and fraudulent experts, *The RAND Journal of Economics* **28**(1): 107–119.

Fattore, G. and Torbica, A. (2006). Inpatient reimbursement system in italy: How do tariffs relate to costs?, *Health Care Management Science* **9**(3): 251–258.

Glaeser, E. L. (2003). Introduction, *in* Glaeser, E.L. (ed.), *The Governance of Not-for-Profit Organizations*, University of Chicago Press, pp. 1–43.

Hansmann, H. (1988). Ownership of the firm, *Journal of Law, Economics, and Organization* **4**(2): 267–304.

Hart, O., Shleifer, A. and Vishny, R. (1997). The proper scope of government: Theory and an application to prisons, *Quarterly Journal of Economics* **112**(4): 1127–1161.

ISTAT (2001). Istituzioni Non Profit in Italia - anno 1999, Collana Informazioni, Roma.

ISTAT (2004). Censimento 2001. Imprese, Istituzioni e Unità Locali, Collana Informazioni, Roma.

Langiano, T. (1997). *DRG: Strategie, Valutazione, Monitoraggio*, Il Pensiero Scientifico Editore.

Laville, J. L., Borzaga, C., Defourny, J., Evers, A., Lewis, J., Nyssens, M. and Pestoff, V. (1999). Third system: a european definition, *Technical report*, Paper produced in the course of the framework of the pilot action Third System and Employment of the European Commission.

Newhouse, J. (1970). Toward a Theory of Nonprofit Institutions, *American Economic Review* **60**(1): 64–74.

Pauly, M. (1980). *Doctors and Their Workshops: Economic Models of Physician Behavior*, University of Chicago Press.

Pauly, M. (1987). Nonprofit firms in medical markets, *The American Economic Review* **77**(2): 257–262.

Pauly, M. and Redisch, M. (1973). The not-for-profit hospital as a physicians cooperative, *American Economic Review* **63**(1): 87–99.

Salamon, L. M. and Anheier, H. K. (1992). In search of the non-profit sector. I: The question of definitions, *Voluntas* **3**: 125–151.

Silverman, E. and Skinner, J. (2001). Are for-profit hospitals really different? medicare upcoding and market structure, *Working Paper 8133*, National Bureau of Economic Research.
URL: *http://www.nber.org/papers/w8133*

Sloan, F. (2000). Not-for-profit ownership and hospital behavior, *in* A. Culyer, J. Newhouse and J. Kenneth (eds), *Handbook of health economics*, Vol. 1B, Elsevier New York, North Holland, pp. 1141–1174.

Smith, D. G., Clement, J. P. and Wheeler, J. R. (1995). Philanthropy and hospital financing, *Health Services Research* **30**(5): 615–635.

Steinberg, R. (1986). The revealed objective functions of nonprofit firms, *Rand Journal of Economics* **17**(4): 508–526.

Thomsen, S. and Rose, C. (2004). Foundation ownership and financial performance: Do companies need owners?, *European Journal of Law and Economics* **18**(3): 343–364.

Weisbrod, B. (1991). *The Nonprofit Economy*, Harvard University Press.

In: Handbook of Business and Finance
Editors: M. Bergmann and T. Faust, pp. 321-322

ISBN: 978-1-60692-855-4
© 2010 Nova Science Publishers, Inc.

EXPERT COMMENTARY

Margee Hume[*] and Gillian Sullivan-Mort
Department of Marketing, Griffith University

Decreased government financial support and increased competition for donors, grants and sponsor support has increased the pressure on cultural arts organizations to raise funds from ticket sales to improve financial returns on show performances. With the primary objective of cultural arts organizations needing to reposition to audience development and increased ticket fro survival, any supportive practices and recommendations are welcome. Until recently, it has been believed that the success of the performing arts service offering was dependent on the ability of the show/service to evoke emotion and arouse subjective reactions overlooking issues of service encounter delivery and other more functional needs of performing art consumers. Moreover, it is evident in the past that the marketing efforts focused on subscriptions, venue management and attendance have not met organizational profit performance objectives and new strategies need to be identified. The performing arts have been trapped in measuring performance not in ticket sales but in overall artistic effectiveness and contribution to the arts. It is important to value artistic effectiveness but not at the neglect of the consumer and audience development. Marketing approaches that seek to nurture greater contact between the audience and the core service need to be introduced. With strategies addressing the entire service offering from pre-arrival to post-departure inclusive of all contacts with all facilitating and supplementary services. Overall, the performing arts researchers and practitioners need to focus on a balanced approach of artistic and technical show quality and the more functional dimensions of service quality, audience experience, process and satisfaction. This practice should improve and develop retention and repurchase for further survival. At a summary level, there is a critical need for performing arts managers to increase efforts to understand their markets and customers (current and potential) and the necessary engagement that must occur with their respective organisations and their service offerings. The need for professional managers in non-profit organisations, particularly the performing arts, who possess the requisite graduate management training and experience, must be emphasised. Loyalty, "a love of the arts" and/or longevity of involvement, whilst

---

[*] E-mail address: m.hume@griffith.edu.au, Nathan Campus Nathan Qld 4111.

desirable credentials, should be secondary attributes to engaging and/or employing management professionals to guide the performing arts organisations through the increasing competitive entertainment landscape. Moreover, focusing the design and delivery of the performing arts service from a practice of cultural exhibition to a consumer-driven service offering is a fundamental that must transform performing arts organisations to ensure their future survival.

INDEX

A

absorption, 283, 285, 287
academic, 96, 108, 163
academics, 165
access, xii, 3, 9, 13, 45, 46, 47, 48, 51, 64, 69, 172, 175, 179, 219, 220, 268, 283, 284, 293, 294, 295, 296, 297, 302, 311
accessibility, 52
accommodation, 311
accountability, 55, 66
accounting, 52, 61, 70, 150
acculturation, 46, 50, 70
accuracy, 14, 278
ACE, 165
ACF, 9
achievement, 4
acquisitions, vii, xi, 24, 27, 31, 43, 128, 259, 273, 274
acute, 20
adaptability, 45
adaptation, ix, 21, 22, 48, 51, 68, 69, 74, 101
adjustment, 46, 104, 105, 106, 117, 119, 120, 223
administration, 51, 177, 179, 182
administrative, 16, 51, 55, 110, 251
administrators, 153, 311
adolescence, 120, 122
adolescents, 119, 120, 121
adulthood, 101, 102, 103, 106, 107, 118, 122
advertisement, 176, 177
advertising, 185
aesthetics, 179
affiliates, 2, 22, 24, 32
Africa, 2, 102, 173, 184, 187
age, 20, 33, 53, 57, 61, 64, 102, 108, 110, 120, 153, 181, 188, 197, 205, 206, 207, 208, 210, 211, 213, 214, 226, 271, 303
agents, 55, 244, 249, 250
aggregation, 7, 277
aging, 122, 268
aging society, 268
agricultural, 18, 135, 252, 253, 254, 287

agricultural market, 254
agriculture, xi, 18, 197, 242, 243, 252, 254, 257, 287, 289
aid, 51, 313
AIDS, 121
air, 30, 271
algorithm, 134
allocative efficiency, 283
alpha, 56, 109, 110, 133
Alps, 269, 272, 276
alternative, xiii, 24, 28, 44, 50, 54, 61, 65, 66, 67, 69, 71, 95, 129, 131, 136, 184, 244, 250, 252, 254, 263, 288, 289, 290, 309, 315
alternatives, 77, 127, 129, 144, 188, 257
alters, 149, 179
altruism, 102, 105, 111, 113, 114, 115, 119
ambiguity, 51, 106, 110, 111, 113, 114, 117
ambivalent, 46
ambulance, 311
American Cancer Society, 245
American culture, 5
American Revolution, 172
American Stock Exchange, 197, 225
analysts, 12
annual rate, 261
antagonistic, 18
antecedents, 84, 91, 92, 97, 307
anxiety, 105
APEC, 1, 28, 39
API, vii, viii, 41, 42, 43, 44, 45, 46, 47, 48, 49, 50, 51, 53, 54, 55, 56, 57, 61, 62, 63, 64, 65, 66, 67, 68, 69, 70, 71
application, 11, 47, 70, 81, 92, 177, 178, 184, 243, 318
applied research, 126
arbitrage, 149, 170, 287
archetype, 85
Argentina, 290
argument, vii, ix, xi, 3, 5, 6, 9, 14, 21, 23, 67, 88, 123, 131, 152, 173, 212, 220, 242, 243, 249, 251, 310, 311
Armenia, 2
articulation, 173
artificial intelligence, 173, 185

324 Index

artistic, viii, 79, 82, 83, 87, 88, 91, 92, 93, 96, 321
ASEAN, 13, 18, 28
Asia, vii, 1, 2, 3, 4, 5, 7, 8, 9, 11, 13, 15, 17, 19, 20, 21, 22, 23, 25, 27, 28, 29, 30, 31, 32, 33, 34, 35, 36, 37, 38, 39
Asian, vii, 1, 2, 3, 4, 5, 7, 10, 15, 16, 19, 20, 21, 22, 23, 25, 26, 28, 29, 30, 32, 33, 34, 35, 38
Asian countries, vii, 1, 2
Asian cultures, 19
Asian management, 3, 32, 34
aspiration, 29, 287
assessment, 7, 9, 29
assets, ix, 2, 24, 25, 29, 47, 48, 49, 52, 53, 54, 56, 57, 74, 76, 147, 149, 150, 151, 152, 153, 156, 157, 158, 159, 161, 163, 165, 177, 192, 194, 196, 198, 206, 207, 208, 210, 211, 212, 213, 214, 218, 283, 296
assimilation, 47
assumptions, 46, 52, 104, 129, 131, 171, 173, 184, 185, 186, 242
asymmetric information, 149, 170
asymmetry, 221, 247, 250, 297
Athens, 187
Atlas, 174
ATM, 263
atmosphere, 105, 252
attitudes, 23, 104, 105
attractiveness, 93
Australia, 1, 17, 27, 32, 33, 36, 38, 39, 99, 125, 166, 168
Austria, 102
authority, 14, 19, 103
Autocorrelation, 63
automobiles, 150, 157
autonomy, ix, 123, 124, 125, 126, 128, 130, 131, 132, 133, 136, 137, 138, 139, 140, 141, 145, 264, 312
availability, 61, 67, 69, 119, 219, 244, 289, 290
averaging, 66
avoidance, 10, 14, 55
awareness, 102, 104, 184, 185
Azerbaijan, 2

B

baggage, 183
bail-out, 11
balance sheet, ix, 147, 149, 159, 163
bandwidth, 289
Bangladesh, 1, 2
bankers, 149
banking, 26, 148, 156, 163, 307
banking industry, 307
bankruptcy, 147, 149, 152, 153, 170, 196, 303
banks, 16, 148, 149, 157, 158, 163, 192, 194, 218, 306
bargaining, x, 14, 32, 50, 74, 205, 217, 219, 221, 222, 229, 231

barrier, 286
barriers, 23, 46, 47, 49, 51, 72, 283, 288
basic research, 133
basis points, 158, 159
behavior, 46, 50, 75, 82, 104, 105, 109, 192, 195, 242, 243, 246, 249, 250, 251, 254, 286, 309, 310, 317, 318
behaviours, 12, 91
Beijing, 290
Belgium, 24
beliefs, 45, 105, 246, 303
benchmark, 7, 134, 135, 136
benchmarking, 7
benchmarks, 5
benefits, viii, x, xii, 6, 9, 24, 41, 42, 44, 45, 46, 48, 49, 50, 51, 66, 67, 68, 70, 95, 105, 127, 130, 152, 163, 177, 178, 192, 195, 217, 218, 246, 249, 274, 281, 284, 291, 302, 310
Bhutan, 1
bias, 52, 56, 61, 74, 132, 135, 142, 313
biotechnology, 72, 76, 197, 199, 226
birth, 110, 313
blindness, 122
blocks, 28
blogs, 184
blue-collar workers, 19
board members, 229
bond market, 148
bondholders, 153
bonding, 296
bonus, 10, 129
borrowers, 148
Boston, 31, 33, 36, 41, 142, 154
bottlenecks, 128
boundary conditions, 44, 69
boundedly rational, 251
Brazil, ix, 123, 125, 132, 135, 140, 141, 290
Brazilian, 125
break-even, 311
Bronfenbrenner, ix, 101, 104, 119
Brooklyn, 185, 186
brutality, 9
Buddha, 14
Buddhism, 2, 8, 10, 11, 13, 15, 19
Buddhist, 10, 16, 18
building blocks, 29
Burma, 12
burnout, 109, 119, 121
business environment, 7, 44, 260
business management, 4, 153
bust, 35

C

Cambodia, 1
campaigns, 251
Canada, 34, 145, 166, 168, 171
candidates, 86, 87, 88, 96

Index 325

capacity, viii, xii, 41, 43, 47, 48, 49, 50, 51, 69, 70, 71, 72, 75, 78, 127, 128, 130, 131, 138, 139, 245, 281, 283, 284, 285, 286, 290, 291
capitalism, 16, 257
capitalist, 192, 297
career development, vii, 23, 38
career success, xii, 301
caregiving, 102
case study, 38, 39, 78, 97, 133, 172, 173, 174, 278
cash flow, 72, 147, 153, 192, 194, 195, 218, 220, 312, 315, 316
Catholic, 14, 247, 313
Catholic school, 247
cation, 246
Caucasus, 2
causal reasoning, 264
causal relationship, 118, 254, 262, 263
Cayman Islands, 165
cement, 38
Census, 310
Central Intelligence Agency, 8, 10, 11, 13, 14, 16, 18, 32
CEO, 93, 95, 192, 302, 303, 305, 306, 307
ceramic, 273
certification, 5
CFI, 136
channels, 46
chemical industry, 135
children, 102, 120, 246
Chile, 23, 28
China, 1, 2, 4, 8, 9, 10, 11, 12, 13, 17, 18, 20, 21, 22, 23, 24, 25, 30, 32, 33, 34, 37, 38, 39, 147, 191, 217, 289, 290
China Daily, 38
Christianity, 11, 19
Christians, 12
citizens, 55, 242
citizenship, 17, 187
civil service, 55
civil society, 119
civil war, 9, 102
classes, 150, 152, 157, 158
classical, 10
classification, 53, 197, 312, 313
clients, 110, 124, 294
close relationships, 16
clusters, 289, 290, 295
codes, 23, 52, 315
coding, 174, 178
cognition, 32, 263
cognitive, 48, 51, 55, 297
cognitive dimension, 297
coherence, 119
cohesion, 120
collaboration, ix, 6, 43, 44, 45, 46, 47, 48, 51, 55, 69, 70, 71, 72, 76, 123, 124, 180, 184, 297
collateral, 157, 193
collective bargaining, 9, 14, 19, 20
collectivism, 8, 13, 18, 20, 248

colleges, 288, 289
colonial rule, 13
colonialism, 172, 187
colonization, x, 171, 172, 184
Columbia, 36, 144, 215
Columbia University, 215
combined effect, 125
commercialization, 133
commodity, 177
commons, 187
communication, 45, 46, 47, 49, 51, 55, 93, 124, 144, 174, 175, 176, 177, 179, 180, 181, 182, 183, 184, 185, 187, 197, 267, 269, 282, 285, 288
communication technologies, 282
Communist Party, 9
communities, 102, 122, 184, 187
community, 8, 12, 83, 103, 105, 106, 109, 110, 116, 121, 182, 186, 249, 253, 311
community psychology, 121
comparative advantage, 45, 52, 71, 148
compassion, 102
compatibility, 47
compensation, 10, 109, 116, 231, 305, 306, 307
competence, 74, 127, 128, 129, 287, 299
competency, 33, 45, 71
competition, x, xii, 7, 26, 36, 74, 83, 95, 126, 128, 129, 130, 131, 133, 134, 138, 141, 142, 180, 186, 217, 219, 222, 281, 289, 290, 311, 312
competitive advantage, 7, 15, 26, 30, 31, 34, 44, 72, 73, 75, 76, 127, 144, 281, 290, 291
competitiveness, 7, 10, 131, 144, 282
competitor, 7
complement, 44, 70, 124, 126, 127
complementarity, 71, 127, 249, 297
complexity, 4, 11, 43, 51, 57, 70, 71, 75, 84, 92, 94, 174, 312, 315
compliance, 17, 23, 129
components, 55, 56, 82, 90, 109, 110, 121, 127, 151, 185, 270, 271, 273, 282, 283
composites, 176
composition, 67, 68, 72, 96, 192, 196, 197, 205, 219, 229
compounds, 265
comprehension, 93, 94
computer graphics, 175
computer software, 199
computing, 53, 108, 109, 171, 172, 187, 188
concentration, 84, 150
conception, 243
conceptual model, 125, 126, 131
conceptualization, 77, 173, 174, 179, 180, 183, 184, 186
conceptualizations, 173, 185
conditioning, 271
confidence, 55, 73, 161, 195, 207
configuration, 43, 44, 70, 71, 125, 126, 313
conflict, 11, 46, 48, 90, 106
conflict resolution, 46
confrontation, 1, 18

326 Index

Confucianism, 2, 8, 13, 19
Confucius, 14, 34
conjecture, 96
Connecticut, 170
consciousness, 268, 271
consensus, viii, 79, 86, 97, 177, 263, 296
Constitution, 12
constraints, 23, 45, 51, 69, 83, 172, 194, 206, 207, 244, 249, 250, 253, 282, 286, 296, 307
construction, 135, 184, 197, 250, 307
consultants, 21
consumer satisfaction, 99
consumers, viii, 79, 81, 82, 83, 86, 87, 88, 91, 94, 96, 97, 242, 243, 246, 247, 248, 253, 255, 310, 321
consumption, 82, 83, 84, 87, 88, 91, 93, 95, 97, 98, 179, 242, 244, 245, 246, 249, 267
consumption patterns, 95
content analysis, xi, 259, 262, 263, 264, 266, 268, 270, 271, 275
context cultures, 23
contingency, 6, 33
continuity, 38
contract enforcement, 55
contracts, 22, 127, 192, 251
control, vii, x, 6, 9, 13, 14, 16, 17, 19, 20, 24, 25, 26, 29, 32, 34, 37, 52, 53, 55, 56, 57, 63, 66, 67, 73, 78, 103, 105, 117, 124, 125, 127, 129, 130, 141, 143, 144, 149, 156, 183, 192, 194, 195, 196, 206, 207, 208, 212, 214, 217, 218, 219, 220, 222, 223, 224, 229, 233, 235, 237, 245, 246, 247, 252, 268, 270, 296, 304, 306, 310, 311, 312
convergence, vii, 1, 6, 7, 17, 35, 73, 174
conversion, 230, 317
coordination, vii, ix, 43, 44, 46, 48, 51, 68, 70, 71, 73, 123, 124, 125, 126, 127, 128, 129, 138, 139, 140
Copenhagen, 41
corporate governance, 223, 307, 315
corporate performance, 259, 263, 264, 301
corporate scandals, 302, 303, 304, 305
corporate social responsibility, 36
corporations, 73, 143, 145, 148, 163, 287, 291, 302, 306
correlation, xi, 63, 66, 110, 113, 114, 115, 116, 117, 118, 152, 192, 224, 259, 261, 264, 266, 284, 315
correlation coefficient, xi, 261, 266
correlations, 111, 113, 114, 115, 117, 118, 135, 209
corruption, 12, 16, 55
cost of debt, 151
cost of equity, 151, 152, 157
Costa Rica, 290
cost-effective, 14
costs, ix, 15, 20, 42, 45, 46, 48, 49, 50, 69, 70, 73, 95, 125, 127, 128, 129, 131, 138, 139, 144, 147, 149, 150, 151, 152, 153, 158, 165, 193, 218, 220, 245, 251, 252, 254, 282, 287, 290, 305, 312, 314, 317
country of origin, 5, 22, 27, 28, 54, 55, 56, 66
couples, 83

coupling, 129
courts, 55, 153
coverage, 88, 267, 303
covering, 2, 311
CPC, 9
CPI, 12
creativity, 118, 184, 270
credentials, 89, 322
credibility, 55, 294
credit, vii, 148, 149, 150, 151, 157, 158
credit card, vii, 148
credit rating, 150, 157
creditors, 149, 152, 153, 159, 165
crime, 55
critical analysis, 175
critical value, 63, 135, 137
criticism, xii, 301, 302, 303
cronyism, 13
cross-border, 7, 24, 27, 74
cross-country, 55
cross-cultural, 7, 35, 78, 187
cross-sectional, 63
crowding out, ix, xi, 123, 241, 252, 254
CT scan, 263
cues, 305
cultivation, 183
cultural artifacts, 171, 179, 186
cultural character, 8, 13, 20
cultural differences, 3, 43, 55, 77
cultural heritage, 11, 179, 183
cultural norms, 18
Cultural Revolution, 9
cultural values, 5, 14, 15, 104
culture, vii, x, 1, 3, 4, 5, 7, 8, 9, 10, 11, 15, 17, 19, 23, 29, 30, 31, 32, 35, 37, 46, 55, 73, 171, 173, 175, 179, 180, 181, 182, 183, 184, 188, 269, 270
currency, 1, 157
current balance, 157
current ratio, 153
customers, xii, 45, 81, 83, 85, 86, 87, 89, 91, 93, 94, 95, 96, 99, 177, 242, 261, 262, 263, 264, 268, 269, 270, 272, 274, 301, 302, 303, 304, 305, 310, 321
cyberspace, 172
cycles, 45
Czech Republic, 7

D

data collection, 174
data communication, 288
data set, 193, 196, 219, 226, 237
database, 52, 53, 132, 150, 156, 157, 304
data-mining, 185
de novo, 43
debt, vii, 52, 53, 57, 147, 148, 150, 151, 152, 154, 157, 158, 159, 165, 170, 194, 196, 197, 204, 230
debts, 150
decentralization, 125, 139

Index 327

decision makers, 85, 303
decision making, 220, 229, 297
decisions, 11, 52, 61, 63, 87, 94, 99, 141, 177, 178, 183, 195, 221, 296, 297, 305, 307
defense, 286
deficit, 242, 274
deficits, 243
definition, vii, viii, xi, xii, 2, 43, 79, 86, 87, 90, 91, 93, 95, 96, 188, 225, 248, 259, 260, 261, 262, 263, 264, 265, 266, 269, 270, 271, 273, 274, 275, 278, 312, 313, 318
deflate, 63
degrees of freedom, 136
delivery, 81, 82, 83, 84, 85, 86, 87, 89, 91, 92, 93, 94, 95, 96, 98, 321, 322
demand, xiii, 56, 124, 128, 179, 245, 287, 288, 309
democracy, 10, 11, 12, 13, 17
Democratic Progressive Party (DPP), 17
demographic change, 20
Denmark, 12
Department of Education, 41
dependent variable, 53, 54, 61, 65, 114, 136, 206, 228, 266, 304, 315, 316
deposits, 169
designers, 176
desire, 88, 93, 95, 105, 109, 233
detection, 132
developing countries, xii, 173, 247, 253, 281, 282, 283, 284, 285, 289, 290, 291
developmental psychology, 120
deviation, 226
differentiation, 6, 21, 32
diffusion, 3, 6, 24, 28, 30, 31, 127, 129, 143, 282, 286
diffusion process, 24
digitization, 282
direct investment, 286
direct measure, 148
disabled, 248
discipline, 80
disclosure, 170
discomfort, 17
discourse, 184, 187
Discover, 154
discretionary, 153
dispersion, 43, 70, 71, 253, 254, 255
dissatisfaction, 86
disseminate, 246, 285
distortions, 283
distribution, 26, 43, 54, 114, 204, 226, 274, 314
divergence, vii, 1, 6, 35, 46
diversification, 71, 74, 75, 76, 77, 220, 269, 273
diversity, 12, 20, 47, 57, 66, 68, 71, 73, 76, 77, 94, 106, 109, 187, 188
division, xi, 13, 23, 38, 132, 163, 241, 243, 244, 245, 247, 249, 250, 253, 254, 264, 265, 274, 304
division of labor, xi, 241, 243, 244, 245, 247, 249, 250, 253, 254
doctors, 311

dominance, 252, 311
dominant strategy, 68
donors, 82, 247, 251, 321
doors, 298
downsizing, xii, 301, 302, 304, 305
dream, 268
duality, vii, 1, 72
duration, 52, 53, 84, 127, 260
duties, 286, 288

E

earnings, 192, 218, 247, 282, 288, 305
earth, 269, 271, 272
East Asia, 2
Eastern Europe, 241
ecological, ix, 101, 104, 106, 107, 108, 111, 113, 114, 116, 117, 118, 119, 187
ecological systems, ix, 101, 104, 106, 107, 108, 111, 113, 114, 116, 117, 118
ecology, 119, 120, 267, 317
econometrics, 74
economic change, 76
economic crisis, 18
economic development, 15, 20, 43, 44, 45, 56, 245, 257, 291
economic efficiency, 310
economic growth, 2, 16, 18, 29, 34, 74, 217, 282, 286, 287, 296
economic incentives, 315
economic institutions, 257
economic integration, 28
economic performance, 310
economic policy, 22
economic problem, 15
economic reform, 9
economic reforms, 9
economic resources, 102, 121
economic systems, 8, 9
economics, vii, x, xi, 50, 78, 127, 140, 241, 242, 243, 248, 249, 250, 254, 256, 257, 317, 318
economies of scale, 43, 70, 131, 139, 153, 252
Eden, 44, 55, 70, 71, 73, 77
educated women, 116, 118, 119
Education, 32, 36, 39, 41, 104, 110, 111, 112, 115, 120, 123, 188, 289, 299
educational objective, 179
educators, 180
efficiency seeking, 125
elaboration, 184
elderly, 116, 117, 119, 246
elders, 14
election, 17
electronic materials, 270
email, 294
emotion, 82, 83, 85, 86, 87, 91, 96, 98, 321
emotional, viii, 79, 81, 82, 83, 84, 87, 88, 91, 92, 102, 104, 109

Index

emotions, 97, 268
employees, xii, 2, 3, 5, 6, 10, 11, 13, 17, 18, 19, 20, 22, 23, 28, 29, 30, 52, 86, 119, 177, 251, 262, 263, 264, 272, 274, 301, 302, 303, 304, 305, 310, 311
employers, 7, 11, 13, 14, 15, 16, 17, 18, 19, 301, 302, 304, 305, 306
employment, 2, 13, 14, 17, 23, 25, 29, 30, 31, 35, 36, 37, 108, 110, 116, 176, 181, 252, 283, 298, 303, 311
employment status, 110
empowered, 102, 103, 116
empowerment, ix, 101, 103, 104, 105, 106, 107, 108, 109, 111, 113, 114, 115, 116, 117, 118, 119, 121, 122
encouragement, 117
endogeneity, 61, 77
endorsements, 77
end-users, 184, 273
energy, 106, 197, 260, 267, 269, 271, 286, 289
engagement, 89, 176, 180, 181, 182, 183, 184, 321
England, 102, 119, 165, 166, 168
enlargement, 139
Enron, 149, 153, 170, 302, 306, 307
enterprise, 9, 10, 18, 20, 38, 73, 75, 143, 255, 268, 294, 296, 310
entertainment, 83, 87, 89, 91, 93, 95, 96, 98, 260, 267, 268, 322
enthusiasm, 178, 179
entrepreneurs, x, 192, 218, 241, 242, 243, 246, 247, 248, 254, 295, 296, 297, 299
entrepreneurship, 99, 142, 153, 246, 294, 295, 296, 297, 300, 309
entropy, 314
environment, ix, xii, 5, 6, 10, 11, 16, 22, 26, 34, 45, 46, 47, 74, 103, 104, 105, 106, 117, 119, 123, 124, 149, 195, 196, 218, 255, 267, 268, 269, 271, 293, 294
environmental factors, 103
environmental protection, 269, 271, 273
environmental resources, 116
equality, 10, 132
equilibrium, 193, 206, 231
equipment, 53, 175, 183, 265, 267, 271, 273, 274, 287
equity, vii, 6, 24, 27, 30, 54, 57, 148, 149, 150, 151, 152, 156, 157, 158, 159, 160, 161, 163, 165, 192, 194, 195, 196, 197, 198, 205, 207, 215, 218, 222, 223, 224, 225, 228, 230, 231, 232, 234, 235, 237, 306
equity market, 157
estimating, 149
estimators, 63
ethics, 305
ethnic groups, 11, 12, 13, 14
ethnicity, 187
ethnocentrism, 129
etiquette, 8
Europe, 2, 18, 28, 29, 120, 187, 317
European Commission, 318

European Union, 28, 257
evolution, 8, 9, 32, 36, 49, 69, 142, 144, 269, 291, 300
exchange markets, 225
exchange rate, 1
exchange relationship, x, 241, 243, 244, 249, 297
execution, 130, 268
exercise, 128, 205, 247, 310
exosystem, 104
expertise, 69, 76, 172, 175, 176, 180, 183, 192, 218, 270, 296, 298
exploitation, 75, 317
exports, xii, 281, 282, 286, 287, 288, 290
exposure, 125, 138, 158, 206
external financing, 302
extrapolation, 132
extrinsic rewards, 106
eyes, 247

F

fabric, 12, 16
face-to-face interaction, 51
factor analysis, 56, 66
failure, viii, 6, 42, 70, 245, 286, 303
faith, 14
familial, 8
family, ix, 8, 9, 10, 25, 101, 105, 106, 108, 109, 113, 114, 116, 117, 118, 119, 120, 121, 132, 252, 254, 311
family life, 106, 109
family members, 105, 119
family support, ix, 101, 106, 109, 113, 114, 116, 117, 118
famine, 9
farming, 289
farms, 252, 254
FAS, 149
fast food, 7
FDI, 2, 3, 15, 16, 17, 18, 28, 77, 283, 285, 287
FDI inflow, 2, 285
February, 142, 143
Federal Reserve, 238, 307
Federal Reserve Bank, 238, 307
feedback, 41
feelings, 98, 105, 109, 117
fees, 150, 151, 153
feminist, 103
Filipino, 15
film, 175
finance, xii, 16, 94, 150, 157, 165, 170, 192, 221, 294, 296, 297, 301
Financial Accounting Standards Board, 169, 170
financial capital, 295, 296
financial crisis, 39
financial distress, 306
financial institution, 148, 150, 151, 153, 157, 158, 161, 163, 169, 192, 218

financial institutions, 148, 151, 153, 157, 158, 163, 192, 218
financial markets, 148
financial performance, vii, viii, 34, 41, 45, 46, 48, 50, 51, 53, 56, 61, 64, 65, 66, 67, 68, 69, 264, 302, 303, 319
financial resources, xii, 61, 293
financial support, 41, 82, 321
financing, vii, x, 149, 150, 152, 153, 157, 159, 165, 191, 192, 193, 194, 196, 197, 200, 201, 205, 206, 209, 210, 212, 214, 215, 218, 221, 229, 230, 237, 247, 274, 296, 300, 312, 318
Finland, 12
firewalls, 132
firm size, 56, 57, 68, 127
firms, vii, viii, ix, x, xi, xii, 2, 7, 11, 14, 15, 18, 21, 22, 25, 26, 27, 29, 30, 31, 33, 36, 41, 42, 43, 44, 45, 50, 52, 53, 54, 55, 56, 57, 61, 63, 64, 67, 68, 69, 70, 71, 72, 73, 74, 75, 77, 97, 123, 124, 127, 128, 129, 138, 144, 149, 152, 153, 158, 192, 194, 197, 218, 226, 241, 242, 243, 244, 245, 246, 247, 248, 250, 251, 252, 254, 257, 260, 283, 284, 285, 286, 287, 289, 290, 299, 301, 302, 303, 304, 306, 307, 309, 310, 311, 312, 314, 318
fishing, 197, 289
fixed costs, 128, 138, 139
flexibility, 10, 11, 15, 16, 45, 50, 75, 127, 128, 129, 130, 175
flow, 3, 27, 30, 72, 220, 285, 294, 312, 315, 316
fluctuations, 223, 232
fluid, 274
focusing, 18, 31, 42, 82, 87, 89, 92, 93, 95, 222, 313, 316, 322
food, 7
Ford, 154
foreign direct investment, 44, 49, 70, 76
foreign firms, 11, 22, 32
foreign investment, 16, 18, 287
forestry, 197, 200, 203, 204, 263, 289
Fort Worth, 170
framing, 174
France, 135, 167, 181, 182, 247
fraud, 302, 306, 307
free trade, 288
freedom, 16, 55, 129, 131, 136, 248
freight, 260
frequency distribution, 314
frustration, 106
Fuji Electric, 270, 272, 276
fulfillment, 94, 247
functional analysis, 119
functional aspects, 83
funding, x, 83, 150, 157, 158, 183, 197, 199, 200, 201, 202, 217, 219, 297, 312
fundraising, 180, 251
funds, 82, 151, 165, 192, 196, 197, 200, 201, 202, 205, 206, 207, 213, 214, 218, 219, 220, 247, 317, 321
fusion, 267, 271

G

gender, 103, 121
gender role, 103
General Electric, 30
general knowledge, 284
General Motors, 150, 157, 302
generalization, 140
generation, 144, 172, 173, 185, 244, 283, 284
Geneva, 144
genre, 94, 95, 96
geography, 73
Georgia, 2, 187
Germany, 125, 135, 166, 167, 168, 241
gift, 180, 181
gifts, 181
glass, 32
global competition, 260
global economy, 69, 287, 291
global leaders, 34
global management, 24, 25, 30, 31
global markets, 128, 131, 138, 140
globalization, 2, 3, 7, 28, 30, 33, 34, 36, 38, 44, 124, 173, 187, 188, 291
GNP, 287
goal attainment, 81
goals, xiii, 3, 46, 82, 84, 92, 97, 105, 106, 118, 177, 179, 183, 309, 310, 315
God, 188
goods and services, 124, 295
governance, 45, 49, 50, 55, 57, 74, 76, 95, 125, 129, 142, 223, 229, 237, 243, 246, 250, 251, 253, 254, 297, 306, 309, 314, 315, 316
government, xii, xiii, 9, 11, 12, 13, 14, 16, 17, 18, 19, 20, 22, 23, 30, 55, 82, 83, 97, 124, 132, 245, 281, 284, 285, 287, 288, 290, 309, 310, 312, 313, 315, 316, 318, 321
government intervention, 16, 17
GPs, 311
grains, 148
grants, 82, 83, 321
graph, 185
Great Britain, 13, 22
Greece, 293
gross domestic product, 2, 4, 564, 132, 282, 289
grounding, xi, 241
groups, xi, 4, 8, 10, 11, 12, 13, 14, 18, 20, 22, 25, 29, 87, 102, 103, 109, 121, 198, 234, 241, 245, 246, 253, 263, 312, 316
growth, vii, xi, xii, 2, 16, 18, 25, 29, 34, 42, 71, 72, 74, 77, 83, 85, 96, 102, 106, 109, 111, 112, 113, 114, 115, 148, 156, 158, 161, 192, 193, 194, 196, 197, 199, 205, 207, 208, 209, 217, 218, 224, 259, 260, 261, 262, 263, 266, 267, 268, 269, 270, 271, 273, 274, 275, 277, 278, 282, 286, 287, 288, 289, 290, 291, 296
growth rate, xi, 148, 156, 161, 224, 259, 261, 266, 268, 270, 271, 273, 274, 275, 277, 290

growth time, 112
Guangdong, 9
guardian, 12
guidance, 10, 118, 177
guilt, 105
guilt feelings, 105
guilty, 102

H

Haifa, 41
handling, 61, 194, 196, 250, 251
harm, xi, 15, 241, 253, 254, 303, 305
harmony, xi, 15, 241, 253, 254
Harvard, 31, 33, 34, 36, 72, 73, 76, 98, 99, 119, 142,
    188, 257, 278, 317, 319
hazards, 55, 192, 193, 195, 222
healing, 121
health, xiii, 11, 96, 102, 106, 197, 199, 226, 286,
    309, 311, 312, 313, 314, 315, 317, 318
health care, xiii, 289, 309, 311, 313, 314, 315
heart, 6, 126, 245, 268
Hebrew, 119, 120, 121
hedge funds, 165
hedonic, 87
hedonism, 82
helplessness, 103
heme, 312
heterogeneity, 57, 61, 63
heterogeneous, 93, 175, 193
heteroskedasticity, 212, 235
high growth potential, 194, 218
high risk, 192, 193, 195, 205, 210, 218, 222, 231
high school, 108
high scores, 19
higher education, 104, 116, 118, 119
high-tech, 17, 26, 131, 192, 194, 218, 231, 285, 290,
    299
hip, 34
hiring, 5, 15, 16, 50, 302
Hispanic, 15
Holland, 2, 318
homogeneity, 153
Hong Kong, 1, 2, 8, 21, 22, 147, 169, 191, 217, 290
horizon, 139, 291
hospital, xiii, 246, 309, 310, 311, 312, 313, 314, 315,
    316, 318
hospital care, 246, 310, 311
hospitalization, 311
hospitals, 246, 247, 310, 311, 312, 313, 314, 315,
    316, 317, 318
host, vii, ix, 2, 5, 23, 25, 28, 33, 123, 124, 125, 130,
    139, 140, 285, 291
House, 14, 293
household, 117
households, 243

HRM, vii, 1, 3, 4, 5, 6, 7, 8, 9, 10, 11, 13, 14, 15, 16,
    17, 19, 20, 21, 22, 23, 24, 25, 26, 27, 28, 29, 30,
    31, 32, 33, 34, 35, 36, 37, 38, 39
human, vii, ix, 1, 3, 4, 5, 8, 10, 14, 30, 31, 32, 33, 34,
    35, 37, 38, 85, 90, 94, 96, 101, 104, 119, 122, 244,
    249, 263, 267, 284, 285, 289, 294, 295, 296, 299,
    302
human capital, 284, 296, 299, 302
human development, 104, 119, 289
human resource development, 14
human resource management (HRM), vii, 1, 3, 4, 5,
    10, 30, 31, 32, 33, 34, 35, 36, 37, 38, 39, 96, 143,
    301
human resources, 8, 14, 90, 94
humanity, 12
humiliation, 9
hybrid, 50, 256
hybrids, 129, 250
hypothesis, xi, 30, 56, 63, 64, 66, 72, 75, 137, 139,
    159, 163, 222, 235, 237, 259, 260, 264, 304, 316
hypothesis test, 137

I

IBM, x, 171, 175, 176, 177, 178, 179, 181, 183, 263,
    290, 302
ice, 83, 178
ICM, 315
ICT, x, xii, 38, 171, 172, 173, 174, 175, 177, 178,
    179, 183, 184, 185, 186, 281, 282, 283, 285, 286,
    288, 291
identification, 85
identity, 187, 188, 250, 266, 316
ideology, 12, 106, 172, 176, 178
idiosyncratic, 48
imagery, 176
images, 264, 267
imagination, 268
imaging, 267, 270
IMF, 11
imitation, 6, 7, 16, 33
imperialism, 188
implementation, viii, 9, 55, 79, 81, 93, 180, 263
imports, 286, 287
in situ, 50
in transition, 16, 20, 39, 77
inactive, 53
incentive, xi, 29, 55, 105, 124, 130, 153, 192, 193,
    218, 219, 231, 241, 243, 250, 251, 254, 257, 310,
    315, 317
incentives, xi, 124, 125, 126, 129, 131, 145, 153,
    222, 241, 244, 246, 247, 250, 251, 254, 285, 310,
    311, 315
inclusion, 63, 66, 173
income, vii, x, xii, 52, 53, 147, 148, 150, 163, 165,
    196, 217, 218, 219, 220, 222, 223, 224, 233, 234,
    235, 237, 252, 301, 302, 303, 304, 305, 311
incomes, 287

Index

increased competition, 82, 282, 321
independence, 55, 103, 286
independent variable, 65, 88, 114, 118, 135, 136, 158, 159, 206, 213, 223, 224, 231, 235, 266, 315
India, xii, 2, 4, 8, 10, 11, 12, 13, 22, 23, 32, 33, 36, 281, 282, 283, 285, 286, 287, 288, 289, 290, 291, 292
Indian, 10, 11, 13, 15, 16, 32, 37, 282, 286, 287, 288, 289, 291
Indiana, 119
Indians, 10, 13, 20, 287
indication, 177, 178, 195, 207
indicators, 55, 56, 57, 65, 66, 68, 74, 133, 134, 135, 136, 196, 224, 289
indices, 15, 136
indigenous, 15, 22, 35, 173, 283, 284, 285, 287
individualism, 10, 13, 15, 17, 20, 243, 248
individuality, 55
Indonesia, vii, 1, 2, 4, 11, 12, 13, 14, 20, 22, 29, 36, 37
industrial, 4, 7, 8, 9, 11, 15, 17, 20, 21, 33, 35, 37, 128, 135, 139, 260, 270, 273, 274, 282, 286
industrial policy, 139
industrial relations, 4, 7, 8, 9, 11, 17, 20, 21, 33, 35, 37
industrial restructuring, 33
industrial sectors, 135, 282
industrialization, 15, 18, 286, 287
industrialized countries, 74
industry, xii, 6, 7, 11, 13, 19, 24, 26, 27, 32, 52, 53, 56, 61, 68, 69, 71, 72, 75, 76, 77, 83, 94, 95, 132, 135, 142, 156, 159, 163, 169, 184, 192, 197, 198, 200, 201, 202, 204, 205, 218, 219, 220, 221, 223, 226, 260, 262, 269, 270, 271, 273, 281, 283, 284, 285, 286, 287, 288, 289, 290, 291, 304, 306, 307, 310, 312, 316
inefficiency, 310
infancy, 13
infant mortality, 289
infant mortality rate, 289
inferences, 262, 263
inflation, 213, 235
information asymmetry, 221, 247, 250, 297
information exchange, 302
information processing, xi, 241, 254, 269
information sharing, 184
Information System, 291
information technology, 52, 129, 188, 197, 231, 260, 282, 287
Information Technology, 224, 236
infrastructure, xii, 13, 29, 125, 253, 254, 255, 281, 284, 285, 286, 287, 288, 289, 290
inherited, 1, 11, 173, 179
initial public offerings, 52
initiation, 134, 136
innovation, xii, 42, 45, 72, 74, 76, 77, 124, 125, 127, 130, 131, 138, 144, 176, 184, 262, 267, 270, 271, 281, 284, 286, 291, 299, 307
innovation output, 42

insight, 84, 87, 92, 117, 119, 159, 174, 243
inspection, 185
instability, 74, 78
institutional response, 248
institutionalization, 5, 6, 21, 27, 170
institutions, xii, 4, 5, 8, 11, 19, 20, 22, 23, 30, 31, 163, 165, 243, 244, 246, 249, 250, 257, 288, 301, 313
instruments, 61, 204, 205, 251, 268
insurance, 26, 150, 157
intangible, 7, 83, 84, 86, 194, 206, 207, 208, 210, 213
intangible attributes, 84
integration, 5, 6, 14, 21, 28, 32, 37, 76, 99, 119, 124, 143, 242, 254, 257, 267, 275, 287
integrity, 219
Intel, 290
intellectual capital, 294
intelligence, 7, 33, 268
intensity, 56, 61, 64, 117, 138, 282, 288
intentions, viii, 79, 99
interaction, 12, 26, 28, 45, 47, 51, 63, 64, 65, 66, 67, 75, 105, 106, 140, 171, 173, 180, 187, 243, 248, 249, 282, 294, 295, 296, 297
interaction effect, 63, 64, 65, 66, 67, 140
interaction effects, 63, 66, 140
interactions, 47, 48, 63, 64, 65, 66, 68, 86, 87, 104, 184, 249, 294, 295, 296
interactivity, 175, 282
interest rates, 170
interface, 98, 176, 187, 296
intermediaries, 192, 194, 218
internal organization, 129, 244
internationalization, vii, 41, 42, 43, 44, 46, 47, 48, 50, 51, 55, 61, 63, 64, 68, 69, 70, 71, 73, 74, 291
Internet, x, 143, 171, 172, 173, 174, 179, 180, 181, 182, 183, 184, 185, 198, 199, 200, 202, 265
interpersonal relations, 51
interpersonal relationships, 51
interpretation, 22, 54, 174, 243, 254
interrelationships, 88, 90
interval, 114
intervention, 16, 17, 145, 196, 313
interview, 87, 174, 178, 180, 189, 262
interviews, viii, 21, 52, 79, 86, 87, 88, 90, 91, 93, 95, 174, 262
intrinsic, xi, 82, 106, 116, 153, 241, 251, 252, 254
intrinsic motivation, xi, 241, 251, 252, 254
intrinsic value, 153
inventories, 150, 157
investment, vii, x, xii, 2, 6, 9, 16, 18, 22, 44, 49, 70, 74, 76, 151, 153, 165, 192, 193, 194, 195, 196, 197, 198, 199, 200, 201, 204, 205, 206, 207, 208, 209, 210, 211, 212, 213, 214, 217, 218, 219, 220, 221, 222, 223, 225, 226, 228, 281, 285, 286, 287, 291, 297, 302, 307
investment bank, 151, 165, 302
investors, x, 11, 150, 156, 157, 192, 195, 210, 217, 218, 219, 225, 237, 274, 296, 297, 302

332 Index

ions, 35, 45, 55, 89, 132, 257, 311
IPO, 73, 75, 194, 196, 197, 198, 199, 204, 205, 206, 207, 208, 218, 222, 223, 224, 225, 226, 227, 228, 229, 230, 231, 232, 233, 234, 236, 238, 302
IPOs, 192, 196, 197, 218, 225, 238
Iran, 2
Iraq, 12
Ireland, 32, 102, 166, 167, 289
iron, 33
Islam, 11, 13, 14
Islamic, 13
Islamism, 2, 19
island, 14, 17
isomorphism, 5, 6, 7, 33, 46, 297
Israel, ix, 2, 41, 101, 102, 103, 110, 120, 121, 289
Italy, 166, 167, 169, 309, 310, 311, 312, 313, 314, 316

J

January, 110, 273
Japan, 2, 8, 22, 38, 135, 167, 169, 173, 259, 277, 279, 286
Japanese, 4, 9, 18, 19, 22, 23, 24, 25, 27, 28, 31, 35, 36, 37, 75, 142, 172, 173, 181, 260, 261, 264, 265, 268, 270, 271, 276, 278, 279
Jefferson, 106, 119
Jerusalem, 41, 120, 121
job creation, 282
jobs, 19, 29, 110, 119
joint ventures, 21, 31, 32, 37, 42, 57, 72, 74, 75, 76, 78
Jordan, 2
judgment, 95, 305
Jung, 9, 103, 121
justice, 11, 12, 144
justification, 206, 233

K

killing, 9
King, 10
KMT, 9, 17
knowledge acquisition, 295, 299
knowledge economy, 17, 27
knowledge transfer, 27, 28, 30, 32, 74, 77, 129
knowledge-based economy, 17
koji, 259
Korea, 20, 31, 168, 286, 287
Korean, 8, 25, 125

L

labor, xi, 120, 241, 244, 253, 282, 285, 287, 289, 290, 302
labor force, 282, 285, 287, 289

labour, vii, 1, 2, 6, 9, 11, 15, 17, 18, 20, 22, 23, 29, 30, 37, 38
labour market, 2, 20
land, 10, 11, 18
landscapes, 188
language, 73, 178, 179, 181, 183, 185
large-scale, 289, 290
later life, ix, 101, 102, 116, 117
Latin America, 23, 28, 132, 247, 290
Latin American countries, 23, 290
law, 15, 17, 55, 180, 181
laws, 5, 6, 9, 11, 15, 22, 23
lawsuits, xii, 301, 302, 303, 304, 305, 306
layering, 182
layoffs, 303
LCDs, 75
lead, 6, 25, 26, 46, 61, 71, 84, 86, 88, 102, 128, 136, 139, 157, 177, 195, 210, 212, 218, 219, 221, 226, 268, 270, 271, 283, 294, 295, 297
leadership, 14, 21, 103, 120, 177, 179, 180, 251
leadership abilities, 103
leadership style, 21
learning, viii, xii, 35, 41, 43, 44, 45, 46, 47, 48, 49, 50, 51, 67, 69, 70, 71, 72, 73, 74, 75, 76, 77, 83, 125, 138, 144, 193, 263, 281, 283, 284, 285, 286, 291
learning process, 44, 283, 285
legal systems, 51
legislation, 9, 13, 15, 17, 20
legislative, 313
Leibniz, 241
lending, 148, 153, 159, 169, 175, 192, 194, 218
lens, 31
liberalization, 11, 286, 287
licensing, 53, 286, 287
life cycle, 103, 104, 120
life satisfaction, 106
lifestyle, 267
lifetime, 106
likelihood, 51, 63, 68, 127, 134, 139, 316
Likert scale, 133
limitation, 14, 118, 194
limitations, xi, 3, 55, 71, 80, 118, 242, 243, 244, 247, 249, 254
limited liability, 147
Lincoln, 6, 19
line graph, 185
linear, 53, 56, 63, 64, 65, 150, 314
linear regression, 150
linkage, 264, 273, 275, 278, 284
links, ix, 90, 104, 123, 182, 297
liquid asset ratio, 159
liquid assets, 153
liquidity, 149, 150, 153, 157, 158, 159, 163, 165
liquidity ratio, 153
literacy, 289
literacy rates, 289
living environment, 267, 268
loans, vii, 148, 149

local community, 253
localization, 6, 22, 24, 26, 27, 29, 30, 31, 124, 173, 187
location, 26, 29, 44, 54, 73, 74, 282, 315
locus, 76, 294
logistics, 153
London, 10, 31, 32, 33, 34, 35, 36, 37, 38, 72, 74, 120, 142, 143, 188, 291, 292, 299
longevity, 76, 89, 117, 321
longitudinal study, 75
long-term, 8, 17, 18, 52, 53, 57, 71, 74, 139, 150, 251
losses, 64, 103, 153, 192
love, 8, 85, 89, 321
Lovelock, 82, 84, 85, 88, 89, 90, 91, 99
low power, 20, 267
low risk, 6
low-income, 245
low-tech, 131
loyalty, 8, 13, 30, 92
LTD, 150, 167, 168, 169

M

Macau, 2, 8
machine learning, 185
machinery, 135
machines, 185
macrosystem, 104
magnetic, 274
Mainland China, 1, 8, 21
mainstream, 3, 254
maintenance, 88, 178, 249, 250
Malaysia, vii, 1, 2, 4, 12, 13, 14, 20, 22, 23, 29, 36, 38, 289, 290
maltreatment, 119
management, vii, viii, 1, 3, 4, 5, 6, 7, 8, 9, 10, 13, 14, 15, 16, 17, 18, 19, 20, 21, 22, 23, 24, 25, 27, 28, 29, 30, 31, 32, 33, 34, 35, 36, 37, 38, 43, 44, 70, 78, 80, 81, 82, 85, 87, 88, 89, 90, 91, 92, 93, 96, 97, 129, 130, 135, 139, 140, 142, 143, 144, 149, 150, 153, 157, 177, 179, 197, 207, 220, 221, 225, 229, 245, 260, 263, 265, 268, 283, 288, 303, 304, 306, 307, 316, 321, 322
management practices, vii, 1, 3, 5, 6, 9, 16, 20, 21, 22, 23, 24, 27, 30
mandates, 130, 144
Manhattan, 72
man-made, 9
manpower, 38, 288
manufacturer, 269, 273, 274
manufacturing, 14, 16, 18, 23, 26, 32, 33, 37, 53, 75, 144, 153, 197, 268, 271, 274, 282, 287
Maori, 173
marital status, 110
market, ix, 3, 6, 7, 10, 20, 24, 25, 26, 31, 42, 45, 48, 50, 52, 57, 69, 74, 76, 83, 89, 92, 93, 97, 123, 124, 125, 126, 127, 128, 129, 130, 131, 133, 135, 136,

137, 138, 139, 140, 142, 143, 149, 157, 158, 159, 163, 192, 196, 197, 208, 209, 217, 220, 225, 242, 243, 244, 245, 246, 248, 249, 250, 252, 253, 254, 257, 260, 261, 263, 269, 270, 271, 274, 276, 277, 283, 284, 286, 289, 294, 296, 302, 307, 309, 310, 311, 317, 318
market failure, 242, 244, 245, 246, 249, 254, 257, 309
market segment, 93, 260
market share, 83, 97, 263
market structure, 318
market value, 42, 217, 261, 274, 277
marketing, viii, 42, 53, 68, 79, 80, 81, 82, 83, 84, 85, 86, 87, 88, 89, 90, 91, 93, 94, 96, 97, 98, 99, 135, 142, 153, 178, 321
marketing strategy, 83
markets, ix, 44, 45, 46, 69, 71, 89, 91, 123, 125, 126, 128, 129, 130, 131, 133, 138, 139, 140, 141, 143, 148, 150, 157, 225, 246, 250, 257, 264, 282, 283, 286, 311, 318, 321
martial law, 17
masculinity, 10
masking, 47
Massachusetts, 142
matrix, 136
mature economies, 20
Mauritius, 290
meanings, 296, 297
measure of value, 96
measurement, 14, 75, 77, 91, 94, 96, 135, 148, 170, 269
measures, 52, 54, 55, 56, 66, 71, 81, 85, 86, 89, 93, 94, 106, 111, 133, 135, 142, 156, 197, 273, 288, 314
media, xii, 55, 174, 175, 176, 187, 188, 267, 269, 301, 303, 305
median, 198, 201, 202, 245
medical care, 317
medical services, 316
medication, 311
membership, 11, 82, 122, 251
memory, 269
men, 103, 110, 121
mergers, vii, xi, 24, 27, 31, 128, 170, 259, 273
merit-based, 10
mesosystem, 104
messages, 263, 294
meta-analysis, 77
metric, 165
metropolitan area, 304
Mexico, 23, 28, 290
Microsoft, 290
microsystem, ix, 101, 104, 105, 106, 108, 113, 114, 116, 117
Middle East, 2
middle-aged, 116, 117
midlife, 101, 102, 103, 106, 107, 118
migrants, 29
migration, 29

miniaturization, 269
mining, xi, 259, 263, 278
Minnesota, 188
minority, 8, 188, 195
minority groups, 8
mirror, 286
misappropriation, 45
missions, xi, 241, 245, 247, 251, 253, 260, 263
MIT, 74, 187, 215, 238
Mitsubishi, 276
mixed economy, 313
mixing, 24
mobility, 29, 269
modeling, ix, 61, 123, 125, 134, 140
models, 4, 54, 56, 57, 61, 63, 64, 65, 67, 87, 136, 148, 159, 169, 171, 173, 184, 206, 225, 242, 266, 310, 313
moderates, 51
moderators, 66, 69
modules, 128, 130
money, 149, 175, 183, 192, 194, 218, 221, 245, 295
monopoly, 287
moral hazard, 148, 193, 195, 222, 296
Morocco, 290
mortality, 289
mortgage, vii, 147, 148, 150, 157
mortgages, vii, 148, 157
Moscow, 188
mothers, 102
motivation, x, xi, 105, 107, 118, 119, 139, 241, 242, 243, 246, 247, 248, 251, 252, 254, 255
motives, ix, 82, 97, 101, 104, 105, 106, 109, 111, 112, 113, 114, 115, 117, 118, 220, 252
motors, 273, 274
movement, 17, 18, 119, 173, 176, 177, 181, 182, 185
multicultural, 26
multiculturalism, 188
multidimensional, 91, 92, 103, 173
multidisciplinary, 85
multi-ethnic, 13, 14
multimedia, 267, 269, 271
multinational companies, vii, ix, 2, 3, 5, 6, 16, 17, 19, 20, 21, 33, 38, 123, 141, 143
multinational corporations, vii, 29, 33, 34, 139, 142, 143, 144
multinational enterprises, 144, 283
multinational firms, 35, 44, 77, 143
multiple regression, xi, 259, 266, 275
multiple regression analyses, 266
multiplicity, 11
multivariate, 53, 68, 132
music, 7, 15
musicians, 83
Muslim, 12, 13, 14, 120
Muslims, 11
mutual funds, 165
Myanmar, 2, 12
myopia, 75

N

NAFTA, 28
narratives, 172
NASDAQ, 197, 225
nation, 1, 11, 12, 16, 17, 18, 19, 20, 28, 282
national, viii, xii, 3, 4, 5, 6, 7, 8, 17, 18, 19, 20, 24, 27, 28, 35, 38, 41, 42, 43, 44, 45, 46, 47, 48, 49, 50, 51, 52, 54, 55, 56, 66, 67, 68, 69, 70, 71, 74, 75, 97, 121, 171, 176, 178, 180, 182, 183, 184, 185, 188, 281, 284, 286, 301, 311, 312
national culture, 3, 5, 8, 20, 24, 27, 35, 44, 46, 50, 75
national economies, 301
National Gallery, 176, 185
National Health Service, 311, 312
nationality, 24, 27, 29, 311
natural, 156, 158, 161, 178, 185, 219, 315
naturalization, 179
NEC, 260, 263, 276
negative relation, 209, 232
neglect, 321
negligence, 16
Nepal, 2
nepotism, 13
net income, xii, 52, 53, 301, 302, 303, 305
Netherlands, 165, 167, 188, 281
network, viii, 27, 42, 45, 46, 47, 48, 49, 51, 64, 67, 69, 70, 71, 72, 73, 75, 77, 124, 126, 128, 129, 140, 141, 142, 243, 244, 267, 268, 269, 271, 285, 294, 295, 296, 297, 298, 313
network density, 42
networking, 124, 271, 294
New Frontier, 172, 178, 179, 183, 187
new media, 174, 175, 187, 188
New York, 35, 36, 37, 76, 97, 120, 121, 122, 144, 145, 169, 170, 185, 187, 188, 189, 197, 225, 238, 256, 257, 299, 304, 307, 318
New York Stock Exchange, 197, 225
New York Times, 185, 188
New Zealand, 99
newspapers, 132
next generation, 180, 267
NFI, 136
NGO, 313
NGOs, 253, 257
non-linear, 68
non-profit, vii, 80, 81, 83, 89, 95, 313, 318, 321
normal, 114
normal distribution, 114
norms, 18, 45, 104, 109, 118, 294, 295
North America, 28, 173, 185, 274
not-for-profit, x, 241, 310, 318
null hypothesis, 163
nurses, 314
nursing, 102, 246
nursing care, 246
nursing home, 246

O

objectivity, 264
obligation, 13
obligations, 153, 297, 315
observations, 53, 68, 132, 134, 174, 178, 209, 210, 212, 226, 231, 233, 234, 311
obsolete, 11
obstetricians, 311
Oceania, 2
OCR, 265
OECD, 253, 256
offshore, 287, 288, 289, 290
older people, 120
olive, 187
online, 173, 174, 175, 180, 181, 182, 183, 184, 186, 187
on-the-job training, 19
openness, 180, 182, 183, 184, 287
operations research, 85, 126
opportunism, xi, 241, 250, 251, 252, 254, 257
opposition, 250
optical, 274
optimization, 70
oral, 189, 294
organic, 248
organization, ix, x, xi, xii, 4, 5, 6, 9, 18, 19, 24, 38, 39, 47, 69, 76, 77, 101, 102, 105, 106, 108, 110, 111, 113, 114, 116, 117, 118, 119, 144, 241, 242, 243, 244, 245, 246, 247, 248, 249, 250, 251, 252, 253, 254, 257, 262, 263, 264, 275, 295, 301, 302, 303, 304, 305, 310, 311, 313, 314, 315, 316, 317
organizational behavior, 55, 262
organizational culture, 76
organizations, vii, ix, 3, 5, 6, 7, 9, 13, 16, 34, 36, 37, 77, 82, 97, 102, 103, 110, 116, 118, 119, 122, 123, 128, 130, 133, 139, 141, 142, 245, 247, 248, 253, 256, 257, 260, 301, 302, 303, 304, 305, 306, 310, 311, 312, 313, 315, 316, 317, 321
orientation, 8, 15, 17, 18, 103, 139
orthography, 268
oscillator, 273
outliers, 68, 132
out-of-pocket, 310
outsourcing, ix, xii, 11, 123, 124, 125, 126, 127, 128, 130, 131, 133, 134, 136, 137, 138, 139, 140, 281, 283, 286, 288, 289, 290
oversight, 81
ownership, xiii, 10, 21, 24, 25, 27, 32, 73, 76, 150, 192, 196, 197, 205, 306, 309, 310, 313, 314, 315, 316, 317, 318, 319
ownership structure, 76, 192, 196, 205, 310, 313, 314, 317

P

Pacific, 1, 28, 31, 32, 33, 34, 35, 36, 37, 38, 39, 75, 279
pain, 9
Pakistan, 2, 15, 23, 35
paper, xi, xii, 10, 41, 75, 80, 87, 88, 90, 110, 124, 138, 142, 143, 147, 148, 149, 150, 165, 169, 170, 187, 188, 191, 193, 194, 215, 218, 219, 238, 242, 243, 244, 245, 247, 248, 249, 250, 251, 252, 253, 281, 285, 291, 302, 303, 307, 309, 313, 315, 316, 317, 318
paradox, 46, 47, 76
parameter, 63, 136
parenting, 120
parents, 120, 246
Paris, 172, 175, 181, 184, 188, 256
partnership, 147, 150, 156, 177, 178, 188
partnerships, 73, 77, 128, 253
passenger, 260
passive, 121
pathways, 86, 90, 96
patients, 121, 312, 314, 315, 316
payroll, 14
PCs, 289
peer, 124, 128, 129, 130, 140
peers, 220
penalty, 163, 194, 305
pensioners, 121
per capita, 2, 56, 287
per capita income, 287
perception, 86, 90, 91, 94, 98, 178, 234, 302, 305
perceptions, 12, 31, 91, 93, 105, 108, 116, 117
performance, vii, viii, xi, xii, 6, 10, 13, 14, 15, 16, 19, 21, 26, 31, 33, 34, 35, 38, 39, 41, 42, 43, 44, 45, 46, 47, 48, 50, 51, 53, 56, 57, 61, 63, 64, 65, 66, 67, 68, 69, 70, 71, 72, 73, 74, 75, 76, 77, 78, 81, 82, 83, 86, 91, 93, 94, 95, 98, 116, 118, 124, 125, 129, 138, 139, 142, 144, 150, 152, 153, 156, 157, 159, 165, 193, 195, 196, 197, 198, 206, 207, 208, 209, 219, 223, 224, 226, 238, 257, 259, 260, 261, 263, 264, 268, 273, 274, 275, 278, 282, 285, 286, 302, 303, 304, 305, 306, 310, 319, 321
performance appraisal, 15
performance indicator, 260, 263
performers, 95
permit, 55, 124, 139, 243
personal, 19, 21, 82, 102, 103, 105, 106, 109, 111, 113, 114, 116, 118, 121, 175, 176, 177, 180, 181, 246, 296
personal benefit, 105
personal communication, 175, 176, 177, 180, 181
personality, 84, 103, 104, 119
personality traits, 104
petroleum, 260
pharmaceutical, 135
philanthropic, 102, 180
philanthropy, 119

Index

Philippines, vii, 1, 2, 4, 12, 13, 14, 15, 20, 22, 23, 29, 31, 34, 35
philosophy, 5, 8, 13, 182, 264
phone, 132
physicians, 311, 314, 316, 318
planning, 38, 94, 124, 126, 182, 183, 312
plants, 23, 37
plastic, 273
platforms, 125
play, 19, 20, 29, 86, 88, 92, 94, 96, 98, 153, 183, 185, 193, 196, 212, 219, 221, 222, 228, 232, 235, 246, 285, 294, 298
PLC, 165, 166, 167, 168
pleasure, 9
pluralism, 11, 313
pneumonia, 315
police, 55
political democracy, 72
political stability, 55, 65
politicians, 16
politics, 74, 121, 188
polytechnics, 289
pools, 69, 152, 157
poor, xii, 26, 46, 83, 150, 157, 253, 254, 255, 281, 290, 303
population, 1, 2, 4, 8, 11, 13, 14, 16, 17, 18, 20, 61, 109, 116, 118, 181, 182, 245, 253, 254, 255, 287, 289, 311
population density, 253, 254, 255
population group, 109
portfolio, vii, viii, 41, 42, 43, 44, 45, 47, 48, 49, 50, 51, 53, 55, 56, 57, 61, 63, 64, 66, 68, 69, 71, 130, 150, 152, 157, 159, 194, 220
portfolios, viii, 42, 43, 44, 45, 53, 61, 63, 68, 69, 70, 71, 72, 75, 152, 220, 226
Portugal, 166
positive attitudes, 46
positive correlation, xi, 113, 156, 259, 261, 275, 315
positive relation, 92, 130, 137, 139, 234
positive relationship, 92, 130, 137, 139, 234
poverty, 15, 289
poverty line, 289
power, 8, 10, 13, 15, 16, 18, 19, 20, 30, 32, 50, 55, 74, 78, 119, 121, 192, 195, 207, 223, 230, 252, 267, 269, 271, 273, 289, 311
powers, 188
pragmatic, 177
prediction, 221, 235
predictors, 61, 85, 87, 89, 92, 94, 122, 306
pre-existing, 311
preference, 4, 193, 199, 201
pregnancy, 120
premium, 157, 290
premiums, 46
present value, 316
president, 15
pressure, 3, 6, 17, 18, 20, 22, 82, 106, 124, 149, 206, 212, 321
prestige, 105, 246, 306, 310

prevention, 121, 311
price changes, 317
prices, 129, 307
primacy, 10
principal component analysis, 135
priorities, 20, 46, 180, 182, 288
prisons, 318
private, 16, 18, 25, 55, 148, 192, 194, 195, 218, 246, 249, 287, 297, 302, 304, 310, 311, 312, 313, 315, 316
private benefits, 192, 195, 218, 246
private enterprises, 287
private good, 246, 249
private ownership, 25
private property, 16
private sector, 18, 55
proactive, 18, 139
probability, 136, 314, 315
procedural justice, 144
producers, 83, 253, 255
product design, 126, 133, 285
product market, 45
production, 125, 143, 221, 244, 245, 246, 249, 252, 254, 257, 268, 282, 285, 309, 312
production networks, 143
productivity, 6, 10, 13, 34, 244, 282
profit, xi, 82, 95, 195, 210, 224, 241, 242, 244, 245, 246, 248, 254, 261, 264, 277, 321
profit margin, 264
profitability, 42, 53, 54, 64, 65, 68, 71, 81, 82, 84, 97, 157, 268
profits, 6, 192, 195, 210, 218, 242, 247, 310, 313, 315, 316, 317
program, 41, 81, 85, 86, 89, 90, 91, 93, 95, 96, 254
programming, 4, 5, 176
promote, 15, 19, 55, 103, 285, 288
property, 245, 310
property rights, 16, 310
proposition, 153, 248, 283, 285, 295, 315
prosocial behavior, 119
prosperity, 2
protection, 9, 20, 74, 222, 269, 271, 273, 286
prototype, 126, 133
prototyping, 133, 134
proxy, 55
prudence, 11
PSB, 168
psyche, 10
public, x, xii, 11, 18, 25, 53, 55, 102, 151, 175, 181, 182, 192, 194, 196, 214, 217, 219, 225, 226, 232, 245, 246, 247, 251, 264, 265, 284, 301, 302, 303, 304, 305, 309, 310, 311, 312, 313, 314, 315, 316
public companies, 192, 194, 214, 217
public expenditures, 312
public goods, 245, 247
public markets, 151
punishment, 129
purification, 86

Q

qualitative research, 91, 92, 187, 189
quality control, 177, 178
quality of life, 273, 290
quality of service, 246
quantum, 145
quartile, 132
quartz, 273
query, 174, 177
questioning, 84
questionnaire, 108, 109, 110, 132, 133, 135, 143, 262
questionnaires, 132, 262

R

R&D investments, 53
race, 13
racial issue, 13
radar, 188
radical, 34, 243, 305
RandD, 30, 42, 45, 53, 56, 61, 64, 75, 77, 194, 206, 207, 208, 210, 211, 213, 214
random, 63, 223
range, xi, 4, 44, 71, 84, 102, 106, 118, 131, 172, 182, 183, 259, 265, 266, 267, 269, 270, 272, 273, 275, 303
ratings, 148, 157
rationality, 33, 43, 70
reading, 19
real estate, 165
reality, vii, x, 6, 14, 34, 73, 175, 183, 187, 191, 193, 214, 219, 220, 221, 237, 248
reasoning, 17, 128, 130, 133, 248, 264, 283, 284
reciprocity, 18, 175, 178, 246, 296
recognition, 46, 105, 295
reconstruction, 248
recovery, 152
recreation, 129
recruiting, 290, 307
recycling, 271
redistribution, 313
reduction, 11, 45, 128, 154, 231, 237, 251, 288, 305, 310
redundancy, 56
refining, 129
reflection, 46, 64, 181, 255, 306
reforms, 9, 11, 38, 102
refugees, 120
regional, vii, 1, 16, 24, 28, 29, 30, 31, 33, 67, 132, 286, 289, 290, 311, 312
regression, xi, xii, 75, 111, 114, 115, 116, 158, 194, 206, 209, 210, 212, 219, 222, 223, 231, 232, 233, 234, 235, 237, 259, 266, 272, 273, 275, 316
regression analysis, 114, 266, 272, 275
regression equation, 115, 116, 158

regressions, 63, 158, 161, 162, 163, 164, 194, 196, 208, 209, 210, 212, 213, 219, 222, 223, 224, 231, 235, 304, 315
regular, 95, 151, 244, 248
regulation, xiii, 287, 309, 314
regulations, 5, 6, 9, 11, 14, 15, 17, 22, 23, 53, 55, 139, 315
regulators, 149, 153
regulatory capital, 149, 150, 170
reimbursement, 310, 314, 317
reinforcement, 16, 139
relationship, vii, viii, xi, xii, 18, 19, 22, 41, 42, 44, 48, 50, 51, 64, 68, 77, 79, 80, 83, 84, 85, 88, 89, 91, 92, 98, 99, 104, 105, 106, 118, 124, 125, 126, 130, 131, 137, 139, 140, 172, 176, 177, 178, 181, 185, 193, 206, 209, 210, 212, 214, 232, 234, 237, 249, 254, 259, 260, 261, 262, 263, 264, 266, 273, 278, 284, 297, 305, 311
relationships, vii, viii, ix, x, xii, 5, 16, 23, 38, 41, 42, 49, 51, 53, 68, 75, 81, 84, 85, 86, 88, 92, 96, 98, 104, 107, 119, 123, 124, 125, 126, 127, 136, 140, 148, 173, 180, 192, 212, 218, 237, 241, 243, 244, 265, 293, 294, 295, 296, 297, 303
relevance, 89, 140, 249, 252, 254
reliability, 52, 94, 109, 110, 133, 134, 135, 263, 268, 270
religion, 13, 15, 20, 188
religions, 11, 16
religiosity, 108, 110
religious groups, 246
remediation, 174, 175, 176, 179
rent, 128, 284
reputation, 42, 149, 170, 288, 296, 300, 301, 302, 304, 305, 307, 312, 315, 316
resale, 53
research, vii, viii, ix, xi, xiii, 1, 3, 4, 6, 8, 14, 20, 21, 23, 28, 32, 37, 41, 42, 43, 44, 49, 50, 53, 54, 68, 69, 70, 71, 78, 79, 80, 81, 82, 83, 84, 85, 86, 87, 88, 89, 90, 91, 92, 93, 94, 95, 96, 104, 106, 108, 111, 113, 116, 117, 118, 120, 123, 124, 125, 126, 128, 129, 130, 132, 133, 138, 139, 140, 142, 144, 165, 169, 172, 173, 174, 182, 187, 188, 189, 241, 242, 243, 245, 254, 255, 259, 260, 262, 263, 265, 268, 270, 271, 286, 291, 305, 309, 311, 312, 313
research and development, 286
research design, 95, 118, 187
researchers, viii, 68, 71, 79, 80, 81, 83, 84, 85, 96, 102, 103, 104, 105, 132, 180, 321
reservoirs, 295
residential, 157
residuals, 68
resistance, 51, 187
resolution, x, 46, 51, 191
resource allocation, 69, 139, 248
resource management, vii, 1, 3, 4, 5, 30, 31, 32, 33, 34, 35, 36, 37, 38, 96, 268
resources, viii, xii, 6, 7, 8, 14, 24, 30, 31, 32, 38, 42, 45, 46, 47, 48, 49, 51, 56, 61, 64, 68, 69, 70, 71, 73, 85, 90, 94, 102, 103, 104, 105, 106, 113, 116,

117, 121, 127, 129, 130, 219, 220, 221, 237, 283, 284, 285, 287, 288, 293, 294, 295, 296, 298, 312, 315
responsibilities, 51, 83, 102, 103, 117, 132, 192, 195, 218
responsiveness, 6, 7, 45
restructuring, xii, 38, 281
retail, 26
retention, vii, 1, 14, 30, 85, 96, 98, 99, 109, 110, 149, 158, 163, 321
retirement, 102, 303
retirement age, 303
returns, 42, 43, 69, 71, 77, 82, 93, 94, 152, 165, 192, 218, 321
revenue, 42, 52, 54, 196, 222, 224, 231, 237
rewards, ix, 26, 101, 105, 106, 108, 109, 110, 111, 113, 114, 116, 117, 118, 129, 219, 232
righteousness, 8
rigidity, 69
risk, ix, x, 12, 45, 69, 76, 124, 147, 149, 150, 151, 152, 153, 154, 156, 157, 158, 159, 163, 165, 170, 192, 194, 195, 196, 200, 201, 202, 206, 207, 209, 210, 212, 214, 217, 218, 219, 220, 221, 222, 223, 231, 232, 235, 237, 311
risk factors, 206, 209, 210, 212, 214, 223, 231
risk sharing, x, 195, 200, 201, 202, 209, 217, 218, 219, 220, 221, 222, 223, 235, 237
risks, x, 18, 149, 150, 191, 193, 194, 195, 196, 206, 210, 214, 215, 219, 220, 222, 223, 231, 232, 237
RMSEA, 136
robotics, 173
robustness, 61, 65, 67
ROE, 154, 155, 156, 160, 161, 162, 164, 198
ROI, 264
routines, viii, 41, 42, 43, 47, 48, 49, 50, 51, 68, 69, 70, 71, 78, 283
Royal Dutch Shell, 290
royalties, 53
R-squared, 161, 162, 164
rubber, 13
rule of law, 55
rural, xi, 242, 243, 253, 254, 255, 257, 289, 290
rural areas, 253, 254, 255, 289, 290
rural development, xi, 242, 243, 253, 254, 257
Russia, 171, 177, 183, 188
Russian, 175, 176, 177, 178, 179, 183, 188
Rutherford, 170

S

safeguards, 49, 51
safety, 11, 21, 267
salaries, 290
sales, xi, 25, 29, 54, 72, 82, 207, 259, 260, 261, 266, 268, 270, 271, 274, 275, 277, 321
sample, ix, 52, 53, 54, 56, 61, 86, 101, 108, 110, 118, 123, 132, 134, 135, 136, 153, 154, 157, 158, 159,

163, 193, 196, 197, 200, 201, 202, 214, 225, 226, 237, 301, 304, 314, 316
sampling, 61, 118
SAR, 147
satisfaction, viii, ix, 80, 81, 82, 83, 84, 85, 86, 88, 91, 92, 93, 94, 96, 97, 98, 99, 101, 106, 109, 116, 118, 120, 121, 269, 270, 272, 321
saturation, 288
savings, 152, 158, 282
scarcity, 288
scatter, 265
scholarship, viii, 80, 81, 88, 89
school, 108, 121, 247
scientific knowledge, 45
scores, 8, 19, 108, 132, 260, 261, 265
scripts, 86
search, 51, 77, 128, 133, 141, 185, 219, 251, 257, 265, 278, 304, 318
search engine, 265, 278
searching, 53, 251
second language, 179
secondary education, 108
securities, ix, 147, 148, 150, 157, 192, 194, 196, 204, 205, 218, 230, 303
security, 21, 22, 118, 148, 194, 197, 204, 265, 273
seed, 194, 197, 198, 199, 201, 205, 207, 224, 226
segmentation, 89, 93
selecting, 7, 17, 296
selectivity, 61
self image, 121
self-concept, 264
self-esteem, ix, 101, 104, 105, 106, 107, 109, 111, 113, 114, 116, 117, 118
self-expression, 116
self-help, 253
self-worth, 109
semantic, x, 171, 185, 266
semiconductor, 76, 197, 273
semiconductors, 26
Senegal, 290
sensation, 176
sensing, 267, 270
sensitivity, 30, 183
sensors, 274
separation, x, 56, 152, 153, 177, 241, 242, 254
series, viii, xi, 56, 79, 109, 150, 154, 156, 157, 259, 278
service provider, 86, 270
service quality, viii, 80, 81, 82, 83, 84, 85, 86, 87, 88, 91, 92, 93, 94, 96, 97, 98, 321
services, viii, ix, xii, xiii, 26, 42, 55, 79, 80, 81, 82, 83, 84, 85, 88, 89, 91, 93, 94, 96, 97, 99, 101, 102, 103, 118, 119, 124, 126, 129, 130, 133, 138, 172, 180, 185, 197, 246, 247, 262, 263, 264, 266, 269, 270, 272, 281, 282, 283, 285, 286, 287, 288, 289, 290, 291, 295, 301, 302, 304, 306, 309, 310, 311, 312, 313, 314, 317, 321
severity, 194, 206
Shanghai, 24, 191, 217, 290

Index

shape, viii, 24, 41, 68, 71, 77, 102, 172, 269, 297, 298, 303
shaping, 172, 173, 178, 179, 311
shareholders, 192, 195, 196, 197, 205, 207, 209, 211, 212, 213, 214, 215, 316
shares, 19, 24, 205, 218, 222, 223, 224, 225, 230, 231, 232, 234, 235, 237, 273, 274
sharing, x, 47, 48, 49, 51, 73, 175, 184, 195, 196, 200, 201, 202, 207, 209, 215, 217, 218, 219, 220, 221, 222, 223, 224, 230, 234, 235, 237
Shell, 176
shock, 311
short period, 16
short supply, 45
shortage, 29, 128
short-term, xi, 8, 15, 71, 126, 139, 150, 192, 251, 259, 273, 275
SIC, 52, 53, 56, 57, 60, 61
sigmoid, viii, 41, 42, 43, 44, 48, 64, 65, 68, 70, 71
sign, 154, 159, 315
signaling, 148, 152, 306
signalling, 252, 294, 297
signals, 294, 305, 311
significance level, 63, 68, 136, 261
signs, 159, 212
Silicon Valley, 288
similarity, 57, 76, 182, 294
simulation, 149, 173
Singapore, vii, 1, 2, 4, 8, 12, 13, 16, 17, 18, 19, 20, 22, 23, 29, 35, 36, 38, 39, 289
sites, 124, 174, 184, 187
skill shortages, 14
skills, 10, 45, 46, 102, 104, 108, 116, 117, 220, 282, 283, 285, 287, 288, 302, 306
SMEs, 21, 39, 75
smiles, 18
social activities, 119
social awareness, 104
social capital, xii, 293, 294, 295, 296, 297, 298, 299, 300
social context, 36, 295
social control, 26
social environment, 295
social exchange, 46, 77, 296
social group, 103
social influence, 19, 97
social justice, 12
social network, xii, 184, 186, 293, 294
social norms, 45, 109, 118
social obligations, 297
social order, 249, 250
social organization, 102
social relations, 18, 106, 295, 297
social relationships, 297
social resources, 102, 295
social responsibility, 33, 36
social sciences, 103, 187
social services, 102, 118, 309
social situations, 295

social skills, 102
social structure, 10, 73
social support, 109
social systems, 1, 295
social theory, 72
social units, 295
social welfare, 102, 313
social work, 121
socialist, 313
socialization, 118, 124
socioeconomic, xii, 249
sociological, 130
software, viii, xii, 11, 42, 52, 54, 61, 63, 68, 69, 71, 75, 134, 174, 176, 180, 181, 184, 226, 265, 278, 281, 282, 285, 287, 288, 289, 290, 291
solar, 273
solar panels, 273
solutions, 6, 14, 15, 45, 129, 177, 267, 268, 269, 270, 271
solvency, 56, 61, 64
Somalia, 12
South Africa, 102
South Asia, 4
South Korea, 1, 2, 4, 125
Southeast Asia, 33, 35, 38
sovereignty, 28
Soviet Union, 2
SPA, 166, 167
Spain, 166, 301
spatial, 44, 288, 289
special education, 103
specialization, 50, 130, 139, 244, 249, 312, 314
specific knowledge, 27
specificity, 8, 252
spectrum, 20
speed, 127, 144, 145, 274
spheres, xii, 104, 281, 290
spillovers, 74, 283, 284, 285, 286, 291
spindle, 273, 274
spiritual, 10
sponsor, 82, 119, 321
Sri Lanka, 2
St. Petersburg, 171, 188
stability, 2, 9, 13, 15, 55, 56, 65, 263
staffing, 28, 37
stages, 15, 20, 54, 102, 116, 118, 126, 133, 139, 186, 192, 194, 195, 196, 198, 199, 205, 206, 207, 208, 209, 210, 211, 213, 214, 220, 222, 223, 224, 226, 294
stakeholder, xi, 241
stakeholder groups, xi, 241
stakeholders, 30, 247, 251, 252, 253, 269, 272, 297, 311
Standard and Poor's, 52, 150, 156
standard deviation, 56, 64, 65, 132, 134, 159, 223, 225, 226, 230, 232, 237
standard error, 63, 212, 315
standardization, 5, 6, 21, 22, 24, 27, 29, 30, 31, 282

340 Index

standards, 5, 6, 7, 17, 22, 45, 83, 85, 114, 149, 177, 178, 179, 183, 268, 289
state intervention, 288
state-owned, 9, 20, 21, 25
statistics, 57, 137, 156, 158, 161, 185, 266, 272, 305
statutory, 170
STD, 150
steel, 76
stock, 52, 74, 193, 197, 204, 220, 225, 261, 283, 284, 303, 306
stock exchange, 197, 225
stock price, 52, 261
storage, 269
strain, 289
strategic, 3, 6, 11, 14, 15, 16, 17, 19, 20, 24, 32, 33, 34, 37, 53, 57, 64, 73, 74, 76, 77, 78, 83, 91, 92, 93, 94, 96, 99, 127, 130, 131, 139, 144, 153, 183, 265, 286
strategic management, 14
strategic planning, 94, 183
strategies, vii, 1, 3, 5, 7, 19, 21, 22, 26, 27, 31, 34, 61, 73, 75, 78, 82, 83, 84, 88, 94, 96, 122, 127, 144, 180, 181, 182, 194, 263, 264, 285, 286, 291, 321
strength, 42, 63, 68, 102, 103, 271, 294, 299
stress, 16, 106, 117
stressors, 103, 104, 105
strikes, 285
structural equation model, 86, 144
Structural Equation Modeling, 79, 86, 142, 144
structuring, 176, 250
students, 18, 135
subjective, viii, 79, 82, 83, 84, 88, 91, 92, 262, 321
subjectivity, 97
sub-prime, 153
subsistence, 289
substitutes, 159
substitution, 159, 165, 246
Sumatra, 12
superiority, 178, 193, 264
supervision, 252, 310, 312
supervisors, 19
suppliers, ix, 123, 129, 243, 246, 283, 287
supply, 53, 120, 125, 254, 268, 271, 284, 288, 315
supply chain, 125
surgery, 311
surplus, 151
surprise, x, 191, 193
survival, 5, 25, 76, 77, 83, 85, 89, 96, 124, 252, 321, 322
sustainability, xii, 85, 178, 184, 187, 281, 290
Sweden, 67, 97, 135
switching, 69, 251
symbols, 208, 263
sympathy, 246
symptoms, 63
synchronization, 263
syndicated, 195, 221, 226
synthesis, 174

systems, ix, 1, 4, 7, 10, 11, 13, 17, 32, 38, 44, 45, 46, 51, 55, 101, 104, 106, 107, 108, 111, 113, 114, 116, 117, 118, 121, 129, 177, 267, 268, 271, 285, 286, 295, 313

T

Taiwan, vii, 1, 2, 4, 8, 9, 12, 17, 18, 20, 21, 22, 24, 29, 32, 34, 35, 36, 38, 39, 274
talent, 38, 307
tangible, 7, 71, 86, 192, 218
tangible resources, 71
Tanzania, 187
Taoism, 8
target population, 116
targets, 218, 289, 290
tariffs, 288, 312, 317
tax incentive, 83
tax incentives, 83
taxes, 288
teaching, 14, 18, 181, 312
technical change, 283, 284
technical efficiency, 283
technicians, 83
technological change, 292
technological revolution, xii, 281, 290
technology, x, 3, 6, 45, 57, 68, 73, 124, 127, 133, 135, 141, 144, 171, 172, 174, 175, 176, 177, 178, 180, 182, 183, 184, 187, 188, 193, 196, 197, 219, 231, 232, 262, 265, 268, 269, 270, 271, 273, 274, 282, 283, 284, 285, 286, 287, 288, 290
technology transfer, 288
Tel Aviv, 119, 120, 121
telecommunication, 269, 285, 289
telecommunications, 32, 96, 269, 273, 289
telephone, 289
temporal, 94
tension, 13, 117
tenure, 260
territorial, 313
territory, 12, 17
terrorism, 21
Texas, 41, 215
text mining, xi, 263, 278
Thai, 17, 18, 19, 22, 23
Thailand, vii, 1, 2, 4, 8, 12, 13, 18, 19, 22, 23, 29, 34, 35, 36, 37, 38, 274, 291
The Economist, 292
theory, xi, xii, 4, 5, 7, 71, 72, 76, 80, 81, 84, 85, 86, 89, 90, 91, 104, 121, 125, 138, 140, 174, 175, 187, 188, 189, 193, 194, 218, 219, 220, 221, 224, 241, 242, 243, 244, 245, 246, 247, 249, 250, 253, 254, 255, 256, 257, 264, 281, 295, 306, 307
thinking, 3, 8, 30, 173
Thomson, 33, 189
threat, 18
threatening, xii, 192, 195, 281, 290
threshold, 47, 48, 69, 213, 235

time, xi, 5, 9, 10, 16, 18, 20, 29, 45, 63, 65, 75, 84,
94, 104, 105, 106, 109, 110, 111, 112, 113, 114,
115, 118, 121, 124, 128, 132, 139, 157, 175, 176,
180, 183, 196, 197, 198, 222, 229, 243, 245, 247,
248, 254, 259, 287, 290, 291, 295, 299, 302, 309,
312, 313
time series, xi, 259
time use, 121
timing, 192, 224, 226, 287
TIR, 166
title, 154, 182, 304
Tokyo, 259, 260, 276, 278, 279
tolerance, 18, 55, 95, 213
top management, 260, 263, 303, 304, 307, 316
Toshiba, 273, 276
total employment, 2, 25, 29
tourism, 181
Toyota, 6, 73
toys, 26
tracking, 52
trade, 7, 18, 28, 30, 150, 248, 249, 286, 288
trade policy, 286
trade union, 7, 30
trading, 16, 252, 306, 307
trading partners, 252
tradition, 149, 163, 172
traffic, 185
training, vii, 1, 10, 11, 13, 14, 15, 16, 17, 19, 22, 23,
26, 38, 89, 118, 177, 283, 285, 288, 313, 321
training programs, 14
traits, 1, 119
trajectory, 50, 51
tranches, 149, 150, 153, 157
transaction costs, 50, 127, 251, 252, 254
transactions, 53, 157, 244, 250, 296
transcripts, 178
transfer, 5, 23, 24, 25, 30, 32, 37, 46, 48, 50, 51, 55,
69, 70, 72, 76, 77, 124, 153, 288, 297
transformation, 16, 17, 35, 246
transformations, 184
transition, 69, 71, 172
transnational, 2, 3, 27, 33, 142
transparency, 12, 34
transparent, 12, 16
transplant, 21
transportation, 45, 55, 197, 260, 267, 282
traps, 45, 71
travel, 51
Treasury, 148
trend, xi, 24, 173, 184, 185, 259, 266, 269, 275, 278,
311
trial, 35, 69
trial and error, 69
triangulation, 75
triggers, 192
trust, 19, 42, 46, 48, 49, 51, 73, 94, 98, 147, 152,
157, 294, 295, 296
trusts, 165, 312
trustworthiness, 245, 246, 247, 248, 255

Tunisia, 290
turnover, 14, 17, 22, 23, 30, 34, 35, 38, 120, 129,
192, 195, 305, 306, 307
Tuscany, 313
typology, 34, 121

U

uncertainty, 10, 14, 18, 45, 46, 55, 76, 128, 192, 195,
218, 311
unemployment, 13, 14
unemployment rate, 13, 14
uniform, 311
unions, 9, 11, 14, 15, 18, 20
United Kingdom, 25, 38, 135, 167, 168, 247, 291,
292
United Nations, 132, 144, 292
United States, 55, 56, 67, 71, 78, 102, 165, 166, 167,
168, 169, 172, 175, 192, 193, 197, 217, 225, 290,
312
univariate, 132
universality, 8
universe, 4
universities, ix, 123, 124, 133, 141, 246, 284, 289
updating, 53

V

vaccination, 312
validity, 133, 135, 255
values, 5, 8, 9, 10, 12, 13, 14, 15, 16, 17, 18, 19, 20,
23, 29, 35, 45, 46, 53, 55, 56, 57, 61, 63, 74, 104,
105, 135, 136, 137, 173, 269, 271, 272, 297, 304,
314
variable, xi, 25, 27, 53, 54, 56, 57, 61, 65, 66, 67,
109, 114, 132, 158, 159, 161, 163, 194, 206, 207,
208, 210, 212, 222, 223, 224, 225, 228, 259, 264,
266, 275, 304, 314, 315, 316
variables, ix, 3, 23, 24, 27, 29, 31, 52, 53, 54, 56, 63,
64, 65, 67, 85, 101, 103, 104, 105, 106, 107, 108,
111, 113, 114, 115, 116, 117, 118, 134, 163, 206,
207, 212, 219, 223, 224, 225, 232, 233, 234, 235,
237, 266, 272, 314
variance, 52, 55, 109, 110, 114, 116, 135, 213, 235
variation, xii, 56, 63, 70, 184, 206, 281, 290
varimax rotation, 56
vehicles, 147
vein, 114, 119, 127, 184
Venezuela, 290
venture capital, vii, x, xii, 191, 192, 193, 196, 199,
214, 217, 218, 219, 220, 229, 230, 237, 293, 294,
296, 297, 298, 299, 302
venue, 82, 83, 91, 92, 95, 321
Venus, 181
vertical integration, 257, 275
veterinary medicine, 312
Vietnam, 2, 4

Index

Vietnamese, 17
violence, 55, 65
violent, 55
virtual reality, 175, 187
visible, 15, 282
vision, 179, 180, 181, 182, 183, 184, 188, 289
visual images, 267
vocabulary, 185
voice, 55, 65, 174
volatility, 149, 152
volunteerism, 106, 119, 122
voting, 196, 205, 223

W

wages, 251, 252, 282, 287
Wall Street Journal, 305
warfare, 9
warrants, 81, 84, 197
weakness, 103
wealth, 149, 152, 156, 165
web, x, 132, 143, 171, 172, 173, 174, 175, 176, 177, 178, 179, 180, 182, 183, 184, 185, 186, 188, 189
Web 2.0, x, 171, 172, 173, 184, 185, 186, 188
web-based, 184

websites, 52, 54, 171, 173, 174, 175, 176, 182, 183, 184, 185
welfare, 1, 9, 13, 17, 20, 102, 310, 311, 313, 317
welfare economics, 317
well-being, 102, 106, 116, 271
WG, 36
wholesale, 26
windows, 66, 176
wisdom, 8, 10
wives, 102, 103
women, ix, 12, 101, 102, 103, 104, 105, 106, 107, 108, 110, 111, 113, 114, 115, 116, 117, 118, 119, 120, 188
word of mouth, 26
workers, 9, 10, 11, 13, 19, 20, 23, 29, 283, 287, 307
workforce, vii, 1, 3, 13, 20, 28, 29
workplace, 11, 12, 13, 15, 16, 20, 105, 106, 119, 122
World Bank, 11, 55, 56, 74, 187
World Wide Web, 175, 184
writing, 182, 288
WTO, 9

Y

yield, 139, 151, 157, 248, 253